ADVERSE CHILDHOOD EXPERIENCES

ADVERSE CHILDHOOD EXPERIENCES

Using Evidence to Advance Research, Practice, Policy, and Prevention

---

Edited by

GORDON J.G. ASMUNDSON

TRACIE O. AFIFI

Academic Press is an imprint of Elsevier
125 London Wall, London EC2Y 5AS, United Kingdom
525 B Street, Suite 1650, San Diego, CA 92101, United States
50 Hampshire Street, 5th Floor, Cambridge, MA 02139, United States
The Boulevard, Langford Lane, Kidlington, Oxford OX5 1GB, United Kingdom

Notices
Knowledge and best practice in this field are constantly changing. As new research and experience broaden our understanding, changes in research methods, professional practices, or medical treatment may become necessary.

Practitioners and researchers must always rely on their own experience and knowledge in evaluating and using any information, methods, compounds, or experiments described herein. In using such information or methods they should be mindful of their own safety and the safety of others, including parties for whom they have a professional responsibility.

To the fullest extent of the law, neither the Publisher nor the authors, contributors, or editors, assume any liability for any injury and/or damage to persons or property as a matter of products liability, negligence or otherwise, or from any use or operation of any methods, products, instructions, or ideas contained in the material herein.

Library of Congress Cataloging-in-Publication Data
A catalog record for this book is available from the Library of Congress

British Library Cataloguing-in-Publication Data
A catalogue record for this book is available from the British Library

ISBN 978-0-12-816065-7

For information on all Academic Press publications
visit our website at https://www.elsevier.com/books-and-journals

Publisher: Nikki Levy
Acquisition Editor: Joslyn Chaiprasert-Paguio
Editorial Project Manager: Barbara Makinster
Production Project Manager: Bharatwaj Varatharajan
Cover Designer: Miles Hitchen

Typeset by SPi Global, India

Dedication

To my children, Taerjan and Aleiia, who inspire me daily.

Gordon J.G. Asmundson

To Tarek, Amelie, and Sloan
My parents
Children who have endured adversity.

Tracie O. Afifi

Contents

Section II

4 ACEs and mental health outcomes

Julia L. Sheffler, Ian Stanley and Natalie Sachs-Ericsson

5 ACEs and physical health outcomes

Kelsey D. Vig, Michelle M. Paluszek and Gordon J.G. Asmundson

6 ACEs, sexual violence, and sexual health

Christine Wekerle, Martine Hébert, Isabelle Daigneault,
Elisabeth Fortin-Langelier and Savanah Smith

7 ACEs and violence in adulthood

Tamara L. Taillieu, Isabel Garces Davila and Shannon Struck

Section III

Section IV

11 Global perspective on ACEs

Greta M. Massetti, Karen Hughes, Mark A. Bellis and James Mercy

12 Effective prevention of ACEs

Brian Brennan, Natalie Stavas, Philip Scribano

13 Neurodevelopmental mechanisms linking ACEs with psychopathology

Margaret A. Sheridan and Katie A. McLaughlin

14 ACEs and resilience: Methodological and conceptual issues

Assaf Oshri, Erinn K. Duprey, Sihong Liu and Andrea Gonzalez

15 ACEs and trauma-informed care

Caroline C. Piotrowski

16 Safe, stable, nurturing environments for children

Melissa T. Merrick, Katie A. Ports, Angie S. Guinn and Derek C. Ford

17 Current knowledge and future directions for the ACEs field

Tracie O. Afifi and Gordon J.G. Asmundson

Contributors

Tracie O. Afifi Departments of Community Health Sciences and Psychiatry, University of Manitoba, Winnipeg, MB, Canada

Gordon J.G. Asmundson Department of Psychology, University of Regina, Regina, SK, Canada

Mark A. Bellis College of Human Sciences, Bangor University, Bangor; World Health Organization Collaborating Centre for Investment in Health and Well-being, Public Health Wales, Cardiff, United Kingdom

Brian Brennan The Children's Hospital of Philadelphia, Philadelphia, PA; Uniformed Services University, F. Edward Hebert School of Medicine, Bethesda, MD, United States

Michael Chmielewski Southern Methodist University, Dallas, TX, United States

Isabelle Daigneault University of Montreal, Montreal, QC, Canada

Isabel Garces Davila Department of Community Health Sciences, Max Rady College of Medicine, Rady Faculty of Health Sciences, University of Manitoba, Winnipeg, MB, Canada

Shanta R. Dube Department of Population Health Sciences, School of Public Health, Georgia State University, Atlanta, GA, United States

Erinn K. Duprey Department of Human Development and Family Science, The Youth Development Institute, The University of Georgia, Athens, GA; The Offord Center, McMaster University, Hamilton, ON, United States

Derek C. Ford Division of Violence Prevention, National Center for Injury Prevention and Control, Centers for Disease Control and Prevention, Atlanta, GA, United States

Elisabeth Fortin-Langelier University of Montreal, Montreal, QC, Canada

Andrea Gonzalez Department of Human Development and Family Science, The Youth Development Institute, The University of Georgia, Athens, GA; The Offord Center, McMaster University, Hamilton, ON, United States

Tricia Gower Southern Methodist University, Dallas, TX, United States

Angie S. Guinn Division of Violence Prevention, National Center for Injury Prevention and Control, Centers for Disease Control and Prevention, Atlanta, GA, United States

Martine Hébert University of Quebec at Montreal, Montreal, QC, Canada

Margret Herbert Independent Researcher Work

George W. Holden Southern Methodist University, Dallas, TX, United States

Karen Hughes College of Human Sciences, Bangor University, Bangor; World Health Organization Collaborating Centre for Investment in Health and Well-being, Public Health Wales, Cardiff, United Kingdom

Joanne Lacroix Independent Researcher Work

Sihong Liu Department of Human Development and Family Science, The Youth Development Institute, The University of Georgia, Athens, GA; The Offord Center, McMaster University, Hamilton, ON, United States

Harriet L. MacMillan Department of Pediatrics, University of Calgary, Calgary, AB; Department of Psychiatry & Behavioural Neurosciences, McMaster University; Offord Centre for Child Studies, Hamilton, ON, Canada

Greta M. Massetti Division of Violence Prevention, Centers for Disease Control and Prevention, Atlanta, GA, United States

Katie A. McLaughlin Harvard University, Cambridge, MA, United States

John D. McLennan Department of Pediatrics, University of Calgary, Calgary, AB; Children's Hospital of Eastern Ontario-Research Institute, Ottawa, ON, Canada

Jill R. McTavish Department of Psychiatry & Behavioural Neurosciences, McMaster University; Offord Centre for Child Studies, Hamilton, ON, Canada

James Mercy Division of Violence Prevention, Centers for Disease Control and Prevention, Atlanta, GA, United States

Melissa T. Merrick Division of Violence Prevention, National Center for Injury Prevention and Control, Centers for Disease Control and Prevention, Atlanta, GA, United States

Assaf Oshri Department of Human Development and Family Science, The Youth Development Institute, The University of Georgia, Athens, GA; The Offord Center, McMaster University, Hamilton, ON, United States

Michelle M. Paluszek Department of Psychology, University of Regina, Regina, Canada

Caroline C. Piotrowski Department of Community Health Sciences, University of Manitoba; Children's Hospital Research Institute of Manitoba, Winnipeg, MB, Canada

Katie A. Ports Division of Violence Prevention, National Center for Injury Prevention and Control, Centers for Disease Control and Prevention, Atlanta, GA, United States

Natalie Sachs-Ericsson Department of Psychology, Florida State University, Tallahassee, FL, United States

Philip Scribano Perelman School of Medicine, University of Pennsylvania; Division of General Pediatrics, Center for Child Protection and Health, The Children's Hospital of Philadelphia, Philadelphia, PA, United States

Julia L. Sheffler Florida State University College of Medicine, Tallahassee, FL, United States

Margaret A. Sheridan University of North Carolina, Chapel Hill, NC, United States

Savanah Smith McMaster University, Hamilton, ON, Canada

Ian Stanley Department of Psychology, Florida State University, Tallahassee, FL, United States

Natalie Stavas The Children's Hospital of Philadelphia; Perelman School of Medicine, University of Pennsylvania, Philadelphia, PA, United States

Shannon Struck Department of Community Health Sciences, Max Rady College of Medicine, Rady Faculty of Health Sciences, University of Manitoba, Winnipeg, MB, Canada

Tamara L. Taillieu Department of Community Health Sciences, Max Rady College of Medicine, Rady Faculty of Health Sciences, University of Manitoba, Winnipeg, MB, Canada

Lil Tonmyr Public Health Agency of Canada, Ottawa, ON, Canada

Kelsey D. Vig Department of Psychology, University of Regina, Regina, Canada

Christine Wekerle McMaster University, Hamilton, ON, Canada

Preface

For many years, we have been interested in understanding varied aspects of childhood adversity in order to assist in the development of effective and accessible preventive and therapeutic interventions that might help reduce the prevalence of such experiences and their negative impacts on the mental and physical health of children and adults. As a consequence of these interests and our related empirical work, as well as indications of an increasing interest in adverse childhood experiences (ACEs) from clinicians, researchers, and policy makers, Elsevier approached us in 2017 with the idea of putting together a book that would cut across the interests of these audiences. This edited book is the result.

ACEs were first defined in the literature in 1998 as childhood exposures to emotional maltreatment, physical abuse, sexual abuse, and household dysfunction (e.g., exposure to violence against a mother or step mother and household members with problems with drugs or alcohol, depression or mental illness, suicide attempts, and incarceration). Over the last two decades, this literature has expanded to demonstrate the high prevalence of ACEs in the general population and the links between ACEs and mental and physical health outcomes, risky behaviors, and violence in adulthood. While we have learned a lot about ACEs over the past two decades, there are still many unanswered questions, such as what other experiences should be included as ACEs, is there evidence that screening for ACEs in a healthcare facility or by healthcare professionals leads to beneficial outcomes, how can we foster resilience following ACEs, and what can we do to effectively prevent ACEs from occurring in the first place. Likewise, while translation into practical preventive and therapeutic intervention strategies that may improve individual and societal health have been ongoing, much remains to be learned. To date, there have been few books published in the area of ACEs and, of those available, most have focused on treatment and recovery from ACEs. It is our hope that this book, written by some of the foremost experts, will further facilitate recognition and dissemination of ACEs-relevant empirical evidence in a manner that advances best clinical practices, prevention, research, and policy.

This book provides an overview that defines ACEs and lays the foundation for understanding their prevalence and co-occurrence, reviews the evidence linking ACEs and negative outcomes in youth and adults, addresses current controversies in the field, and uses the current evidence to inform policy and healthcare practice in efforts to prevent ACEs and to improve the health of those with an ACEs history. As such, the book is organized into four broad sections.

Section 1 covers the history of the original ACE Study and an overview of current efforts to address and prevent childhood trauma (Chapter 1: Twenty Years and Counting: The Past, Present, and Future of ACEs Research by Dube), various ACEs data collection systems and prevalence estimates (Chapter 2: ACEs: Definitions, Measurement, and Prevalence by Ford, Merrick, and Guinn), and inconsistencies in the ACEs definition and recommendations for its expansion (Chapter 3: Considerations for Expanding the Definition of ACEs by Afifi).

Section 2 focuses on the current state of knowledge regarding the outcomes of ACEs, including the impact of childhood adversity on mental health (Chapter 4: ACEs and Mental Health Outcomes by Sheffler, Stanley, and Sachs-Ericsson), the impact of childhood adversity on physical health (Chapter 5: ACEs and Physical Health Outcomes by Vig, Paluszek, and Asmundson), intimate partner and sexual violence (Chapter 6: ACEs, Sexual Violence, and Sexual Health by Wekerle, Hébert, Daigneault, Fortin-Langelier, and Smith), and adult violence (Chapter 7: ACEs and Violence in Adulthood by Taillieu, Garces Davila, and Struck).

Section 3 highlights several current controversies and new developments in the ACEs field, including the issue of whether or not to implement routine screening for ACEs (Chapter 8: Routine Screening for ACEs: Should We or Shouldn't We? by McLennan, McTavish, and MacMillan) and strategies for improving ACEs research (Chapter 9: Methodological Considerations in ACEs Research by Holden, Gower, and Chmielewski).

The fourth and final section is unique in its coverage of issues pertinent to policy, prevention, and the future of ACEs research, including chapters on the public health issues associated with ACEs (Chapter 10: The Public Health Issues of ACEs in Canada by Tonmyr, Lacroix, and Herbert), understanding the prevalence and outcomes of ACEs globally (Chapter 11: Global Perspective on ACEs by Massetti, Hughes, Bellis, and Mercy), preventive strategies (Chapter 12: Effective Prevention of ACEs by Brennan, Staves, and Scribano), neuroscience and ACEs-related neural adaptations (Chapter 13: ACEs and Neural Development by Sheridan and McLaughlin), ACEs-related resilience (Chapter 14: ACEs and Resilience: Methodological and Conceptual Issue by Oshri, Duprey, Liu, and Gonzalez), delivery of care (Chapter 15: ACEs and Trauma-Informed Care by Piotrowski), and providing children with positive relationships and environments (Chapter 16: Safe, Stable, Nurturing Environments for Children by Merrick, Ports, Guinn, and Ford). This final section, and the book, concludes with a chapter that sets the stage for the ACEs research agenda moving forward (Chapter 17: Current Knowledge and Future Directions for the ACEs Field by Afifi and Asmundson).

The selection of these chapters illustrates our current state of knowledge regarding the pervasive negative outcomes of ACEs on early and later life as well as the advances and obstacles faced by researchers, clinicians, and policy makers as they strive to develop and implement evidence-based preventive and intervention strategies. As such, this book will have broad applications. It will be useful as a primary text for clinical psychology, psychiatry, pediatrics, and community health residency programs. It will serve as a valuable supplement for advanced undergraduate and graduate students studying family violence, child maltreatment, abnormal psychology, social work, public health, and related topics. And, it should prove an invaluable resource for researchers, scholars, healthcare professionals, social welfare workers, child advocates, and policy makers working with those affected by ACEs.

Our hope, ultimately, is that this book will assist ACEs researchers in identifying and tackling the most pressing matters requiring empirical attention and that it will aid clinicians and policy makers in their efforts to deliver highly effective evidence-based strategies to prevent or reduce ACEs-related human suffering and enhance quality of life.

Gordon J.G. Asmundson
University of Regina, Regina, SK, Canada
Tracie O. Afifi
University of Manitoba, Winnipeg, MB, Canada

SECTION I

CHAPTER

1

Twenty years and counting: The past, present, and future of ACEs research

Shanta R. Dube

Department of Population Health Sciences, School of Public Health, Georgia State University, Atlanta, GA, United States

Introduction

A little over two decades ago, the Centers for Disease Control and Prevention (CDC) and Kaiser Permanente in San Diego launched the landmark CDC-Kaiser ACE Study (Felitti et al., 1998). This groundbreaking study of adverse childhood experiences (ACEs) documented the contribution of early-life stress and trauma to the leading and actual causes of death in the US across the lifespan. Since being launched, numerous ACEs efforts across various disciplines have focused on crossvalidation through study replications and research translation. Realizing that ACEs are widespread, multiple systems and settings are now actively applying the research findings.

The ACE Study was conducted among an adult cohort born between 1900 and 1978 who retrospectively assessed their childhood adversities. One of the most striking findings from the ACE Study is that within the cohort, all generations with one or more early-life adversities were at greater risk for substance abuse, mental illness, and perpetrating violence compared to those reporting no ACEs. Thus, ACEs science provides empirical support on the importance of breaking the intergenerational cycle of these early-life exposures. By virtue of these findings, a *dual-* or *multigenerational* approach emphasizes the importance

Adverse Childhood Experiences
https://doi.org/10.1016/B978-0-12-816065-7.00001-X

of recognizing ACEs among adults to promote their healing and recovery, in order to prevent future exposure to the next generation of children. This chapter outlines the history of the CDC-Kaiser ACE Study, citing the original published studies. Current efforts to address and prevent early childhood trauma along with proposed future directions are discussed.

Past: Initial clinical observations leading to the ACE Study

In the early 1990s, Felitti (1993) conducted a case-control study to examine how life events correlated with obesity among adults entering a weight management program compared to a control group of nonobese, slender adults. Through interviews, the study indicated that the prevalence of childhood abuse (e.g., sexual and physical), early parental loss, and parental alcoholism was higher among obese adults compared to nonobese, slender adults. The study also revealed that obesity among adults served as their *protection* from unwanted attention and excess food intake as a means to cope with emotional distress. His research also documented the correlation between current depression and current family and marital problems in obese adults compared to nonobese, slender adults. The findings from this initial observational study served as a springboard for the ACE Study (Felitti et al., 1998), which would be one of the most extensive epidemiological studies to examine the long-term health consequences of multiple, co-occurring forms of childhood abuse, childhood neglect, and related household stressors.

From 1995 to 1997, over 17,000 adult health maintenance organization (HMO) members who made appointments for an overall health assessment took part in the ACE Study across two separate waves. Two weeks after their clinic visit at Kaiser Permanente's Department of Preventive Medicine in San Diego, California, individuals were sent the Family Health History Questionnaire (Felitti et al., 1998) to complete in the privacy of their home. In the first wave, the Family Health History Questionnaire included eight categories of ACEs. Assessment included three forms of abuse (i.e., physical, emotional, and sexual) and exposure to five types of household dysfunction while growing up (i.e., witnessing mother being treated violently, living with substance abuse in the home, living with mentally ill household member, absence of household member due to incarceration, and parental discord/divorce).

Felitti et al. (1998) examined seven of the eight ACEs—physical abuse, emotional abuse, sexual abuse, growing up in a home exposed to untreated mental illness, household substance abuse, witnessing mother treated violently, and absence of household member due to incarceration—in relationship to the actual and leading causes of death in the US. In the second wave of the ACE Study, measures of physical and emotional neglect were added, increasing the total number of childhood adversities examined to a total of 10 (Dube et al., 2001).

The CDC-Kaiser ACE Study led to the following summary findings:

(1) Childhood exposure to abuse, neglect, domestic violence, and related household stressors are widespread and commonly occur across all populations. In the Kaiser Permanente study cohort that was predominately White, well-educated adults with good healthcare, close to two-thirds of the respondents reported experiencing at least one adversity, and close to 40% reported two or more ACEs (Felitti et al., 1998). Additionally, 1 in 6 men and 1 in 4 women experienced childhood sexual abuse (CSA), with the contribution of CSA to depression, substance use, and marital problems in adulthood being similar for both genders, highlighting the importance in recognizing that all children, girls and boys, are vulnerable to this form of abuse (Dube et al., 2005).

(2) Childhood exposure to abuse, neglect, domestic violence, and related household stressors are an interrelated group of commonly occurring adverse childhood experiences. When exposed to any one category of ACEs, 81% to 98% of respondents reported experiencing one or more additional childhood adversities and 58% to 90% of respondents reported experiencing two or more ACEs (Dong et al., 2004). By enumerating the total number of childhood adversities reported, the ACEs score provided evidence of dose-response relationships between childhood adversities and numerous health, social, and behavioral outcomes (Felitti et al., 1998).

(3) Childhood exposure to abuse, neglect, domestic violence, and related household stressors contribute to important social, behavioral, and health outcomes across the lifespan. ACEs are associated with a wide range of health problems that begin in adolescence as behavioral risks and continue into adulthood as a disease, behavioral risks, and social outcomes of importance in society today (see Fig. 1). The Life Course Epidemiology Model (Ben-Shlomo & Kuh, 2002), which includes recognition of these experiences as nonbiological exposures with an intergenerational cycle, is an essential framework by which the long-term impact of ACEs must be studied.

(4) Childhood exposure to abuse, neglect, domestic violence, and related household stressors contribute to health outcomes that transcend a 100 years of social and secular trends to change behaviors and prevent disease (Dube, Anda, Felitti, Dong, & Giles, 2003). Study participants born between 1900 and 1978 who reported ACEs had an increased odds of alcohol problems, smoking, illicit drug use, sexual

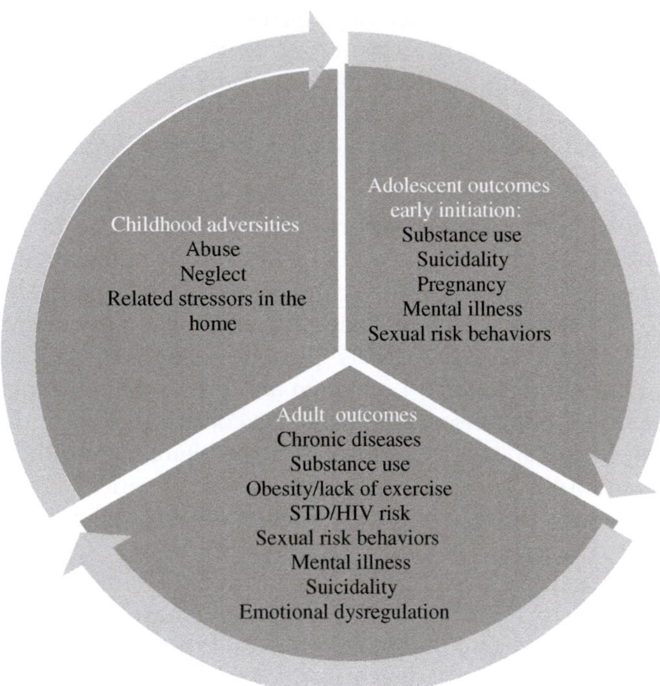

FIG. 1 The cycle and impact of ACEs across the lifespan and generations.

risk behaviors, and mental illness across four separate birth cohorts from 1900 to 1978 (Dube et al., 2003). The findings from this particular study support the supposition that ACEs have a strong influence on health, despite the time period when individuals were born.

(5) Childhood exposure to abuse, neglect, domestic violence, and related household stressors early in the lifespan impact healthy neurobiological development. Prenatally and in early childhood, neural pathways in the brain are rapidly developing based on sensory exposure to experiences both positive and negative. Persons exposed to early life trauma are more likely to have greater limbic irritability than persons not exposed to early life trauma, as measured by brain-wave abnormalities using electroencephalograms (Teicher et al., 2003). Compared to nonabused individuals, magnetic resonance imaging has revealed that severely sexually abused women have reductions in hippocampal volumes and that intracranial and cerebral volumes among maltreated children also show reductions compared to nonmaltreated children (Driessen et al., 2000).

Present: Increasing integration of ACEs science

Raising awareness: ACEs research, surveillance, and assessments

As a result of the overwhelming scientific evidence documenting the neurodevelopmental impact of ACEs, the American Academy of Pediatrics (AAP) released a policy statement calling for the pediatric community to heed the science and address and prevent childhood toxic stress (American Academy of Pediatrics, 2012a, 2012b). The World Health Organization (2011) also recognizes the importance of ACEs science to support the Global ACE Research Network that assesses ACEs across different countries (http://www.who.int/violence_injury_prevention/violence/activities/adverse_childhood_experiences/en/).

The ACEs science was also integral to informing the 2014 Substance Abuse Mental Health Services Administration (SAMHSA, 2014) Tip 57: Trauma-Informed Care (TIC) In Behavioral Health (http://www.samhsa.gov/nctic/trauma-interventions). As outlined by the TIC framework, ACEs are not the only form of childhood trauma that can occur. For example, other exposures may include natural disasters, community violence, peer victimization, living in poverty, and loss, to name a few. Finkelhor, Shattuck, Turner, and Hamby (2015) make a valid recommendation to revise the ACEs inventory and include other forms of childhood adversities, to provide a better measure of predicting mental and physical health problems. The TIC framework also emphasizes the use of specific principles and strategies when working with populations. The TIC framework follows these principles: (1) Realizing that trauma is widespread (2) recognizing the symptoms of trauma, and (3) resisting retraumatization by responding with support, safety, collaboration, nonjudgment, and nurturance (http://www.samhsa.gov/nctic/trauma-interventions).

Surveillance is a critical public health practice for gathering credible evidence to assess the burden of ACEs in the population. For example, 10 years after the launch of the original ACE Study, the Behavioral Risk Factor Surveillance System (BRFSS) ACEs Optional Module was developed to provide state health departments a tool to assess estimates of ACEs in the adult population. The BRFSS is a state-based surveillance system administered yearly to gather data on leading indicators for health and chronic disease. While the initial development of the ACEs module included all 10 ACEs, cognitive testing and programmatic decisions were made to cut the questionnaire due to length. Therefore, the final BRFSS ACEs Optional Module includes only the original eight ACEs from Wave I. From 2009 to 2017, multiple US states have administered the ACEs BRFSS questionnaire (Centers for Disease Control and Prevention, 2003).

Applying public health practice through the surveillance of ACEs across populations provides states with the data needed to assess the burden of the problem and inform policies and programs. In 2009, only six states administered the ACEs BRFSS questionnaire. Currently, all but about eight states have administered it at some point in time between 2009 and 2017 (see Fig. 2A and B).

Various sectors have utilized formal ACEs assessments, not for diagnosis, but rather for increasing knowledge about the populations they serve. Informal ACEs assessments are also increasingly occurring in educational settings as part of TIC implementation. While conducting ACEs assessments is still very controversial (Dube, 2018; Finkelhor, 2017), there is a general sense of the importance of understanding trauma exposures to help individuals and organizations increase the realization and awareness about how widespread ACEs are in populations. For example, a study among medical school residents indicated that 80% believed that screening for ACEs should be part of their role (Tink, Tink, Turin, & Kelly, 2017).

The field must not view ACEs assessments as diagnostic tools, but rather a window through which to understand health from the perspective of the individual. The CDC-Kaiser ACE Study was launched, based on the early clinical observations made by Felitti (1993). Unbeknownst to him, he utilized Arthur Kleinman's Explanatory Model of Illness (Kleinman, Loustaunua, & Sobo, 1997) to understand obesity and being overweight from the perspective of the patients. A purely objective view of the individual tells about the disease, whereas a subjective view provides the *why* and, thus, reinforces the need to understand that these types of experiences can impact well-being.

Promoting acceptance: Policy to address and prevent ACEs

ACEs science has caught the attention of policymakers. According to the May 2018 report by the US Association of State and Territorial Health Officials (ASTHO), several states have included statutory language to address and prevent ACEs in four sectors, including child welfare, education, justice, and healthcare. In 2011, Washington included legislative language that required a multisector stakeholder planning group to convene around prevention of ACEs. While Washington was the first state, California and Vermont have up to seven initiatives that focus on addressing and preventing ACEs. According to ASTHO tracking, California is proposing funding for systems-approaches to provide children exposed to ACEs needed supports for their well-being. Currently, most southern US states (with exception to Florida) have not incorporated legislation related to ACEs or TIC.

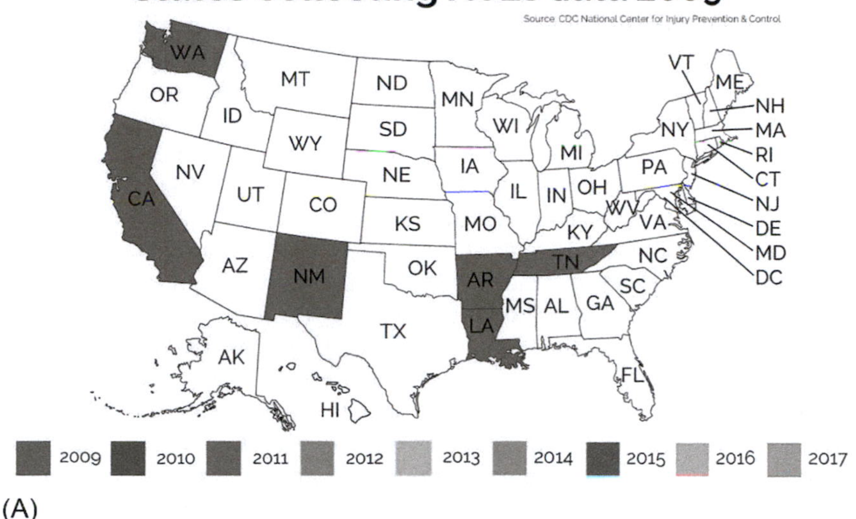

(A)

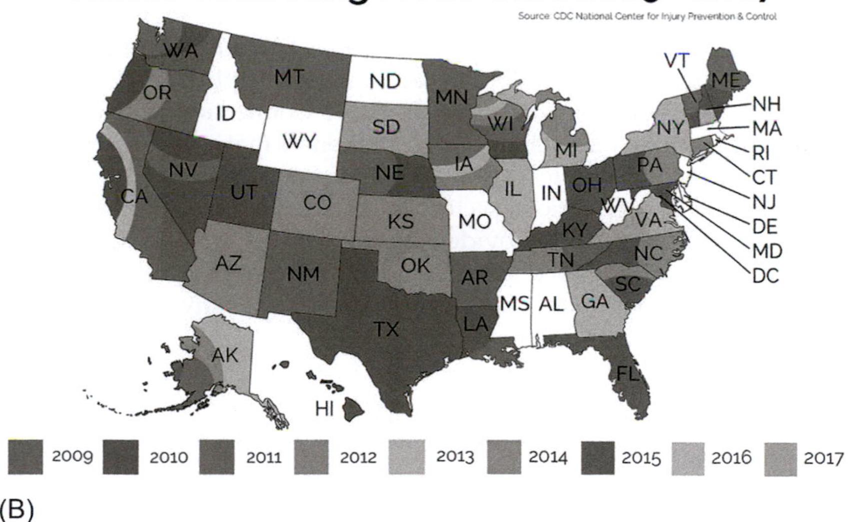

(B)

FIG. 2 (A) Six states that administered the ACEs BRFSS questionnaire in 2009. (B) States that administered the ACEs BRFSS questionnaire between 2009 and 2017. Figures obtained by permission from ACEs Connection (https://acesconnection.com/g/state-aces-action-group/blog/behavioral-risk-factor-surveillance-system-brfss).

Active adoption: Efforts to address and prevent ACEs

There is a plethora of grassroots efforts underway that actively adopt ACEs science. Rather than a purely top-down approach, communities and systems of care apply ACEs science to educate and inform systems that work with children. To begin with, there is a growing interest and recognition that assessment of ACEs is a needed component when delivering TIC. Researchers have systematically investigated the feasibility of various ACEs assessments across different populations and settings and found them acceptable to administer (Bethell et al., 2017). Pediatricians who reported conducting ACEs assessments were more likely to do so if they believed they could influence parenting behaviors (Kerker et al., 2016). They were also more likely to assess ACEs because they believed that it is within the bounds of pediatric care (Kerker et al., 2016). Dr. Nadine Burke-Harris has actively adopted the ACEs science (https://centerforyouthwellness.org/translating-aces-science/). Her early awareness and acceptance of ACEs as the root factors of disease and poor health in her patient population are why assessments of childhood adversities are a regular practice in her clinic. Lastly, parenting interventions focused on improving caregiver-child attachment utilize ACEs assessments among both the parent and child as an early intervention to prevent the intergenerational cycle (Murphy et al., 2014, 2016).

To document the wave of ACEs science adoption both nationally and internationally, Jane Stevens founded and launched ACEs Connection in 2012 (https://acesconnection.com). ACEs Connection is a web-based community open to researchers and practitioners that provides users with the latest information on tools, training, and practices used to address and prevent ACEs across various sectors and settings. Through the dissemination of the information provided on this web platform, ACEs science best practices can be shared and discussed. The grassroots efforts include training educational staff on how to build safe, supportive, and nurturing learning environments in school settings.

Future of ACEs science

There is a tremendous momentum toward increasing awareness, acceptance, and adoption of the ACEs science at present. Specific areas of continued research, education, training, and practice will be needed, as outlined in the following content.

Research

Timing, intensity, and frequency of ACEs exposure. Research must continue to investigate all 10 ACEs, along with other types of childhood adversities such as growing up in poverty, peer violence, and community violence.

Additional research on the timing of when ACEs occur, the intensity, and frequency during various developmental stages will provide the field with additional insights into mechanisms through which early-life adversity impacts health across the lifespan. Research is also needed to further understand the specificity of pregnant women's exposure to adversity-related stressors and their impact on the developing fetus.

Resiliency, assets, and dimensions of well-being. In addition to assessing ACEs and associated health outcomes, measures of resiliency, assets, and multiple dimensions of well-being are essential in providing a more complete picture of coping and adaptation. This was an understated limitation of the CDC-Kaiser ACEs Study; indeed, while two-thirds of the participants in the ACE Study experienced ACEs, there were only two studies published (Dube, Felitti, & Rishi, 2013; Hillis et al., 2010) that examined protective or health-promoting factors. In an analysis of Wave II CDC-Kaiser data, Hillis et al. (2010) investigated the contribution of childhood family strengths (i.e., family closeness, support, loyalty, protection, love, importance, and responsiveness to health needs) to adolescent pregnancy and psychosocial consequences. The results indicated that, in the presence of ACEs, these factors were strongly protective against teenage pregnancy, early initiation of sexual activity, and long-term psychosocial consequences. Using the same data set, Dube et al. (2013) examined evidence-based protective and health promoting factors (i.e., physical activity, smoking abstinence, educational attainment, and social/emotional support) in association with health-related quality of life among adults who reported at least one adversity. We found that physical and mental health was statistically significantly better for those who indicated regular physical activity, smoking abstinence, having at least two or more persons to talk to about their feelings, and those with at least a high school diploma. A similar analysis was conducted using the 2010 BRFSS (Dube & Rishi, 2017), to examine mentally unhealthy days (MUDS) and physically unhealthy days (PUDS) as the outcome. We found that, among adults who reported at least one adversity, the mean number of MUDS and PUDS was statistically significantly lower for those who indicated they exercise regularly, abstain from smoking, frequently engage in social support, and obtained a high school diploma or higher. Future research must consider not only the contribution of ACEs to risk behaviors and adverse health outcomes, but also understand among those who have experienced ACEs and early trauma, the means by which they positively coped and adapted to early-life stress and trauma.

Education and training

Health professional curriculum. Medical schools, public health schools, allied health profession schools, and mental health and counseling curriculum have not fully integrated ACEs science and TIC instruction.

The lack of training in professional schools does a disservice to population health sciences. More effort is needed to ensure that ACEs science and TIC training integrates into medical school and other allied health curricula.

Trauma-informed competency. Education and training that follows the SAMHSA TIC framework require adults who work with children not only to realize trauma is widespread and recognize the symptoms of trauma, but also to understand in themselves their reactions to safe and threatening situations. Focused on adult learning theories, The Why and How of Trauma-Informed Care© (Dube, 2017) is a curriculum focused on increasing knowledge about *why* trauma-informed care is needed. The *how* focuses on helping adults to engage in self-reflective learning and practice to become better aware of their reactions to stress (Mezirow, 1991; Schacter, 1992; Taylor, 1996) and provide them with evidence-based practices for self-care. Often overlooked, self-care is an essential tool for resisting re-traumatization in the TIC framework (Dube, 2017).

Practice

Use of a dual- or multigenerational approach. The large proportion of adults (i.e., two-thirds) who experienced at least one childhood adversity are testament to the importance of understanding that the occurrence of ACEs is far more common than is realized. The large proportion of adults with at least one childhood adversity also emphasizes the importance of tertiary prevention of ACEs-related outcomes in adults as a critical effort to prevent the exposures from occurring in children (Dube et al., 2013; Dube & Rishi, 2017). For example, outcomes associated with ACEs, such as substance use problems (e.g., alcohol problems), are symptoms of trauma that may perpetuate the same ACEs to the next generation, giving rise to the intergenerational cycle of these exposures (Dube, Anda, Felitti, Edwards, & Croft, 2002). For example, an ACEs score of four or more was associated with a threefold increase in the likelihood of marrying an individual with alcohol problems after controlling for history of parental alcoholism (Dube et al., 2002). Childhood abuse, neglect, and related stressors commonly occur in families with alcohol problems, and they significantly increase the risk of personal problems with alcohol or marriage to individuals with alcohol problems later in life, heightening the likelihood that the intergenerational cycle of ACEs will occur (Dube et al., 2002).

There are no vaccinations or antibiotics to prevent or treat ACEs; therefore, in addition to primary and secondary prevention in children and adolescents, models of healing and recovery (Cortez et al., 2011; Todahl, Walters, Bharwdi, & Dube, 2014) are needed for tertiary prevention of outcomes associated with ACEs among adult survivors. Primary prevention of ACEs must necessarily include the tertiary prevention of ACEs outcomes in adult caregivers (Sanders & Hall, 2018). To break the intergenerational cycle of ACEs, we must also give attention to adults with ACEs histories who raise or work with children.

Implementing integrative health approaches. Medical science has made tremendous strides to influence longevity and disease prognosis. However, it is reductionist, costly, and creates societal dependence. Taking a step back, we can discover the steps needed in the journey to heal, recover, and move toward health and well-being across generations. Mind-body sciences provide tools through which we can build resiliency and promote healing and recovery. Research studies on the 5000 year old practices of Ayurveda, Yoga, Pranayama (breathing), meditation, and mindfulness have documented their promise in reducing symptoms of stress and promoting resiliency (Baer, 2003; Cherkin, Sherman, Balderson, et al., 2016; Jacobs, Benson, & Friedman, 1996; Lazar et al., 2000; Nahin, Boineau, Khalsa, Stussman, & Weber, 2016; Newberg, Pourdehnad, Alavi, & d'Aquili, 2003; Rhodes, Spinazzola, & van der Kolk, 2016; Smith et al., 2011; van der Kolk et al., 2014). Inherently, mindfulness naturally becomes a part of TIC approaches, which require adult learners to utilize reflective practice and learning (Mezirow, 1991; Taylor, 1996) to address and prevent ACEs and their outcomes at the primary, secondary, and tertiary levels.

Summary

The groundbreaking ACEs Study research has informed policy and practice across multiple disciplines and sectors, especially with regards to implementing TIC. The next several decades will rely on research to increase our knowledge about the specific developmental mechanisms through which these early-life stressors act and the tangible ways to promote resiliency and healing. The integration of ACEs science and innovative best practices for TIC as standard curriculum in educational institutions will be essential and transformational for addressing population health. Considering that ACEs often go unresolved among adults who work with or raise children will emphasize the importance of taking comprehensive approach that includes integrating *three-level* prevention of ACEs across multiple generations.

Disclosure statement

The author has no financial conflicts of interest to report.

Any contents taken from this chapter must be properly cited: Shanta R. Dube, 2018©.

References

American Academy of Pediatrics. (2012a). Policy statement: early childhood adversity, toxic stress, and the role of the pediatrician: translating developmental science into lifelong health. *Pediatrics, 129*(1), e224–e231. http://pediatrics.aappublications.org/content/129/1/e224.long?trendmd-shared=0. Reaffirmed July 2016a.

American Academy of Pediatrics. (2012b). Technical report: the lifelong effects of early childhood adversity and toxic stress. *Pediatrics, 129*(1), e232–e246. http://pediatrics.aappublications.org/content/129/1/e232. Reaffirmed July 2016b.

Baer, R. A. (2003). Mindfulness training as a clinical intervention: a conceptual and empirical review. *Clinical Psychology: Science and Practice, 10*, 125–143.

Ben-Shlomo, Y., & Kuh, D. (2002). A life course approach to chronic disease epidemiology: conceptual models, empirical challenges and interdisciplinary perspectives. *International Journal of Epidemiology, 31*(2), 285–293.

Bethell, C. D., Carle, A., Hudziak, J., Gombojav, N., Powers, K., Wade, R., & Braveman, P. (2017). Methods to assess adverse childhood experiences of children and families: toward approaches to promote child well-being in policy and practice. *Academic Pediatrics, 17*, S51–S69.

Centers for Disease Control and Prevention. (2003). Public health surveillance for behavioral risk factors in a changing environment. Recommendations from the behavioral risk factor surveillance team. *Morbidity and Mortality Weekly Report. Recommendations and Reports, 52*, 1–12.

Cherkin, D. C., Sherman, K. J., Balderson, B. H., et al. (2016). Effects of mindfulness-based stress reduction vs cognitive-behavioral therapy and usual care on back pain and functional limitations among adults with chronic low back pain: a randomized clinical trial. *JAMA, 315*(12), 1240–1249.

Cortez, P., Dumas, T., Joyce, J., Olson, D., Peters, S., Todahl, J., … Wilde, R. (2011). Survivor voices: co-learning, re-connection, and healing through community action research and engagement (CARE). *Progress in Community Health Partnerships: Research, Education and Action, summer 2011*, 133–142.

Dong, M., Loo, C., Dube, S. R., Williamson, D. F., Thompson, T., Giles, W. H., … Anda, R. F. (2004). Interrelatedness of multiple adverse childhood experiences. *Child Abuse and Neglect, 28*(7), 771–784.

Driessen, M., Herrmann, J., Stahl, K., Zwaan, M., Meier, S., Hill, A., … Petersen, D. (2000). Magnetic resonance imaging volumes of the hippocampus and the amygdala in women with borderline personality disorder and early traumatization. *Archives of General Psychiatry, 57*, 1115–1122.

Dube, S. R., Anda, R. F., Felitti, V. J., Croft, J. B., Edwards, V. J., & Giles, W. H. (2001). Growing up with parental alcohol abuse: exposure to childhood abuse, neglect and household dysfunction. *Child Abuse and Neglect, 25*(12), 1627–1640.

Dube, S. R., Anda, R. F., Felitti, V. J., Edwards, V. J., & Croft, J. B. (2002). Adverse childhood experiences and personal alcohol abuse as an adult. *Addictive Behaviors, 27*(5), 713–725.

Dube, S. R., Anda, R. F., Felitti, V. J., Dong, M., & Giles, W. H. (2003). The impact of adverse childhood experiences on health problems: evidence from four birth cohorts dating back to 1900. *Preventive Medicine, 37*(3), 268–277.

Dube, S. R., Anda, R. F., Whitfield, C. L., Brown, D. W., Felitti, V. J., Dong, M., & Giles, W. H. (2005). Long-term consequences of childhood sexual abuse by gender of victim. *American Journal of Preventive Medicine, 28*, 430–438.

Dube, S. R., Felitti, V. J., & Rishi, S. (2013). Moving beyond childhood adversity: association between salutogenic factors and subjective well-being among adult survivors of trauma. In K. Rutkowski & M. Linden (Eds.), *Hurting memories and beneficial forgetting*. London, England: Elsevier, Inc, ISBN: 978-0-12-398393-0.

Dube, S. R., & Rishi, S. (2017). Utilizing the salutogenic paradigm to investigate well-being among adult survivors of childhood sexual abuse and other adversities. *Child Abuse and Neglect, 26*. https://doi.org/10.1016/j.chiabu.2017.01.026. pii: S0145-2134(17)30037-6. [Epub ahead of print].

Dube, S. R. (2017). *Understanding the why and how of trauma-informed practices*. In: *Georgia Head Start Association conference Spring 2017. Oral presentation, May 11, 2017, St. Simons Island, GA*.

Dube, S. R. (2018). Continuing conversations about adverse childhood experiences (ACEs) screening: a public health perspective. *Child Abuse & Neglect*, https://doi.org/10.1016/j.chiabu.2018.03.007.

Felitti, V. J. (1993). Childhood sexual abuse, depression, and family dysfunction in adult obese patients: a case control study. *Southern Medical Journal*, *86*, 732–736.

Felitti, V. J., Anda, R. F., Nordenberg, D., Williamson, D. F., Spitz, A. M., Edwards, V., … Marks, J. S. (1998). Relationship of childhood abuse and household dysfunction to many of the leading causes of death in adults. *American Journal of Preventive Medicine, 14*, 245–258.

Finkelhor, D. (2017). Screening for adverse childhood experiences (ACEs): Cautions and suggestions. *Child Abuse & Neglect*. https://doi.org/10.1016/j.chiabu.2017.07.016.

Finkelhor, D., Shattuck, A., Turner, H., & Hamby, S. (2015). A revised inventory of adverse childhood experiences. *Child Abuse & Neglect*, *48*, 13–21.

Hillis, S. D., Anda, R. F., Dube, S. R., Felitti, V. J., Marchbanks, P. A., Macaluso, M., & Marks, J. S. (2010). The protective effect of family strengths in childhood against adolescent pregnancy and its long-term psychosocial consequences. *The Permanente Journal*, *14*, 18–27.

Jacobs, G. D., Benson, H., & Friedman, R. (1996). Topographic EEG mapping of the relaxation response. *Biofeedback and Self Regulation*, *21*(2), 121–129.

Kerker, B. D., Storfer-Isser, A., Szilagyi, M., Stein, R. E. K., Garner, A., O'Connor, K. G., … Horwitz, S. M. (2016). Do pediatricians ask about adverse childhood experiences in pediatric primary care? *Academic Pediatrics*, *16*(2), 154–160. https://doi.org/10.1016/j.acap.2015.08.002.

Kleinman, A., Loustaunua, M. O., & Sobo, E. J. (1997). *The cultural context of health, illness, and medicine*. Westport, CT: Bergin & Garvey.

Lazar, S. W., Bush, G., Gollub, R. L., Fricchione, G. L., Khalsa, G., & Benson, H. (2000). Functional brain mapping of the relaxation response and meditation. *Neuroreport*, *11*(7), 1581–1585.

Mezirow, J. (1991). *Transformative dimensions of adult learning*. San Francisco: Jossey-Bass.

Murphy, A., Steele, M., Dube, S. R., Bate, J., Bonuck, K., Meissner, P., … Steele, H. (2014). Adverse childhood experiences (ACEs) questionnaire and adult attachment interview (AAI): implications for parent child relationships. *Child Abuse and Neglect*, *8*(2), 224–233. https://doi.org/10.1016/j.chiabu.2013.09.004.

Murphy, A., Steele, H., Steele, M., Allman, B., Kastner, T., & Dube, S. R. (2016). Adverse childhood experiences: implications for trauma informed behavioral health care. In R. Briggs (Ed.), *Integrated early childhood behavioral health in primary care: A guide to implementation and evaluation*. Switzerland: Springer International Publishing Switzerland, ISBN: 978-3-319-31813-4.

Nahin, R. L., Boineau, R., Khalsa, P. S., Stussman, B. J., & Weber, W. J. (2016). Evidence-based evaluation of complementary health approaches for pain management in the United States. *Mayo Clinic Proceedings*, *91*(9), 1292–1306.

Newberg, A., Pourdehnad, M., Alavi, A., & d'Aquili, E. G. (2003). Cerebral blood flow during meditative prayer: preliminary findings and methodological issues. *Perceptual and Motor Skills*, *97*(2), 625–630.

Rhodes, A., Spinazzola, J., & van der Kolk, B. (2016). Yoga for adult women with chronic PTSD: a long-term follow-up study. *Journal of Alternative and Complementary Medicine*, *22*(3), 189–196. https://doi.org/10.1089/acm.2014.0407 [Epub 2016 Feb 10].

Sanders, M. R., & Hall, S. L. (2018). Trauma-informed care in the newborn intensive care unit: promoting safety, security and connectedness. *Journal of Perinatology*, *38*, 3–10.

Schacter, D. L. (1992). Implicit knowledge: new perspectives on unconscious processes. *Proceedings of the National Academy of Science*, *89*, 1113–1117.

Smith, B. W., Ortiz, J. A., Steffen, L. E., Tooley, E. M., Wiggins, K. T., Yeater, E. A., et al. (2011). Mindfulness is associated with fewer PTSD symptoms, depressive symptoms, physical symptoms, and alcohol problems in urban firefighters. *Journal of Consulting and Clinical Psychology*, *79*, 613–617.

Substance Abuse and Mental Health Administration. (2014). https://store.samhsa.gov/system/files/sma14-4816.pdf (Accessed December 27, 2018).

Taylor, E. W. (1996). Transformative learning theory: a neurobiological perspective of the role of emotions and unconscious ways of knowing. *International Journal of Lifelong Education*, *20*(3), 218–236. http://www.samhsa.gov/nctic/trauma-interventions. (Accessed December 24, 2018).

Teicher, M. H., Andersen, S. L., Polcari, A., Anderson, C. M., Navalta, C. P., & Kim, D. M. (2003). The neurobiological consequences of early stress and childhood maltreatment. *Neuroscience and Biobehavioral Reviews*, *27*(1–2), 33–44.

Tink, W., Tink, J. C., Turin, T. C., & Kelly, M. (2017). Adverse childhood experiences: survey of resident practice, knowledge, and attitude. *Family Medicine*, *49*, 7–13.

Todahl, J. L., Walters, E., Bharwdi, D., & Dube, S. R. (2014). Trauma healing: a mixed methods study of personal and community-based healing. *Journal of Aggression, Maltreatment & Trauma*, *23*(4), 611–632.

van der Kolk, B. A., Stone, L., West, J., Rhodes, A., Emerson, D., Suvak, M., & Spinazzola, J. (2014). Yoga as an adjunctive treatment for posttraumatic stress disorder: a randomized controlled trial. *The Journal of Clinical Psychiatry*, *75*(6), e559–e565. https://doi.org/10.4088/JCP.13m08561.

World Health Organization. (2011). *Adverse childhood experiences international questionnaire (ACE-IQ)*. Available at: http://www.who.int/violence_injury_prevention/violence/activities/adverse_childhood_experiences/en/. (Accessed December 24, 2018).

CHAPTER

2

ACEs: Definitions, measurement, and prevalence☆

Katie A. Ports, Derek C. Ford, Melissa T. Merrick, Angie S. Guinn

Division of Violence Prevention, National Center for Injury Prevention and Control, Centers for Disease Control and Prevention, Atlanta, GA, United States

Introduction

Childhood experiences, both positive and negative, have a tremendous impact on lifelong health and opportunity. They provide the building blocks for future learning, behavior, and health, providing the brain a sturdy foundation for future development. Early adverse experiences like child abuse, neglect, or substance abuse in the household can impede the progress of a strong foundation, affecting brain architecture and optimal development (Shonkoff, 2016). While some degree of adversity is a normal and essential part of human development, exposure to frequent and prolonged adversity can result in a toxic stress response (Shonkoff, 2016). Toxic stress can disrupt the development of brain architecture and other organ systems, increasing the risk for unhealthy coping behaviors, disease, and cognitive impairment throughout the life course (Shonkoff, 2016). These broad effects on health and well-being make early childhood experiences an important public health issue.

Childhood experiences, trauma, and maltreatment have long been associated with healthy development across diverse fields (e.g., developmental psychology, pediatrics, child welfare, social work). However, it was not until the late 1990s when researchers from the Centers for Disease Control and Prevention (CDC) and Kaiser Permanente collaborated on a

☆ The findings and conclusions in this report are those of the authors and do not necessarily represent the official position of the Centers for Disease Control and Prevention.

https://doi.org/10.1016/B978-0-12-816065-7.00002-1

study that highlighted the connections between childhood adversity and adult health outcomes (Felitti et al., 1998). As a result, childhood adversity gained recognition as an important public health issue. Much of the foundational research in this area has been referred to as adverse childhood experiences or ACEs. ACEs is a term used to refer to a collection of potentially traumatic exposures that individuals may experience during childhood ages 0 to 18 years. Exposure to ACEs is related to increased risk for a host of negative health outcomes and can limit life opportunities, including educational attainment and employment (Felitti et al., 1998; Gilbert et al., 2015; Metzler, Merrick, Klevens, Ports, & Ford, 2017), which have far-reaching impacts beyond a single time-period, person, or generation. The wide-ranging health and social consequences of ACEs underscore the importance of preventing ACEs before they happen.

Preventing public health issues, including ACEs, requires defining the problem, measuring the problem, and then using data to inform action. ACEs data can help identify the size and nature of the problem, how to best direct prevention resources, and allow researchers and policy makers to monitor the ultimate impact of any interventions (such as a new program or policy). Researchers, practitioners, communities, states, and countries around the world are collecting ACEs data, but what is included as ACEs varies by study, population of interest, and time, among other things. In this chapter, an overview of several ACEs data collection systems, including the CDC-Kaiser Permanente ACE Study and the Behavioral Risk Factor Surveillance System, will be provided. Prevalence of ACEs, as determined from these surveys, as well as directions for future research and implications for policy and practice will also be discussed.

Measuring ACEs

CDC and Kaiser Permanente ACE Study

In a seminal investigation of the impact of childhood adversity on subsequent physical and mental health, researchers conducting the CDC-Kaiser Permanente ACE Study asked adults to retrospectively report on their experiences occurring prior to 19 years of age (Felitti et al., 1998). In this ACE Study, 10 ACEs categories comprising three overall domains of ACEs were measured: *Child Abuse* (physical, emotional, and sexual abuse), *Neglect* (physical and emotional neglect), *and Household Challenges* (mental illness in the household, substance abuse in the household, divorce/separation, parental incarceration, and mother treated violently). The ACEs questions were included in two waves of data collection occurring in 1995 and 1997; however, neglect items were only included in the second wave of data collection in 1997 (Dong et al., 2004). These 10 ACEs categories were constructed from 28 survey items, which were selected and adapted from several validated measures of sexual history, violence, and traumatic childhood experiences, including the Wyatt Sex History Questionnaire (Wyatt, 1985), the Conflict Tactics Scales (CTS; Straus & Gelles, 1990), and the Childhood Trauma Questionnaire (CTQ; Bernstein et al., 1994). The preambles, item content, and response options for each item can be found in Table 1.

Typically, responses to the survey items are converted to reflect a dichotomous exposure to ACEs—never exposed versus exposed. Exposure to these ACEs is operationalized here. These definitions have been used extensively in previously published ACE Study manuscripts (e.g., Felitti et al., 1998; Ports et al., 2016).

TABLE 1 ACEs Items Included in the CDC-Kaiser ACE Study

Item	Preamble and content	ACE category
During your first 18 years of life:		
1	Did you live with anyone who was a problem drinker or alcoholic?[a]	Household Substance Abuse
2	Did you live with anyone who used street drugs?[a]	Household Substance Abuse
3	Was anyone in your household depressed or mentally ill?[a]	Household Mental Illness
4	Did anyone in your household attempt to commit suicide?[a]	Household Mental Illness
5	Were your parents ever separated or divorced?[a]	Parental Separation/Divorce
6	Did anyone in your household ever go to prison?[a]	Incarcerated Household Member
While you were growing up, during your first 18 years of life:		
7	You didn't have enough to eat.[d]	Physical Neglect[b]
8	You know there was someone to take care of you and protect you.[d]	Physical Neglect[b]
9	Your parents were too drunk or high to take care of the family.[d]	Physical Neglect[b]
10	You had to wear dirty clothes.[d]	Physical Neglect[b]
11	There was someone to take you to the doctor if you needed it.[d]	Physical Neglect[b]
12	There was someone in your family who helped you feel important or special.[d]	Emotional Neglect[b]

Continued

TABLE 1 ACE Items Included in the CDC-Kaiser ACE Study—cont'd

Item	Preamble and content	ACE category
13	You felt loved.[d]	Emotional Neglect[b]
14	People in your family looked out for each other.[d]	Emotional Neglect[b]
15	People in your family felt close to each other.[d]	Emotional Neglect[b]
16	Your family was a source of strength and support.[d]	Emotional Neglect[b]
Sometimes parents or other adults hurt children. While you were growing up, during your first 18 years of life, how often did a parent, stepparent, or adult living in your home:		
17	Swear at you, insult you, or put you down?[c]	Emotional Abuse
18	Act in a way that made you afraid that you might be physically hurt?[c]	Emotional Abuse
19	Actually push, grab, shove, slap you or throw something at you?[c]	Physical Abuse
20	Hit you so hard that you had marks or were injured?[c]	Physical Abuse
Sometimes physical blows occur between parents. While you were growing up in your first 18 years of life, how often did your father (or stepfather) or mother's boyfriend do any of these things to your mother (or stepmother)?		
21	Push, grab, slap or throw something at her?[c]	Household Physical Violence
22	Kick, bite, hit her with a fist, or hit her with something hard?[c]	Household Physical Violence
23	Repeatedly hit her over at least a few minutes?[c]	Household Physical Violence
24	Threaten her with a knife or a gun, or use a knife or gun to hurt her?[c]	Household Physical Violence
Some people, while growing up in their first 18 years of life, had a sexual experience with an adult or someone at least 5 years older than themselves. These experiences may have involved a relative family friend or stranger. During the first 18 years of life, did an adult or older relative, family friend or stranger ever:		
25	Touch or fondle your body in a sexual way?[a]	Sexual Abuse
26	Have you touch their body in a sexual way?[a]	Sexual Abuse
27	Attempt to have any type of sexual intercourse (oral, anal, or vaginal) with you?[a]	Sexual Abuse
28	Actually have any type of sexual intercourse with you (oral, anal, or vaginal) with you?[a]	Sexual Abuse

[a] *Dichotomous scale—yes/no.*
[b] *Collected during Wave II only.*
[c] *Likert scale—never, once or twice, sometimes, often, very often.*
[d] *Likert scale—never true, rarely true, sometimes true, often true, very often true.*
Source: Ports, K. A., Ford, D. C., & Merrick, M. T. (2016). Adverse childhood experiences and sexual victimization in adulthood. Child Abuse & Neglect, 51, 313–22.

Child abuse items

Three categories of child abuse were measured—emotional abuse, physical abuse, and sexual abuse. Exposure to emotional abuse was deemed present if the participant responded (a) "often" or "very often" to item 17 in Table 1, *Swear at you, insult you, or put you down?* or (b) "sometimes," "often," or "very often" to item 18, *Act in a way that made you afraid that you might be physically hurt*? Exposure to one or both of the items indicated exposure to emotional abuse. Exposure to physical abuse was similarly established for items 19 and 20. Four dichotomous (yes/no) items adapted from the Wyatt Sex History Questionnaire (Wyatt, 1985) were used to assess sexual victimization during childhood. A person was determined to have experienced child sexual abuse if they responded affirmatively to one or more of these items—items 25, 26, 27, and 28 in Table 1.

Child neglect items

Both physical and emotional neglect were measured. The Physical Neglect subscale of the CTQ (Bernstein et al., 1994) was used to define whether someone experienced childhood physical neglect. This subscale comprises five items that are rated on a 1 ("never") to 5 ("very often") Likert scale. The responses to items 8 and 11 (Table 1) were reverse coded to match the negative valence of the remaining items. The responses to all five items were then summed together to estimate a physical neglect score, which ranges from 5 to 25. Individuals with a score of 10 or more fall in the moderate to extreme range. Individuals retrospectively reporting the moderate to extreme level of childhood physical neglect were considered to be exposed to physical neglect.

Similarly, the Emotional Neglect subscale of the CTQ (Bernstein et al., 1994) was used to define the presence of child emotional neglect. This subscale also comprises five items that are rated on a 1 ("never") to 5 ("very often") Likert scale. The responses to these items were summed together to compute an emotional neglect score, which ranges from 5 to 25. Individuals with a score of 15 or more fall in the moderate to extreme range. Individuals retrospectively reporting the moderate to extreme level of child emotional neglect were considered to be exposed to emotional neglect.

Household challenges

Five different household challenges were measured, including substance abuse, mental illness, mother treated violently, parental separation/divorce, and incarceration. Items 1 and 2 in Table 1 were used to assess whether the respondent lived with a household member who was a problem drinker or used street drugs. An affirmative response to one or both of these items indicated exposure to substance abuse in the household. Similarly, a "yes" response to either items 3 or 4 in Table 1, *Was anyone in your household mentally ill or depressed*? or *Did anyone in your household attempt to commit suicide*? indicated exposure to mental illness in the household. Four dichotomous (yes/no) items adapted from the CTS (Straus & Gelles, 1990) were used to assess the presence of household physical violence among the participant's parents. An individual was considered to be exposed to household physical violence if he or she responded affirmatively to one or more of these items—items 21–24 in Table 1. A "yes" response to item 5 in Table 1, *Were your parents ever separated or divorced*? indicated exposure to parental divorce, and a "yes" response to item 6 in Table 1, *Did anyone in your household ever go to prison*?, indicated exposure to the incarceration of a household member.

Behavioral risk factor surveillance system ACEs module

Following the success of the Kaiser-CDC ACE Study in demonstrating multiple associations between early adversity and health (Felitti et al., 1998), the CDC developed a brief ACEs module for use on the Behavioral Risk Factor Surveillance System (BRFSS). The BRFSS, coordinated by the CDC, is a state- and territory-based telephone survey aimed at tracking state-specific behavioral health risks in the US. Information from this survey is used to improve preventative health practices for chronic diseases, injuries, and infectious diseases. The survey is conducted in each state using a random-digit dialing (RDD) sampling protocol to contact respondents. RDD is a method for selecting people for involvement in telephone surveys by generating telephone numbers at random within residential area codes and exchanges (CDC, 2013). Once contacted, BRFSS interviewers ask respondents a series of questions regarding their health and health behaviors. Whereas many of these health-related questions are included in the questionnaire across every state, several items comprising additional modules are optional, and it is at the discretion of each state whether or not they will be included during a given data collection year. The ACEs items were among these optional modules from 2009 to 2012. Since 2013, the ACEs items have been included as state-added questions without the support of CDC. From 2009 to 2018, 43 states plus Washington D.C. have included ACEs items on their state survey.

Items for the BRFSS ACEs module were derived from those used in the CDC-Kaiser study. In consideration of respondent burden, much of the content from the original survey questions was reduced, resulting in an 11-item ACEs measure for use as a public health surveillance instrument. However, unlike the version administered during the CDC-Kaiser study, which assessed 10 distinct ACEs, the BRFSS ACEs excluded physical and emotional neglect items from the surveillance instrument, bringing the total number of individual ACEs measured to eight—physical abuse, emotional abuse, sexual abuse, witnessing intimate partner violence, living with a household member with mental illness, substance abuse in the household, having an incarcerated household member, and parental separation or divorce. The preambles, item content, and response options for each item can be found in Table 2.

Similar to the CDC-Kaiser measure, responses to the items on the BRFSS ACEs module are typically converted to reflect a dichotomous exposure to ACEs. For each item, responses indicating "no" or "never" are

TABLE 2 Behavioral Risk Factor Surveillance System Adverse Childhood Experiences Module Items

Item	Content	ACE type
Looking back before you were 18 years of age...		
1	Did you live with anyone who was depressed, mentally ill, or suicidal?[a]	Household Mental Illness
2	Did you live with anyone who was a problem drinker or alcoholic?[a]	Household Alcohol Abuse
3	Did you live with anyone who used illegal street drugs or who abused prescription medications?[a]	Household Substance Abuse
4	Did you live with anyone who served time or was sentenced to serve time in a prison, jail, or other correctional facility?[a]	Incarcerated Family Member
5	Were your parents separated or divorced?[a]	Parental Separation/Divorce
6	How often did your parents or adults in your home ever slap, hit, kick, punch or beat each other up?[b]	Household Physical Violence
7	Before age 18, how often did a parent or adult in your home ever hit, beat, kick, or physically hurt you in any way?[b]	Physical Abuse
8	How often did a parent or adult in your home ever swear at you, insult you, or put you down?[b]	Emotional Abuse
9	How often did anyone at least 5 years older than you or an adult, ever touch you sexually?[b]	Sexual Abuse
10	How often did anyone at least 5 years older than you or an adult, try to make you touch them sexually?[b]	Sexual Abuse
11	How often did anyone at least 5 years older than you or an adult, force you to have sex?[b]	Sexual Abuse

[a] *Dichotomous scale—yes/no.*

[b] *Likert scale—none, once, more than once.*

Source: Ford, D. C., Merrick, M. T., Parks, S. E., Breiding, M. J., Gilbert, L. K., Dhingra, S. S., …, Thompson, W. W. (2014). Examination of the factorial structure of adverse childhood experiences and recommendations for three subscale scores. Psychology of Violence, 4(4), 432–444.

considered to mean that the individual has never been exposed to that ACEs type. All other response options are considered to indicate exposure to the ACEs type being measured by that item. For example, the response options for the intimate partner violence item, *How often did your parents or adults in your home ever slap, hit, kick, punch, or beat each other up?*, consist of several categories, including "never," "once," and "more than once." The response options for this item and similar items were collapsed into "Never exposed" and "Exposed," reflecting exposure status. It is also worth noting that while each item in the BRFSS ACEs module assesses a distinct ACEs type, the assessment of sexual abuse is the lone exception. Exposure to sexual abuse is measured using separate items assessing whether or not the respondent experiences three different means of sexual abuse: being fondled, being forced to touch the perpetrator in a sexual manner, and being forced to engage in sexual intercourse. An affirmative response to one or more of these three items indicates exposure to sexual abuse. These definitions have been used extensively in previously published ACE Study work (e.g., Ford et al., 2014; Gilbert et al., 2015; Merrick, Ford, Ports, & Guinn, 2018).

Other ACEs measures

Both the CDC-Kaiser ACE Study and the BRFSS ACEs module require adults to retrospectively report on their childhood experiences; but, several studies have assessed ACEs among samples of youth. For example, the National Survey of Children's Exposure to Violence (NatSCEV) has used RDD to construct a sample of 4500 households with children ages birth to 17 years whereby one target child is randomly selected from each eligible household. Interviewers conduct a short interview with the caregiver and then conduct the main interview with the target child. For children younger than 10 years, proxy interviews with the adult in the household who is most familiar with the child's activities are conducted. The NatSCEV collects a breadth of data on childhood experiences that include ACEs exposures, such as abuse (emotional, physical, and sexual), neglect (physical and emotional), mental illness in the household, peer victimization (nonsibling), exposure to community violence, socioeconomic status, someone close had a bad accident or illness, parents always arguing, among others (Finkelhor, Hamby, Ormrod, & Turner, 2009; Finkelhor, Shattuck, Turner, & Hamby, 2013).

The National Survey of Children's Health (NSCH) is conducted by the U.S. Census Bureau for the Maternal and Child Health Bureau, Health Resources and Services Administration. This nationally representative survey examines the physical and emotional health of children ages 0 to 17 years, including several ACEs items: socioeconomic hardship, divorce/parental separation, substance abuse in the household, victim/witness of neighborhood violence, mental illness in the household, witnessed domestic violence, parent served time in jail, race/ethnicity discrimination, and death of a parent (Bethell, Davis, Gombojav, Stumbo, & Powers, 2017). The NSCH does not include indicators of child abuse and neglect, which are often leading drivers of poor health outcomes (e.g., Merrick et al., 2017). However, the NSCH does provide information on the health and well-being of children at a given time through the items that assess community-level ACEs (e.g., witnessing neighborhood violence) and adverse conditions (e.g., socioeconomic hardship) that put children at risk of experiencing additional ACEs.

There have been numerous replications and adaptions of the ACE Study since the 1990s. Beyond the large surveillance systems mentioned, researchers and practitioners have used the ACE Study questions or similar items both in research studies and in clinical settings, adapting the items as necessary to meet the need of the populations they are working with. As such, there are many additional types of childhood adversity that are measured to understand the experiences of children and improve the predictive ability of ACEs on health outcomes across the life course (Cronholm et al., 2015; Finkelhor et al., 2013; Mersky, Janczewski, & Topitzes, 2017; Ports et al., 2019). For example, Wade, Shea, Rubin, and Wood (2014) identified additional ACEs experienced by low-income urban youth in Philadelphia, including negative peer relationships, economic hardship, and discrimination. A follow-up study in Philadelphia demonstrated that nearly 14% of youth experienced only these additional ACEs, and their exposure to ACEs might have gone unrecognized if only the original ACEs were measured (Cronholm et al., 2015). Therefore, including additional types of adversities can help researchers and practitioners more accurately represent the level of adversity experienced across various sociodemographic groups (Cronholm et al., 2015). Greater detail about expanding the definition of ACEs is provided in Chapter 3.

The ACEs score

The ACEs measures, including the CDC-Kaiser Study, BRFSS, and NSCH, provide information about the prevalence of exposure to each of the measured adverse experiences. From this information, researchers can construct an ACEs score or a general measure of childhood adversity and challenging household environment whereby the cumulative impact of multiple types of adversity can be explored. An ACEs score is the total sum of the different types of ACEs reported by participants used to assess cumulative childhood stress (Felitti et al., 1998; Ford et al., 2014). In the CDC-Kaiser Study, respondents could be exposed to a range of ACEs from 0 (unexposed) to 10 (exposed to all ACE types). This number differs from study to study, depending on which ACEs items are included. While it may not include every type of traumatic event that a child can experience, an ACEs score does give researchers and practitioners an overall sense of what was going on in a person's life and household during their first 18 years, and provides a glimpse into the accumulation of adversity that can contribute to a toxic stress response.

Using an ACEs score, scientists have been able to operationalize childhood adversity into a simple framework that can be used to investigate the relationship between childhood adversity and later outcomes that expand beyond mental health outcomes. This frame has provided critical opportunities for the field of public health to understand and prioritize upstream prevention efforts that assure children have access to safe, stable, nurturing relationships and environments (CDC, 2014; Garner et al., 2012; Shonkoff, 2016). ACEs scores have also shed important light on a general dose-response relationship between exposure and outcomes. For example, research consistently reveals that as the ACEs score goes up so does the risk of adverse outcomes, including physical and mental health problems, engagement in risky health behaviors, limited life opportunities, and premature death (Brown et al., 2009; Felitti et al., 1998; Merrick et al., 2017; Metzler et al., 2017). This body of work has propelled ACEs forward as a major public health problem that warrants further attention as a mechanism to address and prevent many of the leading causes of death.

ACEs prevalence across populations

Data from the CDC-Kaiser ACE Study were collected in two waves, resulting in a sample of 17,337 adults (Felitti et al., 1998). The sample comprised adult members of Kaiser Permanente, a large healthcare maintenance organization in southern California. In this sample, 63.9% of adults had one or more ACEs and 12.5% had four or more (CDC, 2016). Exposure to each of the ACEs ranged from 4.7% of respondents indicating that they had an incarcerated household member to 28.3% of respondents indicating that they had experienced physical abuse (CDC, 2016). Approximately 10.6% of the sample experienced emotional abuse, 12.7% witnessed their mother treated violently, 19.4% experienced mental illness in the household, 20.7% experienced sexual abuse, 23.3% experienced parental divorce or separation, and 26.9% experienced substance abuse in the household. It is important to note that neglect items were not added until the second wave of data collection and, subsequently, the childhood neglect prevalence estimates reflects a smaller sample size of 8639 adults. Of adults in the second wave, 14.8% experienced emotional neglect and 9.9% experienced physical neglect.

It is important to remember that the CDC-Kaiser ACE Study was conducted on a mostly non-Hispanic White, middle-class sample from southern California and, as such, the experiences of adversity may be different across different populations. However, even among more representative samples, such as the BRFSS, the prevalence of ACEs is similar. For example, in a recent analysis of BRFSS ACEs data from 2011 to 2014 that included a sample of 180,062 adults from 23 states, 61.5% of adults had one or more ACEs and 15.8% had four or more. Exposure to each of the ACEs ranged from 7.9% of respondents indicating that they had an incarcerated household member to 34.4% of respondents indicating that they had experienced emotional abuse (Merrick et al., 2018). Approximately 11.6% of the sample experienced sexual abuse, 16.5% experienced mental illness in the household, 17.5% witnessed intimate partner violence, 17.9% experienced physical abuse, 27.6% experienced parental divorce or separation, and 27.6% experienced substance abuse in the household (Merrick et al., 2018).

According to the NSCH data, 46.3% of all children have at least one adversity, and exposure to different types of ACEs ranges from 3.3% of children experiencing the death of their parent/guardian to 25.5% experiencing socioeconomic hardship (Bethell et al., 2017). The NSCH estimates are comparatively lower than estimates that include samples of adults. This is likely due to the fact that they are surveying children and, thus, not measuring ACEs over the entire age range of 0 to 18 years. As noted previously, the NSCH also measures different types of ACEs, which may influence prevalence estimates.

ACEs by demographic characteristics

Given the prevalence, ACEs affect most people in some manner; but, some groups are at increased risk because of structural and social conditions that influence how they interact with their environments (Andersen & Blosnich, 2013; Cronholm et al., 2015; Merrick et al., 2018; Sedlak et al., 2010). Numerous studies have documented inequities in ACEs exposure by race and ethnicity (e.g., Cronholm et al., 2015; Kenney & Singh, 2016; Sacks & Murphey, 2018). More specifically, these studies demonstrate that compared to non-Hispanic White samples, minoritized racial and ethnic populations tend to experience more ACEs. Similar findings exist across many sociodemographic categories, including sexual orientation (e.g., Andersen & Blosnich, 2013) and socioeconomic status (Sedlak et al., 2010).

Importantly, demographic groupings (e.g., race, class, gender) do not cause ACEs; rather, minoritized groups often experience increased social and economic challenges and health risks. Such environments can make it difficult for some families to provide safe, stable, and nurturing relationships and places groups of people at increased risk for experiencing ACEs and the negative outcomes associated with exposure to childhood adversity.

Moreover, experiencing early adversity can be a social determinant in and of itself. In other words, exposure to ACEs can affect educational attainment, employment, and poverty—outcomes that can reverberate across generations. As such, it is important to acknowledge the temporal relationship of ACEs and socioeconomic outcomes as well as the conditions that make it difficult for some children and families to thrive.

Co-occurrence of ACEs

Using data from the original study, Dong et al. (2004) estimated that 87% of respondents who had experienced one adversity in childhood reported exposure to at least one additional adverse experience. This finding highlights the co-occurrence of early adversity. It is not just that individuals experience one childhood adversity and are thereby subsequently at risk of poor outcomes. They often experience multiple ACEs, which have an additive impact on their future health and well-being (e.g., Dong et al., 2004; Felitti et al., 1998). Other researchers have documented the risk for experiencing multiple types of violence (e.g., Finkelhor, Ormrod, & Turner, 2007) or poly-victimization. Notably, Finkelhor et al. (2009) estimated that approximately 22% of children in the NatSCEV sample experienced four or more different kinds of victimization in the past year, and that poly-victimization was highly predictive of trauma symptoms.

Considerations for ACEs measurement and directions for future research

ACEs scores provide an example of how to understand the complicated science linking childhood adversity to later health and well-being. However, there are several limitations to the ACEs score that should be noted. First, ACEs items and scores are relatively simplistic measures of adversity. For example, ACEs items do not consider important dimensions of exposure, including age of exposure, perpetrator, chronicity, severity, and a host of other dimensions that influence the impact of ACEs on later health. In addition, ACEs scores mask the unequal impact of individual ACEs on later outcomes. Some ACEs may be more traumatic and can have a greater impact on outcomes (e.g., Merrick et al., 2017; Ports et al., 2016), but an ACEs score treats all exposures as equal. For example, in an ACEs score, indicating having divorced/separated parents is equivalent to a score of 1, which is also true for someone who indicates that they were physically abused. Subsequently, scientists have encouraged the use of ACEs factors (Ford et al., 2014; Mersky et al., 2017) as a way to measure the unique contribution of ACEs categories (e.g., physical and emotional abuse versus household challenges). Research documenting the characteristics of exposure and the unique contribution of specific ACEs factors and even individual ACEs on outcomes may be better able to predict effects of exposure and thereby improve how we intervene to lessen harm from exposure to ACEs.

Another notable limitation is that the ACEs questionnaires do not comprise an exhaustive list of potential childhood traumas. There are many adverse events that can influence health and well-being across the lifespan, including economic hardship, historical trauma (e.g., group trauma that extends across generations as a result of adversity, including colonization, dislocation, and racism), bullying, peer victimization, spanking, teen dating violence, and exposure to community violence (Afifi et al., 2017; Cronholm et al., 2015; Finkelhor et al., 2013). For some populations, the magnitude and burden of these additional ACEs (in addition to the more traditional ACEs) may be unequal and, as such, researchers and practitioners may want to consider what ACEs are salient and culturally relevant in the communities that they are working with. For example, practicing cultural humility, an intentional self-reflection on personal experiences and cultural influences, along with reflection on what one knows and does not know about another person's unique values, experiences, and goals, can reduce false assumptions regarding the needs and experiences of a child and family (Tervalon & Murray-Garcia, 1998) and, in turn, may promote a more comprehensive approach to prevention and intervention.

In addition, there may be mediators of the relationship between childhood experiences and adult health status other than the risk factors typically examined. Not all individuals who experience ACEs go on to have impairment, risky behavior, or any other long-term negative outcomes. The likelihood of negative outcomes from exposure to ACEs may be affected by many factors, including severity, developmental timing, and the presence of protective factors. When children's positive experiences (e.g., social connectedness, supportive parent) outweigh their negative experiences, they may be more likely to have positive outcomes later in life (Schofield, Lee, & Merrick, 2013). However, we tend to know less about protective factors and how they prevent or mitigate adverse experiences. These gaps represent our incomplete, but growing, understanding of the risk and protective factors that influence the relationship between ACEs and later health and well-being. Chapters 15 and 16 provide additional information on protective factors in the context of preventing ACEs and intervening after exposure occurs.

ACEs studies often rely on self-reported data, with its obvious limitations. Notably, child abuse and related injuries are often sensitive and potentially provoke anxiety for a respondent to report, which may influence respondents' willingness to answer in a forthcoming manner (Tourangeau & Yan, 2007). Because respondents are often asked to retrospectively report on their exposure to ACEs, memory bias or coping mechanisms as a result of enduring abuse (e.g., repression) may influence the accuracy of the individual's self-report (Edwards, Fivush, Anda, Felitti, & Nordenberg, 2001). In fact, longitudinal studies of adults with documented adolescent abuse have shown that their retrospective reports of the abuse often underestimate the actual occurrence (Della Femina, Yeager, & Lewis, 1990; Williams, 1994). Alone, cross-sectional ACEs surveillance data and/or retrospective self-reporting can only demonstrate general associations between childhood exposures and health risk behaviors, health status, and diseases in adulthood. Longitudinal studies that incorporate ACEs have the potential to help us understand the causal role of ACEs on health and well-being across lifespans and generations.

Importantly, asking adults about traumatic experiences years and sometimes decades later does not provide opportunities to intervene early to minimize risk and change trajectories. Nor does it provide an opportunity for researchers to understand current trends in exposure. Furthermore, experiencing a childhood adversity does not mean that an individual experienced trauma and needs intervention. Those wishing to incorporate ACEs into their research or practice should be mindful that ACEs are not deterministic; that is, exposure does not mean that an individual will have negative health outcomes and, subsequently, assessing trauma symptoms in addition to or in place of ACEs could be beneficial. Finally, the ACEs items included in this chapter were used for public health surveys; as such, they were not designed or intended for clinical samples, and are not always appropriate for use as a screening tool. Additional research is needed to identify and validate appropriate ACEs items for inclusion in practice settings.

Implications for policy and practice

Despite limitations, ACEs data can provide a concise picture of how ACEs occur nationally, in communities, and even within families and individuals. As noted earlier, researchers have harnessed ACEs data to demonstrate that childhood adversities are common. Furthermore, research consistently demonstrates that as the number of ACEs increases, the risk for health problems increases in a strong and graded fashion (Felitti et al., 1998; Gilbert et al., 2015). Research also shows that ACEs themselves are strongly interrelated (Dong et al., 2004; Finkelhor et al., 2007) and those who reported multiple categories of ACEs were likely to have multiple health risk factors later in life (Felitti et al., 1998; Gilbert et al., 2015). The ACE Study, along with other research in the area of trauma, child maltreatment, toxic stress, and brain development, has raised public awareness about the high prevalence and impact of negative life events in children's lives. This has helped redefine the way clinicians, researchers, policymakers, and the public understand the intersections between exposure to adversity and mental and physical health outcomes, including academic achievement, opioid misuse, suicidality, and poverty (e.g., AAP Council on Community Pediatrics, 2016; Metzler et al., 2017).

ACEs data can help identify the needs of individuals, families, and communities. The data can also be used to understand how to intervene to lessen harms after exposure to ACEs occur, as well as the steps that can be taken to prevent ACEs within communities. Recently, CDC developed technical packages to assist communities take advantage of the best available evidence to prevent violence in childhood and adolescence across the different levels of the social ecology (CDC, 2018). For example, strategies highlighted in the technical package to prevent child abuse and neglect, one type of adversity, include policies that strengthen economic supports to families (e.g., tax credits and subsidized childcare) and providing quality care and education early in life (Fortson, Klevens, Merrick, Gilbert, & Alexander, 2016). Similar strategies also exist for preventing youth violence (David-Ferdon et al., 2016). A detailed description of prevention activities is provided in Chapter 16. However, it is important to note that continued monitoring of ACEs can serve as an indicator of how well ACEs prevention and intervention strategies are working, and may highlight gaps, opportunities for improvement, and necessary adaptations.

Conclusion

ACEs are a serious public health issue with far-reaching consequences; but, they are preventable. Monitoring ACEs across populations can help assess the impact of prevention efforts and direct adaptations to prevention strategies to ensure that all children reach their full health and life potential. Together we can prevent ACEs by adopting and promoting appropriate, evidence-based policies, social norms, and programmatic strategies and approaches that create neighborhoods and communities where every child has safe, stable, nurturing relationships and environments and, ultimately, a world where every child can thrive (CDC, 2014, 2018).

References

AAP Council on Community Pediatrics. (2016). Poverty and child health in the United States. *Pediatrics*, *137*(4), e20160339.

Afifi, T. O., Ford, D., Gershoff, L., Merrick, M. T., Grogan-Kaylor, A., Ports, K. A., … Bennett, R. P. (2017). Spanking and impairment in adult mental health: evidence for adversity. *Child Abuse and Neglect*, *71*, 24–31.

Andersen, J. P., & Blosnich, J. (2013). Disparities in adverse childhood experiences among sexual minority and heterosexual adults: results from a multi-state probability-based sample. *PLoS One*, *8*(1), e54691.

Bernstein, D. P., Fink, L., Handelsman, L., Foote, J., Lovejov, M., Wenzel, K., … Ruggiero, J. (1994). Initial reliability and validity of a new retrospective measure of child abuse and neglect. *American Journal of Psychiatry*, *151*, 1132–1136.

Bethell, C. D., Davis, M. B., Gombojav, N., Stumbo, S., & Powers, K. (2017). *Issue brief: Adverse childhood experiences among US children, child and adolescent health measurement initiative*. Johns Hopkins Bloomberg School of Public Health. Retrieved from: cahmi.org/projects/adverse-childhood-experiences-aces.

Brown, D. W., Anda, R. F., Tiemeier, H., Felitti, V. J., Edwards, V., Croft, J. B., & Giles, W. H. (2009). Adverse childhood experiences and the risk of premature mortality. *American Journal of Preventive Medicine*, *37*(5), 389–396.

Centers for Disease Control and Prevention. (2013). *The BRFSS data user guide*. Atlanta, Georgia: U.S. Department of Health and Human Services, Centers for Disease Control and Prevention. Available from: https://www.cdc.gov/brfss/data_documentation/pdf/UserguideJune2013.pdf.

Centers for Disease Control and Prevention, Kaiser Permanente. (2016). *The ACE study survey data*. [Unpublished Data]. Atlanta, Georgia: U.S. Department of Health and Human Services, Centers for Disease Control and Prevention. Available from: https://www.cdc.gov/violenceprevention/acestudy/about.html.

Centers for Disease Control and Prevention. (2014). *Essentials for childhood: Steps to create safe, stable, nurturing relationships and environments*. Atlanta, Georgia: U.S. Department of Health and Human Services, Centers for Disease Control and Prevention. Available from: http://www.cdc.gov/violenceprevention/pdf/essentials_for_childhood_framework.pdf.

Centers for Disease Control and Prevention. (2018). *Technical packages for violence prevention: Using evidence-based strategies in your violence prevention efforts*. Atlanta, Georgia: U.S. Department of Health and Human Services, Centers for Disease Control and Prevention. Available from: https://www.cdc.gov/violenceprevention/pub/technical-packages.html.

Cronholm, P. F., Forke, C. M., Wade, R., Bair-Merrit, M. H., Davis, M., Harkins-Schwarz, M., … Fein, J. A. (2015). Adverse childhood experiences: expanding the concept of adversity. *American Journal of Preventive Medicine*, *49*(3), 354–361.

David-Ferdon, C., Vivolo-Kanto, A. M., Dahlberg, L. L., Marshall, K. J., Rainford, N., & Hall, J. E. (2016). *A comprehensive technical package for the prevention of youth violence and associated risk behaviors*. Atlanta, GA: National Center for Injury Prevention and Control, Centers for Disease Control and Prevention.

Della Femina, D., Yeager, C. A., & Lewis, D. O. (1990). Child abuse: adolescent records vs. adult recall. *Child Abuse & Neglect*, *14*, 227–231.

Dong, M., Anda, R. F., Felitti, V. J., Dube, S. R., Williamson, D. F., Thompson, T. J., … Giles, W. H. (2004). The interrelatedness of multiple forms of childhood abuse, neglect, and household dysfunction. *Child Abuse Neglect*, *28*(7), 771–784.

Edwards, V. J., Fivush, R., Anda, R. F., Felitti, V. J., & Nordenberg, D. F. (2001). Autobiographical memory disturbances in childhood abuse survivors. In J. J. Freyd & A. P. DePrince (Eds.), *Trauma and cognitive science: A meeting of minds, science, and human experience*. Binghamton, NY: Haworth Press.

Felitti, V. J., Anda, R. F., Nordenberg, D., Williamson, D. F., Spitz, A. M., Edwards, V., … Marks, J. S. (1998). Relationship of childhood abuse and household dysfunction to many of the leading causes of death in adults: the adverse childhood experiences (ACE) study. *American Journal of Preventive Medicine*, *14*, 245–258.

Finkelhor, D., Hamby, S. L., Ormrod, R. K., & Turner, H. A. (2009). Violence, abuse, and crime exposure in a national sample of children and youth. *Pediatrics*, *124*(5), 1–14.

Finkelhor, D., Ormrod, R. K., & Turner, H. A. (2007). Poly-victimization: a neglected component in child victimization. *Child Abuse and Neglect*, *31*, 7–26.

Finkelhor, D., Shattuck, A., Turner, H., & Hamby, S. (2013). Improving the adverse childhood experiences study scale. *JAMA Pediatrics*, *167*(1), 70–75.

Ford, D. C., Merrick, M. T., Parks, S. E., Breiding, M. J., Gilbert, L. K., Dhingra, S. S., ... Thompson, W. W. (2014). Examination of the factorial structure of adverse childhood experiences and recommendations for three subscale scores. *Psychology of Violence*, *4*(4), 432–444.

Fortson, B. L., Klevens, J., Merrick, M. T., Gilbert, L. K., & Alexander, S. P. (2016). *Preventing child abuse and neglect: A technical package for policy, norm, and programmatic activities.* Atlanta, GA: National Center for Injury Prevention and Control, Centers for Disease Control and Prevention.

Garner, A. S., Shonkoff, J. P., Committee on Psychosocial Aspects of Child and Family Health, Committee on Early Childhood, Adoption, and Dependent Care, Section on Developmental and Behavioral Pediatrics. (2012). Early childhood adversity, toxic stress, and the role of the pediatrician: translating developmental science into lifelong health. *Pediatrics*, *129*(1), e224–e231.

Gilbert, L. K., Breiding, M. J., Merrick, M. T., Thompson, W. W., Ford, D. C., Dhingra, S. S., & Parks, S. E. (2015). Childhood adversity and adult chronic disease: an update from ten states and the District of Columbia, 2010. *American Journal of Preventive Medicine*, *48*(3), 345–349.

Kenney, M. K., & Singh, G. K. (2016). *Adverse childhood experiences among American Indian/Alaska native children: the 2011–2012 National Survey of Children's Health.* Cairo: Scientifica. 7424239. Available from: https://www.hindawi.com/journals/scientifica/2016/7424239/.

Merrick, M. T., Ford, D. C., Ports, K. A., & Guinn, A. S. (2018). Adverse childhood experiences in 23 states: results from the behavioral risk factor surveillance system 2011-2014. *JAMA Pediatrics*, *172*(11), 1038–1044.

Merrick, M. T., Ports, K. A., Ford, D. C., Afifi, T. O., Gershoff, E. T., & Grogan-Kaylor, A. (2017). Unpacking the impact of adverse childhood experiences on adult mental health. *Child Abuse & Neglect*, *69*, 10–19.

Mersky, J. P., Janczewski, C. E., & Topitzes, J. (2017). Rethinking the measurement of adversity: moving toward second-generation research on adverse childhood experiences. *Child Maltreatment*, *22*(1), 58–68.

Metzler, M., Merrick, M. T., Klevens, J., Ports, K. A., & Ford, D. C. (2017). Adverse childhood experiences and life opportunities: shifting the narrative. *Children and Youth Services Review*, *72*, 141–149.

Ports, K. A., Ford, D. C., & Merrick, M. T. (2016). Adverse childhood experiences and sexual victimization in adulthood. *Child Abuse & Neglect*, *51*, 313–322.

Ports, K. A., Holman, D. M., Guinn, A., Pampati, S., Dyer, K., Merrick, M. T., ...& Metzler, M. (2019). Association between adverse childhood experiences and leading risk factors for cancer in adulthood. *Journal of Pediatric Nursing*, *44*, 81–96.

Schofield, T. J., Lee, R. D., & Merrick, M. T. (2013). Safe, stable, nurturing relationships as a moderator of intergenerational continuity of child maltreatment: a meta-analysis. *The Journal of Adolescent Health*, *53*(4 Suppl), S32–S38.

Sacks, V., & Murphey, D. (2018). *The prevalence of adverse childhood experiences, nationally, by state, and by race or ethnicity*. Child Trends Issue Brief. Available from: https://www.childtrends.org/publications/prevalence-adverse-childhood-experiences-nationally-state-race-ethnicity/.

Sedlak, A. J., Mettenburg, J., Basena, M., Peta, I., McPherson, K., & Greene, A. (2010). *Fourth national incidence study of child abuse and neglect (NIS-4)*. Washington, DC: US Department of Health and Human Services. Available from: http://www.acf.hhs.gov/sites/default/files/opre/nis4_report_congress_full_pdf_jan2010.pdf.

Shonkoff, J. P. (2016). Capitalizing on advances in science to reduce the health consequences of early childhood adversity. *JAMA Pediatrics*, *170*(10), 1003–1007.

Straus, M. A., & Gelles, R. J. (1990). *Physical violence in American families: Risk factors and adaptations to violence in 8,145 families*. New Brunswick, NJ: Transaction Press.

Tervalon, M., & Murray-Garcia, J. (1998). Cultural humility versus cultural competence: a critical distinction in defining physician training outcomes in multicultural education. *Journal of Health Care for the Poor and Underserved*, *9*(2), 117–125.

Tourangeau, R., & Yan, T. (2007). Sensitive questions in surveys. *Psychological Bulletin*, *133*, 859.
Wade, R. J., Shea, J. A., Rubin, D., & Wood, J. (2014). Adverse childhood experiences of low-income urban youth. *Pediatrics*, *134*(1), e13–e20.
Williams, L. M. (1994). Recall of childhood trauma: a prospective study of women's memories of child sexual abuse. *Journal of Consulting and Clinical Psychology*, *62*, 1167–1176.
Wyatt, G. E. (1985). The sexual abuse of Afro-American and White-American women in childhood. *Child Abuse & Neglect*, *9*, 507–519.

CHAPTER

3

Considerations for expanding the definition of ACEs

Tracie O. Afifi

Departments of Community Health Sciences and Psychiatry, University of Manitoba, Winnipeg, MB, Canada

Introduction

Physical abuse, sexual abuse, emotional abuse, physical neglect, emotional neglect, violence against a mother, parental divorce, household member having problems with substances, household member having problems with mental illness, and incarceration of a household member comprise the 10 adverse childhood experiences (ACEs) assessed in the original ACE Study (Dube et al., 2003; Felitti et al., 1998). This is not a comprehensive list of adverse experiences that can occur in childhood and, therefore, researchers, clinicians, and others working in the field have added and removed experiences while still using the term ACEs. In this chapter, an overview of the original ACEs, inconsistencies in defining ACEs in research, and ACEs from a global perspective are provided. Directions for future research, including recommendations for expanding the definition of ACEs and implications on policy and practice of an expanded ACEs list, are also discussed.

The original 10 ACEs

The literature on childhood adversity is large and dates back many decades. However, it has been more recent, over the past 20 years since the 1998 publication of the ACE Study by Felitti et al. (1998), that the term *adverse childhood experiences*, or *ACEs* in abbreviated form, has been more consistently used in the literature to refer to a specific set of experiences. The original Wave I of the ACE Study included three types of child abuse (i.e., physical abuse, sexual abuse, and emotional abuse) and five types of house-

Adverse Childhood Experiences
https://doi.org/10.1016/B978-0-12-816065-7.00003-3

hold dysfunction or challenges (i.e., violence against a mother, household member having problems with substances, household member having problems with mental illness, incarceration of a household member and parental separation or divorce; Felitti et al., 1998; Anda et al., 1999). In Wave II of the original ACE Study, two additional adverse experiences were added (i.e., physical neglect and emotional neglect) to total 10 ACEs (Dube et al., 2003).

Importantly, there has not been any theoretical or empirical evidence published that indicates why these specific 10 constructs were chosen to be included in the Wave I and II data collection of the original ACE Study. As described in Chapters 2 and 9, the items used to measure these constructs in the original ACE Study were taken from a variety of preexisting scales to create what is now commonly referred to as the ACEs instrument or ACEs questionnaire. Despite the lack of rigorous tool development to indicate adequate validity and reliability of the measurement or empirical data to determine the underlying factor structure of the items, this list of 10 ACEs has become mainstream in the academic literature and, more recently, in the general media. One reason for this uptake despite the lack of measurement rigor is likely because the tool is freely available, short, and easy to administer. As well, the large and growing ACEs literature indicates that these individual 10 ACEs, as well as a count of the number of ACEs experienced, are consistently associated with numerous poor mental and physical health outcomes and other at-risk behaviors such as smoking and drug use (e.g., Anda et al., 1999; Bellis, Lowey, Leckenby, Hughes, & Harrison, 2014; Dube et al., 2001, 2003; Felitti et al., 1998; Hughes, Lowey, Quigg, & Bellis, 2016; Hillis, Anda, Felitti, Nordenberg, & Marchbanks, 2000; Merrick et al., 2017). It is not contested that these experiences are traumatic and it is appropriate to call them ACEs. However, it is also true that this list is not a complete list of adverse experiences that could occur during childhood, nor was it ever intended to be such a list.

Although there is more consistency in the use of the term ACEs in the literature over the past two decades, there remains diversity in how this term is applied in research. Assessment of ACEs is not consistent across studies (Liming & Grube, 2018). This may be due to terms like child abuse, child maltreatment, and childhood adversity also being inconsistently used in research. For example, some studies have used the term *adverse childhood experiences,* but have only included measures of child maltreatment (Afifi et al., 2008). Inconsistencies may also be due to the lack of available data, with some studies using the term *adverse childhood experiences* or *ACEs,* but including only some indicators of child abuse, neglect, and household challenges or dysfunction from the original list of 10 (e.g., Tonmyr, Med, Mery, & Harriet, 2005). Finally, other studies have included some of the original 10 ACEs, but also expand this list to include additional adverse experiences such as being sent away, parental unemployment, witnessing injury or murder, being threatened or held captive (e.g., Schilling, Aseltine, & Gore, 2007), community violence (e.g., Hambrick, Rubens, Brawner, & Taussig, 2018), and parental death (e.g., Berg, Acharya, Shi, & Michael, 2018). It may or may not be important for all studies using the term *adverse childhood experiences* or *ACEs* to be measuring exactly the same experiences or be restricted to a specific list of events. However, we are now at a point in the ACEs field where we should reconsider the definition of ACEs and contemplate the utility of expanding what is typically considered as a childhood adversity. Best practice for reconsidering ACEs would be a process that includes selecting potentially new ACEs informed by theory or findings from previous research. This could be followed by empirical examinations of the current 10 ACEs along with new potential ACEs to provide indicators of validity.

If one was tasked with generating a list of adverse experiences that occur in childhood, like the original 10 ACEs items, it would include experiences of child maltreatment and household challenges or dysfunction. It may also include other types of adverse experiences occurring in childhood that are known from other research to be traumatic but not typically included in ACEs studies. Such an exercise could generate a list much larger than the 10 original ACEs. Expanding the ACEs list may have merit, including being more comprehensive, which may in turn better inform policy and practice. However, an expanded list also introduces new challenges. For example, the length of the list could be debated. Having a longer and more extensive list may seem ideal; but, it would create numerous challenges for data collection, such as respondent burden (i.e., respondents' perception that the questionnaire is too difficult, time consuming, or emotionally stressful; Lavrakas, 2008). It would be best to have a list large enough to be inclusive of other known childhood adversities, yet still small enough in size to have practical utility when conducting research.

Defining ACEs from a global perspective

To date, most of ACEs research has been conducted in the US with a small number of studies using data from Canada and other countries worldwide. Conceptualizing ACEs from a global perspective may also be important when expanding the definition of ACEs. Having one tool that could measure ACEs in any country may lead to greater knowledge of ACEs worldwide and have utility for international comparisons. This was the intention of an international ACEs research network led by the World Health Organization (WHO), which steered the development of the Adverse Childhood Experiences International Questionnaire (ACE-IQ; WHO, 2011a, 2011b, 2011c). The ACE-IQ was designed to be administered to individuals aged 18 years and older and included an expanded list of ACEs (WHO, 2011a, 2011b, 2011c). The ACE-IQ includes nine of the original 10 ACEs with the tenth childhood adversity, emotional neglect, assessed in a limited capacity. Notably, the wording of the constructs and the response categories on the ACE-IQ is different than what is included on the ACE Questionnaire. The ACE-IQ expanded the ACEs to also include marriage (i.e., age and consent), parental death, peer violence or bullying, witnessing community violence, and exposure to war or collective violence (WHO, 2011a, 2011b, 2011c). This tool was developed to be brief, with the recommendation that it should be integrated into larger health surveys worldwide (WHO, 2011a, 2011b, 2011c).

The ACE-IQ has been used in a number of studies, including research from Kenya (Kiburi, Molebatsi, Obondo, & Kuria, 2018), Lebanon (Naal, El Jalkh, & Haddad, 2018), Saudi Arabia (Almuneef, ElChoueiry, Saleheen, & Al-Eissa, 2017; Almuneef, Qayad, Aleissa, & Albuhairan, 2014), and Baghdad (AlShawi & Lafta, 2014). Interestingly, there is no consistency in what ACEs are included in these published studies and how the data are computed and analyzed varies. As well, it has been argued that the ACE-IQ should be modified to match the culture context of the population to which it is being administered (Quinn et al., 2018). Such a practice may be important, but could also introduce changes to the tool that would limit comparability across studies. Clearly, the ACE-IQ has merit; but, it also has practical challenges with administration across countries, including language translation and cultural sensitivity. To date, there have not been any studies published on the reliability and validity of the ACE-IQ. Further work is needed to understand the psychometric data and internal consistencies of the tool.

Directions for future research: Recommendations and cautions for expanding the definition of ACEs

Recommendations to broaden what is considered an adverse experience during childhood and included in ACEs research is not a new concept. Researchers in the field have made a number of recommendations based on empirical evidence. This work is summarized here.

Using a representative sample of children from the US collected in 2008, Finkelhor and colleagues selected additional adverse experiences known to be related to poor health and well-being outcomes and used statistical models to compare how these experiences were linked to distress compared to the original ACEs (Finkelhor, Turner, Shattuck, & Hamby, 2013). Based on data from this study, the authors recommended that parental divorce and incarceration be removed from the ACEs list and that additional ACEs be added. The additional ACEs recommendations included property victimization (e.g., robbery, theft, or vandalism), peer victimization (e.g., assault, intimidation, or emotional victimization), exposure to community violence (e.g., witnessing assault, experiencing household theft, someone close murdered, experiencing riot, or being in a war zone), low socioeconomic status, someone close in an accident for suffered illness, below-average grades, parents always arguing, and no close friends (Finkelhor et al., 2013). Finkelhor and colleagues extended this work using a telephone survey of youth aged 10 to 17 years from the US conducted in 2013–14 (Finkelhor, Shattuck, Turner, & Hamby, 2015). Using data from this study, it was recommended that the original 10 ACEs remain, and an additional four ACEs be added, in this case low socioeconomic status, peer victimization (siblings and nonsiblings), social isolation, and exposure to community violence.

Based on empirical evidence, it has also been recommended that spanking be included as an adverse experience (Afifi et al., 2017). The original ACEs study included a question on spanking; however, spanking had not been analyzed in previous studies using these data. Spanking was assessed using the following question: *Sometimes parents spank their children as a form of discipline. While you were growing up during your first 18 years of life, how often were you spanked?* (Afifi et al., 2017). Using the original ACE Study data, a factor analysis found that spanking loaded on the same factor as physical abuse and emotional abuse. When items load on the same factor, in this case, spanking, physical abuse, and emotional abuse, it indicates that these experiences have a similar underlying construct (Tabachnick & Fidell, 2013). Furthermore, data from this study indicated that spanking was associated with increased odds of suicide attempts, moderate to heavy drinking, and street drug use independent of experiencing physical or emotional abuse (Afifi et al., 2017). This indicates that spanking has shared variance (i.e., is empirically similar) with physical and emotional abuse; but, it also accounts for additional unique variance for understanding adult mental and behavioral health impairment. Based on these findings, it was recommended that spanking should be considered a form of childhood adversity and that it should be further addressed in efforts to prevent violence.

Although not empirically examined, a revised ACEs tool called the Center for Youth Wellness ACE Questionnaire has been developed as a tool for health professionals (Bucci et al., 2015). In addition to the original 10 ACEs, this tool also includes parental death; foster care; child separated from primary caregiver through deportation or immigration; child had serious medical procedure or life-threatening illness; harassment or bullying at school; verbal or physical abuse in a dating relationship; seeing or hearing violence in the neighborhood; child being detained, arrested, or incarcerated; and child treated badly because of race, sexual orientation, place of birth, disability, or religion.

Based on what we know from research findings to date, expanding the list of ACEs beyond the original 10 would likely provide a better assessment of childhood adversity and, thereby, lead to a better understanding of poor outcomes across the lifespan. However, it should be noted that very few studies have been conducted to address the issue of expanding the list of ACEs. All recommendations for an expanded inventory of ACEs should be developed using empirical evidence showing how adverse experiences are correlated and group together.

Based on the current state of knowledge, an expanded list of ACEs to be empirically assessed and considered in future research is presented in Table 1. This list collates current recommendations for expanding the list of ACEs to be used as a potential starting point for future ACEs tool development or conceptualization of ACEs and empirical testing. Some of the "new" ACEs (i.e., ACEs beyond the original 10) that are listed in Table 1 have evidence that they are empirically related to the original 10 ACEs or related to the same poor outcomes as other ACEs. This is the

TABLE 1 Recommendations for an Expanded List of ACEs to be Empirically Assessed in Future Research

Child maltreatment	Household challenges	Peer victimization	Community violence
1. Physical abuse	6. Parental substance use		
2. Sexual abuse	7. Parental mental illness		
3. Emotional abuse	8. Parental incarceration		
4. Physical neglect	9. Parental divorce or separation		
5. Emotional neglect	*Mother treated violently (Suggested replacement with items 10 and 11)*		
ADDITIONAL ACES TO CONSIDER			
10. Exposure to physical violence in the home	13. Poverty	20. Physical bullying	27. Seen physical fighting
11. Exposure to verbal violence/abuse in the home	14. Parental death	21. Verbal bullying	28. Seen or heard stabbing or threat of stabbing with a weapon
12. Spanking	15. Sibling death	22. Cyberbullying	29. Seen or heard shooting or threat of shooting with a gun

TABLE 1 Recommendations for an Expanded List of ACEs to be Empirically Assessed in Future Research—cont'd

Child maltreatment	Household challenges	Peer victimization	Community violence
	16. Foster care	23. Physical dating violence	
	17. Sibling violence	24. Verbal dating violence/abuse	
	18. Major childhood illness	25. Sexual dating violence	
	19. Long-term separation from due to deployment or immigration	26. Peer rejection (no close friendships)	

Notes:

(1) Items 10 and 11 could replace mother treated violently.

(2) Empirical data supports the additions of items: 12 (Afifi et al., 2017), 13, 17, 20, 21, 26, 27, 28, 29 (Finkelhor et al., 2013, 2015).

(3) Other known childhood adversities without empirical examination for fit with ACEs: 14; 16; 18; 19; 23; 24 (Lee Oh et al., 2018).

(4) Other possible considerations based on previous data showing the items to be traumatic, but not typically called a childhood adversity: 15 (Alhujailli & Karwowski, 2019; Hébert, Blais, & Lavoie, 2017; Jonas, Scanlon, Rusch, Ito, & Joselow, 2018).

case for poverty, sibling violence, physical and verbal bullying, peer rejections, community violence (Finkelhor et al., 2013, 2015), and spanking (Afifi et al., 2017). Other ACEs included in Table 1 have been recognized as types of childhood adversity, but have not been examined empirically with regard to fit with the original ACEs (e.g., foster care, major childhood illness, long-term separation because of deployment or immigration, and physical dating violence and verbal dating violence/abuse such as name calling, yelling, criticism, and humiliation; Lee Oh et al., 2018). As well, there are other traumatic experiences that occur in childhood, such as the death of a sibling (Jonas et al., 2018), cyberbullying (Alhujailli & Karwowski, 2019), and sexual dating violence (Hébert et al., 2017), which have been shown to be stressful and related to poor outcomes but not commonly labeled as ACEs. To advance the field, careful consideration and tool development would be necessary to improve how constructs are measured if an expanded ACEs inventory was adopted.

A critique of the original ACEs is that the list is not comprehensive (Finkelhor et al., 2013). Even though the expanded list presented in Table 1 may lead to a broader scope of ACEs, it would also not be comprehensive and overtime would require further revisions to remain relevant. Notably, Finkelhor et al. (2015) have cautioned against investing too much effort into developing tools that add and remove ACEs in an attempt to develop an instrument with increased predictive ability; indeed, equally, or perhaps more important, is the development and testing of interventions that reduce or prevent childhood adversity.

Implications for policy and practice

Expanding the definitions of ACEs beyond the original 10 experiences would have implications for policy and practice. If the list of ACEs presented in Table 1 did prove to be empirically validated, it would represent a broader assessment of ACEs that may help to better inform policy and clinical practice on what experiences in childhood are related to poor outcomes. However, a larger list would introduce practical issues, especially in research. It is often the case that asking more questions in a study is not always feasible. On the other hand, not gleaning all relevant information regarding a particular circumstance also leaves researches with an incomplete picture of variables involved and foregoes a complete understanding of pertinent issues at hand. Importantly, policy and practice decisions should be evidence-based or at the very least evidence-informed. Therefore, improving the original ACEs items with a more updated and comprehensive assessment of ACEs that is derived using empirically sound techniques could potentially play a significant role in advancing the field.

Conclusion

Expanding what is considered a childhood adversity using data-driven techniques and then using this expanded list more consistently in research would have great benefits for the field of ACEs overall. However, revising and expanding the list of ACEs is not an easy task. Although it is beyond the scope of this chapter to validate a new list, recommendations for an expanded list of ACEs to be empirically assessed in future research have been provided, based on current knowledge in the field. Further work in this area, starting with the recommendations for an expanded list of ACEs outlined in Table 1 and then progressing to empirical testing to determine whether or not there is evidence to support an expanded list, is encouraged. Along with this work, implications on policy and practice of an expanded ACEs list also require careful consideration.

References

Afifi, T. O., Enns, M. W., Cox, B. J., Asumndson, G. J. G., Stein, M. B., & Sareen, J. (2008). Population attributable fractions of psychiatric disorders and suicide ideation and attempts associated with adverse childhood experiences. *American Journal of Public Health, 98*, 946–952.

Afifi, T. O., Ford, D., Gershoff, E. T., Merrick, M., Grogan-Kaylor, A., Ports, K. A., ... Peters, R. (2017). Spanking and adult mental health impairment: the case for the designation of spanking as an adverse childhood experience. *Child Abuse & Neglect*, *71*, 24–31. https://doi.org/10.1016/j.chiabu.2017.01.014.

Alhujailli, A., & Karwowski, W. (2019). Emotional and stress responses to cyberbullying. In G. Di Bucchianico (Ed.), *Advances in intelligent systems and computing*: Vol. 776. Advances in design for inclusion. AHFE 2018. Cham: Springer. https://doi.org/10.1007/978-3-319-94622-1_4.

Almuneef, M., ElChoueiry, N., Saleheen, S., & Al-Eissa, M. (2017). Gender-based disparities in the impact of adverse childhood experiences on adult health: findings from a national study in the Kingdom of Saudi Arabia. *International Journal for Equity in Health*, *16*, 1–9. https://doi.org/10.1186/s12939-017-0588-9.

Almuneef, M., Qayad, M., Aleissa, M., & Albuhairan, F. (2014). Adverse childhood experiences, chronic diseases, and risky health behaviors in Saudi Arabian adults: a pilot study. *Child Abuse & Neglect*, *38*(11), 1787–1793. https://doi.org/10.1016/j.chiabu.2014.06.003.

AlShawi, A., & Lafta, R. (2014). Relation between childhood experiences and adults' self-esteem: a sample from Baghdad. *Qatar Medical Journal*, *2014*. https://doi.org/10.5339/qmj.2014.14.

Anda, R. F., Croft, J. B., Felitti, V. J., Nordenberg, D., Giles, W. H., Williamson, D. F., & Giovino, G. (1999). Adverse childhood experiences and smoking during adolescence and adulthood. *Journal of the American Medical Association*, *282*, 1652–1658. https://doi.org/10.1001/jama.282.17.1652.

Bellis, M. A., Lowey, H., Leckenby, N., Hughes, K., & Harrison, D. (2014). Adverse childhood experiences: retrospective study to determine their impact on adult health behaviours and health outcomes in a UK population. *Journal of Public Health (Oxford, England)*, *36*, 81–91. https://doi.org/10.1093/pubmed/fdt038.

Berg, K. L., Acharya, K., Shi, C., & Michael, S. (2018). Delayed diagnosis and treatment among children with autism who experience adversity. *Journal of Autism and Developmental Disorders*, *48*, 45–54. https://doi.org/10.1007/s10803-017-3294-y.

Bucci, M., Wang, L. G., Koita, K., Purewal, S., Marques, S. S., & Harris, N. B. (2015). *ACE-questionnaire: User guide*. San Francisco, CA: Center for Youth Wellness.

Dube, S. R., Anda, R. F., Felitti, V. J., Chapman, D. P., Williamson, D. F., Giles, W. H., & Page, P. (2001). Childhood abuse, household dysfunction, and the risk of attempted suicide findings from the adverse childhood experiences study. *Journal of the American Medical Association*, *286*, 3089–3096. https://doi.org/10.1001/jama.286.24.3089.

Dube, S. R., Felitti, V. J., Dong, M., Chapman, D. P., Giles, W. H., & Anda, R. F. (2003). Childhood abuse, neglect, and household dysfunction and the risk of illicit drug use: the adverse childhood experiences study. *Pediatrics*, *111*, 564–572. https://doi.org/10.1542/peds.111.3.564.

Felitti, V. J., Anda, R. F., Nordenberg, D., Williamson, D. F., Spitz, A. M., Edwards, V., ... Marks, J. S. (1998). Relationship of child abuse and household dysfunction to many of the leading causes of death in adults. The adverse childhood experiences (ACE) study. *American Journal of Preventive Medicine*, *14*, 245–258. https://doi.org/10.1016/S0749-3797(98)00017-8.

Finkelhor, D., Shattuck, A., Turner, H., & Hamby, S. (2015). A revised inventory of adverse childhood experiences. *Child Abuse & Neglect*, *48*, 13–21. https://doi.org/10.1016/j.chiabu.2015.07.011.

Finkelhor, D., Turner, H. A., Shattuck, A., & Hamby, S. L. (2013). Violence, crime, and abuse exposure in a national sample of children and youth an update. *JAMA Pediatrics*, *167*, 614–621. https://doi.org/10.1001/jamapediatrics.2013.42.

Hambrick, E. P., Rubens, S. L., Brawner, T. W., & Taussig, H. N. (2018). Do sleep problems mediate the link between adverse childhood experiences and delinquency in preadolescent children in foster care? *Journal of Child Psychology and Psychiatry*, *2*, 140–149. https://doi.org/10.1111/jcpp.12802.

Hébert, M., Blais, M., & Lavoie, F. (2017). Prevalence of teen dating victimization among a representative sample of high school students in Quebec. *International Journal of Clinical and Health Psychology, 17*, 225–233. https://doi.org/10.1016/j.ijchp.2017.06.001.

Hillis, S. D., Anda, R. F., Felitti, V. J., Nordenberg, D., & Marchbanks, P. A. (2000). Adverse childhood experiences and sexually transmitted diseases in men and women: a retrospective study. *Pediatrics, 106*, 1–6. https://doi.org/10.1542/peds.106.1.e11. Objective, A.

Hughes, K., Lowey, H., Quigg, Z., & Bellis, M. A. (2016). Relationships between adverse childhood experiences and adult mental well-being: results from an English national household survey. *BMC Public Health, 16*, 1–11. https://doi.org/10.1186/s12889-016-2906-3.

Jonas, D., Scanlon, C., Rusch, R., Ito, J., & Joselow, M. (2018). Bereavement after a child's dead. *Child and Adolescent Psychiatric Clinics of North America, 27*, 579–590. https://doi.org/10.1016/j.chc.2018.05.010.

Kiburi, S. K., Molebatsi, K., Obondo, A., & Kuria, M. W. (2018). Adverse childhood experiences among patients with substance use disorders at a referral psychiatric hospital in Kenya. *BMC Psychiatry, 18*, 1–12. https://doi.org/10.1186/s12888-018-1780-1.

Lavrakas, P. J. (2008). *Encyclopedia of survey research methods*. Thousand Oaks, CA: Sage Publications, Inc.https://doi.org/10.4135/9781412963947.

Lee Oh, D., Jerman, P., Boparai, S. K. P., Koita, K., Briner, S., Bucci, M., & Harris, N. B. (2018). Review of tools for measuring exposure to adversity in children and adolescents. *Journal of Pediatric Health Care, 32*, 564–583. https://doi.org/10.1016/j.pedhc.2018.04.021.

Liming, K. W., & Grube, W. A. (2018). Wellbeing outcomes for children exposed to multiple adverse experiences in early childhood: a systematic review. *Child and Adolescent Social Work Journal, 35*, 317–335. https://doi.org/10.1007/s10560-018-0532-x.

Merrick, M. T., Ports, K. A., Ford, D. C., Afifi, T. O., Gershoff, E. T., & Grogan-Kaylor, A. (2017). Unpacking the impact of adverse childhood experiences on adult mental health. *Child Abuse & Neglect, 69*, 10–19. https://doi.org/10.1016/j.chiabu.2017.03.016.

Naal, H., El Jalkh, T., & Haddad, R. (2018). Adverse childhood experiences in substance use disorder outpatients of a Lebanese addiction center. *Psychology, Health & Medicine, 23*(9), 1137–1144. https://doi.org/10.1080/13548506.2018.1469781.

Quinn, M., Caldara, G., Collins, K., Owens, H., Ozodiegwu, I., Loudermilk, E., & Stinson, J. (2018). Methods for understanding childhood trauma: modifying the adverse childhood experiences international questionnaire for cultural competency. *International Journal of Public Health, 63*, 149–151. https://doi.org/10.1007/s00038-017-1058-2.

Schilling, E. A., Aseltine, R. H., & Gore, S. (2007). Adverse childhood experiences and mental health in young adults: a longitudinal survey. *BMC Public Health, 7*, 1–10. https://doi.org/10.1186/1471-2458-7-30.

Tabachnick, B. G., & Fidell, L. S. (2013). *Using multivariate statistics*. New Jersey: Pearson Education Inc.

Tonmyr, L., Med, E. J., Mery, L. S., & Harriet, L. (2005). The relationship between childhood adverse experiences and disability due to physical health problems in a community sample of women. *Women & Health, 41*, 23–35. https://doi.org/10.1300/J013v41n04.

World Health Organization (WHO). (2011a). *Adverse childhood experiences international questionnaire (ACE-IQ)*. Retrieved from: http://www.who.int/violence_injury_prevention/violence/activities/adverse_childhood_experiences/questionnaire.pdf?ua=1. on 19 July 2018.

World Health Organization (WHO). (2011b). *Adverse childhood experiences international questionnaire (pilot study review and finalization meeting)*. Retrieved from: http://www.who.int/violence_injury_prevention/violence/activities/adverse_childhood_experiences/global_research_network_may_2011.pdf. on 19 July 2018.

World Health Organization (WHO). (2011c). *Adverse childhood experiences international questionnaire (ACE-IQ) rationale for ACE-IQ*. Retrieved from: http://www.who.int/violence_injury_prevention/violence/activities/adverse_childhood_experiences/introductory_materials.pdf?ua=1. on 19 July 2018.

SECTION II

CHAPTER

4

ACEs and mental health outcomes

Julia L. Sheffler[a], *Ian Stanley*[b], *Natalie Sachs-Ericsson*[b]

[a]Florida State University College of Medicine, Tallahassee, FL, United States, [b]Department of Psychology, Florida State University, Tallahassee, FL, United States

Introduction

Over the past several decades, considerable research has accumulated documenting the long-term negative sequelae of adverse childhood experiences (ACEs). Most notably, childhood abuse has been linked to mental health conditions in adulthood (e.g., Afifi et al., 2008; Bergen, Martin, Richardson, Allison, & Roeger, 2004; Edwards, Holden, Felitti, & Anda, 2003; Kessler et al., 2010; MacMillan et al., 2001; Polusny & Follette, 1995), including disorders within the internalizing (e.g., anxiety, depression; Merrick et al., 2017; Sareen et al., 2013) and externalizing (e.g., antisocial personality, substance dependence; Dube et al., 2006; Toth, Cicchetti, & Kim, 2002) domains. In this chapter, we first review the possible biopsychosocial mechanisms through which ACEs lead to the development of psychopathology. Secondly, we review the literature linking ACEs with mental disorders and thereafter discuss the relationship between ACEs and psychosocial problems across the lifespan. Finally, we discuss implications for clinical practice, for policy, and future research directions.

Underlying mechanisms

There are several possible mechanisms through which childhood adversity may confer risk for psychopathology. ACEs represent early and often chronic stressors, which lead to biological and behavioral dysregulation, as

https://doi.org/10.1016/B978-0-12-816065-7.00004-5

well as problematic psychological coping strategies—each of which greatly increases the risk for developing an array of psychiatric disorders. While the specific biopsychosocial pathways to later psychological and social problems may vary from person to person, "sensitization to stress" appears to be one common mechanism. Stress sensitization due to early adversity has been well documented (Bandoli et al., 2017; Hammen, 1991; McLaughlin, Conron, Koenen, & Gilman, 2010; Rudolph & Flynn, 2007) and is likely due to disruption in core areas of development, as outlined by the biopsychosocial model. This model highlights the notion that biological, psychological, and social factors are inextricably intertwined in both normal and pathological development (see Borrell-Carrió, Suchman, & Epstein, 2004). The influence of ACEs on each area of the biopsychosocial model is outlined below.

Biological processes

ACEs are associated with neurophysiological changes in the development of the brain, such that individuals with high levels of ACEs may be more physiologically and psychologically sensitive to subsequent stressors. Multiple models have been posited to explain the processes by which ACEs change a person's physiological response to stressful situations. The neuroimmune network hypothesis presents a synthesis of the existing literature (Nusslock & Miller, 2016). This model states that individuals exposed to early adversity have sensitized corticoamygdala neural circuitry, which is associated with increased vigilance and heightened reactivity to threatening stimuli. The amygdala acts as an initial trigger for the body's response to stress, with mobilizing influences on the sympathetic nervous system and the hypothalamic-pituitary-adrenocortical (HPA) axis. In this way, ACEs increase physiological arousal in response to subsequent life stressors throughout adulthood (Miller, Chen, & Parker, 2011).

A downstream effect of heightened amygdala sensitivity, in response to ACEs exposure, is increased inflammation due to glucocorticoid insensitivity. Research demonstrates that individuals who have experienced high levels of ACEs have higher levels of inflammatory biomarkers (Danese & McEwen, 2012). Chronic low-grade inflammation has been implicated in various psychological (e.g., depression, substance use) and physical (e.g., metabolic, allergic, cardiovascular diseases; see Nusslock & Miller, 2016) health problems. Further, Nusslock and Miller (2016) posit that the relationship between the threat circuitry (i.e., corticoamygdala) and such immune/inflammatory signaling may be bidirectional. In their model of childhood adversity, cross-sensitization of both systems amplifies inflammation and neural threat responses through a positive feedback loop (Nusslock & Miller, 2016). In sum, the neuroimmune network hypothesis suggests that "low grade inflammatory activity, which acts together with genetics, lifestyle, and other exposures" predisposes individuals with ACEs to develop and maintain mental and physical health problems across the lifespan (p. 9; Nusslock & Miller, 2016).

This model is highly consistent with prior models of biological embedding, which posit that ACEs get "programmed" through epigenetic markings, affecting proinflammatory tendencies and interacting with genetic predispositions and behavioral factors to foster later disease (Miller et al., 2011). Thus, ACEs not only modify the structure and reactivity of the brain, but also influence neuroimmunological dysregulation and associated inflammation. These factors further influence the expression of genetic factors (Schwaiger et al., 2016). Changes in the structure and signaling of the brain appear to also influence behaviors through altered reward processing (Miller, Maletic, & Raison, 2009; Nusslock & Miller, 2016) and impaired self-regulation (Obradović, 2016). These biological changes further interact with behavioral risks.

Behavioral processes

Early adversity shapes how children interact with and perceive their environment and the people around them. Behaviorally, individuals who experience high levels of early stress are at increased risk to develop more dysfunctional coping mechanisms, engage in behaviors that damage health, and foster difficult social relationships in adulthood. For example, maltreated children tend to perceive their environment as more threatening and unpredictable, leading them to adopt more avoidant and disengaged coping strategies (Danese & McEwen, 2012). While these strategies may be functional in childhood (Briere, 2002), habitual use of such strategies may be detrimental in adulthood. Avoidant coping encompasses a wide range of psychological and behavioral strategies, including drug and alcohol use, negative eating patterns, and avoidance of stressful experiences, people, and situations. Avoidance in the face of a stressor diminishes the capacity for mastering a problematic situation. Research consistently demonstrates that ACEs are associated with these avoidant coping strategies which, in turn, contribute to negative health behaviors (Dube, Felitti, Dong, Giles, & Anda, 2003).

In addition to increased use of maladaptive coping strategies, ACEs are also associated with decreased use of adaptive coping skills (i.e., active coping, emotional support, planning, and reframing; Helitzer, Graeber, LaNoue, & Newbill, 2015). For example, one study found that individuals who reported that ACEs had a negative impact on their lives in adulthood were significantly (1) less likely to use adaptive coping strategies and (2) more likely to use maladaptive coping strategies (Helitzer et al., 2015). Importantly, active coping strategies are associated with more successful outcomes in the face of new stressors (Sandler, Kim-Bae, & MacKinnon, 2000; Sandler, Tein, Mehta, Wolchik, & Ayers, 2000). Thus, early adversity shapes how a person learns to interact with and cope with other people and environmental stressors.

These maladaptive coping mechanisms appear to develop not only through environmental learning, but also through neurophysiological changes to reward circuits (Kim et al., 2013) and executive functioning areas of the brain (Kim et al., 2013). For example, Evans and Kim (2013) explain that low-income children often have multiple self-regulatory deficits, including poorer attention, decreased inhibition, and difficulty in delaying gratification. Additionally, Nusslock and Miller (2016) hypothesize that inflammation dampens reward sensitivity, leading to high-risk behaviors (e.g., drug, alcohol use, overeating) that serve, in part, as an attempt to either increase positive emotions or dampen the experience of negative emotions. There is some evidence for this hypothesis from studies examining childhood maltreatment and low childhood socioeconomic status, both of which are associated with increased drug and alcohol misuse, decreased physical activity, and poorer diets (Felitti et al., 1998; Miller et al., 2011). Therefore, behavioral coping strategies may be inextricably linked with the neurophysiological changes associated with ACEs.

Psychological

ACEs also have a significant impact on how a person views themselves within their environment. A negative self-schema may have rippling effects on one's ability to recover from stress (Segal, 1988). Childhood abuse experiences, in particular, may lead a person to have more negative interpretations of stressful life events (Liu, Choi, Boland, Mastin, & Alloy, 2013) and more negative internalized self-schemas (Gibb & Abela, 2008; Sachs-Ericsson, Verona, Joiner, & Preacher, 2006). These processes lead to an increase in (1) negative affect, (2) the likelihood of a behavioral response that exacerbates a problematic situation, and (3) risk for internalizing and externalizing mental disorders.

There is some evidence that childhood verbal and emotional abuse confer risk for development of a negative cognitive style (Sachs-Ericsson et al., 2006), which is a risk factor for depression (Alloy, Abramson, & Francis, 1999; Sachs-Ericsson, Joiner, Cougle, Stanley, & Sheffler, 2015). Negative cognitive style (Abramson, Metalsky, & Alloy, 1989) has been defined as a characteristic way of attributing the causes of negative life events to stable and global factors and making self-critical judgments of one's character (Alloy et al., 2004; Seligman, Abramson, Semmel, & Von Baeyer, 1979), as well as having dysfunctional attitudes and maladaptive self-schemas (Beck & Steer, 1987). One aspect of a negative cognitive style is self-criticism (Beck, Epstein, & Harrison, 1983). Such negative cognitive styles are strongly associated with poor emotion regulation (Gross, 1998), which is a transdiagnostic feature of numerous mental disorders (Nemeroff, 2016), such as mood disorders, posttraumatic stress disorder (PTSD), substance use, and personality disorders (see Hofmann, Sawyer, Fang, & Asnaani, 2012).

Summary of underlying mechanisms

In sum, ACEs disrupt the development of adaptive emotion regulation processes in each of the areas of the biopsychosocial model. Psychologically, ACEs appear to alter interpretations of threat in the environment, negative cognitive styles, and beliefs about self-worth, which influence coping strategies enacted and the biological response to stress. Biologically, ACEs alter processes in the amygdala and prefrontal cortex—areas that play vital roles in the processing and response to stressful stimuli (Kim et al., 2013). Finally, behaviorally, these changes lead to maladaptive coping mechanisms that further the neuroimmune dysregulation (Nusslock & Muller, 2016). Ultimately, each of these psychosocial, behavioral, and biological factors works independently and interactively to increase risk for the development of mental disorders. The complexity of this network demonstrates why early adversity may lead to such a variety of psychological sequelae.

ACEs and mental disorders

ACEs broadly contribute to overall risk for developing a wide range of mental disorders (Edwards et al., 2003; Kessler et al., 2010; Polusny & Follette, 1995). Afifi et al. (2008) found that the estimated attributable fractions for mental disorders related to having experienced any childhood adversity (i.e., childhood sexual or physical abuse, exposure to intimate partner violence) ranged from 22% to 32% among women and 20% to 24% among men. Indeed, other similar models suggest that childhood adversity is associated with almost 45% of childhood-onset disorders, and up to 32% of later-onset disorders (Green et al., 2010). Thus, the effects of ACEs are clearly persistent through adulthood. Notably, ACEs have a particularly strong link with mood and anxiety disorders.

Mood and anxiety disorders

One of the most consistent relationships identified is between early adversity and the development of mood and anxiety disorders in adolescence and adulthood (De, Demyttenaere, & Bruffaerts, 2013; Heim, Newport, Mletzko, Miller, & Nemeroff, 2008; Heim, Shugart, Craighead, & Nemeroff, 2010; Liu, Jager-Hyman, Wagner, Alloy, & Gibb, 2012; Sachs-Ericsson, Sheffler, Stanley, Piazza, & Preacher, 2017; Sareen et al., 2013). For example, researchers found that people who were verbally abused had 1.6 times as many symptoms of depression and anxiety as those who had not been verbally abused, and were twice as likely to have suffered a mood or anxiety disorder over their lifetime (Sachs-Ericsson et al., 2006).

Further, one study of active duty military personnel found that number of ACEs (i.e., childhood physical abuse, childhood sexual abuse, economic deprivation, exposure to domestic violence, parental divorce/separation, parental substance abuse problems, hospitalization as a child, and apprehension by a child protection service) was associated with the occurrence of a mood and anxiety disorders in the previous year (Sareen et al., 2013). Metaanalyses have confirmed that a history of childhood physical or sexual abuse significantly increases the risk for depression and anxiety disorders (Li, D'Arcy, & Meng, 2016; Lindert et al., 2014). For instance, Li et al. (2016) concluded that a 10%–25% reduction in child abuse and neglect could potentially prevent 31.4–80.3 million depression and anxiety cases worldwide.

For mood disorders specifically, the number of ACEs a person experiences is associated with increases in recent and lifetime depressive disorders (Chapman et al., 2004). Chapman et al. (2004) note that, of the ACEs examined (i.e., emotional, physical, and sexual abuse, battered mother, household substance abuse, parental divorce/separation, criminal household member, and mental illness in the household), emotional abuse demonstrated the strongest relationship to later depressive symptoms. In addition to the relationship between ACEs and mood disorders, ACEs are also associated with poorer psychosocial functioning among individuals with depression and bipolar disorders. Lu, Mueser, Rosenberg, and Jankowski (2008) demonstrated that, among individuals with a major mood disorder, ACEs were associated with number of suicide attempts, earlier first hospitalization, adult physical or sexual victimization and PTSD, riskier health behaviors, increased likelihood of a substance use disorder (SUD) diagnosis, greater medical service utilization, poorer self-reported health, and increased risk of being homeless.

The effects of ACEs on the development and course of anxiety disorders are similar to those of mood disorders. Further, the effects of ACEs continue to influence mood and anxiety disorders across the lifespan, with an increased number of ACEs associated with higher odds of having an anxiety disorder even in older adulthood (Raposo, Mackenzie, Henriksen, & Afifi, 2014). Of the various ACEs in the literature, childhood physical and sexual abuse and a history of family violence specifically appear to show the strongest relationships with later anxiety disorders (De et al., 2013; Lindert et al., 2014; Mancini, Van Ameringen, & Macmillan, 1995). Early sexual abuse is associated with higher rates of generalized anxiety disorder, social anxiety disorder, and panic disorder (Cougle, Timpano, Sachs-Ericsson, Keough, & Riccardi, 2010), as well as developing a specific phobia or agoraphobia (Fergusson, Horwood, & Lynskey, 1996). Given the mechanisms through which ACEs increase physiological and psychosocial dysfunction in response to new stressors, it is unsurprising that ACEs would contribute to maladaptive anxiety, hypervigilance, and worry.

PTSD

ACEs contribute to the development of PTSD through both direct and indirect pathways. First, experiencing an early trauma could directly contribute to the development of PTSD, wherein the childhood experience may serve as an index trauma per *DSM*-5 Criterion A (APA, 2013). Additionally, ACEs increase the likelihood of developing PTSD in response to stressors later in life (Cloitre et al., 2009; Kaplow, Dodge, Amaya-Jackson, & Saxe, 2005; Sachs-Ericsson, Rushing, Stanley, & Sheffler, 2016). There are a number of factors related to ACEs and the subsequent development of PTSD. For example, early abuse increases the risk for revictimization (Stein, Jang, Taylor, Vernon, & Livesley, 2002), and studies have suggested that trauma has a cumulative effect in increasing risk for PTSD (Cougle, Resnick, & Kilpatrick, 2009). Additionally, individuals exposed to ACEs have heightened reactivity to new stressors (Smid, Kleber, Rademaker, van Zuiden, & Vermetten, 2013), as well as altered neuroimmune functioning (Nusslock & Miller, 2016). Thus, individuals with increased ACEs are at increased risk for the development of PTSD following significant stressors in adulthood (McLaughlin et al., 2010).

Substance use

SUDs occur at much higher rates among individuals with ACEs. As previously noted, it is likely that substance use is adopted as a form of coping. For example, Jester, Steinberg, Heitzeg, and Zucker (2015) found that alcohol consumption in young adulthood is a strategy adopted by individuals who have experienced early trauma to decrease negative affect. They demonstrated that, for individuals who reported early trauma, the expectancy that alcohol would help them cope was a significant mediator between early trauma and later alcohol use. Further, multiple studies have shown that the number of ACEs a person experiences has a graded relationship to alcohol use, and an associate with beginning to drink alcohol earlier in life (Chatterjee et al., 2018; Dube et al., 2006; Dube, Anda, Felitti, Edwards, & Croft, 2002). Gender also influences the occurrence of alcohol use disorders. In general, men, compared to women, have a higher risk for developing an alcohol use disorder; notably, however, as the number of ACEs increases, the gender gap narrows (Evans, Grella, & Upchurch, 2017).

The relationship between ACEs and drug and polysubstance use is similar to that seen between ACEs and alcohol use. For example, Dube et al. (2003) found that for each childhood adversity experienced, the likelihood of earlier drug use increased, as did lifetime illicit substance use. ACEs are also associated with increased polysubstance use (Brockie, Dana-Sacco, Wallen, Wilcox, & Campbell, 2015) and increased likelihood of being diagnosed with a SUD (Giordano, Ohlsson, Kendler, Sundquist, & Sundquist, 2014). Regardless of the number of ACEs, polysubstance use remains higher in men than women (Evans et al., 2017). Notably, however, a SUD is similarly probable in men and women, although women's probability for a disorder exceeds men's as the number of ACEs increases (Evans et al., 2017).

Personality disorders

ACEs are frequently associated with the development of personality disorders. Battle et al. (2004) found that up to 82% of individuals with a diagnosed personality disorder (i.e., borderline, schizotypal, avoidant, or obsessive-compulsive) reported either abuse or neglect as a child. Of the personality disorders, borderline personality disorder (BPD) is most consistently associated with childhood maltreatment (Battle et al., 2004). As noted, ACEs are associated with deficits in emotional regulation skills (Carvalho Fernando et al., 2014; Cloitre, Miranda, Stovall-McClough, & Han, 2005) that contribute to the development of personality disorders, particularly BPD. Linehan's (1993; see also Crowell, Beauchaine, & Linehan, 2009) biosocial model of BPD proposes that invalidating and inconsistent environments (i.e., abusive or neglectful childhood experience) are etiologically related to BPD. This model is supported by recent findings that ACEs influence stress regulation in individuals with BPD, and that this relationship is moderated by problematic attachment-related regulatory processes (Ehrenthal, Levy, Scott, & Granger, 2018). Thus, early relationships, which may be disrupted by ACEs, serve as a possible pathway to the development of a personality disorder in adulthood.

Eating disorders

The association between eating disorders and ACEs, especially early abuse experiences, is well documented (Caslini et al., 2016; Danese & Tan, 2013; Sachs-Ericsson, Medley, Kendall–Tackett, & Taylor, 2011; Shin & Miller, 2012; Speranza et al., 2003). Guillaume et al. (2016) found a dose-response relationship between the number of childhood trauma subtypes (i.e., sexual and physical abuse, physical neglect, and emotional abuse and neglect) and the severity of eating disorder characteristics, demonstrating that childhood traumas are additive in their impact on disordered eating. Additionally, Isohookana, Marttunen, Hakko, Riipinen, and Riala (2016) found that the type of childhood adversity may influence the eating pathology in adolescents. For example, adolescent girls with a history of sexual abuse were more likely to be obese and to use extreme weight loss behaviors, girls who witnessed intimate partner violence between parents or whose parent(s) died were more likely to excessively exercise, and parental unemployment was associated with obesity and being underweight.

Investigators have examined the mechanisms underlying the association between exposure to ACEs and the development of eating pathology. Disordered eating mediates the relationship between traumatic childhood experiences and higher body mass index in adulthood (Bakalar et al., 2018). Further, the relationship between ACEs (i.e., emotional, physical, and sexual abuse and neglect) and emotional eating is mediated by depressive symptoms and, more prominently, emotion dysregulation (Michopoulos et al., 2015). Thus, the relationship between ACEs and eating disorders may be driven by the same maladaptive coping that contributes to emotion regulation difficulties, while the type of disorder developed may depend on the specific type of childhood adversity, social experience, and internalized self-schemas.

Sachs-Ericsson et al. (2011) point to the importance of considering the interplay between genetics, parental psychopathology, exposure to ACEs, and the development of eating disorder symptoms. Using structural equation modeling, they demonstrated that parental pathology, including both symptoms of internalizing disorders and externalizing disorders, directly contributed to child abuse as well as to symptoms of binge eating disorders. Additionally, exposure to abuse (e.g., sexual or physical abuse) predicted binge symptoms and partially mediated associations between parental psychopathology and binge-eating behaviors. In this regard, other studies have found important interactive effects of exposure to ACEs, genetics, and development of eating disorder symptoms. For example, Akkermann et al. (2012) demonstrated that the effect of a number of ACEs (i.e., physical, sexual and emotional abuse or neglect, parental pathology, and parental death) on binge eating and on drive for thinness was moderated by the serotonin transporter gene, and this effect was more pronounced for individuals who experienced childhood sexual abuse in particular. The researchers concluded that exposure to ACEs may heighten susceptibility to serotonergic dysregulation following stress and, in turn, increase vulnerability to disturbed eating behaviors. Thus, both emotional and biological dysregulation due to ACEs appear to contribute to the development of eating pathology.

Psychotic disorders

A metaanalysis demonstrated that ACEs (i.e., all forms of childhood abuse and neglect, parental death or separation, bullying by peers, and being taken into care) are associated with an almost two-fold increase in the persistence of psychotic experiences and symptoms (Trotta, Murray, & Fisher, 2015). Researchers have found that heightened stress reactivity is a key mechanism linking ACEs to the development of psychotic experiences in adulthood (Cristóbal-Narváez et al., 2016). In combination with genetic vulnerabilities, psychotic symptoms may develop through the previously discussed neuroimmunological pathways, which sensitize individuals to stress and disrupt dopaminergic pathways. One hypothesis for psychotic experience posits that psychosis occurs due to the attribution of salience to irrelevant internal and external cues, and salience processing is associated with elevated dopamine levels in the striatum (Schmidt et al., 2017). Notably, however, recent research examining genotypes known to affect dopamine levels failed to find an association between the genotypes examined and psychosis related to ACEs (Trotta et al., 2018). Thus, these hypotheses require further empirical assessment.

Obsessive-compulsive disorder

There is some evidence linking ACEs to obsessive-compulsive disorder (OCD), although the relationship diminishes once other anxiety and depression symptoms are included in the models (Briggs & Price, 2009; Mathews, Kaur, & Stein, 2008). Among those with OCD, a history of ACEs does increase risk for comorbidity (Visser, van Oppen, van Megen, Eikelenboom, & van Balkom, 2014), particularly with affective, substance use, and eating disorders, but not anxiety disorders (Visser et al., 2014). There also appear to be some indirect effects of ACEs on the development of OCD. ACEs are associated with increased gray matter in the caudate nucleus and, moreover, increased volume and metabolism in this area is consistently associated with OCD (Benedetti et al., 2012). ACEs also influence psychological correlates of OCD, such as experiential avoidance (Briggs & Price, 2009) and increased conscientiousness (Mathews et al., 2008). Thus, there appears to be more evidence for an indirect pathway between ACEs and later obsessive-compulsive symptoms, though further research is needed.

Sleep disorders

Sleep problems are an important symptom associated with a wide range of physical and mental health conditions. Kajeepeta, Gelaye, Jackson, and Williams (2015) review of the literature linking ACEs with sleep disorders suggests that a history of childhood adversity is associated with sleep apnea, narcolepsy, nightmares, sleep paralysis, and other sleep disorders. Specifically, childhood sexual assault appears to carry significantly increased risk for insomnia and subjective sleep disturbances later in adulthood (Lind, Aggen, Kendler, York, & Amstadter, 2016). This developing literature is important, as sleep problems are increasingly recognized as a transdiagnostic risk factor (Harvey & Buysse, 2017), which may also hamper quality of life.

Suicidal ideation, plans, and attempts

In addition to the effects of ACEs on the mental disorders enumerated earlier, research has also identified ACEs as risk factors for suicidal thoughts and behaviors. For instance, in a retrospective cohort study of 17,337 primary care patients, Dube et al. (2001) found that the presence of at least one childhood adversity was associated with a two- to five-fold risk of reporting a lifetime suicide attempt. Remarkably, participants with seven or more ACEs were 31.1 times more likely to report a suicide attempt history. These findings highlight that more ACEs are associated with greater suicide risk. Complementing these findings, utilizing data from the National Comorbidity Survey-Replication (NCS-R), Afifi et al. (2008) found that the proportion of suicide ideation and attempts attributable to child physical abuse, sexual abuse, and exposure to intimate partner violence (i.e., population attributable fractions) were 16% and 50%, respectively, for women and 21% and 33%, respectively, for men. Indeed, the potential effects of ACEs on suicide-related outcomes have been widely reported (see Kalmakis & Chandler, 2015, for review).

To elucidate potential mechanisms whereby ACEs relate to suicidal thoughts and behaviors, we will now turn to a brief discussion of a leading theoretical framework—the interpersonal theory of suicide (ITS). The ITS, originally developed by Joiner (2005) and expanded upon by Van Orden et al. (2010), proposes that suicidal ideation develops when one simultaneously experiences intractable feelings of thwarted belongingness (cf. loneliness) and perceived burdensomeness (i.e., an incorrect mental calculation that one's death is worth more than one's life to others). It is conceivable that the experience of ACEs, particularly interpersonal ACEs such as emotional abuse, might contribute to the development and maintenance of these constructs and, in turn, lead to suicidal ideation (cf. Sachs-Ericsson, Stanley, Sheffler, Selby, & Joiner, 2017). Further, the theory posits that individuals who think about suicide will make a suicide attempt if they also experience the capability for suicide, which is a consequence partially of genetics (Smith et al., 2012), but also of exposure to painful and provocative events (e.g., physical or sexual abuse).

This ITS has garnered strong empirical support (see Chu et al., 2017), including in relation to ACEs. For instance, utilizing cross-sectional data from the National Comorbidity Survey (NCS), Joiner et al. (2007) found that childhood abuse demonstrated significant associations with lifetime suicide attempts, and consistent with the hypotheses of the ITS, that the effects were strongest for childhood physical and violent sexual abuse as opposed to molestation and verbal abuse. That is, although all forms of childhood abuse are clinically relevant regarding suicide-related outcomes, the results of Joiner et al. (2007) suggest that more violent forms of abuse may confer greater risk for suicide attempts in part due to an increased capability for suicide. Sachs-Ericsson, Stanley, et al. (2017) extended these findings by examining baseline (NCS-1) and 10-year follow-up (NCS-2) data from the NCS. The authors found that nonviolent and violent abuse reported at baseline predicted suicide attempts by 10-year follow-up and that rates of new-onset suicide attempts were higher for those experiencing violent abuse. The authors additionally found that whereas nonviolent abuse exerted its effect on suicide attempts via mental disorders, violent abuse demonstrated a direct link to suicide attempts, which the authors hypothesized might reflect a manifestation of the capability for suicide.

Earlier, we have highlighted how childhood abuse is one form of adversity that contributes to suicide risk. It is important to emphasize that other ACEs (e.g., parental psychopathology; Mok et al., 2016) also confer risk for suicide. Moreover, there appears to be a dose-response with regard to the number of ACEs experienced and suicide risk (Merrick et al., 2017). Importantly, the effects of ACEs on suicide risk appear to persist into late life, with multiple biopsychosocial pathways implicated in the long-term pathogenesis of suicide-related outcomes (see Sachs-Ericsson et al., 2016, for review). In part due to the aforementioned findings, the National Action Alliance for Suicide Prevention and the US Surgeon General identified the prevention of ACEs as a critical path for suicide risk mitigation (US Department of Health and Human Services, & Office of the Surgeon General, 2012).

Summary

Overall, the literature demonstrates a link between ACEs and the development of a variety of later mental disorders and symptoms, encompassing PTSD, OCD, personality disorders, psychotic disorders, mood and anxiety disorders, eating disorders, sleep problems, SUDs, and suicidality. It is important to acknowledge, however, that counts of ACEs are still infrequently examined relative to specific forms of adversity (e.g., childhood abuse). Thus, the current review of the literature may not fully account for the potential influence of overall adverse environment on later mental health outcomes. Regardless, it is clear from the current evidence that mental disorders may arise due to singular types of childhood adversities as well as more complex interactions between multiple forms of ACEs (i.e., multifinality and equifinality).

Psychosocial functioning and quality of life

Functional impairment is a key criterion for a cluster of symptoms to be considered a mental disorder (APA, 2013). Thus, it is important to consider how ACEs disrupt psychosocial functioning and quality of life for people with and without mental health conditions. First, children exposed to ACEs are less resilient when faced with new challenges, and this decrease in resilience appears to co-occur with more difficulties in school (i.e., more likely to repeat a grade, less engaged in school; Bethell, Newacheck, Hawes, & Halfon, 2014). In adulthood, Nurius, Green, Logan-Greene, and Borjaa (2015) found that ACEs influence psychological well-being, psychological distress, and impairment in daily activities. The authors demonstrate that these relationships are also moderated by adult stress levels (Nurius et al., 2015). Psychological well-being, regardless of the presence of a mental disorder, is clearly influenced by stress levels and resiliency resources to respond effectively to new stressors.

In addition to reduced well-being and quality of life factors, ACEs and related mental health conditions are also associated with significant impairments in psychosocial functioning beginning early in life. For example, Giovanelli, Reynolds, Mondi, and Ou (2016) found that children with four or more ACEs were less likely to graduate high school, had riskier health behaviors, and were less likely to hold skilled jobs as adults. Further, individuals with a greater number of ACEs are more likely to have juvenile arrests and felony charges (Giovanelli et al., 2016). Roos et al. (2016) similarly found that childhood maltreatment increases the risk for incarceration/criminal justice involvement, as well as victimization. Notably, these relationships remained significant after controlling for other sociodemographic risk factors. Even among homeless families, it is exposure to maltreatment rather than family dysfunction that is predictive of children's socioemotional problems (Narayan et al., 2017). Such studies demonstrate the persistent effects of ACEs on social functioning across the lifespan and provide insight into how ACEs may contribute to intergenerational cycles of poverty.

Prevention and intervention

Given the substantial individual and societal burden of ACEs-related mental conditions, we next discuss the developing literature on prevention and intervention strategies for the sequelae of ACEs. This is especially important considering that among individuals with mental disorders, those with a history of abuse have a more chronic course and may respond more poorly to currently available treatments (Lu et al., 2008). Yet, it is equally important to acknowledge that many individuals are resilient in the face of early adversity (Logan-Greene, Green, Nurius, & Longhi, 2014). Thus, there are potentially modifiable mechanisms supporting such resilience that might offer points for intervention.

It is important to first concede that, in childhood and adolescence, there are significant barriers to the implementation of early intervention programs due to the dysfunction that is often inherent in the child's family and social structure (Saxe, Ellis, Fogler, Hansen, & Sorkin, 2017); yet, some early interventions show promise. Kinniburgh, Blaustein, Spinazzola, and van der Kolk (2005) provide a framework identifying the key areas an effective treatment should address, including "safety, self-regulation, self-reflective information processing, traumatic experience integration, relational engagement or attachment, and positive affect enhancement" (p. 424). These goals for treatment are aligned with core processes that may be disrupted by ACEs. Bethell, Gombojav, Solloway, and Wissow (2016) indicate that mindfulness-based, mind-body approaches to intervention hold promise for addressing multiple processes simultaneously, thereby improving the social and emotional well-being of children and adolescents. Such mindfulness-based approaches might provide cost-effective interventions that could be implemented at any stage of development.

In adulthood, ACEs may be better addressed through treatment styles with particular emphasis on transdiagnostic factors. For example, Chandler, Roberts, and Chiodo (2015) tested a strengths-based intervention for increasing resilience and positive health behaviors in college students exposed to ACEs, finding that the intervention promoted improved health behaviors after four 1-hour sessions. More recently, interventions specifically designed to target emotion regulation skills are being examined. Cameron, Carroll, and Hamilton (2018) evaluated the ACE Overcomers program, which was specifically designed to help individuals exposed to ACEs improve their social functioning, emotion regulation, and self-efficacy. The authors found that participation in the 12-session program was associated with significant improvements in "emotion regulation skills, psychological resilience, mental health, quality of life, and physical health problems" in a sample of outpatient adults (p. 430; Cameron et al., 2018). These findings encouragingly demonstrate that relatively brief, structured interventions may broadly affect each component of the biopsychosocial model influenced by ACEs.

Implications for public policy

ACEs are distributed across the social economic status gradients (Halfon, Larson, Son, Lu, & Bethell, 2017). Therefore, a broad community-based approach is necessary (i.e., individuals, families, communities, and the larger society; Larkin, Felitti, & Anda, 2014; Ports et al., 2017). Increased funding for intervention and prevention programs is needed to attenuate the consequences of ACEs, as well as to potentially prevent the occurrence of ACEs. Although potentially more challenging to implement, early-years interventions that are effective could yield large social and economic returns on investment in the long run (Caspi et al., 2017).

Importantly, the proportion of child victims who are not coming to the attention of practitioners is unclear. Thus, collaborative efforts are needed to build a framework for public health surveillance that can be used to define the global health burden of ACEs, define unmet needs, and develop strategies to address such needs (Anda, Butchart, Felitti, & Brown, 2010; Finkelhor, Turner, Shattuck, & Hamby, 2015). Community outreach programs should adopt evidence-based strategies for early intervention (Anda et al., 2010). Community outreach should consider providing parent training for high-risk parents and the provision of mental health treatment when appropriate, making available programs proven to be effective in mitigating the deleterious effects of ACEs. To better identify families and children in need, healthcare policy should consider recommendations to primary care physicians for universal ACEs screening as a means of surveillance (Dube, 2018; although, see Chapter 8). As Dube (2018) suggests, such a surveillance tool may help to inform and guide both healthcare practice and policy. To accomplish this, we need to move forward integrating ACEs-related research with public policy (Bethell et al., 2017).

Future directions

While there remain many avenues to explore to better develop our understanding of the psychological sequela of ACEs, the literature may most benefit from methodological improvements. McLaughlin (2016) outlines specific needs for future research. First, she posits that ACEs are inconsistently defined across the literature, and early adversity is often used synonymously with early trauma. Because of inconsistencies in definitions, ACEs are measured differently across studies and often fail to include important adversities. For example, in addition to the ACEs set forth by the original ACE Study (Felitti et al., 1998), Finkelhor et al. (2015) identified peer victimization, peer isolation/rejection, and community violence exposure as important contributors to the prediction of mental and physical health problems. Although they present a more representative inventory, it is important to consider additional ACEs, such as childhood racial or ethnic discrimination, that contribute to important outcomes across the lifespan (Bethell et al., 2017). Improvements in the assessment of ACEs may have significant implications for improving the specificity of our research models when examining the links between ACEs and later mental health disorders. For example, it is possible that ACEs that activate the stress response may result in different neurodevelopmental outcomes than those associated with neglect or deprivation (McLaughlin, Sheridan, & Lambert, 2014).

McLaughlin (2016) further stresses the need to better identify mechanisms within the individual and the environment that link ACEs to the onset of psychopathology (i.e., multifinality). This is particularly relevant regarding the empirical examination of the pathways proposed in the neuroimmune network hypothesis. This and similar models provide clear descriptions of the cascade of biological changes that follow early adversity; however, explicit longitudinal investigations are needed. Further, research incorporating the complex interplay of genetic, psychological, and environmental factors may improve the validity of such models. Within these models, it will be important to distinguish whether the mechanisms linking the type of childhood adversity with psychopathology are general or specific (McLaughlin, 2016).

Ultimately, the final steps in ACEs research will be understanding how to effectively prevent the occurrence of ACEs and to implement effective interventions for those exposed. This step may require broad changes in public and health policy to effectively assess patients and to provide a cost- and time-efficient intervention options. Further evaluation of current interventions and widescale assessment of public policy changes will be key for effectively mitigating the burden ACEs place on the individual and health care systems as a whole.

References

Abramson, L. Y., Metalsky, G. I., & Alloy, L. B. (1989). Hopelessness depression: a theory-based subtype of depression. *Psychological Review*, *96*(2), 358.

Afifi, T. O., Enns, M. W., Cox, B. J., Asmundson, G. J., Stein, M. B., & Sareen, J. (2008). Population attributable fractions of psychiatric disorders and suicide ideation and attempts associated with adverse childhood experiences. *American Journal of Public Health*, *98*(5), 946–952.

Akkermann, K., Kaasik, K., Kiive, E., Nordquist, N., Oreland, L., & Harro, J. (2012). The impact of adverse life events and the serotonin transporter gene promoter polymorphism on the development of eating disorder symptoms. *Journal of Psychiatric Research*, *46*(1), 38–43. https://doi.org/10.1016/j.jpsychires.2011.09.013.

Alloy, L. B., Abramson, L. Y., & Francis, E. L. (1999). Do negative cognitive styles confer vulnerability to depression? *Current Directions in Psychological Science*, *8*(4), 128–132.

Alloy, L. B., Abramson, L. Y., Gibb, B. E., Crossfield, A. G., Pieracci, A. M., Spasojevic, J., & Steinberg, J. A. (2004). Developmental antecedents of cognitive vulnerability to depression: review of findings from the cognitive vulnerability to depression project. *Journal of Cognitive Psychotherapy*, *18*(2), 115–134.

Anda, R. F., Butchart, A., Felitti, V. J., & Brown, D. W. (2010). Building a framework for global surveillance of the public health implications of adverse childhood experiences. *American Journal of Preventive Medicine*, *39*(1), 93–98.

APA. (2013). *Diagnostic and statistical manual of mental disorders* (5th ed.). Washington, DC: American Psychiatric Association [DSM-5].

Bakalar, J. L., Barmine, M., Druskin, L., Olsen, C. H., Quinlan, J., Sbrocco, T., & Tanofsky-Kraff, M. (2018). Childhood adverse life events, disordered eating, and body mass index in US Military service members. *International Journal of Eating Disorders*, *51*(5), 465–469.

Bandoli, G., Campbell-Sills, L., Kessler, R. C., Heeringa, S. G., Nock, M. K., Rosellini, A. J., … Stein, M. B. (2017). Childhood adversity, adult stress, and the risk of major depression or generalized anxiety disorder in US soldiers: a test of the stress sensitization hypothesis. *Psychological Medicine*, *47*(13), 2379–2392.

Battle, C. L., Shea, M. T., Johnson, D. M., Yen, S., Zlotnick, C., Zanarini, M. C., … McGlashan, T. H. (2004). Childhood maltreatment associated with adult personality disorders:

findings from the collaborative longitudinal personality disorders study. *Journal of Personality Disorders*, *18*(2), 193–211.

Beck, A. T., & Steer, R. A. (1987). *Manual for the revised Beck depression inventory*. San Antonio, TX: Psychological Corporation.

Beck, A. T., Epstein, N., & Harrison, R. (1983). Cognitions, attitudes and personality dimensions in depression. *British Journal of Cognitive Psychotherapy*, *1*(1), 1–16.

Benedetti, F., Poletti, S., Radaelli, D., Pozzi, E., Giacosa, C., Ruffini, C., ... Smeraldi, E. (2012). Caudate gray matter volume in obsessive-compulsive disorder is influenced by adverse childhood experiences and ongoing drug treatment. *Journal of Clinical Psychopharmacology*, *32*(4), 544–547.

Bergen, H. A., Martin, G., Richardson, A. S., Allison, S., & Roeger, L. (2004). Sexual abuse, antisocial behaviour and substance use: gender differences in young community adolescents. *Australian and New Zealand Journal of Psychiatry*, *38*(1–2), 34–41.

Bethell, C. D., Newacheck, P., Hawes, E., & Halfon, N. (2014). Adverse childhood experiences: assessing the impact on health and school engagement and the mitigating role of resilience. *Health Affairs*, *33*(12), 2106–2115.

Bethell, C., Gombojav, N., Solloway, M., & Wissow, L. (2016). Adverse childhood experiences, resilience and mindfulness-based approaches. *Child and Adolescent Psychiatric Clinics of North America*, *25*(2), 139–156. https://doi.org/10.1016/j.chc.2015.12.001.

Bethell, C. D., Carle, A., Hudziak, J., Gombojav, N., Powers, K., Wade, R., & Braveman, P. (2017). Methods to assess adverse childhood experiences of children and families: toward approaches to promote child well-being in policy and practice. *Academic Pediatrics*, *17*(7), S51–S69.

Borrell-Carrió, F., Suchman, A. L., & Epstein, R. M. (2004). The biopsychosocial model 25 years later: principles, practice, and scientific inquiry. *Annals of Family Medicine*, *2*(6), 576–582.

Briere, J. (2002). Treating adult survivors of severe childhood. In J. E. B. Myers, L. Berliner, & J. Briere, et al. (Eds.), *The APSAC handbook on child maltreatment* (pp. 175–202). Newbury Park, CA: Sage Publications.

Briggs, E. S., & Price, I. R. (2009). The relationship between adverse childhood experience and obsessive-compulsive symptoms and beliefs: the role of anxiety, depression, and experiential avoidance. *Journal of Anxiety Disorders*, *23*(8), 1037–1046.

Brockie, T., Dana-Sacco, G., Wallen, G., Wilcox, H., & Campbell, J. (2015). The relationship of adverse childhood experiences to PTSD, depression, poly-drug use and suicide attempt in reservation-based native American adolescents and young adults. *American Journal of Community Psychology*, *55*(3/4), 411–421. https://doi.org/10.1007/s10464-015-9721-3.

Cameron, L. D., Carroll, P., & Hamilton, W. K. (2018). Evaluation of an intervention promoting emotion regulation skills for adults with persisting distress due to adverse childhood experiences. *Child Abuse & Neglect*, *79*, 423–433.

Carvalho Fernando, S., Beblo, T., Schlosser, N., Terfehr, K., Otte, C., Löwe, B., ... Wingenfeld, K. (2014). The impact of self-reported childhood trauma on emotion regulation in borderline personality disorder and major depression. *Journal of Trauma & Dissociation*, *15*(4), 384–401. https://doi.org/10.1080/15299732.2013.863262.

Caslini, M., Bartoli, F., Crocamo, C., Dakanalis, A., Clerici, M., & Carrà, G. (2016). Disentangling the association between child abuse and eating disorders: a systematic review and meta-analysis. *Psychosomatic Medicine*, *78*(1), 79–90.

Caspi, A., Houts, R. M., Belsky, D. W., Harrington, H., Hogan, S., Ramrakha, S., ... Moffitt, T. E. (2017). Childhood forecasting of a small segment of the population with large economic burden. *Nature Human Behaviour*, *1*(1), 0005.

Chandler, G. E., Roberts, S. J., & Chiodo, L. (2015). Resilience intervention for young adults with adverse childhood experiences. *Journal of the American Psychiatric Nurses Association*, *21*(6), 406–416.

Chapman, D. P., Whitfield, C. L., Felitti, V. J., Dube, S. R., Edwards, V. J., & Anda, R. F. (2004). Adverse childhood experiences and the risk of depressive disorders in adulthood. *Journal of Affective Disorders*, *82*(2), 217–225.

Chatterjee, D., McMorris, B., Gower, A. L., Forster, M., Borowsky, I. W., & Eisenberg, M. E. (2018). Adverse childhood experiences and early initiation of marijuana and alcohol use: the potential moderating effects of internal assets. *Substance Use & Misuse*, 1–9.

Chu, C., Buchman-Schmitt, J. M., Stanley, I. H., Hom, M. A., Tucker, R. P., Hagan, C. R., … Joiner, T. E. (2017). The interpersonal theory of suicide: a systematic review and meta-analysis of a decade of Cross-National Research. *Psychological Bulletin*, https://doi.org/10.1037/bul0000123.

Cloitre, M., Miranda, R., Stovall-McClough, K. C., & Han, H. (2005). Beyond PTSD: emotion regulation and interpersonal problems as predictors of functional impairment in survivors of childhood abuse. *Behavior Therapy*, *36*(2), 119–124.

Cloitre, M., Stolbach, B. C., Herman, J. L., Kolk, B.v.d., Pynoos, R., Wang, J., & Petkova, E. (2009). A developmental approach to complex PTSD: childhood and adult cumulative trauma as predictors of symptom complexity. *Journal of Traumatic Stress*, *22*(5), 399–408. https://doi.org/10.1002/jts.20444.

Cougle, J. R., Timpano, K. R., Sachs-Ericsson, N., Keough, M. E., & Riccardi, C. J. (2010). Examining the unique relationships between anxiety disorders and childhood physical and sexual abuse in the National Comorbidity Survey-Replication. *Psychiatry Research*, *177*(1–2), 150–155. https://doi.org/10.1016/j.psychres.2009.03.008.

Cougle, J. R., Resnick, H., & Kilpatrick, D. G. (2009). Does prior exposure to interpersonal violence increase risk of PTSD following subsequent exposure? *Behaviour Research and Therapy*, *47*(12), 1012–1017.

Cristóbal-Narváez, P., Sheinbaum, T., Ballespí, S., Mitjavila, M., Myin-Germeys, I., Kwapil, T. R., & Barrantes-Vidal, N. (2016). Impact of adverse childhood experiences on psychotic-like symptoms and stress reactivity in daily life in nonclinical young adults. *PLoS One*, *11*(4), e0153557.

Crowell, S. E., Beauchaine, T. P., & Linehan, M. M. (2009). A biosocial developmental model of borderline personality: elaborating and extending linehan's theory. *Psychological Bulletin*, *135*(3), 495.

Danese, A., & McEwen, B. S. (2012). Adverse childhood experiences, allostasis, allostatic load, and age-related disease. *Physiology & Behavior*, *106*(1), 29–39.

Danese, A., & Tan, M. (2013). Childhood maltreatment and obesity: systematic review and meta-analysis. *Molecular Psychiatry*, *19*, 544. https://doi.org/10.1038/mp.2013.54.

De, M. V., Demyttenaere, K., & Bruffaerts, R. (2013). The relationship between adverse childhood experiences and mental health in adulthood. A systematic literature review. *Tijdschrift voor Psychiatrie*, *55*(4), 259–268.

Dube, S. R., Anda, R. F., Felitti, V. J., Chapman, D. P., Williamson, D. F., & Giles, W. H. (2001). Childhood abuse, household dysfunction, and the risk of attempted suicide throughout the life span: findings from the adverse childhood experiences study. *JAMA*, *286*(24), 3089–3096.

Dube, S. R., Anda, R. F., Felitti, V. J., Edwards, V. J., & Croft, J. B. (2002). Adverse childhood experiences and personal alcohol abuse as an adult. *Addictive Behaviors*, *27*(5), 713–725.

Dube, S. R. (2018). Continuing conversations about adverse childhood experiences (ACEs) screening: a public health perspective. *Child Abuse and Neglect*, *85*, 180–184.

Dube, S. R., Felitti, V. J., Dong, M., Chapman, D. P., Giles, W. H., & Anda, R. F. (2003). Childhood abuse, neglect, and household dysfunction and the risk of illicit drug use: the adverse childhood experiences study. *Pediatrics*, *111*(3), 564–572.

Dube, S. R., Felitti, V. J., Dong, M., Giles, W. H., & Anda, R. F. (2003). The impact of adverse childhood experiences on health problems: evidence from four birth cohorts dating back to 1900. *Preventive Medicine*, *37*(3), 268–277. https://doi.org/10.1016/S0091-7435(03)00123-3.

Dube, S. R., Miller, J. W., Brown, D. W., Giles, W. H., Felitti, V. J., Dong, M., & Anda, R. F. (2006). Adverse childhood experiences and the association with ever using alcohol and initiating alcohol use during adolescence. *Journal of Adolescent Health*, *38*(4), https://doi.org/10.1016/j.jadohealth.2005.06.006. 444.e441–444.e410.

Edwards, V. J., Holden, G. W., Felitti, V. J., & Anda, R. F. (2003). Relationship between multiple forms of childhood maltreatment and adult mental health in community respondents: results from the adverse childhood experiences study. *American Journal of Psychiatry, 160*(8), 1453–1460.

Ehrenthal, J. C., Levy, K. N., Scott, L. N., & Granger, D. A. (2018). Attachment-related regulatory processes moderate the impact of adverse childhood experiences on stress reaction in borderline personality disorder. *Journal of Personality Disorders, 32*(Supplement), 93–114.

Evans, G. W., & Kim, P. (2013). Childhood poverty, chronic stress, self-regulation, and coping. *Child Development Perspectives, 7*(1), 43–48.

Evans, E. A., Grella, C. E., & Upchurch, D. M. (2017). Gender differences in the effects of childhood adversity on alcohol, drug, and polysubstance-related disorders. *Social Psychiatry and Psychiatric Epidemiology, 52*(7), 901–912.

Felitti, V. J., Anda, R. F., Nordenberg, D., Williamson, D. F., Spitz, A. M., Edwards, V., … Marks, J. S. (1998). Relationship of childhood abuse and household dysfunction to many of the leading causes of death in adults: the adverse childhood experiences (ACE) study. *American Journal of Preventive Medicine, 14*(4), 245–258.

Fergusson, D. M., Horwood, L. J., & Lynskey, M. T. (1996). Childhood sexual abuse and psychiatric disorder in young adulthood. II. Psychiatric outcomes of childhood sexual abuse. *Journal of the American Academy of Child & Adolescent Psychiatry, 35*(10), 1365–1374.

Finkelhor, D., Turner, H. A., Shattuck, A., & Hamby, S. L. (2015). Prevalence of childhood exposure to violence, crime, and abuse: results from the national survey of children's exposure to violence. *JAMA Pediatrics, 169*(8), 746–754.

Gibb, B., & Abela, J. (2008). Emotional abuse, verbal victimization, and the development of children's negative inferential styles and depressive symptoms. *Cognitive Therapy and Research, 32*(2), 161–176. https://doi.org/10.1007/s10608-006-9106-x.

Giordano, G. N., Ohlsson, H., Kendler, K. S., Sundquist, K., & Sundquist, J. (2014). Unexpected adverse childhood experiences and subsequent drug use disorder: a Swedish population study (1995–2011). *Addiction (Abingdon, England), 109*(7), 1119–1127. https://doi.org/10.1111/add.12537.

Giovanelli, A., Reynolds, A. J., Mondi, C. F., & Ou, S. R. (2016). Adverse childhood experiences and adult well-being in a low-income, urban cohort. *Pediatrics*. peds-2015.

Green, J. G., McLaughlin, K. A., Berglund, P. A., Gruber, M. J., Sampson, N. A., Zaslavsky, A. M., & Kessler, R. C. (2010). Childhood adversities and adult psychiatric disorders in the national comorbidity survey replication I: associations with first onset of DSM-IV disorders. *Archives of General Psychiatry, 67*(2), 113–123.

Gross, J. J. (1998). The emerging field of emotion regulation: an integrative review. *Review of General Psychology, 2*(3), 271–299.

Guillaume, S., Jaussent, I., Maimoun, L., Ryst, A., Seneque, M., Villain, L., … Courtet, P. (2016). Associations between adverse childhood experiences and clinical characteristics of eating disorders. *Scientific Reports, 6*, 35761.

Halfon, N., Larson, K., Son, J., Lu, M., & Bethell, C. (2017). Income inequality and the differential effect of adverse childhood experiences in US children. *Academic Pediatrics, 17*(7), S70–S78.

Hammen, C. (1991). Generation of stress in the course of unipolar depression. *Journal of Abnormal Psychology, 100*(4), 555–561.

Harvey, A. G., & Buysse, D. J. (2017). *Treating sleep problems: A transdiagnostic approach.* Guilford Publications.

Heim, C., Newport, D. J., Mletzko, T., Miller, A. H., & Nemeroff, C. B. (2008). The link between childhood trauma and depression: insights from HPA axis studies in humans. *Psychoneuroendocrinology, 33*(6), 693–710. https://doi.org/10.1016/j.psyneuen.2008.03.008.

Heim, C., Shugart, M., Craighead, W. E., & Nemeroff, C. B. (2010). Neurobiological and psychiatric consequences of child abuse and neglect. *Developmental Psychobiology, 52*(7), 671–690. https://doi.org/10.1002/dev.20494.

Helitzer, D., Graeber, D., LaNoue, M., & Newbill, S. (2015). Don't step on the Tiger's tail: a mixed methods study of the relationship between adult impact of childhood adversity and use of coping strategies. *Community Mental Health Journal, 51*(7), 768–774. https://doi.org/10.1007/s10597-014-9815-7.

Hofmann, S. G., Sawyer, A. T., Fang, A., & Asnaani, A. (2012). Emotion dysregulation model of mood and anxiety disorders. *Depression and Anxiety, 29*(5), 409–416.

Isohookana, R., Marttunen, M., Hakko, H., Riipinen, P., & Riala, K. (2016). The impact of adverse childhood experiences on obesity and unhealthy weight control behaviors among adolescents. *Comprehensive Psychiatry, 71*, 17–24.

Jester, J. M., Steinberg, D. B., Heitzeg, M. M., & Zucker, R. A. (2015). Coping expectancies, not enhancement expectancies, mediate trauma experience effects on problem alcohol use: a prospective study from early childhood to adolescence. *Journal of Studies on Alcohol and Drugs, 76*(5), 781–789.

Joiner, T. E. (2005). *Why people die by suicide*. Cambridge, MA: Harvard University Press.

Joiner, T. E., Sachs-Ericsson, N. J., Wingate, L. R., Brown, J. S., Anestis, M. D., & Selby, E. A. (2007). Childhood physical and sexual abuse and lifetime number of suicide attempts: a persistent and theoretically important relationship. *Behaviour Research and Therapy, 45*(3), 539–547. https://doi.org/10.1016/j.brat.2006.04.007.

Kajeepeta, S., Gelaye, B., Jackson, C. L., & Williams, M. A. (2015). Adverse childhood experiences are associated with adult sleep disorders: a systematic review. *Sleep Medicine, 16*(3), 320–330.

Kalmakis, K. A., & Chandler, G. E. (2015). Health consequences of adverse childhood experiences: a systematic review. *Journal of the American Association of Nurse Practitioners, 27*(8), 457–465.

Kaplow, J. B., Dodge, K. A., Amaya-Jackson, L., & Saxe, G. N. (2005). Pathways to PTSD, part II: sexually abused children. *The American Journal of Psychiatry, 162*(7), 1305–1310. https://doi.org/10.1176/appi.ajp.162.7.1305.

Kessler, R. C., McLaughlin, K. A., Green, J. G., Gruber, M. J., Sampson, N. A., Zaslavsky, A. M., … Benjet, C. (2010). Childhood adversities and adult psychopathology in the WHO World Mental Health Surveys. *The British Journal of Psychiatry, 197*(5), 378–385.

Kim, P., Evans, G. W., Angstadt, M., Ho, S. S., Sripada, C. S., Swain, J. E., … Phan, K. L. (2013). Effects of childhood poverty and chronic stress on emotion regulatory brain function in adulthood. *Proceedings of the National Academy of Sciences, 110*(46), 18442–18447.

Kinniburgh, K., Blaustein, M., Spinazzola, J., & van der Kolk, B. (2005). Attachment, self-regulation and competency: a comprehensive intervention framework for children with complex trauma. *Psychiatric Annals, 35*(5), 424–430.

Larkin, H., Felitti, V. J., & Anda, R. F. (2014). Social work and adverse childhood experiences research: implications for practice and health policy. *Social Work in Public Health, 29*(1), 1–16. https://doi.org/10.1080/19371918.2011.619433.

Li, M., D'Arcy, C., & Meng, X. (2016). Maltreatment in childhood substantially increases the risk of adult depression and anxiety in prospective cohort studies: systematic review, meta-analysis, and proportional attributable fractions. *Psychological Medicine, 46*(4), 717–730. https://doi.org/10.1017/s0033291715002743.

Lind, M. J., Aggen, S. H., Kendler, K. S., York, T. P., & Amstadter, A. B. (2016). An epidemiologic study of childhood sexual abuse and adult sleep disturbances. *Psychological Trauma Theory Research Practice and Policy, 8*(2), 198.

Lindert, J., von Ehrenstein, O., Grashow, R., Gal, G., Braehler, E., & Weisskopf, M. (2014). Sexual and physical abuse in childhood is associated with depression and anxiety over the life course: systematic review and meta-analysis. *International Journal of Public Health, 59*(2), 359–372. https://doi.org/10.1007/s00038-013-0519-5.

Linehan, M. M. (1993). *Cognitive-behavioral treatment of borderline personality disorder*. New York, NY: Guilford Press.

Liu, R. T., Choi, J. Y., Boland, E. M., Mastin, B. M., & Alloy, L. B. (2013). Childhood abuse and stress generation: the mediational effect of depressogenic cognitive styles. *Psychiatry Research*, *206*(2–3), 217–222. https://doi.org/10.1016/j.psychres.2012.12.001.

Liu, R. T., Jager-Hyman, S., Wagner, C. A., Alloy, L. B., & Gibb, B. E. (2012). Number of childhood abuse perpetrators and the occurrence of depressive episodes in adulthood. *Child Abuse & Neglect*, *36*(4), 323–332. https://doi.org/10.1016/j.chiabu.2011.11.007.

Logan-Greene, P., Green, S., Nurius, P. S., & Longhi, D. (2014). Distinct contributions of adverse childhood experiences and resilience resources: a cohort analysis of adult physical and mental health. *Social Work in Health Care*, *53*(8), 776–797.

Lu, W., Mueser, K. T., Rosenberg, S. D., & Jankowski, M. K. (2008). Correlates of adverse childhood experiences among adults with severe mood disorders. *Psychiatric Services*, *59*(9), 1018–1026.

MacMillan, H. L., Fleming, J. E., Streiner, D. L., Lin, E., Boyle, M. H., Jamieson, E., … Beardslee, W. R. (2001). Childhood abuse and lifetime psychopathology in a community sample. *American Journal of Psychiatry*, *158*(11), 1878–1883.

Mancini, C., Van Ameringen, M., & Macmillan, H. (1995). Relationship of childhood sexual and physical abuse to anxiety disorders. *Journal of Nervous and Mental Disease*, *183*(5), 309–314.

Mathews, C. A., Kaur, N., & Stein, M. B. (2008). Childhood trauma and obsessive-compulsive symptoms. *Depression and Anxiety*, *25*(9), 742–751.

McLaughlin, K. A., Conron, K. J., Koenen, K. C., & Gilman, S. E. (2010). Childhood adversity, adult stressful life events, and risk of past-year psychiatric disorder: a test of the stress sensitization hypothesis in a population-based sample of adults. *Psychological Medicine*, *40*(10), 1647–1658.

McLaughlin, K. A. (2016). Future directions in childhood adversity and youth psychopathology. *Journal of Clinical Child & Adolescent Psychology*, *45*(3), 361–382.

McLaughlin, K. A., Sheridan, M. A., & Lambert, H. K. (2014). Childhood adversity and neural development: deprivation and threat as distinct dimensions of early experience. *Neuroscience & Biobehavioral Reviews*, *47*, 578–591.

Merrick, M. T., Ports, K. A., Ford, D. C., Afifi, T. O., Gershoff, E. T., & Grogan-Kaylor, A. (2017). Unpacking the impact of adverse childhood experiences on adult mental health. *Child Abuse & Neglect*, *69*, 10–19. https://doi.org/10.1016/j.chiabu.2017.03.016.

Mok, P. L. H., Pedersen, C. B., Springate, D., Astrup, A., Kapur, N., Antonsen, S., … Webb, R. T. (2016). Parental psychiatric disease and risks of attempted suicide and violent criminal offending in offspring. *JAMA Psychiatry*, *73*(10), 1015. https://doi.org/10.1001/jamapsychiatry.2016.1728.

Michopoulos, V., Powers, A., Moore, C., Villarreal, S., Ressler, K. J., & Bradley, B. (2015). The mediating role of emotion dysregulation and depression on the relationship between childhood trauma exposure and emotional eating. *Appetite*, *91*, 129–136.

Miller, G. E., Chen, E., & Parker, K. J. (2011). Psychological stress in childhood and susceptibility to the chronic diseases of aging: moving toward a model of behavioral and biological mechanisms. *Psychological Bulletin*, *137*(6), 959–997. https://doi.org/10.1037/a0024768.

Miller, A. H., Maletic, V., & Raison, C. L. (2009). Inflammation and its discontents: the role of cytokines in the pathophysiology of major depression. *Biological Psychiatry*, *65*(9), 732–741.

Narayan, A. J., Kalstabakken, A. W., Labella, M. H., Nerenberg, L. S., Monn, A. R., & Masten, A. S. (2017). Intergenerational continuity of adverse childhood experiences in homeless families: unpacking exposure to maltreatment versus family dysfunction. *American Journal of Orthopsychiatry*, *87*(1), 3.

Nemeroff, C. B. (2016). Paradise lost: the neurobiological and clinical consequences of child abuse and neglect. *Neuron*, *89*(5), 892–909. https://doi.org/10.1016/j.neuron.2016.01.019.

Nurius, P. S., Green, S., Logan-Greene, P., & Borjaa, S. (2015). Life course pathways of adverse childhood experiences toward adult psychological well-being: a stress process analysis. *Child Abuse & Neglect*, *45*, 143–153. https://doi.org/10.1016/j.chiabu.2015.03.008.

Nusslock, R., & Miller, G. E. (2016). Early-life adversity and physical and emotional health across the lifespan: a neuroimmune network hypothesis. *Biological Psychiatry*, *80*(1), 23–32.

Obradović, J. (2016). Physiological responsivity and executive functioning: implications for adaptation and resilience in early childhood. *Child Development Perspectives*, *10*(1), 65–70.

Polusny, M. A., & Follette, V. M. (1995). Long-term correlates of child sexual abuse: theory and review of the empirical literature. *Applied and Preventive Psychology*, *4*(3), 143–166.

Ports, K. A., Merrick, M. T., Stone, D. M., Wilkins, N. J., Reed, J., Ebin, J., & Ford, D. C. (2017). Adverse childhood experiences and suicide risk: toward comprehensive prevention. *American Journal of Preventive Medicine*, *53*(3), 400–403.

Raposo, S. M., Mackenzie, C. S., Henriksen, C. A., & Afifi, T. O. (2014). Time does not heal all wounds: older adults who experienced childhood adversities have higher odds of mood, anxiety, and personality disorders. *The American Journal of Geriatric Psychiatry*, *22*(11), 1241–1250.

Roos, L. E., Afifi, T. O., Martin, C. G., Pietrzak, R. H., Tsai, J., & Sareen, J. (2016). Linking typologies of childhood adversity to adult incarceration: findings from a nationally representative sample. *American Journal of Orthopsychiatry*, *86*(5), 584.

Rudolph, K. D., & Flynn, M. (2007). Childhood adversity and youth depression: influence of gender and pubertal status. *Development and Psychopathology*, *19*(2), 497–521.

Sandler, I. N., Tein, J. Y., Mehta, P., Wolchik, S., & Ayers, T. (2000). Coping efficacy and psychological problems of children of divorce. *Child Development*, *71*(4), 1099–1118.

Sandler, I. N., Kim-Bae, L. S., & MacKinnon, D. (2000). Coping and negative appraisal as mediators between control beliefs and psychological symptoms in children of divorce. *Journal of Clinical Child Psychology*, *29*(3), 336–347.

Sachs-Ericsson, N., Verona, E., Joiner, T., & Preacher, K. J. (2006). Parental verbal abuse and the mediating role of self-criticism in adult internalizing disorders. *Journal of Affective Disorders*, *93*(1–3), 71–78.

Sachs-Ericsson, N., Medley, A. N., Kendall–Tackett, K., & Taylor, J. (2011). Childhood abuse and current health problems among older adults: the mediating role of self-efficacy. *Psychology of Violence*, *1*(2), 106.

Sachs-Ericsson, N. J., Sheffler, J. L., Stanley, I. H., Piazza, J. R., & Preacher, K. J. (2017). When emotional pain becomes physical: adverse childhood experiences, pain, and the role of mood and anxiety disorders. *Journal of Clinical Psychology*, https://doi.org/10.1002/jclp.22444.

Sachs-Ericsson, N., Joiner, T. E., Cougle, J. R., Stanley, I. H., & Sheffler, J. L. (2015). Combat exposure in early adulthood interacts with recent stressors to predict PTSD in aging male veterans. *The Gerontologist*, *56*(1), 82–91.

Sachs-Ericsson, N. J., Rushing, N. C., Stanley, I. H., & Sheffler, J. (2016). In my end is my beginning: developmental trajectories of adverse childhood experiences to late-life suicide. *Aging & Mental Health*, *20*(2), 139–165.

Sachs-Ericsson, N. J., Stanley, I. H., Sheffler, J. L., Selby, E., & Joiner, T. E. (2017). Non-violent and violent forms of childhood abuse in the prediction of suicide attempts: direct or indirect effects through psychiatric disorders. *Journal of Affective Disorders*, *215*, 15–22. https://doi.org/10.1016/j.jad.2017.03.030.

Sareen, J., Henriksen, C. A., Bolton, S. L., Afifi, T. O., Stein, M. B., & Asmundson, G. J. G. (2013). Adverse childhood experiences in relation to mood and anxiety disorders in a population-based sample of active military personnel. *Psychological Medicine*, *43*(1), 73–84.

Saxe, G. N., Ellis, B. H., Fogler, J., Hansen, S., & Sorkin, B. (2017). Comprehensive care for traumatized children: an open trial examines treatment using trauma systems therapy. *Psychiatric Annals*, *35*(5), 443–448.

Schmidt, A., Antoniades, M., Allen, P., Egerton, A., Chaddock, C. A., Borgwardt, S., … McGuire, P. (2017). Longitudinal alterations in motivational salience processing in ultra-high-risk subjects for psychosis. *Psychological Medicine*, *47*(2), 243–254.

Schwaiger, M., Grinberg, M., Moser, D., Zang, J. C., Heinrichs, M., Hengstler, J. G., … Kumsta, R. (2016). Altered stress-induced regulation of genes in monocytes in adults with a history of childhood adversity. *Neuropsychopharmacology*, *41*(10), 2530.

Seligman, M. E., Abramson, L. Y., Semmel, A., & Von Baeyer, C. (1979). Depressive attributional style. *Journal of Abnormal Psychology*, *88*(3), 242.

Segal, Z. V. (1988). Appraisal of the self-schema construct in cognitive models of depression. *Psychological Bulletin*, *103*(2), 147.

Shin, S. H., & Miller, D. P. (2012). A longitudinal examination of childhood maltreatment and adolescent obesity: results from the national longitudinal study of adolescent health study. *Child Abuse & Neglect*, *36*(2), 84–94. https://doi.org/10.1016/j.chiabu.2011.08.007.

Smid, G. E., Kleber, R. J., Rademaker, A. R., van Zuiden, M., & Vermetten, E. (2013). The role of stress sensitization in progression of posttraumatic distress following deployment. *Social Psychiatry and Psychiatric Epidemiology*, *48*(11), 1743–1754.

Smith, A. R., Ribeiro, J. D., Mikolajewski, A., Taylor, J., Joiner, T. E., & Iacono, W. G. (2012). An examination of environmental and genetic contributions to the determinants of suicidal behavior among male twins. *Psychiatry Research*, *197*(1–2), 60–65.

Speranza, M., Atger, F., Corcos, M., Loas, G., Guilbaud, O., Stéphan, P., … Lang, F. (2003). Depressive psychopathology and adverse childhood experiences in eating disorders. *European Psychiatry*, *18*(8), 377–383.

Stein, M. B., Jang, K. L., Taylor, S., Vernon, P. A., & Livesley, W. J. (2002). Genetic and environmental influences on trauma exposure and posttraumatic stress disorder symptoms: a twin study. *American Journal of Psychiatry*, *159*(10), 1675–1681.

Toth, S. L., Cicchetti, D., & Kim, J. (2002). Relations among children's perceptions of maternal behavior, attributional styles, and behavioral symptomatology in maltreated children. *Journal of Abnormal Child Psychology*, *30*(5), 487–501.

Trotta, A., Iyegbe, C., Yiend, J., Dazzan, P., David, A. S., Pariante, C., & Fisher, H. L. (2018). Interaction between childhood adversity and functional polymorphisms in the dopamine pathway on first-episode psychosis. *Schizophrenia Research*, *205*, 51–57.

Trotta, A., Murray, R. M., & Fisher, H. L. (2015). The impact of childhood adversity on the persistence of psychotic symptoms: a systematic review and meta-analysis. *Psychological Medicine*, *45*(12), 2481–2498.

US Department of Health and Human Services, & Office of the Surgeon General. (2012). National strategy for suicide prevention 2012: goals and objectives for action. In *A report of the US Surgeon General and of the National Action Alliance for Suicide Prevention*. Washington, DC: US Department of Health and Human Services.

Van Orden, K. A., Witte, T. K., Cukrowicz, K. C., Braithwaite, S. R., Selby, E. A., & Joiner, T. E., Jr. (2010). The interpersonal theory of suicide. *Psychological Review*, *117*(2), 575.

Visser, H. A., van Oppen, P., van Megen, H. J., Eikelenboom, M., & van Balkom, A. J. (2014). Obsessive-compulsive disorder; chronic versus non-chronic symptoms. *Journal of Affective Disorders*, *152*, 169–174.

Further reading

Fairburn, C. G., Doll, H. A., Welch, S. L., Hay, P. J., Davies, B. A., & O'connor, M. E. (1998). Risk factors for binge eating disorder: a community-based, case-control study. *Archives of General Psychiatry*, *55*(5), 425–432.

Oppenheimer, R., Howells, K., Palmer, R. L., & Chaloner, D. A. (1986). *Adverse sexual experience in childhood and clinical eating disorders: a preliminary description*. In *Anorexia nervosa and bulimic disorders* (pp. 357–361).

CHAPTER

5

ACEs and physical health outcomes

Kelsey D. Vig, Michelle M. Paluszek, Gordon J.G. Asmundson
Department of Psychology, University of Regina, Regina, SK, Canada

Introduction

Considerable evidence linking adverse childhood experiences (ACEs) to compromised physical health across the developmental spectrum has emerged over the past several decades; indeed, various forms of childhood adversity have been linked to increased odds of a host of chronic health conditions. While there are some contradictory findings, the majority of the evidence confirms the pervasively negative impact of ACEs on physical health. The purpose of this chapter is severalfold. First, we provide an overview of the potential mechanisms underlying the linkage between childhood adversity and poor physical health. Second, we summarize the evidence pertaining to the nature and mediators of poor physical health following experiences of childhood adversity. Third, we explore various implications of current knowledge for health service utilization, therapeutic intervention, and prevention. Finally, we conclude with a brief outline of policy implications as well as a summary of areas that we believe to be in need of additional empirical scrutiny.

Mechanisms

The mechanisms through which childhood adversity leads to poor physical health outcomes overlap with the pathways connecting childhood adversity and psychopathology (see Chapter 4). Chronic and/or extreme stressors like ACEs lead to biological, psychological, and behavioral dysregulations that have negative consequences on both mental and

https://doi.org/10.1016/B978-0-12-816065-7.00005-7

physical health. Two important concepts that researchers have developed to describe how stress negatively impacts physical health are allostatic load (McEwen, 1998) and biological embedding (Hertzman, 1999). These concepts are described and followed by an overview of specific psychological, behavioral, and biological processes involved.

Allostatic load and biological embedding

Allostatic load refers to the physiological consequences of chronic or repeated activation of the stress response system (McEwen, 1998), which comprises the nervous and endocrine systems. Chronic stress affects the structure and function of the nervous and endocrine systems, changing how these systems operate at rest and in response to future stress and threat (McEwen, 2008). Given the interrelated nature of the systems of the body, changes in the nervous and endocrine systems lead to additional changes in other systems of the body, particularly the immune system. Allostatic load, in short, leads to wear and tear on the body that serves to increase susceptibility to a number of physical health conditions, including metabolic and cardiovascular diseases (CVD; Danese & McEwen, 2012; McEwen, 2003).

The concept of allostatic load is not specific to the effects of early life stress on physical health; rather, it describes the negative impact of stress on physical health occurring throughout the lifespan. To better capture the unique features of ACEs and explain how stress in early life leads to poor health outcomes in later life, researchers are increasingly considering allostatic load together with biological embedding (Barboza Solís et al., 2015; Berens, Jensen, & Nelson, 2017; Danese & McEwen, 2012). Biological embedding occurs when life experiences promote long-term and stable changes to an individual's biology and developmental trajectory which, in turn, impact physical health, emotional well-being, and behavior (Hertzman, 2012). Building from the concept of biological embedding, Miller, Chen, and Parker (2011) formulated a biological embedding of childhood adversity model. According to this model, stress experienced as a child "gets under the skin" (p. 960) and leads to biological changes that interact with behavioral tendencies to increase susceptibility to diseases throughout the lifespan. In other words, ACEs affect physical health over time through both behavioral and biological processes.

Behavioral and related psychological processes

ACEs are associated with an increased tendency to engage in high-risk health behaviors, such as disordered eating and substance use (e.g., Fuemmeler, Dedert, McClernon, & Beckham, 2009; Mersky, Topitzes, & Reynolds, 2013). The relationship appears to follow a dose-response pattern, with increasing frequency of ACEs predicting greater odds of engaging in risky health behaviors (Campbell, Walker, & Egede, 2016; Felitti et al., 1998). Researchers have posited that individuals who have experienced childhood adversity engage in risky health behaviors more often due to increased behavioral impulsivity (Lovallo, 2013) and the tendency to rely on maladaptive (e.g., self-blame, disengagement) rather than adaptive (e.g., active coping, emotional support, planning, reframing) coping strategies (Helitzer, Graeber, LaNoue, & Newbill, 2015). Impulsivity and maladaptive coping strategies are associated with a negative cognitive style (i.e., dysfunctional attitudes and maladaptive self-schemas that lead one to attribute the causes of negative life events to stable and global factors) and negative self-schema (i.e., judging oneself negatively), both of which are associated with catastrophic thinking, poor emotion regulation, and, in what amounts to a reciprocal vicious cycle, a host of maladaptive behaviors and psychological disorders.

Across the general population, health behaviors like eating habits and substance use predict morbidity and mortality from a variety of causes, such as hypertension, obesity, CVD, and diabetes (Haskell, 2003; Lichtenstein et al., 2006; World Health Organization, 2003). In samples of adults who have experienced childhood adversity, those who engage in more health promoting behaviors (e.g., physical activity, smoking abstinence) report having better physical health (Dube, Felitti, & Rishi, 2013) and fewer days where they feel that their physical health is not good (Dube & Rishi, 2017) when compared to those who engage in fewer health-promoting behaviors. Despite associations between ACEs, health behaviors, and physical health, the tendency to engage in fewer health-promoting behaviors and more high-risk health behaviors does not entirely account for the association between ACEs and poor physical health outcomes. Indeed, many studies have controlled for health behaviors and still observe an association between childhood adversity and poor physical health (e.g., Afifi et al., 2016; Danese et al., 2009; Dong, Dube, Felitti, Giles, & Anda, 2003).

Biological processes

As noted, allostatic load promotes alterations in the nervous and endocrine systems that, over time, negatively impact physical health. These alterations and associated consequences can stem from a variety of forms of chronic stress, including childhood adversity; yet, it is noteworthy that the biological alterations and subsequent poor physical health stemming from ACEs do not generalize to all chronic stressors. While chronic stress occurring across the lifespan has been associated with biological alterations and poor physical health outcomes, many empirically supported models posit that childhood adversity has unique physiological consequences because the stress occurs during a sensitive period of development (e.g., Ben-Shlomo

& Kuh, 2002; Miller et al., 2011). For example, the biological embedding of childhood adversity model posits that stress during sensitive periods causes systems of the body to operate differently, a phenomenon known as biological programming (Miller et al., 2011). The model emphasizes the biological programming of immune cells, which affects the endocrine and autonomic nervous systems and behavioral functioning, leading to a state of chronic inflammation. Research examining the effect of ACEs on the nervous system (i.e., the brain) is discussed in Chapters 4 and 13 and, therefore, will not be repeated here.

Of all the biological alterations that have been associated with ACEs, support for immune system dysregulation is the most robust. Researchers have demonstrated that, compared to individuals with no ACEs, individuals who report experiencing childhood adversity display greater baseline levels of inflammatory biomarkers (Baumeister, Akhtar, Ciufolini, Pariante, & Mondelli, 2016; Danese, Pariante, Caspi, Taylor, & Poulton, 2007; Lin, Neylan, Epel, & O'Donovan, 2016) and greater increases in inflammatory biomarkers in response to stress (Gouin, Glaser, Malarkey, Beversdorf, & Kiecolt-Glaser, 2012; Pace et al., 2006). Furthermore, a history of childhood adversity has been associated with increased inflammatory gene expression in older adults (Levine, Cole, Weir, & Crimmins, 2015). The precise time at which concentrations of inflammatory biomarkers increase remains a topic of debate (i.e., whether the concentrations are increased in childhood as well, or only in adulthood; Slopen, Koenen, & Kubzansky, 2012).

The findings of increased inflammatory biomarkers following ACEs have led researchers to propose that adversity in childhood results in a proinflammatory phenotype that increases odds of poor health (Ehrlich, Ross, Chen, & Miller, 2016; Elwenspoek, Kuehn, Muller, & Turner, 2017). Inflammation is a risk factor for a variety of chronic physical health conditions, including cancer, CVD, and metabolic disorders (Chung et al., 2009; Libby, 2007). Interestingly, inflammation may also contribute to accelerated cellular aging by reducing telomere length (Fagundes, Glaser, & Kiecolt-Glaser, 2013). Telomeres, the caps that protect the ends of chromosomes, shorten as cells age (Nemeroff, 2016). Several studies examining ACEs and telomere length support the hypothesis that childhood adversity is associated with reduced telomere length (e.g., Elwenspoek et al., 2017; Ridout et al., 2018).

ACEs are also associated with disruptions in the endocrine system, and in the hypothalamic-pituitary-adrenal (HPA) axis in particular (Miller et al., 2011; Strüber, Strüber, & Roth, 2014). HPA axis dysregulation is thought to lead to poor health by inducing metabolic deficits (Maniam, Antoniadis, & Morris, 2014) and increasing allostatic load (Berens et al., 2017). The exact nature of the HPA axis dysregulation remains unclear, as studies have provided evidence for both hyper- and hypoactivity (e.g., Carpenter,

Shattuck, Tyrka, Geracioti, & Price, 2011; Heim, Newport, Bonsall, Miller, & Nemeroff, 2001; Rinne et al., 2002). One group of researchers has proposed a two-pathway model to explain the discrepant findings for the effects of ACEs on HPA axis functioning (Strüber et al., 2014). According to the model, oxytocin and serotonin concentrations at the time of childhood adversity moderate the effects of stress on HPA axis functioning. Other moderating variables that have been proposed to explain findings of both HPA axis hyper- and hypoactivity following ACEs include the nature and number of ACEs, whether subsequent traumatic events occur in later life, and family psychiatric history (Nemeroff, 2016).

Summary

ACEs are associated with biological, behavioral, and psychological dysregulations that collectively impact physical health. Empirically supported models propose that early childhood adversity programs immune cell functioning, leading to a state of chronic inflammation that affects the body at large, increasing allostatic load and making the individual more susceptible to chronic physical health conditions. Moreover, individuals with ACEs engage in more high-risk health behaviors and fewer health-promoting behaviors, tend to rely on negative coping strategies, and have a negative cognitive style, further increasing risk of poor health outcomes.

Specific physical health conditions and risk factors

Research consistently demonstrates that ACEs are associated with poorer overall physical health outcomes. Researchers using prospective study designs have demonstrated that experiencing multiple childhood adversities is associated with a 57%–80% increased risk of premature mortality (Brown et al., 2009; Kelly-Irving et al., 2013). Adults with ACEs are more likely to have a physical disorder (Afifi et al., 2016; Afifi, Mota, MacMillan, & Sareen, 2013), report more physical symptoms, have more medical diagnoses (Springer, Sheridan, Kuo, & Carnes, 2007; Walker et al., 1999), and have worse overall health (Mersky et al., 2013). The original ACE Study by Felitti and colleagues in 1998 was the first large-scale effort to understand the effects of childhood adversity on physical health in later life. The physical health conditions assessed in that study included ischemic heart disease, stroke, diabetes, chronic obstructive pulmonary disease (COPD), liver disease, cancer, and skeletal fractures. The findings of the study determined that adults who experienced four or more ACEs were significantly more likely to have all of the assessed physical health conditions as compared to adults without ACEs. The results indicated a strong dose-response relationship between ACEs and most physical health conditions after adjusting for sociodemographic variables, with more exposure to childhood adversity associated with an increased likelihood of having all physical health conditions except stroke and diabetes. Further analysis of the original ACE Study data and other research examining associations between childhood adversity and specific physical health outcomes is reviewed, including results from two prominent metaanalyses of 37 (Hughes et al., 2017) and 24 (Wegman & Stetler, 2009) related studies. Unless otherwise stated, all comparison groups are made up of participants who reported no ACEs.

Cardiovascular conditions

Evidence for an association between ACEs and CVD is substantial. Further analysis of data from the original ACE Study indicated that all types of assessed ACEs, with the exception of parental marital discord, were associated with an increased risk of ischemic heart disease (Dong et al., 2004). Moreover, the risk of ischemic heart disease increased as the number of ACEs increased. Results from a study comparing individuals who were and were not separated from their parents and evacuated abroad to temporary foster care during World War II similarly demonstrated that individuals who were evacuated as children were twice as likely to have CVD compared to those who were not evacuated (Alastalo et al., 2009). In their respective metaanalyses, Wegman and Stetler (2009) found a medium-sized association between child abuse and cardiovascular disorders and Hughes et al. (2017) reported that adults with four or more ACEs were twice as likely to have CVD. Interestingly, researchers using longitudinal data have determined that the association between childhood adversity and CVD risk in adulthood is mediated by health behaviors, lack of medical or dental care, financial stress, maternal relationship, and educational attainment (Doom, Mason, Suglia, & Clark, 2017).

Metabolic disorders

Numerous studies examining ACEs and metabolic disorders demonstrate that childhood adversity is associated with an increased risk of type 2 diabetes and obesity in adulthood (Alastalo et al., 2009; Rich-Edwards et al., 2010; Thomas, Hyppönen, & Power, 2008), supporting the conclusions of the original ACE Study (Felitti et al., 1998; Williamson, Thompson, Anda, Dietz, & Felitti, 2002). Researchers who completed a metaanalysis of 41 studies examining ACEs and obesity showed that individuals who experienced adversity as children are 1.36 times more likely to be obese as adults (Danese & Tan, 2014). The association was not attributable to adult health behaviors (e.g., smoking, physical activity). Further metaanalytic work suggests that associations between metabolic conditions, including obesity and diabetes, are small to moderate in size (Hughes et al., 2017; Wegman & Stetler, 2009).

Other physical health conditions

A variety of other physical health conditions have received less empirical attention in the ACEs literature. Wegman and Stetler (2009) noted that child abuse was strongly associated with neurological conditions, whereas child abuse and gastrointestinal disorders shared medium associations. When specifically examining the effects of multiple ACEs and physical health outcomes, Hughes et al. (2017) reported that individuals with four or more ACEs were significantly more likely to have sexually transmitted infections (STIs), cancer, and liver/digestive diseases. Using follow-up medical-record data from the original ACE Study, researchers have shown that the number of ACEs is positively associated with the likelihood of hospitalization for an autoimmune disease (Dube et al., 2009). Original ACE Study data were also used to show that adults with five or more ACEs are more than two and a half times more likely to have COPD (Anda et al., 2008). Similarly, in their metaanalyses, Hughes et al. (2017) reported that adults with four or more ACEs are three times more likely to have a respiratory disease, and Wegman and Stetler (2009) noted a moderately sized association between respiratory conditions and child abuse. Finally, empirical evidence supports an association between ACEs and musculoskeletal conditions; however, effect size estimates vary from modest to strong depending on the specific outcome variable (Davis, Luecken, & Zautra, 2005; Wegman & Stetler, 2009).

Risk factors for poor physical health

Some researchers have suggested that ACEs affect a variety of risk factors for poor physical health. Researchers have shown that early adolescents who have experienced adversity have higher heart rate, body mass index (BMI), and waist circumference (Pretty, O'Leary, Cairney, & Wade, 2013) and adults with ACEs are more likely to be hypertensive (Alastalo et al., 2009; Riley, Wright, Jun, Hibert, & Rich-Edwards, 2010). Results from a prospective study indicate that exposure to more ACEs is associated with having more metabolic risk factors for age-related diseases (e.g., hypertension, hypercholesteremia, overweight) in early adulthood (Danese et al., 2009). In contrast, researchers examining samples of adult women have reported that ACEs are not associated with CVD risk factors (e.g., BMI, blood pressure; Anderson et al., 2018; Bleil et al., 2013).

Discrepant results may be attributable to moderating variables, such as sex or the frequency, severity, chronicity, and type of adversity experienced in childhood. For example, women who experienced more severe abuse (e.g., severe sexual and physical abuse in childhood and adolescence) appear more likely to develop hypertension compared to women with less severe forms of abuse exposure (e.g., mild physical or sexual abuse only; Riley et al., 2010). Another possible explanation for discrepant results when examining risk factors for poor physical health is that effects are difficult to detect when considering risk factors individually. Studies examining cumulative measures of risk may provide more consistent evidence of an association between ACEs and increased risk for poor physical health. For example, a prospective study of middle-aged women examined child abuse and incidence of metabolic syndrome (MetS), a collection of risk factors for CVD and diabetes (Midei, Matthews, Chang, & Bromberger, 2013). An individual is diagnosed with MetS if s/he has at least three of the following: central obesity, hypertension, hyperglycemia, and abnormal cholesterol or triglyceride levels. The researchers determined that, at baseline, experiencing child abuse was not associated with an increased likelihood of MetS diagnosis. Childhood sexual and emotional abuse also were not associated with incident MetS at 7-year follow-up. However, women who experienced physical abuse in childhood were twice as likely to have developed MetS by the 7-year follow-up. Additionally, some researchers have combined multiple physiological measures (e.g., blood pressure, cortisol concentrations, BMI) to create an index of allostatic load that estimates overall biological dysregulation. Results from retrospective work and a 30-year prospective study indicate that experiencing child abuse is associated with increased allostatic load in adulthood (Barboza Solís et al., 2015; Carroll et al., 2013; Widom, Horan, & Brzustowicz, 2015). Similar studies with other forms of childhood adversity have yet to be conducted.

Summary

ACEs are associated with an increased likelihood of poor physical health in general and an elevated risk of many specific chronic physical conditions. Research has most consistently supported associations between ACEs and an increased risk of age-related physical health conditions such as CVD and metabolic disorders. Notably, similar findings have emerged in the literature examining associations between posttraumatic stress disorder and physical health outcomes (e.g., Sareen et al., 2007; Sareen, Cox, Clara, & Asmundson, 2005; Vig, El-Gabalawy, & Asmundson, 2018). Research examining ACEs and risk factors for chronic physical health conditions is less consistent, possibly due to the effects of moderating variables or as a result of considering risk factors individually instead of using cumulative measures of risk.

Clinical implications

The physical health consequences of ACEs highlight the widespread and devastating lifelong impact of childhood adversity. The increased prevalence of physical health conditions among individuals with ACEs influences health service usage and costs and creates a need for interventions to prevent the incidence of ACEs and mitigate their potential health effects. Accordingly, implications for health service utilization, prevention and therapeutic intervention, and public policy are described.

Health service utilization

The negative physical health outcomes associated with ACEs have a significant impact on the healthcare system. Using self-report and examination of healthcare records from both clinical samples and the general population, researchers have shown that adults who report ACEs have more frequent primary care visits (Bellis et al., 2017; Bonomi et al., 2008; Chartier, Walker, & Naimark, 2010; Finestone et al., 2000), health professional visits (e.g., dentists, medical specialists, physiotherapists; Bonomi et al., 2008; Chartier, Walker, & Naimark, 2007; Chartier et al., 2010), emergency room visits (Arnow et al., 1999; Bellis et al., 2017; Bonomi et al., 2008), surgeries (Finestone et al., 2000), hospitalizations (Bellis et al., 2017; Bellis, Lowey, Leckenby, Hughes, & Harrison, 2013; Finestone et al., 2000), and higher prescription medication use (Anda, Brown, Felitti, Dube, & Giles, 2008) than adults without ACEs. Evidence also indicates that these health service utilization patterns may extend to chronic illness populations, with researchers from one study finding that women with fibromyalgia report greater medication use for pain if they had a history of abuse (Alexander et al., 1998).

Poorer physical health linked to a history of ACEs is also associated with increased healthcare expenditures (Tang et al., 2006), likely due to the patterns of increased health service use noted. Indeed, a number of researchers have demonstrated that women with a history of physical and sexual abuse have substantially greater healthcare costs than women who do not have a history of abuse (Bonomi et al., 2008; Hulme, 2000; Tang et al., 2006; Walker et al., 1999). Annual healthcare costs after adjusting for age and education were 36% higher among women who experienced both physical and sexual abuse, 22% higher for women with physical abuse only, and 16% higher for women with sexual abuse only (Bonomi et al., 2008). Over the lifespan, average childhood and adult medical costs for an individual with a history of childhood maltreatment are estimated to be over $40,000 in the US (Fang, Brown, Florence, & Mercy, 2012). In short, ACEs place a substantial burden on service care providers and financial resources.

Prevention and treatment

The extent to which ACEs influence physical health problems and healthcare utilization is contingent on the measures put in place to prevent and respond to cases of ACEs (Norman et al., 2012; Turner, Thomas, & Brown, 2016). However, as mentioned in other chapters of this book, implementation of preventive strategies is not easily achieved. Effective prevention necessitates support and integration on a multisystem scale, involving families, the community, child care, educational institutions, justice, and healthcare (Berens et al., 2017; Chartier et al., 2010; Oral et al., 2016).

A potential approach to prevention involves application of universal screening procedures to identify at-risk or exposed individuals and to thereafter allocate these individuals to appropriate services that may circumvent development of negative mental and physical health outcomes; however, such universal screening (described in more detail in Chapter 8) is not without controversy and is currently lacking sufficient evidence to support implementation. Routine screening by healthcare providers may be worth considering, especially given findings that individuals with ACEs are often in contact with healthcare providers (discussed earlier in this chapter) and early placement into interventions is critical for treatment success (Boparai et al., 2018). As is the case with universal screening proposals, additional evidence of the effectiveness of routine screening by health providers is warranted. One concern is the lack of established evidence-based interventions for individuals with ACEs, as screening practices are of limited use if there are no effective interventions to provide to those who screen positive (Dube, 2018; Finkelhor, 2018; National Research Council, 1999).

As suggested by Finkelhor (2018), it may be better to develop and evaluate programs that prevent ACEs from occurring in the first place than to invest in screening programs to identify those at-risk or already exposed to ACEs. As a collective, such programs focus on improving parenting skills, parent-child relationships, and overall familial functioning (Chartier et al., 2010; also see Chapter 12); for example, the Nurse-Family Partnership has demonstrated evidence for improving positive parent-child interactions, lowering rates of child maltreatment, and improving child health outcomes in the long term (DuMont et al., 2008; MacMillan et al., 2009). A recent review suggests that early behavioral preventive interventions may target physiological mechanisms that give rise to physical health problems by normalizing cortisol levels and reducing the impact of adversity on brain development (Boparai et al., 2018).

The complete cessation of ACEs is an ideal venture; but, the reality is that this is an aspirational target and, as such, having effective treatments that mitigate mental and physical health problems in those exposed to ACEs is critical. Chapter 4 describes two interventions relevant to our discussion, including a strengths-based intervention for adults reporting ACEs (Chandler, Roberts, & Chiodo, 2015), which resulted in increased physical activity, and the ACEs Overcomers program, which targets emotion regulation and reduced the number of depressive symptoms, somatic symptoms, and sick days in young adults reporting ACEs (Cameron, Carroll, & Hamilton, 2018). In a review of psychosocial treatments for adults with ACEs (Korotana, Dobson, Pusch, & Josephson, 2016), cognitive-behavioral therapies had the strongest evidence for improving mental health and reducing risky health behaviors, with expressive writing and mindfulness-based interventions also showing potential. In that same review, however, only five of 99 studies assessed effects on neurological systems, healthcare utilization, or physical health outcomes. None of the studies examined physiological mechanisms implicated in the trajectory of ACEs.

Further appraisal of the literature corroborates the paucity of interventions examining these important outcomes. Yet, some existing interventions may be well suited to address physical health problems and the physiological underpinnings of ACEs across the lifespan, though further investigation is warranted. For example, mindfulness-based interventions and mind-body approaches have been found to be beneficial in reducing physical health problems (Gaylord et al., 2011; Smith et al., 2011), modifying physiological factors (Bergen-Cico, Possemato, & Pigeon, 2014; Carlson, Speca, Patel, & Goodey, 2003), and lowering stress symptoms (Carlson et al., 2003; Carlson, Speca, Patel, & Goodey, 2004), though outcomes have yet to be thoroughly explored in samples with ACEs. Likewise, researchers have demonstrated that various forms of exercise (e.g., moderate-intensity aerobic training, resistance training) have significant mental and physical health benefits (e.g., Asmundson et al., 2013; LeBouthillier & Asmundson, 2017); however, this line of investigation has yet to be pursued in children, adolescents, and adults reporting ACEs. The development and evaluation of therapeutic interventions for attenuating the potential physical health consequences of ACEs are still nascent; but, promising avenues of study exist.

Public policy implications

Policy goals should be directed at increasing awareness of the findings of ACEs-related research demonstrating pervasive negative effects of child adversity on health behavior and physical health outcomes, providing evidence-based prevention and therapeutic intervention strategies, and improving resources and opportunities in the community to improve health on a larger scale (Dube, 2018; Kagi & Regala, 2012; Metzler, Merrick, Klevens, Ports, & Ford, 2017). These goals can be achieved in several ways, such as through incorporation of knowledge gained from ACEs-related research into public awareness campaigns and training models for healthcare professions (Djeddah, Facchin, Ranzato, & Romer, 2000; Dube, 2018). Likewise, increased financial support for the development and implementation of evidence-based prevention strategies and therapeutic interventions that target general as well as physical health outcomes, all in the context of systematic evaluation of outcomes and cost benefits (Oral et al., 2016) is key (Hughes et al., 2017; Norman et al., 2012). Finally, policy changes that help families have access to affordable health services, affordable housing, quality and low-cost child care, employment opportunities, and social supports will help optimize conditions for child development (Berens et al., 2017; Chartier et al., 2010; Metzler et al., 2017). Setting ACEs as a public health priority is the first step to catalyze these multifaceted approaches.

Summary

The implications of the link between childhood adversity and poor physical health in later life for intervention and policy are complex. ACEs lead to higher healthcare utilization and need to be addressed through evidence-based prevention and treatment efforts, as well as public policy. The current state of the literature on prevention suggests that some early behavioral interventions have encouraging findings; but, screening procedures are lacking the empirical support needed to justify implementation. The evidence base for therapeutic intervention is also still developing and requires more thorough examination of neurological, physiological, healthcare usage, and physical health outcomes. To address ACEs on a broader scale, public policy needs to strengthen collaboration between different sectors, while also disseminating findings from ACEs research and increasing supports and resources for families.

Future directions

As outlined earlier, the current state of the evidence provides relatively consistent support for the association between ACEs and poor physical health outcomes. The most notable gaps in the literature include a thorough understanding of the physiological mechanisms driving the association and empirically supported prevention and therapeutic intervention strategies. These gaps are likely interrelated as effective prevention and therapeutic intervention should be informed by knowledge of the processes by which ACEs lead to poor physical (and mental) health.

As other researchers have acknowledged (e.g., Miller et al., 2011), more research examining the biological changes that occur in the time between ACEs and the development of physical illnesses is needed to clarify the specific processes that mediate the association. The exact nature of HPA axis dysfunction and its role in poor physical health also remains unclear. More research is needed to determine how early in the lifespan the damaging effects of childhood adversity on health occur and the approximate age range during which stress has uniquely detrimental effects on physiological functioning.

Additional research is needed to identify and understand the effects of potential moderating variables, including the effects of sex, resiliency factors, and ACEs type. For example, researchers evaluating associations between nonsexual ACEs (i.e., physical and emotional abuse and neglect) and physical health have reported that individuals with this type of childhood adversity are at increased risk for STIs, arthritis, ulcers, and headaches or migraines compared to those without ACEs (Norman et al., 2012). The researchers stated that the evidence for associations between nonsexual ACEs and type 2 diabetes, hypertension, CVD, neurological disorders, respiratory diseases, and cancer was weak and inconsistent; yet, in metaanalyses that include both sexual and nonsexual ACEs, many of the same conditions show moderate or strong associations with ACEs (Hughes et al., 2017; Wegman & Stetler, 2009).

An improved understanding of the mediating processes and timeline, as well as moderating variables, that characterize the association between ACEs and physical health outcomes will facilitate development of effective intervention programs. For example, if inflammation is the primary mechanism by which childhood adversity translates to poor health and the detrimental effects occur within a year of the adverse experience, treatments that aim to reduce inflammation may only be effective if administered shortly after the adverse experience. This example is purely speculative; however, it highlights how more research is needed to establish effective interventions that short-circuit the likelihood of childhood adversity leading to poor physical health.

Conclusion

Childhood adversity has the potential to have significant and pervasive negative effects on health behaviors and physical health across the lifespan. While mechanisms and the specificity of their association with ACEs remain to be better understood and explanatory models further refined, what is clear is that exposure to ACEs increases the likelihood of high-risk health behaviors and compromised physical health for conditions ranging from STIs to cardiovascular conditions to metabolic disorders and a host of other chronic health conditions. Emerging evidence also implicates ACEs in premature aging. These negative physical health outcomes exert a significant toll on the individual as well as the healthcare system. Prevention and therapeutic interventions are available, but await additional empirical scrutiny, further development of collaborations between different sectors to foster evidence-based implementation, and, ultimately, more accessible supports for children and adults whose health has been compromised as a consequence of ACEs.

References

Afifi, T. O., MacMillan, H. L., Boyle, M., Taillieu, T., Cheung, K., Turner, S., & Sareen, J. (2016). Child abuse and physical health conditions in Canada. *Health Reports, 27*, 19–27. https://doi.org/10.1503/cmaj.131792.

Afifi, T. O., Mota, N., MacMillan, H. L., & Sareen, J. (2013). Harsh physical punishment in childhood and adult physical health. *Pediatrics, 132*, e333–e340. https://doi.org/10.1542/peds.2012-4021d.

Alastalo, H., Räikkönen, K., Pesonen, A. K., Osmond, C., Barker, D. J., Kajantie, E., … Eriksson, J. G. (2009). Cardiovascular health of Finnish war evacuees 60 years later. *Annals of Medicine, 41*, 66–72. https://doi.org/10.1080/07853890802301983.

Alexander, R. W., Aaron, L. A., Alberts, K. R., Martin, M. Y., Stewart, K. E., Bradley, L. A., … Triana-Alexander, M. (1998). Sexual and physical abuse in women with fibromyalgia: association with outpatient health care utilization and pain medication usage. *Arthritis & Rheumatism: Official Journal of the American College of Rheumatology, 11*, 102–115. https://doi.org/10.1002/art.1790110206.

Anda, R. F., Brown, D. W., Dube, S. R., Bremner, J. D., Felitti, V. J., & Giles, W. H. (2008). Adverse childhood experiences and chronic obstructive pulmonary disease in adults. *American Journal of Preventive Medicine, 34*, 396–403. https://doi.org/10.1016/j.amepre.2008.02.002.

Anda, R. F., Brown, D. W., Felitti, V. J., Dube, S. R., & Giles, W. H. (2008). Adverse childhood experiences and prescription drug use in a cohort study of adult HMO patients. *BMC Public Health, 8*, 1471–1479. https://doi.org/10.1186/1471-2458-8-198.

Anderson, E. L., Fraser, A., Caleyachetty, R., Hardy, R., Lawlor, D. A., & Howe, L. D. (2018). Associations of adversity in childhood and risk factors for cardiovascular disease in mid-adulthood. *Child Abuse & Neglect, 76*, 138–148. https://doi.org/10.1016/j.chiabu.2017.10.015.

Arnow, B. A., Hart, S., Scott, C., Dea, R., O'Connell, L., & Taylor, C. B. (1999). Childhood sexual abuse, psychological distress, and medical use among women. *Psychosomatic Medicine, 61*, 762–770. https://doi.org/10.1097/00006842-199911000-00008.

Asmundson, G. J. G., Fetzner, M. G., DeBoer, L. B., Powers, M. B., Otto, M. W., & Smits, J. A. J. (2013). Let's get physical: a contemporary review of the anxiolytic effects of exercise for anxiety and its disorders. *Depression and Anxiety, 30*, 362–373.

Barboza Solís, C., Kelly-Irving, M., Fantin, R., Darnaudéry, M., Torrisani, J., Lang, T., & Delpierre, C. (2015). Adverse childhood experiences and physiological wear-and-tear in midlife: findings from the 1958 British birth cohort. *Proceedings of the National Academy of Sciences, 112*(7), E738–E746.

Baumeister, D., Akhtar, R., Ciufolini, S., Pariante, C. M., & Mondelli, V. (2016). Childhood trauma and adulthood inflammation: a meta-analysis of peripheral C-reactive protein, interleukin-6 and tumour necrosis factor-α. *Molecular Psychiatry, 21*, 642–649. https://doi.org/10.1038/mp.2015.67.

Bellis, M., Hughes, K., Hardcastle, K., Ashton, K., Ford, K., Quigg, Z., & Davies, A. (2017). The impact of adverse childhood experiences on health service use across the life course using a retrospective cohort study. *Journal of Health Services Research & Policy*, *22*, 168–177. https://doi.org/10.1177/1355819617706720.

Bellis, M. A., Lowey, H., Leckenby, N., Hughes, K., & Harrison, D. (2013). Adverse childhood experiences: retrospective study to determine their impact on adult health behaviours and health outcomes in a UK population. *Journal of Public Health*, *36*, 81–91. https://doi.org/10.1093/pubmed/fdt038.

Ben-Shlomo, Y., & Kuh, D. (2002). A life course approach to chronic disease epidemiology: conceptual models, empirical challenges and interdisciplinary perspectives. *International Journal of Epidemiology*, *31*, 285–293. https://doi.org/10.1093/intjepid/31.2.285.

Berens, A. E., Jensen, S. K., & Nelson, C. A. (2017). Biological embedding of childhood adversity: from physiological mechanisms to clinical implications. *BMC Medicine*, *15*(135), 1–12. https://doi.org/10.1186/s12916-017-0895-4.

Bergen-Cico, D., Possemato, K., & Pigeon, W. (2014). Reductions in cortisol associated with primary care brief mindfulness program for veterans with PTSD. *Medical Care*, *52*, S25–S31. https://doi.org/10.1097/mlr.0000000000000224.

Bleil, M. E., Adler, N. E., Appelhans, B. M., Gregorich, S. E., Sternfeld, B., & Cedars, M. I. (2013). Childhood adversity and pubertal timing: understanding the origins of adulthood cardiovascular risk. *Biological Psychology*, *93*, 213–219. https://doi.org/10.1016/j.biopsycho.2013.02.005.

Bonomi, A. E., Anderson, M. L., Rivara, F. P., Cannon, E. A., Fishman, P. A., Carrell, D., … Thompson, R. S. (2008). Health care utilization and costs associated with childhood abuse. *Journal of General Internal Medicine*, *23*, 294–299. https://doi.org/10.1007/s11606-008-0516-1.

Boparai, S. K. P., Au, V., Koita, K., Oh, D. L., Briner, S., Harris, N. B., & Bucci, M. (2018). Ameliorating the biological impacts of childhood adversity: a review of intervention programs. *Child Abuse & Neglect*, *81*, 82–105. https://doi.org/10.1016/j.chiabu.2018.04.014.

Brown, D. W., Anda, R. F., Tiemeier, H., Felitti, V. J., Edwards, V. J., Croft, J. B., & Giles, W. H. (2009). Adverse childhood experiences and the risk of premature mortality. *American Journal of Preventive Medicine*, *37*, 389–396. https://doi.org/10.1016/j.amepre.2009.06.021.

Cameron, L. D., Carroll, P., & Hamilton, W. K. (2018). Evaluation of an intervention promoting emotion regulation skills for adults with persisting distress due to adverse childhood experiences. *Child Abuse & Neglect*, *79*, 423–433. https://doi.org/10.1016/j.chiabu.2018.03.002.

Campbell, J. A., Walker, R. J., & Egede, L. E. (2016). Associations between adverse childhood experiences, high-risk behaviors, and morbidity in adulthood. *American Journal of Preventive Medicine*, *50*, 344–352. https://doi.org/10.1016/j.amepre.2015.07.022.

Carlson, L. E., Speca, M., Patel, K. D., & Goodey, E. (2003). Mindfulness-based stress reduction in relation to quality of life, mood, symptoms of stress, and immune parameters in breast and prostate cancer outpatients. *Psychosomatic Medicine*, *65*, 571–581. https://doi.org/10.1097/01.PSY.0000074003.35911.41.

Carlson, L. E., Speca, M., Patel, K. D., & Goodey, E. (2004). Mindfulness-based stress reduction in relation to quality of life, mood, symptoms of stress and levels of cortisol, dehydroepiandrosterone sulfate (DHEAS) and melatonin in breast and prostate cancer outpatients. *Psychoneuroendocrinology*, *29*, 448–474. https://doi.org/10.1016/S0306-4530(03)00054-4.

Carpenter, L. L., Shattuck, T. T., Tyrka, A. R., Geracioti, T. D., & Price, L. H. (2011). Effect of childhood physical abuse on cortisol stress response. *Psychopharmacology*, *214*, 367–375. https://doi.org/10.1007/s00213-010-2007-4.

Carroll, J. E., Gruenewald, T. L., Taylor, S. E., Janicki-Deverts, D., Matthews, K. A., & Seeman, T. E. (2013). Childhood abuse, parental warmth, and adult multisystem biological risk in the Coronary Artery Risk Development in Young Adults study. *Proceedings of the National Academy of Sciences*, *110*(42), 17149–17153. https://doi.org/10.1073/pnas.1315458110.

Chandler, G. E., Roberts, S. J., & Chiodo, L. (2015). Resilience intervention for young adults with adverse childhood experiences. *Journal of the American Psychiatric Nurses Association*, *21*, 406–416. https://doi.org/10.1177/1078390315620609.

Chartier, M. J., Walker, J. R., & Naimark, B. (2007). Childhood abuse, adult health, and health care utilization: results from a representative community sample. *American Journal of Epidemiology*, *165*, 1031–1038. https://doi.org/10.1093/aje/kwk113.

Chartier, M. J., Walker, J. R., & Naimark, B. (2010). Separate and cumulative effects of adverse childhood experiences in predicting adult health and health care utilization. *Child Abuse & Neglect*, *34*, 454–464. https://doi.org/10.1016/j.chiabu.2009.09.020.

Chung, H. Y., Cesari, M., Anton, S., Marzetti, E., Giovannini, S., Seo, A. Y., ... Leeuwenburgh, C. (2009). Molecular inflammation: underpinnings of aging and age-related diseases. *Ageing Research Reviews*, *8*, 18–30. https://doi.org/10.1016/j.arr.2008.07.002.

Danese, A., & McEwen, B. S. (2012). Adverse childhood experiences, allostasis, allostatic load, and age-related disease. *Physiology & Behavior*, *106*, 29–39. https://doi.org/10.1016/j.physbeh.2011.08.019.

Danese, A., Moffitt, T. E., Harrington, H., Milne, B. J., Polanczyk, G., Pariante, C. M., ... Caspi, A. (2009). Adverse childhood experiences and adult risk factors for age-related disease: depression, inflammation, and clustering of metabolic risk markers. *Archives of Pediatrics & Adolescent Medicine*, *163*, 1135–1143. https://doi.org/10.1001/archpediatrics.2009.214.

Danese, A., Pariante, C. M., Caspi, A., Taylor, A., & Poulton, R. (2007). Childhood maltreatment predicts adult inflammation in a life-course study. *Proceedings of the National Academy of Sciences*, *104*, 1319–1324. https://doi.org/10.1073/pnas.0610362104.

Danese, A., & Tan, M. (2014). Childhood maltreatment and obesity: systematic review and meta-analysis. *Molecular Psychiatry*, *19*, 544–554. https://doi.org/10.1038/mp.2013.54.

Davis, D. A., Luecken, L. J., & Zautra, A. J. (2005). Are reports of childhood abuse related to the experience of chronic pain in adulthood?: a meta-analytic review of the literature. *The Clinical Journal of Pain*, *21*, 398–405. https://doi.org/10.1097/01.ajp.0000149795.08746.31.

Djeddah, C., Facchin, P., Ranzato, C., & Romer, C. (2000). Child abuse: current problems and key public health challenges. *Social Science & Medicine*, *51*, 905–915. https://doi.org/10.1016/s0277-9536(00)00070-8.

Dong, M., Dube, S. R., Felitti, V. J., Giles, W. H., & Anda, R. F. (2003). Adverse childhood experiences and self-reported liver disease: new insights into the causal pathway. *Archives of Internal Medicine*, *163*, 1949–1956. https://doi.org/10.1001/archinte.163.16.1949.

Dong, M., Giles, W. H., Felitti, V. J., Dube, S. R., Williams, J. E., Chapman, D. P., & Anda, R. F. (2004). Insights into causal pathways for ischemic heart disease: adverse childhood experiences study. *Circulation*, *110*, 1761–1766. https://doi.org/10.1161/01.cir.0000143074.54995.7f.

Doom, J. R., Mason, S. M., Suglia, S. F., & Clark, C. J. (2017). Pathways between childhood/adolescent adversity, adolescent socioeconomic status, and long-term cardiovascular disease risk in young adulthood. *Social Science & Medicine*, *188*, 166–175. https://doi.org/10.1016/j.socscimed.2017.06.044.

Dube, S. R. (2018). Continuing conversations about adverse childhood experiences (ACEs) screening: a public health perspective. *Child Abuse & Neglect*, *85*, 180–184. https://doi.org/10.1016/j.chiabu.2018.03.007.

Dube, S. R., Fairweather, D., Pearson, W. S., Felitti, V. J., Anda, R. F., & Croft, J. B. (2009). Cumulative childhood stress and autoimmune diseases in adults. *Psychosomatic Medicine*, *71*, 243–250. https://doi.org/10.1097/PSY.0b013e3181907888.

Dube, S. R., Felitti, V. J., & Rishi, S. (2013). Moving beyond childhood adversity: association between salutogenic factors and subjective well-being among adult survivors of trauma. In K. Rutkowski & M. Linden (Eds.), *Hurting memories and beneficial forgetting* (pp. 139–151). London, UK: Elsevier, Inc.

Dube, S. R., & Rishi, S. (2017). Utilizing the salutogenic paradigm to investigate well-being among adult survivors of childhood sexual abuse and other adversities. *Child Abuse & Neglect*, *66*, 130–141. https://doi.org/10.1016/j.chiabu.2017.01.026.

DuMont, K., Mitchell-Herzfeld, S., Greene, R., Lee, E., Lowenfels, A., Rodriguez, M., & Dorabawila, V. (2008). Healthy families New York (HFNY) randomized trial: effects on early child abuse and neglect. *Child Abuse & Neglect, 32*, 295–315. https://doi.org/10.1016/j.chiabu.2007.07.007.

Ehrlich, K. B., Ross, K. M., Chen, E., & Miller, G. E. (2016). Testing the biological embedding hypothesis: is early life adversity associated with a later proinflammatory phenotype? *Development and Psychopathology, 28*, 1273–1283. https://doi.org/10.1017/S0954579416000845.

Elwenspoek, M. M., Kuehn, A., Muller, C. P., & Turner, J. D. (2017). The effects of early life adversity on the immune system. *Psychoneuroendocrinology, 82*, 140–154. https://doi.org/10.1016/j.psyneuen.2017.05.012.

Fagundes, C. P., Glaser, R., & Kiecolt-Glaser, J. K. (2013). Stressful early life experiences and immune dysregulation across the lifespan. *Brain, Behavior, and Immunity, 27*, 8–12. https://doi.org/10.1016/j.bbi.2012.06.014.

Fang, X., Brown, D. S., Florence, C. S., & Mercy, J. A. (2012). The economic burden of child maltreatment in the United States and implications for prevention. *Child Abuse & Neglect, 36*, 156–165. https://doi.org/10.1016/j.chiabu.2011.10.006.

Felitti, V. J., Anda, R. F., Nordenberg, D., Williamson, D. F., Spitz, A. M., Edwards, V., & Marks, J. S. (1998). Relationship of childhood abuse and household dysfunction to many of the leading causes of death in adults: the adverse childhood experiences (ACE) study. *American Journal of Preventive Medicine, 14*, 245–258. https://doi.org/10.1016/S0749-3797(98)00017-8.

Finestone, H. M., Stenn, P., Davies, F., Stalker, C., Fry, R., & Koumanis, J. (2000). Chronic pain and health care utilization in women with a history of childhood sexual abuse. *Child Abuse & Neglect, 24*, 547–556. https://doi.org/10.1016/S0145-2134(00)00112-5.

Finkelhor, D. (2018). Screening for adverse childhood experiences (ACEs): cautions and suggestions. *Child Abuse & Neglect, 85*, 174–179. https://doi.org/10.1016/j.chiabu.2017.07.016.

Fuemmeler, B. F., Dedert, E., McClernon, F. J., & Beckham, J. C. (2009). Adverse childhood events are associated with obesity and disordered eating: results from the U. S. Population-based survey of young adults. *Journal of Traumatic Stress, 22*, 329–333. https://doi.org/10.1002/jts.20421.

Gaylord, S. A., Palsson, O. S., Garland, E. L., Faurot, K. R., Coble, R. S., Mann, J. D., … Whitehead, W. E. (2011). Mindfulness training reduces the severity of irritable bowel syndrome in women: results of a randomized controlled trial. *The American Journal of Gastroenterology, 106*, 1678–1688. https://doi.org/10.1038/ajg.2011.184.

Gouin, J. P., Glaser, R., Malarkey, W. B., Beversdorf, D., & Kiecolt-Glaser, J. K. (2012). Childhood abuse and inflammatory responses to daily stressors. *Annals of Behavioral Medicine, 44*, 287–292. https://doi.org/10.1016/j.bbi.2012.06.014.

Haskell, W. L. (2003). Cardiovascular disease prevention and lifestyle interventions: effectiveness and efficacy. *Journal of Cardiovascular Nursing, 18*, 245–255. https://doi.org/10.1097/00005082-200309000-00003.

Heim, C., Newport, D. J., Bonsall, R., Miller, A. H., & Nemeroff, C. B. (2001). Altered pituitary-adrenal axis responses to provocative challenge tests in adult survivors of childhood abuse. *American Journal of Psychiatry, 158*, 575–581. https://doi.org/10.1176/appi.ajp.158.4.575.

Helitzer, D., Graeber, D., LaNoue, M., & Newbill, S. (2015). Don't step on the tiger's tail: a mixed methods study of the relationship between adult impact of childhood adversity and use of coping strategies. *Community Mental Health Journal, 51*, 768–774. https://doi.org/10.1007/s10597-014-9815-7.

Hertzman, C. (1999). The biological embedding of early experience and its effects on health in adulthood. *Annals of the New York Academy of Sciences, 896*, 85–95. https://doi.org/10.1111/j.1749-6632.1999.tb08107.x.

Hertzman, C. (2012). Putting the concept of biological embedding in historical perspective. *Proceedings of the National Academy of Sciences, 109*(S2), 1–8. https://doi.org/10.1073/pnas.1202203109.

Hughes, K., Bellis, M. A., Hardcastle, K. A., Sethi, D., Butchart, A., Mikton, C., … Dunne, M. P. (2017). The effect of multiple adverse childhood experiences on health: a systematic review and meta-analysis. *The Lancet Public Health*, *2*, e356–e366. https://doi.org/10.1016/S2468-2667(17)30118-4.

Hulme, P. A. (2000). Symptomatology and health care utilization of women primary care patients who experienced childhood sexual abuse. *Child Abuse & Neglect*, *24*, 1471–1484. https://doi.org/10.1016/S0145-2134(00)00200-3.

Kagi, R., & Regala, D. (2012). Translating the adverse childhood experiences (ACE) study into public policy: progress and possibility in Washington state. *Journal of Prevention & Intervention in the Community*, *40*, 271–277. https://doi.org/10.1080/10852352.2012.707442.

Kelly-Irving, M., Lepage, B., Dedieu, D., Bartley, M., Blane, D., Grosclaude, P., … Delpierre, C. (2013). Adverse childhood experiences and premature all-cause mortality. *European Journal of Epidemiology*, *28*, 721–734. https://doi.org/10.1007/s10654-013-9832-9.

Korotana, L. M., Dobson, K. S., Pusch, D., & Josephson, T. (2016). A review of primary care interventions to improve health outcomes in adult survivors of adverse childhood experiences. *Clinical Psychology Review*, *46*, 59–90. https://doi.org/10.1016/j.cpr.2016.04.007.

LeBouthillier, D. M., & Asmundson, G. J. G. (2017). The efficacy of aerobic exercise and resistance training as transdiagnostic interventions for anxiety-related disorders and constructs: a randomized controlled trial. *Journal of Anxiety Disorders*, *52*, 43–52.

Levine, M. E., Cole, S. W., Weir, D. R., & Crimmins, E. M. (2015). Childhood and later life stressors and increased inflammatory gene expression at older ages. *Social Science & Medicine*, *130*, 16–22. https://doi.org/10.1016/j.socscimed.2015.01.030.

Libby, P. (2007). Inflammatory mechanisms: the molecular basis of inflammation and disease. *Nutrition Reviews*, *65*, S140–S146. https://doi.org/10.1111/j.1753-4887.2007.tb00352.x.

Lichtenstein, A. H., Appel, L. J., Brands, M., Carnethon, M., Daniels, S., Franch, H. A., … Karanja, N. (2006). Diet and lifestyle recommendations revision 2006. *Circulation*, *114*, 82–96. https://doi.org/10.1161/circulationaha.106.176158.

Lin, J. E., Neylan, T. C., Epel, E., & O'Donovan, A. (2016). Associations of childhood adversity and adulthood trauma with C-reactive protein: a cross-sectional population-based study. *Brain, Behavior, and Immunity*, *53*, 105–112. https://doi.org/10.1016/j.bbi.2015.11.015.

Lovallo, W. R. (2013). Early life adversity reduces stress reactivity and enhances impulsive behavior: implications for health behaviors. *International Journal of Psychophysiology*, *90*, 8–16. https://doi.org/10.1016/j.ijpsycho.2012.10.006.

MacMillan, H. L., Wathen, C. N., Barlow, J., Fergusson, D. M., Leventhal, J. M., & Taussig, H. N. (2009). Interventions to prevent child maltreatment and associated impairment. *The Lancet*, *373*, 250–266. https://doi.org/10.1016/S0140- 6736(08)61708-0.

Maniam, J., Antoniadis, C., & Morris, M. J. (2014). Early-life stress, HPA axis adaptation, and mechanisms contributing to later health outcomes. *Frontiers in Endocrinology*, *5*(73), 1–12. https://doi.org/10.3389/fendo.2014.00073.

McEwen, B. S. (1998). Protective and damaging effects of stress mediators. *New England Journal of Medicine*, *338*, 171–179. https://doi.org/10.1056/nejm199801153380307.

McEwen, B. S. (2003). Mood disorders and allostatic load. *Biological Psychiatry*, *54*, 200–207. https://doi.org/10.1016/S0006-3223(03)00177-X.

McEwen, B. S. (2008). Central effects of stress hormones in health and disease: understanding the protective and damaging effects of stress and stress mediators. *European Journal of Pharmacology*, *583*, 174–185. https://doi.org/10.1016/j.ejphar.2007.11.071.

Mersky, J. P., Topitzes, J., & Reynolds, A. J. (2013). Impacts of adverse childhood experiences on health, mental health, and substance use in early adulthood: a cohort study of an urban, minority sample in the US. *Child Abuse & Neglect*, *37*, 917–925. https://doi.org/10.1016/j.chiabu.2013.07.011.

Metzler, M., Merrick, M. T., Klevens, J., Ports, K. A., & Ford, D. C. (2017). Adverse childhood experiences and life opportunities: shifting the narrative. *Children and Youth Services Review*, *72*, 141–149. https://doi.org/10.1016/j.childyouth.2016.10.021.

Midei, A. J., Matthews, K. A., Chang, Y. F., & Bromberger, J. T. (2013). Childhood physical abuse is associated with incident metabolic syndrome in mid-life women. *Health Psychology*, *32*, 121–127. https://doi.org/10.1037/a0027891.

Miller, G. E., Chen, E., & Parker, K. J. (2011). Psychological stress in childhood and susceptibility to the chronic diseases of aging: moving toward a model of behavioral and biological mechanisms. *Psychological Bulletin*, *137*, 959–997. https://doi.org/10.1037/a0024768.

National Research Council. (1999). Public health screening programs. In M. A. Stoto, D. A. Almario, & M. C. McCormick (Eds.), *Reducing the odds: Preventing perinatal transmission of HIV in the United States* (pp. 21–35). Washington, DC: National Academies Press.

Nemeroff, C. B. (2016). Paradise lost: the neurobiological and clinical consequences of child abuse and neglect. *Neuron*, *89*, 892–909. https://doi.org/10.1016/j.neuron.2016.01.019.

Norman, R. E., Byambaa, M., De, R., Butchart, A., Scott, J., & Vos, T. (2012). The long-term health consequences of child physical abuse, emotional abuse, and neglect: a systematic review and meta-analysis. *PLoS Medicine*, *9*(11), e1001349 https://doi.org/10.1371/journal.pmed.1001349.

Oral, R., Ramirez, M., Coohey, C., Nakada, S., Walz, A., Kuntz, A., … Peek-Asa, C. (2016). Adverse childhood experiences and trauma informed care: the future of health care. *Pediatric Research*, *79*, 227–233. https://doi.org/10.1038/pr.2015.197.

Pace, T. W., Mletzko, T. C., Alagbe, O., Musselman, D. L., Nemeroff, C. B., Miller, A. H., & Heim, C. M. (2006). Increased stress-induced inflammatory responses in male patients with major depression and increased early life stress. *American Journal of Psychiatry*, *163*, 1630–1633. https://doi.org/10.1176/appi.ajp.163.9.1630.

Pretty, C., O'Leary, D. D., Cairney, J., & Wade, T. J. (2013). Adverse childhood experiences and the cardiovascular health of children: a cross-sectional study. *BMC Pediatrics*, *13*(208), 1–8. https://doi.org/10.1186/1471-2431-13-208.

Rich-Edwards, J. W., Spiegelman, D., Hibert, E. N. L., Jun, H. J., Todd, T. J., Kawachi, I., & Wright, R. J. (2010). Abuse in childhood and adolescence as a predictor of type 2 diabetes in adult women. *American Journal of Preventive Medicine*, *39*, 529–536. https://doi.org/10.1016/j.amepre.2010.09.007.

Ridout, K. K., Levandowski, M., Ridout, S. J., Gantz, L., Goonan, K., Palermo, D., … Tyrka, A. R. (2018). Early life adversity and telomere length: a meta-analysis. *Molecular Psychiatry*, *23*, 858–871. https://doi.org/10.1038/mp.2017.26.

Riley, E. H., Wright, R. J., Jun, H. J., Hibert, E. N., & Rich-Edwards, J. W. (2010). Hypertension in adult survivors of child abuse: observations from the nurses' Health Study II. *Journal of Epidemiology & Community Health*, *64*, 413–418. https://doi.org/10.1136/jech.2009.095109.

Rinne, T., De Kloet, E. R., Wouters, L., Goekoop, J. G., DeRijk, R. H., & van den Brink, W. (2002). Hyperresponsiveness of hypothalamic-pituitary-adrenal axis to combined dexamethasone/corticotropin-releasing hormone challenge in female borderline personality disorder subjects with a history of sustained childhood abuse. *Biological Psychiatry*, *52*, 1102–1112. https://doi.org/10.1016/s0006-3223(02)01395-1.

Sareen, J., Cox, B. J., Clara, I., & Asmundson, G. J. G. (2005). The relationship between anxiety disorders and physical disorders in the US national comorbidity survey. *Depression and Anxiety*, *21*, 193–202.

Sareen, J., Cox, B. J., Stein, M. B., Afifi, T. O., Fleet, C., & Asmundson, G. J. G. (2007). Physical and mental comorbidity, disability, and suicidal behavior associated with posttraumatic stress disorder in a large community sample. *Psychosomatic Medicine*, *69*, 242–248.

Slopen, N., Koenen, K. C., & Kubzansky, L. D. (2012). Childhood adversity and immune and inflammatory biomarkers associated with cardiovascular risk in youth: a systematic review. *Brain, Behavior, and Immunity*, *26*, 239–250. https://doi.org/10.1016/j.bbi.2011.11.003.

Smith, B. W., Ortiz, J. A., Steffen, L. E., Tooley, E. M., Wiggins, K. T., Yeater, E. A., … Bernard, M. L. (2011). Mindfulness is associated with fewer PTSD symptoms, depressive symptoms, physical symptoms, and alcohol problems in urban firefighters. *Journal of Consulting and Clinical Psychology*, *79*, 613–617. https://doi.org/10.1037/a0025189.

Springer, K. W., Sheridan, J., Kuo, D., & Carnes, M. (2007). Long-term physical and mental health consequences of childhood physical abuse: results from a large population-based sample of men and women. *Child Abuse & Neglect, 31,* 517–530. https://doi.org/10.1016/j.chiabu.2007.01.003.

Strüber, N., Strüber, D., & Roth, G. (2014). Impact of early adversity on glucocorticoid regulation and later mental disorders. *Neuroscience & Biobehavioral Reviews, 38,* 17–37. https://doi.org/10.1016/j.neubiorev.2013.10.015.

Tang, B., Jamieson, E., Boyle, M., Libby, A., Gafni, A., & MacMillan, H. (2006). The influence of child abuse on the pattern of expenditures in women's adult health service utilization in Ontario, Canada. *Social Science & Medicine, 63,* 1711–1719. https://doi.org/10.1016/j.socscimed.2006.04.015.

Thomas, C., Hyppönen, E., & Power, C. (2008). Obesity and type 2 diabetes risk in midadult life: the role of childhood adversity. *Pediatrics, 121,* e1240–e1249. https://doi.org/10.1542/peds.2007-2403.

Turner, R. J., Thomas, C. S., & Brown, T. H. (2016). Childhood adversity and adult health: evaluating intervening mechanisms. *Social Science & Medicine, 156,* 114–124. https://doi.org/10.1016/j.socscimed.2016.02.026.

Vig, K. D., El-Gabalawy, R., & Asmundson, G. J. G. (2018). Stress and comorbidity of physical and mental health conditions. In K. Harkness & E. P. Hayden (Eds.), *The Oxford handbook of stress and mental health.* New York, NY: Oxford University Press.

Walker, E. A., Gelfand, A., Katon, W. J., Koss, M. P., Von Korff, M., Bernstein, D., & Russo, J. (1999). Adult health status of women with histories of childhood abuse and neglect. *The American Journal of Medicine, 107,* 332–339. https://doi.org/10.1016/s0002-9343(99)00235-1.

Wegman, H. L., & Stetler, C. (2009). A meta-analytic review of the effects of childhood abuse on medical outcomes in adulthood. *Psychosomatic Medicine, 71,* 805–812. https://doi.org/10.1097/psy.0b013e3181bb2b46.

Widom, C. S., Horan, J., & Brzustowicz, L. (2015). Childhood maltreatment predicts allostatic load in adulthood. *Child Abuse & Neglect, 47,* 59–69. https://doi.org/10.1016/j.chiabu.2015.01.016.

Williamson, D. F., Thompson, T. J., Anda, R. F., Dietz, W. H., & Felitti, V. (2002). Body weight and obesity in adults and self-reported abuse in childhood. *International Journal of Obesity, 26,* 1075–1082. https://doi.org/10.1038/sj.ijo.0802038.

World Health Organization. (2003). *Diet, nutrition and the prevention of chronic diseases.* (WHO Technical Report No. 916). Retrieved from: http://www.who.int/dietphysicalactivity/publications/trs916/en/.

Further reading

Kalmakis, K. A., & Chandler, G. E. (2015). Health consequences of adverse childhood experiences: a systematic review. *Journal of the American Association of Nurse Practitioners, 27,* 457–465. https://doi.org/10.1002/2327-6924.12215.

Teicher, M. H., & Samson, J. A. (2016). Annual research review: enduring neurobiological effects of childhood abuse and neglect. *Journal of Child Psychology and Psychiatry, 57,* 241–266. https://doi.org/10.1111/jcpp.12507.

CHAPTER

6

ACEs, sexual violence, and sexual health

Christine Wekerle[a], *Martine Hébert*[b], *Isabelle Daigneault*[c], *Elisabeth Fortin-Langelier*[c], *Savanah Smith*[a]

[a]**McMaster University, Hamilton, ON, Canada,**
[b]**University of Quebec at Montreal, Montreal, QC, Canada,**
[c]**University of Montreal, Montreal, QC, Canada**

Unprecedented global forces are shaping the health and wellbeing of the largest generation of 10 to 24 year olds in human history. Population mobility, global communications, economic development, and the sustainability of ecosystems are setting the future course for this generation and, in turn, humankind. **Patton et al., 2016**, *p. 2423.*

Trauma is a time traveler, an ouroboros that reaches back and devours everything that came before. ***Junot Diaz (https://www.newyorker.com/magazine/2018/04/16/the-silence-the-legacy-of-childhood-trauma).***

I'm ground in joy; I'm not grounded in the trauma anymore. ***Tarana Burke,*** *founder of #MeToo movement disclosing sexual violence.*

Introduction

More than ever, world conversation is currently confronting the reality of sexual violence (SV) and resultant trauma, as well as reckoning with the traumatic environment as a prevalent setting for such violence to ensue. With the adverse childhood experiences (ACEs) initiative, the high prevalence of at least 10 potentially traumatic single events, series of events,

https://doi.org/10.1016/B978-0-12-816065-7.00006-9

or everyday living environments are compellingly understood as a public health pandemic (Felitti et al., 1998).

While the cost of SV*any sexual act, attempt to obtain a sexual act, unwanted sexual comments or advances, or acts to traffic, or otherwise directed, against a person's sexuality using coercion, by any person regardless of their relationship to the victim, in any setting, including but not limited to home and work* (WHO, 2002, p. 149)—can never be truly estimated, its prevalence across all age groups and all genders points to an epidemic truth to which most would prefer to participate in an individual and group gaze aversion. However, in the 21st century, we are decidedly in a reality of reckoning, and we are responsible for the rippling impacts across communities. Given that all countries in the world, except the US, are signatory to the United Nations Convention on the Rights of the Child (UNCRC), it is an alarming political back-step that Ontario, Canada, has closed the rights defender, the provincial advocate's office. November 29, 2019 is the 30th anniversary of the UNCRC, demanding forward, progressive action.

Writer, Junot Diaz, a child abuse victim himself, and who in adult life has had challenges relating to allegations of SV perpetration, points to the symbol of the ouroboros, a mythical figure that continuously encircles: "I take responsibility for my past. That is the reason I made the decision to tell the truth of my rape and its damaging aftermath. This conversation is important and must continue. I am listening to and learning from women's stories in this essential and overdue cultural movement. We must continue to teach all men about consent and boundaries"; https://www.nytimes.com/2018/05/04/books/junot-diaz-accusations.html. The ouroboros may serve well as a metaphor for the potential for the cycle of violence victimization, the knowledge that in maltreatment from attachment figures, both the victim and victimizer roles are learned (e.g., Wekerle, Wolfe, Cohen, Bromberg, & Murray, 2018) or the dynamic dialectic between trauma and resilience. Developmentally, perhaps the greatest challenge for child survivors of abuse is when they begin to navigate adult roles. Adolescents negotiate such relating risks at a time where there is also a push for autonomy strivings, with the potential for an over-reliance on the self, especially in maltreating homes where adult caregivers have been unreliable, unresponsive, or absent. This may add to the risk potential of adverse environments when youth are unwilling to disclose adversity or become less inclined to reach out to less familiar adult resources (GBD 2015 Risk Factors Collaborators, 2016). For example, Canadian population research on physical and sexual abuse and exposure to intimate partner violence (EIPV) found that 67% of adults identified that they never disclosed to anyone, including family and friends (Burczycka, 2017). The 2017 Ontario Student Drug and Health Survey found that about 35% of high school youth reported that they had experienced one or more traumatic events (Boak, Hamilton, Adlaf, Henderson, & Mann, 2018), suggesting the widespread prevalence of self-described trauma. A recent study found that adolescents' confidence or doubts about whether the individuals in their relationships would be there for them when they needed them mediated the relationship between their history of ACEs and depression, anxiety, stress, and self-reported well-being (Corcoran & McNulty, 2018). In recognition of a number of needs, including their relative high population growth, the increasing mental health concerns, including suicide rates and the level of trauma that they experience while growing up, adolescents are a key target within the current global health strategy (World Health Organization and Calouste Gulbenkian Foundation, 2014).

While child maltreatment has long gained attention, the ACEs approach has gained public health policy traction as a key means of providing trauma-informed, and hence more client-centered and efficient, care (for more information on trauma-informed care, please see Chapter 15). The ACEs model seeks to quantify risk along a set of potentially traumatic events occurring within a youth's household or directly to youth. The ACEs have put a spotlight on 10 adversities that represent four household/caregiver risks (e.g., divorce, incarceration, substance abuse, mental illness) and six violence experiences/exposures (e.g., physical, emotional, and sexual abuse, physical and emotional neglect, EIPV; Felitti et al., 1998). For most experiences, these are not single-time events and, as such, accumulate as toxic stress to the neurobiological basis underlying the transmission of multigenerational and epigenetic trauma (Flaherty et al., 2014). While the threshold of four or more ACEs is often used to gage adult impairment outcome likelihoods, a threshold of three or more ACEs is suggested as a marker for parent-child difficulties, even though with youth, one childhood adversity may impact development deleteriously (Dube, Felitti, Dong, Giles, & Anda, 2003). It is unclear what threshold is meaningful for various populations of youth. A greater differential was observed at the four or more ACEs level between child welfare/Child Protective Services (CPS) and population levels, with 51% vs. 13% (Stambaugh et al., 2013). In a large study of youth in residential treatment, Briggs et al. (2012) categorized the number of traumatic events—77% with one or more trauma events, 27% experienced four to five traumas, and 31% experienced five or more traumas—suggesting that polyvictimization is particularly prevalent in CPS samples. Four polyvictimization pathways have been suggested, including (1) living in a family that experiences violence and conflict, (2) having a family with problems that tend to limit a child's supervision by caretakers and/or results in a child's emotional needs not being met, (3) living in or moving into a dangerous neighborhood, and (4) being a minor with pre-existing issues that increase risky behavior and, thereby, the likelihood of victimization (Finkelhor, Turner, Hamby, & Ormrod, 2011).

In this chapter, we focus on the concerns arising from SV as a broad-scale trauma, ranging from sexual harassment to rape. SV has high toxicity potential due to its invasiveness physically and psychologically. SV is perhaps better conceptualized as a potential set of traumatic experiences that tend to overlap, co-occurring or occurring sequentially (Wekerle & Kerig, 2017). This would include such extended actions as with "grooming" behaviors where showing pornography may precede or co-occur fondling (Craven, Brown, & Gilchrist, 2006; McAlinden, 2006). Group contexts, such as "hazing" behaviors of humiliation, may involve SV as part of sports identity consolidation (McGlone & Schaefer, 2008). Youth gang membership may require initiation behaviors that include sex crimes (Knox, 2004). Those who have experienced SV may experience internalized sex-related stigma (Feiring, Simon, & Cleland, 2009; Gibson & Leitenberg, 2001), as well as internalized homophobia in LGBTQ2S+ populations (Arreola, Neilands, & Díaz, 2009; Gold, Marx, & Lexington, 2007) However, it is hoped that it is, or becomes, clear to victims that none of the stigma, guilt, shame, and blame belongs to the victim; indeed, sexual abuse is the result of a perpetrator choice and the culpability remains with them. Sadly, the perpetrator's decision to prey on a child or youth means that the burden of suffering and recovery remain with the victim. This has implications not only for the victim, but also for their future roles, such as parenting. For example, Ehrensaft, Knous-Westfall, Cohen, and Chen (2015) investigated the association between mothers and fathers having experienced physical and/or sexual abuse while they were minors, and their parenting practices. Having been sexually victimized predicted lower availability, less time spent with the child, and child-rearing in lower-quality neighborhoods (e.g., fewer parks and public facilities). This points to the ACEs context as potentially conferring a cycle of socioeconomic disadvantage and victimization risk. Given that different forms of SV are discussed in this chapter, this broader term will be utilized for denoting outcomes (e.g., sexual dating violence), and child sexual abuse (CSA) will be used to denote the childhood adversity of focal interest. In this chapter, we focus on CSA in particular, in the context of other ACEs and high childhood adversity populations. We consider issues in perpetration, victimization, and sexual health-related issues (e.g., pregnancy, sexually transmitted infections [STIs]), and then consider select populations of high-risk youth (i.e., CPS-involved, street-involved, Indigenous, and lesbian, gay, bisexual and transsexual, gender-queer, nonbinary, two-spirit, and other [LGBTQ2S+] nonheteronormative groups of youth). Finally, we consider future directions and relevance of the ACEs approach for clinical research and prevention-oriented policy.

Child sexual abuse as a key childhood adversity

The original 10-item ACEs questionnaire (Felitti et al., 1998) has a single item on CSA, and has been integrated into the US Center for Disease Control and Prevention's Behavior Risk Factor Surveillance Study

(BRFSS). Merrick, Ford, Ports, and Guinn (2018) report on BRFSS data from over 200,000 adult participants in 23 states. Approximately 62% reported one or more ACEs. The World Health Organization ACE International Questionnaire (ACE-IQ) has four items: (1) *Did someone touch or fondle you in a sexual way when you did not want them to?*, (2) *Did someone make you touch their body in a sexual way when you did not want them to?*, (3) *Did someone attempt oral, anal, or vaginal intercourse with you when you did not want them to?*, and (4) *Did someone actually have oral, anal, or vaginal intercourse with you when you did not want them to?* (WHO, 2016). The response options are "refused," "never," "once," "a few times," and "many times," and the stem refers to *certain things YOU may have experienced when you were growing up, during the first 18 years of your life...* Country-specific data utilizing this tool are becoming increasingly available (Almuneef, Qayad, Aleissa, & Albuhairan, 2014; Bellis et al., 2014; Tran, Dunne, Vo, & Luu, 2015). Prevalence, then, may be considered from a variety of sources, recognizing that SV is considered under-reported due to a range of factors (e.g., stigma, threats to disclosing, not labeling the abuse as such, the challenges for adolescence in connecting item wording to their experiences; Wekerle, Goldstein, Tanaka, & Tonmyr, 2017). In a meta-analysis of over 200 studies, CSA had a prevalence of 17.7% worldwide, with higher rates of female victimization as compared to males (Stoltenborgh, van Ijzendoorn, Euser, & Bakermans-Kranenburg, 2011). From crime statistics, nearly half of violent crimes involving female victims under the age of 12 years are sexual in nature (Statistics Canada, 2013). For male CSA victims, the use of restraint is high. In an online study of males experiencing CSA, five CSA factors (i.e., age at first abuse, number of abusers, use of physical force, penetration, injury) were associated with the number of ACEs indicators these males experienced. Higher ACEs males (reporting an average 4.7 ACEs) were more likely to be polyvictims who experienced CSA with physical injury or perpetrator use of weapons (Easton, 2012).

While some analyses suggest that no single childhood adversity was the dominant driver of negative consequences (e.g., Cecil, Viding, Fearon, Glaser, & McCrory, 2017), and that high ACEs (four or more) are linked to is an increased risk of engagement in relationship violence (over sevenfold) and STIs (over fivefold) (Hughes et al., 2017), there is evidence for the deleterious impact of SV. Minors who experience physical abuse, or both physical and sexual abuse, have reduced educational outcomes in adulthood (Tanaka, Georgiades, Boyle, & MacMillan, 2015). Cheung et al. (2018) found a sixfold increase in past 30-day suicidal ideation for CSA, as compared to emotional abuse (Odds ratio [OR] = 2.7), EIPV (OR = 3.2), or physical abuse (OR = 3.2). Mental health functions as a mediator in the CSA-romantic relationship link for young adults (e.g., Tardiff-Williams, Tanaka, Boyle, & MacMillan, 2015) indicating that, for adolescents' entry into sexual relationships (and risk to sexual health), the trauma experiences related to the body and to engaging in sex may confer particular risk. Simon, Smith, Fava, and Feiring (2015) found that, six years after CSA discovery, most youth and young adults reported more posttrauma negative changes than positive changes. Negative posttrauma change was linked with greater abuse stigmatization, posttraumatic stress disorder (PTSD), sexual problems, and teen dating violence (TDV). Similarly, Afifi et al. (2015) found that experiencing three forms of child abuse—CSA, physical abuse, and EIPV—had the greatest odds for child welfare involvement. One of the challenges for victims is the concern in terms of repeating the trauma and engaging themselves in SV as the perpetrator.

ACEs and issues in SV perpetration

A substantial body of research attests to the findings that chronic ACEs impair the development of the adolescent brain and decrease the victim's ability to utilize and react to emotional, cognitive, and sensory information (i.e., emotion dysregulation), which increases their risk of problems in interpersonal relationships (Layne et al., 2014; Stettler & Katz, 2017; van der Kolk, 2005). Individuals with high ACEs tend to have increased interpersonal difficulties as a result, in part, of emotional dysregulation stemming from their trauma experiences (Poole, Dobson, & Pusch, 2018). In fact, by middle childhood, those who have been exposed to multiple ACEs may begin demonstrating externalizing (e.g., physical aggression, bullying) and internalizing (e.g., anxiety, fear, lack of socialization with others) behaviors (Hunt, Slack, & Berger, 2017). Youth who are involved in crime tend to have high exposure to ACEs and engage in maladaptive coping strategies (e.g., substance use) that contribute to their delinquent behavior (Craig, Intravia, Wolff, & Baglivio, 2017).

Ybarra and Thompson (2018) reported on the epidemiology of SV among youth, finding that the average age of engagement is 15 to 16 years with harassment in person or online being the most common form of adolescent perpetration. Rape had a relatively low prevalence (4%). Over 80% of perpetrators reported aggressive behaviors and exposure to adult IPV contributed to a sixfold increase in the youths' SV perpetration. This overall antisocial behavior is echoed in other work. CSA victims are more likely to engage in all types of criminal offending, including sexual offending (Paplia, Ogloff, Cutajar, & Mullen, 2018). Some studies show that ACEs are linked to perpetration of SV (Casey et al., 2016; Drury et al., 2017; Levenson & Socia, 2016; Levenson, Willis, & Prescott, 2016; Voith, Anderson, & Cahill, 2017). A study of adult male sex offenders found that offenders had more than three times higher rates of CSA, over four times higher rates of emotional neglect and parental divorce, nearly twice the odds of physical abuse, and 13 times higher rates of verbal abuse, in comparison to the general population of males with no offending history

(Levenson et al., 2016). In a small-scale US study of female sex offenders, half reported experiencing three times the rate of CSA, four times higher rates of verbal abuse, and over three times higher rates of emotional abuse and familial incarceration, compared to the general population of females (Levenson, Willis, & Prescott, 2014). High ACEs scores are also associated with perpetration on younger victims, sexual contact, higher levels of violence and aggression, as well as arrests related to nonsexual offenses (Levenson et al., 2016). A 2017 study of federal sex offenders indicated that high ACEs were common among the population, who averaged 4.7 paraphilias, including pedophilia, pornography addiction, exhibitionism, voyeurism, and other paraphilias (Drury et al., 2017). With evidence that SV victimization is increased in juvenile justice populations (e.g., Chaplo, Kerig, Modroski, & Bennett, 2017), ACEs research tied to prevention programming is critical to pursue. The importance of applying a trauma-informed lens is advanced in the understanding that offending, for both boys and girls, is linked to polyvictimization via processes of emotional avoidance and dysregulation (Kerig & Modrowski, 2018).

ACEs and issues in SV

For youth with CSA experiences, other forms of victimization are likely, as CSA may occur as a direct form or occur as secondary to parental neglect (i.e., lack of monitoring, exposure to dangerous persons). Polyvictimization increases the likelihood that youth will be exposed to SV multiple times and to multiple perpetrators, as they have previously had their agency denied and acts of opposition diminished, which can alter their experience and knowledge of their own rights and freedoms (Wekerle & Kerig, 2017). Having experienced childhood adversity also puts individuals at risk for SV in adulthood. Adults who report one childhood adversity are 1.77 times more likely to experience SV in adulthood and those who report five or more ACEs are 8.32 times more likely to experience SV in adulthood, with CSA identified as the largest ACEs risk factor for SV (Ports, Ford, & Merrick, 2016). Duke, Pettingell, McMorris, and Borowsky (2010) examined how ACEs predicted TDV perpetration for boys and girls. Physical abuse and sexual abuse by a household member, witnessing physical abuse between family members, and experiencing problems engendered by alcohol or drug use of a household member predicted TDV perpetration for boys and girls, but presented a greater risk for boys. Having experienced sexual and physical abuse was the greatest predictor of perpetration, regardless of gender. A US representative national sample of youth showed that sexual assault, rape, having been flashed by a peer or adult, and having been sexually harassed was associated with a higher risk of overall TDV victimization (Hamby, Finkelhor, & Turner, 2012). Results also showed that having experienced property crime, physical gang assault or bias-motivated attack, internet harassment, or sexual internet harassment was also associated with TDV victimization. A recent meta-analysis has shown that psychological abuse, sexual abuse, physical abuse, neglect, and witnessing IPV predict adolescent and emerging adult victimization in domestic violence (Hébert et al., 2017; Hébert, Blais, & Lavoie, 2017). In a study of female university students, Walsh, DiLillo, and Messman-Moore (2012) found that two specific aspects of emotion dysregulation put victims of CSA at risk for potential sexual re-victimization—limited or maladaptive emotion regulation strategies and trouble with impulse control. While the onus for violence victimization resides fully on the perpetrator, it seems that the victim's ability to assess, exit, or otherwise defend against potentially dangerous situations in adolescent relational contexts may be impaired, a potential outcome of prior victimizations. This may be especially salient in CSA where protest behaviors are ignored or quashed by the perpetrator via direct threats and injury as well as PTSD symptoms such as avoidance or numbing.

ACEs and issues in sexual health

Everyday stressors can trigger trauma-related maladaptive coping strategies, including various forms of escape avoidance as self-regulation. Adolescents who have been exposed to ACEs have been shown to have a higher likelihood of engaging in sexual activities that may put them at risk for STIs, unwanted pregnancy, and SV. The original ACE Study found that the number of ACEs a female aged 25 years or over had experienced was positively associated with having sexual intercourse before the age of 15 years, perceiving oneself as being at risk of contracting Human Immunodeficiency Virus (HIV)/Acquired Immune Deficiency Syndrome (AIDS), and having 30 or more sexual partners (Hillis, Anda, Felitti, & Marchbanks, 2001). For males, all ACEs were significantly associated with involvement in an adolescent pregnancy. Having experienced physical abuse, sexual abuse, or witnessing IPV as a child had a strong positive relationship with impregnating a teenager (Anda et al., 2001, 2002). Sexually abused youth have been shown to be significantly younger at the time of first consensual sex, and have more sexual partners; however, this effect was shown to be more prevalent for male victims (Negriff, Schneiderman, & Trickett, 2015). Compared with single CSA exposure, two or more incidents of CSA, or exposure to both incest and extrafamilial sexual abuse, had stronger associations with early puberty and adolescent pregnancy in females as well as pregnancy involvement in males (Brown, Cohen, Chen, Smailes, & Johnson, 2004; Saewyc, Magee, & Pettingell, 2004). Other study results have indicated that both sexual and physical abuse were associated with an increased risk of teenage pregnancy, and that the strongest effect was found when they co-occurred, indicating increased risk of teenage pregnancy with the accumulation of ACEs (Madigan, Wade, Tarabulsy, Jenkins, & Shouldice, 2014). One study that considered the CSA-sexual motives and sexual risk-taking relationship found that, for both male and female CSA youth, sexual activity was motivated by a need for coping to deal with negative affect (Wekerle et al., 2017).

Individuals who have experienced ACEs have been shown to be more likely to engage in sexual intercourse earlier than their peers. The literature on adolescent sexual and reproductive health refers to the age of first consensual intercourse as their sexual debut (Golden, Furman, & Collibee, 2016). A recent study by Brown, Masho, Perera, Mezuk, and Cohen (2015) found that males and females who had experienced neglect were 2.7 and 31.5 times, respectively, more likely to have a sexual debut before the age of 13 years (Brown et al., 2015). Male and female victims of CSA were 9.9 and 90.5 times, respectively, more likely to have a sexual debut before the age of 13 years. Finally, males and females with parental psychopathology or incarceration were 3.46 and 30 times, respectively, more likely to have their sexual debut before the age of 13 years. Having a younger sexual debut has been associated with psychological maladjustment, delinquency, reduced chances of participation in postsecondary education, increased number of sexual partners, increased rates of STIs, early pregnancy, having sex under the influence of drugs or alcohol, forcing a partner to have sex, sexual risk-taking, single parenthood, decreased stability in marriage, poverty, and depression in women (Armour & Haynie, 2007; Donahue, Lichtenstein, Långström, & D'Onofrio, 2013; Kugler, Vasilenko, Butera, & Coffman, 2017; O'Donnell, O'Donnell, & Stueve, 2001; Parkes, Wight, Henderson, & West, 2010; Rector, Johnson, Noyes, & Martin, 2003). There is also some evidence that ACEs are related to reproductive health problems through their association with elevated mental health problems, such as depression and perceived stress (Meltzer-Brody et al., 2013; Nelson & Lepore, 2013; Nelson, Uscher-Pines, Staples, & Grisso, 2010). Recent research suggests that the presence of anxiety symptoms may mediate the relationship between ACEs and sexual risk-taking behavior (Wong, Choi, Chan, & Fong, 2017).

ACEs have been associated with increased reproductive health problems among adolescents and young adults. Three categories of reproductive health outcomes have been documented in relation to ACEs. These include (1) adolescent pregnancies, (2) genitourinary health problems such as vulvovaginitis, pathological vaginal discharge, dyspareunia or enuresis, and (3) STIs or HIV/AIDS. Each of these categories of reproductive outcomes and their associations with ACEs are discussed below.

Increased adolescent pregnancy in females (Anda et al., 2001; Brown et al., 2004; Copping, Campbell, & Muncer, 2013; Madigan et al., 2014; Noll, Shenk, & Putnam, 2009; Putnam-Hornstein, Cederbaum, King, Cleveland,

& Needell, 2013; Saewyc et al., 2004) and pregnancy involvement in adolescent males have been associated with exposure to varied ACEs (Anda et al., 2001; Homma, Wang, Saewyc, & Kishor, 2012; Negriff et al., 2015; Saewyc et al., 2004). In female adolescents, previous abortions and current STI status were more frequent for those with documented child welfare involvement than those without (Cederbaum, Putnam-Hornstein, Sullivan, Winetrobe, & Bird, 2015). One review found that 10 of the 15 studies on CSA and other types of maltreatment showed that ACEs were significantly associated with more frequent adolescent pregnancy (Blinn-Pike, Berger, Dixon, Kuschel, & Kaplan, 2002), while a meta-analysis documenting the relationship between witnessing IPV and adolescent pregnancy identified inconclusive results due to a number of study limitations, including low methodological quality and wide variations in outcome measures (van Rosmalen-Nooijens, Lahaije, Wong, Prins, & Lagro-Janssen, 2017). Also assessing the relationship between IPV and pubertal timing, the aforementioned meta-analysis found that there was no significant relationship (van Rosmalen-Nooijens et al., 2017).

Studies on the relationship between CSA and genitourinary health problems have indicated that they are more common among abused adolescent girls than in those who have not been abused (Champion et al., 2005; Haydon, Hussey, & Halpern, 2011; Ohene, Halcon, Ireland, Carr, & McNeely, 2005; Upchurch & Kusunoki, 2004). In female children and adolescents, a matched-cohort prospective study with more than 1700 participants found that, compared with the general population, there is a 1.4 to 2.1 increased risk of genitourinary health problems following CSA (Vezina-Gagnon, Bergeron, Frappier, & Daigneault, 2017). Finally, CSA was also associated with higher anxiety symptoms, which were in turn associated with genitopelvic pain in adolescent girls (Santerre-Baillargeon, Vézina-Gagnon, Daigneault, Landry, & Bergeron, 2017).

Study results have also consistently linked varied ACEs with increased risk of STIs (Cederbaum et al., 2015; Champion et al., 2007; Haydon et al., 2011; Kelly & Koh, 2006; Nelson et al., 2010; Norman et al., 2012; Richter et al., 2014). However, one large matched-cohort prospective study found that sexually abused adolescent males and females receiving child welfare services were not significantly more likely to have contracted STIs compared to those of the general population (Vezina-Gagnon et al., 2017), which the authors explained by the relatively younger age of participants (average of 19 years old) and their unknown sexual activity compared with previously cited studies whose participants were older and almost all or all sexually active. A South African study of HIV-infected adolescents found that half of participants reported experiencing eight or more ACEs, and those reporting eight ACEs in comparison to three were three times as likely to report highly risky sexual behavior within the past year (Kidman, Nachman, Dietrich, & Violari, 2018).

A number of limitations remain in the knowledge base relating ACEs with these three reproductive health outcomes. Most important, there are still too few boys and adolescent males that are included, which limits our understanding of their reproductive health risks following ACEs (Anda et al., 2001; Champion et al., 2005; Homma et al., 2012; Landry & Bergeron, 2011; Postma, Bicanic, van der Vaart, & Laan, 2013; Saewyc et al., 2004; Upchurch & Kusunoki, 2004; Vezina-Gagnon et al., 2017). As well, no study has included a cumulative measure of ACEs to document dose-response associations with genitourinary problems among youth or adults. Although studies on adult populations have revealed that increased ACEs exposure is related with a greater risk of STIs, with elevated odds of HIV infection, perceiving oneself as being at risk of AIDS, and higher risk of reinfection with STIs (Champion et al., 2007; Dube et al., 2003; Hillis, Anda, Felitti, Nordenberg, & Marchbanks, 2000; Reisner, Falb, & Mimiaga, 2011), to our knowledge there are no studies conducted with adolescents that assess the effect of cumulative ACEs on risk of STIs/HIV.

Specific at-risk youth populations

Child welfare-involved youth

Children in the foster care system are exposed to significantly more ACEs than their peers, which makes them increasingly vulnerable to sexual exploitation (Turney & Wildeman, 2017). A recent UK study found that 46% of foster care youth stated they had "had sex" before the age of 12 years (before they are even able to consent to any form of sexual activity; Roberts et al., 2018). Foster care youth also had the lowest rates of contraception use (Roberts et al., 2018). Polyvictimization increases the risk of youth being exposed to SV in multiple contexts (Wekerle & Kerig, 2017). In comparison to children who live with both biological parents, those who are living separate from both parents (e.g., foster care youth, adopted youth, youth in diaspora) are 10 times more likely to be sexually abused (Sedlak et al., 2010). In a recent study of homeless youth, 66% percent of participants had an ACEs score of four or higher, and 32.1% reported having been molested or raped (Middleton, Gattis, Frey, & Roe-Sepowitz, 2018). Of these youth, 41.2% reported being victims of sex trafficking (Middleton et al., 2018).

Foster care is identified as "training" for future exploitation as children are frequently moved around and bringing income to the foster home in which they are living (Walker, 2013). These youth are at an increased risk of being subjected to sexual exploitation due to their previous histories of abuse and neglect, movement from home to home, and lack of stable interpersonal relationships—a phenomenon referred to as the *foster care to prostitution pipeline*. According to the National Center for Missing and Exploited Children (NCMEC), over 18,500 "endangered runaways" were reported in 2016, of whom one in six were likely victims of child sex trafficking and 86% of those went missing while they were under the protection of social services (http://www.missingkids.org/footer/media/keyfacts#aboutncmec). Similarly, in 2013, the FBI conducted a nationwide raid to recover child victims of sex trafficking. Of victims recovered, 60% were lured from group homes or foster care homes, and many were not even reported missing by their foster parents (possibly due to a cease in funding; https://www.npr.org/templates/story/story.php?storyId=207901614).

Some foster homes expose children to abusive and exploitative situations as well. Youth in foster care often crave close, protective familial relationships that they have not been previously able to attain within their own families. Pimps and sex traffickers bait victims by creating promises of a family-style relationship. These vulnerabilities may be preyed upon by opportunistic adults. Youth aging-out of foster care are also at-risk for sexual exploitation, as they are at an increased risk of homelessness and may not have the tools or resources to support themselves without the financial aid and guidance of social services and caseworkers (Cecka, 2015). A poll of foster care youth found that foster parents often have unapproved, unregistered adults living in their homes, and almost 40% had been confronted with sexual advances while in foster care, with 20% having been approached by a foster parent with sexual advances (http://nationalpolicycouncil.org/; Vulnerability to Predators & Sex Trafficking, 2012).

Street-involved youth

High ACEs youth may resort to selling sexual services in exchange for cash to provide themselves with basic necessities such as food, clothing, or shelter—referred to as "survival sex" (Roos et al., 2013). Runaway youth receiving services at a US Child and Youth Advocacy Centre (CAYC) were more likely to have experienced severe sexual abuse, higher levels of emotional distress, self-harm, made a past-year suicide attempt, more sexual partners, substance abuse, and to have STIs than nonrunaways; however, fewer CAYC females were pregnant and reported more positive social connections to caring adults (Edinburgh, Harpin, Garcia, & Saewyc, 2013). Resilience factors, such as arts engagement, are less likely to have been experienced by these CSA runaways (Edinburgh et al., 2013).

Indigenous youth

Indigenous youth become increasingly vulnerable to sexual exploitation as they travel from rural to larger urban city centers for school, work, and leisure where they may be targeted by pimps. Aboriginal girls are highly represented in the sex trade in Canada, ranging from 14% to 60% of sex workers (Assistant Deputy Ministers' Committee, 2001). The number of Indigenous youth exploited in major cities is alarmingly high. For example, in Vancouver, Canada, 60% of sexually exploited youth are Indigenous (Urban Native Youth Association, 2002). Indigenous youth experience higher rates of traditional ACEs, including sexual abuse, physical abuse, and substance abuse in the home, likely a result of colonization and intergenerational trauma (Brockie, Dana-Sacco, Wallen, Wilcox, & Campbell, 2015; Kenney & Singh, 2016; Warne & Lajimodiere, 2015). However, they also experience multiple other adverse experiences that affect their vulnerability to sexual exploitation and should arguably be represented on a more relevant ACEs list, such as intergenerational trauma, housing instability, systemic racism, lack of access to clean water and food instability, poverty, community violence, social exclusion and isolation, high community unemployment, and lack of transportation to urban areas and services (Sethi, 2007). A 2010 study of Vancouver youth age 14 to 26 years who self-identified as drug users found that being female, of Aboriginal ethnicity, and being addicted to drugs (e.g., crack cocaine) were significantly associated with having sex in exchange for money, drugs, shelter, clothing, or food (Chettiar, Shannon, Wood, Zhang, & Kerr, 2010).

Sexual minority youth

In addition to traditional ACEs, LGBTQ2S+ youth may often sustain adverse experiences in relation to their sexual orientation. Heteronormative discrimination is a subtle form of peer or family victimization associated with a two times higher risk of TDV victimization (Blais et al., 2017). Traditional ACEs have also been associated with TDV victimization in lesbian, gay, bisexual, and transsexual youth, but have been rarely examined in this subpopulation. Among the various ACEs, only child maltreatment (Stults, Javdani, Greenbaum, Kapadia, & Halkitis, 2015) and sexual abuse in the family (Langenderfer-Magruder, Walls, Whitfield, Brown, & Barrett, 2016) have been studied in sexual minority groups and have been shown to increase the probability of being a victim of TDV by 2.18 times and 2.67 times, respectively.

Sexual minority youth are more likely to have experienced a higher prevalence of co-occurring ACEs than their peers as well as social stigma due to their sexual orientation, putting them at risk for negative mental health outcomes, substance abuse, sexual risk-taking behaviors, earlier sexual debut, homelessness and, in turn, sexual exploitation (Andersen & Blosnich, 2013; Austin, Herrick, & Proescholdbell, 2016; Brown et al., 2015; Clements-Nolle et al., 2018; Liles, Blacker, Landini, & Urquiza, 2016; Stettler & Katz, 2017). According to the BRFSS survey of US adults ($n = 22{,}071$), gay males and lesbians were more than twice as likely to report physical, sexual, or emotional abuse as a child and bisexuals were nearly three times as likely to report sexual abuse as a child in comparison to heterosexual adults (Andersen & Blosnich, 2013). Perpetrators may also take advantage of sexual minority youths' sexual development in their grooming tactics. They may tell victims that they are trying to aid them in developing their sexual identity and knowledge or that they were favored as victims because they were identified as homosexual (Wekerle & Black, 2017). This may be especially true of black LGBTQ2S+ youth who not only intersect two minority statuses, but also have a higher prevalence of ACEs than their peers (Ports et al., 2017). Sexual minority individuals are more likely to witness, perpetrate, and be victimized by extreme forms of violence in adolescence (Russell, Franz, & Driscoll, 2001). Since sexual minority youth are exposed to more ACEs, they are at a greater risk for deficits in emotion regulation that contribute to mental health issues (Stettler & Katz, 2017). Men who have sexual relations with men who have a history of CSA are more likely to report being HIV positive, engaging in unprotected sex, having casual sexual partners, and having sex under the influence of alcohol or drugs (Lloyd & Operario, 2012).

Directions for future research

The theory of toxic stress and developmental traumatology has driven greater understanding in the brain-based vulnerabilities ensuing from chronically, relationally unhealthy environments (De Bellis, 2001; Franke, 2014). The ACEs are a driver of economics and well-being, and a high priority for prevention (e.g., De Bellis, 2001; Shonkoff et al., 2012). Normatively, the "fight, flight, freeze, faint" threat response system reflects the *individual's response* to stress. However, the "tend and befriend" relational system emphasizes the *social response* to stress, where seeking safety in the company of safe, nurturing others or within a known group, is a protection and stress reduction strategy. However, excessively high levels of stress hormones and prolonged exposure to stress dysregulates the body's systems yielding "wear and tear" effects on organs, including the brain (Lupien, McEwen, Gunnar, & Heim, 2009). It is evident that further research is needed in many of the ACEs relationships, especially in terms of determining the mechanisms that explain the relationship between varied ACEs and health outcomes (Cederbaum et al., 2015; also see Chapters 4 and 5).

It is important to note that the WHO (2005) defines mental health not only as the absence of impairment, but as the presence of well-being, which involves health promotion, posttraumatic growth, resilience, and functionality in day-to-day living; as such, there is a need for ACEs research to focus on flourishing. Many people with a significant ACEs history do well. In investigating flourishing in a community survey of adults, 69% with any type of abuse were rated as flourishing, whereas 80% of nonabused adults were flourishing in mental health domains (Afifi et al., 2016). These findings point back to the windows of opportunity in adolescence as potentially yielding a triple dividend: (1) ameliorating ACEs effects in adolescence, (2) addressing preventable problems of adolescent SV and STIs, as well as (3) setting up a healthier context for future parenting. It is necessary to conduct research through an intersectional lens to understand how the experiences of victims of CSA and SV differ due to the underlying social and political structures that have the potential to create privilege for some and oppression for others (Hankivsky, 2014). For male victims, socially constructed masculinity norms (i.e., self-sufficiency and emotional control, acting tough, and rigid gender roles; Ragonese, Shand, & Barker, 2018) may prevent them from ever disclosing their abuse and seeking help to cope with their trauma symptoms. Addressing CSA and SV impacts, such as posttraumatic stress symptoms and resilience directly, is a relevant route going forward in understanding the ACEs framework as a model for intervention. Given that maltreatment is linked with global and multiple neuropsychological deficits *unrelated* to current posttraumatic stress symptoms or psychopathology (De Bellis, Woolley, & Hooper, 2013), it is important to consider nontrauma impairment. For example, to our knowledge, no known program specifically addresses ACEs to prevent TDV (De Koker, Mathews, Zuch, Bastien, & Mason-Jones, 2014; De La Rue, Polanin, Espelage, & Pigott, 2017). This suggests that ACEs research would benefit from a lifespan perspective and cohort designs in concert with broad-scale intervention models. Recent guidelines relevant to the ACEs-SV trauma connection include: (1) responding to children and adolescents who have been sexually abused (https://www.who.int/reproductivehealth/publications/violence/clinical-response-csa/en/), (2) guidance on ethical considerations in planning and reviewing research studies on sexual and reproductive health in adolescents (http://www.who.int/reproductivehealth/publications/adolescence/ethical-considerations-srh-research-in-adolescents/en/), (3) guidelines for psychological practice with boys and men (https://www.apa.org/about/policy/boys-men-practice-guidelines.pdf), and (4) terminology guidelines for the protection of children from sexual exploitation and sexual abuse (http://luxembourgguidelines.org). Currently, a there is major need for research in SV centers on trafficking with the increasing vulnerabilities to youth from migration and the online environment. Trauma-informed learning environments can support a trajectory of opportunities for engaging in good citizenry, labor market engagement, well-being and resilience.

Implications for policy and practice

Early childhood education programs can buffer against negative mental health and behavioral impacts and allow for the added benefit of experiencing nonviolent, invested care, and enriching environments (Stepleton, McIntosh, & Corrington, 2010). Three domains of healthy communities are: (1) equitable economic and educational opportunity, (2) the physical built environment, and (3) the social and cultural environment (Pinderhughes, Davis, & Williams, 2015). Collective efficacy is the group action version of individual self-efficacy that involves confidence in effecting safety, from neighborhood or crime watch to "someone will see, hear, or know and tell" about crime and child abuse and neglect (i.e., prosocial social norms, safe adults to confide in, informal respite care, paying attention to violence sounds) to information community cohesion (i.e., block parties, neighborhood welcome). This social cohesion would be expected to facilitate more social ties and greater access to social support. Further, this neighborhood knowledge of adults knowing children and children knowing adults may build natural mentorship processes and resource alliances.

To address the broader context and target community resilience, the Communities That Care (CTC; Arthur, Glaser, & Hawkins, 2005; Brown, Hawkins, Arthur, Briney, & Abbott, 2007; Hawkins et al., 2008) model promotes positive youth development in socioeconomic disadvantaged (i.e., high crime) urban neighborhoods (http://www.communitiesthatcare.net/how-ctc-works/social-development-strategy/). Key objectives are to reduce early entry into substance use and alter trajectories toward delinquency. The alternative to developing problem lifestyles is investment in school and education. The CTC advocates for the use of five socialization and social competence strategies: (1) providing prosocial opportunities, (2) focusing on skills development, (3) supporting recognition of mastery, (4) acknowledging bonding efforts, and (5) consistency with clear standards of behavior. This approach has led to higher school bonding, more youth graduating high school on time, and having better economic status in young adulthood. Further study has indicated that short-term effects may be less dramatic than longer-term effects (McCauley et al., 2016), and that the level of impact varies across communities (Monahan, Hawkins, & Abbott, 2013). The benefit-cost ratio in the CTC was $8.23 per dollar invested (Kuklinski, Fagan, Hawkins, Briney, & Catalano, 2015). Within the CTC sample, foster care youth were found to be at high risk, reporting use of all illicit substances measured, controlling for confounds, as compared to nonfoster home residents, and especially for females (McDonald, Marsical, Yan, & Brook, 2014). Collective efficacy and strong community approaches, such as those involved in the CTC, reveal the protective impacts on fewer youth with firearms, lowered delinquency and aggression, lowered youth suicidality, and lowered TDV (Browning, Gardner, Maimon, & Brooks-Gunn, 2014). The burden for SV prevention cannot fall on the child, and proactive approaches appropriately contextualize the shared responsibility for minors and the community standard of protection. When paired with appropriate community-based proactive approaches, as well as early intervention approaches for high ACEs youth, including the provision of evidence-based treatment for SV (for a discussion of trauma-focused cognitive behavior therapy, see Wekerle et al., 2018), the ACEs screening approach may lead to more positive parenting, community engagement, and reductions in ACEs prevalence and, hence, their broad impact.

We come back to the reality that adolescence is a time of risk for relating, but also that it is a window of opportunity to support youth with high ACEs on a wellness trajectory. It remains important to meet youth where they are at and accept the reality that disclosure is a process and one that may be initiated online, as seen in the recent #MeToo phenomenon. Research shows that by ages 16 to 17 years, 85% of youth own a smartphone, spending an average of 6 to 9 hours online per day (Common Sense Media, 2015; Steeves, 2014). Adolescents are living in two worlds, the physical and the virtual, with spillover from one to the other. Most youth feel they spend too much idle time on their smartphones (PEW Research Center, 2018); but, this is an opportunity. What if a fraction of this time was spent on developing resilience skills and enhancing emotion regulation strategies? Youth with SV backgrounds may be able to incrementally build their resilience while negotiating the risk and relating terrain of their twin realities. The model of disruptive innovations points to the utility in developing simpler, cost-effective innovations that offer only the most prevalent features of treatment and are able to serve a vast population at once (Rotheram-Borus, Swendeman, & Chorpita, 2012). Technology-based interventions provide opportunity to provide resilience-bolstering tools to adolescents who have experienced adversity in a timely and confidential manner. We have focused on our learning from SV and resilience to build a daily tool to support youth attending to and experiencing more positives in their daily living, being able to build increasing self-agency in crafting a life worth living. Counteracting the adverse living environments with constructive, safe, self-care online living environments merits our further intervention research attention.

Conclusion

Victims of ACEs, mainly those who have experienced maltreatment and CSA victimization, show a greater risk of offending, being revictimized, and experiencing sexual health-related issues. However, their victimization trajectory can be interrupted because, importantly, not all youth who have experienced ACEs will later be victims or impaired in very sustained ways. What is most critical moving forward is that we do not denigrate rights-based approaches to support youth in preventing their own SV perpetration, and that ACEs prevention remains focused on child maltreatment prevention. Due to the additional risks of SV and the wide range of contexts within which it manifests, a trauma-informed approach must reach an intersectional perspective that considers how such factors as gender socialization norms and mental health help-seeking impacts the trajectories of risk and resilience. Evaluation of the programs offered to vulnerable youth also showed that something can collectively be done to prevent SV victimization, a major public health issue; however, SV has not been as effectively addressed as child injury prevention. Sexually violated children, with some gender differences, clearly point to injury impacts and impacts on sexual health. Adolescence is a critical opportunity for preventative education and trauma-focused treatment to be considered as part of a resilience in youth approach.

In sum, ACEs are a critical information source for action, and matching intervention to ACEs profiles is the key focus going forward. This is perhaps not as sizeable a task as it may seem, with technology facilitating access and uptake of "in-time" intervention that is mindful of resilience promotion, alongside symptom reduction or management. Evidence-based policy means that the requisite quality research has been undertaken and synthesized with a long-term view for the health and wellbeing to all children and their successive generations.

Acknowledgments

We would like to thank Ronald Chung and Hailey Smith for their research support. The authors would like to acknowledge the Canadian Institutes of Health Research, Institute of Gender and Health, and Public Health Agency of Canada funding our team grant in boys and men's health. For more information on publications from this team, see: https://www.researchgate.net/project/Understanding-health-risks-and-promoting-resilience-in-male-youth-with-sexual-violence-experience-CIHR-Team-Grant-TE3-138302.

For an award winning CIHR Institute of Human Development and Child and Youth Health research-to-action videos on this grant, see:

Child Sexual Abuse Prevention: https://youtu.be/k1qvzGhOWU4.

The Maltreatment and Adolescent Pathways Study: https://www.youtube.com/watch?v=3Zes-PJi2OY.

References

Afifi, T. O., MacMillan, H. L., Taillieu, T., Cheung, K., Turner, S., Tonmyr, L., & Hovdestad, W. (2015). Relationship between child abuse exposure and reported contact with child protection organizations: results from the Canadian Community Health Survey. *Child Abuse & Neglect*, *46*, 198–206. https://doi.org/10.1016/j.chiabu.2015.05.001.

Afifi, T. O., MacMillan, H. L., Taillieu, T., Turner, S., Cheung, K., Sareen, J., & Boyle, M. H. (2016). Individual- and relationship-level factors related to better mental health outcomes following child abuse: results from a nationally representative Canadian sample. *Canadian Journal of Psychiatry*, *61*(12), 776–788. https://doi.org/10.1177/0706743716651832.

Almuneef, M., Qayad, M., Aleissa, M., & Albuhairan, F. (2014). Adverse childhood experiences, chronic diseases, and risky health behaviors in Saudi Arabian adults: a pilot study. *Child Abuse & Neglect*, *38*(11), 1787–1793. https://doi.org/10.1016/j.chiabu.2014.06.003.

Anda, R. F., Chapman, D. P., Felitti, V. J., Edwards, V., Williamson, D. F., Croft, J. B., & Giles, W. H. (2002). Adverse childhood experiences and risk of paternity in teen pregnancy. *Obstetrics & Gynecology*, *100*(1), 37–45. https://doi.org/10.1016/S0029-7844(02)02063-X.

Anda, R. F., Felitti, V. J., Chapman, D. P., Croft, J. B., Williamson, D. F., Santelli, J., … Marks, J. S. (2001). Abused boys, battered mothers, and male involvement in teen pregnancy. *Pediatrics*, *107*(2), e19. https://doi.org/10.1542/peds.107.2.e19.

Andersen, J. P., & Blosnich, J. (2013). Disparities in adverse childhood experiences among sexual minority and heterosexual adults: results from a multi-state probability sample. *PLoS One*, *8*(1), e54691. https://doi.org/10.1371/journal.pone.0054691.

Arreola, S. G., Neilands, T. B., & Díaz, R. (2009). Childhood sexual abuse and the sociocultural context of sexual risk among adult Latino gay and bisexual men. *American Journal of Public Health*, *99*(Suppl. 2), S432–S438. https://doi.org/10.2105/AJPH.2008.138925.

Armour, S., & Haynie, D. L. (2007). Adolescent sexual debut and later delinquency. *Journal of Youth and Adolescence*, *36*(2), 141–152. https://doi.org/10.1007/s10964-006-9128-4.

Arthur, M. W., Glaser, R. R., & Hawkins, J. D. (2005). Steps towards community-level resilience: community adoption of science-based prevention programming. In R. D. V. Peters, B. Leadbeater, & R. J. McMahon (Eds.), *Resilience in children, families, and communities: Linking context to practice and policy* (pp. 177–194). New York: Kluwer.

Assistant Deputy Ministers' Committee on Prostitution and the Sexual Exploitation of Youth. (2001). *Sexual exploitation of youth in British Columbia*. Victoria, British Columbia: Ministry of Attorney General, Ministry for Children and Families, and Ministry of Health and Ministry Responsible for Seniors.

Austin, A., Herrick, H., & Proescholdbell, S. (2016). Adverse childhood experiences related to poor adult health among lesbian, gay, and bisexual individuals. *American Journal of Public Health*, *106*(2), 314–320. https://doi.org/10.2105/AJPH.2015.302904.

Bellis, M. A., Hughes, K., Leckenby, N., Jones, L., Baban, A., Kachaeva, M., … Terzic, N. (2014). Adverse childhood experiences and associations with health-harming behaviours in young adults: surveys in eight eastern European countries. *Bulletin of the World Health Organization*, *92*, 641–655. https://doi.org/10.2471/BLT.13.129247.

Blais, M., Bergeron, F.-A., Hébert, M., Fernet, M., Godbout, N., & Lavoie, F. (2017). *La violence dans les relations amoureuses des jeunes de la diversité sexuelle et de genre: Une recension narrative.*

Blinn-Pike, L., Berger, T., Dixon, D., Kuschel, D., & Kaplan, M. (2002). Is there a causal link between maltreatment and adolescent pregnancy? A literature review. *Perspectives on Sexual and Reproductive Health*, *34*(2), 68–75. https://doi.org/10.1363/3406802.

Boak, A., Hamilton, H. A., Adlaf, E. M., Henderson, J. L., & Mann, R. E. (2018). *The mental health and well-being of Ontario students, 1991–2017: Detailed findings from the Ontario Student Drug Use and Health Survey (OSDUHS) (CAMH Research Document Series No. 47).* Toronto, ON: Centre for Addiction and Mental Health.

Briggs, E. C., Greeson, J. K., Layne, C. M., Fairbank, J. A., Knoverek, A. M., & Pynoos, R. S. (2012). Trauma exposure, psychosocial functioning, and treatment needs of youth in residential care: preliminary findings from the NCTSN core data set. *Journal of Child & Adolescent Trauma*, *5*(1), 1–15. https://doi.org/10.1080/19361521.2012.646413.

Brockie, T. N., Dana-Sacco, G., Wallen, G. R., Wilcox, H. C., & Campbell, J. C. (2015). The relationship of adverse childhood experiences to PTSD, depression, poly-drug use and suicide attempt in reservation-based Native American adolescents and young adults. *American Journal of Community Psychology*, *3–4*, 411–421. https://doi.org/10.1007/s10464-015-9721-3.

Brown, E. C., Hawkins, J. D., Arthur, M. W., Briney, J. S., & Abbott, R. D. (2007). Effects of communities that care on prevention services systems: findings from the community youth development study at 1.5 years. *Prevention Science*, *8*(3), 180–191. https://doi.org/10.1007/s11121-007-0068-3.

Brown, J., Cohen, P., Chen, H., Smailes, E., & Johnson, J. G. (2004). Sexual trajectories of abused and neglected youths. *Journal of Developmental and Behavioral Pediatrics*, *25*(2), 77–82. https://doi.org/10.1097/00004703-200404000-00001.

Browning, C. R., Gardner, M., Maimon, D., & Brooks-Gunn, J. (2014). Collective efficacy and the contingent consequences of exposure to life-threatening violence. *Developmental Psychology*, *50*(7), 1878–1890. https://doi.org/10.1037/a0036767.

Brown, M. J., Masho, S. W., Perera, R. A., Mezuk, B., & Cohen, S. A. (2015). Sex and sexual orientation disparities in adverse childhood experiences and early age at sexual debut in the United States: results from a nationally representative sample. *Child Abuse & Neglect*, *46*, 89–102. https://doi.org/10.1016/j.chiabu.2015.02.019.

Burczycka, M. (2017). *Section 1: Profile of Canadian adults who experienced childhood maltreatment*. Ottawa: Statistics Canada. 2017 Feb 21 [cited 2018 Oct]. Available from: https://www150.statcan.gc.ca/n1/pub/85-002-x/2017001/article/14698/01-eng.htm.

Casey, E. A., Masters, N. T., Beadnell, B., Hoppe, M. J., Morrison, D. M., & Wells, E. A. (2016). Predicting sexual assault perpetration among heterosexually active young men. *Violence Against Women*, *23*(1), 3–27. https://doi.org/10.1177/1077801216634467.

Cecil, C. A. M., Viding, E., Fearon, P., Glaser, D., & McCrory, E. J. (2017). Disentangling the mental health impact of childhood abuse and neglect. *Child Abuse & Neglect*, *63*, 106–119. https://doi.org/10.1016/j.chiabu.2016.11.024.

Cecka, D. M. (2015). *The civil rights of sexually exploited youth in foster care. Vol. 117* (pp. 1225–1271). Law Faculty Publications (University of Richmond- School of Law).1225–1271. Retrieved from: https://scholarship.richmond.edu/cgi/viewcontent.cgi?article=2078&context=law-faculty-publications.

Cederbaum, J. A., Putnam-Hornstein, E., Sullivan, K., Winetrobe, H., & Bird, M. (2015). STD and abortion prevalence in adolescent mothers with histories of childhood protection involvement. *Perspectives on Sexual and Reproductive Health*, *47*(4), 187–193. https://doi.org/10.1363/47e4215.

Champion, J. D., Piper, J. M., Holden, A. E., Shain, R. N., Perdue, S., & Korte, J. E. (2005). Relationship of abuse and pelvic inflammatory disease risk behavior in minority adolescents. *Journal of the American Association of Nurse Practitioners*, *17*(6), 234–241. https://doi.org/10.1111/j.1041-2972.2005.00038.x.

Champion, J. D., Shain, R. N., Korte, J. E., Holden, A. E. C., Piper, J. M., Perdue, S. T., & Guerra, F. A. (2007). Behavioral interventions and abuse: secondary analysis of reinfection in minority women. *International Journal of STD & AIDS*, *18*(11), 748–753. https://doi.org/10.1258/095646207782212180.

Chaplo, S. D., Kerig, P. K., Modroski, C. A., & Bennett, D. C. (2017). Gender differences in the associations among sexual abuse, posttraumatic stress symptoms, and delinquent behaviors in a sample of detained adolescents. *Journal of Child and Adolescent Trauma*, *10*(1), 29–39. https://doi.org/10.1007/s40653-016-0122-z.

Chettiar, J., Shannon, K., Wood, E., Zhang, R., & Kerr, T. (2010). Survival sex work involvement among street-involved youth who use drugs in a Canadian setting. *Journal of Public Health*, *32*(3), 322–327. https://doi.org/10.1093/pubmed/fdp126.

Cheung, K., Taillieu, T., Turner, S., Fortier, J., Sareen, J., MacMillan, H. L., … Afifi, T. O. (2018). Individual-level factors related to better mental health outcomes following child maltreatment among adolescents. *Child Abuse & Neglect*, *79*, 192–202. https://doi.org/10.1016/j.chiabu.2018.02.007.

Clements-Nolle, K., Lensch, T., Baxa, A., Gay, C., Larson, S., & Yang, W. (2018). Sexual identity, adverse childhood experiences, and suicidal behaviors. *Journal of Adolescent Health*, *62*(2), 198–204. https://doi.org/10.1016/j.jadohealth.2017.09.022.

Common Sense Media. (2015). *The common sense census: Media use by teens and tweens*. Common Sense Media. Retrieved from: https://www.commonsensemedia.org/research/the-common-sense-census-media-use-by-tweens-and-teens.

Copping, L. T., Campbell, A., & Muncer, S. (2013). Violence, teenage pregnancy, and life history ecological factors and their impact on strategy-driven behavior. *Human Nature*, *24*(2), 137–157. https://doi.org/10.1007/s12110-013-9163-2.

Corçoran, M., & McNulty, M. (2018). Examining the role of attachment in the relationship between childhood adversity, psychological distress and subjective well-being. *Child Abuse & Neglect*, *76*, 297–309. https://doi.org/10.1016/j.chiabu.2017.11.012.

Craig, J. M., Intravia, J., Wolff, K. T., & Baglivio, M. T. (2017). What can help? Examining levels of substance (non)use as a protective factor in the effect of ACEs on crime. *Youth Violence and Juvenile Justice*, 1–20. https://doi.org/10.1177/1541204017728998.

Craven, S., Brown, S., & Gilchrist, E. (2006). Sexual grooming of children: review of literature and theoretical considerations. *Journal of Sexual Aggression*, *12*(3), 287–299. https://doi.org/10.1080/13552600601069414.

De Bellis, M. D. (2001). Developmental traumatology: the psychobiological development of maltreated children and its implications for research, treatment, and policy. *Development and Psychopathology*, *13*(3), 539–564. https://doi.org/10.1017/S0954579401003078.

De Bellis, M. D., Woolley, D. P., & Hooper, S. R. (2013). Neuropsychological findings in pediatric maltreatment: relationship of PTSD, dissociative symptoms, and abuse/neglect indices to neurocognitive outcomes. *Child Maltreatment*, *18*(3), 171–183. https://doi.org/10.1177/1077559513497420.

De Koker, P., Mathews, C., Zuch, M., Bastien, S., & Mason-Jones, A. J. (2014). A systematic review of interventions for preventing adolescent intimate partner violence. *Journal of Adolescent Health*, *54*(1), 3–13. https://doi.org/10.1016/j.jadohealth.2013.08.008.

De La Rue, L., Polanin, J. R., Espelage, D. L., & Pigott, T. D. (2017). A meta-analysis of school-based interventions aimed to prevent or reduce violence in teen dating relationships. *Review of Educational Research*, *87*(1), 7–34. https://doi.org/10.3102/0034654316632061.

Donahue, K. L., Lichtenstein, P., Långström, N., & D'Onofrio, B. M. (2013). Why does early sexual intercourse predict subsequent maladjustment? Exploring potential familial confounds. *Health Psychology*, *32*(2), 180–189. https://doi.org/10.1037/a0028922.

Drury, A., Heinrichs, T., Elbert, M., Tahja, K., DeLisi, M., & Caropreso, D. (2017). Adverse childhood experiences, paraphilias, and serious criminal violence among federal sex offenders. *Journal of Criminal Psychology*, *7*(2), 105–119. https://doi.org/10.1108/JCP-11-2016-0039.

Dube, S. R., Felitti, V. J., Dong, M., Giles, W. H., & Anda, R. F. (2003). The impact of adverse childhood experiences on health problems: evidence from four birth cohorts dating back to 1900. *Preventive Medicine*, *37*(3), 268–277. https://doi.org/10.1016/S0091-7435(03)00123-3.

Duke, N. N., Pettingell, S. L., McMorris, B. J., & Borowsky, I. W. (2010). Adolescent violence perpetration: associations with multiple types of adverse childhood experiences. *Pediatrics*, *125*(4), e78–786. https://doi.org/10.1542/peds.2009-0597.

Easton, S. D. (2012). Understanding adverse childhood experiences (ACE) and their relationship to adult stress among male survivors of childhood sexual abuse. *Journal of Prevention & Intervention in the Community*, *40*(2), 291–303. https://doi.org/10.1080/10852352.2012.707446.

Edinburgh, L. D., Harpin, S. B., Garcia, C. M., & Saewyc, E. M. (2013). Differences in abuse and related risk and protective factors by runaway status for adolescents seen at a U.S. child advocacy centre. *International Journal of Child and Adolescent Resilience*, *1*(1), 4–16. Retrieved from: https://www.ncbi.nlm.nih.gov/pmc/articles/PMC4716834/pdf/nihms5382.pdf.

Ehrensaft, M. K., Knous-Westfall, H. M., Cohen, P., & Chen, H. (2015). How does child abuse history influence parenting of the next generation? *Psychology of Violence*, *5*(1), 16–25. https://doi.org/10.1037/a0036080.

Felitti, V. J., Anda, R. F., Nordenberg, D., Williamson, D. F., Spitz, A. M., Edwards, V., … Marks, J. S. (1998). Relationship of childhood abuse and household dysfunction to many of the leading causes of death in adults: the adverse childhood experiences (ACE) study. *American Journal of Preventative Medicine, 14*(4), 245–258. https://doi.org/10.1016/S0749-3797(98)00017-8.

Feiring, C., Simon, V. A., & Cleland, C. M. (2009). Childhood sexual abuse, stigmatization, internalizing symptoms, and the development of sexual difficulties and dating aggression. *Journal of Consulting and Clinical Psychology, 77*(1), 127–137. https://doi.org/10.1037/a0013475.

Finkelhor, D., Turner, H. A., Hamby, S. L., & Ormrod, R. K. (2011). *Poly-victimization: Children's exposure of multiple types of violence, crime, and abuse*. Washington, DC: US Government Publishing Company.

Flaherty, E. G., Thompson, R., Dubowitz, H., Harvey, E. M., English, D. J., Everson, M. D., … Runyan, D. K. (2014). Adverse childhood experiences and child health in early adolescence. *JAMA Pediatrics, 167*(7), 622–629. https://doi.org/10.1001/jamapediatrics.2013.22.

Franke, H. A. (2014). Review: toxic stress: effects, prevention and treatment. *Children, 1*, 390–402. https://doi.org/10.3390/children1030390.

GBD 2015 Risk Factors Collaborators. (2016). Global, regional, and national comparative risk assessment of 79 behavioral, environmental and occupational, and metabolic risks or clusters of risks, 1990–2015: a systematic analysis for the Global Burden of Disease Study 2015. *Lancet, 388*(10053), 1659–1724. https://doi.org/10.1016/S0140-6736(16)31679-8.

Gibson, L. E., & Leitenberg, H. (2001). The impact of child sexual abuse and stigma on methods of coping with sexual assault among undergraduate women. *Child Abuse & Neglect, 25*(10), 1343–1361. https://doi.org/10.1016/S0145-2134(01)00279-4.

Gold, S. D., Marx, B. P., & Lexington, J. M. (2007). Gay male sexual assault survivors: the relations among internalized homophobia, experiential avoidance, and psychological symptom severity. *Behaviour Research and Therapy, 45*(3), 549–562. https://doi.org/10.1016/j.brat.2006.05.006.

Golden, R. L., Furman, W., & Collibee, C. (2016). The risks and rewards of sexual debut. *Developmental Psychology, 52*(11), 1913–1925. https://doi.org/10.1037/dev0000206.

Hamby, S., Finkelhor, D., & Turner, H. (2012). Teen dating violence: co-occurrence with other victimizations in the National Survey of Children's Exposure to Violence (NatSCEV). *Psychology of Violence, 2*(2), 111–124. https://doi.org/10.1037/a0027191.

Hankivsky, O. (2014). *Intersectionality*. The Institute for Intersectionality Research & Policy, SFU. https://www.sfu.ca/iirp/documents/resources/101_Final.pdf.

Hawkins, J. D., Catalano, R. F., Arthur, M. W., Egan, E., Brown, E. C., Abbott, R. D., & Murray, D. M. (2008). Testing communities that care: the rationale, design, and behavioral baseline equivalence of the community youth development study. *Prevention Science, 9*(3), 178–190. https://doi.org/10.1007/s11121-008-0092-y.

Haydon, A. A., Hussey, J. M., & Halpern, C. T. (2011). Childhood abuse and neglect and the risk of STDs in early adulthood. *Perspectives on Sexual and Reproductive Health, 43*(1), 16–22. https://doi.org/10.1363/4301611.

Hébert, M., Blais, M., & Lavoie, F. (2017). Prevalence of teen dating victimization among a representative sample of high school students in Quebec. *International Journal of Clinical and Health Psychology, 17*(3), 225–233. https://doi.org/10.1016/j.ijchp.2017.06.001.

Hébert, M., Daspe, M.È., Lapierre, A., Godbout, N., Blais, M., Fernet, M., & Lavoie, F. (2017). A meta-analysis of risk and protective factors for dating violence victimization: the role of family and peer interpersonal context. *Trauma, Violence & Abuse*, 1–17. https://doi.org/10.1177/1524838017725336.

Hillis, S. D., Anda, R. F., Felitti, V. J., & Marchbanks, P. A. (2001). Adverse childhood experiences and sexual risk behaviors in women: a retrospective cohort study. *Family Planning Perspectives, 33*(5), 206–211. https://doi.org/10.2307/2673783.

Hillis, S. D., Anda, R. F., Felitti, V. J., Nordenberg, D., & Marchbanks, P. A. (2000). Adverse childhood experiences and sexually transmitted diseases in men and women: a retrospective study. *Pediatrics, 106*(1), E11. https://doi.org/10.1542/peds.106.1.e11.

Homma, Y., Wang, N. R., Saewyc, E., & Kishor, N. (2012). The relationship between sexual abuse and risky sexual behavior among adolescent boys: a meta-analysis. *Journal of Adolescent Health*, *51*(1), 18–24. https://doi.org/10.1016/j.jadohealth.2011.12.032.

Hughes, K., Bellis, M. A., Hardcastle, K. A., Sethi, D., Butchart, A., Mikton, C., … Dunne, M. P. (2017). The effect of multiple adverse childhood experiences on health: a systematic review and meta-analysis. *The Lancet Public Health*, *2*(8), e356–e366. https://doi.org/10.1016/S2468-2667(17)30118-4.

Hunt, T. K. A., Slack, K. S., & Berger, L. M. (2017). Adverse childhood experiences and behavioral problems in middle childhood. *Child Abuse & Neglect*, *67*, 391–402. https://doi.org/10.1016/j.chiabu.2016.11.005.

Kelly, P., & Koh, J. (2006). Sexually transmitted infections in alleged sexual abuse of children and adolescents. *Journal of Paediatrics and Child Health*, *42*(7–8), 434–440. https://doi.org/10.1111/j.1440-1754.2006.00893.x.

Kenney, M. K., & Singh, G. K. (2016). Adverse childhood experiences among American Indian/Alaska native children: the 2011-2012 national survey of children's health. *Scientifica*, *2016*, 1–14. https://doi.org/10.1155/2016/7424239.

Kerig, P. K., & Modrowski, C. A. (2018). Testing gender-differentiated models of the mechanisms linking polyvictimization and youth offending: numbing and callousness versus dissociation and borderline traits. *Journal of Trauma & Dissociation*, *19*(3), 347–361. https://doi.org/10.1080/15299732.2018.1441355.

Kidman, R., Nachman, S., Dietrich, J., & Violari, A. (2018). Childhood adversity increases the risk of onward transmission from perinatal HIV-infected adolescents and youth in South Africa. *Child Abuse & Neglect*, *79*, 98–106. https://doi.org/10.1016/j.chiabu.2018.01.028.

Knox, G. W. (2004). Females and gangs: sexual violence, prostitution, and exploitation. *Journal of Gang Research*, *11*(3), 1–15.

Kugler, K. C., Vasilenko, S. A., Butera, N. M., & Coffman, D. L. (2017). Long-term consequences of early sexual initiation on young adult health: a causal inference approach. *The Journal of Early Adolescence*, *37*(5), 662–676. https://doi.org/10.1177/0272431615620666.

Kuklinski, M. R., Fagan, A. A., Hawkins, J. D., Briney, J. S., & Catalano, R. F. (2015). Benefit-cost analysis of a randomized evaluation of communities that care: monetizing intervention effects on the initiation of delinquency and substance use through grade 12. *Journal of Experimental Criminology*, *11*(2), 165–192. https://doi.org/10.1007/s11292-014-9226-3.

Landry, T., & Bergeron, S. (2011). Biopsychosocial factors associated with dyspareunia in a community sample of adolescent girls. *Archives of Sexual Behavior*, *40*(5), 877–889. https://doi.org/10.1007/s10508-010-9637-9.

Langenderfer-Magruder, L., Walls, N. E., Whitfield, D. L., Brown, S. M., & Barrett, C. M. (2016). Partner violence victimization among lesbian, gay, bisexual, transgender, and queer youth: associations among risk factors. *Child and Adolescent Social Work Journal*, *33*(1), 55–68. https://doi.org/10.1007/s10560-015-0402-8.

Layne, C. M., Greeson, J. K. P., Ostrowski, S. A., Kim, S., Reading, S., Vivrette, R. L., … Pynoos, R. S. (2014). Cumulative trauma exposure and high risk behavior in adolescence: findings from the national child traumatic stress network core data set. *Psychological Trauma: Theory, Research, Practice, and Policy*, *6*(S1), S40–S49. https://doi.org/10.1037/a0037799.

Levenson, J. S., & Socia, K. M. (2016). Adverse childhood experiences and arrest patterns in a sample of sexual offenders. *Journal of Interpersonal Violence*, *31*(10), 1883–1911. https://doi.org/10.1177/0886260515570751.

Levenson, J. S., Willis, G. M., & Prescott, D. S. (2014). Adverse childhood experiences in the lives of female sex offenders. *Sexual Abuse*, *27*(3), 258–283. https://doi.org/10.1177/1079063214544332.

Levenson, J. S., Willis, G. M., & Prescott, D. S. (2016). Adverse childhood experiences in the lives of male sex offenders: implications for trauma-informed care. *Sexual Abuse*, *28*(4), 340–359. https://doi.org/10.1177/1079063214535819.

Liles, B. D., Blacker, D. M., Landini, J. L., & Urquiza, A. J. (2016). A California multidisciplinary juvenile court: serving sexually exploited and at-risk youth. *Behavioral Sciences & the Law*, *34*(1), 234–245. https://doi.org/10.1002/bsl.2230.

Lloyd, S., & Operario, D. (2012). HIV risk among men who have sex with men who have experienced childhood sexual abuse: systematic review and meta-analysis. *AIDS Education and Prevention*, *24*(3), 228–241. https://doi.org/10.1521/aeap.2012.24.3.228.

Lupien, S. J., McEwen, B. S., Gunnar, M. R., & Heim, C. (2009). Effects of stress throughout the lifespan on the brain, behaviour and cognition. *Nature Reviews Neuroscience*, *10*, 434–445. https://doi.org/10.1038/nrn2639.

Madigan, S., Wade, M., Tarabulsy, G., Jenkins, J. M., & Shouldice, M. (2014). Association between abuse history and adolescent pregnancy: a meta-analysis. *Journal of Adolescent Health*, *55*(2), 151–159. https://doi.org/10.1016/j.jadohealth.2014.05.002.

McAlinden, A.-M. (2006). 'Setting 'Em Up': personal, familial and institutional grooming in the sexual abuse of children. *Social & Legal Studies*, *15*(3), 339–362. https://doi.org/10.1177/0964663906066613.

McDonald, T. P., Marsical, E. S., Yan, Y., & Brook, J. (2014). Substance use and abuse for youths in foster care: results from the communities that care normative database. *Journal of Child & Adolescent Substance Abuse*, *23*(4), 262–268. https://doi.org/10.1080/1067828X.2014.912093.

McCauley, E., Gudmundsen, G., Schloredt, K., Martell, C., Rhew, I., Hubley, S., & Dimidjian, S. (2016). The adolescent behavioral activation program: adapting behavioral activation as a treatment for depression in adolescence. *Journal of Clinical Child & Adolescent Psychology*, *45*(3), 291–304. https://doi.org/10.1080/15374416.2014.979933.

McGlone, C., & Schaefer, G. R. (2008). After the haze: legal aspects of hazing. *The Entertainment and Sports Law Journal*, *6*(1), 2. https://doi.org/10.16997/eslj.64.

Meltzer-Brody, S., Bledsoe-Mansori, S. E., Johnson, N., Killian, C., Hamer, R. M., Jackson, C., … Thorp, J. (2013). A prospective study of perinatal depression and trauma history in pregnant minority adolescents. *American Journal of Obstetrics and Gynecology*, *208*(3), 211.e211–211.e217. https://doi.org/10.1016/j.ajog.2012.12.020.

Merrick, M. T., Ford, D. C., Ports, K. A., & Guinn, A. S. (2018). Prevalence of adverse childhood experiences from the 2011-2014 behavioral risk factor surveillance system in 23 states. *JAMA Pediatrics*, *172*(11), 1038–1044. https://doi.org/10.1001/jamapediatrics.2018.2537.

Middleton, J. S., Gattis, M. N., Frey, L. M., & Roe-Sepowitz, D. (2018). Youth experiences survey (YES): exploring the scope and complexity of sex trafficking in a sample of youth experiencing homelessness. *Journal of Social Service Research*, *44*(2), 141–157. https://doi.org/10.1080/01488376.2018.1428924.

Monahan, K. C., Hawkins, J. D., & Abbott, R. D. (2013). The application of meta-analysis within a matched-pair randomized control trial: an illustration testing the effects of communities that care on delinquent behavior. *Prevention Science*, *14*(1), 1–17. https://doi.org/10.1007/s11121-012-0298-x.

Negriff, S., Schneiderman, J. U., & Trickett, P. K. (2015). Child maltreatment and sexual risk behavior: maltreatment types and gender differences. *Journal of Developmental & Behavioral Pediatrics*, *36*(9), 708–716. https://doi.org/10.1097/DBP.0000000000000204.

Nelson, D. B., & Lepore, S. J. (2013). The role of stress, depression, and violence on unintended pregnancy among young urban women. *Journal of Women's Health*, *22*(8), 673–680. https://doi.org/10.1089/jwh.2012.4133.

Nelson, D. B., Uscher-Pines, L., Staples, S. R., & Grisso, J. A. (2010). Childhood violence and behavioral effects among urban pregnant women. *Journal of Women's Health*, *19*(6), 1177–1183. https://doi.org/10.1089/jwh.2009.1539.

Noll, J. G., Shenk, C. E., & Putnam, K. T. (2009). Childhood sexual abuse and adolescent pregnancy: a meta-analytic update. *Journal of Pediatric Psychology*, *34*(4), 366–378. https://doi.org/10.1093/jpepsy/jsn098.

Norman, R. E., Byambaa, M., De, R., Butchart, A., Scott, J., & Vos, T. (2012). The long-term health consequences of child physical abuse, emotional abuse, and neglect: a systematic review and meta-analysis. *PLoS Medicine*, *9*(11), e1001349. https://doi.org/10.1371/journal.pmed.1001349.

O'Donnell, L., O'Donnell, C. R., & Stueve, A. (2001). Early sexual initiation and subsequent sex-related risks among urban minority youth: the reach for health study. *Family Planning Perspectives*, *33*(6), 268–275. https://doi.org/10.2307/3030194.

Ohene, S.-A., Halcon, L., Ireland, M., Carr, P., & McNeely, C. (2005). Sexual abuse history, risk behavior, and sexually transmitted diseases: the impact of age at abuse. *Sexually Transmitted Diseases*, *32*(6), 358–363. https://doi.org/10.1097/01.olq.0000154505.68167.d1.

Paplia, N., Ogloff, J. R. P., Cutajar, M., & Mullen, P. E. (2018). Child sexual abuse and criminal offending: gender-specific effects and the role of abuse characteristic and other adverse outcomes. *Child Maltreatment*, *23*(4), 399–416. https://doi.org/10.1177/1077559518785779.

Parkes, A., Wight, D., Henderson, M., & West, P. (2010). Does early sexual debut reduce teenagers' participation in tertiary education? Evidence from the SHARE longitudinal study. *Journal of Adolescence*, *33*(5), 741–754. https://doi.org/10.1016/j.adolescence.2009.10.006.

Patton, G. C., Sawyer, S. M., Santelli, J. S., Ross, D. A., Afifi, R., Allen, N. B., … Viner, R. M. (2016). Our future: a lancet commission on adolescent health and wellbeing. *The Lancet*, *387*(10036), 2423–2478. https://doi.org/10.1016/s0140-6736(16)00579-1.

PEW Research Center. (2018). *How teens and parents navigate screen time and device distractions*. PEW Research Center. Retrieved from: http://www.pewinternet.org/2018/08/22/how-teens-and-parents-navigate-screen-time-and-device-distractions/.

Pinderhughes, H., Davis, R., & Williams, M. (2015). *Adverse community experiences and resilience: A framework for addressing and preventing community trauma*. Oakland, CA: Prevention Institute.

Poole, J. C., Dobson, K. S., & Pusch, D. (2018). Do adverse childhood experiences predict adult interpersonal difficulties? The role of emotion dysregulation. *Child Abuse & Neglect*, *80*, 123–133. https://doi.org/10.1016/j.chiabu.2018.03.006.

Ports, K. A., Lee, R. D., Raiford, J., Spikes, P., Manago, C., & Wheeler, D. P. (2017). Adverse childhood experiences and health and wellness outcomes among black men who have sex with men. *Journal of Urban Health*, *94*(3), 375–383. https://doi.org/10.1007/s11524-017-0146-1.

Ports, K. A., Ford, D. C., & Merrick, M. T. (2016). Adverse childhood experiences and sexual victimization in adulthood. *Child Abuse & Neglect*, *51*, 313–322. https://doi.org/10.1016/j.chiabu.2015.08.017.

Postma, R., Bicanic, I., van der Vaart, H., & Laan, E. (2013). Pelvic floor muscle problems mediate sexual problems in young adult rape victims. *The Journal of Sexual Medicine*, *10*(8), 1978–1987. https://doi.org/10.1111/jsm.12196.

Putnam-Hornstein, E., Cederbaum, J. A., King, B., Cleveland, J., & Needell, B. (2013). A population-based examination of maltreatment history among adolescent mothers in California. *Journal of Adolescent Health*, *53*(6), 794–797. https://doi.org/10.1016/j.jadohealth.2013.08.004.

Ragonese, C., Shand, T., & Barker, G. (2018). *Masculine norms and men's health: Making the connections: Executive summary*. Washington, DC: Promundo-US.

Rector, R. E., Johnson, K. A., Noyes, L. R., & Martin, S. (2003). *The harmful effects of early sexual activity and multiple sexual partners among women: A book of charts*. Washington, DC: The Heritage Foundation.

Reisner, S. L., Falb, K. L., & Mimiaga, M. J. (2011). Early life traumatic stressors and the mediating role of PTSD in incident HIV infection among US men, comparisons by sexual orientation and race/ethnicity: results from the NESARC, 2004–2005. *Journal of Acquired Immune Deficiency Syndromes*, *57*(4), 340–350. https://doi.org/10.1097/QAI.0b013e31821d36b4.

Richter, L., Komarek, A., Desmond, C., Celentano, D., Morin, S., Sweat, M., ... Coates, T. (2014). Reported physical and sexual abuse in childhood and adult HIV risk behavior in three African countries: findings from project accept (HPTN-043). *AIDS and Behavior, 18*(2), 381–389. https://doi.org/10.1007/s10461-013-0439-7.

Roberts, L., Long, S. J., Young, H., Hewitt, G., Murphy, S., & Moore, G. F. (2018). Sexual health outcomes for young people in state care: cross-sectional analysis of a national survey and views of social care professionals in wales. *Children and Youth Services Review, 89*, 281–288. https://doi.org/10.1016/j.childyouth.2018.04.044.

Roos, L. E., Mota, N., Afifi, T. O., Katz, L. Y., Distasio, J., & Sareen, J. (2013). Relationship between adverse childhood experiences and homelessness and the impact of axis I and II disorders. *American Journal of Public Health, 103*(S2), s275–s281. https://doi.org/10.2105/AJPH.2013.301323.

Rotheram-Borus, M. J., Swendeman, D., & Chorpita, B. F. (2012). Disruptive innovations for designing and diffusing evidence-based interventions. *American Psychologist, 67*(6), 463–476. https://doi.org/10.1037/a0028180.

Russell, S. T., Franz, B. T., & Driscoll, A. K. (2001). Same-sex romantic attraction and experiences of violence in adolescence. *American Journal of Public Health, 91*(6), 903–906. Retrieved from: https://www.ncbi.nlm.nih.gov/pmc/articles/PMC1446466/pdf/11392932.pdf.

Saewyc, E. M., Magee, L. L., & Pettingell, S. E. (2004). Teenage pregnancy and associated risk behaviors among sexually abused adolescents. *Perspectives on Sexual and Reproductive Health, 36*(3), 98–105. https://doi.org/10.1111/j.1931-2393.2004.tb00197.

Santerre-Baillargeon, M., Vézina-Gagnon, P., Daigneault, I., Landry, T., & Bergeron, S. (2017). *Anxiety mediates the relation between childhood sexual abuse and genito-pelvic pain in adolescent girls*. In *Paper presented at the annual meeting of the Society for Sex Therapy & Research, Montréal, Québec*.

Sedlak, A. J., Mettenburg, J., Basena, M., Petta, I., McPherson, K., Greene, A., & Li, S. (2010). *Fourth national incidence 3 study of child abuse and neglect (NIS-4): Report to congress, executive summary*. Washington, DC: U.S. Department of Health and Human Services, Administration for Children and Families.

Sethi, A. (2007). Domestic sex trafficking of aboriginal girls in Canada: issues and implications. *First Peoples Child and Family Review, 3*(3), 57–71. Retrieved from: http://journals.sfu.ca/fpcfr/index.php/FPCFR/article/view/50/88.

Shonkoff, J. P., Garner, A. S., Committee on Psychosocial Aspects of Child and Family Health; Committee on Early Childhood, Adoption, and Dependent Care; & Section on Developmental and Behavioral Pediatrics. (2012). The lifelong effects of early childhood adversity and toxic stress. *Pediatrics, 129*(1), e232–e246. https://doi.org/10.1542/peds.2011-2663.

Simon, V. A., Smith, E., Fava, N., & Feiring, C. (2015). Positive and negative posttraumatic change following childhood sexual abuse are associated with youths' adjustment. *Child Maltreatment, 20*(4), 278–290. https://doi.org/10.1177/1077559515590872.

Stambaugh, L. F., Ringeisen, H., Casanueva, C. C., Tueller, S., Smith, K. E., & Dolan, M. (2013). *Adverse childhood experiences in NSCAW. OPRE Report #2013-26*. Washington, DC: Office of Planning, Research and Evaluation, Administration for Children and Families, U.S. Department of Health and Human Services.

Statistics Canada. (2013). *Measuring violence against women: Statistical trends*. Ottawa, Ontario: Statistics Canada. https://www150.statcan.gc.ca/n1/en/pub/85-002-x/2013001/article/11766-eng.pdf?st=S0kUY7bv [Catalogue No. 85-002-X].

Steeves, V. (2014). *Young Canadians in a wired world, phase III: Trends and recommendations*. Ottawa, Ontario: MediaSmarts. Retrieved from: http://mediasmarts.ca/ycww.

Stepleton, K., McIntosh, J., & Corrington, B. (2010). *Allied for better outcomes: Child welfare and early childhood*. Washington, DC: Center for the Study of Social Policy.

Stettler, N. M., & Katz, L. F. (2017). Minority stress, emotion regulation, and the parenting of sexual-minority youth. *Journal of GLBT Family Studies*, *13*(4), 380–400. https://doi.org/10.1080/1550428X.2016.1268551.

Stoltenborgh, M., van Ijzendoorn, M. H., Euser, E. M., & Bakermans-Kranenburg, M. J. (2011). A global perspective on child sexual abuse: meta-analysis of prevalence around the world. *Child Maltreatment*, *16*(2), 79–101. https://doi.org/10.1177/1077559511403920.

Stults, C. B., Javdani, S., Greenbaum, C. A., Kapadia, F., & Halkitis, P. N. (2015). Intimate partner violence and substance use risk among young men who have sex with men: the P18 cohort study. *Drug and Alcohol Dependence*, *2*(2), 54–62. https://doi.org/10.1016/j.drugalcdep.2015.06.008.

Tanaka, M., Georgiades, K., Boyle, M. H., & MacMillan, H. L. (2015). Child maltreatment and educational attainment in young adulthood: results from the Ontario child health study. *Journal of Interpersonal Violence*, *30*(2), 195–214. https://doi.org/10.1177/0886260514533153.

Tardiff-Williams, C. Y., Tanaka, M., Boyle, M. H., & MacMillan, H. L. (2015). The impact of childhood abuse and current mental health on young adult intimate relationship functioning. *Journal of Interpersonal Violence*, *32*(22), 3420–3447. https://doi.org/10.1177/0886260515599655.

Tran, Q. A., Dunne, M. P., Vo, T. V., & Luu, N. H. (2015). Adverse childhood experiences and the health of university students in eight provinces of Vietnam. *Asia-Pacific Journal of Public Health*, *27*(8S), 26S–32S. https://doi.org/10.1177/1010539515589812.

Turney, K., & Wildeman, C. (2017). Adverse childhood experiences among children placed in and adopted from foster care: evidence from a nationally representative survey. *Child Abuse & Neglect*, *64*, 117–129. https://doi.org/10.1016/j.chiabu.2016.12.009.

Upchurch, D. M., & Kusunoki, Y. (2004). Associations between forced sex, sexual and protective practices, and sexually transmitted diseases among a national sample of adolescent girls. *Women's Health Issues*, *14*(3), 75–84. https://doi.org/10.1016/j.whi.2004.03.006.

Urban Native Youth Association. (2002). *Full circle*. Vancouver, British Columbia: Urban Native Youth Association.

van der Kolk, B. A. (2005). Developmental trauma disorder: toward a rational diagnosis for children with complex trauma histories. *Psychiatric Annals*, *35*(5), 401–408. https://doi.org/10.3928/00485713-20050501-06.

van Rosmalen-Nooijens, K., Lahaije, F. A. H., Wong, S., Prins, J. B., & Lagro-Janssen, A. L. M. (2017). Does witnessing family violence influence sexual and reproductive health of adolescents and young adults? A systematic review. *Psychology of Violence*, *7*(3), 343–374. https://doi.org/10.1037/vio0000113.

Vezina-Gagnon, P., Bergeron, S., Frappier, J. Y., & Daigneault, I. (2017). Genitourinary health of sexually abused girls and boys: a matched-cohort Study. *Journal of Pediatrics*, *194*, 171–176. https://doi.org/10.1016/j.jpeds.2017.09.087.

Voith, L. A., Anderson, R. E., & Cahill, S. P. (2017). Extending the ACEs framework: examining relations between childhood abuse and later victimization and perpetration with college men. *Journal of Interpersonal Violence*, *2017*, 1–26. https://doi.org/10.1177/0886260517708406.

Walker, K. (2013). *Ending the commercial sexual exploitation of children: a call for multi-system collabora-tion \in California*. Child Welfare Council. Retrieved from: http://www.chhs.ca.gov/Child%20Welfare/Ending%20CSEC%20-%20A%20Call%20for%20Multi-System%20Collaboration%20in%20CA%20-%20February%202013.pdf.

Walsh, K., DiLillo, D., & Messman-Moore, T. L. (2012). Lifetime sexual victimization and poor risk perception: does emotional dysregulation account for the links? *Journal of Interpersonal Violence*, *27*(15), 3054–3071. https://doi.org/10.1177/0886260512441081.

Warne, D., & Lajimodiere, D. (2015). American Indian health disparities: psychological influences. *Social and Personality Psychology Compass*, *9*(10), 567–579. https://doi.org/10.1111/spc3.12.

Wekerle, C., & Black, T. (2017). Gendered violence: advancing evidence-informed research, practice and policy in addressing sex, gender, and child sexual abuse. *Child Abuse & Neglect*, *66*, 166–170. https://doi.org/10.1016/j.chiabu.2017.03.010.

Wekerle, C., Goldstein, A. L., Tanaka, M., & Tonmyr, L. (2017). Childhood sexual abuse, sexual motives, and adolescent risk-taking among males and females receiving child welfare services. *Child Abuse & Neglect*, *66*, 101–111. https://doi.org/10.1016/j.chiabu.2017.01.013.

Wekerle, C., & Kerig, P. K. (2017). Sexual and non-sexual violence against children and youth: current issues in gender, trauma and resilience. *Journal of Child and Adolescent Trauma*, *10*(1), 3–8. https://doi.org/10.1007/s40653-017-0130-7.

Wekerle, C., Wolfe, D. A., Cohen, J. A., Bromberg, D. S., & Murray, L. (2018). *Childhood maltreatment* (2nd ed.). Hogrefe Publishing.

Wong, J. Y., Choi, E. P., Chan, C. K., & Fong, D. Y. (2017). Controlling anxiety mediates the influence of childhood adversities on risky sexual behaviors among emerging adults. *The Journal of Sex Research*, *54*(8), 1018–1025. https://doi.org/10.1080/00224499.2017.1278569.

World Health Organization (WHO). (2002). *World report on violence and health*. Geneva, Switzerland: World Health Organization.

World Health Organization (WHO). (2005). *Promoting mental health: Concepts, emerging evidence, practice: report of the World Health Organization, Department of Mental Health and Substance Abuse in collaboration with the Victorian Health Promotion Foundation and the University of Melbourne*. Geneva, Switzerland: World Health Organization.

World Health Organization (WHO). (2016). Violence and injury prevention: Adverse childhood experiences international questionnaire (ACE-IQ). Retrieved from: http://www.who.int/violence_injury_prevention/violence/activities/adverse_childhood_experiences/en/.

World Health Organization and Calouste Gulbenkian Foundation. (2014). *Social determinants of mental health*. Retrieved from World Health Organization Website: http://www.who.int/mental_health/publications/gulbenkian_paper_social_determinants_of_mental_health/en/.

Ybarra, M. L., & Thompson, R. E. (2018). Predicting the emergence of sexual violence in adolescence. *Prevention Science*, *19*(4), 403–415. https://doi.org/10.1007/s11121-017-0810-4.

Further reading

Centers for Disease Control and Prevention. (2016). *Understanding teen dating violence*. Atlanta, GA. Retrieved from: http://www.cdc.gov/violenceprevention/pdf/teen-dating-violence-fact sheet-a.pdf.

Department for Children Schools and Families (DCSF). (2009). *Safeguarding children and young people from sexual exploitation: Supplementary guidance to working together to safeguard children*. United Kingdom: HM Government.

Fagan, A. A., Wright, E. M., & Pinchevsky, G. M. (2014). The protective effects of neighbourhood collective efficacy on adolescent substance use and violence following exposure to violence. *Journal of Youth and Adolescence*, *43*(9), 1498–1512. https://doi.org/10.1007/s10964-013-0049-8.

World Health Organization. (1999). *Report of the consultation on child abuse prevention*. Geneva, Switzerland: World Health Organization.

World Health Organization. (2017). *Responding to children and adolescents who have been sexually abused: WHO clinical guidelines*. Geneva, Switzerland: World Health Organization.

World Health Organization. (2018). *Guidance on ethical considerations in planning and reviewing research studies on sexual and reproductive health in adolescents*. Geneva, Switzerland: World Health Organization.

CHAPTER

7

ACEs and violence in adulthood

Tamara L. Taillieu, Isabel Garces Davila, Shannon Struck

Department of Community Health Sciences, Max Rady College of Medicine, Rady Faculty of Health Sciences, University of Manitoba, Winnipeg, MB, Canada

Introduction

Adverse childhood experiences (ACEs) are generally conceptualized into two broad categories: child maltreatment ACEs (i.e., physical abuse, sexual abuse, emotional abuse, emotional neglect, physical neglect, and exposure to intimate partner violence (IPV)) and household dysfunction ACEs (e.g., household substance use, household mental illness, parental separation/divorce, and parental incarceration; Dube et al., 2003; Felitti et al., 1998). Exposure to ACEs is common (Felitti et al., 1998), and ACEs tend to co-occur (Dong et al., 2004; Dube et al., 2003; Levenson, Willis, & Prescott, 2016). ACEs increase the risk of mental health problems, substance use problems, physical health conditions, and suicidal behaviors and decrease quality of life across the lifespan (Dube et al., 2001, 2003; Dube, Anda, Felitti, Edwards, & Croft, 2002; Felitti et al., 1998). Dose-response effects have also been noted in the literature, with exposure to increasing numbers of ACEs corresponding to incremental increase in the risk of adverse outcomes (Dube et al., 2001, 2003; Felitti et al., 1998; Whitfield, Anda, Dube, & Felitti, 2003). Another potential longer-term outcome of exposure to ACEs is an increased risk of being a perpetrator or victim of violence in adulthood. Violent behavior poses a serious public health problem for society (Bland, Lambie, & Best, 2018). This chapter reviews research on the links between ACEs, including both child maltreatment ACEs and household dysfunction ACEs, and violence in adulthood. Specifically, this

https://doi.org/10.1016/B978-0-12-816065-7.00007-0

chapter will review links between ACEs in childhood and physical, sexual, and emotional violence in adult relationships as well other forms of interpersonal violence in adulthood. The chapter will conclude with suggested directions for future research and implications for policy and practice.

Physical violence in relationships

In the US, it is estimated that 30.6% of women and 31.0% of men have experienced some form of physical violence from an intimate partner in their lifetime (Smith et al., 2018). Further, 21.4% of women and 14.9% of men report having experienced severe physical violence from an intimate partner (Smith et al., 2018). This section will briefly review research on the association between ACEs and physical violence in adult relationships.

Child maltreatment ACEs

Most of the research on the relationship between child maltreatment ACEs and physical violence in relationships focuses on the impact of childhood physical abuse and/or exposure to IPV and adult outcomes. A recent systematic review ($N = 9$ studies) indicated that significant associations exist between childhood exposure to IPV and adult IPV perpetration (Kimber, Adham, Gill, McTavish, & MacMillan, 2018). This review found that exposure to IPV in childhood was strongly related to perpetrating IPV as an adult (Kimber et al., 2018). However, although all studies included in the review controlled for physical child abuse, consideration of other types of maltreatment (e.g., neglect, verbal/emotional abuse, sexual abuse) was inconsistent across studies. Support for the relationship between exposure to IPV and physical child abuse and physical violence in adult relationships has been found in both prospective, longitudinal (Abajobi, Kisely, Williams, Clavarino, & Najman, 2017; Ehrensaft et al., 2003; Herrenkohl & Jung, 2016; Ireland & Smith, 2009), and nationally representative (Afifi, Mota, Sareen, & MacMillan, 2017; Madruga, Viana, Abdalla, Caetano, & Laranjeira, 2017; McKinney, Caetano, Ramisetty-Mikler, & Nelson, 2009) studies.[1]

[1] In epidemiological research, odds ratios measure of the strength of the association between an exposure (e.g., exposure to ACEs) and an outcome (e.g., physical violence in adulthood). An odds ratio greater than 1.0 indicates that the odds of experiencing the outcome are greater in the exposed group (e.g., individuals with an ACEs history) than the odds of experiencing the outcome in the unexposed group (e.g., individuals without and ACEs history). Adjusted odds ratios represent the strength of the association between the exposure (e.g., ACEs history) and outcome (e.g., physical violence in adulthood) after the effects of other important covariates (e.g., indicators of socioeconomic disadvantage) that may affect the relationship have been considered. That is, adjusted odds ratios represent the strength of the association between an exposure and an outcome over and above the effects of additional covariates included in analyses.

In a 20-year prospective study (*N*=543), childhood exposure to IPV (combined official reports and self-reported child maltreatment measures) was associated with significantly increased odds of perpetrating past-year physical and/or sexual IPV (AOR [adjusted odds ratio]=2.34) and being a victim of IPV (AOR=2.68; Ehrensaft et al., 2003). That is, after adjustment for sociodemographic covariates, power assertive discipline, family functioning, adolescent conduct problems, substance use, and other types of childhood maltreatment, exposure to IPV during childhood was strongly associated with perpetrating IPV and being a victim of IPV in adulthood. Multivariate analyses (i.e., analyses adjusting for all the covariates listed above) also indicated that childhood physical abuse was associated with injury to partner (AOR=4.77) and injury from a partner (AOR=3.56). Childhood sexual abuse and neglect were not associated with IPV perpetration, injury, or victimization in adulthood (Ehrensaft et al., 2003). The relationship between exposure to IPV in childhood and being a victim of IPV, independent of child physical abuse experiences (assessed as covariate), has also been noted in a nationally representative Brazilian sample (Madruga et al., 2017). In the Brazilian study, exposure to IPV in childhood was not associated with perpetrating IPV in adulthood. It could be that childhood physical abuse is more strongly associated with IPV perpetration while exposure to IPV is associated with both IPV victimization and perpetration. However, results from a prospective longitudinal study from Australia (*N*=3322) found that all types of substantiated child maltreatment (i.e., physical abuse, sexual abuse, emotional abuse, and neglect) were associated with physical IPV victimization (AORs ranged from 1.76 to 2.76) in early adulthood, after adjustment for several potential confounders, including adolescent aggression and exposure to violence in the home (Abajobi et al., 2017). Because exposure to IPV was included as a covariate rather than as a specific form of child maltreatment in this study, the effects of exposure to IPV on physical violence in adult relationships cannot be determined as parameter estimates for covariates were not provided.

Substantiated cases of child maltreatment likely represent more severe forms of child maltreatment, and could be one of the reasons for differences in findings across prospective studies. Herrenkohl and Jung (2016) found that child maltreatment that had been reported to child protection agencies (but not parent self-reported perpetration of child maltreatment) was associated with sexual IPV perpetration, IPV perpetration resulting in injury, and the total number of types of IPV perpetrated (i.e., physical, injury, sexual, and psychological) in a prospective study following a sample of children (*N*=457) from the 1970s into adulthood. In this study, reported child maltreatment was not associated with any type of IPV victimization in adulthood or physical IPV in the absence of injury. So, it could also be that disparate prospective findings are due to differences in the severity of physical IPV in adulthood (e.g., injurious vs. noninjurious physical violence). Prospectively assessed exposure to severe physical IPV in childhood has been shown to be related to minor (AOR=1.65) and severe (AOR=1.72) physical IPV in adulthood, after controlling for socioeconomic disadvantage, family transitions, and child physical abuse (official reports) in a sample of 1000 urban youth followed into early adulthood (Ireland & Smith, 2009). Exposure to less severe forms of IPV in childhood was not associated with physical IPV in adulthood. This lends some support to the idea that the severity of child maltreatment exposure might impact the relationship between ACEs and adult outcomes. However, substantiated child physical abuse (likely representing more severe cases) was also not associated with adult IPV outcomes in this study (Ireland & Smith, 2009). Importantly, although exposure to nonsevere IPV and child physical abuse were not associated with adult IPV outcomes, in models adjusting for relevant covariates (i.e., socioeconomic disadvantage and family transitions), they were associated with other problematic outcomes during adolescence, including arrest, general crime, violent crime, and externalizing problem behaviors.

In some studies, even less severe forms of physical violence experienced in childhood have been shown to be related to IPV in adulthood. For example, Afifi, Mota, et al. (2017) found that childhood experience of harsh physical punishment (i.e., pushing, grabbing, shoving, hitting, and being slapped without causing marks, bruises, or injury) was significantly associated with IPV perpetration (AOR=1.7), IPV victimization (AOR=1.7), and reciprocal IPV (defined as situations where both partners perpetrate IPV against each other in the relationship) (AOR=1.4) in a nationally representative US sample after adjustment for current sociodemographic covariates, any other type of child maltreatment, and a family history of dysfunction. A similar finding was reported in Ehrensaft et al.'s (2003) prospective study in that power assertive discipline experienced in childhood was associated with significantly increased odds of IPV perpetration (AOR=1.18), after adjustment for several confounding variables, including adolescent conduct problems and other types of child maltreatment. Finally, McKinney et al. (2009) found that male partner's experiences of moderate physical child abuse (defined as being hit with an object) were associated with increased odds of past-year nonreciprocal male-to-female IPV (AOR=3.1) in models adjusting for relevant covariates (i.e., sociodemographic covariates, substance use, childhood exposure to IPV and severe physical abuse, and approval of IPV).

Household dysfunction ACEs

Few studies have examined the relationship between household dysfunction ACEs and physical IPV in adulthood. In a nationally representative study of the US general population (N=34,402), any household dysfunction in childhood (i.e., household alcohol or drug use, incarceration, mental illness, suicide attempts/deaths) was associated with increased odds of past-year physical and/or sexual IPV perpetration (AOR = 1.3) and reciprocal IPV (AOR = 1.8), after adjusting for sociodemographic covariates and other types of child maltreatment (Afifi, Mota, et al., 2017). Any household dysfunction in childhood was not associated with past-year IPV victimization in this study. This study did not disentangle the specific effects of different types of household dysfunction ACEs, so it remains unclear which specific household dysfunctions might be associated with an increased risk of perpetrating IPV in adulthood.

Other studies focus on the relationship between a specific type of childhood adversity exposure and physical violence in adult relationships. For example, in a 30-year longitudinal New Zealand birth cohort study ($N = 1265$), a significant but modest association was found between parental separation/divorce before the age of 15 years and perpetration of past 12-month physical IPV in adulthood, after adjustment for a number of other social, family, and contextual factors, including several other ACEs (i.e., parental alcohol/illicit drug use, parental depression/anxiety, parental criminality, sexual abuse, and physical punishment/maltreatment) (Fergusson, McLeod, & Horwood, 2014). Parental separation/divorce was not significantly associated with IPV victimization. Although precise estimates for these additional ACEs covariates were not provided in the article, the authors indicated that childhood physical punishment/maltreatment and childhood conduct problems were also significantly associated with IPV perpetration. Relationships held for both males and females, and regardless of time of parental separation/divorce.

Childhood exposure to paternal substance abuse and household member incarceration have also been examined in relation to IPV in adulthood. In a sample of men in treatment for domestic violence ($N = 74$), paternal substance abuse was found to exert comparable effects to child maltreatment (i.e., physical abuse and exposure to IPV) on respondents' severity of IPV perpetration, and significantly increased the explained variance in multivariate models (Corvo & Carpenter, 2000). In a convenience sample of college students ($N = 284$), multivariate analyses indicated that incarceration of a household member during the students' childhood was associated with increased odds (AOR = 4.20) of perpetrating physical IPV in early adulthood (Nikulina, Gelin, & Zwilling, 2017).

Interestingly, all of the studies examining the relationship between household dysfunction ACEs and physical violence in adult relationships have found that household dysfunction ACEs are associated with the perpetration of physical violence in relationships, but not with victimization. Because research on the effects of specific household dysfunction ACEs is sparse, definitive conclusions on how these adverse experiences relate to the physical violence in adult relationships cannot be made.

Cumulative effects of ACEs

Research has also examined the relationship between the cumulative effects of ACEs on physical violence in adult relationships. Findings from the original ACE Study indicated that a statistically significant dose-response relationship exists between the total number of child abuse exposures (i.e., physical abuse, sexual abuse, and exposure to violence against mother) and the risk of physical IPV in adulthood (Whitfield et al., 2003). That is, increasing number of child abuse exposures were associated with incrementally increased odds of IPV victimization among women and IPV perpetration among men (Whitfield et al., 2003). This study did not adjust for other forms of child maltreatment or household dysfunctions in analyses, even though data on other ACEs were available; so, it remains unknown as to how the inclusion of additional ACEs would have influenced results. As well, IPV perpetration among women and IPV victimization among men were not assessed in this study.

In a crosscultural study of men receiving substance use treatment in Brazil ($N=281$) and England ($N=223$), a greater number of ACEs (i.e., sexual abuse, physical abuse, witnessing IPV, father never/rarely home, mother never/rarely home, being looked after/adopted, neglect, parental death, parental separation/divorce, and being told weak or lazy) were associated with the perpetration of physical (and sexual) IPV in adulthood (Gilchrist, Radcliffe, Noto, & D'Oliveira, 2017). However, in a sample of college students ($N=284$), no cumulative effects of ACEs (i.e., physical abuse, sexual abuse, emotional abuse, emotional neglect, physical neglect, witnessing IPV, or living with a mentally ill, substance abusing, or incarcerated family member) and past-year physical IPV victimization or perpetration were noted after adjusting for sociodemographic covariates and individual ACEs (Nikulina et al., 2017). In this study, a range of ACEs were associated with types of IPV perpetration and victimization at the bivariate level; however, in multivariate models (i.e., models adjusting for sociodemographic covariates and other ACEs that were significant at the bivariate level), only witnessing IPV (AOR=5.49), incarceration of a household member (AOR=4.20), and physical abuse in childhood (AOR=1.96, nonsignificant trend) remained significantly associated with physical IPV perpetration in early adulthood.

Nikulina et al. (2017) suggest that it might be a few specific types of ACEs (e.g., physical abuse, exposure to IPV, family member incarceration) that drive the association in cumulative models examining risk for IPV perpetration or victimization. Alternatively, differences in sample recruitment (e.g., convenience vs. representative sample), participant characteristics (e.g., sex differences, age range), and/or the types of ACEs included in the measure (e.g., child maltreatment vs. household dysfunction) might also help to explain discrepant findings. It is important to replicate the current work with longitudinal studies (e.g., administrative health data, surveys with other populations), in which the cumulative effect of ACEs, as well as the independent effects of specific ACEs, could be monitored through several years while also adjusting for participant characteristics (e.g., sex, age, socioeconomic status).

Summary

Support for the relationship between exposure to IPV and physical abuse in childhood and physical violence in adult relationships has been found in prospective, longitudinal, and nationally representative studies (Abajobi et al., 2017; Afifi, Mota, et al., 2017; Ehrensaft et al., 2003; Ireland & Smith, 2009; Madruga et al., 2017; McKinney et al., 2009), even after adjustment for many important covariates (e.g., sociodemographic covariates, family functioning variables, other types of child maltreatment). There is also some evidence that childhood physical abuse may be more strongly associated with IPV perpetration than IPV victimization, while exposure to IPV seems to be associated with both IPV victimization and perpetration (Ehrensaft et al., 2003). Importantly, less severe forms of physical violence exposure in childhood (e.g., harsh physical punishment, power assertive discipline) have also been associated with IPV in adult relationships (Afifi, Mota, et al., 2017; Ehrensaft et al., 2003). Other types of child maltreatment ACEs (i.e., sexual abuse, neglect, and emotional maltreatment) are less frequently considered in research on physical violence in adult relationships. Thus, the extent to which childhood sexual abuse, neglect, or emotional maltreatment are associated with physical violence in adult relationships largely remains unknown. Similarly, few studies have examined the relationship between household dysfunction ACEs and physical IPV in adulthood, although preliminary research suggests that specific household dysfunction ACEs (e.g., parental separation/divorce, parental substance use, parental incarceration; Corvo & Carpenter, 2000; Fergusson et al., 2014; Nikulina et al., 2017) might be particularly relevant to consider in research on physical IPV in adult relationships.

Sexual violence in relationships

In the US, it is estimated that 18.3% of women and 8.2% of men have experienced contact sexual violence from an intimate partner in their lifetime (Smith et al., 2018). These lifetime estimates increase to 43.6% of women and 24.8% of men when contact sexual violence from nonintimate partners is included in the measure (Smith et al., 2018). This section will briefly review research on the association between ACEs and sexual violence in adulthood. Since very little research examines the relationship between ACEs and sexual violence specific to adult intimate relationships, this section is based on research examining sexual offending and sexual victimization more broadly defined.

Child maltreatment ACEs

Most of the attention in research on the relationship between ACEs and sexual violence in adulthood has focused on child sexual abuse. The sexually abused-sexual abuser hypothesis suggests a specific link between child sexual abuse history and sexual offending in adulthood (Jespersen, Lalumière, & Seto, 2009; Leach, Stewart, & Smallbone, 2016). Research has shown that adult sex offenders constitute a disproportionate number of individuals who have experienced child sexual abuse, but not necessarily other types of child maltreatment, compared with samples of other types of offenders (Jespersen et al., 2009). Metaanalytic results support this assertion, showing that adult sex offenders have significantly higher odds of reporting a child sexual abuse history (Odds Ratio [OR] = 3.36) than adult nonsex offenders (Jespersen et al., 2009). Further, sex offenders targeting child victims are significantly more likely to report a child sexual abuse history than sex offenders targeting adult victims (Jespersen et al., 2009). As well, metaanalytic findings indicate no significant difference in histories of childhood physical abuse or emotional abuse and neglect between sex offenders and other types of offenders, suggesting a unique link between child sexual abuse and sexual offending in adulthood (Jespersen et al., 2009). Similar relationships have been reported in a sample of male college student (N = 423); that is, only a history of child sexual abuse, but not childhood physical or emotional abuse, was associated with sexual violence perpetration and victimization in intimate relationships (Voith, Anderson, & Cahill, 2017).

However, other studies have found only limited support for the sexually abused-sexual abuser hypothesis. For example, a prospective, longitudinal birth cohort study of N = 37,282 men with a documented child maltreatment history and at least one criminal conviction by age 25 years found no specific association between child sexual abuse history and sexual offending in early adulthood (Leach et al., 2016). In this study, child sexual abuse, physical abuse, and emotional abuse/neglect were all associated with any criminal offense (vs. no offense: AORs = 1.49, 1.17, and 1.12, respectively) and sexual offenses (vs. other types of offenses; AORs = 1.26, 1.36, and 1.25, respectively); but, there were no significant differences in child maltreatment histories between those convicted of a sexual offense relative to a violent criminal offense (Leach et al., 2016). The authors highlight that proportionately few of the sexually abused boys (3%) went on to become sexual offenders, and proportionately few sexual offenders (4%) had a documented history of child sexual abuse, a finding that has also been documented elsewhere (Jespersen et al., 2009; Ogloff, Cutajar, Mann, & Mullen, 2012: Salter et al., 2003).

Less research exists with regard to other types of child maltreatment and sexual offenses in adulthood. In a longitudinal study of male childhood sex abuse victims ($N=224$), 11.6% went on to commit sexual offenses, primarily against children (Salter et al., 2003). In this study, material/physical neglect (OR = 3.4), lack of supervision (OR = 3.0), and sexual abuse by a female perpetrator (OR = 3.0) were associated with an increased risk of committing sexual offenses. This study also assessed child physical abuse, witnessing intrafamilial violence, rejection by carers/emotional abuse, and discontinuity of care (i.e., parental separations and periods in foster care/children's home). All of these ACEs were elevated in the victim-abuser group; but, differences did not reach statistical significance. Note this study was not limited to offenses committed as an adult, only after documented child sexual abuse (mean age of first offense 14 years). In a study examining the effects of child maltreatment ACEs among male sex offenders ($N=679$), in addition to having increased odds of reporting childhood sexual abuse (OR = 3.22), sex offenders also had increased odds of having experienced childhood physical abuse (OR = 1.71), verbal abuse (OR = 13.88), emotional neglect (OR = 4.26), physical neglect (OR = 1.58), and witnessed violence against mother (OR = 2.43) compared to general population estimates for men (Levenson et al., 2016). Both of these studies were limited in that only bivariate relationships were assessed, thereby limiting knowledge of the independent effects of each type of child maltreatment and other forms of household dysfunction on later sexual offending.

Research examining the relationship between ACEs and sexual offending among females is also not well developed as the vast majority of studies are based on samples of male sex offenders. In a small sample of convicted female offenders ($n=61$ sex offenders and $n=81$ nonsex offenders), sex offenders reported more frequent instances of childhood sexual abuse and had longer durations of childhood sexual abuse than nonsex offenders (Christopher, Lutz-Zois, & Reinhardt, 2007). Duration of sexual abuse seemed to be a much stronger predictor of sexual offending than experiences of childhood sexual abuse alone. No significant differences were found between sex offenders and nonsex offenders with regard to childhood physical or emotional abuse (Christopher et al., 2007). It is also important to note that sexual offenders in this study had all committed sexual offenses against children (vs. adults), and findings may not be applicable to female perpetrated sexual violence against an adult partner.

Metaanalytic findings have also indicated that a history of childhood sexual abuse is associated with an increased risk of sexual victimization in adulthood among women; indeed, between 15% and 79% of female child sexual abuse victims report sexual revictimization in adulthood (Roodman & Clum, 2001). In a study using data from the original ACE

Study, childhood sexual abuse (AOR=2.37), physical abuse (AOR=1.43), emotional abuse (AOR=1.39), and emotional neglect (AOR=1.49) remained independently associated with self-reported sexual victimization after adjustment for sociodemographic covariates and all types of ACEs among women (including household dysfunction ACEs) (Ports, Ford, & Merrick, 2016). The relationship between physical neglect and exposure to IPV in childhood and adult sexual victimization were not significant in adjusted models (Ports et al., 2016).

Household dysfunction ACEs

Research has shown that at the bivariate level, each individual type of adverse experience (i.e., using the original 10 item scale) was associated with increased adult sexual victimization, including parental separation/divorce and household member mental illness, substance use, and incarceration (Ports et al., 2016). After adjustment for sociodemographic covariates and individual types of ACEs, the only household dysfunction ACEs (in addition to several child maltreatment ACEs) that remained independently associated with adult sexual victimization were household mental illness (AOR=1.72) and incarcerated household member (AOR=1.50). The authors note that although childhood sexual abuse appeared to be the strongest risk factor (AOR=2.37 in adjusted model), other ACEs need to be considered in sexual violence prevention efforts as they are also associated with adult sexual victimization.

Household dysfunction ACEs have also been shown to be related to sexual offending in a sample of male offenders (*N*=679) attending a sex offender treatment program (Levenson et al., 2016). This study compared ACEs exposure among male sex offenders to general population estimates for men, finding that male sex offenders had significantly increased odds of both childhood maltreatment ACEs (i.e., physical abuse, sexual abuse, emotional abuse, emotional neglect, physical neglect, and exposure to IPV) and household dysfunction ACEs, including coming from a broken home (OR=4.26), household member substance use (OR=2.81), household member mental illness/attempted suicide (OR=2.01), and incarcerated family member (OR=6.83; Levenson et al., 2016). This study was limited to bivariate associations; thus, the independent effects of each type of ACE on sexual offending remain unknown.

Cumulative effects of ACEs

Cumulative effects of ACEs on sexual offending and sexual victimization have also been reported in the literature. For example, using the original ACE Study data, Ports et al. (2016) found that an increasing number of ACEs was associated with increased odds of sexual victimization in adulthood. In this study, the odds associated with reporting adult sexual victimization ranged from 1.77 for respondents reporting one childhood adversity to 8.32 for respondents reporting five or more ACEs (Ports et al., 2016). In a prospective, longitudinal birth cohort study of males with a documented child maltreatment history ($N=38{,}282$), polyvictimization (i.e., exposure to multiple types of childhood maltreatment) was significantly associated with sexual offending, violent offending, and general (i.e., nonsexual, nonviolent) offending (Leach et al., 2016). There is also some indication that total ACEs scores are associated with characteristics of the type of sex offense committed by male sex offenders. Specifically, Levenson et al. (2016) reported significantly higher ACEs scores (10-item scale) among sex offenders with victims less than 12 years of age (mean: 4.2 vs. 2.9), who had used violence or force in the commission of a sex offense (mean: 4.9 vs. 3.2), used a weapon in a sex crime (mean: 5.3 vs. 3.4), or who injured a victim in a sex crime (mean: 5.4 vs. 3.4). Higher ACEs scores were also found among sex offenders with contact versus noncontact sex offenses (mean: 3.4 vs. 2.2) in this study. Therefore, higher ACEs scores appear to be associated with more violent sexual offending than lower ACE scores.

Summary

Most of the research on the relationship between ACEs and sexual violence in adulthood has focused on childhood sexual abuse. Research indicates that adult sex offenders have significantly higher odds of reporting childhood sexual abuse compared to adult nonsex offenders (Jespersen et al., 2009; Voith et al., 2017). It is also important to recognize that proportionately few individuals reporting childhood sexual abuse go on to perpetrate sexual violence in adulthood (Jespersen et al., 2009; Leach et al., 2016; Ogloff et al., 2012; Salter et al., 2003). Research on female offenders is not well developed as most studies have focused on male sex offenders. However, a history of childhood sexual abuse has been found to be associated with an increased risk of sexual victimization in adulthood among women (Ports et al., 2016; Roodman & Clum, 2001). Research suggests that other types of child maltreatment ACEs (i.e., physical abuse, neglect, emotional maltreatment, and exposure to IPV) are also important to consider when examining the relationship between ACEs and sexual violence (both perpetration and victimization) in adulthood (Leach et al., 2016; Levenson et al., 2016; Ports et al., 2016; Salter et al., 2003). Fewer studies have examined the relationship between household dysfunction ACEs and sexual violence in adulthood. However, preliminary findings indicate that household dysfunction ACEs (independently and cumulatively) may be associated with both sexual offending and sexual victimization in adulthood (Levenson et al., 2016; Ports et al., 2016).

Emotional violence in relationships

In the US, 36.4% of women and 34.3% of men report having experienced emotional/psychological violence from an intimate partner in their lifetime (Smith et al., 2018). However, research examining the relationship between ACEs and emotional/psychological violence in adulthood as a specific, unique outcome is rare (Cascardi, Jouriles, & Temple, 2017). For example, only seven studies were found that directly examined the relationship between ACEs and emotional/psychological violence in adulthood (Abajobi et al., 2017; Cascardi et al., 2017; Gilchrist, Radcliffe, et al., 2017; Gilchrist, Canfield, Radcliffe, & D'Oliveira, 2017; Herrenkohl & Jung, 2016; Taft, Schumm, Marshall, Panuzio, & Holtzworth-Munroe, 2008; Voith et al., 2017). Studies examining the relationship between ACEs and emotional/psychological violence in adulthood remain an important avenue for future research.

Child maltreatment ACEs

In a prospective, longitudinal study from Australia ($N = 3322$), substantiated childhood physical abuse (AOR = 1.84), emotional abuse (AOR = 3.19), and neglect (AOR = 2.64) were associated with significantly increased odds of emotional IPV victimization in early adulthood, after adjustment for several potential confounders (e.g., other early negative life events, violence in home, adolescent aggressive behaviors; Abajobi et al., 2017). Substantiated childhood sexual abuse was not significantly associated with emotional IPV victimization in multivariate models (Abajobi et al., 2017). In contrast, in a prospective, longitudinal study of child welfare involved ($n = 249$) and nonchild welfare involved ($n = 208$) preschool aged children from Pennsylvania (followed for approximately 35 years), neither officially reported childhood maltreatment (indicated by child welfare involvement during sample recruitment) nor parent-reported perpetration of childhood physical or emotional abuse (preschool assessment) were associated with psychological IPV perpetration or victimization in adulthood (Herrenkohl & Jung, 2016). In this study, the only variables associated with the perpetration of psychological IPV in adulthood were general violence victimization and approval of dating violence during the adolescent period. Approval of dating violence during adolescence was also associated with being the victim of psychological IPV in adulthood. This study did not account for childhood maltreatment that occurred after the preschool period, which may have underestimated maltreatment exposure in this sample.

In a study examining the correlates of psychological IPV in a sample of undergraduate students ($N = 504$), self-reported childhood physical and emotional abuse were significantly correlated with past 6-month psychological IPV perpetration at the bivariate level (Cascardi et al., 2017). However, these relationships became nonsignificant in multivariate models that adjusted for insecure attachment, hostility, and anger levels (Cascardi et al., 2017). In this study, only being female, insecure attachment, and anger were uniquely correlated with psychological IPV perpetration (Cascardi et al., 2017). Bivariate analyses also indicated that both childhood physical and emotional abuse were significantly correlated with insecure attachment and anger; therefore, it could be that childhood experiences are indirectly associated with perpetrating psychological IPV in adulthood through their influence on attachment patterns and anger. In a sample of college men ($N=423$), self-reported childhood physical abuse (AOR = 1.68), but not childhood emotional or sexual abuse, was associated with significantly increased odds of perpetrating past-year psychological IPV (Voith et al., 2017); however, both childhood physical (AOR = 1.63) and emotional (AOR = 1.70) abuse were associated with increased odds of past-year psychological IPV victimization. Only a limited number of covariates (i.e., age and sexual orientation) were included in multivariate analyses, which could potentially explain differences in findings from other studies. In a community sample of physically violent ($n=102$) and nonviolent ($n=62$) men, bivariate correlations indicated that childhood exposure to IPV and parental rejection, but not child physical abuse, were associated with the perpetration of psychological IPV in adulthood (Taft et al., 2008). Results from structural equation modeling indicated that only parental rejection was associated with IPV abuse outcomes, and these effects were indirect through posttraumatic stress disorder (PTSD) symptoms and social information processing deficits (Taft et al., 2008).

Household dysfunction ACEs

The association between specific household dysfunction ACEs and emotional/psychological violence in adulthood has largely been ignored in research to date. Future research examining associations between household dysfunction ACEs and emotional/psychological violence in adult relationships is clearly warranted.

Cumulative effects of ACEs

In a crosscultural study examining the relationship between ACEs (total score) and the perpetration of IPV among men receiving substance use treatment in England ($N=281$) and Brazil ($N=223$), total number of ACEs (assessed with a 10-item modified ACEs scale) was not significantly associated with the perpetration of emotional IPV in adulthood (Gilchrist, Radcliffe, et al., 2017). Findings from this study are limited, however, in that findings from clinical samples in Brazil and England may not generalize to other populations. In another study using the same sample, total number of ACEs was found to be associated with the perpetration of controlling behaviors in both Brazil (AOR=1.45) and England (AOR=1.23), after adjustment for several significant covariates and confounding variables in both countries (Gilchrist, Canfield, et al., 2017). Controlling behaviors were also significantly associated with the perpetration of physical and sexual IPV. The seven items used to assess controlling behaviors in this study (e.g., restricting access to family/friends, wanting to know partner's whereabouts, suspicion/jealousy) seem to represent behaviors that can be considered psychologically abusive as coercive control over a partner is often considered a key component of abusive behavior (Johnson, 1995).

Summary

To date, the research on the relationship between ACEs and emotional/psychological violence in adulthood remains limited. Few studies include emotional/psychological violence in adulthood as a specific outcome and most existing research is based on nonrepresentative samples (Cascardi et al., 2017; Gilchrist, Canfield, et al., 2017; Gilchrist, Radcliffe, et al., 2017; Taft et al., 2008; Voith et al., 2017). Further, inconsistent findings have been reported in the literature. For example, some studies have found that specific types of child maltreatment ACEs (e.g., physical abuse, emotional abuse, and neglect) are associated with emotional/psychological IPV in adulthood (Abajobi et al., 2017; Voith et al., 2017), while other studies find no significant relationship between childhood maltreatment ACEs (Herrenkohl & Jung, 2016) or specific types of child maltreatment ACEs (e.g., sexual abuse) (Abajobi et al., 2017; Voith et al., 2017) and emotional/psychological IPV in adulthood. Research also suggests that the relationship between ACEs and emotional/psychological IPV in adulthood may be indirect via the effect of ACEs on the development of insecure attachment, anger, PTSD, or social information processing deficits, which, in turn, increase the risk of perpetrating emotional/psychological violence in adulthood (Cascardi et al., 2017; Taft et al., 2008). Finally, research on the relationship between household dysfunction ACEs and emotional/psychological violence in adulthood has not been adequately examined in the literature to date.

Other forms of interpersonal violence

Most often the relationship between ACEs and other forms of interpersonal violence (nonintimate partner) is assessed by examining involvement with the criminal justice system. This section will briefly review research on the relationship between ACEs and other forms of interpersonal violence in adulthood, with most of the focus centering on the commission of violent crimes.

Child maltreatment ACEs

In a longitudinal study comparing children with documented histories of child maltreatment ($n=908$) to a nonmaltreated control group ($n=208$), being abused or neglected as a child increased the likelihood of committing a violent crime in adulthood by 30% (Widom & Maxfield, 2001). Individuals with a childhood physical abuse or neglect history were more likely to be arrested for a violent crime in adulthood than individuals with a documented history of childhood sexual abuse (Widom & Maxfield, 2001). Inverse relationships between childhood sexual abuse and violent crime perpetration have been reported in samples of incarcerated adult males in both the US (Cuadra, Jaffe, Thomas, & DiLillo, 2014) and China (Wang et al., 2012). In a sample of homeless individuals with mental illness ($N=1888$), childhood physical abuse, emotional abuse, and physical neglect but not sexual abuse or emotional neglect were all associated with criminal justice system involvement (Edalati et al., 2017). It is not clear why childhood sexual abuse may be associated with lower risk of violent crime in adulthood. Wang et al. (2012) speculate that the shame associated with experiences of childhood sexual abuse may lead to more internalized consequences (e.g., depression, anxiety, suicidal behaviors) than externalizing problem behaviors (Wang et al., 2012). However, a prospective, longitudinal study from Australia (follow-up period of 45 years) reported a strong association between a documented childhood sexual abuse history and being charged with both sexual (OR=7.59) and violent (OR=8.22) criminal offenses in adulthood compared to matched controls (Ogloff et al., 2012).

Wang et al. (2012) found that childhood physical abuse, but not sexual abuse, was significantly associated with violent crime perpetration (vs. other types on nonviolent crimes), a finding that lends support to social learning and cycle of violence explanations. In contrast, Cuadra et al. (2014) found that no individual type of childhood maltreatment was associated with nonsexual violent offending or nonsexual, nonviolent criminal offending. Although some types of childhood maltreatment (i.e., physical abuse, emotional abuse, and physical neglect) were associated with overall criminality, others types were not (i.e., sexual abuse and emotional neglect; Cuadra et al., 2014). These findings seem to suggest overall general (vs. specific) effects, whereby all forms of child maltreatment are harmful and share similar elements that lead to similar outcomes in adulthood.

In a population-based study from Sweden, any self-reported history of childhood maltreatment was associated with adult convictions for a violent crime (AOR=1.98) compared to nonmaltreated controls (Forsman

& Långström, 2012). In this study, AORs became nonsignificant when maltreated twins were compared to nonmaltreated twins, suggesting substantial confounding by genetic or family environmental factors. The authors concluded that childhood maltreatment is a weak causal predictor for adult violent offending; therefore, decreasing childhood maltreatment might reduce violent offending less than previously thought. Instead, prevention strategies need to address the overlapping genetic and/or familial environmental liability for abusive and violent behaviors (Forsman & Långström, 2012). This study did not disentangle the effects of different types of childhood maltreatment, which could have also influenced study results given that there is some indication that the type of adulthood offending may be related to the type of maltreatment experienced earlier in life. For example, in a small Finnish sample of young offenders ($N=89$; ages 16–22 years), childhood physical abuse (both self-reported and official child protection reports) predicted violent offending, self-reported emotional abuse predicted vandalism, and self-reported neglect predicted property offenses (Haapasalo & Moilanen, 2004).

A smaller body of research exists with regard to associations between ACEs and risk of non-IPV victimization experiences in adulthood. In a longitudinal sample of new mothers ($N=477$), women with a childhood maltreatment history had significantly increased odds of experiencing a sexual assault, physical assault with a weapon, and physical assault without a weapon compared to women without a childhood maltreatment history (Parks, Kim, Day, Garza, & Larkby, 2011). This study did not disentangle the specific types of childhood maltreatment with specific types of adult victimization experiences; so, it is unclear whether specific types of childhood maltreatment were associated with specific types of adult victimization (e.g., physical or sexual) in this study. In a prospective case-control study (followed to middle adulthood), all types of officially reported childhood maltreatment (i.e., physical abuse, sexual abuse, and neglect) increased the risk of physical (OR = 2.56) and sexual (OR = 2.28) criminal victimization, but not of property crime, relative to nonmaltreated controls (McIntyre & Widom, 2011). Note that the authors used a lifetime criminal victimization measure; so, victimizations could have occurred during childhood or adolescence rather than exclusively during adulthood. All types of childhood maltreatment have also been found to be related to victimization risk (i.e., victim of robbery, threatened, physical assault, and sexual assault) in a large sample of homeless adults with mental illness (Edalati et al., 2017). Thus, although childhood maltreatment ACEs appear to increase the risk of violent victimization in adulthood, whether the effects of childhood maltreatment are general (i.e., lead to all types of victimization) or specific (i.e., specific types of child maltreatment lead to specific outcomes) remains unknown.

Household dysfunction ACEs

Most of the research on the relationship between household dysfunction ACEs and other forms of interpersonal violence in adulthood focus on the effects of parental incarceration or parental mental illness on offspring criminal offending. Information on other types of household dysfunction ACEs remains largely unexamined in research to date. With regard to the relationship between parental incarceration on offspring violent offending, data from the National Longitudinal Study of Adolescent Health (N=15,587) found that parental incarceration during childhood was associated with increased odds of offspring self-reported arrest (maternal incarceration AOR=1.71; paternal incarceration AOR=1.50), conviction (maternal incarceration AOR=1.87; paternal incarceration AOR=1.59), and incarceration (maternal incarceration AOR=1.92; paternal incarceration AOR=1.81) after the age of 18 years (Burgess-Proctor, Huebner, & Durso, 2016). Effects were most pronounced for same-sex parent-child dyads, and persisted after adjustment for childhood physical abuse, sexual abuse, and several other criminogenic factors. Although this study excluded convictions for minor traffic offenses, outcome measures (i.e., arrests, convictions, and incarceration) were not limited to violent crimes. The relationship between a history of parental incarceration and physical violence perpetration specifically (i.e., physically attacking someone with the idea of seriously hurting them) has been reported among college students (Muftic & Smith, 2018).

A Swedish adoption study found evidence for both genetic and environmental risk in the etiology of violent criminal offending in adulthood (Kendler et al., 2014). Multivariate analyses implicated several environmental (i.e., adoptive parent low education, medical hospitalization, or death) and genetic (i.e., biological parent violent crime, alcohol use disorders, maternal divorce, maternal young age at birth, maternal low education, or biological sibling violent crime) risk factors for offspring violent offending; however, they also noted differences in the type of ACEs and type of offending in adulthood. For example, parental alcohol use disorders seemed to be more strongly related to violent (vs. nonviolent) criminal offending, whereas parental mental illness seemed to be a weak predictor of later violent offending, as the effects of parental mental illness became nonsignificant in multivariate models.

Other studies have found support for the relationship between parental mental illness and offspring violent offending in adulthood. For example, a large, random sample of the Danish population followed offspring (N=412,117) less than 15 years old from 1981 to 2006 to examine the relationship between parental mental illness (before offspring age of 15 years) and offspring sexual and violent offense convictions (after offspring age of 15 years; Dean et al., 2012). Offspring of parents with a diagnosed mental illness had a higher rate of violent and/or sexual convictions than offspring of parents without a diagnosed mental illness, after adjustment for sociodemographic covariates and parental history of criminality. Relationships held for both male and female offspring, and across maternal and paternal mental disorders. The authors suggested that there is likely a shared genetic vulnerability for mental disorders and violent criminal behaviors. Similarly, Mok et al. (2016) found that parental psychiatric disorders increased the risk of violent criminal offending (convictions) among offspring in a population-based Danish cohort. Relationships were especially pronounced for antisocial personality disorder, cannabis misuse, and parental suicide attempts. In addition, similar to Dean et al. (2012), risk was most pronounced in cases where both parents (vs. one parent) had a diagnosed mental disorder or suicide attempt (Mok et al., 2016). In both studies, mood disorders conferred a much lower, albeit significant, risk for offspring criminal offending. Both of these studies did not consider other types of ACEs in their analyses.

Cumulative effects of ACEs

In a large sample of homeless adults with mental illness, a cumulative measure of total number of ACEs (10-item scale) indicated that exposure to increasing number of ACEs was associated with increased criminal justice system involvement (AOR = 1.04) and violent victimizations (AOR = 1.11) after adjustment for sociodemographics (Edalati et al., 2017). Total number of ACEs were also associated with significantly increased odds of violent victimization (AOR = 1.09) after adjustment for PTSD and alcohol and drug dependence.

Summary

Childhood physical abuse and neglect have been found to increase the likelihood of committing a violent crime in adulthood (Cuadra et al., 2014; Edalati et al., 2017; Wang et al., 2012; Widom & Maxfield, 2001). As well, it appears that childhood emotional abuse, but not emotional neglect, is related to criminality in adulthood (Cuadra et al., 2014; Edalati et al., 2017). Research is not conclusive on the relationship between childhood sexual abuse and violent crimes in adulthood, with some studies reporting nonsignificant (Edalati et al., 2017) or inverse (Cuadra et al., 2014; Wang et al., 2012) relationships between childhood sexual abuse and the risk of violent crime perpetration in adulthood. Less is known about the relationship between ACEs and non-IPV violent victimizations in adulthood. Preliminary evidence suggests that a history of maltreatment in childhood increases the risk of violent victimization in adulthood (Edalati et al., 2017; McIntyre & Widom, 2011; Parks et al., 2011); however, it remains unclear whether specific types of maltreatment are associated with specific types of adult victimization. Research on household dysfunction ACEs has largely focused on the relationship between childhood exposure to parental incarceration and/or parental mental illness on adult violent offending. Both types of childhood exposures have been associated with an increased likelihood of violent offending in adulthood (Dean et al., 2012; Kendler et al., 2014; Mok et al., 2016; Muftic & Smith, 2018). As well, some researchers have speculated that there may be a shared genetic vulnerability in the development of both mental disorders and violent offending (Dean et al., 2012; Kendler et al., 2014). Less is known about the relationship between other types of household dysfunction ACEs (e.g., parental separation/divorce, parental substance abuse), or the cumulative effects of ACEs, on violent offending in adulthood.

Directions for future research

Most of the research that has been conducted to date on the relationship between ACEs and violence in adulthood has focused on childhood maltreatment ACEs, particularly links between childhood physical abuse, exposure to IPV, and sexual abuse and later violence perpetration and/or victimization. Less is known about the relationship between other types of child maltreatment ACEs (e.g., emotional abuse, emotional neglect, physical neglect) or the impact of household dysfunction ACEs (e.g., parental separation/divorce, mental illness, substance abuse, incarceration) on violence outcomes in adulthood. To better understand the intergenerational effects of ACEs on violence in adulthood, consideration of under-researched childhood adversities should be incorporated into future research. Also, given the strong correlation between experiencing co-occurring ACEs, both specific and cumulative effects ACEs models should be considered. Relatedly, different types of violence in adulthood also tend to co-occur. It is important to address whether different types of adult violence have a single etiology or if they have different etiologies and distinct correlates (Cascardi et al., 2017).

Much of the research concerning less studied types of ACEs (e.g., emotional abuse and neglect, household dysfunctions) and specific adult violence outcomes (e.g., sexual violence, emotional violence, other interpersonal violence) is based on nonrepresentative samples, including samples of college or university students, treatment seeking clinical samples, and samples of individuals convicted of violent crimes. Although these studies provide useful information, findings may not generalize to the wider population. Given the substantial proportion of the general population exposed to ACEs (Felitti et al., 1998), effects of exposures to childhood adversities on adult violence outcomes at the population level need to be determined. Also, many studies use dichotomous assessments of ACEs (present vs. absent) and do not consider severity, duration, or age of onset in analyses (Edalati et al., 2017; Jespersen et al., 2009; Ports et al., 2016), all of which may impact longer-term outcomes. Further, many studies only assess substantiated forms of childhood maltreatment and/or are based on outcome data on officially reported crime. Over-reliance on official reporting may underestimate true exposure and outcome rates, as many cases of childhood maltreatment, sexual violence, and violent criminal offending never get reported to official agencies (Leach et al., 2016).

It is also important for research to examine moderators and mediators in the relationship between ACEs and violence in adulthood. This will help to identify for whom intervention is most necessary as well as to identify targeted intervention points. For example, some studies find sex differences in the relationship between ACEs and adult violence (Brown, Perera, Masho, Mezuk, & Cohen, 2015; McIntyre & Widom, 2011; McKinney et al., 2009; Widom & Maxfield, 2001), while others do not (Dean et al., 2012; Fergusson et al., 2014). However, sex differences are rarely considered in analyses. Further, the almost exclusive focus on women as victims and men as perpetrators is another important limitation of the extant research. Several mediating variables, including depressive symptoms (Madruga et al., 2017), adolescent conduct disorder (Ehrensaft et al., 2003), insecure attachment (Cascardi et al., 2017; Grady, Levenson, & Bolder, 2017), emotion dysregulation (Berzenski & Yates, 2010), PTSD (Brown et al., 2015; Taft et al., 2008), substance use (Brown et al., 2015), and social information processing deficits (Taft et al., 2008), have all been identified in the literature. To reduce physical, sexual, emotional/psychological, and other forms of interpersonal violence, researchers, practitioners, and policy makers need to understand the mechanisms and pathways through which ACEs lead to violence in adulthood (Grady et al., 2017).

Finally, researchers have also suggested that it may be time to rethink the conceptualization of ACEs. For example, many other experiences not frequently conceptualized as a childhood adversity have been found to be associated with negative long-term outcomes, including less severe forms of physical violence (e.g., spanking), peer victimization, peer isolation/rejection, community violence, and socioeconomic disadvantage (Afifi, Ford, et al., 2017; Finkelhor, Shattuck, Turner, & Hamby, 2015; Ports et al., 2016). All of these potential ACEs seem particularly relevant for understanding the etiology of violent behavior in adulthood. Many of these experiences are much more common and, hence, likely have a greater impact at the population level than some of the more traditional ACEs.

Policy and practice implications

The prevention of childhood maltreatment, other types of childhood disadvantages, and violence clearly remain important public health priorities. Reducing violence in all of its forms is important because even less severe forms of physical violence (e.g., harsh physical punishment, power assertive discipline) and nonphysical forms of violence (e.g., emotional maltreatment, neglect) are associated with violence in adulthood. Macrolevel stressors such as poverty, community violence, food insecurity, and housing instability all need to be examined with regard to how they contribute to both ACEs and later violence (Grady et al., 2017). However, developing the most effective intervention programs and services for those who have experienced ACEs is also necessary to promote better health and well-being, including the reduction of violence in adulthood.

It is important to recognize the interconnectedness between various types of ACEs in prevention and intervention efforts. Coordinated strategies to prevent multiple forms of childhood adversity at the same time are necessary to strengthen the public health impact of violence prevention efforts (Ports et al., 2016). As Bland et al. (2018) note, interventions targeting any particular type of childhood adversity may be less effective in reducing later violence than interventions designed to decrease the temperamental and neurobiological risk factors for violent behaviors. It is also necessary to target high-risk children (e.g., early conduct problems) and families (e.g., household substance use or mental illness) early to redirect developmental trajectories that are associated with violence later in life. Promoting the development of protective factors—graduation from high school, the provision of meaningful employment opportunities, and fostering healthy interpersonal and community attachments—has been found to mediate the relationship between ACEs and later violent outcomes (Bland et al., 2018); thus, interventions designed to assist children exposed to ACEs in achieving important life goals may also be important in reducing violence in adulthood.

Interventions should also recognize the unique needs of child victims and adult survivors of ACEs. For example, providing positive role models and ensuring a healthy environment, especially in homes with parental alcohol use, mental illness, or violence, may be important for children facing adverse experiences, whereas adult survivors may require programs aimed at decreasing high-risk behaviors (e.g., substance use), increasing personal safety, and fostering healthy attitudes and expectations about gender roles and relationships (Yuan, Koss, Polacca, & Goldman, 2006). In all cases, ACEs need to be recognized and addressed in intervention efforts aimed at reducing all forms of violence in adult relationships (Grady et al., 2017; Levenson et al., 2016).

Conclusion

All children need safe, stable, and nurturing environments. Preventing and reducing exposure to ACEs is necessary to help not only promote such environments, but given evidence that all types of ACEs are associated with violence in adulthood, to reduce violence at the population level.

References

Abajobi, A. A., Kisely, S., Williams, G. M., Clavarino, A. M., & Najman, J. M. (2017). Substantiated childhood maltreatment and intimate partner violence victimization in young adulthood: a birth cohort study. *Journal of Youth and Adolescence*, *46*, 165–179.

Afifi, T. O., Ford, D., Gershoff, E. T., Merrick, M., Grogan-Kaylor, A., Ports, K. A., … Bennett, R. P. (2017). Spanking and adult mental health impairment: the case for the designation of spanking as an adverse childhood experience. *Child Abuse & Neglect*, *71*, 24–31.

Afifi, T. O., Mota, N., Sareen, J., & MacMillan, H. L. (2017). The relationship between harsh physical punishment and child maltreatment in childhood and intimate partner violence in adulthood. *BMC Public Health*, *17*(493), 1–10.

Berzenski, S. R., & Yates, T. M. (2010). A developmental process analysis of the contribution of childhood emotional abuse to relationship violence. *Journal of Aggression, Maltreatment & Trauma*, *19*(2), 180–203.

Bland, V. J., Lambie, I., & Best, C. (2018). Does child neglect contribute to violent behavior in adulthood? A review of possible links. *Clinical Psychology Review*, *60*, 126–135.

Brown, M. J., Perera, R. A., Masho, S. W., Mezuk, B., & Cohen, S. A. (2015). Adverse childhood experiences and intimate partner aggression in the US: sex differences and similarities in psychosocial mediation. *Social Science & Medicine*, *131*, 48–57.

Burgess-Proctor, A., Huebner, B. M., & Durso, J. M. (2016). Comparing the effects of maternal and paternal incarceration on adult daughters' and sons' criminal justice system involvement: a gendered pathways analysis. *Criminal Justice and Behavior*, *43*(8), 1034–1055.

Cascardi, M., Jouriles, E. N., & Temple, J. R. (2017). Distinct and overlapping correlates of psychological and physical partner violence perpetration. *Journal of Interpersonal Violence*, 1–24.

Christopher, K., Lutz-Zois, C. J., & Reinhardt, A. R. (2007). Female sexual-offenders: personality pathology as a mediator of the relationship between childhood sexual abuse history and sexual abuse perpetration against others. *Child Abuse & Neglect*, *31*, 871–883.

Corvo, K., & Carpenter, E. H. (2000). Effects of parental substance abuse on current levels of domestic violence: a possible elaboration of intergenerational transmission processes. *Journal of Family Violence*, *15*(2), 123–135.

Cuadra, L. E., Jaffe, A. E., Thomas, R., & DiLillo, D. (2014). Child maltreatment and adult criminal behavior: does criminal thinking explain the association? *Child Abuse & Neglect*, *38*, 1399–1408.

Dean, K., Mortensen, P. B., Stevens, H., Murray, R. M., Walsh, E., & Agerbo, E. (2012). Criminal convictions among offspring with parental history of mental disorder. *Psychological Medicine*, *42*, 571–581.

Dong, M., Anda, R. F., Felitti, V. J., Dube, S. R., Williamson, D. F., Thompson, T. J., … Giles, W. H. (2004). The interrelatedness of multiple forms of childhood abuse, neglect, and household dysfunction. *Child Abuse & Neglect*, *28*, 771–784.

Dube, S. R., Anda, R. F., Felitti, V. J., Chapman, D. P., Williamson, D. F., & Giles, W. H. (2001). Childhood abuse, household dysfunction, and the risk of attempted suicide throughout the life span. *JAMA*, *286*, 3089–3096.

Dube, S. R., Anda, R. F., Felitti, V. J., Edwards, V. J., & Croft, J. B. (2002). Adverse childhood experiences and personal alcohol abuse as an adult. *Addictive Behaviors*, *27*(5), 713–725.

Dube, S. R., Felitti, V. J., Dong, M., Chapman, D. P., Giles, W. H., & Anda, R. F. (2003). Childhood abuse, neglect, and household dysfunction and the risk of illicit drug use: the Adverse Childhood Experiences Study. *Pediatrics*, *111*(3), 564–572.

Edalati, H., Nicholls, T. L., Crocker, A. G., Roy, L., Somers, J. M., & Patterson, M. L. (2017). Adverse childhood experiences and the risk of criminal justice system involvement and victimization among homeless adults with mental illness. *Psychiatric Services*, *68*, 1288–1295.

Ehrensaft, M. K., Cohen, P., Brown, J., Smailes, E., Chen, H., & Johnson, J. G. (2003). Intergenerational transmission of partner violence: a 20-year prospective study. *Journal of Consulting and Clinical Psychology*, *71*(4), 741–753.

Felitti, V. J., Anda, R. F., Nordenberg, D., Williamson, D. F., Spitz, A. M., Edwards, V., … Marks, J. S. (1998). Relationship of childhood abuse and household dysfunction to many of the leading causes of death in adults: The Adverse Childhood Experiences (ACE) Study. *American Journal of Preventive Medicine*, *14*(4), 245–258.

Fergusson, D. M., McLeod, G. F. H., & Horwood, L. J. (2014). Parental separation/divorce in childhood and partnership outcomes at age 30. *Journal of Child Psychology and Psychiatry*, *55*(4), 352–360.

Finkelhor, D., Shattuck, A., Turner, H., & Hamby, S. (2015). A revised inventory of adverse childhood experiences. *Child Abuse & Neglect*, *48*, 13–21.

Forsman, M., & Långström, N. (2012). Child maltreatment and adult violent offending: population-based twin study addressing the 'cycle of violence' hypothesis. *Psychological Medicine*, *42*, 1977–1983.

Gilchrist, G., Canfield, M., Radcliffe, P., & D'Oliveira, A.F.P.L. (2017). Controlling behaviours and technology-facilitated abuse perpetrated by men receiving substance use treatment in England and Brazil: prevalence and risk factors. *Drug and Alcohol Review*, *36*, 52–63.

Gilchrist, G., Radcliffe, P., Noto, A. R., & D'Oliveira, A.F.P.L. (2017). The prevalence and factors associated with ever perpetrating intimate partner violence by men receiving substance use treatment in Brazil and England: a cross-cultural comparison. *Drug and Alcohol Review*, *36*, 34–51.

Grady, M. D., Levenson, J. S., & Bolder, T. (2017). Linking adverse childhood effects and attachment: a theory of etiology for sexual offending. *Trauma, Violence & Abuse*, *18*(4), 433–444.

Haapasalo, J., & Moilanen, J. (2004). Official and self-reported childhood abuse and adult crime of young offenders. *Criminal Justice and Behavior*, *31*(2), 127–149.

Herrenkohl, T. I., & Jung, H. (2016). Effects of child abuse, adolescent violence, peer approval and pro-violence attitudes on intimate partner violence in adulthood. *Criminal Behaviour and Mental Health*, *26*, 304–314.

Ireland, T. O., & Smith, C. A. (2009). Living in partner-violent families: developmental links to antisocial behavior and relationship violence. *Journal of Youth and Adolescence*, *38*, 323–339.

Jespersen, A. F., Lalumière, M. L., & Seto, M. C. (2009). Sexual abuse history among adult sex offenders and non-sex offenders: a meta-analysis. *Child Abuse & Neglect*, *33*, 179–192.

Johnson, M. P. (1995). Patriarchal terrorism and common couple violence: two forms of violence against women. *Journal of Marriage and Family*, *57*(2), 283–294.

Kendler, K. S., Lönn, S. L., Morris, N. A., Sundquist, J., Långström, N., & Sundquist, K. (2014). A Swedish national adoption study of criminality. *Psychological Medicine*, *44*, 1913–1925.

Kimber, M., Adham, S., Gill, S., McTavish, J., & MacMillan, H. L. (2018). The association between child exposure to intimate partner violence (IPV) and perpetration of IPV in adulthood: a systematic review. *Child Abuse & Neglect*, *76*, 273–286.

Leach, C., Stewart, A., & Smallbone, S. (2016). Testing the sexually abused-sexual abuser hypothesis: a prospective longitudinal birth cohort study. *Child Abuse & Neglect*, *51*, 144–153.

Levenson, J. S., Willis, G. M., & Prescott, D. S. (2016). Adverse childhood experiences in the lives of male sex offenders: implications for trauma-informed care. *Sexual Abuse: A Journal of Research and Treatment*, *28*(4), 340–359.

Madruga, C. S., Viana, M. C., Abdalla, R. R., Caetano, R., & Laranjeira, R. (2017). Pathways from witnessing parental violence during childhood to involvement in intimate partner violence in adult life: the roles of depression and substance use. *Drug and Alcohol Review*, *36*, 107–114.

McIntyre, J. K., & Widom, C. S. (2011). Childhood victimization and crime victimization. *Journal of Interpersonal Violence*, *26*(4), 640–663.

McKinney, C. M., Caetano, R., Ramisetty-Mikler, S., & Nelson, S. (2009). Childhood family violence and perpetration and victimization of intimate partner violence: findings from a national population-based study of couples. *Annals of Epidemiology*, *19*, 25–32.

Mok, P. L., Pedersen, C. B., Springate, D., Astrup, A., Kapur, N., Antonsen, S., … Webb, R. T. (2016). Parental psychiatric disease and risks of attempted suicide and violent criminal offending in offspring: a population-based cohort study. *JAMA Psychiatry*, *73*(10), 1015–1022.

Muftic, L. R., & Smith, M. (2018). Sex, parental incarceration, and violence perpetration among a sample of young adults. *Journal of Interpersonal Violence*, *33*(2), 316–338.

Nikulina, V., Gelin, M., & Zwilling, A. (2017). Is there a cumulative association between adverse childhood experiences and intimate partner violence in emerging adulthood? *Journal of Interpersonal Violence*, 1–28. https://doi.org/10.1177/0886260517741626.

Ogloff, J. R. P., Cutajar, M. C., Mann, E., & Mullen, P. (2012). Child sexual abuse and subsequent offending and victimisation: a 45 year follow-up study. *Trends and Issues in Crime and Criminal Justice*, *440*, 1–6.

Parks, S. E., Kim, K. H., Day, N. L., Garza, M. A., & Larkby, C. A. (2011). Lifetime self-reported victimization among low-income urban women: the relationship between childhood maltreatment and adult violent victimization. *Journal of Interpersonal Violence*, *26*(6), 1111–1128.

Ports, K. A., Ford, D. C., & Merrick, M. T. (2016). Adverse childhood experiences and sexual victimization in adulthood. *Child Abuse & Neglect*, *51*, 313–322.

Roodman, A. A., & Clum, G. A. (2001). Revictimization rates and method variance: a meta-analysis. *Clinical Psychology Review*, *21*(2), 188–204.

Salter, D., McMillan, D., Richards, M., Talbot, T., Hodges, J., Bentovim, A., … Skuse, D. (2003). Development of sexually abusive behaviour in sexually victimised males: a longitudinal study. *Lancet*, *361*, 471–476.

Smith, S. G., Zhang, X., Basile, K. C., Merrick, M. T., Wang, J., Krenshaw, M.-J., & Chen, J. (2018). *National intimate partner and sexual violence survey: 2015 data brief*. Atlanta, GA: Centers for Disease Control and Prevention. Retrieved from: https://www.cdc.gov/violenceprevention/nisvs/2015NISVSdatabrief.html.

Taft, S. T., Schumm, J. A., Marshall, A. D., Panuzio, J., & Holtzworth-Munroe, A. (2008). Family-of-origin maltreatment, posttraumatic stress disorder symptoms, social information processing deficits, and relationship abuse perpetration. *Journal of Abnormal Psychology*, *117*(3), 637–646.

Voith, L. A., Anderson, R. E., & Cahill, S. P. (2017). Extending the ACEs framework: examining the relations between childhood abuse an later victimization and perpetration with college men. *Journal of Interpersonal Violence*, 1–26. https://doi.org/10.1177/0886260517708400.

Wang, Y., Xu, K., Cao, G., Qian, M., Shook, J., & Ai, A. L. (2012). Child maltreatment in an incarcerated sample in China: prediction for crime types in adulthood. *Children and Youth Services Review*, *34*, 1553–1559.

Whitfield, C. L., Anda, R. F., Dube, S. R., & Felitti, V. J. (2003). Violent childhood experiences and the risk of intimate partner violence in adults: assessment in a large health maintenance organization. *Journal of Interpersonal Violence*, *18*(2), 166–185.

Widom, C. S., & Maxfield, M. G. (2001). *An update on the "cycle of violence"*. Washington, DC: National Institute of Justice.

Yuan, N. P., Koss, M. P., Polacca, M., & Goldman, D. (2006). Risk factors for physical assault and rape among six Native American tribes. *Journal of Interpersonal Violence*, *21*(12), 1566–1590.

SECTION III

CHAPTER

8

Routine screening of ACEs: Should we or shouldn't we?

John D. McLennan[*,†], *Jill R. McTavish*[‡,§], *Harriet L. MacMillan*[*,‡,§]

[*]Department of Pediatrics, University of Calgary, Calgary, AB, Canada, [†]Children's Hospital of Eastern Ontario-Research Institute, Ottawa, ON, Canada, [‡]Department of Psychiatry & Behavioural Neurosciences, McMaster University, Hamilton, ON, Canada, [§]Offord Centre for Child Studies, Hamilton, ON, Canada

Introduction

There is an extensive literature that identifies key dimensions to consider when deciding whether to proceed with disease screening and, more broadly, health problem screening. Key *process* objectives of health problem screening are to (1) identify those problems that would not otherwise be identified within existing health and social service systems, and/or (2) identify problems earlier in their progression than would otherwise be the case. The key *outcome* objective is to improve the health of those identified as a function of the screening program; that is, identification should not be an end in and of itself.

Screening for adverse childhood experiences (ACEs) does not entail identifying health problems, but rather identifying risk factors (e.g., having experienced child abuse) which are associated with the increased likelihood of health problems (Hughes et al., 2017). As such, this shift to risk-factor screening requires a refocusing of the key *process* objectives; that is, to identify *high-risk groups* who would not otherwise be identified within the existing health and social service systems and/or identify such groups earlier than would otherwise be the case. While the process objectives require modification, the key *outcome* objective is the same as for health problem screening—improving health outcomes for those identified through the screening program.

Adverse Childhood Experiences
https://doi.org/10.1016/B978-0-12-816065-7.00008-2

What questions need to be answered favorably when deciding whether or not to implement a specific risk factor screening program?

There are many factors to consider when deciding whether to implement a screening program for a given disease or health problem. A recent systematic review and consensus process identified 12 key principles to inform decision making as to whether to proceed with a given screening program. These have been divided into three domains, including disease/health problem principles, test/intervention principles, and program/system principles (Dobrow, Hagens, Chafe, Sullivan, & Rabeneck, 2018). For the purpose of this chapter, we draw on some of these key principles, as well as others. We reframe some of these principles as questions in need of answers to guide decision making as to whether to implement screening for the proposed risk factors. We first present the questions and associated concepts with some examples and then apply the questions specifically to what is known about ACEs screening. The questions are summarized in Table 1. We suggest this as a starting place and not an exhaustive consideration of all potentially relevant variables that may influence the appropriateness of a given risk factor screening program.

TABLE 1 Questions to Assist in Evaluating the Appropriateness of Proceeding With a Given Risk Factor Screening Program

I. Does an evidence-based intervention exist that has been demonstrated to improve outcomes for the identified high-risk group?
II. Will the evidence-based intervention be available to the high-risk group identified through screening?
III. What is the accuracy of the screening approach in identifying the high-risk group that is anticipated to benefit from intervention?
IV. What harms may result from screening?
V. What are findings from experimental trials using the screening approach?
VI. Have other critical domains been considered for the proposed screening program?

I. Does an evidence-based intervention exist that has been demonstrated to improve outcomes for the identified high-risk group?

The existence of a relevant evidence-based intervention is sometimes erroneously taken as a given and is not an explicit principle within the screening guide referred to above (although the concept is embedded in the "postscreening test options" principle [Dobrow et al., 2018]). This question has been articulated before when considering mass screening

(Mant & Fowler, 1990) and we would argue that this principle is foundational, as screening and identification in and of itself is not expected to improve health outcomes. If there is no evidence-based intervention for the identified high-risk group, such a screening program would raise ethical concerns given the potential harm for labeling a group as "high risk" and not providing an effective intervention to achieve a positive benefit-to-risk tradeoff (Goldenberg et al., 2016; Shickle & Chadwick, 1994).

An illustrative example could be a proposal to screen young children for signs of excessive disruptive behaviors, characteristics that may identify children at risk for conditions such as attention-deficit/hyperactivity disorder (Charach, McLennan, Bélanger, & Nixon, 2017). Screening could entail parents completing standardized questionnaires that identify whether a child has elevated levels of attention and disruptive behaviors. Those identified as "high-risk" from this process could be systematically linked to evidence-based parent training programs, an intervention that has evidence for improved outcomes for such populations (Charach et al., 2013).

II. Will the evidence-based intervention be available to the high-risk group identified through screening?

The existence of an evidence-based intervention in and of itself is not sufficient. Such an intervention needs to be available to those identified from the screening program. It is problematic if a screening program makes an unverified assumption that the existing health or social service systems will effectively deliver evidence-based interventions to identified high-risk groups. The system may not provide relevant evidence-based interventions and, if it does, it may not have the capacity to address the needs of individuals newly identified as potentially benefiting from such interventions. Given the substantial existing demands on health services in the public sector, this is an important consideration if no new intervention resources are planned as part of the proposed screening program. Extending the example above, it would be important to determine the system capacity and resources to expand the availability of evidence-based parenting programs to address early childhood disruptive behavior problems identified through screening.

III. What is the accuracy of the screening approach in identifying the high-risk group that is anticipated to benefit from intervention?

This question addresses more directly the properties of the screening tool and process for its use. Determining screening test performance characteristics is one of the key principles of screening (Dobrow et al., 2018). Sensitivity, specificity, positive predictive values, and negative predictive values are common accuracy outcomes that are used to evaluate screening tools (see Fig. 1). However, recent research suggests that these values

		Does the index test predict depression?		
	Total population	Positive index test outcome	Negative index test outcome	
The person has depression? (reference standard)	Condition positive (The person has depression)	True positive	False negative (Type II error)	**Sensitivity** = # True positive / (Sum of condition positive)
	Condition negative (The person does not have depression)	False positive (Type I error)	True negative	**Specificity** = # True negatives / (Sum of condition negative)
		Positive predictive value = # True positives / (Sum of test outcome positive)	**Negative predictive value** = # True negative / (Sum of test outcome negative)	

FIG. 1 Equations for calculating sensitivity, specificity, positive and negative predictive value using depression screening as the example.

are easily misinterpreted and may not accurately reflect the effects of the screening tool in the population of interest (Mustafa et al., 2015). Instead, rates for true positives, true negatives, false positives, and false negatives may give practitioners a clearer picture of how many people who should have been identified will be missed by a screening tool (false negatives) and how many will be falsely identified by the screening tool (false positives). These numbers have clearer implications, as those who are missed may not receive the interventions that may provide benefit, and those who are falsely identified may suffer an unnecessary or intrusive intervention response. For example, a metaanalysis of diagnostic accuracy studies for poststroke depression concluded that none of the identification tools were able to identify this condition with few false positives (Meader, Moe-Byrne, Llewellyn, & Mitchell, 2014).

It is important to recognize that poor study quality leads to reduced confidence in all accuracy outcomes, including rates of sensitivity, specificity, positive or negative predictive values, and false positives/negatives. Several tools are available, such as QUADAS-II, to assess the quality of diagnostic accuracy studies (Whiting et al., 2011). For example, diagnostic accuracy studies usually involve a sample population of individuals who undergo (1) assessment with an index test (e.g., depression screener) followed by (2) assessment with a reference standard (e.g., clinical interview by a qualified provider). In studies with large sample sizes, it is appropriate to apply the reference standard to a random subsample of the population who were screened negative by the index test. In some studies, the same reference standard is not applied to all of the sample population, or even to a random subsample. These studies are said to suffer from verification bias. Using the example of poststroke depression, verification bias could occur if only the people who screened positive by a depression screener were later evaluated by a clinical interview. In this case, the sensitivity values are compromised as it is unclear if the people who screened negative for depression actually have depression (false negatives), since they were not evaluated by the reference standard.

IV. What harms may result from screening?

Potential harms are often not considered when evaluating the appropriateness for implementing a new screening program; however, it is essential to consider such aspects as a core component of screening principles (Dobrow et al., 2018). There are different mechanisms that can lead to harm. One is the potential adverse impact of a person being labeled as "high-risk." Some of the more substantial examinations on labeling come from work on delinquency and the potential adverse consequences of the label itself (Liberman, Kirk, & Kim, 2014). More recent work has extended potential risks of being labeled as "high risk" to the condition of psychosis (Rüsch et al., 2014). Other risks include the potential anxiety resulting from having a positive test from a disease screener (Brodersen & Siersma, 2013). This is particularly problematic for false positives as there is the lack of potential benefit to compensate from this potential harm.

A second mechanism for harm is related to the next steps following a positive screen. Typically, a positive screen leads to additional assessment or testing. In some disease-screening procedures, an initial low-invasive and low-cost screener is used, followed by a more invasive and higher cost component to assess those who screen positive. An example would be colon cancer screening using a fecal occult blood test followed by colonoscopy of those who screen positive.

An important related dimension to consider is opportunity cost. Any intervention (including screening processes and any follow-up assessment) involves resources. As there is a finite pool of resources in the public health sector (or other relevant service sectors), the implementation of a new screening program means less resources (e.g., time, personnel) are available for other services. If the new screening program has no net benefits (i.e., even if there are no direct adverse impacts), this can still result in a net harm as there was a lost opportunity for using the resources for an effective intervention. Opportunity costs are one component of the more general principle of conducting an economic evaluation of proposed screening programs (Dobrow et al., 2018).

V. What are findings from experimental trials using the screening approach?

Positive responses to the earlier questions are not sufficient to ensure that a screening program will result in positive gains for the participants. Experimental trials of screening approaches are the most rigorous way of determining if the proposed screening approach does more good than harm. Such designs allow for the control of multiple factors, which is not possible with other study designs. While such trials can be costly and time consuming, they provide the strongest level of evidence for decision making.

Experiments examining the evidence for effectiveness of screening for intimate partner violence (IPV) may be an important example to inform considerations related to ACEs screening. A recent Cochrane systematic review identified 13 studies that used randomized or quasirandomized controlled trials to evaluate a range of IPV screening tools (e.g., Woman Abuse Screening Tool, Abuse Assessment Screen, Partner Violence Screen) compared to usual care or another comparison (O'Doherty et al., 2015). Included studies assessed the impact of IPV screening on a range of outcomes, such as identification, information giving, referral, uptake of services, and recurrence of IPV. While these studies suggest that screening tools improve *detection* of women experiencing IPV in certain settings (e.g., antenatal care), but not others (e.g., hospital-based primary care), there was *no improvement* in women's health outcomes, including reduction of IPV.

While trials should incorporate measures to detect potential harms from screening tools, this is rarely done. Only one of the IPV screening studies set out to assess potential harms of screening among women with and without a history of IPV; however, this assessment only extended 3 months (MacMillan et al., 2009). Other studies assessed potentially related outcomes, such as acceptability, comfort levels, and positive and negative reactions, with no negative outcomes found, although the studies only evaluated these outcomes immediately following the intervention (O'Doherty et al., 2015).

VI. Have other critical domains been considered for the proposed screening program?

It is beyond the scope of this chapter to review all possible relevant domains that should be considered for proposed screening programs. We refer the reader to the comprehensive set of screening principles described in the previously referenced paper by Dobrow et al. (2018). However, we will briefly flag two additional questions: (1) is the screening program coordinated, and where possible integrated, with the broader health and social service systems and (2) is the screening program "...clinically, socially and ethically acceptable to screening participants..." (Dobrow et al., 2018; p. E427).

New health initiatives, screening or otherwise, are not implemented within a vacuum. Rather, they are embedded within existing health and social service systems. Consideration should be given to what is already being provided in the system for those who might be identified through screening. Perhaps a subgroup of such individuals will already be receiving services through other routes that are appropriate and less stigmatizing.

Continuing with a previous example, the parent of a child with disruptive behaviors, on their own initiative or following the recommendation of others (i.e., not through the screening program), may already be participating in an evidence-based parenting program. This needs to be factored in when modeling the potential benefits of implementing a new screening program within an existing service system. Furthermore, values and preferences of multiple stakeholders must be considered for the various components of the screening program. Screening components are many and include recruitment, testing, information access, among others (Dobrow et al., 2018).

How does the proposal for ACEs screening fair on this set of questions?

In this section, we apply these same six questions specifically to ACEs screening to determine the pattern of responses to inform deliberations on the appropriateness of proceeding with ACEs screening programs at this time.

I. Does an evidence-based intervention exist that has been demonstrated to improve outcomes for groups with elevated ACEs scores identified through ACEs screening?

There are important challenges in trying to answer this question about ACEs screening. First, there is currently no single evidence-based intervention or group of interventions that have been shown to improve health outcomes among groups scoring high on ACEs. This is partly related to the broad array of exposures that ACEs include, which may result in at least two sources of heterogeneity. First, those scoring high on ACEs can have substantially different exposures. For one group, a high ACEs score may result from exposure to physical, emotional, and/or sexual abuse, while another group may have no abuse experience, but screen positive on items asking about exposure to others in the household who have had health and social problems (e.g., mental illness, drug abuse, incarceration). These different types of exposures might lead to different intervention needs.

Second, exposure to the same cluster of ACEs may result in substantially different health problems, which again could lead to different intervention needs. For example, a subgroup scoring high on ACEs secondary to exposure to abuse may meet criteria for posttraumatic stress disorder (PTSD). This subgroup may benefit from being linked to a specific evidence-based intervention such as trauma-focused cognitive behavioral therapy (TF-CBT) (de Arellano et al., 2014). However, for accurate linkage, a second-stage screening or assessment process would be needed to identify whom among those scoring high on ACEs screeners meet criteria for

PTSD. An alternative process would be to screen for PTSD (rather than ACEs) to help identify persons with PTSD from past abuse exposures that are being missed. However, not all who have had past abuse will have PTSD and past abuse is only one part of ACEs screening. It is not then obvious what evidence-based interventions will be offered to those who have past abuse with no current PTSD and for those with high ACEs scores secondary to other risk exposures (e.g., having lived with others who have serious health and social problems).

Some of the findings highlighted as related to elevated ACEs scores include medical problems such as obesity and cardiovascular disease (Felitti et al., 1998; also see Chapter 5). If these are primary concerning health outcomes for the high-risk group identified through ACEs screening, then one might consider whether the identified high-risk groups should be tracked into evidence-informed interventions to reduce cardiovascular risk, such as diet and exercise programs (Artinian et al., 2010). However, if this was a core objective, it would seem more efficient to screen for more immediate and direct cardiovascular risk factors (e.g., current obesity, elevated blood pressure). Again, it is not obvious why one would employ a screener that identifies heterogenous high-risk groups if the aim is to link them with specific evidence-based interventions to improve health outcomes.

II. Will the evidence-based intervention (assuming one or more are identified) be available to those scoring high (or "positive") on ACEs screeners?

Answering this second question is hampered by unanswered aspects for the preceding question. However, if we extend the earlier example whereby TF-CBT is to be offered to those with PTSD, there should be assurance that the intervention will be available. Access to evidence-based interventions may be extremely limited within public health and mental health services depending on the jurisdiction. It would be important to verify, for example, how available TF-CBT is for persons already identified as having PTSD in the service systems. This consideration would need to be extended to other interventions identified as evidence-based for persons with high ACEs screens.

III. What is the accuracy of ACEs screening approaches in identifying a high-risk group that is anticipated to benefit from intervention?

The first wave of the landmark ACE Study was conducted from 1995 to 1996 at Kaiser Permanente, a large US-managed care organization, and entailed sending an ACEs questionnaire to 13,494 adults who had received a standardized medical evaluation (8056 questionnaires [i.e., 59.7%] were returned with usable data) (Felitti et al., 1998). For this study, ACEs questions were drawn from a variety of sources, such as the Conflict Tactics Scale (Straus & Gelles, 1978) for questions about emotional abuse, physical abuse, and exposure to IPV; Wyatt's Sexual History Questionnaire (Wyatt, 1985) for questions about contact sexual abuse; and the National Health Interview Survey for questions about exposure to alcohol or drug abuse (National Center for Health Statistics, 1991). Additional questions were created for the purposes of the study, including questions about mental illness among others in the household, questions about parental separation or divorce, and questions about incarcerated household members. All questions addressed experiences that occurred during the first 18 years. This study suggests a graded dose–response relationship between exposure to one or more ACEs and increased health risks, with exposure to four or more ACEs leading to a 4- to 12-fold increase in certain health risks, such as depression or suicide attempt (Felitti et al., 1998).

What has become widely known as the ACE Study received considerable policy attention and has resulted in much debate about the relevance of screening for ACEs. However, screening tools for ACEs are still in their infancy and we are not aware of any peer-reviewed published research that has evaluated their diagnostic accuracy (i.e., their ability to accurately detect people with ACEs). For example, Finkelhor and colleagues have designed the popular ACEs scale based on the original study (Finkelhor, Shattuck, Turner, & Hamby, 2013), as well as a revised ACEs scale (Finkelhor, Shattuck, Turner, & Hamby, 2015). Questions from both surveys draw from an enhanced version of the Juvenile Victimization Questionnaire (Finkelhor, Hamby, Ormrod, & Turner, 2005), as well as other questions from unvalidated sources. Studies evaluating the ACEs scale indicate that certain ACEs (e.g., low socioeconomic status) are predictive of health status, while others (e.g., peer victimization and maltreatment) are predictive of psychological stress (Finkelhor et al., 2015). In spite of these predictive abilities, Finkelhor (2018) cautions against the use of the ACEs scale as a prospective screening tool for the following reasons: (1) lack of evidence-based programs for addressing those with high ACEs scores, including programs attempting to reduce recurrence of child maltreatment or to address the health outcomes of this exposure, (2) lack of research about acceptability (e.g., would screening for ACEs be experienced as intrusive?), (3) potential for overtreatment, and (4) potential harms and complications resulting from mandatory reporting obligations. Some of these potential harms can be further understood by examining the current diagnostic accuracy research related to screening for exposure to child maltreatment, a major component of ACEs scales.

McTavish et al. (n.d.) recently conducted an update of a systematic review by Bailhache, Leroy, Pillet, and Salmi (2013) related to the accuracy of tools for identifying children exposed to potential maltreatment. They identified 25 cross-sectional studies evaluating a range of tools for identification of child maltreatment, including multiple types of maltreatment (4 studies), sexual abuse (4 studies), emotional abuse (1 study), and physical abuse (15 studies, which included abusive head trauma [10 studies]). Included in these studies are the evaluations of two recently examined screening tools, the SPUTOVAMO tool and the Escape tool. Use of the SPUTOVAMO tool is currently mandatory in emergency department settings in the Netherlands. It is used to identify suspicion of maltreatment with a positive answer to one or more of five questions (e.g., delay in seeking help without satisfactory explanation?) (Schouten et al., 2017). The Escape tool is very similar in design and structure to the SPUTOVAMO tool (Dinpanah & Akbarzadeh Pasha, 2017; Louwers et al., 2014).

McTavish et al. (n.d.) noted that all studies included in the review were rated as at high risk of bias and all but one study evaluating screening of child maltreatment suffered from serious verification bias. The latter study (Sittig et al., 2016) evaluated the effectiveness of the SPUTOVAMO tool in identifying exposure to potential physical abuse or neglect in all children under 8 years of age who presented to an emergency department with a physical injury. Using the findings from this study, and assuming a child maltreatment incidence of 2% (the lower range of incidence rates for emergency room settings) (Louwers, Affourtit, Moll, De Koning, & Korfage, 2010), the SPUTOVAMO tool may miss zero per 100,000 children who were potentially exposed to physical abuse and 334 per 100,000 children who were potentially exposed to neglect. This same tool may lead to 13,230 children per 100,000 being misidentified as potentially physically abused and 13,034 children per 100,000 being misidentified as potentially neglected (McTavish et al., n.d.). The existence of false negatives suggests that those children exposed to maltreatment who need intervention may not have access to the services they need. False positives suggest that several children who are not maltreated are undergoing potentially intrusive intervention responses, such as investigation by child protection services. Given the limited evidence about the benefits of screening for child maltreatment, recent guidance from the WHO mhGAP update does not recommend screening for child maltreatment (WHO, 2015).

IV. What harms may result from ACEs screening?

We are not aware of any assessments to date attempting to assess whether ACEs screening efforts have led to any harm. As noted earlier, there is potential for adverse impacts related to screening in general, and ACEs screening in particular. For example, what is the impact on the person identified as screening high on ACEs? Emphasis on the association of high ACEs values with several health problems, including increased prevalence of mental health conditions (see Chapter 4), could lead to adverse effects such as excessive anxiety or poor decision making based on being labeled as at high risk for health and mental health outcomes. A second area of potential negative impact depends on what is being recommended for those scoring high on ACEs screeners. Unless this is made explicit as part of proposed ACEs screening programs, it is not possible to systematically consider additional risks for harm. An example is whether individuals with high ACEs scores will be referred for a comprehensive mental health assessment. If so, the cost and impact of this should be considered for those not ultimately needing this step (i.e., false positives). Third, it is important to consider the cautions of potential harms identified by Finkelhor (2018) summarized earlier.

V. What are findings from experimental trials using the ACEs screening approach?

To our knowledge, there have been no published experimental trials evaluating ACEs screening programs or the use of ACEs screening tools. Future research trials could help determine if ACEs screening programs result in net health benefits.

VI. Have other critical domains been considered for ACEs screening?

As noted earlier, not all the important domains related to screening are considered in this chapter; but, we will consider two additional domains flagged earlier. The first is considering how screening will be coordinated or integrated within existing health and social service systems. Within this domain, one important aspect to consider is to what degree persons with ACEs have already received or are receiving appropriate interventions (independent of the proposed ACEs screening). While this will vary by jurisdiction, it would seem extreme to assume that no persons with ACEs have had some intervention already, such as mental health intervention related to sequelae from past abuse. They may have sought such help themselves or been identified within the existing health and social service systems (i.e., not connected with ACEs screening). The potential gain from screening would only apply to those not otherwise identified (or not identified in a timely manner).

The other domain introduced earlier is the acceptability of ACEs screening programs to different stakeholders. We are not aware of any peer-reviewed publications that have explicitly examined this dimension about ACEs. Indeed, even for studies of child maltreatment, there has been very little research evaluating the acceptability of screening tools. For example, one study evaluated the acceptability of the "Hague Protocol," where nurses and doctors in the Netherlands attempted to detect child maltreatment in the emergency department based on parental characteristics (e.g., substance use) (Diderich, Fekkes, Dechesne, Buitendijk, & Oudesluys-Murphy, 2015). The authors suggest that most parents who agreed to be interviewed were positive about the screening protocol and would revisit the emergency departments for the same complaints in the future. However, the authors noted that it was very difficult to convince parents to take part in the interview, which may be an indicator of a lack of acceptability for the protocol. To date, the acceptability of screening procedures for ACEs remains unknown.

Directions for future research

Relevant research questions can be developed to address proposed service and policy initiatives when the objectives and assumptions of those service and policy initiatives are clearly articulated. To move forward, it will be important for greater clarity on what proponents of ACEs screening hope to accomplish and how they propose to achieve these aims. Research can then more directly answer the question about effectiveness and specifically whether the benefits outweigh the risks.

Using the questions outlined in this chapter, which are derived from well-considered principles of health screening, could be informative. For example, if those advocating for ACEs screening can more clearly identify the intended target groups, this will inform the search for relevant evidence-based interventions. It will also provide the opportunity to determine if such evidence-based interventions can be made available for the population so identified. Clarity regarding targeted groups would also guide advances in examining accuracy of the screening tools. Unless the target group is clearly identified, the examination of critical variables such as false positives and false negatives cannot move forward. Assuming that all these components are in place, it is still critical to require formal evaluation through screening trials, preferably through randomized controlled trials, as even the most well-intentioned efforts with strong supporting evidence do not necessarily translate into improved health outcomes, nor ensure that benefits outweigh harms.

It should be emphasized that while our aim has been to highlight some of the most important questions to consider, we have not provided an exhaustive list of relevant questions to inform decisions about health screening. Other questions could certainly be generated from the complete list of principles of health screening (Dobrow et al., 2018), which would identify additional areas to consider for future research.

Implications for policy and practice

Based on the evidence to date, it is important for practitioners and policy makers to understand that screening for ACEs is not justified. There should be an awareness of the importance of ACEs, and their association with physical and mental health problems; but, these are not sufficient reasons to implement screening. The current emphasis should be on development of evidence-based interventions for conditions associated with ACEs, and identification of effective approaches to preventing ACEs. These undertakings do not require routine screening for ACEs, but would entail important investment to address ACEs.

Conclusion

At this time, we conclude that there is insufficient evidence to support the routine implementation of ACEs screening in the population. This should not be misconstrued as suggesting that ACEs are not important. It is essential that society aim to reduce the prevalence of ACEs in the population and to support those who have experienced negative sequelae as a function of ACEs. There is, however, no compelling evidence that ACEs screening will contribute to realizing these aims.

References

Artinian, N. T., Fletcher, G. F., Mozaffarian, D., Kris-Etherton, P., Van Horn, L., Lichtenstein, A. H., … Burke, L. E. (2010). Interventions to promote physical activity and dietary lifestyle changes for cardiovascular risk factor reduction in adults: a scientific statement from the American Heart Association. *Circulation*, *122*(4), 406–441.

Bailhache, M., Leroy, V., Pillet, P., & Salmi, L.-R. (2013). Is early detection of abused children possible? A systematic review of the diagnostic accuracy of the identification of abused children. *BMC Pediatrics*, *13*(1), 202.

Brodersen, J., & Siersma, V. (2013). Long-term psychosocial consequences of false-positive mammography screening. *Annals of Family Medicine*, *11*(2), 106–115.

Charach, A., Carson, P., Fox, S., Ali, M. U., Beckett, J., & Lim, C. G. (2013). Interventions for preschool children at high risk for ADHD: a comparative effectiveness review. *Pediatrics*, *131*(5), e1584–e1604.

Charach, A., McLennan, J. D., Bélanger, S. A., & Nixon, M. K. (2017). A joint statement from the Canadian Academy of Child and Adolescent Psychiatry and the Canadian Paediatric Society: screening for disruptive behaviour problems in preschool children in primary health care settings. *Journal of the Canadian Academy of Child and Adolescent Psychiatry*, *26*(3), 172–178.

de Arellano, M. A. R., Lyman, D. R., Jobe-Shields, L., George, P., Dougherty, R. H., Daniels, A. S., … Delphin-Rittmon, M. E. (2014). Trauma-focused cognitive-behavioral therapy for children and adolescents: assessing the evidence. *Psychiatric Services*, *65*(5), 591–602.

Diderich, H. M., Fekkes, M., Dechesne, M., Buitendijk, S. E., & Oudesluys-Murphy, A. M. (2015). Detecting child abuse based on parental characteristics: Does the Hague protocol cause parents to avoid the emergency department? *International Emergency Nursing*, *23*(2), 203–206.

Dinpanah, H., & Akbarzadeh Pasha, A. (2017). Potential child abuse screening in emergency department: a diagnostic accuracy study. *Emergency (Tehran, Iran)*, *5*(1), e8.

Dobrow, M. J., Hagens, V., Chafe, R., Sullivan, T., & Rabeneck, L. (2018). Consolidated principles for screening based on a systematic review and consensus process. *Canadian Medical Association Journal*, *190*(14), E422–E429.

Felitti, V. J., Anda, R. F., Nordenberg, D., Williamson, D. F., Spitz, A. M., Edwards, V., … Marks, J. S. (1998). Relationship of childhood abuse and household dysfunction to many of the leading causes of death in adults. The adverse childhood experiences (ACE) study. *American Journal of Preventive Medicine*, *14*(4), 245–258.

Finkelhor, D. (2018). Screening for adverse childhood experiences (ACEs): cautions and suggestions. *Child Abuse & Neglect*, *85*, 174–179.

Finkelhor, D., Hamby, S. L., Ormrod, R., & Turner, H. (2005). The juvenile victimization questionnaire: reliability, validity, and national norms. *Child Abuse & Neglect*, *29*(4), 383–412.

Finkelhor, D., Shattuck, A., Turner, H., & Hamby, S. (2013). Improving the adverse childhood experiences study scale. *JAMA Pediatrics*, *167*(1), 70–75.

Finkelhor, D., Shattuck, A., Turner, H., & Hamby, S. (2015). A revised inventory of adverse childhood experiences. *Child Abuse & Neglect*, *48*, 13–21.

Goldenberg, A. J., Comeau, A. M., Grosse, S. D., Tanksley, S., Prosser, L. A., Ojodu, J., … Green, N. S. (2016). Evaluating harms in the assessment of net benefit: a framework for newborn screening condition review. *Maternal and Child Health Journal*, *20*(3), 693–700.

Hughes, K., Bellis, M. A., Hardcastle, K. A., Sethi, D., Butchart, A., Mikton, C., … Dunne, M. P. (2017). The effect of multiple adverse childhood experiences on health: a systematic review and meta-analysis. *The Lancet Public Health*, *2*(8), e356–e366.

Liberman, A. M., Kirk, D. S., & Kim, K. (2014). Labeling effects of first juvenile arrests: secondary deviance and secondary sanctioning. *Criminology*, *52*(3), 345–370.

Louwers, E.C.F.M., Affourtit, M. J., Moll, H. A., De Koning, H. J., & Korfage, I. J. (2010). Screening for child abuse at emergency departments: a systematic review. *Archives of Disease in Childhood*, *95*(3), 214–218.

Louwers, E.C.F.M., Korfage, I. J., Affourtit, M. J., Ruige, M., van den Elzen, A. P. M., de Koning, H. J., & Moll, H. A. (2014). Accuracy of a screening instrument to identify potential child abuse in emergency departments. *Child Abuse & Neglect*, *38*(7), 1275–1281.

MacMillan, H. L., Wathen, C., Jamieson, E., Boyle, M., Shannon, H., Ford-Gilboe, M., … McNutt, L. (2009). Screening for intimate partner violence in health care settings: a randomized trial. *JAMA*, *302*(5), 493–501.

Mant, D., & Fowler, G. (1990). Mass screening: theory and ethics. *BMJ*, *300*, 916–918.

McTavish, J. R., Gonzalez, A., MacGregor, J. C. D., McKee, C., Santesso, N., & MacMillan, H. L. (n.d.). Identification of child maltreatment: An update of a systematic review. Unpublished manuscript.

Meader, N., Moe-Byrne, T., Llewellyn, A., & Mitchell, A. J. (2014). Screening for poststroke major depression: a meta-analysis of diagnostic validity studies. *Journal of Neurology, Neurosurgery, and Psychiatry*, *85*(2), 198–206.

Mustafa, R. A., Wiercioch, W., Santesso, N., Cheung, A., Prediger, B., Baldeh, T., … Schünemann, H. J. (2015). Decision-making about healthcare related tests and diagnostic strategies: user testing of GRADE evidence tables. *PLoS One*, *10*(10), e0134553.

National Center for Health Statistics. (1991). *Exposure to alcoholism in the family*. Washington, DC: U.S. Department of Health and Human Services.

O'Doherty, L., Hegarty, K., Ramsay, J., Davidson, L. L., Feder, G., & Taft, A. (2015). Screening women for intimate partner violence in healthcare settings. *The Cochrane Database of Systematic Reviews*, *7*, CD007007.

Rüsch, N., Corrigan, P. W., Heekeren, K., Theodoridou, A., Dvorsky, D., Metzler, S., … Rössler, W. (2014). Well-being among persons at risk of psychosis: the role of self-labeling, shame, and stigma stress. *Psychiatric Services*, *65*(4), 483–489.

Schouten, M. C. M., Van Stel, H. F., Verheij, T. J. M., Houben, M. L., Russel, I. M. B., Nieuwenhuis, E. E. S., & Van De Putte, E. M. (2017). The value of a checklist for child abuse in out-of-hours primary care: to screen or not to screen. *PLoS One*, *12*(1), 1–12.

Shickle, D., & Chadwick, R. (1994). The ethics of screening: is "screeningitis" an incurable disease? *Journal of Medical Ethics*, *20*(1), 12–18.

Sittig, J. S., Uiterwaal, C.S.P.M., Moons, K. G. M., Russel, I. M. B., Nievelstein, R. A. J., Nieuwenhuis, E. E. S., & Van De Putte, E. M. (2016). Value of systematic detection of physical child abuse at emergency rooms: a cross-sectional diagnostic accuracy study. *BMJ Open*, *6*(3), 1–7.

Straus, M., & Gelles, R. J. (1978). *Physical violence in American families: Risk factors and adaptation to violence in 8,145 families*. New York, NY: John Wiley & Sons.
Whiting, P. F., Rutjes, A. W. S., Westwood, M. E., Mallett, S., Deeks, J. J., Reitsma, J. B., ... Bossuyt, P. M. M. (2011). QUADAS-2: a revised tool for the quality assessment of diagnostic accuracy studies. *Annals of Internal Medicine*, *155*(8), 529–536.
World Health Organization (WHO). (2015). *Update of the mental health gap action programme (mhGAP) guideline for mental, neurological and substance use disorders*. May 20, 2018, Retrieved from: http://apps.who.int/iris/bitstream/10665/204132/1/9789241549417_eng.pdf?ua=1.
Wyatt, G. E. (1985). The sexual abuse of Afro-American and white-American women in childhood. *Child Abuse & Neglect*, *9*(4), 507–519.

CHAPTER

9

Methodological considerations in ACEs research

George W. Holden, Tricia Gower, Michael Chmielewski

Southern Methodist University, Dallas, TX, United States

Introduction

To date, researchers examining adverse childhood experiences (ACEs) have made valuable contributions to our understanding of the effects of childhood adversity on the subsequent physical and mental health in adults (e.g., Anda et al., 2006; Edwards, Holden, Felitti, & Anda, 2003; Felitti et al., 1998). However, the accuracy of ACEs research and the utility of the instrument are at least partly dependent on how well childhood adversities are assessed. In this chapter, we examine the different manifestations of the ACEs instruments and the evidence about their psychometric qualities. We then discuss general methodological issues associated with ACEs instruments. We also briefly review alternative instruments that assess ACEs, make recommendations for future research concerning how ACEs instruments could be improved, and end with a discussion of some research implications.

Multiple manifestations of the ACEs instrument

The original ACEs instrument

What is known as the ACEs instrument is actually a subset of the questions in a lengthy questionnaire called the Family Health History Survey (FHH; CDC, 2016). That survey consists of 148 questions assessing demographic information, a wide variety of lifestyle and health issues (e.g., smoking, drinking, street drugs), as well as living situations, family context, and

https://doi.org/10.1016/B978-0-12-816065-7.00009-4

functioning. There are also questions about current mental health. Embedded in the FHH instrument are 17 questions (also called items) that address negative experiences during the first 18 years of life.

In the initial data collection effort, called Wave I of the ACEs Study, Felitti et al. (1998) collected data on eight types of adverse experiences, but only included seven ACEs in this first publication. Three of the types (also called domains or categories in some publications) addressed manifestations of child abuse—physical, sexual, and emotional. Physical and emotional abuse were assessed with two questions each, and sexual abuse was assessed with four questions. The remaining five categories addressed family or household dysfunction or challenges with violence directed at mother or stepmother (four questions), exposure to alcohol or substance abuse (two questions), mental illness (two questions), incarceration (one question), and parental separation or divorce (one question). These categories formed two general classes of problems—child abuse and family or household challenges. We label this version of the ACEs the *original* instrument.

An *expanded original* instrument, one that grew from 17 questions to 28 questions, was given to participants in Wave II of the ACEs Study (Dube, Williamson, Thompson, Felitti, & Anda, 2004). The new instrument maintained the two classes of problems (i.e., child abuse and family or household challenges), but expanded the number of types of adverse experiences to 10. The two new categories were emotional neglect (five questions) and physical neglect (five questions).

The questions in the *original* instrument appeared in one of two response formats: a dichotomous "yes/no" response scale or an ordinal response rating scale. Of the 28 questions used in Wave II, 10 were responded to dichotomously (i.e., questions regarding household mental illness, substance abuse, incarceration, and sexual abuse). However, 18 questions (i.e., those regarding interparental violence, emotional and physical neglect, and emotional and physical abuse) were responded to using a 5-point Likert-type rating scale concerning frequency (*never* to *very often*) or truth (*never true* to *very often true*). These ordinal scale responses were then dichotomized into whether the problem had been present or absent.

As Felitti and colleagues (Anda et al., 2006; Felitti et al., 1998) reported, the *original* ACEs questions were simply lifted from previously published surveys. For example, the physical and psychological abuse questions as well as the questions assessing violence against mothers came from the Conflict Tactics Scale (CTS; Straus, 1979). Emotional and physical neglect questions were drawn from the Childhood Trauma Questionnaire-Short Form (CTQ-SF; Bernstein et al., 1994). Sexual contact questions were adapted from the Wyatt Sexual History Questionnaire, and the exposure to substance abuse question came from questions developed by Schoenborn (1991).

Modified ACEs measures

Since the first ACEs publication appeared in the late 1990s (Felitti et al., 1998), a number of modifications of the *original* instrument have been made. Bethell et al. (2017) found 14 different ACEs instruments. We identified six additional versions. Of those 20 versions, the most common modification consists of adding more content areas, as will be discussed later. Although many of these modified instruments capture similar constructs, they often contain questions with slightly revised wording. For example, a question in the *original* instrument was *During your first 18 years of life, did you live with anyone who used street drugs?* That question became *Did you live with anyone who used illegal street drugs or who abused prescription medications?* in the Behavioral Risk Factor Surveillance Survey (BRFSS; Ford et al., 2014).

To catalog all the derivatives of the ACEs questionnaire goes beyond the scope of this chapter; instead, we will focus on illustrating the alternative instruments by discussing the versions that have appeared in multiple publications. Of the 20 manifestations of ACEs instruments that we are aware of, six instruments have each appeared in three or more journal publications. The *original*, *expanded original*, and six modifications vary on four dimensions: the length, the number of categories assessed, the wording of questions, and the types of rating scales used (see Table 1). We briefly describe the six different versions.

The three shortest scales range in length from 8 to 11 questions. The ACE-Abuse Short Form (ACE-ASF) comprises eight items focused solely on physical, emotional, and sexual child abuse as well as spanking, and "being punched or beaten up" (Brett, Espeleta, Lopez, Leavens, & Leffingwell, 2018; Espeleta, Brett, Ridings, Leavens, & Mullins, 2018; Meinck et al., 2017). A 9-item scale, called the National Survey of Children's Health-Adverse Childhood Experiences (NSCH-ACEs), leaves out questions about child abuse and neglect; but, like the *original* ACEs instrument, it includes questions concerning financial hardship, loss of a biological parent, household mental illness, substance abuse, and domestic violence (Bethell et al., 2017; Bethell, Newacheck, Hawes, & Halfon, 2014; Heard-Garris, Davis, Szilagyi, & Kan, 2018). The NSCH-ACEs expands into new adversity content areas as well by including questions about racial discrimination and neighborhood violence. Notably, this instrument comes in two formats, including one for self-reports and one for concurrent parent-reports. A third short instrument is the 11-item BRFSS (Bensley, Van Eenwyk, & Simmons, 2000, 2003; Ford et al., 2014). This scale includes questions adapted from the *original* ACEs instrument but uses three, rather than two, questions to assess child sexual abuse.

Three more extensive ACEs instruments have also been developed. A 17-item measure that borrowed heavily from the BRFSS is labeled the Childhood Experiences Survey (CES; Mersky & Janczewski, 2018; Mersky, Janczewski, & Nitkowski, 2018; Mersky et al., 2017). This survey, designed

TABLE 1 Eight ACEs Instruments, Their Formats, and Psychometric Properties

Instrument and source	Format	ACE score	Reliability	Validity
Original ACEs Instrument Felitti et al., 1998	7 categories, 17 questions	0–7	–	EV[a]
Expanded Original ACEs Instrument Dube et al., 2004	10 categories, 28 questions	0–10	A[h]; TRT[a]	PV[h]
ACE Abuse Short-Form (ACE-ASF) Meinck, Cosma, Mikton, & Baban, 2017	3 categories, 8 questions	0–8	A[b]	EFA[b]; CFA[b]; PV[b]
Behavioral Risk Factor Surveillance Survey (BRFSS) Ford et al., 2014	8 categories, 11 questions	0–8	A[c]; IT-r[c]	CFA[c]
ACE-Screener Wingenfeld et al., 2011	10 categories, 10 questions	0–10	A[d]; II-r[d]	PV[d]; CvgV[d]
National Survey of Children's Health-ACEs (NSCH-ACEs) Bethell et al., 2017	9 categories, 9 questions	0–9	II-r[e]; IT-r[e]	CFA[e]; LCA[e]; PV[e]
ACE-International Questionnaire (ACE-IQ) Kazeem, 2015	13 categories, 43 questions	0–13	A[f]	CvgV[f]
Childhood Experiences Survey Expanded CES Mersky, Janczewski, & Topitzes, 2017	17 categories, 17 questions	0–17	A[g]; TRT[g]	EFA[g]; PV[g]

[a]*Dube et al. (2004).*
[b]*Meinck et al. (2017).*
[c]*Ford et al. (2014).*
[d]*Wingenfeld et al. (2011).*
[e]*Bethell et al. (2017).*
[f]*Kazeem (2015).*
[g]*Mersky et al. (2017).*
[h]*Murphy et al. (2014).*
Notes. A = Cronbach's *alpha*; CFA = confirmatory factor analysis; CvgV = convergent validity; EFA = exploratory factor analysis; LCA = latent class analysis; II-r = item-item correlation; IT-r = item-total correlation; PV = predictive validity; TRT = test-retest reliability.

to assess a broad range of ACEs, includes eight BRFSS questions, two questions about physical and emotional neglect, and seven questions assessing frequent family financial problems, food insecurity, homelessness, prolonged parental absence, death of a parent or sibling, frequent peer victimization, and violent crime victimization. A longer instrument, a 21-item version to assess ACEs, is named the Philadelphia ACEs Survey (Bethell et al., 2017; Cronholm et al., 2015; Wade et al., 2016). In order to augment its applicability to urban populations, it includes questions about experiencing racism, witnessing violence, being bullied, living in foster care, and residing in unsafe neighborhoods. The most lengthy instrument is the ACE-International Questionnaire (ACE-IQ) (Almuneef, ElChoueiry, Saleheen, & Al-Eissa, 2017; Almuneef, Qayad, Aleissa, & Albuhairan, 2014; Kazeem, 2015). Created from the BRFSS, it was expanded to assess 13 categories of adversity based on 43 questions. In addition to the eight categories from its parent instrument (with questions reworded, such as spanking and slapping), the survey includes emotional and physical neglect, bullying, community violence, and war (or collective violence). Among the eight instruments listed in Table 1, the only two that share the identical core set of items are the BRFSS and the CES. Nine of items use the exact same wording.

Psychometric properties of the ACEs instruments

How good are the ACEs instruments? Good survey questions are clear and specific, thereby avoiding ambiguity and misinterpretations (e.g., Holden & Edwards, 1989). Items should not be "double-barreled," ensuring that the respondent is answering only one question at a time. Many of the ACEs instruments can be critiqued for failing to follow those basic rules. For example, respondents are asked whether something happen "often" or "very often" without a definition of what that adverb means. Several questions contain multiple parts and clearly violate the admonition about double-barreled items; for example, the question about parental loss in a common version of the ACEs instrument includes three very different causes, including divorce, abandonment, or "some other reason." Another limitation is that the type of adversity is sometimes confounded with the severity of an abusive act; for example, items from the physical abuse item include both mild forms of physical abuse (i.e., "push," "grab") and very severe forms ("hit so hard... you were injured"). One can evidently critique some of the items on many of the ACEs instruments. But, ultimately, the appropriate assessment of the quality of an instrument lies in its construct validity.

Construct validity, the extent to which a measure assesses the idea that it is intended to capture (in this case, ACEs), is the key for comprehensively evaluating the quality of any instrument (Chmielewski, Sala, Tang, & Baldwin, 2016; Clark & Watson, 1995; Cronbach & Meehl, 1955; Loevinger, 1957; Strauss & Smith, 2009). Indeed, this form of validity subsumes all forms of reliability and validity. High-quality instruments, by definition, must be both reliable and valid.

In the simplest terms, the reliability of a measure refers to its consistency. Different types of consistency (e.g., consistency between items, consistency over time) are assessed by one or more indices of reliability. The index for an instrument's consistency in responses between items (i.e., internal consistency) is Cronbach's *alpha*. Test-retest reliability measures the consistency with which the items are answered in the same way over time. Validity is more complex. The four major types of validity are content, criterion (which includes concurrent and predictive), convergent, and discriminant (sometimes referred to as divergent) (e.g., see Taylor & Asmundson, 2008). In addition, there are numerous other forms of validity (e.g., structural, known-groups) that also fall under construct validity.

We start this section by reviewing the psychometric properties of the *original* ACEs instrument and then the alternate versions. The *original* ACEs instrument, as mentioned earlier, borrowed items from previously established surveys. Only two of those established instruments—the CTS (Straus, 1979) and the CTQ-SF (Bernstein, Ahluvalia, Pogge, & Handelsman, 1997; Bernstein et al., 1994)—have strong psychometric properties. However, one should not assume that the evidence for the psychometric properties of items taken from previously developed instruments remains the same in a new instrument.

The *original* as well as the *expanded original* ACEs instruments have received little psychometric evaluation. The one exception we located was a study by Murphy and colleagues (Murphy et al., 2014), who assessed one index of reliability and one type of validity. They reported that the *expanded original* ACEs instrument had good internal consistency ($\alpha = 0.88$) as well as good predictive validity with adult attachment classifications. Given the popularity of the ACEs concept, it is surprising that there have not been more tests of the *original* or *expanded original* instrument. Evidently, the psychometrics of the *original* ACEs instrument needs further psychometric scrutiny. However, in each of the six other versions of the ACEs, there is at least one study providing psychometric information. We now summarize the available data on the reliability and validity of all the eight instruments listed in Table 1.

Reliability

Data about reliability can be found for seven of the eight versions of the ACEs instruments listed in Table 1. The most common form of reliability assessed in these instruments is internal consistency, as measured by Cronbach's *alpha* or item-total correlations. In general, the recommended minimum Cronbach's *alpha* is 0.70 with above 0.80 being preferable (Clark & Watson, 1995; Nunnally & Bernstein, 1994). Evidence for internal consistency is available for six instruments. The ACE-ASF total scale, using a sample of 1733 adolescents, had adequate internal consistency ($\alpha = 0.71$;

Meinck et al., 2017). The CES also has also demonstrated adequate internal consistency ($\alpha = 0.81$; Mersky et al., 2017), as has the ACE-IQ (Kazeem, 2015). The BRFSS, in a nationally representative sample of more than 85,000 mostly white middle-aged adults, had an overall *alpha* of 0.80 with item-total correlations ranging from 0.45 to 0.80 (Ford et al., 2014). In another nationally representative sample of almost 95,700 parents of children aged 0 to 17 years, the NSCH-ACEs were found to have lower item-total correlations than the BRFSS, with a range from 0.13 to 0.49 (Bethell et al., 2017). Overall, the internal consistency of the ACEs instruments is typically in the acceptable range.

The other major type of reliability for surveys is test-retest reliability. However, evidence for test-retest reliability can be found for only two of the eight ACEs instruments. Using a subsample of 658 individuals who completed the *expanded original* survey in both Waves I (collected in 1995) and II (collect 2 years later), Dube et al. (2004) found Cohen's *kappa* coefficients ranged from only 0.46 to 0.86. The only other instrument with test-retest reliability data is the CES. The *kappa* coefficients between items across an average of 9 months ranged from 0.41 to 0.82 (Mersky et al., 2017). In evaluating these coefficients, it is essential to remember that the participants were adults at both assessment times. As such, it is impossible for the experiences they had as children to change over the test-retest interval. They either were or were not abused as children, their parents either did or did not engage in intimate partner violence, and so forth. Therefore, ideally, the test-retest coefficients should be 1.0 or close to it (Chmielewski et al., 2016; Chmielewski & Watson, 2009). Although coefficients in the 0.80 range are recognized to reflect an acceptable level of measurement error, those instruments with a test-retest coefficient below 0.70 are clearly problematic. In summing up the reliability evidence, the ACEs instruments appear to have acceptable to good internal consistency but more data are needed regarding their test-retest reliability.

Validity

Validity evidence is available for all eight instruments listed in Table 1. We found evidence for five types of validity, assessed in a variety of ways. For example, reports of predictive validity can be found in five studies, convergent validity in two studies, and structural validity (e.g., exploratory and/or confirmatory factor analysis) in four studies. Predictive validity is exemplified by the dose-response relations frequently reported in the ACEs literature regarding emotional, mental, or behavioral health costs of childhood adversities (e.g., Bethell et al., 2017; Mersky et al., 2017). There is also evidence for concurrent and convergent validity. Concurrent criterion validity has been shown with the ACE-ASF by including such variables as quality of life, life satisfaction, self-perceived health, bullying victimization and perpetration, and behavior problems (Meinck et al., 2017). Convergent validity evidence was found in a sample of 253 Nigerian prisoners, wherein Kazeem (2015) reported that correlations between the ACE-IQ and the CTQ ranged from 0.49 to 0.72.

Like the reliability assessments, we found some evidence in only eight studies about the validity of the ACEs instruments. Thinking about the construct validity of the instruments, as formed by both reliability and validity assessments, there are far too few investigations into the psychometric properties. Internal consistency, as assessed by Cronbach's *alphas*, was the most commonly reported form of reliability. Fewer studies document the validity of the instruments. Of the eight instruments listed in Table 1, the instrument with the most psychometric properties assessed and reported is the NSCH-ACEs (Bethell et al., 2017). That publication lists five properties. Two of the instruments have four psychometric properties identified, three instruments have three properties, and the other two instruments have either two or one published psychometric properties.

Which instrument is the best one? The answer to that question is, of course, it depends. It depends on what types of adverse experiences need to be covered, what depth of questioning is desired, how many items can be included, and how much evidence is available concerning its psychometric properties. The instrument that assesses the most types of ACEs is the expanded CES (Mersky et al., 2017). It yields scores of up to 17. The longest instrument, containing 43 items, is the ACE-IQ. Not surprisingly, it provides the most thorough assessment of ACEs, with a total adversity score of up to 13. However, the psychometric information available for it is limited to internal consistency and convergent validity. The instrument with the most psychometric information is the NSCH-ACEs; but, it contains only nine items about adverse experiences in childhood.

The answer to the question of which instrument to use depends on such considerations as the focus of the study, the context, and the time that is available to answer the adversity items. All of the instruments appear to be at least adequate for a rudimentary assessment of certain ACEs. Our view is that more extensive assessments provide richer information and, therefore, are preferable.

Methodological issues of ACEs instruments

In reviewing the ACEs instruments, a number of methodological issues and concerns can be raised. For example, the *original* ACEs survey was not created using optimal strategies for instrument development (e.g., see Clark & Watson, 1995; Loevinger, 1957; Strauss & Smith, 2009). This requires, among other things, that researchers begin by identifying the full potential array of ACEs. Then researchers need to conduct structural analyses to empirically test this array and identify the domains that should be included in the ACEs instrument. An iterative process of testing, revising, and retesting the item pool is also required. Simultaneously, researchers must ensure that items are not tapping into other related constructs (e.g., neuroticism, negative affect, current depression). In addition, test-retest analyses need to be designed into the scale development process to ensure the final measure has adequate test-retest reliability. Importantly, each stage of scale development should involve multiple large samples (e.g., community, hospital patient, student) to examine the replicability of results and ensure the scales are generalizable.

Rather than adopting that approach, the approach adopted for many ACEs instruments was to borrow one or more items from other instruments. We found only one ACEs-related instrument, the Maltreatment and Abuse Chronology of Exposure Scale (MACE) (Teicher & Parigger, 2015), that was developed by investigators who followed the optimal approach for constructing scales. Another concern is the practice of condensing 28 items into a 10-item ACEs score. By aggregating different types of adversity into single items, the precision of the ACEs score is reduced. Third, as mentioned earlier, the psychometric properties of many of the instruments have not been adequately tested.

In addition to concerns about the creation and evaluation of the instruments, there are four methodological issues that merit discussion. Three of these concern additional subtypes of validity. First, does the instrument demonstrate measurement invariance, i.e., is the instrument equally appropriate for assessing adversity from a variety of individuals? Second, does the instrument comprehensively assess the many forms of childhood adversity? This is an issue of content validity. Specifically, are some key sources of trauma missing from the instruments? Third, what is the underlying factor structure of childhood adversities? This is the issue of the structural validity of the instruments. A fourth more general but critical methodological issue concerns the accuracy of adult retrospective memories of childhood adversity. Each of these issues are discussed now.

Measurement invariance

Measurement invariance refers to whether an instrument is interpreted in the same way across different groups of individuals. For example, if participants react differently to the wording or the content of a measure, the instrument will not be equivalent to individuals from diverse backgrounds. Without evidence of measurement invariance across different demographic groups, the instrument may be susceptible to measurement errors.

A key way to ensure equivalent interpretation of the instrument across groups is to avoid ambiguity and to phrase items such that they focus on specific and concrete behaviors (Pinto, Correia, & Maia, 2014). Simple and clear language is preferable. Items also need to avoid colloquialisms and, instead, use language that will be consistently interpreted across ages, sex, ethnicity, regions of a country, socioeconomic groups, and, if possible, cultures. As an example, the *original* ACEs instrument contains a problematic item: *Did an adult or person at least 5 years older ever touch or fondle you in a sexual way*? (italics added). The phrase "in a sexual way" is not specific enough to represent an objective behavior and, therefore, may lead to ambiguity in interpretation across participants.

Little effort has been devoted to testing the measurement invariance of the ACEs instruments. We found three studies that provide some evidence for invariance. The BRFSS has evidence for both configural (i.e., the factor structure is equivalent across groups) and metric (i.e., factor loadings are constrained equally across groups, but intercepts are allowed to differ) invariance across age and sex of respondent (Ford et al., 2014). Additionally, the ACE-ASF has metric, but not scalar (i.e., factor loadings and intercepts are constrained across groups), invariance (Meinck et al., 2017). A 13-item measure of ACEs pulled from the Panel Study of Income Dynamics also demonstrated invariance across boys and girls (Olofson, 2018). Although these studies do provide some support for the measurement invariance of ACEs instruments, there are still many ACEs instruments and participant characteristics that have yet to be evaluated for measurement invariance. This psychometric deficit limits the potential to make accurate comparisons between different groups of participants.

The lack of measurement invariance raises questions about some of the findings of the ACEs studies. For example, data from the NSCH-ACEs instrument indicate that black and Hispanic children are exposed to greater adversity than white children, even though the instrument has not been evaluated for measurement invariance across race (Slopen et al., 2016). Additional investigations testing the different ACEs instruments and using multiple samples are needed to confirm measurement invariance.

The assessment of adversities

The strength of the ACEs instruments is that they provide a quick snapshot of an individual's childhood adversities; but, a single, narrowly focused snapshot is limited. The *original* ACEs instrument assessed only seven categories of adversity. Subsequent instruments have expanded the view to give a wider angle assessment of adversity, such as including poverty, exposure to community violence, and discrimination. By omitting commonly experienced adversities, ACEs measures may underestimate differences in cumulative adversities. Other negative childhood experiences that are beginning to be recognized in ACEs instruments include physical punishment (Afifi et al., 2017), being bullied, peer victimization, experiencing isolation and peer rejection, living in foster care, being

TABLE 2 Types of Adverse Experiences Assessed in ACEs Instruments

Child maltreatment	Environmental adversities

• Physical abuse
• Physical punishment
• Sexual abuse
• Emotional abuse
• Exposed to mother's physical abuse
• Victimized by peer (bullying)
• Victimized by peer social isolation
• Victim of violent crime
• Discrimination
	• Mental illness in the family
	• Substance abuse in the family
	• Incarcerated family members
	• Parental separation/divorce
	• Economic hardship
	    • Food insecurity
	    • Homelessness
	• Violence exposure
	    • Neighborhood violent
	    • Living in war zone
	• Death of a parent/sibling

confronted with serious accidents or illnesses, disasters, or living in a war zone (Cronholm et al., 2015; Finkelhor, Shattuck, Turner, & Hamby, 2013; Mersky et al., 2017) (see Table 2).

Two other key dimensions of adversity that typically go unrecognized in these instruments are severity and chronicity. Each adversity in the existing instruments receives the same unweighted score and then the scores are added together. However, this cumulative scoring does not account for variations in severity by type of adverse experiences. For instance, parental separation is likely a less traumatic experience than being abused (Finkelhor et al., 2013; Green et al., 2010); but both of these ACEs receive equal weight in the cumulative score. In fact, in cases of high conflict marriages, parental separation or diverse can be beneficial for children's well-being (Arkes, 2017).

Even though evidence for a dose-response relation between ACEs and health outcomes consistently emerges irrespective of the specific adversities involved, weighting of the particular adversities based on their severity may improve the predictive power of a given instrument (Schilling, Aseltine, & Gore, 2008). For example, compared with other ACEs, emotional abuse and physical neglect have been found to be most detrimental to brain development (Teicher et al., 2018). Additionally, certain adverse events, such as the death of a family member or abuse, are more detrimental to mental health outcomes than other negative experiences (Kilpatrick et al., 2013).

Weighting adversity by severity is a complex task; indeed, large and well-defined samples are required to determine appropriate weights. But, the increased precision will likely result in improved predictive validity. For example, when the Cumulative Childhood Adversity Scale was scored using "effect proportional" weighting based on effect sizes, the prediction of psychopathology was improved (Schilling et al., 2008). An alternative approach is to use a regression weighting approach, which combines adversities according to their severity. This strategy increases the explanatory power of the instrument to predict health outcomes (e.g., Schilling et al., 2008).

Related to the severity is the timing and chronicity of the adversity. At what age did it start and how long did it continue? The ACEs instruments typically use "before age 18 years" as the timeline to respond to events occurring. However, failure to account for the child's specific phase of development results in the omission of valuable predictive information. For instance, according to one study, preschoolers (4- to 5-year-old children) and preadolescents (8- to 9-year-old youth) have been found to be most susceptible to the effects of neglect on subsequent psychopathology (Schalinski et al., 2016). Chronic sexual abuse yields a greater likelihood of psychopathology than a single incident of sexual abuse (Molnar, Buka, & Kessler, 2001); but, that information is ignored in the instruments. In fact, allostatic or stress theory posits that chronicity of exposure to adversity results in poorer outcomes (e.g., Danese & McEwen, 2012). Separating ACEs by their onset would also afford the ability to capture the temporal co-occurrence of ACEs and, by accounting for chronicity, the ACEs score could more accurately predict adverse health outcomes. It is likely that the effects of cumulative adversity are not linear, although such an assumption underlies the typical ACEs scoring approach. Instead, there may be a positive curvilinear relation between ACEs and outcomes, as happens when an individual becomes sensitized to adversity following cumulative exposure (Schilling et al., 2008).

To fully capture an individual's susceptibility to childhood adversity, protective factors also need to be recognized. Children may be buffered from the negative effects of ACEs by certain individual, family, and environmental factors, including at least one nurturing parent, multiple forms of social support, higher socioeconomic status, more education, and access to neighborhood resources (Wade, Shea, Rubin, & Wood, 2014). These types of resiliency factors have only received preliminary attention in the context of ACEs studies (e.g., Bethell, Gombojav, Solloway, & Wissow, 2016). Investigators should include the assessment of protective factors along with ACEs (e.g., Bethell et al., 2017).

Factor structure

An integral issue concerning the assessment of adversities is factor structure. Do all the adversities load onto one factor or multiple factors? To date, ACEs instruments have either not been evaluated for factor structure, or, if they have, discrepant findings have emerged. For example, a three-factor structure emerged with the 11-item BRFSS (Ford et al., 2014). The factors were physical/emotional abuse, sexual victimization, and household dysfunction. However, when Mersky et al. (2017) added neglect items to the instrument, they found a two-factor structure (i.e., child maltreatment and household dysfunction). With the shorter 8-item ACE-ASF, a two-factor structure of physical/emotional abuse and sexual abuse emerged (Meinck et al., 2017). Olofson and colleagues (2017) also found two factors with their 13-item ACEs measure. Using exploratory factor analysis on the 17-item CES, a four-factor solution was identified and comprised emotional/physical neglect, interpersonal victimization with household problems, family loss and separation, and poverty (Mersky et al., 2017). These variations in factor structure highlight a problem with the ACEs questionnaires; specifically, the central dimensions of the adverse experiences are still unclear. The factor structures, ranging from two to four, highlight the need for careful evaluations of the structure of ACEs using confirmatory factor analyses.

Retrospective recall

All of the ACEs instruments use self-reported retrospective memories. That approach provides a fast, convenient, and economical way to get a snapshot of negative childhood experiences. But, are those reports veridical? The ACEs instruments have two fundamental types of threats to their accuracy: biases associated with self-reports and errors from relying on retrospective memories.

Depending on the type of question posed, self-reports can be susceptible to a variety of biases, both within and between participants, due to such processes as social desirability, demand characteristics, or expectancy effects (e.g., Schwarz, 2007). This problem is potentially particularly acute if someone is asked to disclose traumatic events (Meinck et al., 2017). Demographic characteristics, most notably gender and education, can affect the accuracy of the self-report of ACEs. For example, gender stereotypes and shame may lead men to underreport sexual abuse (Ayalon, 2015). Lower levels of education are associated with greater inconsistency of reports over time, something also attributed to limited literacy or experience with surveys (Ayalon, 2015; Brener, Collins, Kann, Warren, & Williams, 1995).

Collecting retrospective memories and assuming they are veridical reports of childhood events is even more problematic. There are many reasons to suspect that some recollections are inaccurate. To recall childhood adversities with clarity, the informant must first correctly encode the incident or experience. Then, after a gap of years or even decades, the informant must retrieve that memory. The process relies on language ability, which changes over development. As Conway and Pleydell-Pearce (2000) and others (Ayalon, 2015; Fergusson, Horwood, & Woodward, 2000; Thomson and Jaque, 2017; Widom, Raphael, & DuMont, 2004) make clear, autobiographical memories are based not just on encoding and retrieval processes but on many factors, including the individual's age and knowledge base, the severity of the hardships, subconscious processes, and current wellbeing. Due to those types of findings, memory is commonly recognized to be largely reconstructive rather than veridical (e.g., Hemmer & Steyvers, 2009). To be sure, determining whether a retrospective memory is accurate is a complex issue (e.g., Widom & Shepard, 1996). The key question for future researchers is not whether or not retrospective reports are accurate, but how best to maximize their accuracy.

Directions for future research: Recommendations for methodological improvements

The ACEs instruments afford clinicians and researchers with valuable insights into the detrimental effects of childhood adversity on long-term health outcomes. However, to become more accurate and scientifically useful instruments, the instruments need to have well documented and strong psychometric properties. Unfortunately, too little psychometric data are available for most ACEs measures. Thus, our first of four recommendations for future research is that researchers devote more attention to the reliability and validity of the ACEs instruments. One of the instruments with the most psychometric data is the CES. Mersky et al. (2017) provide data about its internal consistency, test-retest reliability, validity, and factor structure. Another instrument that has considerable psychometric information to support it is the BRFSS; however, evaluation of its test-retest reliability and factor structure is missing. All instruments need evaluation of their measurement invariance.

A second recommendation concerns ACEs surveys and retrospective memory. It is important to examine the test-retest reliability of ACEs instruments across a variety of time intervals and participant ages. This type of investigation will help to guide researchers to the best age range for assessing the retrospective reports of adverse experiences and a better understanding of how to increase the accuracy of reports.

Third, we recommend revising ACEs measures in several ways. One improvement would be to develop a scoring method that more fully captures the quality of the participants' experiences with adversity, including the severity, duration, and distress associated with the adversities. The current cumulative scoring approach is overly simplistic and the technique of assigning weights to particular experiences merits systematic attention. It is also important to consider adding contextual variables that may prove to mediate or moderate the impact of adversities.

Our final recommendation is the need to conduct an empirical study that would compare the utility of a brief ACEs measure, a longer ACEs measure, and an alternative, detailed instrument of childhood adversity. The goal of this investigation would be to determine how many items are necessary to provide a valid (i.e., predictive validity) assessment of ACEs. Are the 10 categories used in the *original revised* ACEs survey sufficient or is it necessary to use the 17 category scheme of the CES to capture a full understanding of negative childhood experiences? Coupled with new psychometric data, results of such a study would be informative as to which instrument to use.

Ideally, a new generation of ACEs measures should be created. These would be guided by the principles of construct validity from the initial stages of scale creation (see Clark & Watson, 1995) and, as previously noted, would include sophisticated psychometric analyses (e.g., structural analyses, Item Response Theory), an iterative process of testing and rewriting items, and the use of numerous large samples. Only through this process can researchers have confidence that the ACEs instruments are providing the best possible assessment of childhood adversities.

Implications for policy and practice

Methodological chapters typically do not address policy issues and we will not stray from that common practice; but, we raise an important practice question—should an alternative instrument be used? Researchers interested in studying childhood adversity should consider using one of several previously developed instruments that assess childhood maltreatment. The advantage of most of the ACEs instruments is that they are short and easy to complete, providing an economical avenue for data collection; however, as discussed, there is much information missing. If a fuller understanding of childhood adversity is desired and there are adequate resources and time, alternative measures that are psychometrically stronger and more fully capture childhood adversities might be considered. We mention five surveys that have established and good psychometric properties.

The Conflicts Tactics Scale-Revised (CTS2; Straus, 2004) should be considered as a viable alternative to the ACEs instruments in order to obtain a more complete understanding of child maltreatment. This 79-item parent-report survey measures psychological aggression, physical assault, sexual coercion, physical injury, and negotiation. It has extensive psychometric evaluation across diverse samples, and has been found to have adequate internal consistency as well as discriminant and concurrent validity (Straus, 2004; Straus & Mickey, 2012).

Another extensive survey designed to measure child maltreatment is the CTQ (Bernstein et al., 1994), a 70-item measure that assesses retrospective reports of emotional, physical, and sexual abuse, as well as physical and emotional neglect. The CTQ has low-to-good internal consistency ($\alpha = 0.61$–0.95) and criterion-related validity with samples of adolescent psychiatric patients, adult substance abusers, as well as community samples (Bernstein et al., 2003; Klinitzke, Romppel, Häuser, Brähler, & Glaesmer, 2012; Scher, Stein, Asmundson, McCreary, & Forde, 2001).

For researchers interested in assessing a greater breadth of victimization and adversity, the Juvenile Victimization Questionnaire (JVQ; Finkelhor, Hamby, Ormrod, & Turner, 2005) is a well-validated option. The JVQ is a 34-item instrument that measures conventional crime, child maltreatment, peer and sibling victimization, sexual victimization, and indirect victimization. The psychometric properties include good internal consistency ($\alpha = 0.80$), test-retest reliability, and some forms of validity (construct and criterion-related validity) (e.g., Finkelhor et al., 2005; Pereda, Gallardo-Pujol, & Guilera, 2018).

Another strong instrument for assessing certain forms of child maltreatment is The ISPCAN Child Abuse Screening Tool-Retrospective version (ICAST-R) (Dunne et al., 2009). It contains 15 primary items about potential physical, sexual, and emotional abusive events, with follow-up questions about the frequency of the acts, the timing of the events, and perpetrator characteristics. It was carefully developed in four phases, including input from child maltreatment experts from 28 countries. The instrument also comes in a child report form (Zolotor et al., 2009).

A final example of a good alternative to an ACEs instrument is the MACE (Teicher & Parigger, 2015), developed with the intention of improving on the limitations of the *original* ACEs measure and the CTQ. It consists of 52 questions that assess degree and timing of exposure to sexual abuse, physical abuse, emotional abuse, nonverbal emotional abuse, witnessing violence to siblings, peer emotional abuse, peer physical abuse, emotional neglect, and physical neglect. Positive responses to an item prompt specification of its occurrence within every single year of life up to age 18 years. The MACE yields a score reflecting the multiplicity of childhood adversities (ranges from 0 to 10) as well as a score indicating their overall severity (ranges from 0 to 100; Schalinski et al., 2016). It also stands out by its careful development. Item Response Theory was used to evaluate 75 questions from previously developed questionnaires. The instrument has strong test-retest reliability ($r = 0.91$) and convergent validity with the *original* ACEs questionnaire and the CTQ. The scores also showed larger correlations with symptom measures than the *original* ACEs or the CTQ, indicating good predictive validity (Teicher & Parigger, 2015).

In sum, new instruments to assess children's adverse experiences are appearing in the literature with some regularity. At least two recently developed instruments (i.e., ICAST-R, MACE) are psychometrically strong and cover a wider spectrum of potential adverse experiences than the *original* ACEs measure. We encourage investigators to consider using these instruments, if possible, due to the rich quality of information that can be gleaned from them.

Conclusion

We identified eight versions of the ACEs instrument and describe their psychometric evidence. Internal consistency data were available for most of the instruments; but there is little test-retest reliability information. Limited validity data have been published. The most common form, predictive validity, was found for only about half of the surveys. In addition to needing more psychometric evidence, we raised three methodological issues that merit consideration. We then made three recommendations for ways that researchers could improve the quality of ACEs instruments. Five established instruments, all considerably longer than most of the ACEs instruments, are mentioned as alternative ways of collecting data about childhood adversities. In sum, there is no question that the ACEs studies are having a significant impact on how we think about early adversity. It is now time to improve the ACEs instruments so they can provide more precise insights into the relations between childhood experiences and adult physical as well as mental health.

References

Afifi, T. O., Ford, D., Gershoff, E. T., Merrick, M., Grogan-Kaylor, A., Ports, K. A., ... Peters Bennett, R. (2017). Spanking and adult mental health impairment: the case for the designation of spanking as an adverse childhood experience. *Child Abuse & Neglect*, *71*, 24–31. https://doi.org/10.1016/j.chiabu.2017.01.014.

Almuneef, M., ElChoueiry, N., Saleheen, H. N., & Al-Eissa, M. (2017). Gender-based disparities in the impact of adverse childhood experiences on adult health: findings from a national study in the Kingdom of Saudi Arabia. *International Journal for Equity in Health*, *16*, 90–99. https://doi.org/10.1186/s12939-017-0588-9.

Almuneef, M., Qayad, M., Aleissa, M., & Albuhairan, F. (2014). Adverse childhood experiences, chronic diseases, and risky health behaviors in Saudi Arabian adults: apilot study. *Child Abuse & Neglect*, *38*, 1787–1793. https://doi.org/10.1016/j.chiabu.2014.06.003.

Anda, R. F., Felitti, V. J., Bremner, J. D., Walker, J. D., Whitfield, C., Perry, B. D., ... Giles, W. H. (2006). The enduring effects of abuse and related adverse experiences in childhood. *European Archives of Psychiatry and Clinical Neuroscience*, *256*, 174–186. https://doi.org/10.1007/s00406-005-0624-4.

Arkes, J. (2017). Separating the harmful versus beneficial effects of marital disruptions on children. *Journal of Divorce & Remarriage*, *58*, 526–541. https://doi.org/10.1080/10502556.2017.1344500.

Ayalon, L. (2015). Retrospective reports of negative early life events over a 4-year period: a test of measurement invariance and response consistency. *The Journals of Gerontology Series B: Psychological Sciences and Social Sciences*, *72*, 901–912. https://doi.org/10.1093/geronb/gbv087.

Bernstein, D. P., Ahluvalia, T., Pogge, D., & Handelsman, L. (1997). Validity of the childhood trauma questionnaire in an adolescent psychiatric population. *Journal of the American Academy of Child & Adolescent Psychiatry*, *36*, 340–348. https://doi.org/10.1097/00004583-199703000-00012.

Bernstein, D. P., Fink, L., Handelsman, L., Foote, J., Lovejoy, M., Wenzel, K., ... Ruggiero, J. (1994). Initial reliability and validity of a new retrospective measure of child abuse and neglect. *American Journal of Psychiatry, 151,* 1132–1136. https://doi.org/10.1176/ajp.151.8.1132.

Bernstein, D. P., Stein, J. A., Newcomb, M. D., Walker, E., Pogge, D., Ahluvalia, T., ... Zule, W. (2003). Development and validation of a brief screening version of the childhood trauma questionnaire. *Child Abuse & Neglect, 27,* 169–190. https://doi.org/10.1016/S0145-2134(02)00541-0.

Bensley, L. S., Van Eenwyk, J., & Simmons, K. W. (2000). Self-reported childhood sexual and physical abuse and adult HIV-risk behaviors and heavy drinking. *American Journal of Preventive Medicine, 18,* 151–158. https://doi.org/10.1016/S0749-3797(99)00084-7.

Bensley, L. S., Van Eenwyk, J., & Simmons, K. W. (2003). Childhood family violence history and women's risk for intimate partner violence and poor health. *American Journal of Preventive Medicine, 25,* 38–44. https://doi.org/10.1016/S0749-3797(03)00094-1.

Bethell, C. D., Carle, A., Hudziak, J., Gombojav, N., Powers, K., Wade, R., & Braveman, P. (2017). Methods to assess adverse childhood experiences of children and families: toward approaches to promote child well-being in policy and practice. *Academic Pediatrics, 17*(7S), S51–S69. https://doi.org/10.1016/j.acap.2017.04.161.

Bethell, C., Gombojav, N., Solloway, M., & Wissow, L. (2016). Adverse childhood experiences, resilience and mindfulness-based approaches: common denominator issues for children with emotional, mental, or behavioral problems. *Child and Adolescent Psychiatric Clinics of North America, 25,* 139–156. https://doi.org/10.1016/j.chc.2015.12.001.

Bethell, C. D., Newacheck, P., Hawes, E., & Halfon, N. (2014). Adverse childhood experiences: assessing the impact on health and school engagement and the mitigating role of resilience. *Health Affairs, 33,* 2106–2115. https://doi.org/10.1377/hlthaff.2014.0914.

Brener, N. D., Collins, J. L., Kann, L., Warren, C. W., & Williams, B. I. (1995). Reliability of the youth risk behavior survey questionnaire. *American Journal of Epidemiology, 141,* 575–580. https://doi.org/10.1016/S1054-139X(02)00339-7.

Brett, E. I., Espeleta, H. C., Lopez, S. V., Leavens, E. L., & Leffingwell, T. R. (2018). Mindfulness as a mediator of the association between adverse childhood experiences and alcohol use and consequences. *Addictive Behaviors, 84,* 92–98. https://doi.org/10.1016/j.addbeh.2018.04.002.

Centers for Disease Control and Prevention. (2016). *Family health history.* Retrieved from: https://www.cdc.gov/violenceprevention/acestudy/pdf/fhhmlorna.pdf.

Chmielewski, M., Sala, M., Tang, R., & Baldwin, A. (2016). Examining the construct validity of affective judgments of physical activity measures. *Psychological Assessment, 28,* 1128. https://doi.org/10.1037/pas0000322.

Chmielewski, M., & Watson, D. (2009). What is being assessed and why it matters: the impact of transient error on trait research. *Journal of Personality and Social Psychology, 97,* 186–202. https://doi.org/10.1037/a0015618.

Clark, L. A., & Watson, D. (1995). Constructing validity: basic issues in objective scale development. *Psychological Assessment, 7,* 309–319. https://doi.org/10.1037/1040-3590.7.3.309.

Conway, M. A., & Pleydell-Pearce, C. W. (2000). The construction of autobiographical memories in the self-memory system. *Psychological Review, 107,* 261–288. https://doi.org/10.1037/0033-295X.107.2.261.

Cronbach, L. J., & Meehl, P. E. (1955). Construct validity in psychological tests. *Psychological Bulletin, 52,* 281–302. https://doi.org/10.1037/h0040957.

Cronholm, P. F., Forke, C. M., Wade, R., Bair-Merritt, M. H., Davis, M., Harkins-Schwarz, M., ... Fein, J. A. (2015). Adverse childhood experiences: expanding the concept of adversity. *American Journal of Preventive Medicine, 49,* 354–361. https://doi.org/10.1016/j.amepre.2015.02.001.

Danese, A., & McEwen, B. S. (2012). Adverse childhood experiences, allostasis, allostatic load, and age-related disease. *Physiology & Behavior, 106,* 29–39. https://doi.org/10.1016/j.physbeh.2011.08.019.

Dube, S. R., Williamson, D. F., Thompson, T., Felitti, V. J., & Anda, R. F. (2004). Assessing the reliability of retrospective reports of adverse childhood experiences among adult HMO members attending a primary care clinic. *Child Abuse & Neglect*, *28*, 729–737. https://doi.org/10.1016/j.chiabu.2003.08.009.

Dunne, M. P., Zolotor, A. J., Runyan, D. K., Andreva-Miller, I., Choo, W. Y., Dunne, S. K., … Youssef, R. (2009). ISPCAN Child Abuse Screening Tools Retrospective version (ICAST-R): delphi study and field testing in seven countries. *Child Abuse & Neglect*, *33*, 815–825. https://doi.org/10.1016/j.chiabu.2009.09.005.

Edwards, V. J., Holden, G. W., Felitti, V. J., & Anda, R. F. (2003). Relationship between multiple forms of childhood maltreatment and adult mental health in community respondents: results from the adverse childhood experiences study. *American Journal of Psychiatry*, *160*, 1453–1460. https://doi.org/10.1176/appi.ajp.160.8.1453.

Espeleta, H. C., Brett, E. I., Ridings, L. E., Leavens, E. L. S., & Mullins, L. L. (2018). Childhood adversity and adult health-risk behaviors: examining the roles of emotion dysregulation and urgency. *Child Abuse & Neglect*, *82*, 92–101. https://doi.org/10.1016/j.chiabu.2018.05.027.

Felitti, V. J., Anda, R. F., Nordenberg, D., Williamson, D. F., Spitz, A. M., Edwards, V., … Marks, J. S. (1998). Relationship of childhood abuse and household dysfunction to many of the leading causes of death in adults: the adverse childhood experiences (ACE) study. *American Journal of Preventive Medicine*, *14*, 245–258. https://doi.org/10.1016/S0749-3797(98)00017-8.

Fergusson, D. M., Horwood, L. J., & Woodward, L. J. (2000). The stability of child abuse reports: a longitudinal study of the reporting behaviour of young adults. *Psychological Medicine*, *30*, 529–544. https://doi.org/10.1017/S0033291799002111.

Finkelhor, D., Hamby, S. L., Ormrod, R., & Turner, H. (2005). The Juvenile Victimization Questionnaire: reliability, validity, and national norms. *Child Abuse & Neglect*, *29*, 383–412. https://doi.org/10.1016/j.chiabu.2004.11.001.

Finkelhor, D., Shattuck, A., Turner, H., & Hamby, S. (2013). Improving the adverse childhood experiences study scale. *JAMA Pediatrics*, *167*, 70–75. https://doi.org/10.1001/jamapediatrics.2013.420.

Ford, D. C., Merrick, M. T., Parks, S. E., Breiding, M. J., Gilbert, L. K., Edwards, V. J., … Thompson, W. W. (2014). Examination of the factorial structure of adverse childhood experiences and recommendations for three subscale scores. *Psychology of Violence*, *4*, 432–444. https://doi.org/10.1037/a0037723.

Green, J. G., McLaughlin, K. A., Berglund, P. A., Gruber, M. J., Sampson, N. A., Zaslavsky, A. M., & Kessler, R. C. (2010). Childhood adversities and adult psychiatric disorders in the national comorbidity survey replication. I. Associations with first onset of DSM-IV disorders. *Archives of General Psychiatry*, *67*, 113–123. https://doi.org/10.1001/archgenpsychiatry.2009.186.

Heard-Garris, N., Davis, M. M., Szilagyi, M., & Kan, K. (2018). Childhood adversity and parent perceptions of child resilience. *BMC Pediatrics*, *18*, 204. https://doi.org/10.1186/s12887-018-1170-3.

Hemmer, P., & Steyvers, M. (2009). A Bayesian account of reconstructive memory. *Topics in Cognitive Science*, *1*, 189–202. https://doi.org/10.1111/j.1756-8765.2008.01010.x.

Holden, G. W., & Edwards, L. A. (1989). Parental attitudes toward child rearing: instruments, issues, and implications. *Psychological Bulletin*, *106*, 29–58. https://doi.org/10.1037/0033-2909.106.1.29.

Kazeem, O. T. (2015). A validation of the adverse childhood experiences scale in Nigeria. *Research on Humanities and Social Sciences*, *5*, 18–23. https://doi.org/10.1016/j.chiabu.2017.08.016.

Kilpatrick, D. G., Resnick, H. S., Milanak, M. E., Miller, M. W., Keyes, K. M., & Friedman, M. J. (2013). National estimates of exposure to traumatic events and PTSD prevalence using DSM-IV and DSM-5 criteria. *Journal of Traumatic Stress*, *26*, 537–547. https://doi.org/10.1002/jts.21848.

Klinitzke, G., Romppel, M., Häuser, W., Brähler, E., & Glaesmer, H. (2012). The German Version of the Childhood Trauma Questionnaire (CTQ): psychometric characteristics in a representative sample of the general population. *Psychotherapie, Psychosomatik, Medizinische Psychologie*, *62*, 47–51. https://doi.org/10.1055/s-0031-1295495.

Loevinger, J. (1957). Objective tests as instruments of psychological theory. *Psychological Reports*, *3*, 635–694. https://doi.org/10.2466/PR0.3.7.635-694.

Meinck, F., Cosma, A. P., Mikton, C., & Baban, A. (2017). Psychometric properties of the adverse childhood experiences abuse short form (ACE-ASF) among Romanian high school students. *Child Abuse & Neglect*, *72*, 326–337. https://doi.org/10.1016/j.chiabu.2017.08.016.

Mersky, J. P., & Janczewski, C. E. (2018). Racial and ethnic differences in the prevalence of adverse childhood experiences: findings from a low-income sample of US women. *Child Abuse & Neglect*, *76*, 480–487. https://doi.org/10.1016/j.chiabu.2017.12.012.

Mersky, J. P., Janczewski, C. E., & Nitkowski, J. C. (2018). Poor mental health among low income women in the US: the roles of adverse childhood and adult experiences. *Social Science & Medicine*, *206*, 14–21. https://doi.org/10.1016/j.socscimed.2018.03.043.

Mersky, J. P., Janczewski, C. E., & Topitzes, J. (2017). Rethinking the measurement of adversity: moving toward second-generation research on adverse childhood experiences. *Child Maltreatment*, *22*, 58–68. https://doi.org/10.1177/1077559516679513.

Molnar, B. E., Buka, S. L., & Kessler, R. C. (2001). Child sexual abuse and subsequent psychopathology: results from the national comorbidity survey. *American Journal of Public Health*, *91*, 753–760. https://doi.org/10.2105/AJPH.91.5.753.

Murphy, A., Steele, M., Dube, S. R., Bate, J., Bonuck, K., Meissner, P., … Steele, H. (2014). Adverse childhood experiences (ACEs) questionnaire and adult attachment interview (AAI): implications for parent child relationships. *Child Abuse & Neglect*, *38*, 224–233. https://doi.org/10.1016/j.chiabu.2013.09.004.

Nunnally, J. C., & Bernstein, I. H. (1994). *Psychometric theory*. New York: McGraw-Hill.

Olofson, M. W. (2018). A new measurement of adverse childhood experiences drawn from the panel study of income dynamics child development supplement. *Child Indicators Research*, *11*, 629–647. http://dx.doi.org/10.1007_s12187-017-9455-x.

Pereda, N., Gallardo-Pujol, D., & Guilera, G. (2018). Good practices in the assessment of victimization: the Spanish adaptation of the juvenile victimization questionnaire. *Psychology of Violence*, *8*, 76–86. https://doi.org/10.1037/vio0000075.

Pinto, R., Correia, L., & Maia, Â. (2014). Assessing the reliability of retrospective reports of adverse childhood experiences among adolescents with documented childhood maltreatment. *Journal of Family Violence*, *29*, 431–438. https://doi.org/10.1007/s10896-014-9602-9.

Schalinski, I., Teicher, M. H., Nischk, D., Hinderer, E., Müller, O., & Rockstroh, B. (2016). Type and timing of adverse childhood experiences differentially affect severity of PTSD, dissociative and depressive symptoms in adult inpatients. *BMC Psychiatry*, *16*, 295. https://doi.org/10.1186/s12888-016-1004-5.

Scher, C. D., Stein, M. B., Asmundson, G. J. G., McCreary, D. R., & Forde, D. R. (2001). The childhood trauma questionnaire in a community sample: psychometric properties and normative data. *Journal of Traumatic Stress*, *14*, 843–857.

Schilling, E. A., Aseltine, R. H., & Gore, S. (2008). The impact of cumulative childhood adversity on young adult mental health: measures, models, and interpretations. *Social Science & Medicine*, *66*, 1140–1151. https://doi.org/10.1016/j.socscimed.2007.11.023.

Schoenborn, C. A. (1991). *Exposure to alcoholism in the family: United States, 1988*. In *Advance data from vital and health statistics, issue 205* (pp. 1–13). Washington, DC: National Center for Health Statistics.

Schwarz, N. (2007). Retrospective and concurrent self-reports: the rationale for real-time data capture. In A. A. Stone, S. S. Shiffman, A. Atienza, & L. Nebeling (Eds.), *The science of real-time data capture: Self-reports in health research* (pp. 11–26). New York: Oxford University Press.

Slopen, N., Shonkoff, J. P., Albert, M. A., Yoshikawa, H., Jacobs, A., Stoltz, R., & Williams, D. R. (2016). Racial disparities in child adversity in the US: interactions with family immigration history and income. *American Journal of Preventive Medicine, 50*, 47–56. https://doi.org/10.1016/j.amepre.2015.06.013.

Straus, M. A. (1979). Measuring intrafamily conflict and violence: the conflict tactics (CT) scales. *Journal of Marriage and Family, 41*, 75–88. https://doi.org/10.2307/351733.

Straus, M. A. (2004). Cross-cultural reliability and validity of the revised conflict tactics scales: a study of university student dating couples in 17 nations. *Cross-Cultural Research, 38*, 407–432. https://doi.org/10.1177/1069397104269543.

Straus, M. A., & Mickey, E. L. (2012). Reliability, validity, and prevalence of partner violence measured by the conflict tactics scales in male-dominant nations. *Aggression and Violent Behavior, 17*, 463–474. https://doi.org/10.1016/j.avb.2012.06.004.

Strauss, M. E., & Smith, G. T. (2009). Construct validity: advances in theory and methodology. *Annual Review of Clinical Psychology, 5*, 1–25. https://doi.org/10.1146/annurev.clinpsy.032408.153639.

Taylor, S., & Asmundson, G. J. G. (2008). Internal and external validity in clinical research. In D. McKay (Ed.), *Handbook of research methods in abnormal and clinical psychology* (pp. 23–34). Thousand Oaks, CA: Sage.

Teicher, M. H., Anderson, C. M., Ohashi, K., Khan, A., McGreenery, C. E., Bolger, E. A., ... Vitaliano, G. D. (2018). Differential effects of childhood neglect and abuse during sensitive exposure periods on male and female hippocampus. *NeuroImage, 169*, 443–452. https://doi.org/10.1016/j.neuroimage.2017.12.055.

Teicher, M. H., & Parigger, A. (2015). The 'maltreatment and abuse chronology of exposure' (MACE) scale for the retrospective assessment of abuse and neglect during development. *PLoS One, 10*, e0117423. https://doi.org/10.1371/journal.pone.0117423.

Thomson, P., & Jaque, S. V. (2017). Adverse childhood experiences (ACE) and adult attachment interview (AAI) in a non-clinical population. *Child Abuse & Neglect, 70*, 255–263. https://doi.org/10.1016/j.chiabu.2017.06.001.

Wade, R., Jr., Cronholm, P. F., Fein, J. A., Forke, C. M., Davis, M. B., Harkins-Schwarz, M., ... Bair-Merritt, M. H. (2016). Household and community-level adverse childhood experiences and adult health outcomes in a diverse urban population. *Child Abuse & Neglect, 52*, 135–145. https://doi.org/10.1016/j.chiabu.2015.11.021.

Wade, R., Shea, J. A., Rubin, D., & Wood, J. (2014). Adverse childhood experiences of low-income urban youth. *Pediatrics, 134*, e13–e20. https://doi.org/10.1542/peds.2013-2475.

Widom, C. S., Raphael, K. G., & DuMont, K. A. (2004). The case for prospective longitudinal studies in child maltreatment research: commentary on Dube, Williamson, Thompson, Felitti, and Anda (2004). *Child Abuse & Neglect, 28*, 715–722. https://doi.org/10.1016/j.chiabu.2004.03.009.

Widom, C. S., & Shepard, R. L. (1996). Accuracy of adult recollections of childhood victimization: part 1. Childhood physical abuse. *Psychological Assessment, 8*, 412–421. https://doi.org/10.1037/1040-3590.8.4.412.

Wingenfeld, K., Schäfer, I., Terfehr, K., Grabski, H., Driessen, M., Grabe, H., ... Spitzer, C. (2011). The reliable, valid and economic assessment of early traumatization: first psychometric characteristics of the German version of the Adverse Childhood Experiences Questionnaire (ACE). *Psychotherapie, Psychosomatik, Medizinische Psychologie, 61*, e10–14. https://doi.org/10.1055/s-0030-1263161.

Zolotor, A. J., Runyan, D. K., Dunne, M. P., Jain, D., Péturs, H. R., Ramirez, C., ... Muhammad, T. (2009). ISPCAN child abuse screening tool children's version (ICAST-C): instrument development and multi-national pilot testing. *Child Abuse & Neglect, 33*, 833–841. https://doi.org/10.1016/j.chiabu.2009.09.004.

Further reading

Akhtar, S., Justice, L. V., Morrison, C. M., & Conway, M. A. (2018). Fictional first memories. *Psychological Science, 29*(10), 1612–1619.

Bell, D. C., & Bell, L. G. (2018). Accuracy of retrospective reports of family environment. *Journal of Child and Family Studies*, *27*, 1029–1040. https://doi.org/10.1007/s10826-017-0948-5.

Clements, C. M., Oxtoby, C., & Ogle, R. L. (2008). Methodological issues in assessing psychological adjustment in child witnesses of intimate partner violence. *Trauma, Violence & Abuse*, *9*, 114–127. https://doi.org/10.1177/1524838008315870.

Finkelhor, D. (2018). Screening for adverse childhood experiences (ACEs): Cautions and suggestions. *Child Abuse & Neglect*, *85*, 174–179. https://doi.org/10.1016/j.chiabu.2017.07.016.

Finkelhor, D., Shattuck, A., Turner, H., & Hamby, S. (2015). A revised inventory of adverse childhood experiences. *Child Abuse & Neglect*, *48*, 13–21. https://doi.org/10.1016/j.chiabu.2015.07.011.

Merrick, M. T., Ports, K. A., Ford, D. C., Afifi, T. O., Gershoff, E. T., & Grogan-Kaylor, A. (2017). Unpacking the impact of adverse childhood experiences on adult mental health. *Child Abuse & Neglect*, *69*, 10–19. https://doi.org/10.1016/j.chiabu.2017.03.016.

Spinhoven, P., Penninx, B. W., Hickendorff, M., van Hemert, A. M., Bernstein, D. P., & Elzinga, B. M. (2014). Childhood trauma questionnaire: factor structure, measurement invariance, and validity across emotional disorders. *Psychological Assessment*, *26*, 717–729. https://doi.org/10.1037/pas0000002.

Wang, Q., & Conway, M. A. (2004). The stories we keep: autobiographical memory in American and Chinese middle-aged adults. *Journal of Personality*, *72*, 911–938. https://doi.org/10.1111/j.0022-3506.2004.00285.x.

SECTION IV

CHAPTER

10

The public health issue of ACEs in Canada

Lil Tonmyr, Joanne Lacroix*†*, Margret Herbert*†*

*Public Health Agency of Canada, Ottawa, ON, Canada, †Independent Researcher Work

Introduction

A *Blue Ribbon Committee* in the United Kingdom defined public health as "The science and art of preventing disease, prolonging life and promoting health, through organized effort of society" (Great Britain Committee of Inquiry into the Future Development of the Public Health Function, 1988, p. 1, modified from World Health Organization [WHO], 1952). The human and economic costs of adverse childhood experiences (ACEs)—to individuals, families, communities, and society—make them a serious public health problem. ACEs can have long-term ramifications, as they are related to subsequent physical, mental, cognitive, and social problems (Gilbert et al., 2009).

The concept of ACEs is relatively new in the field of public health (Anda, Butchart, Felitti, & Brown, 2010). Initially, ACEs included seven experiences: (1) psychological abuse, (2) physical abuse, (3) sexual abuse, (4) violence against mother, and living with household members who were (5) substance abusers, (6) mentally ill or suicidal, or (7) ever imprisoned (Felitti et al., 1998). The list has varied between datasets to include neglect, parental death and divorce, among others. Because of changing norms, the inclusion of divorce has been contested (Finkelhor, 2017). The inclusion of other issues is currently the subject of debate (see Chapters 3 and 11).

When discussing ACEs as a public health issue, this chapter provides a Canadian perspective, if possible, with a strong emphasis on maltreatment, owing to its importance and negative outcomes and to the scarcity of Canadian data on other ACEs. Simultaneously, we recognize the contribution of studies conducted in other countries. For example, the World Mental Health Survey led by the World Health Organization (WHO) (initiated in the early 2000s) gathered information on mental illness, substance use,

Adverse Childhood Experiences
https://doi.org/10.1016/B978-0-12-816065-7.00010-0

and behavioral disorders from the general population in 28 countries (Kessler et al., 2009). An American study by Kaiser Permanente (1995–97) collected data from members of Health Maintenance Organizations, who received a physical examination and completed a survey on their childhood experiences and current health status and behaviors (Felitti et al., 1998). For a global perspective on ACEs, see Chapter 11.

This chapter has several purposes. First, we define ACEs as a public health issue, as exemplified by recent analyses of Canadian data. Second, we discuss public health implications of ACEs. Third, we address policy and strategies to prevent ACEs, with a focus on maltreatment. Fourth, we suggest implications for policy and practice. Finally, we conclude by proposing directions for future research.

ACEs as a public health issue

Interest in ACEs grew during the 1990s in a context of increased recognition of the importance of the early years and of children's rights. The United Nations Convention on the Rights of the Child came into force in 1990, setting out the civil, political, economic, social, health, and cultural rights of a child. Countries such as Australia, Belgium, Germany, and Norway established or strengthened policies and programs supporting early childhood development (Lundy, Kilkelly, Byrne, & Kang, 2012).

In Canada, healthy childhood development was designated a key determinant of health. Substantial investments late in the last century allowed provinces and territories to create an array of prevention and intervention programs and services for children and their families (Federal, Provincial and Territorial Advisory Committee on Population Health, 1994). These initiatives were consistent with the Ottawa Charter of Health Promotion, which stressed illness prevention and health promotion through creation of the social conditions that are prerequisites for good health (WHO, 1986). This advanced the view that improvements in health are possible if policymakers and practitioners understand and address the complex social and structural determinants, the influence of which begins during pregnancy and in early childhood (Tonmyr, MacMillan, Jamieson, & Kelly, 2002).

Public health aims to prevent health problems and to extend care and safety to the largest number of people. The public health approach is anchored in the use of an evidence-driven framework to guide responses to issues such as ACEs (Jack, 2010). The framework encompasses four interrelated areas: (1) detecting the scope of a problem, (2) identifying its etiology, (3) developing, implementing, and evaluating programs, and (4) assessing the impact of interventions and services and their cost effectiveness.

This section deals with the first two items in the framework—detecting the problem and identifying its etiology. Items three and four—the development, implementation, and evaluation of programs, and assessments of the impact of interventions and services on the health of a population and their cost effectiveness—are discussed later.

Even before the concept of ACEs was fully delineated, several Canadian surveys and research projects addressed situations now recognized as core ACEs. Dr. Harriet MacMillan of McMaster University championed the inclusion of physical and sexual abuse questions in the cross-sectional Mental Health Supplement (OHSUP) to the Ontario Health Survey (1990–91) (MacMillan et al., 1997). The results yielded an initial evidence base on the prevalence of physical and sexual abuse in Canada's most populous province and increased understanding of risk factors related to adult mental and physical health and the use of health services. The OHSUP questions pursued three paths of inquiry, including prevalence of child abuse, understanding risk and protective factors for maltreatment, and health outcomes associated with child abuse. In addition to retrospective measures of physical and sexual abuse, OHSUP included data on risk factors such as parental educational attainment, and on several other ACEs, such as running away from home as an adolescent and parental substance abuse and mental health problems. These childhood experiences are intertwined; for instance, parental substance abuse increases the likelihood of child abuse, and they both have an impact on subsequent health outcomes.

In 2012, Statistics Canada conducted the cross-sectional Canadian Community Health Survey–Mental Health (CCHS-MH). In addition to childhood physical and sexual abuse, this survey included exposure to intimate partner violence and contact with a child protection organization. According to CCHS-MH data, 32% of the population reported at least one experience of child maltreatment (Afifi et al., 2014). Although no other ACEs were included in the CCHS-MH, the survey increased knowledge about child maltreatment and health outcomes at the national level.

Using OHSUP and CCHS-MH data, researchers have studied relationships between childhood maltreatment and adult health conditions (see Appendix for selected peer-reviewed articles based on CCHS-MH data). These analyses sought to understand how the severity of and the frequency of exposure affect associations between various types of maltreatment and health problems such as diabetes (Afifi et al., 2016; Shields et al., 2016).

The longitudinal National Population Health Survey (NPHS), which began in 1994/1995, captured several ACEs and contained one self-defined question about physical abuse (Shields, Hovdestad, & Tonmyr, 2015). The ACEs measures in this survey are dichotomous and illustrate some of the methodological challenges in ACEs research (see Chapter 10). Analysis of longitudinal data from the NPHS is complicated, and accessing the data has been challenging for researchers, which may explain why few ACEs articles have been based on this survey (Thompson & Xiajiec, 2000).[1]

[1]Provincial studies have added to Canadian evidence of the impact of ACEs on mental and physical health. In an earlier cycle of the Canadian Community Health Survey, questions asked of Saskatchewan and Manitoba residents included self-identified physical abuse. Small-scale retrospective population surveys in Quebec and the longitudinal Ontario Child Health Survey have also contributed to the field.

Public health initiatives such as the Canadian Incidence Study of Reported Child Abuse and Neglect (CIS) (1998, 2003, and 2008) and corresponding provincial and First Nations samples have revealed a clustering of ACEs in a child welfare setting, with direct applicability to policy and practice (Public Health Agency of Canada, 2010). However, CIS data cannot provide information about later health outcomes.

As exemplified in the Appendix, the Canadian evidence base on ACEs, particularly maltreatment, has grown. The surveys followed the public health strategy of measuring the distribution of risk factors and outcomes in the population, using large representative samples. The measures of child maltreatment were behavior-based and used multiple items, thereby bolstering the validity and reliability of the information. Testing was conducted to assess the convergent validity and reliability of the maltreatment items (MacMillan et al., 1997; Tanaka et al., 2012; Walsh, MacMillan, Trocmé, Jamieson, & Boyle, 2008). Inclusion of mediating variables in analyses has indicated associations between child maltreatment and later health problems. For instance, when examining health outcomes, researchers have moved beyond binary variables to models that account for mediating factors such as heavy and persistent smoking (Shields, Hovdestad, Gilbert, & Tonmyr, 2016). The sheer accumulation of evidence mitigates some of the shortcomings of survey data, such as the retrospective and cross-sectional nature of the information, recall bias, and respondents' reluctance to disclose negative experiences. The major limitations of OHSUP and CCHS-MH (and for OHSUP, exposure to intimate partner violence) are that emotional maltreatment and neglect were not assessed.

ACEs are often discussed collectively, a focus that may simplify the message about their potential harm. However, ACEs operate not only independently, but also among themselves. Research has demonstrated that ACEs are overlapping risk factors for health problems in adulthood. While the influence of physical, sexual, and psychological abuse is often stronger than that of other ACEs (Holman et al., 2016), a dose-response effect has been observed, with the risk of negative health outcomes rising with the number of ACEs (Afifi et al., 2014; Holman et al., 2016; Hughes et al., 2017). ACEs and their relationship to negative health outcomes later in life may be thought of as an interconnected web. Hypothetically, initial ACEs occurring early in life, such as poverty, family violence, and parental metal health problems (which may themselves be connected or co-occurring), may be risks for a variety of ACEs that may happen later, such as child neglect, exposure to domestic violence, or loss of a parent through separation or divorce. All of these ACES are risks for later physical and mental health problems. There are many possible combinations and outcomes. As another more evidenced pathway, living in a single-parent household and substance abuse by a parent are each risks for child abuse and neglect (Shields, Tonmyr, & Hovdestad, 2016; Singh, Thornton, & Tonmyr, 2011). In turn, child abuse, single-parent family situations, and parental substance abuse are associated with mental health problems in later life, such as depression and suicidal behaviors, and with physical conditions such as heart disease, obesity, and chronic respiratory difficulty (see Appendix).

An American researcher, Kathleen Kendall Tackett (2002), has described four pathways by which childhood maltreatment can influence subsequent health, including behavioral pathways such as high-risk sexual behavior and eating disorders, social pathways such as inability to form healthy interpersonal relationships, cognitive pathways that shape individuals' sense of control and their perception of their circumstances, and emotional pathways such as depression and posttraumatic stress disorder. As well, relatively recent research suggests that childhood maltreatment can bring about changes in biological pathways and in the nervous system, rendering those who experienced maltreatment vulnerable to illness throughout the life course (Tiwari & Gonzalez, 2018).

In summary, over the last two decades, understanding of the scope and occurrence of ACEs has grown, based on analyses of information from large health databases and population health surveys. Researchers have produced a body of work characterizing relationships and clustering among the various ACEs and linking them to negative health outcomes in adulthood. As the ACEs literature broadens, so will knowledge about how the various ACEs are related to each other. Findings published in a wide range of multidisciplinary journals, including medicine and public health, have reached a large, diverse policy, professional, and public audience.

Implications of a public health approach to ACEs

The discussion in the previous section (and in Chapters 4 and 5) illustrates the long-term consequences of ACEs for physical, mental, cognitive, and social health. For that reason alone, ACEs merit recognition as a public health issue. Some of the negative outcomes associated with ACEs affect substantial proportions of the population and are readily acknowledged as matters of public health. For instance, cancer, heart disease, stroke, respiratory diseases, unintentional injuries, diabetes, and suicide are the leading causes of death in Canada and, cumulatively, are responsible for two-thirds of mortality (Statistics Canada, 2018a, 2018b). These health conditions also impose a considerable morbidity burden. By extension, risk factors (including ACEs) for these causes of death and morbidity are also public health issues.

The relative importance of a risk factor is related to the number and range of negative health outcomes, the severity of these outcomes, and the strength and consistency of the evidence linking the risk factor and the outcomes. Some ACEs, particularly maltreatment, have long been considered public health problems (Krug, Mercy, Dahlberg, & Zwi, 2002; MacMillan, 1998). Through the Youth Risk Behaviour Surveillance System and other initiatives, the Centers for Disease Control and Prevention in the United States demonstrated its acceptance of ACEs as a public health concern (Eaton et al., 2006). In Canada, the Public Health Agency maintains a child maltreatment surveillance system, and a report on family violence by the Chief Public Health Officer clearly positioned child maltreatment as a public health issue (Taylor, 2016).

The question is no longer whether ACEs should be defined as a public health issue but, rather, what does adopting a public health perspective entail? Such an approach signals that the health of the entire community, not just individuals, is of concern. A public health approach starts with information about the prevalence of and risk factors for ACEs. This is followed by the development and testing of interventions, and the prevention of future problems by addressing high-risk circumstances.

Surveillance

Surveillance is fundamental to public health. Surveillance helps to understand the scope of a problem, identify and characterize risk factors, and follow trends over time. Tracking the prevalence of ACEs, risk factors, and health outcomes can provide evidence that efforts to intervene are succeeding or failing. Surveillance of negative outcomes associated with ACEs, such as mental health problems, self-injury and suicide, and chronic diseases, has been undertaken for many decades. By contrast, surveillance of ACEs themselves emerged more recently.

Child abuse is among the most developed and widespread targets of ACEs surveillance. Census data on social determinants of maltreatment, such as family income and family structure, are used extensively as risk factors for ACEs among children in low-income households or in single-parent families. Health and social surveys such as the CCHS gather information on factors as diverse as current and past substance use, history of child maltreatment, depression, suicidal ideation, and obesity.

In the case of the CCHS, a set of core questions is maintained from cycle to cycle, but areas of special focus vary. Repetition of core content items and special themes relevant to ACEs that are revisited periodically can reveal trends over time. However, because various interests compete to have their concerns included, there are always more questions than any survey can accommodate. ACEs, particularly maltreatment, bring another layer of complexity. This, along with strategies developed to overcome obstacles and to take advantage of opportunities such as data linkage, will be explored in the next section.

Building the evidence

A public health approach requires pilot projects (of programs, practices, and even policy initiatives) that are rigorously evaluated, preferably with randomized controlled trials (RCTs), before widespread implementation. After implementation, ongoing evaluation is needed to track reduction of risk factors and negative outcomes, and make necessary adjustments. Two public health interventions with proven effectiveness in other countries are being evaluated or considered for testing in RCTs in Canada. The population-based Triple-P Positive Parenting Program attempts to improve parenting (MacMillan et al., 2009). The Nurse-Family Partnership (NFP), a targeted nurse intervention program to assist young, poor mothers in parenting (MacMillan et al., 2009), starts prenatally and continues to the child's second birthday. Evidence suggests that each program has reduced ACEs—the former in the US and the latter in the Netherlands and US (MacMillan et al., 2009; Mejdoubi et al., 2013).

The developer of the NFP, David Olds, advocates rigorous research before the program is implemented in a new setting. He emphasizes the importance of adaptation to local context and a pilot study to examine acceptability by those who would be affected, followed by an RCT. Only after successful trials can the program be implemented more broadly. As well, continued monitoring and research are required to refine the intervention (Jack et al., 2015; Olds, Hill, O'Brien, Racine, & Moritz, 2003). In Canada (specifically, British Columbia, the third largest province), the results of the RCT are eagerly awaited (Catherine et al., 2016). The Canadian RCT is complemented by a process evaluation that provides additional information on lessons learned (Jack et al., 2015) and a study of biological mechanisms linking interventions and behavioral outcomes (Gonzalez et al., 2018).

Research and intervention cannot rest solely on a health orientation, but will benefit from coordinated crossdisciplinary efforts. Programs are often initiated and led by one sector (for instance, health), and with planning, coordination, and partnership with other sectors, may broaden their scope and, ultimately, be more successful. For instance, British Columbia's NFP is a collaborative undertaking by the Ministries of Health and Social Services.

Prevention

Prevention is central to public health (see Chapter 12). In the last 20 years, growing recognition of the pivotal role of early childhood has resulted in programs and interventions to foster child development (Treasury Board of Canada, n.d.). Through the Canada Social Transfer, provinces and territories receive ongoing funding to promote health during pregnancy, birth, and infancy; parenting and family support; learning and care; and community assistance (Treasury Board of Canada, n.d.).

Jurisdictions establish programs according to their needs and priorities. Some programs aim specifically at strengthening parenting skills or preventing child maltreatment, which is consistent with the public health strategy of working upstream and creating conditions favorable to health. However, developing parenting programs to prevent maltreatment and other ACEs is complicated, as is the evaluation of their effectiveness (for example, see Kramer, 1998; McLennan, MacMillan, & Jamieson, 2004). Furthermore, McLennan (2015) challenges the use of lower evidence standards as "better than nothing." He further fears that investments in ineffective programs remove scarce resources for the development and evaluation of others.

Policies and strategies to prevent ACEs

The WHO has described a strategy to prevent violence, based on the ecological view (Krug et al., 2002). The strategy acknowledges the need to work at several levels simultaneously—individual, family, and community (e.g., school), and across sectors and jurisdictions. It emphasizes the need for partnerships with those who contribute to the health of the population, and relies on implementation of policies and allocation of resources aimed at prevention. The premise is that the effectiveness of interventions in any one dimension may be reduced if not supported by measures at other levels.

This strategy for preventing violence, including child maltreatment, is often (though not always) applicable to other ACEs. It is deemed relevant by the mental health field and is seen to include the fundamental elements (i.e., intraperson, family, peer, community, and society) necessary for the promotion of child and youth health (Hertz, Donato, & Wright, 2013; Stiffman et al., 2010). This approach may also be garnering support as a means of dealing with issues beyond ACEs (e.g., radicalization), which are not readily identified as public health concerns (Bhui, Hicks, Lashley, & Jones, 2012).

Canada, like several other countries, has enacted child welfare legislation in response to maltreatment. It allows for assessment and support, and, if necessary, protective action. The identification of children in need of protection has increased with the implementation of legislation; but, it is still necessary to determine the effectiveness of programs that are established to remedy the situation (Tonmyr, Mathews, Shields, Hovdestad, & Afifi, 2018). Programs for children and families, such as NFP and Triple P, can play a dual role in prevention of maltreatment;

specifically, they are fundamental to primary prevention, and can be central to preventing recurrence.

In the WHO strategy, economic vehicles, such as child allowances, tax reduction, and guaranteed income supplements, are tools available to public health. A recent analysis by the Manitoba Centre for Health Policy supports the use of an unconditional prenatal income supplement to promote child development. The study reported a reduction of risk factors associated with ACEs, such as low birthweight and preterm births, and an increase in protective factors, such as breastfeeding (Brownell et al., 2016).

Simply remaining in school has been shown to have potential benefits for the long-term mental health of physically and sexually abused children (Williams, MacMillan, & Jamieson, 2006). For instance, to prevent child sexual abuse, schools may offer relevant instruction to their students (MacMillan et al., 2009). Schools are also focal points for prevention of and response to bullying (not yet included in the conceptualization of ACEs), which has been associated with mental health issues, and even suicide, among youth (Hertz et al., 2013). Beyond schools, interventions at the community level may be preferred when evidence suggests that problems such as maltreatment and substance abuse affect entire communities.

Implications for policy and practice

In the last 20 years, policymakers, researchers, and service providers have embraced prevention and the necessity of working upstream to ensure child and youth well-being. This, in itself, is a major step forward in applying a public health approach to ACEs. However, the use of public health techniques is never without complications, some of which are unique to ACEs. Solutions require discussion far beyond what this chapter can offer. The aim here is to encourage a dialogue to identify ways of reducing, if not entirely removing, obstacles.

First, as outlined earlier, programs are being tested for effectiveness in Canada. Since the early 1990s, child sexual abuse has declined in both Canada and the US; but, reasons for the decline are unclear, and some reasons applicable to one country are not valid in the other (Shields, Tonmyr, & Hovdestad, 2016). Unlike the US, policing and incarcerations have not increased in Canada, where demographic changes, higher employment, and collective values are more likely to be related to the decline in child sexual abuse (Shields, Tonmyr, & Hovdestad, 2016). Therefore, programs that have been successful in some settings may fail in others. Optimum implementation is an immense challenge, and ongoing evaluation is necessary. To ensure the integrity of a program and fidelity to its successful components, a careful balance must be maintained when it is adapted to a new setting (Casillas, Fauchier, Derkash, & Garrido, 2016). Without evidence of effectiveness, it may be that some initiatives should no longer be funded. Perhaps the question is *How do we build the kind of culture where evidence-based interventions are the norm rather than the exception?*

Second, inclusion of questions about ACEs on population surveys is complicated for reasons beyond competition for scarce questionnaire space. Legal liability, ethics, and safety are involved. The security of collected data, protecting respondents' privacy, and avoiding retraumatization of victims are major concerns. For instance, to avoid situations that could endanger the safety of the child or create expectations that help is coming, Statistics Canada often relies on retrospective accounts. Even so, the agency has asked respondents as young as 14 years old about their exposure to maltreatment (Statistics Canada, 2014). A legal review was conducted to allow Statistics Canada to establish a process for refusing parental Access to Information requests if there is risk of harm to the child (Dr. Andrew MacKenzie [Public Health Agency of Canada, Ottawa, ON], personal communication).

The public health strategy is to collect reliable, representative data about the prevalence of risk factors, the impact on the health of individuals and the population, and the cost to health and social systems. Are we willing to compromise this approach in the case of ACEs and settle for less because of the complexity? Survey questions about sensitive topics may be worthwhile for other reasons. A recent metaanalysis found that suicide-related research had benefits, albeit small, to participants (Blades, Stritzke, Page, & Brown, 2018). Responses to surveys have led to disclosures and to protection from further abuse owing to protocols created to support children who report maltreatment (Tonmyr & Hovdestad, 2013). Some countries have successfully collected child maltreatment data and, at the same time, offered counseling and follow-up to respondents, while ensuring their privacy and security (Laurin, Wallace, Draca, Aterman, & Tonmyr, 2018; Tonmyr, Hovdestad, & Draca, 2014).

Third, the concept of ACEs is relatively new. Prevention requires co-ordination across sectors, implementation of measures at the policy and community levels, and interventions with families and individuals. However, little is known about how and the extent to which these elements come together.

Fourth, work remains to be done to determine best practices. In part, this falls within the realm of professional and public education; but, we must consider new ways to ensure that information reaches those who need it to prevent and/or address ACEs. The current trend among editors and publishers of academic papers is to encourage authors to discuss potential applications of their findings. This could be augmented by the preparation of lay summaries of these studies to be disseminated as summaries in professional news and information products and in mass media for the general public.

Fifth, some hesitation in embracing ACEs as a public health issue persists. The roots of public health were in the control of disease and some may continue to view ACEs as social rather than health concerns. Also, the belief that child maltreatment affects only a minuscule portion of the population and, therefore, should not be a matter of public health, remains very much alive. It is not easy to recognize the influence of a particular childhood situation when consequences such as unemployment and poverty do not appear until later in adulthood.

The CCHS finding that more than a third of adults were exposed to childhood maltreatment has shown policymakers the importance of ACEs (Afifi et al., 2014). It is to be hoped that acceptance of ACEs as a pressing matter of public health will grow as evidence linking ACEs to later negative health outcomes accumulates.

Directions for future research

A substantial amount of data demonstrates that specific types of child maltreatment are risks for a wide range of negative outcomes; but, much less is known about the risks posed by other ACEs and the pathways and mechanisms leading to outcomes. ACEs may be thought of as an interconnected web (Hughes et al., 2017; Singh et al., 2011). Some, such as parental substance abuse, are risks for others, such as child physical and sexual abuse (Walsh, MacMillan, & Jamieson, 2003). A greater understanding of which ACEs pose risks for particular outcomes, the relative strength (relative risk) of the various associations, and factors that foster post-ACEs resilience would be helpful (see Chapter 14). This information would advance the development of policy, programs, and professional practice. For children exposed to several ACEs, it would allow professionals to focus treatment, intervention, and services on the ACEs with the largest relative risks and/or that co-occur most frequently. Major crossdisciplinary issues could be identified and used to encourage professional cooperation. Higher-level policy development and scarce resources could be focused on the most important associations, pathways, and outcomes. As well as research exploring relationships among ACEs and later outcomes, applied research is needed to institute programs for primary prevention and early mitigation of ACEs that already exist. The NFP (MacMillan et al., 2009) is an example. Similar applied research would help devise prevention procedures for family and community (group resource) settings. Finally, prevention initiatives should not be limited to the health sector. Additional applied research could identify prevention opportunities in school and social service environments, as well as prospects for interdisciplinary programs.

Conclusion

This chapter demonstrates that ACEs, especially child maltreatment, are a public health issue. Considerable work has been conducted in Canada and beyond; but, we cannot be complacent. Research- and surveillance-informed policy and practice interventions specific to ACEs must be created to improve children's health and subsequent adult health.

Appendix. Selected peer-reviewed articles using ACEs data from the 2012 Canadian Community Health Survey—Mental Health, by topic, 2014–18[2]

Maltreatment

Afifi, T. O., MacMillan, H. L., Boyle, M., Taillieu, T., Cheung, K., & Sareen, J. (2014). Child abuse and mental disorders in Canada. *Canadian Medical Association Journal*. https://doi.org/10.1503/cmaj.13179231792.

- *prevalence of child physical abuse; sexual abuse; exposure to intimate partner violence*

Shields, M., Tonmyr, L., & Hovdestad, W. (2016). Is child sexual abuse declining in Canada? Results from nationally representative retrospective surveys. *Health Promotion and Chronic Disease Prevention in Canada: Research, Policy and Practice*, *36*(11), 252–260.

- *trends in child sexual abuse*

Physical health

Afifi, T. O., MacMillan, H. L., Boyle, M., Cheung, K., Taillieu, T., Turner, S., & Sareen, J. (2016). Child abuse and physical health in adulthood. *Health Reports*, *27*(3), 10–18.

- *asthma; arthritis; back problems; bowel disease; cancer; chronic bronchitis/emphysema/COPD; chronic fatigue syndrome; diabetes; epilepsy; heart disease; high blood pressure; migraine; self-perceived health; stroke*

[2]Some articles are listed under more than one topic.

Badley, E. M., Shields, M. E., O'Donnell, S., Hovdestad, W. E., & Tonmyr, L. (2018). Childhood maltreatment as a risk factor for arthritis: Findings from a population-based survey of Canadian adults. *Arthritis Care and Research.* https://doi.org/10.1002/acr.23776.

- *arthritis*

Brennenstuhl, S., & Fuller-Thomson, E. (2015). The painful legacy of childhood violence: Migraine headaches among adult survivors of adverse childhood experiences. *Headache, 55*(7), 973–983. https://doi.org/10.1111/head.12614.

- *migraine*

England, G., Casey, R., Ferro, M., MacMillan, H., Tonmyr, L., & Gonzalez, A. (2018). Child maltreatment and adult multimorbidity: Results from the Canadian Community Health Survey. *Canadian Journal of Public Health, 109*(4), 561–572. https://doi.org/10.17269/s41997-018-0069-y.

- *chronic pain, chronic physical condition*

Fuller-Thomson, E., & Hollister, B. (2016). Schizophrenia and suicide attempts: Findings from a representative community-based Canadian sample. *Schizophrenia Research and Treatment*. https://doi.org/10.1155/2016/3165243.

- *schizophrenia, suicide attempts*

Fuller-Thomson, E., & Lacombe-Duncan A. (2016). Understanding the association between Chronic Obstructive Pulmonary Disease and current anxiety: a population-based study. *COPD, 13*(5), 622–631. https://doi.org/10.3109/15412555.2015.1132691.

- *chronic obstructive pulmonary disease*

Fuller-Thomson, E., West, K. J., Sulman, J., & Baird, S. L. (2015). Childhood maltreatment is associated with ulcerative colitis but not Crohn's disease: findings from a population-based study. *Inflammatory Bowel Diseases, 21*(11), 2640–2648. https://doi.org/10.1097/MIB.0000000000000551.

- *ulcerative colitis*

Fuller-Thomson, E., Lateef, R., & Sulman, J. (2015). Robust association between inflammatory bowel disease and generalized anxiety disorder: findings from a nationally representative Canadian study. *Inflammatory Bowel Diseases, 21*(10), 2341–2348. https://doi.org/10.1097/MIB.0000000000000518.

- *bowel disease*

Fuller-Thomson, E., Jayanthikumar, J., & Agbeyaka. S. K. (2017). Untangling the association between migraine, pain, and anxiety: examining migraine and generalized anxiety disorders in a Canadian population-based study. *Headache, 57*(3), 375–390.

- *migraine*

Shields, M. E., Hovdestad, W. E., Gilbert, C. P., & Tonmyr, L. E. (2016). Childhood maltreatment as a risk factor for COPD: findings from a population-based survey of Canadian adults. *International Journal of Chronic Obstructive Pulmonary Disease, 11*, 2641–2650.

- *chronic bronchitis/emphysema/COPD*

Shields, M. E., Hovdestad, W. E., Pelletier, C., Dykxhoorn, J. L., O'Donnell, S. C., & Tonmyr, L. (2016). Childhood maltreatment as a risk factor for diabetes: Findings from a population-based survey of Canadian adults. *BMC Public Health, 16*(1), 879.

- *diabetes*

Mental health

Afifi, T. O., MacMillan, H. L., Boyle, M., Taillieu, T., Cheung, K., & Sareen, J. (2014). Child abuse and mental disorders in Canada. *Canadian Medical Association Journal, Canadian Medical Association Journal.* https://doi.org/10.1503/cmaj.13179231792.

- *alcohol abuse or dependence; bipolar disorder; drug abuse or dependence; eating disorders; generalized anxiety disorder; obsessive-compulsive disorder; panic disorder; phobias; post-traumatic stress disorder; suicide attempts; suicidal ideation*

Afifi, T. O., MacMillan, H. L., Taillieu, T., Turner, S., Cheung, K., Sareen, J., & Boyle, M. H. (2016). Individual- and relationship-level factors related to better mental health outcomes following child abuse: results from a nationally representative Canadian sample. *The Canadian Journal of Psychiatry, 61*(12), 776–788.

- *suicidal ideation; any mental health condition*

Baiden, P., Fallon, B., & Antwi-Boasiako, K. (2017). Effect of social support and disclosure of child abuse on adult suicidal ideation: findings from a population-based study. *Primary Care Companion to the Journal of Clinical Psychiatry, 19*(6). https://doi.org/10.4088/PCC.17m02181.

- *suicidal ideation*

Baiden, P., Tarshis, S., Antwi-Boasiako, K., & den Dunnen, W. (2016). Examining the independent protective effect of subjective well-being on severe psychological distress among Canadian adults with a history of child maltreatment. *Child Abuse and Neglect, 58*, 129–140. https://doi.org/10.1016/j.chiabu.2016.06.017

- *severe psychological distress*

Baiden, P., & Fuller-Thomson, E. (2016). Factors associated with achieving complete mental health among individuals with lifetime suicidal ideation. *Suicide & Life-Threatening Behavior, 46*(4), 427–446. https://doi.org/10.1111/sltb.12230.

- *suicidal ideation*

England-Mason, G., Casey, R., Ferro, M., MacMillan, H. L., Tonmyr, L., & Gonzalez, A. (2018). Child maltreatment and adult multimorbidity: Results from the Canadian Community Health Survey. *Canadian Journal of Public Health, 109*(4), 561–572. https://doi.org/ 10.17269/s41997-018-0069-y.

- *mental health condition*

Fuller-Thomson, E., Agbeyaka, S., LaFond, D. M., & Bern-Klug, M. (2016). Flourishing after depression: Factors associated with achieving complete mental health among those with a history of depression. *Psychiatry Research, 242*, 111–120. https://doi.org/10.1016/j.psychres.2016.04.041.

- *depression*

Fuller-Thomson, E., Jayanthikumar, J., & Agbeyaka. S. K. (2017) Untangling the association between migraine, pain, and anxiety: examining migraine and generalized anxiety disorders in a Canadian population-based study. *Headache, 57*(3), 375–390.

- *anxiety*

Fuller-Thomson E., & Lacombe-Duncan A. (2016). Understanding the association between Chronic Obstructive Pulmonary Disease and current anxiety: A population-based study. *COPD*. 13(5):622–31. https://doi.org/10.3109/15412555.2015.1132691.

- *anxiety*

Fuller-Thomson, E., Roane, J. L., & Brennenstuhl, S. (2016). Three types of adverse childhood experiences, and alcohol and drug dependence among adults: an investigation using population-based data. *Substance Use and Misuse, 51*(11), 1451–1461. https://doi.org/10.1080/10826084.2016.1181089.

- *alcohol abuse or dependence; drug abuse or dependence*

Fuller-Thomson, E., Ramzan, N., & Baird, S. L. (2016). Arthritis and suicide attempts: Findings from a large nationally representative Canadian survey. *Rheumatology International, 36*(9), 1237–1248. https://doi.org/10.1007/s00296-016-3498-z.

- *suicide attempts*

Fuller-Thomson, E., Baird, S. L., Dhrodia, R., & Brennenstuhl, S. (2016). The association between adverse childhood experiences (ACEs) and suicide attempts in a population-based study. *Child: Care, Health and Development, 42*(5), 725–734. https://doi.org/10.1111/cch.12351.

- *suicide attempts*

Martin, M. S., Dykxhoorn, J., Afifi, T. O., & Colman, I. (2016). Child abuse and the prevalence of suicide attempts among those reporting suicide ideation. *Social Psychiatry and Psychiatric Epidemiology, 51*(11), 1477–1484. https://doi.org/10.1007/s00127-016-1250-3.

- *suicide attempts*

Meng, X., & D'Arcy, C. (2016). Gender moderates the relationship between childhood abuse and internalizing and substance use disorders later in life: a cross-sectional analysis. *BMC Psychiatry, 16*(1), 401. https://doi.org/10.1186/s12888-016-1071-7.

- *alcohol abuse or dependence; bipolar disorder; depression; drug abuse or dependence; generalized anxiety disorder; hypomania; mania; mood disorder; any kind of internalizing disorder; any kind of externalizing disorder*

Social and health problems

Afifi, T. O., MacMillan, H. L., Boyle, M., Taillieu, T., Cheung, K., & Sareen, J. (2014). Child abuse and mental disorders in Canada. *Canadian Medical Association Journal, Canadian Medical Association Journal.* https://doi.org/10.1503/cmaj.13179231792.

- *attention-deficit/hyperactivity disorder; learning disability*

Baiden, P., den Dunnen, W., & Fallon, B. (2017). Examining the independent effect of social support on unmet mental healthcare needs among Canadians: findings from a population-based study. *Social Indicators Research, 130*(3):1229–1246. https://doi.org/10.1007/s11205-015-1224-y.

- *unmet health care needs*

Baiden, P., Fallon, B., den Dunnen, W., & Boateng, G. O. (2015). The enduring effects of early-childhood adversities and troubled sleep among

Canadian adults: a population-based study. *Sleep Medicine, 16*(6), 760–777. https://doi.org/10.1016/j.sleep.2015.02.527.

- *sleep*

Fuller-Thomson, E., & Lewis, D. A. (2015). The relationship between early adversities and attention-deficit/hyperactivity disorder. *Child Abuse and Neglect, 47*(9), 94–101. https://doi.org/10.1016/j.chiabu.2015.03.005.

- *attention-deficit/hyperactivity disorder*

Fuller-Thomson, E., Lewis, D. A., & Agbeyaka, S. K. (2016). Attention-deficit/hyperactivity disorder casts a long shadow: Findings from a population-based study of adult women with self-reported ADHD. *Child: Care, Health and Development, 42*(6), 918–927. https://doi.org/10.1111/cch.12380.

- *attention-deficit/hyperactivity disorder*

Sampasa-Kanyinga, H., Nilsen, W., & Colman, I. (2018). Child abuse and work stress in adulthood: Evidence from a population-based study. *Preventive Medicine, 108*, 60–66. https://doi.org/10.1016/j.ypmed.2017.12.029.

- *work stress*

Ukah, U. V., Adu, P. A., De Silva, D. A., & Von Dadelszen, P. (2016). The impact of a history of adverse childhood experiences on breastfeeding initiation and exclusivity: Findings from a national population health survey. *Breastfeeding Medicine, 11*(10), 544–550. https://doi.org/10.1089/bfm.2016.0053

- *breastfeeding initiation*

Combined problems

England-Mason, G., Casey, R., Ferro, M., MacMillan, H. L., Tonmyr, L., & Gonzalez, A. (2018). Child maltreatment and adult multimorbidity: results from the Canadian Community Health Survey. *Canadian Journal of Public Health, 109*(4):561–572. 10.17269/s41997-018-0069-y.

- *mental health condition; chronic pain condition; chronic physical condition*

Child protection

Afifi, T. O., MacMillan, H. L., Taillieu, T., Cheung, C., Turner, S., Tonmyr, L., & Hovdestad, W. (2015). Relationship between child abuse exposure and reported contact with child protection organizations: Results from the Canadian Community Health Survey. *Child Abuse and Neglect, 46*, 198–206.

- *contact with child protection*

Afifi, T. O., McTavish, J., Turner, S., MacMillan, H. L., & Wathen, C. N. (2018).The relationship between child protection contact and mental health outcomes among Canadian adults with a child abuse history. *Child Abuse and Neglect, 79*, 22–30.

- *mental health*

Baiden, P., Fallon, B., & Antwi-Boasiako, K. (2017). Effect of social support and disclosure of child abuse on adult suicidal ideation: findings from a population-based study. *Primary Care Companion to the Journal of Clinical Psychiatry, 19*(6). https://doi.org/10.4088/PCC.17m02181.

- *social support and disclosure*

Tonmyr, L., Mathews, B., Shields, M., Hovdestad, W., & Afifi, T.O. (2018). Does mandatory reporting legislation increase contact with child protection? A legal doctrinal review and an analytical examination. *BMC Public Health, 18*(1021), 1–12. Retrieved from: https://doi.org/10.1186/s12889-018-5864-0.

- *increased contact after introduction of mandatory reporting legislation*

Positive mental health indicators

Afifi, T. O., MacMillan, H. L., Taillieu, T., Turner, S., Cheung, K., Sareen, J., & Boyle, M. H. (2016). Individual- and relationship-level factors related to better mental health outcomes following child abuse: results from a nationally representative Canadian sample. *The Canadian Journal of Psychiatry, 61*(12), 776–788.

- *Keyes's well-being and functioning*

Baiden, P., den Dunnen, W., & Fallon, B. (2017). Examining the independent effect of social support on unmet mental healthcare needs among Canadians: findings from a population-based study. *Social Indicators Research, 130*(3):1229–1246. https://doi.org/10.1007/s11205-015-1224-y.

- *social support*

Baiden, P., & Fuller-Thomson, E. (2016). Factors associated with achieving complete mental health among individuals with lifetime suicidal ideation. *Suicide & Life-Threatening Behavior, 46*(4), 427–446. https://doi.org/10.1111/sltb.12230.

- *complete mental health*

Fuller-Thomson, E., Agbeyaka, S., LaFond, D. M., & Bern-Klug, M. (2016). Flourishing after depression: factors associated with achieving complete mental health among those with a history of depression. *Psychiatry Research, 242*, 111–120. https://doi.org/10.1016/j.psychres.2016.04.041.

- *flourishing*

References

Afifi, T. O., MacMillan, H. L., Boyle, M., Cheung, K., Taillieu, T., Turner, S., & Sareen, J. (2016). Child abuse and physical health in adulthood. *Health Reports*, *27*(3), 10–18.

Afifi, T. O., MacMillan, H. L., Boyle, M., Taillieu, T., Cheung, K., & Sareen, J. (2014). Child abuse and mental disorders in Canada. *Canadian Medical Association Journal*, https://doi.org/10.1503/cmaj.13179231792.

Anda, R. F., Butchart, A., Felitti, V. J., & Brown, D. W. (2010). Building a framework for global surveillance of the public health implications of adverse childhood experiences. *American Journal of Preventive Medicine*, *39*(1), 93–98.

Bhui, K. S., Hicks, M. H., Lashley, M., & Jones, E. (2012). A public health approach to understanding and preventing violent radicalization. *BMC Medicine*, *10*(1), 16.

Blades, C. A., Stritzke, W. G. K., Page, A. C., & Brown, J. D. (2018). The benefits and risks of asking research participants about suicide: a meta-analysis of the impact of exposure to suicide-related content. *Clinical Psychology Review*, *64*, 1–12.

Brownell, M. D., Chartier, M. J., Nickel, N. C., Chateau, D., Martens, P. J., Sarkar, J., … Katz, A. (2016). Unconditional prenatal income supplement and birth outcomes. *Pediatrics*, *137*(6). e20152992.

Casillas, K. L., Fauchier, A., Derkash, B. T., & Garrido, E. F. (2016). Implementation of evidence-based home visiting programs aimed at reducing child maltreatment: a meta-analytic review. *Child Abuse and Neglect*, *53*, 64–80.

Catherine, N. L., Gonzalez, A., Boyle, M., Sheehan, D., Jack, S. M., Hougham, K. A., … Waddell, C. (2016). Improving children's health and development in British Columbia through nurse home visiting: a randomized controlled trial protocol. *BMC Health Services Research*, *16*(1), 349.

Eaton, D. K., Kann, L., Kinchen, S., Ross, J., Hawkins, J., Harris, W. A., et al. (2006). Methodology of the youth risk behaviour surveillance—United States, 2005. *MMWR Surveillance Summary*, *55*, 1–108.

Federal, Provincial and Territorial Advisory Committee on Population Health (ACPH). (1994). Strategies for population health. Investigating in the health of Canadians. In *Meeting of the Ministers of Health 1994*. Halifax, N.S., Ottawa: Health Canada.

Felitti, V. J., Anda, R. F., Nordenberg, D., Williamson, D. F., Spitz, A. M., Edwards, V., … Marks, J. S. (1998). Relationship of childhood abuse and household dysfunction to many of the leading causes of death in adults: the adverse childhood experiences (ACE) study. *American Journal of Preventive Medicine*, *14*(4), 245–258.

Finkelhor, D. (2017). Screening for adverse childhood experiences (ACEs): cautions and suggestions. *Child Abuse and Neglect*, https://doi.org/10.1016/j.chiabu.2017.07.016.

Gilbert, R., Widom, C. S., Browne, K., Fergusson, D., Webb, E., & Janson, S. (2009). Burden and consequences of child maltreatment in high-income countries. *Lancet*, *373*(9657), 68–81.

Gonzalez, A., Catherine, N., Boyle, M., Jack, S. M., Atkinson, L., Kobor, M., & MacMillan, H. L. (2018). Healthy foundations study: a randomised controlled trial to evaluate biological embedding of early-life experiences. *BMJ Open*, *8*(1). e018915.

Great Britain Committee of Inquiry into the Future Development of the Public Health Function. (1988). *Public health in England: The report of the committee of inquiry into the future development of the public health function [Cm 289]*. Great Britain: H.M. Stationery Office.

Hertz, M. F., Donato, I., & Wright, J. (2013). Bullying and suicide: a public health approach. *Journal of Adolescent Health, 53*(1), S1–S3.

Holman, D. N., Ports, K. A., Buchanan, N. D., Hawkins, N. A., Merrick, M. T., Metzler, M., & Trivers, K. F. (2016). The association between adverse childhood experiences and risk of cancer in adulthood: a systematic review of the literature. *Pediatrics, 138*(S1), s81–s91.

Hughes, K., Bellis, M. A., Hardcastle, K. A., Sethi, D., Butchart, A., Mikton, C., … Dunne, M. P. (2017). The effect of multiple adverse childhood experiences on health: a systematic review and meta-analysis. *The Lancet Public Health, 2*, e356–e366.

Jack, S. M. (2010). The role of public health in addressing child maltreatment in Canada. *Chronic Diseases and Injuries in Canada, 31*(1), 29–44.

Jack, S. M., Catherine, N., Gonzalez, A., MacMillan, H. L., Sheehan, D., & Waddell, C. (2015). Adapting, piloting and evaluating complex public health interventions: lessons learned from the Nurse-Family Partnership in Canadian public health settings. *Health Promotion and Chronic Disease Prevention in Canada: Research, Policy and Practice, 35*(8–9), 151–159.

Jack, S. M., Sheehan, D., Gonzalez, A., MacMillan, H. L., Catherine, N., & Waddell, C. (2015). British Columbia healthy connections project process evaluation: a mixed methods protocol to describe the implementation and delivery of the Nurse-Family Partnership in Canada. *BMC Nursing, 14*(1), 47.

Kendall Tackett, K. (2002). The health effects of childhood abuse: four pathways by which abuse can influence health. *Child Abuse and Neglect, 26*(6–7), 715–729.

Kessler, R. C., Aguilar-Gaxiola, S., Alonso, J., Chatterji, S., Lee, S., & Üstün, T. B. (2009). The WHO world mental health (WMH) surveys. *Psychiatrie, 6*(1), 5.

Kramer, M. S. (1998). Maternal nutrition, pregnancy outcome and public health policy. *Canadian Medical Association Journal, 159*, 663–665.

Krug, E. G., Mercy, J. A., Dahlberg, L. L., & Zwi, A. B. (2002). The world report on violence and health. *The Lancet, 360*(9339), 1083–1088.

Laurin, J., Wallace, C., Draca, J., Aterman, S., & Tonmyr, L. (2018). Youth self-report of child maltreatment in representative surveys. *Health Promotion and Chronic Disease Prevention in Canada, 38*(2), 37–54.

Lundy, L., Kilkelly, U., Byrne, B., & Kang, J. (2012). *The UN convention on the rights of the child: A study of legal implementation in 12 countries*. UK: UNICEF. (2018 Sept 5) Retrieved from: https://www.qub.ac.uk/research-centres/CentreforChildrensRights/filestore/Filetoupload,368351,en.pdf.

MacMillan, H. L., Fleming, J. E., Trocmé, N., Boyle, M. H., Wong, M., Racine, Y. A., … Offord, D. R. (1997). Prevalence of child physical and sexual abuse in the community: results from the Ontario health supplement. *JAMA, 278*(2), 131–135.

MacMillan, H. L. (1998). Child abuse: a community problem. *Canadian Medical Association Journal, 158*, 1301–1302.

MacMillan, H. L., Wathen, C. N., Barlow, J., Fergusson, D. M., Leventhal, J. M., & Taussig, H. N. (2009). Interventions to prevent child maltreatment and associated impairment. *The Lancet, 373*(9659), 250–266.

McLennan, J. D. (2015). Persisting without evidence is a problem: suicide prevention and other well-intentioned interventions. *Journal of the Canadian Academy of Child and Adolescent Psychiatry, 24*(2), 131–132.

McLennan, J. D., MacMillan, H. L., & Jamieson, E. (2004). Canada's programs to prevent mental health problems in children: the research-practice gap. *CMAJ, 171*(9), 1069–1071.

Mejdoubi, J., van den Heijkant, S., van Leerdam, F. J., Heymans, M. W., Hirasing, R. A., & Crijnen, A. A. (2013). Effect of nurse home visits vs usual care on reducing intimate partner violence in young high-risk pregnant women: a randomized controlled trial. *PLoS One, 8*(10). e78185.

Olds, D. L., Hill, P. L., O'Brien, R., Racine, D., & Moritz, P. (2003). Taking preventive intervention to scale: the Nurse-Family Partnership. *Cognitive and Behavioral Practice, 10*(4), 278–290.

Public Health Agency of Canada. (2010). *Canadian incidence study of reported child abuse and neglect—2008: Major findings*. Ottawa, ON: Public Health Agency.

Shields, M. E., Hovdestad, W. E., Gilbert, C. P., & Tonmyr, L. E. (2016). Childhood maltreatment as a risk factor for COPD: findings from a population-based survey of Canadian adults. *International Journal of Chronic Obstructive Pulmonary Disease*, *11*, 2641–2650.

Shields, M. E., Hovdestad, W. E., Pelletier, C., Dykxhoorn, J. L., O'Donnell, S. C., & Tonmyr, L. (2016). Childhood maltreatment as a risk factor for diabetes: findings from a population-based survey of Canadian adults. *BMC Public Health*, *16*(1), 879.

Shields, M., Hovdestad, W., & Tonmyr, L. (2015). Assessment of the quality of the childhood physical abuse measure in the Canadian national population health survey. *Health Reports*, *26*(5), 3–10.

Shields, M., Tonmyr, L., & Hovdestad, W. (2016). Is child sexual abuse declining in Canada? Results from nationally representative retrospective surveys. *Health Promotion and Chronic Disease Prevention in Canada: Research, Policy and Practice*, *36*(11), 252–260.

Stiffman, A. R., Stelk, W., Horwitz, S. M., Evans, M. E., Outlaw, F. H., & Atkins, M. (2010). A public health approach to children's mental health services: possible solutions to current service inadequacies. *Administration and Policy in Mental Health and Mental Health Services Research*, *37*(1–2), 120–124.

Singh, V. A. S., Thornton, T., & Tonmyr, L. (2011). Determinants of substance abuse in a population of children and adolescents involved with the child welfare system. *International Journal of Mental Health and Addiction*, *9*(4), 382–397.

Statistics Canada. (2014). *The 2014 Ontario child health study. Interviewers manual*. Ottawa, ON.: Statistics Canada. 75411–6626.1.

Statistics Canada. (2018a). *Leading causes of death*. Retrieved from: http://www.statcan.gc.ca/tables-tableaux/sum-som/l01/cst01/hlth36a-eng.htm.

Statistics Canada. (2018b). *Census*. Retrieved from: https://www12.statcan.gc.ca/census-recensement/index-eng.cfm.

Tanaka, M., Wekerle, C., Leung, E., Waechter, R., Gonzalez, A., Jamieson, E., & MacMillan, H. L. (2012). Preliminary evaluation of the childhood experiences of violence questionnaire short form. *Journal of Interpersonal Violence*, *27*(2), 396–407.

Taylor, G. (2016). The Chief Public Health Officer's report on the state of public health in Canada 2016. In *Family violence in Canada*. Ottawa, ON: Public Health Agency of Canada.

Thompson, A., & Xiajiec, C. (2000). Increasing childhood trauma in Canada: findings from the national population health survey, 1994/95. *Canadian Journal of Public Health*, *91*, 197–200.

Tiwari, A., & Gonzalez, A. (2018). Biological alterations affecting risk of adult psychopathology following childhood trauma: a review of sex differences. *Clinical Psychology Review*, https://doi.org/10.1016/j.cpr.2018.01.006.

Tonmyr, L., & Hovdestad, W. E. (2013). Public health approach to child maltreatment. *Paediatrics & Child Health*, *18*(8), 411–413.

Tonmyr, L., Hovdestad, W. E., & Draca, J. (2014). Commentary on Canadian child maltreatment data. *Journal of Interpersonal Violence*, *29*(1), 186–197.

Tonmyr, L., MacMillan, H., Jamieson, E., & Kelly, K. (2002). The population health perspective as a framework for studying child maltreatment outcomes. *Chronic Diseases in Canada*, *23*(4), 123–129.

Tonmyr, L., Mathews, B., Shields, M., Hovdestad, W., & Afifi, T. O. (2018). Does mandatory reporting legislation increase contact with child protection? A legal doctrinal review and an analytical examination. *BMC Public Health*, *18*, 1021. 1–12.

Treasury Board of Canada. n.d. Early childhood development agreement. Retrieved September 15, 2018 from: www.tbs-sct.gc.ca/hidb-bdih/plan-eng.aspx?Hi=43&Org=0&Pl=527.

Walsh, C., MacMillan, H. L., & Jamieson, E. (2003). The relationship between parental substance abuse and child maltreatment: findings from the Ontario health supplement. *Child Abuse and Neglect*, *27*(12), 1409–1425.

Walsh, C. A., MacMillan, H. L., Trocmé, N., Jamieson, E., & Boyle, M. H. (2008). Measurement of victimization in adolescence: development and validation of the childhood experiences of violence questionnaire. *Child Abuse and Neglect*, *32*(11), 1037–1057.

Williams, S., MacMillan, H., & Jamieson, E. (2006). The potential benefits of remaining in school on the long-term mental health functioning of physically and sexually abused children: beyond the academic domain. *American Journal of Orthopsychiatry*, *76*(1), 18.

World Health Organisation. (1952). *Inaugural meeting of the World Health Organization*. Geneva: WHO.

World Health Organisation. (1986). *The Ottawa Charter*. Geneva, Switzerland: WHO.

Further reading

Afifi, T. O., MacMillan, H. L., Taillieu, T., Cheung, K., Turner, S., Tonmyr, L., & Hovdestad, W. (2015). Relationship between child abuse exposure and reported contact with child protection organizations: results from the Canadian community health survey. *Child Abuse and Neglect*, *46*, 198–206.

Afifi, T. O., MacMillan, H. L., Taillieu, T., Turner, S., Cheung, K., Sareen, J., & Boyle, M. H. (2016). Individual- and relationship-level factors related to better mental health outcomes following child abuse: results from a nationally representative Canadian sample. *The Canadian Journal of Psychiatry*, *61*(12), 776–788.

Badley, E. M., Shields, M. E., O'Donnell, S., Hovdestad, W. E., & Tonmyr, L. (2018). Childhood maltreatment as a risk factor for arthritis: findings from a population-based survey of Canadian adults. *Arthritis Care and Research*, https://doi.org/10.1002/acr.23776.

Baiden, P., den Dunnen, W., & Fallon, B. (2017). Examining the independent effect of social support on unmet mental healthcare needs among Canadians: findings from a population-based study. *Social Indicators Research*, *130*(3), 1229–1246. https://doi.org/10.1007/s11205-015-1224-y.

Baiden, P., Fallon, B., & Antwi-Boasiako, K. (2017). Effect of social support and disclosure of child abuse on adult suicidal ideation: findings from a population-based study. *Primary Care Companion to the Journal of Clinical Psychiatry*, *19*(6). https://doi.org/10.4088/PCC.17m02181.

Baiden, P., Tarshis, S., Antwi-Boasiako, K., & den Dunnen, W. (2016). Examining the independent protective effect of subjective well-being on severe psychological distress among Canadian adults with a history of child maltreatment. *Child Abuse and Neglect*, *58*, 129–140. https://doi.org/10.1016/j.chiabu.2016.06.017.

Baiden, P., & Fuller-Thomson, E. (2016). Factors associated with achieving complete mental health among individuals with lifetime suicidal ideation. *Suicide & Life-Threatening Behavior*, *46*(4), 427–446. https://doi.org/10.1111/sltb.12230.

Brennenstuhl, S., & Fuller-Thomson, E. (2015). The painful legacy of childhood violence: migraine headaches among adult survivors of adverse childhood experiences. *Headache*, *55*(7), 973–983. https://doi.org/10.1111/head.12614.

England, G., Casey, R., Ferro, M., MacMillan, H., Tonmyr, L., & Gonzalez, A. (2018). Child maltreatment and adult multimorbidity: results from the Canadian community health survey. *Canadian Journal of Public Health*, *109*(4), 561–572. https://doi.org/10.17269/s41997-018-0069-y.

Fuller-Thomson, E., Agbeyaka, S., LaFond, D. M., & Bern-Klug, M. (2016). Flourishing after depression: factors associated with achieving complete mental health among those with a history of depression. *Psychiatry Research*, *242*, 111–120. https://doi.org/10.1016/j.psychres.2016.04.041.

Fuller-Thomson, E., Baird, S. L., Dhrodia, R., & Brennenstuhl, S. (2016). The association between adverse childhood experiences (ACEs) and suicide attempts in a population-based study. *Child: Care, Health and Development*, *42*(5), 725–734. https://doi.org/10.1111/cch.12351.

Fuller-Thomson, E., & Hollister, B. (2016). Schizophrenia and suicide attempts: findings from a representative community-based Canadian sample. *Schizophrenia Research and Treatment*, https://doi.org/10.1155/2016/3165243.

Fuller-Thomson, E., Jayanthikumar, J., & Agbeyaka, S. K. (2017). Untangling the association between migraine, pain, and anxiety: examining migraine and generalized anxiety disorders in a Canadian population-based study. *Headache*, *57*(3), 375–390.

Fuller-Thomson, E., & Lacombe-Duncan, A. (2016). Understanding the association between chronic obstructive pulmonary disease and current anxiety: a population-based study. *COPD*, *13*(5), 622–631. https://doi.org/10.3109/15412555.2015.1132691.

Fuller-Thomson, E., Lateef, R., & Sulman, J. (2015). Robust association between inflammatory bowel disease and generalized anxiety disorder: findings from a nationally representative Canadian study. *Inflammatory Bowel Diseases*, *21*(10), 2341–2348. https://doi.org/10.1097/MIB.0000000000000518.

Fuller-Thomson, E., & Lewis, D. A. (2015). The relationship between early adversities and attention-deficit/hyperactivity disorder. *Child Abuse and Neglect*, *47*(9), 94–101. https://doi.org/10.1016/j.chiabu.2015.03.005.

Fuller-Thomson, E., Lewis, D. A., & Agbeyaka, S. K. (2016). Attention-deficit/hyperactivity disorder casts a long shadow: findings from a population-based study of adult women with self-reported ADHD. *Child: Care, Health and Development*, *42*(6), 918–927. https://doi.org/10.1111/cch.12380.

Fuller-Thomson, E., Ramzan, N., & Baird, S. L. (2016). Arthritis and suicide attempts: findings from a large nationally representative Canadian survey. *Rheumatology International*, *36*(9), 1237–1248. https://doi.org/10.1007/s00296-016-3498-z.

Fuller-Thomson, E., Roane, J. L., & Brennenstuhl, S. (2016). Three types of adverse childhood experiences, and alcohol and drug dependence among adults: an investigation using population-based data. *Substance Use and Misuse*, *51*(11), 1451–1461. https://doi.org/10.1080/10826084.2016.1181089.

Fuller-Thomson, E., West, K. J., Sulman, J., & Baird, S. L. (2015). Childhood maltreatment is associated with ulcerative colitis but not Crohn's disease: findings from a population-based study. *Inflammatory Bowel Diseases*, *21*(11), 2640–2648. https://doi.org/10.1097/MIB.0000000000000551.

Martin, M. S., Dykxhoorn, J., Afifi, T. O., & Colman, I. (2016). Child abuse and the prevalence of suicide attempts among those reporting suicide ideation. *Social Psychiatry and Psychiatric Epidemiology*, *51*(11), 1477–1484. https://doi.org/10.1007/s00127-016-1250-3.

Meng, X., & D'Arcy, C. (2016). Gender moderates the relationship between childhood abuse and internalizing and substance use disorders later in life: a cross-sectional analysis. *BMC Psychiatry*, *16*(1), https://doi.org/10.1186/s12888-016-1071-7.

Sampasa-Kanyinga, H., Nilsen, W., & Colman, I. (2018). Child abuse and work stress in adulthood: evidence from a population-based study. *Preventive Medicine*, *108*, 60–66. https://doi.org/10.1016/j.ypmed.2017.12.029.

Ukah, U. V., Adu, P. A., De Silva, D. A., & Von Dadelszen, P. (2016). The impact of a history of adverse childhood experiences on breastfeeding initiation and exclusivity: findings from a national population health survey. *Breastfeeding Medicine*, *11*(10), 544–550. https://doi.org/10.1089/bfm.2016.0053.

CHAPTER

11

Global perspective on ACEs☆

Greta M. Massetti[a], *Karen Hughes*[b,c], *Mark A. Bellis*[b,c], *James Mercy*[a]

[a]Division of Violence Prevention, Centers for Disease Control and Prevention, Atlanta, GA, United States, [b]College of Human Sciences, Bangor University, Bangor, United Kingdom, [c]World Health Organization Collaborating Centre for Investment in Health and Well-being, Public Health Wales, Cardiff, United Kingdom

Introduction

Globally, the burden of adverse childhood experiences (ACEs) poses perhaps one of the greatest challenges—and yet some of the greatest opportunities—to impact health and life course outcomes. The biological mechanisms for the associations between ACEs and subsequent mental and physical health problems in adulthood have been established through epidemiological studies as well as basic science. Recent evidence demonstrates that traumatic stress, such as that associated with ACEs, impacts developments in brain architecture (both structure and function; Anda, Butchart, Felitti, & Brown, 2010). Early exposure to toxic stress in childhood, via its impact on the brain, confers lasting changes at the most basic levels of the nervous, endocrine, and immune systems, and such exposures can alter the physical structure of DNA (epigenetic effects; Danese & McEwen, 2012). The ACEs literature has built an expansive and compelling narrative that documents the indelible long-term effects of ACEs on health and well-being throughout the life course (Mercy et al., 2017; Moore et al., 2015; Norman et al., 2012; Raposo, Mackenzie, Henriksen, & Afifi, 2014; Teicher & Samson, 2016). Much of this research has been conducted using samples based in the US, and to some extent other high-income countries (Hughes et al., 2017; Stoltenborgh, Bakermans-Kranenburg, &

☆The findings and conclusions in this report are those of the authors and do not necessarily represent the official position of the Centers for Disease Control and Prevention.

https://doi.org/10.1016/B978-0-12-816065-7.00011-2

van Ijzendoorn, 2013); thus, results of ACEs studies reflect data and findings for high-income populations, primarily in the US. Yet, adverse experiences can and do affect children around the world, and the potential for understanding the burden of ACEs and their impact globally has not fully been tapped.

This chapter will provide an overview of the current understanding of ACEs in a global context. This includes reviewing the data on the prevalence of ACEs across cultures, countries, and contexts; assessing the state of the literature on short- and long-term effects of ACEs globally; and, summarizing what is known about ACEs among vulnerable populations. Discussions of the current quality of research in this area and availability of data are also valuable in understanding what gaps remain in making consistent conclusions from the literature. Quality data and information on ACEs at the global level are critically important in measuring how well the world is doing in protecting its most vulnerable citizens—children—and informing evidence-based strategies to prevent ACEs and related health outcomes. The findings in this chapter seek to shed light on actionable information about ACEs to improve efforts to protect all children in all countries, all contexts, and all communities.

Measurement and definitions in global settings

One issue to address in examining ACEs globally is to understand how well traditional definitions and measures of ACEs translate across settings. This includes translation of findings across cultures, and in settings that reflect low resources and/or low- and middle-income countries. Broadly defined, ACEs are a collection of experiences that may be traumatic to children and youth, including experiencing violence and neglect, witnessing violence in the home or community, and growing up in a household with mental illness, substance abuse, or incarceration of a parent. A significant body of research on adverse experiences in childhood has examined the relationship between individual types or categories of ACEs and their health impacts (Gilbert et al., 2009; Lissau & Sorensen, 1994). Additionally, the frame for ACEs research can also use aggregate assessments of multiple ACEs. In this approach, ACEs are typically measured by summing the number of different ACEs to which an individual is exposed (Dong et al., 2004; Felitti et al., 1998; Ford et al., 2014). Analyses then use the sum score of ACEs to assess the relationship between ACEs and one or more outcomes of interest. Traditional types of ACEs measured in surveys include experiencing violence (including physical abuse, sexual abuse, and neglect) and household challenges (e.g., exposure to domestic violence, living in a household with someone who has a substance abuse disorder) (Dong et al., 2004). Notably, measures of ACEs do not consistently include certain adverse experiences that likely have significant impact on children and youth, such as bullying or teen dating violence. Some ACEs questionnaires include these categories, while others do not (such as the Center for Disease Control and Prevention [CDC] short ACEs tool). This can lead to inconsistencies in measurement and definitions of ACEs in the literature. In addition, the ACEs score does not reflect the frequency or severity of exposures, or the impact on the child.

In addressing the question of translating this definition across contexts and settings, one of the primary definitional challenges involves the transposition of measuring ACEs. The World Health Organization (WHO) ACE-International Questionnaire (ACE-IQ; WHO, 2017) was developed through a deliberate process with input from experts across topics. The questionnaire includes questions about the different types of ACEs (i.e., violence, neglect, and household dysfunction) and is intended to be implemented across countries, contexts, and cultures (WHO, 2011). Some researchers have undertaken efforts to conduct a cultural adaptation of the ACE-IQ; for example, Quinn et al. (2018) collaborated with residents of a low-resource, underserved community in South Africa to conduct focus groups and interviews with community residents to assess the understandability and cultural appropriateness of the ACE-IQ and inform modifications and adaptations of the questionnaire. Documenting the results of such qualitative, methodical approaches to adaptation can inform the implementation of the ACE-IQ across cultures and settings and build the understanding of how the questions perform across cultural contexts.

There are also unique cultural issues that arise in thinking about how to assess certain ACEs, such as child neglect, in contexts of extreme disadvantage. Traditional definitions of child neglect as an adverse experience, and methods for measuring it, are indelibly confounded with material security. For example, common questions to assess child neglect are difficult to disentangle from issues of food insecurity, housing insecurity, and other material resources (Dong et al., 2004; WHO, 2017). These questions often include reference to resources, as noted in the italicized phrase in this example: *How often did your parents/guardians not give you enough food even when they could have easily done so?* (WHO, 2017). For youth whose families have very limited material means, they may have never or very rarely "easily" been provided enough food. Such questions also rely on a youth's perception of the family's access to material goods or resources, which may not always be accurate (Dong, Anda, Dube, Giles, & Felitti, 2003; Dube, Williamson, Thompson, Felitti, & Anda, 2004; Edwards et al., 2001). Because the validity of these measures of physical or resource neglect in low-resource settings is yet to be explored, questions remain as to how these particular ACEs contribute to the burden of overall ACEs in such settings. Emotional neglect, on the other hand, may be relatively more independent of economic resources. However, it has not been extensively measured or examined in low-resource settings or across global contexts.

This lack of consistency in measurement of neglect is reflected in variations in estimates across studies depending on the measures and approach used to assess neglect. One study reflecting data from 21 countries using the WHO World Mental Health Survey Initiative (WMHS; Kessler & Ustun, 2008) found prevalence of neglect to range from 3.6% in low-income and lower-middle-income countries to 5.2% in high-middle-income countries and 4.4% in high-income countries (Kessler et al., 2010). The WMHS data reflect consistency across countries using the same approach to measuring neglect. In contrast, a systematic review and metaanalysis found a combined prevalence of 16.3% for physical neglect and 18.4% for emotional neglect (Stoltenborgh et al., 2013). Thus, the review found different prevalence compared to the WMHS data. This review and metaanalysis also found significantly higher prevalence of neglect in lower-income countries than higher-income countries, suggesting that measures of neglect are associated with, and may reflect access to, material resources. The variation in prevalence of neglect in the literature indicates that more consistency in methodology, measurement, and use of representative samples is needed to effectively measure child neglect. Such methodological precision is necessary to understand to what extent questions about physical neglect reflect differences in material resources. Better data on how emotional neglect contributes to ACEs globally can inform improved crosscultural knowledge of ACEs.

Globally, there is also a gap in measurement of adverse experiences that are not typically captured in ACE measures, yet are likely to impact child well-being and development significantly. We previously noted that ACEs typically include child abuse and neglect, but exclude other forms of violence that can negatively impact youth, such as bullying, teen dating violence, peer-to-peer assault, and community and gang violence (Exner-Cortens, Eckenrode, & Rothman, 2013; Lereya, Copeland, Costello, & Wolke, 2015; Takizawa, Maughan, & Arseneault, 2014). Children and youth are also exposed to natural and manmade disasters, war, and conflict-related violence, which can result in substantial stress that can be associated with severe and long-term mental and/or physical impairment (Amowitz et al., 2002; Joshi & O'Donnell, 2003). For example, findings from one study using WMHS data from Lebanon indicated that about 19% of individuals experienced a traumatic event not related to war in childhood, but 38% experienced a war-related traumatic event in childhood (Itani, Haddad, Fayyad, Karam, & Karam, 2014). In another study of Palestinian children, more than half experienced one or more traumatic events (Khamis, 2015). These exposures also commonly result in secondary impacts—hunger/food instability, housing instability, migration, and acculturation—that in and of themselves constitute significant adverse experiences for children and youth (Bellis, Hardcastle, Hughes, Wood, & Nurse, 2017; Catani, Schauer, & Neuner, 2008; Stark et al., 2017). These effects can be regenerative, in that individuals who have been exposed to violence, trauma, and conflict are, in turn, at greater risk for perpetrating violence and engaging in conflict (Bellis et al., 2017; Catani et al., 2010). Some ACEs measures, such as the WHO ACE-IQ, include questions about exposure to war and conflict-related violence (WHO, 2017); but, not all studies that measure ACEs and not all ACEs questionnaires include such questions. These types of data can be exceptionally valuable to assess these exposures globally.

Prevalence of ACEs globally

Data from global studies provide estimates of the prevalence of ACEs, both for individual childhood experiences or types of experiences, and for combinations of ACEs. Fig. 1 shows a map of countries in which studies assessing cumulative ACEs and their potential impacts have been conducted and published. The map reflects studies identified from a recent comprehensive systematic review and metaanalysis (Hughes et al., 2017), supplemented with an additional search of recent studies and publications. The map shows that, although ACEs data are now available from a significant number of countries, many regions around the world appear to still be lacking this information. For example, there is limited coverage of ACEs data in Central and South America, Western Europe, the Eastern Mediterranean, parts of Asia, and Africa.

One of the major gaps in assessing the prevalence of ACEs involves the lack of nationally representative data on prevalence. Some studies

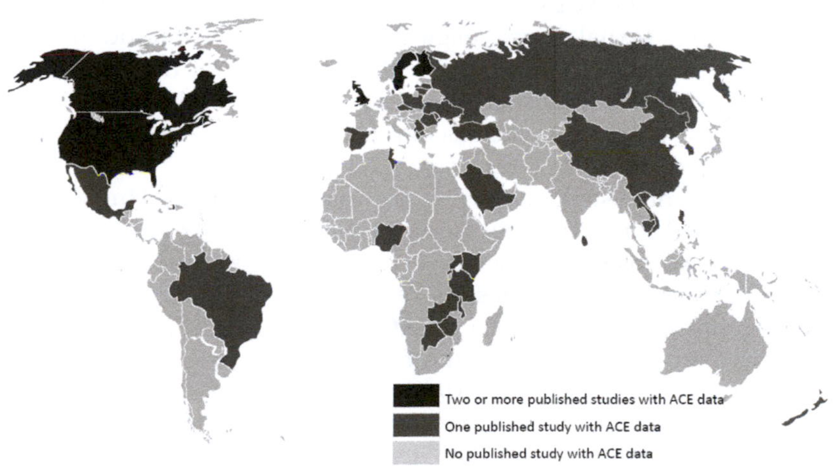

FIG. 1 Global map showing coverage of nationally representative population surveys that have included data on adverse childhood experiences (ACEs).

that have yielded data on ACEs prevalence have used representative samples, while others rely on convenience samples (Hughes et al., 2017). Convenience samples yield valuable information, but may reflect biased estimates if the data are not fully nationally representative (Bornstein, Jager, & Putnick, 2013; Tyrer & Heyman, 2016). One source of nationally representative data comes from the WMHS Initiative (Kessler & Ustun, 2008), which included >50,000 adults from 21 countries. Some countries used nationally representative samples, while others relied on convenience samples from urban areas (Kessler et al., 2010). Response rates averaged about 73% (Heeringa et al., 2008). Measuring 12 types of ACEs retrospectively, prevalence of any childhood adversity was 38.8%, with 59.3%–66.2% of individuals who experienced any ACEs experiencing more than one (Kessler et al., 2010). One interesting finding from the WMHS indicated that the prevalence of ACEs was similar across country income categories, ranging from 38.4% for high-income to 39.1% for low-income and lower-middle-income countries. Despite the similarities in prevalence across income categories, these findings mask wide variation in prevalence across individual countries. Individual country data indicate much larger variation from country to country. For example, among high-income countries, the prevalence for ACEs in Spain was 21% (Perales et al., 2013), whereas it was 57% in the US (Schussler-Fiorenza Rose, Xie, & Stineman, 2014). Such crosscountry variation within income categories indicates the need for more exploration of the factors that may drive differences in prevalence of ACEs, including factors such as inequalities and the concentration of income and trauma within countries. Across country income categories, the most common childhood adversities were parental death, followed by physical abuse. Findings related to the co-occurrence of ACEs revealed that different types of violence (e.g., physical abuse, sexual abuse, neglect, exposure to domestic violence) were highly intercorrelated, along with other types of household challenges such as parental substance use, mental illness, and criminal behavior. In contrast, adversities such as parental death, divorce, and physical illness were less likely to co-occur (Kessler et al., 2010).

A more recent systematic review and metaanalysis by Hughes et al. (2017) compiled comprehensive findings across 37 studies from >250,000 participants. As this review included results across multiple data sources using different surveys, the results reflect broader findings in the literature regarding the prevalence of ACEs globally. Using retrospective experiences reported by adults, the findings reveal significantly higher prevalence of ACEs than the WMHS. The prevalence of any ACEs was 57%, ranging from 33% to 88% across countries. The findings also reflect significant variation across studies in how many ACEs were assessed. This variation likely resulted in variations in prevalence, as measurement of ACEs is likely to vary with the number and types of ACEs measured.

Studies were most likely to include measures of childhood physical abuse, household substance abuse, and childhood sexual abuse. Notably, the review found that ACEs are highly likely to co-occur, and about 13% of participants across studies experienced at least four ACEs.

The Violence Against Children Surveys (VACS), facilitated by the US CDC as part of the global Together for Girls initiative (Chiang et al., 2016), are nationally representative surveys of youth ages 13 to 24 years. The surveys measure a broad range of ACEs in childhood, including sexual, physical, and emotional violence and exposure to domestic violence. Twenty-four surveys have been conducted or are in progress in Africa, Southeast Asia, Eastern Europe, the Caribbean, and Latin America (https://www.cdc.gov/violenceprevention/childabuseandneglect/vacs/index.html), yielding an increasing level of population data on the burden of ACEs across countries and contexts. Reports and publications using VACS data provide valuable information about the prevalence of and risk factors associated with ACEs in multiple countries, and their associations with health. For example, a study by Vander Ende et al. (2016) using Malawi data found that 82.2% of youth were exposed to one or more ACEs and 10.1% experienced four or more. Physical violence was the most common type of adverse experience, with more than two-thirds (64.6%) of youth experiencing it in childhood. The study also found that the odds of perpetration of sexual intimate partner violence in young adulthood increased in a gradient fashion with exposure to increasing numbers of ACEs. Other studies using VACS data have found that ACEs were associated with lifetime experiences of sexually transmitted diseases (STDs), pregnancy complications or miscarriages, unwanted pregnancy, alcohol use, and depression among young adult females in Swaziland (Breiding, Mercy, Gulaid, Reza, & Hleta-Nkambule, 2013; Reza et al., 2009). In Tanzania, females who experienced ACEs were more likely to experience symptoms of sexual risk behaviors, STDs, mental health problems, and alcohol use in young adulthood (Chiang et al., 2015; Vagi et al., 2016). Males who experienced ACEs were more likely to have had an STD diagnosis and symptoms in young adulthood (Vagi et al., 2016). A study on ACEs among males using data from the Haiti, Cambodia, and Kenya surveys found that they were associated with increased odds of alcohol abuse, STDs, mental health problems, and suicidal ideation (Sumner et al., 2016). VACS data provide a rich resource from which information about the prevalence and health consequences of ACEs can be assessed through comprehensive surveys that use rigorous methodology. Recent changes to the standard VACS questionnaire will allow countries to measure a broader range of ACEs, including childhood neglect, exposure to community violence, and additional household challenges. This expansion of coverage of ACEs will further strengthen the availability of population-level global data on ACEs and serve as a key resource to inform science as well as policy and programming strategies for countries implementing the surveys (Chiang et al., 2016).

Table 1 shows the prevalence of any ACEs and 4 or more ACEs by country for studies included in the Hughes et al. (2017) systematic review and metaanalysis, supplemented with studies found through an updated literature search. Although ACEs data are now available from a wide variety of countries and regions, more than half of the studies have been conducted in the US or the United Kingdom. Of note, most ACEs data involve surveying adults sharing information about their experiences in childhood retrospectively. Thus, the data reflect events that could have happened many years prior to the survey.

Prevalence findings across studies and reviews also reflect significant variations in estimates (Hughes et al., 2017; Kessler et al., 2010). There are several potential reasons for these variations. First, as previously discussed, most studies in low- and middle-income countries rely on nonrepresentative samples, which likely reflect biased estimates. They often also exclude individuals who are in vulnerable contexts, such as homeless and institutionalized populations. Without nationally representative data, it is not possible to determine which estimates are closest to the "true" prevalence. Second, variations in measurement of ACEs may result in differences. One such difference involves the number of ACEs assessed. For example, in their comprehensive review, Hughes et al. (2017) included studies that measured between 6 and 12 ACEs. The WMHS assesses 12 ACEs (Kessler et al., 2010). Different questionnaires and question wording can also result in variations in estimates. Finally, different data collection methods, such as in-person versus phone interviews, may result in different estimates (Naicker, Norris, Mabaso, & Richter, 2017; Tourangeau & Yan, 2007).

Despite variations in measurement and differences in prevalence, consistent themes emerge when considering the impact of ACEs on health and other outcomes globally. Across studies, consistently strong associations between ACEs and negative health outcomes emerged for substance use, interpersonal violence, suicidal behavior, sexual risk behaviors, and mental health problems (Hughes et al., 2017; Kessler et al., 2010). In addition, several studies have also found that ACEs are associated with smoking, poor overall health, and chronic diseases such as cancer, heart disease, and respiratory disease (Hughes et al., 2017; also see Chapter 5). These findings are also mirrored in studies that have examined individual ACEs, such as papers from VACS data (Reza et al., 2009; Sumner et al., 2016; Vagi et al., 2016). These findings demonstrate not only the association between individual ACEs and poor health outcomes, but also the consistent increase in risk with increased ACEs exposures (Hughes et al., 2017). The power of the dose-response relationship between ACEs scores and health outcomes constitutes another consistent theme in the literature (Tourangeau & Yan,

TABLE 1 Reported Prevalence of Exposure to Any of the Adverse Childhood Experiences (ACEs) by Study and Location

Country by region	Age	Any ACEs prevalence (%)	≥4 ACEs prevalence (%)	ACEs measure used	Reference[a]
Eastern Mediterranean					
Saudi Arabia	≥18	82%	32%	Self-report, WHO ACE-IQ	Almuneef, Qayad, Aleissa, and Albuhairan (2014)
Tunisia	22 (mean)	72% Females 89% Males	14% Females 27% Males	Self-report, WHO ACE-IQ	El Mhamdi et al. (2017)
Americwas					
Canada	≥15	72%	7%	Self-report, various survey sources	Chartier, Walker, and Naimark (2010)
Canada	18–49	50%	NR	Self-report, National Population Health Survey	Garad et al. (2017)
USA	≥ 18	53%	7%	Self-report, CDC short ACE tool	Cabrera, Hoge, Bliese, Castro, and Messer (2007)
USA	≥18	59%	15%	Self-report, CDC short ACE tool	L. K. Gilbert et al. (2015)
USA	20–81	86%	NR	Self-report, various survey sources	Koss et al. (2003)
USA	48 (mean)	88%	38%	Self-report, derived from CDC short ACE tool	LaNoue, Graeber, de Hernandez, Warner, and Helitzer (2012)
USA	22–24	79%	15%	Administrative records and self-report, Life Events Checklist	Mersky, Topitzes, and Reynolds (2013)
USA	≥21	53%	8%	Self-report, investigator-derived	Miller et al. (2011)
USA	40–79	58%	18%	Self-report, CDC short ACE tool	Mouton, Hargreaves, Liu, Fadeyi, and Blot (2016)
USA	≥19	67%	16%	Self-report, CDC short ACE tool	Ports, Ford, and Merrick (2016)

Continued

TABLE 1 Reported Prevalence of Exposure to Any of the Adverse Childhood Experiences (ACEs) by Study and Location—cont'd

Country by region	Age	Any ACEs prevalence (%)	≥4 ACEs prevalence (%)	ACEs measure used	Reference[a]
USA	NR	76%	32%	Self-report, CDC short ACE tool	Randell, O'Malley, and Dowd (2015)
USA	≥65	43%	NR	Self-report, CDC short ACE tool	Raposo et al. (2014)
USA	20–38	69%	19%	Self-report, CDC short ACE tool	Su et al. (2015)
USA	≥18	67%	20%	Self-report, CDC short ACE tool	Wade et al. (2016)
USA	≥18	57%	14%	Self-report, CDC short ACE tool	Schussler-Fiorenza Rose et al. (2014)
Mexico	18–65	55%	NR	Self-report, WMHS	Benjet, Borges, and Medina-Mora (2010)
Brazil	15	85%	7% Females 3% Males	Self-report, CDC short ACE tool	Soares et al. (2016)
Europe					
Finland	40–54	63%	8%	Self-report, CDC short ACE tool	Harkonmäki et al. (2007)
Finland	30–64	58%	9%	Self-report, derived from CDC short ACE tool	Pirkola et al. (2005)
Sweden	24–28	32%	1%	Administrative records	Bjorkenstam, Vinnerljung, and Hjern (2017)
Denmark	15–33	52%	2%	Administrative records	Dahl et al. (2017)
UK	45–69	33%	1%	Self-report, CDC short ACE tool	Leung, Britton, and Bell (2016)
UK	18–70	47%	12%	Self-report, CDC short ACE tool	Bellis et al. (2014)
UK	18–69	46%	8%	Self-report, CDC short ACE tool	Bellis et al. (2015)
UK	18–69	46%	14%	Self-report, CDC short ACE tool	Bellis et al. (2015)

Country by region	Age	Any ACEs prevalence (%)	≥4 ACEs prevalence (%)	ACEs measure used	Reference[a]
UK	18–69	43%	9%	Self-report, CDC short ACE tool	Ford et al. (2014)
Spain	≥18	21%	0%	Self-report, WMHS	Perales et al. (2013)
Various, Eastern Europe	18–25	53%	7%	Self-report, CDC short ACE tool	Bellis et al. (2014)
Sri Lanka	18–49	NR	31%	Self-report, various survey sources	Fonseka, Minnis, and Gomez (2015)
China	22–23 (means)	68%	10%	Self-report, CDC short ACE tool	Xiao, Dong, Yao, Li, and Ye (2008)
Republic of Korea	19–30	50%	8%	Self-report, WHO ACE-IQ	Kim (2017)
Philippines	≥35	73%	9%	Self-report, CDC short ACE tool	Ramiro, Madrid, and Brown (2010)
Vietnam	18–30	76%	21%	Self-report, WHO ACE-IQ	Tran, Dunne, Vo, and Luu (2015)
New Zealand	21 (mean)	74%	21%	Self-report, investigator-derived	Goodwin, Fergusson, and Horwood (2004)
Kenya	≥18	93%	19%	Self-report, WHO ACE-IQ	Goodman et al. (2017)
Malawi	13–24	82%	10%	Self-report, VACS	Vander Ende et al. (2016)
Nigeria	≥18	46%	NR	Self-report, WMHS	Oladeji, Makanjuola, and Gureje (2010)

NR = not reported; WHO ACE-IQ, World Health Organization ACE-International Questionnaire; VACS, Violence Against Children Surveys; WMHS, World Mental Health Survey Initiative.

[a]*Note: some data sources have resulted in multiple publications on similarly defined subsamples; for these, one sample publication has been selected to minimize overlap. Furthermore, not all studies listed reflect nationally representative data.*

2007). This indicates that the combined effects of multiple stressors convey combined vulnerability in childhood and adolescence. Also of note are the consistencies in relationships between ACEs and specific health outcomes found in studies from different countries and cultures (Hughes et al., 2017). The biological mechanisms that underlie the impact of ACEs on health help explain this consistency, as these effects cut across cultures and national boundaries.

The effects of ACEs on health and other long-term outcomes are not trivial. WMHS data estimate that 30% of adult psychopathology is attributable to ACEs (Kessler et al., 2010). UK data indicate that ACEs account for between 14% and 60% of health and social problems, ranging from poor diet and binge drinking to incarceration and drug use (Bellis et al., 2014). These impacts are not just felt by the individuals who are exposed to childhood adversity, they affect communities and countries as a whole. A study using prevalence data from South Africa found that the total estimated costs of violence against children in that country amounted to 6% of its gross domestic product in 2015 (Fang, Fry, Ganz, Casey, & Ward, 2016). Although the study focused only on the violence components of ACEs, it stands to reason that the economic burden of ACEs could be estimated as even greater. Taken as a whole, the literature on the impact of ACEs on health points to the critical need to interrupt the cycle of ACEs to negative health outcomes, and to build resilience among individuals who have been exposed.

ACEs among vulnerable populations

Despite the growing literature on ACEs globally, significant gaps remain in our knowledge of how adverse experiences affect vulnerable children across the world. There are several specific areas that are notable, including data on children affected by humanitarian crises, data on children with disabilities, and macro drivers of ACEs.

There are currently ongoing severe and widespread humanitarian crises (ACAPS, 2017). Children are often the most vulnerable populations affected by conflict, famine, and other humanitarian issues (Joshi & O'Donnell, 2003; Montgomery & Foldspang, 2005; Stark & Landis, 2016). There are more refugees around the world now than there have ever been (ACAPS, 2017). Many of those are children. What these children have experienced—events that led to displacement, experiences during transit, and living conditions as refugees—have undeniably impacted their lives and left indelible marks in their youth. Yet, comprehensive, quality data on the scope of ACEs among children who are refugees, internally displaced persons, and stateless have not been systematically collected or compiled. A systematic review of population-based surveys of ACEs in humanitarian settings found significant gaps in the literature (Stark & Landis, 2016). Notably, the authors found this field characterized by weak methodology and lack of standardized approaches. These gaps limit the currently available knowledge about the experiences and impacts of ACEs in humanitarian contexts.

Substantial research indicates that children and youth with disabilities are at significantly greater risk for experiencing violence and other adverse experiences (Jones et al., 2012). However, global data on the prevalence of disabilities and the experiences of children with disabilities are limited (Hughes et al., 2017; Winters, Langer, & Geniets, 2017). This information is critical to describe the experiences of one particularly vulnerable population. Information about the prevalence of ACEs globally among children with disabilities, how it differs from the prevalence among youth without disabilities, and what the differences are in the long-term consequences of ACEs can help inform strategies to protect youth with disabilities. A 2012 systematic review and metaanalysis by Jones et al. (2012) assessed the state of the literature on violence against children with disabilities. Though the review focused on the broader violence category of ACEs and did not assess household challenges, the other major type of ACEs, the information is nonetheless valuable at summarizing the experiences of children with disabilities. The review found that there was significant variation in reported prevalence and risk of ACEs among children with disabilities. Overall, children with disabilities were >3.5 times more likely to experience any violence and physical violence, and >2.8 times more likely to experience sexual violence, than typically developing children (Jones et al., 2012). Authors noted significant limitations in the literature due to lack of systematic approaches to measurement of disabilities and violence, and to weaknesses in methodology in unpacking the relationship between the two constructs. Better data on ACEs among youth with disabilities, particularly from nationally representative, population-based studies are needed to clarify the burden of ACEs among this vulnerable group and to identify opportunities for prevention and protection.

Globally, the macrodrivers of ACEs are often known; but, their impacts on children are uncounted. Corruption, inequality, poverty, and political instability—sometimes referred to as adverse environments—can manifest on the daily experiences of children and cause lasting impacts (Stark et al., 2017; Stark & Landis, 2016). Better data on how these types of experiences create the conditions whereby children are more likely to experience ACEs can shed light on opportunities to improve protection. For example, these types of adverse environments can result in increased risk for child abuse and intimate partner violence, demonstrating the transfer of environmental effects into the home (Stark et al., 2017; Stark & Landis, 2016). Data on how these macro drivers result in ACEs for children, both in the immediate and long term, can fill in the narrative of the real-world impacts of such conditions.

Directions for future research

The findings from systematic reviews, metaanalyses, and global research on ACEs reveal important themes in measurement of the prevalence of ACEs globally, as well as some challenges in the current state of the field. First, prevalence data from nationally representative surveys are lacking, indicating that prevalence estimates must be interpreted with caution as they often reflect convenience samples (Bornstein et al., 2013; Tyrer & Heyman, 2016). Second, the majority of studies rely on data collected among adults sharing information about their experiences in childhood. This is a standard approach in the literature, and evidence suggests that such retrospective reports provide accurate and valid accounts of experiences (Dube et al., 2004). However, the absence of more recent data reported among children and youth directly or young adults results in some limitations. Retrospective reports among adults can reflect experiences that took place many years or decades prior to the survey. As such, they do not reflect current status of ACEs and thus have more limited value in informing program and policy strategies to prevent ACEs as well as monitoring changes in the prevalence of ACEs over time. Furthermore, retrospective reports of experiences that may have occurred many years prior to a survey are not reflective of recent events. Results of retrospective results of research on ACEs can benefit from complementing with research with children and youth that reflects more recent experiences. Third, the global research on ACEs also reflects significant gaps in data from various cultures, contexts, and countries. The preponderance of research has been conducted in higher-income countries, primarily in the US and the United Kingdom (Hughes et al., 2017; Kessler & Ustun, 2008). Limited data from low-income or lower-middle-income countries exist. This lack of diversity limits the ability to determine common patterns of ACEs across cultures as well as phenomena that may be unique to particular settings, cultures, or countries. More comprehensive, population data on ACEs from multiple countries can help fill out the global picture of the prevalence of ACEs and associated health outcomes.

Implications for policy and practice

The emergence of global data on ACEs has potential for significant and broad-ranging impact. Importantly, the data have critical implications for prevention of ACEs as a strategic lever for addressing a range of public health and social problems. This is particularly relevant given the consistent and burgeoning research linking ACEs to adverse health and other negative life outcomes around the world (Hughes et al., 2017; Patel, Flisher, Nikapota, & Malhotra, 2008; Stark et al., 2017). Further, ACEs prevention approaches have the ability to underpin multiagency initiatives and crosscutting approaches, resulting in significant potential to broaden the scope of prevention impact (WHO, 2016; also see Chapter 12). Recent innovative modeling approaches have begun to quantify the potential for meaningful impact by addressing preventing ACEs. A study modeling data from South Africa found that preventing violence against children could reduce drug abuse by up to 14%, self-harm by 23%, and alcohol abuse by 14% (Hsiao et al., 2017). Similarly, a study of students in eight eastern European countries identified that preventing ACEs could have reduced drug use by 36%, problem drinking by 51%, and suicide attempt by 83% (Bellis et al., 2014).

On a global basis, we understand very little about why some individuals exposed to ACEs go on to develop health and behavioral problems while others do not. The concept of resilience (protection drawn from individual and community support, cultural connections and other positive factors in children's lives; also see Chapter 14) is poorly studied internationally but is potentially a critical element in understanding how youth exposed to toxic stress from ACEs can build skills and coping strategies within protective environments. A recent systematic review of resilience factors identified biological, psychological, and social mediators for childhood adversity on adult mental health. The review also documented biological/genetic and psychological moderators of the relationship between ACEs and mental health outcomes (Hoppen & Chalder, 2018). Another systematic review found individual-, relationship-, and community-level resilience factors for childhood adversity, and highlighted the potential importance of examining the interrelations between factors (Fritz, de Graaff, Caisley, van Harmelen, & Wilkinson, 2018). These reviews relied almost exclusively on data from studies conducted in high-income countries. Therefore, research is needed in low- and middle-income countries and low-resource contexts to understand the factors that buffer the effects of ACEs across contexts.

The United Nations Sustainable Development Goals (SDGs) established ambitious and aspirational goals for countries to protect children by including two targets related to violence against children, one type or aspect of ACEs (United Nations General Assembly, 2015). The SDGs call for the full elimination—rather than the reduction—of violence and exploitation of children and violence against women and girls. Without more comprehensive, complete, and timely data, it is impossible to determine where countries stand and how they should direct prevention priorities to achieve these targets by 2030. Indeed, better data with direct and actionable implications for programming and policy have the potential to drive national strategies to catalyze change (WHO, 2014). In addition, data can be used to monitor progress and assess trends. One important implication of the status of the literature on ACEs globally, then, is the need for more timely and complete data on ACEs from a broader variety of countries. Relatedly, there is also a need to ensure the data are collected intentionally to inform and guide prevention programs and policies, and that they are collected in such a way as to be sensitive to change.

For more than a decade, CDC in partnership with Together for Girls has been working with country governments to use VACS data to guide comprehensive multisectoral action for preventing and responding to violence (Together for Girls, 2013). This approach has involved building multistakeholder strategies that rely on good-quality data to inform the development and implementation of national action plans based on the best available evidence (Together for Girls, 2015). This approach can serve as a model for coordinated planning and action, linking data to evidence-based strategies. The INSPIRE Technical Package serves as a complementary resource that lays out seven strategies to address violence against children: (1) implementation and enforcement of laws, (2) norms and values, (3) safe environments, (4) parent and caregiver support, (5) income and economic strengthening, (6) response and support services, and (7) education and life skills. Taken together, these strategies are foundational pillars with strong evidence of impact in reducing violence against children and youth and related ACEs (WHO, 2016). INSPIRE serves as a platform for evidence-based action for countries and stakeholders to inform comprehensive prevention strategies with the greatest potential for impact.

Conclusion

Findings from global research on ACEs and their consequences show that, despite significant gaps in data availability, substantial numbers of children are affected by ACEs across the world. These findings indicate that these experiences are likely to constitute major contributors to poor health and life course outcomes in regions across the world (Hughes et al., 2017). Although some crosscultural variations exist (Devries et al., 2018; Hillis, Mercy, Amobi, & Kress, 2016; Hughes et al., 2017; Kessler et al., 2010), consistent patterns in the long-term effects of ACEs suggest that such experiences negatively affect health and development across cultures. The findings in the literature make a strong argument for the need to use the best-quality data to inform implementation and expansion of evidence-based strategies to prevent exposure to adverse experiences among children, and mitigate the effects of such experiences among those who have been exposed (Chiang et al., 2016; Haegerich, David-Ferdon,

Noonan, Manns, & Billie, 2017; WHO, 2016). Improved access to good-quality data on ACEs is essential to measure the burden, target prevention efforts, monitor progress, and drive action toward the 2030 Sustainable Development Agenda (United Nations, 2015). Multicomponent strategies that prevent ACEs through evidence-based approaches have the potential for broad long-term positive impact on a range of indicators of health and well-being (Hawkins et al., 2012; Matjasko et al., 2012). Data-grounded strategies to drive efforts to protect children from ACEs can protect the safety of children in the immediate term (Cluver et al., 2018; Doyle et al., 2018), but also can improve their long-term health and well-being around the world (Hawkins, Kosterman, Catalano, Hill, & Abbott, 2005; Olds et al., 1998; Sandler, Ingram, Wolchik, Tein, & Winslow, 2015; Sandler, Schoenfelder, Wolchik, & MacKinnon, 2011).

Acknowledgments

The findings and conclusions in this report are those of the authors and do not necessarily represent the official position of the Centers for Disease Control and Prevention.

References

Anda, R. F., Butchart, A., Felitti, V. J., & Brown, D. W. (2010). Building a framework for global surveillance of the public health implications of adverse childhood experiences. *American Journal of Preventive Medicine, 39*, 93–98.

Danese, A., & McEwen, B. (2012). Adverse childhood experiences, allostasis, allostatic load, and age-related disease. *Physiology and Behavior, 106*, 29–39.

Fang, X., Fry, D. A., Ganz, G., Casey, T., & Ward, C. L. (2016). *The economic burden of violence against children in South Africa: Report to save the children South Africa*. Georgia State University, and Universities of Cape Town and Edinburgh.

ACAPS. (2017). *Humanitarian overview: An analysis of key crises into 2018*. Retrieved from Geneva.

Almuneef, M., Qayad, M., Aleissa, M., & Albuhairan, F. (2014). Adverse childhood experiences, chronic diseases, and risky health behaviors in Saudi Arabian adults: a pilot study. *Child Abuse & Neglect, 38*(11), 1787–1793. https://doi.org/10.1016/j.chiabu.2014.06.003.

Amowitz, L. L., Reis, C., Lyons, K. H., Vann, B., Mansaray, B., Akinsulure-Smith, A. M., … Iacopino, V. (2002). Prevalence of war-related sexual violence and other human rights abuses among internally displaced persons in Sierra Leone. *Journal of the American Medical Association, 287*(4), 513–521.

Bellis, M. A., Ashton, K., Hughes, K., Ford, K., Bishop, J., & Paranjothy, S. (2015). *Adverse childhood experiences and their impact on health-harming behaviours in the Welsh adult population*. Retrieved from Cardiff.

Bellis, M. A., Hardcastle, K. A., Hughes, K., Wood, S., & Nurse, J. (2017). *Preventing violence, promoting peace: A policy toolkit for preventing interpersonal, collective and extremist violence*. Retrieved from London, UK.

Bellis, M. A., Hughes, K., Leckenby, N., Hardcastle, K. A., Perkins, C., & Lowey, H. (2015). Measuring mortality and the burden of adult disease associated with adverse childhood experiences in England: a national survey. *Journal of Public Health (Oxford, England), 37*(3), 445–454. https://doi.org/10.1093/pubmed/fdu065.

Bellis, M. A., Hughes, K., Leckenby, N., Jones, L., Baban, A., Kachaeva, M., … Terzic, N. (2014). Adverse childhood experiences and associations with health-harming behaviours in young adults: surveys in eight eastern European countries. *Bulletin of the World Health Organization, 92*(9), 641–655. https://doi.org/10.2471/blt.13.129247.

Benjet, C., Borges, G., & Medina-Mora, M. E. (2010). Chronic childhood adversity and onset of psychopathology during three life stages: childhood, adolescence and adulthood. *Journal of Psychiatric Research, 44*(11), 732–740. https://doi.org/10.1016/j.jpsychires.2010.01.004.

Bjorkenstam, E., Vinnerljung, B., & Hjern, A. (2017). Impact of childhood adversities on depression in early adulthood: a longitudinal cohort study of 478,141 individuals in Sweden. *Journal of Affective Disorders, 223*, 95–100. https://doi.org/10.1016/j.jad.2017.07.030.

Bornstein, M. H., Jager, J., & Putnick, D. L. (2013). Sampling in developmental science: situations, shortcomings, solutions, and standards. *Developmental Review, 33*(4), 357–370. https://doi.org/10.1016/j.dr.2013.08.003.

Breiding, M. J., Mercy, J. A., Gulaid, J., Reza, A., & Hleta-Nkambule, N. (2013). A national survey of childhood physical abuse among females in Swaziland. *Journal of Epidemiology and Global Health, 3*(2), 73–81. https://doi.org/10.1016/j.jegh.2013.02.006.

Cabrera, O. A., Hoge, C. W., Bliese, P. D., Castro, C. A., & Messer, S. C. (2007). Childhood adversity and combat as predictors of depression and post-traumatic stress in deployed troops. *American Journal of Preventive Medicine, 33*(2), 77–82. https://doi.org/10.1016/j.amepre.2007.03.019.

Catani, C., Gewirtz, A. H., Wieling, E., Schauer, E., Elbert, T., & Neuner, F. (2010). Tsunami, war, and cumulative risk in the lives of Sri Lankan schoolchildren. *Child Development, 81*(4), 1176–1191.

Catani, C., Schauer, E., & Neuner, F. (2008). Beyond individual war trauma: domestic violence against children in Afghanistan and Sri Lanka. *Journal of Marital and Family Therapy, 34*(2), 165–176. https://doi.org/10.1111/j.1752-0606.2008.00062.x.

Chartier, M. J., Walker, J. R., & Naimark, B. (2010). Separate and cumulative effects of adverse childhood experiences in predicting adult health and health care utilization. *Child Abuse & Neglect, 34*(6), 454–464. https://doi.org/10.1016/j.chiabu.2009.09.020.

Chiang, L. F., Chen, J., Gladden, M. R., Mercy, J. A., Kwesigabo, G., Mrisho, F., … Vagi, K. (2015). HIV and childhood sexual violence: implications for sexual risk behaviors and HIV testing in Tanzania. *AIDS Education and Prevention, 27*(5), 474–487. https://doi.org/10.1521/aeap.2015.27.5.474.

Chiang, L. F., Kress, H., Sumner, S. A., Gleckel, J., Kawemama, P., & Gordon, R. N. (2016). Violence against children surveys (VACS): towards a global surveillance system. *Injury Prevention, 22*(Suppl. 1), i17–i22. https://doi.org/10.1136/injuryprev-2015-041820.

Cluver, L. D., Meinck, F., Steinert, J. I., Shenderovich, Y., Doubt, J., Herrero Romero, R., … Gardner, F. (2018). Parenting for lifelong health: a pragmatic cluster randomised controlled trial of a non-commercialised parenting programme for adolescents and their families in South Africa. *BMJ Global Health, 3*(1). https://doi.org/10.1136/bmjgh-2017-000539.

Dahl, S. K., Larsen, J. T., Petersen, L., Ubbesen, M. B., Mortensen, P. B., Munk-Olsen, T., & Musliner, K. L. (2017). Early adversity and risk for moderate to severe unipolar depressive disorder in adolescence and adulthood: a register-based study of 978,647 individuals. *Journal of Affective Disorders, 214*, 122–129. https://doi.org/10.1016/j.jad.2017.03.014.

Devries, K., Knight, L., Petzold, M., Merrill, K. G., Maxwell, L., Williams, A., … Abrahams, N. (2018). Who perpetrates violence against children? A systematic analysis of age-specific and sex-specific data. *BMJ Paediatrics Open*, 2(1), e000180. https://doi.org/10.1136/bmjpo-2017-000180.

Dong, M., Anda, R. F., Dube, S. R., Giles, W. H., & Felitti, V. J. (2003). The relationship of exposure to childhood sexual abuse to other forms of abuse, neglect, and household dysfunction during childhood. *Child Abuse & Neglect, 27*(6), 625–639.

Dong, M., Anda, R. F., Felitti, V. J., Dube, S. R., Williamson, D. F., Thompson, T. J., … Giles, W. H. (2004). The interrelatedness of multiple forms of childhood abuse, neglect, and household dysfunction. *Child Abuse & Neglect*, *28*(7), 771–784. https://doi.org/10.1016/j.chiabu.2004.01.008.

Doyle, K., Levtov, R. G., Barker, G., Bastian, G. G., Bingenheimer, J. B., Kazimbaya, S., … Shattuck, D. (2018). Gender-transformative Bandebereho couples' intervention to promote male engagement in reproductive and maternal health and violence prevention in Rwanda: findings from a randomized controlled trial. *PLoS One*, *13*(4), e0192756. https://doi.org/10.1371/journal.pone.0192756.

Dube, S. R., Williamson, D. F., Thompson, T., Felitti, V. J., & Anda, R. F. (2004). Assessing the reliability of retrospective reports of adverse childhood experiences among adult HMO members attending a primary care clinic. *Child Abuse & Neglect*, *28*(7), 729–737. https://doi.org/10.1016/j.chiabu.2003.08.009.

Edwards, V. J., Anda, R. F., Nordenberg, D. F., Felitti, V. J., Williamson, D. F., & Wright, J. A. (2001). Bias assessment for child abuse survey: factors affecting probability of response to a survey about childhood abuse. *Child Abuse & Neglect*, *25*(2), 307–312.

El Mhamdi, S., Lemieux, A., Bouanene, I., Ben Salah, A., Nakajima, M., Ben Salem, K., & al'Absi, M. (2017). Gender differences in adverse childhood experiences, collective violence, and the risk for addictive behaviors among university students in Tunisia. *Preventive Medicine*, *99*, 99–104. https://doi.org/10.1016/j.ypmed.2017.02.011.

Exner-Cortens, D., Eckenrode, J., & Rothman, E. (2013). Longitudinal associations between teen dating violence victimization and adverse health outcomes. *Pediatrics*, *131*(1), 71–78. https://doi.org/10.1542/peds.2012-1029.

Felitti, V. J., Anda, R. F., Nordenberg, D., Williamson, D. F., Spitz, A. M., Edwards, V., … Marks, J. S. (1998). Relationship of childhood abuse and household dysfunction to many of the leading causes of death in adults. The adverse childhood experiences (ACE) study. *American Journal of Preventive Medicine*, *14*(4), 245–258.

Fonseka, R. W., Minnis, A. M., & Gomez, A. M. (2015). Impact of adverse childhood experiences on intimate partner violence perpetration among Sri Lankan men. *PLoS One*, *10*(8), e0136321.

Ford, D. C., Merrick, M. T., Parks, S. E., Breiding, M. J., Gilbert, L. K., Edwards, V. J., … Thompson, W. W. (2014). Examination of the factorial structure of adverse childhood experiences and recommendations for three subscale scores. *Psychology of Violence*, *4*(4), 432–444. https://doi.org/10.1037/a0037723.

Fritz, J., de Graaff, A. M., Caisley, H., van Harmelen, A. L., & Wilkinson, P. O. (2018). A systematic review of amenable resilience factors that moderate and/or mediate the relationship between childhood adversity and mental health in young people. *Frontiers in Psychiatry*, *9*, 230. https://doi.org/10.3389/fpsyt.2018.00230.

Garad, Y., Maximova, K., MacKinnon, N., McGrath, J. J., Kozyrskyj, A. L., & Colman, I. (2017). Sex-specific differences in the association between childhood adversity and cardiovascular disease in adulthood: evidence from a National Cohort Study. *The Canadian Journal of Cardiology*, *33*(8), 1013–1019. https://doi.org/10.1016/j.cjca.2017.05.008.

Gilbert, L. K., Breiding, M. J., Merrick, M. T., Thompson, W. W., Ford, D. C., Dhingra, S. S., & Parks, S. E. (2015). Childhood adversity and adult chronic disease: an update from ten states and the District of Columbia, 2010. *American Journal of Preventive Medicine*, *48*(3), 345–349. https://doi.org/10.1016/j.amepre.2014.09.006.

Gilbert, R., Widom, C. S., Browne, K., Fergusson, D., Webb, E., & Janson, S. (2009). Burden and consequences of child maltreatment in high-income countries. *The Lancet*, *373*(9657), 68–81. https://doi.org/10.1016/S0140-6736(08)61706-7.

Goodman, M. L., Hindman, A., Keiser, P. H., Gitari, S., Ackerman Porter, K., & Raimer, B. G. (2017). Neglect, sexual abuse, and witnessing intimate partner violence during childhood predicts later life violent attitudes against children among Kenyan women: evidence of intergenerational risk transmission from cross-sectional data. *Journal of Interpersonal Violence*, 886260516689777. https://doi.org/10.1177/0886260516689777.

Goodwin, R. D., Fergusson, D. M., & Horwood, L. J. (2004). Asthma and depressive and anxiety disorders among young persons in the community. *Psychological Medicine*, *34*(8), 1465–1474.

Haegerich, T. M., David-Ferdon, C., Noonan, R. K., Manns, B. J., & Billie, H. C. (2017). Technical packages in injury and violence prevention to move evidence into practice: systematic reviews and beyond. *Evaluation Review*, *41*(1), 78–108.

Harkonmäki, K., Korkeila, K., Vahtera, J., Kivimäki, M., Suominen, S., Sillanmäki, L., & Koskenvuo, M. (2007). Childhood adversities as a predictor of disability retirement. *Journal of Epidemiology & Community Health*, *61*(6), 479–484.

Hawkins, J. D., Kosterman, R., Catalano, R. F., Hill, K. G., & Abbott, R. D. (2005). Promoting positive adult functioning through social development intervention in childhood: long-term effects from the Seattle social development project. *Archives of Pediatrics & Adolescent Medicine*, *159*(1), 25–31.

Hawkins, J. D., Oesterle, S., Brown, E. C., Monahan, K. C., Abbott, R. D., Arthur, M. W., & Catalano, R. F. (2012). Sustained decreases in risk exposure and youth problem behaviors after installation of the communities that care prevention system in a randomized trial. *Archives of Pediatrics & Adolescent Medicine*, *166*(2), 141–148.

Heeringa, S., Wells, J., Hubbart, F., Mneimneh, Z., Chiu, W., Sampson, N., & Berglund, P. (2008). Sample designs and sampling procedures. In R. C. Kessler & T. B. Ustun (Eds.), *The WHO World Mental Health Surveys: Global perspectives on the epidemiology of mental disorders*. New York, NY: Cambridge University Press.

Hillis, S., Mercy, J., Amobi, A., & Kress, H. (2016). Global prevalence of past-year violence against children: a systematic review and minimum estimates. *Pediatrics*, *137*(3), e20154079. https://doi.org/10.1542/peds.2015-4079.

Hoppen, T. H., & Chalder, T. (2018). Childhood adversity as a transdiagnostic risk factor for affective disorders in adulthood: a systematic review focusing on biopsychosocial moderating and mediating variables. *Clinical Psychology Review*, *65*, 81–151. https://doi.org/10.1016/j.cpr.2018.08.002.

Hsiao, C., Fry, D., Ward, C. L., Ganz, G., Casey, T., Zheng, X., & Fang, X. (2017). Violence against children in South Africa: the cost of inaction to society and the economy. *BMJ Global Health*, *3*, 1–7.

Hughes, K., Bellis, M. A., Hardcastle, K. A., Sethi, D., Butchart, A., Mikton, C., … Dunne, M. P. (2017). The effect of multiple adverse childhood experiences on health: a systematic review and meta-analysis. *The Lancet Public Health*, *2*(8), e356–e366. https://doi.org/10.1016/s2468-2667(17)30118-4.

Itani, L., Haddad, Y. C., Fayyad, J., Karam, A., & Karam, E. (2014). Childhood adversities and traumata in Lebanon: a national study. *Clinical Practice and Epidemiology in Mental Health*, *10*, 116–125. https://doi.org/10.2174/1745017901410010116.

Jones, L., Bellis, M. A., Wood, S., Hughes, K., McCoy, E., Eckley, L., … Officer, A. (2012). Prevalence and risk of violence against children with disabilities: a systematic review and meta-analysis of observational studies. *Lancet*, *380*(9845), 899–907. https://doi.org/10.1016/s0140-6736(12)60692-8.

Joshi, P. T., & O'Donnell, D. A. (2003). Consequences of child exposure to war and terrorism. *Clinical Child and Family Psychology Review*, *6*(4), 275–292. https://doi.org/10.1023/b:ccfp.0000006294.88201.68.

Kessler, R. C., McLaughlin, K. A., Green, J. G., Gruber, M. J., Sampson, N. A., Zaslavsky, A. M., … Williams, D. R. (2010). Childhood adversities and adult psychopathology in the WHO world mental health surveys. *British Journal of Psychiatry*, *197*(5), 378–385. https://doi.org/10.1192/bjp.bp.110.080499.

Kessler, R. C., & Ustun, T. B. (2008). *The WHO world mental health surveys: Global perspectives on the epidemiology of mental disorders*. New York, NY: Cambridge University Press.

Khamis, V. (2015). Coping with war trauma and psychological distress among school-age Palestinian children. *American Journal of Orthopsychiatry*, *85*(1), 72.

Kim, Y. H. (2017). Associations of adverse childhood experiences with depression and alcohol abuse among Korean college students. *Child Abuse & Neglect*, *67*, 338–348. https://doi.org/10.1016/j.chiabu.2017.03.009.

Koss, M. P., Yuan, N. P., Dightman, D., Prince, R. J., Polacca, M., Sanderson, B., & Goldman, D. (2003). Adverse childhood exposures and alcohol dependence among seven native American tribes. *American Journal of Preventive Medicine, 25*(3), 238–244. https://doi.org/10.1016/S0749-3797(03)00195-8.

LaNoue, M., Graeber, D., de Hernandez, B. U., Warner, T. D., & Helitzer, D. L. (2012). Direct and indirect effects of childhood adversity on adult depression. *Community Mental Health Journal, 48*(2), 187–192.

Lereya, S. T., Copeland, W. E., Costello, E. J., & Wolke, D. (2015). Adult mental health consequences of peer bullying and maltreatment in childhood: two cohorts in two countries. *The Lancet Psychiatry, 2*(6), 524–531.

Leung, J. P. K., Britton, A., & Bell, S. (2016). Adverse childhood experiences and alcohol consumption in midlife and early old-age. *Alcohol and Alcoholism, 51*(3), 331–338. https://doi.org/10.1093/alcalc/agv125.

Lissau, I., & Sorensen, T. I. (1994). Parental neglect during childhood and increased risk of obesity in young adulthood. *Lancet, 343*(8893), 324–327.

Matjasko, J. L., Vivolo-Kantor, A. M., Massetti, G. M., Holland, K. M., Holt, M. K., & Cruz, J. D. (2012). A systematic meta-review of evaluations of youth violence prevention programs: common and divergent findings from 25 years of meta-analyses and systematic reviews. *Aggression and Violent Behavior, 17*(6), 540–552.

Mercy, J. A., Hillis, S. D., Butchart, A., Bellis, M. A., Ward, C. L., & Fang, X. (2017). Interpersonal violence: global impact and paths to prevention. In C. N. Mock, et al. (Eds.), *Disease control priorities: Injury Prevention and Environmental Health* (third ed.) (Vol. 7). Washington, DC: World Bank.

Mersky, J. P., Topitzes, J., & Reynolds, A. J. (2013). Impacts of adverse childhood experiences on health, mental health, and substance use in early adulthood: a cohort study of an urban, minority sample in the U.S. *Child Abuse & Neglect, 37*(11), 917–925. https://doi.org/10.1016/j.chiabu.2013.07.011.

Miller, E., Breslau, J., Chung, W. J., Green, J. G., McLaughlin, K. A., & Kessler, R. C. (2011). Adverse childhood experiences and risk of physical violence in adolescent dating relationships. *Journal of Epidemiology & Community Health, 65*, 1006–1013. jech. 2009.105429.

Montgomery, E., & Foldspang, A. (2005). Seeking asylum in Denmark: refugee children's mental health and exposure to violence. *European Journal of Public Health, 15*(3), 233–237. https://doi.org/10.1093/eurpub/cki059.

Moore, S. E., Scott, J. G., Ferrari, A. J., Mills, R., Dunne, M. P., Erskine, H. E., ... Whiteford, H. A. (2015). Burden attributable to child maltreatment in Australia. *Child Abuse & Neglect, 48*, 208–220.

Mouton, C. P., Hargreaves, M. K., Liu, J., Fadeyi, S., & Blot, W. J. (2016). Adult cancer risk behaviors associated with adverse childhood experiences in a low income population in the southeastern United States. *Journal of Health Care for the Poor and Underserved, 27*(1), 68.

Naicker, S. N., Norris, S. A., Mabaso, M., & Richter, L. M. (2017). An analysis of retrospective and repeat prospective reports of adverse childhood experiences from the south African birth to twenty plus cohort. *PLoS One, 12*(7), e0181522. https://doi.org/10.1371/journal.pone.0181522.

Norman, R. E., Byambaa, M., De, R., Butchart, A., Scott, J., & Vos, T. (2012). The long-term health consequences of child physical abuse, emotional abuse, and neglect: a systematic review and meta-analysis. *PLoS Medicine, 9*(11), e1001349.

Oladeji, B. D., Makanjuola, V. A., & Gureje, O. (2010). Family-related adverse childhood experiences as risk factors for psychiatric disorders in Nigeria. *The British Journal of Psychiatry, 196*(3), 186–191. https://doi.org/10.1192/bjp.bp.109.063677.

Olds, D., Henderson, C. R., Jr., Cole, R., Eckenrode, J., Kitzman, H., Luckey, D., ... Powers, J. (1998). Long-term effects of nurse home visitation on children's criminal and antisocial behavior: 15-year follow-up of a randomized controlled trial. *Journal of the American Medical Association, 280*(14), 1238–1244.

Patel, V., Flisher, A. J., Nikapota, A., & Malhotra, S. (2008). Promoting child and adolescent mental health in low and middle income countries. *Journal of Child Psychology and Psychiatry*, *49*(3), 313–334. https://doi.org/10.1111/j.1469-7610.2007.01824.x.

Perales, J., Olaya, B., Fernandez, A., Alonso, J., Vilagut, G., Forero, C. G., ... Haro, J. M. (2013). Association of childhood adversities with the first onset of mental disorders in Spain: results from the ESEMeD project. *Social Psychiatry and Psychiatric Epidemiology*, *48*(3), 371–384. https://doi.org/10.1007/s00127-012-0550-5.

Pirkola, S., Isometsä, E., Aro, H., Kestilä, L., Hämäläinen, J., Veijola, J., ... Lönnqvist, J. (2005). Childhood adversities as risk factors for adult mental disorders. *Social Psychiatry and Psychiatric Epidemiology*, *40*(10), 769–777.

Ports, K. A., Ford, D. C., & Merrick, M. T. (2016). Adverse childhood experiences and sexual victimization in adulthood. *Child Abuse & Neglect*, *51*, 313–322. https://doi.org/10.1016/j.chiabu.2015.08.017.

Quinn, M., Caldara, G., Collins, K., Owens, H., Ozodiegwu, I., Loudermilk, E., & Stinson, J. D. (2018). Methods for understanding childhood trauma: modifying the adverse childhood experiences international questionnaire for cultural competency. *International Journal of Public Health*, *63*(1), 149–151.

Ramiro, L. S., Madrid, B. J., & Brown, D. W. (2010). Adverse childhood experiences (ACE) and health-risk behaviors among adults in a developing country setting. *Child Abuse & Neglect*, *34*(11), 842–855. https://doi.org/10.1016/j.chiabu.2010.02.012.

Randell, K. A., O'Malley, D., & Dowd, M. D. (2015). Association of parental adverse childhood experiences and current child adversity. *JAMA Pediatrics*, *169*(8), 786–787.

Raposo, S. M., Mackenzie, C. S., Henriksen, C. A., & Afifi, T. O. (2014). Time does not heal all wounds: older adults who experienced childhood adversities have higher odds of mood, anxiety, and personality disorders. *The American Journal of Geriatric Psychiatry*, *22*(11), 1241–1250.

Reza, A., Breiding, M. J., Gulaid, J., Mercy, J. A., Blanton, C., Mthethwa, Z., ... Anderson, M. (2009). Sexual violence and its health consequences for female children in Swaziland: a cluster survey study. *Lancet*, *373*(9679), 1966–1972. https://doi.org/10.1016/S0140-6736(09)60247-6.

Sandler, I., Ingram, A., Wolchik, S., Tein, J. Y., & Winslow, E. (2015). Long-term effects of parenting-focused preventive interventions to promote resilience of children and adolescents. *Child Development Perspectives*, *9*(3), 164–171.

Sandler, I. N., Schoenfelder, E. N., Wolchik, S. A., & MacKinnon, D. P. (2011). Long-term impact of prevention programs to promote effective parenting: lasting effects but uncertain processes. *Annual Review of Psychology*, *62*(1), 299–329. https://doi.org/10.1146/annurev.psych.121208.131619.

Schussler-Fiorenza Rose, S. M., Xie, D., & Stineman, M. (2014). Adverse childhood experiences and disability in U.S. adults. *PM & R: The Journal of Injury, Function, and Rehabilitation*, *6*(8), 670–680. https://doi.org/10.1016/j.pmrj.2014.01.013.

Soares, A. L. G., Howe, L. D., Matijasevich, A., Wehrmeister, F. C., Menezes, A. M. B., & Gonçalves, H. (2016). Adverse childhood experiences: prevalence and related factors in adolescents of a Brazilian birth cohort. *Child Abuse & Neglect*, *51*, 21–30. https://doi.org/10.1016/j.chiabu.2015.11.017.

Stark, L., Asghar, K., Yu, G., Bora, C., Baysa, A. A., & Falb, K. L. (2017). Prevalence and associated risk factors of violence against conflict-affected female adolescents: a multi-country, cross-sectional study. *Journal of Global Health*, *7*(1), 010416. https://doi.org/10.7189/jogh.07.010416.

Stark, L., & Landis, D. (2016). Violence against children in humanitarian settings: a literature review of population-based approaches. *Social Science and Medicine*, *152*, 125–137. https://doi.org/10.1016/j.socscimed.2016.01.052.

Stoltenborgh, M., Bakermans-Kranenburg, M. J., & van Ijzendoorn, M. H. (2013). The neglect of child neglect: a meta-analytic review of the prevalence of neglect. *Social Psychiatry and Psychiatric Epidemiology*, *48*(3), 345–355. https://doi.org/10.1007/s00127-012-0549-y.

Su, S., Wang, X., Pollock, J. S., Treiber, F. A., Xu, X., Snieder, H., ... Harshfield, G. A. (2015). Adverse childhood experiences and blood pressure trajectories from childhood to young adulthood: the Georgia stress and heart study. *Circulation*, *131*, 1674–1681. CIRCULATIONAHA. 114.013104.

Sumner, S. A., Mercy, J. A., Buluma, R., Mwangi, M. W., Marcelin, L. H., Kheam, T., … Hillis, S. D. (2016). Childhood sexual violence against boys: a study in 3 countries. *Pediatrics*, *137*(5), https://doi.org/10.1542/peds.2015-3386.

Takizawa, R., Maughan, B., & Arseneault, L. (2014). Adult health outcomes of childhood bullying victimization: evidence from a five-decade longitudinal British birth cohort. *American Journal of Psychiatry*, *171*(7), 777–784.

Teicher, M. H., & Samson, J. A. (2016). Annual research review: enduring neurobiological effects of childhood abuse and neglect. *Journal of Child Psychology and Psychiatry*, *57*(3), 241–266.

Together for Girls. (2013). *The together for girls partnership: Linking violence against children surveys to coordinated and effective action*. Retrieved from Washington, DC.

Together for Girls. (2015). *Considerations for developing comprehensive National Actions to prevent and respond to violence against children*. Retrieved from Washington, DC.

Tourangeau, R., & Yan, T. (2007). Sensitive questions in surveys. *Psychological Bulletin*, *133*(5), 859.

Tran, Q. A., Dunne, M. P., Vo, T. V., & Luu, N. H. (2015). Adverse childhood experiences and the health of university students in eight provinces of Vietnam. *Asia-Pacific Journal of Public Health*, *27*(8 Suppl), 26s–32s. https://doi.org/10.1177/1010539515589812.

Tyrer, S., & Heyman, B. (2016). Sampling in epidemiological research: issues, hazards and pitfalls. *BJPsych Bulletin*, *40*(2), 57–60. https://doi.org/10.1192/pb.bp.114.050203.

United Nations General Assembly. (2015). *Transforming our world: The 2030 agenda for sustainable development*. In *A/RES/70/1* (p. 35).

Vagi, K. J., Brookmeyer, K. A., Gladden, R. M., Chiang, L. F., Brooks, A., Nyunt, M.-Z., … Dahlberg, L. L. (2016). Sexual violence against female and male children in the United Republic of Tanzania. *Violence Against Women*, *22*(14), 1788–1807. https://doi.org/10.1177/1077801216634466.

Vander Ende, K., Mercy, J., Shawa, M., Kalanda, M., Hamela, J., Maksud, N., … Hillis, S. (2016). Violent experiences in childhood are associated with men's perpetration of intimate partner violence as a young adult: a multistage cluster survey in Malawi. *Annals of Epidemiology*, *26*(10), 723–728. https://doi.org/10.1016/j.annepidem.2016.08.007.

Wade, R., Cronholm, P. F., Fein, J. A., Forke, C. M., Davis, M. B., Harkins-Schwarz, M., … Bair-Merritt, M. H. (2016). Household and community-level adverse childhood experiences and adult health outcomes in a diverse urban population. *Child Abuse & Neglect*, *52*, 135–145. https://doi.org/10.1016/j.chiabu.2015.11.021.

Winters, N., Langer, L., & Geniets, A. (2017). Physical, psychological, sexual, and systemic abuse of children with disabilities in East Africa: mapping the evidence. *PLoS One*, *12*(9), e0184541. https://doi.org/10.1371/journal.pone.0184541.

World Health Organization (WHO). (2011). *Adverse childhood experiences international questionnaire: Pilot study review and finalization meeting* Retrieved from:http://www.who.int/violence_injury_prevention/violence/activities/adverse_childhood_experiences/global_research_network_may_2011.pdf.

World Health Organization (WHO). (2014). *Global status report on violence prevention 2014.* . Retrieved from Geneva, Switzerland.

World Health Organization (WHO). (2016). *INSPIRE: Seven strategies for ending violence against children*. Geneva, Switzerland: World Health Organization. https://www.who.int/violence_injury_prevention/violence/inspire/en/.

World Health Organization (WHO). (2017). *Adverse childhood experiences international questionnaire* Retrieved from:http://www.who.int/violence_injury_prevention/violence/activities/adverse_childhood_experiences/en/.

Xiao, Q., Dong, M.-X., Yao, J., Li, W.-X., & Ye, D.-Q. (2008). Parental alcoholism, adverse childhood experiences, and later risk of personal alcohol abuse among Chinese medical students. *Biomedical and Environmental Sciences*, *21*(5), 411–419. https://doi.org/10.1016/S0895-3988(08)60062-8.

CHAPTER

12

Effective prevention of ACEs

Brian Brennan[a,b,*], *Natalie Stavas*[a,c], *Philip Scribano*[c,d]

[a]The Children's Hospital of Philadelphia, Philadelphia, PA, United States, [b]Uniformed Services University, F. Edward Hebert School of Medicine, Bethesda, MD, United States, [c]Perelman School of Medicine, University of Pennsylvania, Philadelphia, PA, United States, [d]Division of General Pediatrics, Center for Child Protection and Health, The Children's Hospital of Philadelphia, Philadelphia, PA, United States

Introduction

Since the original 1998 adverse childhood experiences (ACEs) study (Felitti et al., 1998) was published, the challenge to the medical, social services, legal, and policy communities has been how to prevent the occurrence and/or recurrence of adversities, given the poor health outcomes with which they are associated (Anda et al., 2008; Dong et al., 2004; Shonkoff et al., 2012; also see Chapters 4 and 5). Understanding the root causes of these experiences, and developing a prevention framework, helps the clinician, social worker, or child welfare worker to better target interventions for vulnerable children and families. For any public health prevention effort, the first step is to establish a valid, reliable detection method with targeted screening of patients and families that can then be coupled with proven evidence-based interventions to reduce the long-term negative outcomes from these childhood adversities.

Utility of ACEs screening tools

The usefulness of some of the current ACEs screening tools, initially developed to retrospectively evaluate ACEs using a research design that was

[*] The views expressed in this chapter are those of the author and do not reflect the official policy or position of the Department of the Army, Department of Defense, or the U.S. Government.

https://doi.org/10.1016/B978-0-12-816065-7.00012-4

intended to understand the epidemiology of ACEs (versus a screening tool for clinical use to determine interventions), has significant limitations when clinicians look to prospectively implement them in clinical practice (Finkelhor, Shattuck, Turner, & Hamby, 2013; Prochaska & Norcoss, 2011). While the original ACE Study asked adults to recall adverse experiences in childhood (e.g., psychological abuse, physical abuse, sexual abuse, substance abuse, mental illness, exposure to intimate partner violence, and incarcerated family member in the household) (Felitti et al., 1998), a prospective screening process would require parents of children to self-report these exposures and would be a significant departure from the original intent in the development of the ACEs screen.

This self-reporting could potentially lead to parental self-incrimination and require clinicians, as mandated reporters of child maltreatment, to report parents who honestly and accurately complete the screening tools (Finkelhor, 2017; McKelvey, Selig, & Whiteside-Mansell, 2017). The increasing interest among researchers and clinicians to employ ACEs screening tools in the clinical setting prompted use of a variety of proxy variables for these adverse experiences. The American Academy of Pediatrics' recommendations for screening for sources of sustained, high-intensity adversity (defined as toxic stress) in children stops short of recommending ACEs screening specifically, recommending simply that pediatricians screen for factors that may contribute to toxic stress and are common in their practice (Garner et al., 2012). Specifically, one study substituted foster-care status for sexual abuse history as a stress exposure in their standard questions to patients and their caregivers (McKelvey et al., 2017). Additionally, the 2011/2012 National Survey for Children's Health conducted by the Center for Disease Control frankly omitted questions regarding abuse inflicted by a caregiver due to the known reporting/ascertainment biases associated with this line of questioning (Bright, Knapp, Hinojosa, Alford, & Bonner, 2016).

A proposed, and often utilized, method of blinding the clinician (i.e., mandated reporter) to specifically which ACEs the patients and caregivers are reporting has been to provide an aggregate score of ACEs. This method provides a total number of ACEs to which the child may have been exposed, but does not report specific ACEs. This alleviates the burden of mandatory reporting, but then does not allow for specific targeting of therapies and other interventions to the child or their family (Finkelhor, 2017).

In addition to omitting specific items in the screening process, there have been questions as to whether the original list of ACEs was inclusive of all the adverse experiences associated with poor health outcomes. In a study conducted utilizing data from the National Survey of Children's Exposure to Violence, it was demonstrated that several of the original ACEs, when viewed independently, did not make significant contributions to overall distress (Finkelhor et al., 2013). Issues such as peer rejection, poverty, violence, and exposure to violence outside of the home, as well as poor academic performance, were shown to be as important, if not more important, than the initial set of ACEs in anticipating mental health symptoms (i.e., posttraumatic stress symptoms) (Finkelhor et al., 2013). These issues raise the question of whether current screening tools demonstrate adequate face and construct validity to be used clinically. These and other issues germane to routine screening of ACEs are discussed in detail in Chapter 8 of this volume.

Prevention framework

When discussing prevention and the strategies designed to prevent adverse outcomes, it is recognized that not all populations are at the same risk for adversity. Strategic prevention frameworks have emerged in the literature which identify prevention strategies as being universal, targeted, and indicated. Prevention efforts before occurrence of disease/injury can involve both universal and targeted measures aimed at specific individuals and/or families, communities, and societies, utilizing the social-ecological model as a framework (Magruder, Kassam-Adams, Thoresen, & Olff, 2016; McLeroy, Bibeau, Steckler, & Glanz, 1988). The goal of these interventions is to prevent adversities from occurring. Universal prevention measures are applied to an entire population (whether that be national, local, or neighborhood). Targeted interventions seek out higher than average risk populations within the larger population and offer services. Indicated interventions are specific to the population at risk that has either already shown adverse health consequences related to childhood adversity, or has identified factors that place them at higher risk for childhood adversities. In this chapter we will be exploring universal, targeted, and indicated programs that aim to prevent childhood adversity or prevent the recurrence of adversity. In addition, we will provide a slight shift in utilizing the more recent nomenclature that has emerged in the literature, referring to the concept of social determinants of health. This has appeal as a broader construct to ACEs, and is associated with a growing trend to link various adversities to health and wellbeing as their targeted outcome. It is also appealing as this approach minimizes the risks identified in earlier studies (i.e., the ACEs assessment challenges described previously).

Social determinants of health

Beyond ACEs: A new paradigm to address social needs

Given the inherent limitations in prospective screening tools for ACEs and the uncertainty surrounding whether or not the current ACEs are appropriate or inclusive of the correct set of experiences (Finkelhor, 2017; Finkelhor et al., 2013), more recent approaches to screening children include evaluation of social determinants of health (SDoH). SDoH have been championed as a way to determine allostatic load of adversity, potentially reducing the limitations in screening for ACEs specifically (American Academy of Pediatrics [AAP] Committee on Practice and Ambulatory Medicine and AAP Bright Futures Periodicity Schedule Workgroup, 2017; Gorski & Kuo, 2013). SDoH are defined by the World Health Organization as "the circumstances in which people grow, live, work and age, and the systems put in place to deal with illness" (World Health Organization, 2013, p. 2). These circumstances can include access to healthcare, quality of education and job training, the built environment, housing availability, public safety, and food security, to name a few. The Center for Disease Prevention Office of Disease Prevention and Health Promotion (www.HealthyPeople.gov) categorizes these entities into five categories, or determinants. They are (1) economic stability, (2) neighborhood and built environment, (3) education, (4) social and community context, and (5) health and healthcare (HealthyPeople.gov, 2014).

Systematic reviews of the literature regarding SDoH screening, both in the inpatient and outpatient medical settings, have failed to find a single, comprehensive, well-constructed, screening tool that was validated, though there are many focused screening methodologies used (Morone, 2017; Pai, Kandasamy, Uleryk, & Maguire, 2016). This lack of full spectrum screening across all five SDoH categories has the potential to inadequately risk-stratify children and families, and could impede the most effective allocation of interventions and resources. They do, however, offer promise in providing more insight into the social welfare of the child and family than would otherwise be obtained from a simple, open-ended approach to the social history. One novel approach incorporating SDoH screening has been published describing an enhanced primary care model that includes physician/provider training, social worker integration, and a 20-question Parent Screening Questionnaire (PSQ) (Dubowitz, Feigelman, Lane, & Kim, 2009; Dubowitz, Lane, Semiatin, & Magder, 2012). The PSQ, designed to examine many of the same issues described by SDoH, covers multiple adverse experiences, including substance abuse, maternal depression, and intimate partner violence (Dubowitz et al., 2007; Dubowitz, Prescott, Feigelman, Lane, & Kim, 2008; Lane et al., 2007).

Barriers to screening

In addition to limitations in the validity of current screening tools, there are barriers to SDoH screening reported in the literature. Many providers have indicated that they lack the time, resources, and the requisite risk assessment training to screen for concerns related to social needs

(Beaune et al., 2014; Beck et al., 2016; Beck, Klein, & Kahn, 2012; Klein et al., 2013), whereas others cited SDoH screening as beyond their purview (Dejong et al., 2016). Other providers indicated that they did not screen for SDoH based on their belief that these issues were not remediable (Klein et al., 2013) or that they were not adequately familiar with community resources available for their patients (Beck et al., 2016). Studies have also demonstrated barriers to accurate screening from a patient and caregiver standpoint, citing such issues as caregiver literacy and social desirability biases in addition to the desire to avoid self-incrimination (Beck et al., 2012; Dejong et al., 2016; McKelvey et al., 2017).

Summary

Since the original ACE Study, there have been efforts to create screening tools to identify children at risk for adverse experiences before they occur. Prevention frameworks and more targeted screenings have begun to utilize SDoH to better evaluate children's risk of maltreatment and other adverse experiences; but, at this time, there are no validated screening tools to effectively address all SDoH categories. Barriers exist in the form of caregiver biases and healthcare provider views on screening appropriateness.

ACEs prevention strategies

Program strategies, which target prevention of the multitude of adversities children may experience, are typically unidimensional in their approach, and usually focus on a specific adversity (e.g., child maltreatment prevention, caregiver mental health support). There is no multidimensional programmatic strategy that targets all ACEs as a singular prevention approach. Most evidence-based prevention strategies have centered on caregiver and child support, either in the context of home visitation or parent-enhanced interventions (i.e., positive parenting programs) to populations identified as high risk for the various ACEs. These programs have shown varying degrees of success regarding reduction in maltreatment, improved maternal and child health outcomes, and injury prevention (Aos, Lieb, Mayfield, Miller, & Pennucci, 2004; Corbacho et al., 2017; Glazner, Bondy, Luckey, & Olds, 2004; Karoly et al., 1998b; Olds et al., 1997; Scribano, 2010; Stamuli, Richardson, Duffy, Robling, & Hood, 2015). Enhanced primary care models, which aim to provide more robust assessment and support of social needs, have emerged, also with varying degrees of success (Beck et al., 2016; Dubowitz et al., 2009, 2012). While the current state of ACEs prevention interventions may be limited by lack of implementation success, continued efforts to develop studies with strong implementation science foundations can begin to bridge this knowledge gap in demonstrating effectiveness in many of these well-regarded programs in reducing ACEs risks (Bauer, Damschroder, Hagedorn, Smith, & Kilbourne, 2015; Gottlieb et al., 2018; Holtrop, Rabin, & Glasgow, 2018). In the following sections, we will further explore specific programs that aim to decrease childhood adversity across the social-ecological framework.

Interventions across the social-ecological continuum

As the body of research on the epidemiology and assessment of ACEs grows, so does research on its prevention. The literature now includes interventions that decrease not only childhood adversity, but also covariates of child adversity across the social-ecological continuum from the individual, family, community, society, and public policy to enhance positive outcomes.

Interventions to prevent ACEs occur across this social-ecological framework on different levels. As outlined in Fig. 1, there are multiple overlapping spheres that can affect child health and wellbeing. Every child is born with her/his own unique temperament and health needs. In this context,

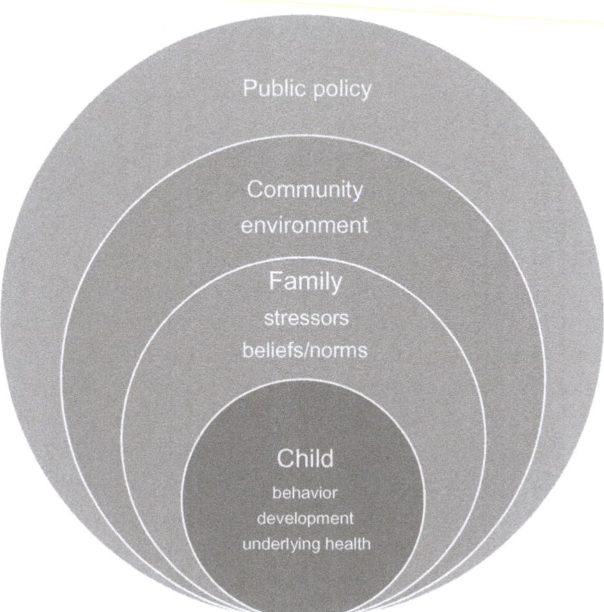

FIG. 1 Dynamic relationship between child, family, community, and social or public policy. Derived from social-ecological framework (McLeroy et al., 1988).

their continued development is influenced by their family stressors and beliefs, their community environment, and public policy. Early intervention (often also referred to as prevention) has been defined as formal attempts by agents outside the family to maintain or improve key outcomes within these spheres, such as birthweight, development, injury prevention, stable housing, food insecurity, and quality of life. The intent is to supplement the family with key resources across domains such as health, education, and social services (Karoly et al., 1998b). Early intervention strategies within the social-ecologic framework that address childhood adversity can occur at multiple points, ideally starting with prevention before occurrence, prevention of recurrence, followed by prevention of impairment. Within the social-ecological prevention framework, we will further explore specific interventions, targeting one or more domains within this interconnected system, with a focus on home visitation, parent-enhanced interventions, enhanced primary care, and community-based support interventions.

Home visitation

Home visiting programs began as a method of providing community-based health services (Council on Child and Adolescent Health, 1998). In 1976, Dr. Kempe, one of the first pediatricians in the medical community to recognize and define child abuse, wrote an article discussing the concept of using health visitors to prevent child maltreatment (Kempe, 1976). In the early 1980s, while associations between maternal-child health and home health visiting had not been demonstrated, countries with extensive home visiting programs generally had lower infant mortality compared to similar countries without home visiting programs (Council on Child and Adolescent Health, 1998). As countries such as Denmark, France, and the United Kingdom expanded their home visiting programs, policy makers in the US viewed such programs as too costly and unnecessary; thus, these programs were not widely implemented (Council on Child and Adolescent Health, 1998; Kamerman & Kahn, 1993). Throughout the 1990s, evidence began to mount regarding the positive benefits of home visitation, including early and regular access to prenatal care (Chapman, Siegel, & Cross, 1990; Olds, Henderson, Tatelbaum, & Chamberlin, 1986), decreased use of physical punishment (Olds, 1992), decreased maternal substance abuse (Olds et al., 1997), and decreased verified incidents of child maltreatment (Olds, 1992; Olds et al., 1986, 1997). In 1998 the American Academy of Pediatrics released a statement reporting the current evidence of home visitation, concluding that home visitations can be an effective strategy to improve the wellbeing of a child but that they are not a "panacea, sufficient unto themselves to reverse or prevent the damaging effects of poverty and inadequate or inexperienced parenting" (Council on Child and Adolescent Health, 1998, p. 488). Around the same time, the RAND

Corporation released a summary statement titled *Investing in our children: What we know and don't know about the costs and benefits of early childhood interventions* (Karoly et al., 1998b). In their report, they looked at 10 targeted early intervention programs and concluded that targeted intervention programs have the potential to improve outcomes for specific populations; however, results were varied and could not be generalizable to all kinds of early intervention and especially not to larger-scale programs (Karoly et al., 1998b).

From this expanding literature, the concept of evidence-based home visiting programs (EBHVP) emerged (Gomby, Culross, & Behrman, 1999). These programs vary widely across design, implementation, cost, and effectiveness (Mikton & Butchart, 2009; Peacock, Konrad, Watson, Nickel, & Muhajarine, 2013; Reynolds, Mathieson, & Topitzes, 2009). To date, home visiting remains one of the most prevalent and well-studied interventions to reduce childhood maltreatment and adversity (Scribano, 2010); although, systematic reviews come to different conclusions on the strength of the evidence that home visitation reduces childhood adversity (Bilukha et al., 2005; Mikton & Butchart, 2009; Olds et al., 1997; Sweet & Appelbaum, 2004). Nevertheless, multiple studies have shown that EBHVP are protective and preventative (Aos et al., 2004; Guttentag et al., 2014) and certain models have shown as much as a 45% reduction in child maltreatment (Gomby et al., 1999; Olds, 2006) as well as a 22% decrease in substantiated reports (Chaiyachati, Gaither, Hughes, Foley-Schain, & Leventhal, 2018).

Although not all EBHVPs are the same in regards to their area of focus, successful programs approach prevention by addressing multiple levels in the social-ecological framework, including addressing the individual child's needs, the family's needs, and providing resources to ensure a safe environment (see Table 1) (Minkovitz, O'Neill, & Duggan, 2016). The ultimate goal of EBHVPs is to enhance parent and community capacity to support families in providing safe, supportive home environments (Minkovitz et al., 2016). When viewed through this lens, home visiting can disrupt the cycle in which early adversity contributes to lifelong impairment in health (Garner, 2013).

In the US, there has been a dramatic scale up of EBHVP after the Patient Protection and Affordable Care Act (commonly shortened as Affordable Care Act) was signed into law in 2010. In this legislation, an amendment of Title V of the Social Security Act authorized the creation of the Maternal, Infant and Early Childhood Home Visiting (MIECHV) program (Adirim & Supplee, 2013; Minkovitz et al., 2016). An appropriation of $1.5 billion over 5 years was issued (and has since been reauthorized in 2018) to be invested into supporting health and development of at-risk children through EBHVP. With the passing of this law, EBHVP came under heighted scrutiny related to its design and outcomes. Specifically, the legislation required that home-visiting programs demonstrate improvement

TABLE 1 Successful Home Visitation Concepts

EBHVP goals	Strategies	Success measures
Mother's personal health	Promoting preventative and prenatal health	Improvement in maternal health
Child's health and development	Offering information and coaching on development	Improvement in newborn/child health
Environment: housing and community violence	Conducting formal assessments	Reduction in crime and intimate partner violence
Family functioning, positive parenting	Modeling parent-child interactions	Reduction in child abuse and neglect
Promote school readiness/mother education	Setting education goals	Improved school readiness and achievement

in the following domains: (1) maternal and newborn health; (2) prevention of abuse, neglect, or maltreatment; (3) improvement in school readiness; (4) reduction in crime and domestic violence; (5) improvements in family economic self-sufficiency; and (6) improvements in the coordination and referrals for other community resources and supports (Adirim & Supplee, 2013). Out of this also came HomVEE (Home Visiting Evidence of Effectiveness, 2018), a federally funded systematic review of the evidence of home visiting models. The goal of this rigorous evaluation of programs was to provide a thorough and transparent review of the home visiting research literature (Adirim & Supplee, 2013; Minkovitz et al., 2016). This review has been applied to dozens of home visiting models and, as of 2017, 18 have been identified as meeting criteria for evidence and effectiveness. A summary of multiple home visitation models as well as the literature supporting them can be found at: http://homvee.acf.hhs.gov.

We will highlight three of the models, which have demonstrated positive outcomes as well as unique strengths, including Nurse Family Partnership (NFP), Healthy Families America (HFA), and Parents as Teachers (PAT). In addition, we highlight several other home visitation models, which have limited literature but are focused on either high-risk family stressors (Early Start) or indicated prevention of child maltreatment (Project Safe Care). Table 2 provides a summary of these programs.

Nurse Family Partnership

NFP is a nurse home visitation program for low-income first-time mothers enrolled during their pregnancy and child's infancy, and continued to age 2 years. Nurses are trained to teach positive health-related behaviors, competent care of children, and maternal, personal development (Social Programs That Work Review: Evidence Summary for the Nurse Family Partnership, 2017). The goal is to build a trusting relationship between

TABLE 2 Summary of Selected Home Visitation Programs

Program	Mission	Objectives	Evidence[b]	Outcomes
Nurse Family Partnership	Provide home visits by nurses for first-time, low-income mothers to improve health outcomes	• Improve maternal/child health • Improve child development • Improve mothers' economic self sufficiency	Supported by multiple RCTs and quasiexperimental studies Meets HHS EBHV[a] criteria	Favorable outcomes reported in: • Maternal/child health • School readiness • Delay in subsequent pregnancy • Reductions in child maltreatment
Healthy Families America	To improve child wellbeing and prevent abuse and neglect through home visitation services	• Reduce child maltreatment • Improve parent child interaction • Promote school readiness	Supported by multiple RCTs and quasiexperimental studies Meets HHS EBHVM criteria	Favorable outcomes reported in: • School readiness • Child health • Positive parenting • Reductions in child maltreatment
Parents as Teachers	Prevent child abuse and neglect and increase school readiness through structured home visits	• Improve parental knowledge of child development • Early detection of developmental delay • Increase school readiness	Supported by 2 RCTs and multiple quasiexperimental studies Meets HHS EBHVM criteria	Favorable outcomes reported in: • School readiness • Positive parenting
Early Start Home Visiting Program	Use home visitation to assess family needs, strengths and challenges	• Improve parenting skills • Encourage economic wellbeing • Reduce child abuse • Support parental mental health	Supported by 1 RCT Meets HHS EBHVM criteria	Favorable outcomes reported in: • School readiness • Positive parenting • Child health
Project Safecare (Augmented)	Parenting intervention to prevent or reduce factors that lead to child abuse and neglect by offering targeted services	• Planned activities training to improve parenting • Infant and child health assessment • Home safety assessment	One RCT, multiple quasiexperimental designs and IS designs Meets HHS EBHVM criteria	Favorable outcomes reported in • Positive parenting • Linkage and referrals

[a] *Department of Health and Human Services Evidence Based Home Visiting Model.*
[b] *For a comprehensive list of all evidence and outcomes data, please visit: https://homvee.acf.hhs.gov.*
HHS-EBHV: Health and Human Services Evidence Based Home Visitation; *IS*: Implementation Science; *RCT*: Randomized Controlled Trial.

nurse and mother with home visits starting in pregnancy (Nurse-Family Partnership—Helping First-Time Parents Succeed, 2018). NFP (along with most home visiting models) target the mother both in her role as a parent and an individual. Multiple randomized control trials (RCT) have been carried out in different populations around the world, including the US, Netherlands, and United Kingdom (Mejdoubi et al., 2011, 2015; Olds et al., 1986, 1997, 1998, 2002). The first RCT—often called the "Elmira" trial—was initiated in the early 1980s in a semirural community in New York State with 300 primarily Caucasian women (Miller, 2015; Olds et al., 1986). This cohort of women and children is perhaps the most studied of all the home visitation programs, as they have been followed for 19 years (Eckenrode et al., 2010; Glazner et al., 2004). Some of the early reported results were compelling, including 43% fewer subsequent pregnancies, and over a 12-month delay in a subsequent pregnancy when compared to the control group (Olds et al., 1986; Olds, Henderson, Tatelbaum, & Chamberlin, 1988). The long-term effects of the NFP intervention in the "Elmira" cohort were evaluated longitudinally over a 15-year period after the first RCT was completed. The group of adolescents that received nurse home visits reported fewer arrests, fewer instances of running away, fewer lifetime sex partners, and fewer cigarettes smoked in a day than those in the control group (Olds et al., 1998). A separate study examining the maternal outcomes in that same 15-year span found that mothers who had nurse home visits were less likely to be perpetrators of abuse and neglect, to have less arrests, and to have less behavioral impairments from drugs (Olds et al., 1997). Longitudinal research from the initial cohort also demonstrated consistent reductions in child maltreatment; however, those outcomes were attenuated when intimate partner violence was present. (Eckenrode et al., 2000)

To examine the impact of NFP on a non-Caucasian population, researchers completed a RCT with primarily low-income African American women in Memphis, Tennessee. They found home visitation by nurses reduced maternal hypertension, childhood injuries, and subsequent births (Kitzman, 1997). A 3-year follow up study showed continued benefits, including longer birth interval between first and second child, and less time being dependent on food stamps (Kitzman et al., 2000). Finally, in a RCT of nearly 800 women and children who were followed for 2 years (with a predominant Hispanic population), mothers who received NFP services had a decrease in smoking, delayed subsequent pregnancies, and increased employment compared to the control group (Olds et al., 2002).

In the Netherlands, a RCT was conducted with 460 women, using the NFP model adapted to the Netherlands. The primary outcome of the study was measures of child maltreatment. In the first 3 years of the study, there was a 42% reduction in child protective service reports between the NFP group and control group (Mejdoubi et al., 2011, 2015). Finally, a study was conducted in the United Kingdom assessing the outcomes of nurse-led visitation programs. This study included 1654 pregnant teenagers who were assigned to receive NFP and a control group that received usual community services. In contrast to other studies, this study found no significant differences in outcomes between the two groups, including birth weight, hospitalizations, or repeat pregnancies (Robling et al., 2016). One possible explanation proposed is that the control group actually received more community services than prior control groups in other populations.

Despite the overwhelming evidence that NFP can have positive impacts on mothers and children, it is important to note that not all studies have shown reproducible outcomes in certain domains. For example, researchers in Pennsylvania evaluated the effects of a state-wide nursing home visiting program on childhood injuries. They found no reductions in serious childhood injuries in families who received home visitation (Matone, O'Reilly, Luan, Localio, & Rubin, 2012). Studies like this underscore the need for strong implementation and dissemination strategies even with programs that have a strong foundational evidence base.

To date, NFP programs have established themselves as effective models with evidence and favorable outcomes in certain domains related to child wellbeing (i.e., school readiness and mother-child relationships). This program has the best evidence for demonstrating child maltreatment prevention (MacMillan et al., 2009) when implemented with good fidelity to the original model.

Healthy Families America

In 1992, the National Committee for Prevention of Child Abuse launched the HFA home visiting program. The goal of this program is to reduce child maltreatment and childhood adversity through strengthening parent-child relationships and healthy attachments. The HFA model includes: (1) initial assessments to identify at-risk families, (2) home visiting services, (3) screening for childhood development, and (4) screening for maternal depression. A targeted prevention approach is utilized to reach at-risk parents, including single parents, families living in poverty, parents with history of ACEs or exposure to substance abuse or intimate partner violence. HFA now has sites across the US and its territories and Canada. To date, HFA has been shown to improve outcomes in some domains, including maternal education (LeCroy & Krysik, 2011), reducing low birth rates (Lee et al., 2009), reducing intimate partner physical violence experiences (Bair-Merritt et al., 2010), and improving child development (Caldera et al., 2007). Other studies have measured overall rates of child maltreatment, finding no difference in physical abuse, but a small improvement in reducing rates of neglect (Duggan et al., 2004). A few studies have evaluated the effects of HFA on adolescent parents, finding a positive impact on parenting stress, intimate partner violence and risky parental behaviors, and a decrease in repeat pregnancy (Jacobs et al., 2016; Ownbey, Ownbey, & Cullen, 2011).

Parents as Teachers

The PAT model has been implemented across the US, in Canada, and internationally (Parents as Teachers, 2018). In contrast to NFP and HFA, PAT is a structured curriculum that can be adapted to local home visiting models and includes a curriculum called Born to Learn, consisting of the four elements of home visits, parent groups, child developmental screening, and referrals to other services (Drotar, Robinson, Jeavons, & Lester Kirchner, 2009). The evidence for this model is supported by quasiexperimental designs (Zigler, Pfannenstiel, & Seitz, 2008). A recent study looked at the impact of voluntary participation in an established statewide home visiting program that implemented a PAT curriculum (Chaiyachati et al., 2018), finding a 22% decreased likelihood of child protective service substantiated reports for child abuse and neglect with families receiving home visiting. The authors also reported, when a substantiated report occurred, it was later in a child's life (although when the home visiting services were still in place), suggesting some effect in preventing earlier adversities. PAT has also partnered with other programs to address specific population needs. For example, PAT partnered with the High 5, Low Fat Program (H5LF) to impact the dietary intake of African American parents (Haire-Joshu et al., 2003). They also partnered with High 5 for Pre-school Kids (H5-KIDS) to evaluate whether a home visiting nutritional program could improve a child's intake of fruits and vegetables. In that study, parents reported participation in H5-KIDS led to an increase in their children's fruits and vegetable intake (Haire-Joshu et al., 2008). PAT has shown the potential benefit of using their home visiting strategy along with community partnership to address complex social issues surrounding childhood adversity. Despite the lack of robust evidence from RCTs, this program has widespread reach, at least in specific populations.

Early Start Home Visiting Program

The Early Start Home Visiting Program is an intensive home visiting program targeted toward families under stress, including social or economic challenges. A RCT compared families receiving Early Start with families receiving standard care (Fergusson, Grant, Horwood, & Ridder, 2005). The families were recruited from a large urban city in New Zealand. In this area, 95% of women who give birth receive a free nursing home visit. At this free nurse visit, families were recruited to join the study. At the time of recruitment, they were randomly assigned to either Early Start or no further intervention. At age 3 years, children enrolled in Early Start had lower childhood injury rates than the control group and fewer hospital admissions for severe abuse. However, there were no differences in the referral rates to child protective service agencies between the two groups (Fergusson et al., 2005). Although this program has achieved international implementation, there are currently no robust data evaluating both short- and long-term outcomes.

Project Safe Care

This home visiting program is an indicated prevention intervention for families where child maltreatment has already occurred and has been substantiated by a child protective services investigation (Gershater-Molko, Lutzker, & Wesch, 2003). It is a 24-week intervention focusing on child health, home safety, and injury prevention (Gershater-Molko, Lutzker, & Wesch, 2002). Some studies have concluded that Safe Care can reduce the recurrence of child maltreatment (Gershater-Molko et al., 2002, 2003); however, due to methodologic weaknesses (i.e., no RCT trials and outcomes were dependent on parent self-report only), firm conclusions about program effectiveness cannot be made.

Summary

When reviewing the literature on the effectiveness of home visitation models, NFP and HFA have shown the most promise for preventing ACEs by promoting the relationships between mother and child and addressing SDoH (MacMillan et al., 2009). These programs have made efforts in ensuring the fidelity of the approach across different demographic characteristics and regions. In theory, programs modeled after NFP and HFA could be effective in preventing child maltreatment. However, the evidence shows that not all home visiting programs have proven effectiveness on reducing rates of child maltreatment (i.e., physical abuse and neglect) (Chaffin, 2004; Chaffin & Friedrich, 2004). A word of caution when evaluating programs is important, as surveillance bias is a vexing problem that may play a role in the results of key outcomes (e.g., reductions in some forms of child maltreatment) and, thus, should be considered whenever reviewing these types of outcomes in prevention interventions (Chaffin & Bard, 2006; Filene, Kaminski, Valle, & Cachat, 2013). As home visiting programs continue to grow in number and scope, program effectiveness should be studied before widespread dissemination is adopted, and attentiveness to the robustness of the study design should be used when interpreting outcomes.

Positive parenting interventions

In the US, it is estimated that between 11% and 20% of children meet diagnostic criteria for a behavioral health disorder (Briggs-Gowan, Horwitz, Schwab-Stone, Leventhal, & Leaf, 2000; Weitzman & Wegner, 2015), and other countries similarly report high rates of childhood behavioral problems (Wichstrøm et al., 2012). Children with behavioral problems are at an increased risk for physical abuse and harsh parenting (Chaffin et al., 2004; Timmer, Urquiza, Zebell, & McGrath, 2005). Parenting behaviors such as corporal punishment can lead to increased behavioral problems in children, low self-esteem, depression, and future physical abuse of their own children (Gershoff & Grogan-Kaylor, 2016; Straus, Sugarman, & Giles-Sims, 1997). Harsh physical punishment, independent of other forms of child maltreatment, is associated with behavioral disorders (Afifi, Mota, Dasiewicz, MacMillan, & Sareen, 2012). Furthermore, early and maladaptive harsh parenting behaviors can lead to lifelong consequences, such as substance abuse and mental health issues (Afifi et al., 2012; Straus et al., 1997; Straus & Kantor, 1994; Weiss, Dodge, Bates, & Pettit, 1992). There is now consensus that safe and nurturing parenting lays the foundations for healthy child development (Barlow et al., 2011; Collins, Maccoby, Steinberg, Hetherington, & Bornstein, 2000; Stack, Serbin, Enns, Ruttle, & Barrieau, 2010). Even in the face of adverse experiences such as poverty, neighborhood deprivation, and low socioeconomic status, children who grow up with nurturing, supportive parenting practices are less likely to develop behavioral problems (Odgers et al., 2012). Parenting strategies during infancy and childhood affect brain development, language, social skills, self-control, capacity to cope, and mental health throughout life (Cecil, Barker, Jaffee, & Viding, 2012; Odgers et al., 2012). Parenting programs have emerged as a way to promote childhood wellbeing and decrease the lifelong consequences of harsh parenting. Multiple evidence-based parenting programs exist (Gershoff, Lee, & Durrant, 2017) and we have selected several to highlight (see Table 3).

The Triple P-Positive Parenting Program

The Triple P was developed from social learning theory and the principles of behavior and cognitive change (Sanders, 2012). This program took 30 years to develop by the collective effort of multiple staff at the University of Queensland (Sanders, Turner, & Markie-Dadds, 2002). The initial goal of Triple P was to be a program delivered in the home, targeting parents of disruptive children, using a tiered, community-based approach. There are now multiple versions of Triple P targeting specific populations, including adolescents, children with disabilities, or other special needs. Triple P aims to improve social, emotional, and behavioral needs of children by enhancing knowledge and confidence in parents (Sanders, Kirby, Tellegen, & Day, 2014). There are five intervention levels that vary according to intensity and delivery. When evaluated, various components of Triple P appear to show improvement in parent reported child behavioral problems, parenting practices, and family characteristics (Prinz, Sanders, Shapiro, Whitaker, & Lutzker, 2009; Sanders et al., 2014; Zubrick et al., 2005). In a metaanalysis, it was reported that each component of Triple P had a positive impact on parenting and in creating nurturing family environments

TABLE 3 Summary of Positive Parenting Interventions

Program	Mission	Objectives	Evidence[a]	Outcomes
Triple P	Reduce mental health problems and behavioral problems in children	• Increase parental knowledge • Increase parental confidence	Multiple RCTs have shown positive effect at community level; however, population-level data remain indeterminate	Favorable outcomes reported in: • Reducing child behavioral problems • Reducing child internalizing and externalizing behaviors • Reduction in child maltreatment reports
PCIT	Improve the quality of the parent-child relationship for young children with behavioral disorders	• Decrease negative behaviors • Decrease severity of maladaptive behaviors • Increase parenting confidence • Decrease the consequences of harsh parenting	Strong evidence by multiple RCTs and metaanalysis	Favorable outcomes reported in: • Reducing harsh parenting • Promoting positive parenting • Reduction in child externalizing behaviors
CARE and PriCARE	Promote the healthy emotional growth of children	• Reduce harsh parenting • Reduce risk of child maltreatment • Improve parent-child relationship	Supported by quasiexperimental studys and one RCT	Favorable outcomes reported in: • Improved parent empathy • Improvement in problem behaviors

[a] *To demonstrate the variability in the strength of the evidence i.e., RCTs vs. quasiexperimental study designs for each intervention.*

on a population level (Prinz et al., 2009). However, a systematic review evaluating 33 studies of Triple P found inconclusive evidence that Triple P works at the population level or has long-lasting outcome effects (Wilson et al., 2012). The authors speculated that their conclusion differed from prior studies due to selection bias, sample size, and lack of control groups. Part of the challenge in the replication of Triple P has been lack of fidelity to implement the model within the social-ecological framework as a community-based intervention with its multicomponents.

Parent Child Interaction Therapy (PCIT)

PCIT is an enhanced parent behavior training program designed to provide parent coaching to improve the parent-child interaction and dynamics in sessions where the parents and children meet together and coaching is performed by a therapist. Parents wear a wireless earphone, and the therapist coaches the parents from behind a one-way mirror (Hakman, Chaffin, Funderburk, & Silovsky, 2009). PCIT has two phases of treatment—child-directed interaction and parent-directed interaction. During these two phases, parents are trained to eliminate the use of harsh parenting practices and criticism, and to use selective attention in response to mild behavioral issues in the child. Ultimately, the goal is to interrupt an escalating cycle of harsh parenting that may lead to child maltreatment, poor parent-child relationships, and worsening child behavioral issues (Baumrind, 1966; Chaffin et al., 2004; Eyberg, Nelson, & Boggs, 2008; Hakman et al., 2009). Originally developed to be a treatment program for parents and children with conduct disorder, it has been adapted for use in a variety of populations, including preschool and school-aged children as well as those who have been physically abused. PCIT has been studied with RCTs (Niec, Barnett, Prewett, & Shanley Chatham, 2016; Thomas & Zimmer-Gembeck, 2012) and has been found to reduce physical abuse recidivism among parents (Hakman et al., 2009; Kennedy, Kim, Tripodi, Brown, & Gowdy, 2016), improve behavioral problems in children (Lenze, Pautsch, & Luby, 2011; Puliafico, Comer, & Pincus, 2012), and promote positive parenting (Shanley & Niec, 2010). While PCIT is primarily viewed as a treatment model, we have included it here due to its evidence in reducing further ACEs, including maltreatment. And, since it is a treatment model, most areas that offer PCIT also require a mental health diagnosis in the child for eligibility, thus limiting its accessibility and full utility as a prevention intervention.

Child Adult Relationship Enhancement (CARE) and PriCARE

CARE is a trauma-informed training program designed to teach parents techniques to support the healthy emotional growth of children (Gurwitch et al., 2016). One of the newer forms of parent-enhanced interventions, it was developed in 2006 using concepts from PCIT, and was initially designed as a primary child maltreatment prevention (Gurwitch et al., 2016). CARE fills a gap in service delivery that exists for children who may not meet the diagnostic criteria for a mental health condition (thus limiting access to PCIT), but who are still at risk for maltreatment; hence, CARE has a primary prevention focus. Out of the CARE model emerged PriCARE, a modified CARE program specifically adapted and incorporated within the primary care office—the child's *medical home*—as a natural environment for this type of intervention, given that parents often discuss with their primary care provider concerns regarding behavioral problems in their children (Schilling et al., 2017). The PriCARE adaptation is a 1.5 hour session each week for 6 weeks, focusing on positive parenting and giving effective commands for parents of preschool children. In 2016, a RCT of the efficacy of PriCARE in an urban primary care clinic was performed (Schilling et al., 2017). The study demonstrated that, compared to controls, parent training in a primary care setting strengthened child-caregiver relationships with improved parent management of externalizing behaviors, improved empathy of their child's needs, reduction in the use of corporal punishment, and reductions in child behavior problems. The authors concluded that PriCARE shows promise in improving parenting constructs and child behavioral symptoms. Although further research is needed, this may be a promising and feasible child maltreatment strategy and incorporates the philosophy of enhancing the medical home as a holistic support system for children and families (Schilling et al., 2017).

Enhanced medical homes

Historically, the mainstay of child maltreatment prevention has rested upon home visiting programs and parent-enhanced programs. Pediatric primary care practices are emerging as another resource for maltreatment prevention, as the benefits of a medical home continue to be recognized. While the US Preventative Services Task Force has concluded that there is insufficient evidence to recommend specific interventions to prevent ACEs in the primary care setting, the AAP continues to recommend screening for risk factors such as maternal depression, substance abuse, and poverty (Weitzman & Wegner, 2015). The AAP also recommends that family and parenting support should begin in the medical home during health promotion anticipatory guidance (Council on Community Pediatrics, 2016). In a medical home adapted for the special needs of high-risk families, parents can be provided with resources to promote resilience and receive services to mitigate the short- and long-term risks of adversity to promote health and wellbeing. Early literacy programs in the medical home (e.g., Reach Out and Read) have been shown to enhance reading readiness (Diener, 2012). The AAP also promotes medical-legal partnership models, which link legal aid to health services in a medical home. A pilot study of a medical-legal partnership found that helping families with legal services improved child health outcomes (Weintraub et al., 2010). Medical homes can also link families to services if pediatricians use validated screening tools. For example, a single question *Do you have difficulty making ends meet at the end of the month?* has up to a 98% sensitivity to a need for linking a family to community resources and services (Brcic et al., 2011).

The Safe Environment for Every Kid (SEEK) model has grown as a promising primary care-based prevention program, which encapsulates the healthcare trends in incorporating social needs assessment and support to families. The goal of this program is to identify psychosocial problems that could place a child at risk for maltreatment (Dubowitz et al., 2012). Initial studies demonstrated that, with adequate staff, training, and administration of the PSQ, they were able to reduce the rates of child maltreatment among high-risk families in their urban clinics with a 31% decrease in the number of reports to child protective services (Dubowitz et al., 2009). A follow-up study based on lower-risk families in a suburban practice setting, utilizing the same model, demonstrated only modest child maltreatment rate reductions (though it did show a reduction in the use of harsh parenting practices), underscoring the importance of targeted prevention interventions (Dubowitz et al., 2012). Reframing the primary care visit to include a more robust social needs component (like the SEEK model) may offer the opportunity to successfully integrate evidence-based prevention programs into primary care settings. Enhanced medical homes can support child maltreatment prevention through early identification of at-risk families, link those families to services, and provide on-going surveillance of health and wellness for child and family.

Community-based interventions

With the exception of some aspects of the Triple P, strategies previously outlined have focused on parent, child, or parent-child interactions. There has been increased attention focused on improving the community environment in which children are born and raised. This emerging focus on community child maltreatment prevention strategies encourages neighbors and members of a community to share a collective responsibility in the protection of children. Studies indicate that neighborhoods can have a significant effect on parenting behaviors and child outcomes (Coulton, Korbin, & Su, 1999; Langford & Ahsan, 2005), demonstrating potential positive effects a neighborhood can have in mitigating childhood adversity. Years of research have repeatedly shown that community factors such as poverty, violent crime, and drug trafficking influence rates of child maltreatment; so, addressing these conditions matters when trying to prevent child maltreatment (Coulton et al., 1999; Daro & Dodge, 2009; Garbarino & Kostelny, 1992; Garbarino & Sherman, 1980; Langford & Ahsan, 2005; Sampson, Raudenbush, & Earls, 1997).

Strengthening Families Initiative

Strengthening Families Initiative (SFI) is designed to enhance the capacity of early intervention centers and child care centers with the goal to build relationships with families so that community centers can more effectively recognize family stress, improve parental resilience, and increase parental knowledge of child development. Established in 2006, through support of the Doris Duke Charitable Foundation, the SFI assists families in fostering protective factors that contribute to child wellbeing. Their five core protective factors include parental resilience, social connections, knowledge of parenting, support in times of need, and emotional competence of children (Daro & Dodge, 2009; Douglass & Klerman, 2012; History of the Center for the Study of Social Policy, 2018). The development of the SFI grew out of literature showing that enrollment in high quality early education programs can have measurable impacts on child wellbeing and the prevention of child maltreatment (Ellenbogen, Klein, & Wekerle, 2014; Follett, 2004; Reynolds, Temple, Robertson, & Mann, 2001; Swick, 2009). Despite the promise of this initiative, it has not been rigorously studied and it remains unknown whether the desired family and child outcomes can be sustainably achieved (Daro & Dodge, 2009).

Strong Communities

The primary emphasis of this program is to change the social norms of attitudes and expectations regarding the collective responsibility that a community has for child welfare. The goal is to foster community competency in understanding how individual and combined efforts can contribute to the complexities of child maltreatment (Daro & Dodge, 2009; The Duke Endowment, 2018). This program uses outreach workers to advance community engagement in efforts, such as hosting community wellness fairs, back to school planning, educating families about the dangers of shaking an infant, and highlighting awareness of child abuse and its prevention during a national, annual effort in April. There have also been efforts to provide direct services to children and families, such as playgroups for children, parent-child activities, financial education, and assistance offering developmental screening. At this time, there are some project implementation data that show a wide range of interest from stakeholders and volunteers have been engaged (Daro & Dodge, 2009). No community-level data currently exist.

Cost outcomes of ACEs prevention interventions

While efforts to provide ACEs prevention interventions in the community have been a popular topic among researchers, basic economics tend to be a key driver for policy change that fosters dissemination of these prevention interventions. Skeptics in the use of universal ACEs screening have raised numerous concerns regarding the cost effectiveness of ACEs screening and prevention programs, citing the costs of the false-positive screenings and overtreatment seen in adult screening programs such as prostate-specific antigen testing and workplace blood pressure-monitoring programs (Finkelhor, 2017; Grimes & Schulz, 2002; McLintock, Foy, House, & Alderson, 2016; Sinyor, Rezmovitz, & Zaretsky, 2016). This becomes significantly more challenging in cases where screening, in the interest of anonymity, provides only a composite score, making it very difficult to associate a specific evidence-based treatment strategy with the generalized high ACEs score (Finkelhor, 2017).

Estimates regarding the long-term, downstream costs of the burden of multiple ACEs and subsequent cost savings of ACEs prevention are few; but, some initial estimates have been promising. One study in Washington State indicated a savings of over $7 million for every 244 foster-care placements prevented (a reasonable proxy for ACEs reduction in targeted and indicated prevention programs) and over $27 million a year when a subset of specific ACEs and ACEs-like events were prevented (e.g., teen pregnancy, school dropout, foster placements, juvenile crimes) (Hall, Porter, Longhi, Becker-Green, & Dreyfus, 2012). Another study from Washington State concluded that the widespread implementation of specific evidence-based programs designed to reduce the number of children placed into foster care could net the state between $317 and $493 million after 5 years (Stephanie, Steve, & Marna, 2008).

Cost analyses of home visitation programs have been studied as well, with varying results. While studies in England have demonstrated no cost benefits compared to existing social programs (Corbacho et al., 2017), more focused studies, metaanalyses, and systematic reviews involving home visitation programs in the US have demonstrated return on investment of approximately $3 for every $1 invested in higher risk families (Glazner et al., 2004; Karoly et al., 1998a; Olds, Henderson, Phelps, Kitzman, & Hanks, 1993; Stamuli et al., 2015). However, in other efforts to determine the cost implications of home visitation interventions from the Washington State Institute for Public Policy, the cost benefit for even the more well-established models (i.e., NFP and HFA) is less robust (Washington State Institute for Public Policy, 2018). As a result, one must be cautious in interpreting cost analyses of these programs, as the methods used to conduct these analyses, the outcomes used to ascribe a cost, and the cost assumptions of the outcomes can vary quite significantly, thus limiting confidence in interpreting summary cost findings of prevention programs.

The future landscape in ACEs prevention

Protecting children from child maltreatment, and preventing impairment when maltreatment has occurred, is a complex task that will not be successful with any one single approach. As outlined in this chapter, there are a variety of potential solutions that have been implemented with varying degrees of success. What we know is that the well-being of a child depends on the building blocks of healthy parental behaviors, a safe community, and the support of public institutions. No single approach can guarantee a successful outcome. It is widely accepted that early support of families, beginning at the time of pregnancy, may reduce child maltreatment and promote wellbeing; however, the best way to implement the right services remains undetermined. Organizations need to be mindful that a prevention plan must be well suited for the family or community in which it is designed. Challenges that should be addressed as prevention opportunities grow include the following:

1. reach those at risk and accurately identify those who will most benefit from a specific service;
2. determine the best intervention for different ethnic and cultural groups, ensuring no language barriers and respecting cultural child-rearing practices when possible;
3. improve the use of technology, exploring how digital health solutions can help reach families in need of services; and
4. balance between family, community, and organization, and policy by identifying how to blend the strengths of different parts of the social-ecological model to prevent child maltreatment.

As our understanding of health promotion and disease prevention across a lifespan advances, a modification to the traditional social-ecological framework—the ecobiodevelopmental framework—is emerging (Shonkoff et al., 2012). This framework further builds on neuroscience, biology, genomics, and social sciences to provide a new perspective on the interaction between experience, environment, and genetic predisposition. It recognizes that it is not adversity alone but also the absence of protective relationships, which leads to poor outcomes. It is now understood that a broad range of multidisciplinary fields and disciplines (e.g., nursing, medicine, genomics, epigenetics, psychology, economics, social work, policy), in collaboration, are necessary to adequately address childhood adversity and its lifelong effects. Successful implementation of effective interventions for health promotion requires not only advocacy but a continued investment in the following (Shonkoff et al., 2012; Starmer, Duby, Slaw, Edwards, & Leslie, 2010):

1. continuous improvement of ongoing, tested home visitation models, such as NFP and HFA;
2. testing of new, multidisciplinary innovative interventions, guided by evidence;
3. training of frontline clinicians to better collaborate with social and policy realms; and
4. commitment from pediatricians to translate research into innovative childhood policies to promote and advocate in society at large.

There are current evidence gaps related to the effectiveness of programs on mitigating physical abuse, sexual abuse, and neglect. Further clinical and population-based trials are necessary to establish the relationship between program implementation and outcome. Clear objective outcome measures are needed without sole reliance on parent or caretaker self-report (MacMillan et al., 2009). Ongoing research needs to address selection bias, ascertainment bias, and the over-reliance of parental self-reports, as well as improvements in defining measures of childhood outcomes related to adversity. As the field of implementation science grows, implementation outcomes such as feasibility, penetration, and fidelity should be incorporated in to program evaluation (Proctor et al., 2011). Efficacy and effectiveness should be simultaneously studied and incorporated into implementation design. Research questions should address which screening tools are appropriate, what implementation methods maximize adoption, how technology can be leveraged to reach high-risk populations, and how payment models can support prevention strategies (Gottlieb et al., 2018).

Preventing childhood adversity is not just a simple solution of parents "doing a better job" but, rather, about creating a culture in which children can thrive in their home, neighborhood, and community. This endeavor will take the continued collaboration of policy makers, clinicians, social workers, community workers, researchers, and, most importantly, families themselves. The progression of prevention is achievable through ongoing collaboration and innovation. As sociologist Robert Wuthnow once stated "the good in society we envision is possible, and the very act of helping each other gives us strength and a common destiny" (Wuthnow, 1991, p. 304).

References

Adirim, T., & Supplee, L. (2013). Overview of the federal home visiting program. *Pediatrics, 132*(Supplement), S59–S64. https://doi.org/10.1542/peds.2013-1021C.

Afifi, T. O., Mota, N. P., Dasiewicz, P., MacMillan, H. L., & Sareen, J. (2012). Physical punishment and mental disorders: results from a nationally representative US sample. *Pediatrics, 130*(2), 184–192. https://doi.org/10.1542/peds.2011-2947.

American Academy of Pediatrics (AAP) Committee on Practice and Ambulatory Medicine and AAP Bright Futures Periodicity Schedule Workgroup. (2017). 2017 recommendations for preventive pediatric health care. *Pediatrics, 139*(4), 0254. https://doi.org/10.1542/peds.2017-0254.

Anda, R. F., Brown, D. W., Dube, S. R., Bremner, J. D., Felitti, V. J., & Giles, W. H. (2008). Adverse childhood experiences and chronic obstructive pulmonary disease in adults. *American Journal of Preventive Medicine, 34*(5), 396–403. https://doi.org/10.1016/j.amepre.2008.02.002.

Aos, S., Lieb, R., Mayfield, J., Miller, M., & Pennucci, A. (2004). *Benefits and costs of prevention and early intervention programs for youth*. Olympia, Washington. Retrieved from: http://www.wsipp.wa.gov.

Bair-Merritt, M. H., Jennings, J. M., Chen, R., Burrell, L., McFarlane, E., Fuddy, L., & Duggan, A. K. (2010). Reducing maternal intimate partner violence after the birth of a child: a randomized controlled trial of the Hawaii Healthy Start Home Visitation Program. *Archives of Pediatrics and Adolescent Medicine, 164*(1), 16–23. https://doi.org/10.1001/archpediatrics.2009.237.

Barlow, J., Smailagic, N., Bennett, C., Huband, N., Jones, H., & Coren, E. (2011). *Individual and group based parenting programmes for improving psychosocial outcomes for teenage parents and their children*. Cochrane.https://doi.org/10.1002/14651858.CD002964.pub2.

Bauer, M. S., Damschroder, L., Hagedorn, H., Smith, J., & Kilbourne, A. M. (2015). An introduction to implementation science for the non-specialist. *BMC Psychology*, *3*(1), 1–12. https://doi.org/10.1186/S40359-015-0089-9.

Baumrind, D. (1966). Effects of authoritative parental control on child behavior. *Child Development*, *37*(4), 887. https://doi.org/10.2307/1126611.

Beaune, L., Leavens, A., Muskat, B., Ford-Jones, L., Rapoport, A., Zlotnik Shaul, R., & Chapman, L. A. (2014). Poverty and pediatric palliative care: what can we do? *Journal of Social Work in End-of-Life & Palliative Care*, *10*(2), 170–185. https://doi.org/10.1080/15524256.2014.906375.

Beck, A. F., Klein, M. D., & Kahn, R. S. (2012). Identifying social risk via a clinical social history embedded in the electronic health record. *Clinical Pediatrics*, *51*(10), 972–977. https://doi.org/10.1177/0009922812441663.

Beck, A. F., Tschudy, M. M., Coker, T. R., et al. (2016). Determinants of health and pediatric primary care practices. *Pediatrics*, *137*(3), 1–11. e20153673.

Bilukha, O., Hahn, R. A., Crosby, A., Fullilove, M. T., Liberman, A., Moscicki, E., & Briss, P. A. (2005). The effectiveness of early childhood home visitation in preventing violence: a systematic review. *American Journal of Preventive Medicine*, *28*(2 Suppl. 1), 11–39. https://doi.org/10.1016/j.amepre.2004.10.004.

Brcic, V., Eberdt, C., Kaczorowski, J., Brcic, V., Eberdt, C., & Kaczorowski, J. (2011). Development of a tool to identify poverty in a family practice setting: a pilot study. *International Journal of Family Medicine*, *2011*, 1–7. https://doi.org/10.1155/2011/812182.

Briggs-Gowan, M. J., Horwitz, S. M. C., Schwab-Stone, M. E., Leventhal, J. M., & Leaf, P. J. (2000). Mental health in pediatric settings: distribution of disorders and factors related to service use. *Journal of the American Academy of Child and Adolescent Psychiatry*, *39*(7), 841–849. https://doi.org/10.1097/00004583-200007000-00012.

Bright, M. A., Knapp, C., Hinojosa, M. S., Alford, S., & Bonner, B. (2016). The comorbidity of physical, mental, and developmental conditions associated with childhood adversity: a population based study. *Maternal and Child Health Journal*, *20*(4), 843–853. https://doi.org/10.1007/s10995-015-1915-7.

Caldera, D., Burrell, L., Rodriguez, K., Crowne, S. S., Rohde, C., & Duggan, A. (2007). Impact of a statewide home visiting program on parenting and on child health and development. *Child Abuse & Neglect*, *31*(8), 829–852. https://doi.org/10.1016/j.chiabu.2007.02.008.

Cecil, C. A. M., Barker, E. D., Jaffee, S. R., & Viding, E. (2012). Association between maladaptive parenting and child self-control over time: cross-lagged study using a monozygotic twin difference design. *British Journal of Psychiatry*, *201*(4), 291–297. https://doi.org/10.1192/bjp.bp.111.107581.

Chaffin, M. (2004). Is it time to rethink healthy start/healthy families? *Child Abuse & Neglect*, *28*(6), 589–595. https://doi.org/10.1016/j.chiabu.2004.04.004.

Chaffin, M., & Bard, D. (2006). Impact of intervention surveillance bias on analyses of child welfare report outcomes. *Child Maltreatment*, *11*(4), 301–312. https://doi.org/10.1177/1077559506291261.

Chaffin, M., & Friedrich, B. (2004). Evidence-based treatments in child abuse and neglect. *Children and Youth Services Review*, *26*(11 SPEC ISS), 1097–1113. https://doi.org/10.1016/j.childyouth.2004.08.008.

Chaffin, M., Silovsky, J. F., Funderburk, B., Valle, L. A., Brestan, E. V., Balachova, T., & Bonner, B. L. (2004). Parent-child interaction therapy with physically abusive parents: efficacy for reducing future abuse reports. *Journal of Consulting and Clinical Psychology*, *72*(3), 500–510. https://doi.org/10.1037/0022-006X.72.3.500.

Chaiyachati, B. H., Gaither, J. R., Hughes, M., Foley-Schain, K., & Leventhal, J. M. (2018). Preventing child maltreatment: examination of an established statewide home-visiting program. *Child Abuse & Neglect*, *79*, 476–484. https://doi.org/10.1016/j.chiabu.2018.02.019.

Chapman, J., Siegel, E., & Cross, A. (1990). Home visitors and child health: analysis of selected programs. *Pediatrics*, *85*(6), 1059–1068.

Collins, W. A., Maccoby, E. E., Steinberg, L., Hetherington, E. M., & Bornstein, M. H. (2000). Contemporary research on parenting. *American Psychologist*, *55*(2), 218–232. https://doi.org/10.1037//0003-066X.55.2.218.

Corbacho, B., Bell, K., Stamuli, E., Richardson, G., Ronaldson, S., Hood, K., & Torgerson, D. (2017). Cost-effectiveness of the family nurse partnership (FNP) programme in England: evidence from the building blocks trial. *Journal of Evaluation in Clinical Practice*, *23*(6), 1367–1374. https://doi.org/10.1111/jep.12799.

Coulton, C. J., Korbin, J. E., & Su, M. (1999). Neighborhoods and child maltreatment: a multi-level study. *Child Abuse & Neglect*, *23*(11), 1019–1040. https://doi.org/10.1016/S0145-2134(99)00076-9.

Council on Child and Adolescent Health. (1998). The role of home-visitation programs in improving health outcomes for children and families. *Pediatrics*, *101*(3), 486–489. Retrieved from: http://pediatrics.aappublications.org/content/101/3/486.full.

Council on Community Pediatrics. (2016). Poverty and child health in the United States. *Pediatrics*, *137*(4), e20160339. https://doi.org/10.1542/peds.2016-0339.

Daro, D., & Dodge, K. A. (2009). Creating community responsibility for child protection: possibilities and challenges. *Future of Children*, *19*(2), 67–93. https://doi.org/10.1353/foc.0.0030.

Dejong, N. A., Wood, C. T., Morreale, M. C., Ellis, C., Davis, D., Fernandez, J., & Steiner, M. J. (2016). Identifying social determinants of health and legal needs for children with special health care needs. *Clinical Pediatrics*, *55*(3), 272–277. https://doi.org/10.1177/0009922815591959.

Diener, M. L. (2012). Kindergarten readiness and performance of latino children participating in reach out and read. *Journal of Community Medicine & Health Education*, *2*, 3. https://doi.org/10.4172/2161-0711.1000133.

Dong, M., Giles, W. H., Felitti, V. J., Dube, S. R., Williams, J. E., Chapman, D. P., & Anda, R. F. (2004). Insights into causal pathways for ischemic heart disease: adverse childhood experiences study. *Circulation*, *110*(13), 1761–1766. https://doi.org/10.1161/01.CIR.0000143074.54995.7F.

Douglass, A., & Klerman, L. (2012). The strengthening families initiative and child care quality improvement: how strengthening families influenced change in child care programs in one state. *Early Education and Development*, *23*(3), 373–392. https://doi.org/10.1080/10409289.2012.666193.

Drotar, D., Robinson, J., Jeavons, L., & Lester Kirchner, H. (2009). A randomized, controlled evaluation of early intervention: the born to learn curriculum. *Child: Care, Health and Development*, *35*(5), 643–649. https://doi.org/10.1111/j.1365-2214.2008.00915.x.

Dubowitz, H., Feigelman, S., Lane, W., & Kim, J. (2009). Pediatric primary care to help prevent child maltreatment: the Safe Environment for Every Kid (SEEK) model. *Pediatrics*, *123*(3), 858–864. https://doi.org/10.1542/peds.2008-1376.

Dubowitz, H., Feigelman, S., Lane, W., Prescott, L., Blackman, K., Grube, L., & Tracy, J. K. (2007). Screening for depression in an urban pediatric primary care clinic. *Pediatrics*, *119*(3), 435–443. https://doi.org/10.1542/peds.2006-2010.

Dubowitz, H., Lane, W. G., Semiatin, J. N., & Magder, L. S. (2012). The seek model of pediatric primary care: can child maltreatment be prevented in a low-risk population? *Academic Pediatrics*, *12*(4), 259–268. https://doi.org/10.1016/j.acap.2012.03.005.

Dubowitz, H., Prescott, L., Feigelman, S., Lane, W., & Kim, J. (2008). Screening for intimate partner violence in a pediatric primary care clinic. *Pediatrics*, *121*(1), e85–e91. https://doi.org/10.1542/peds.2007-0904.

Duggan, A., McFarlane, E., Fuddy, L., Burrell, L., Higman, S. M., Windham, A., & Sia, C. (2004). Randomized trial of a statewide home visiting program: impact in preventing child abuse and neglect. *Child Abuse & Neglect*, *28*(6), 597–622. https://doi.org/10.1016/j.chiabu.2003.08.007.

Eckenrode, J., Campa, M., Luckey, D. W., Henderson, C. R., Cole, R., Kitzman, H., & Olds, D. (2010). Long-term effects of prenatal and infancy nurse home visitation on the life course of youths: 19-year follow-up of a randomized trial. *Archives of Pediatrics and Adolescent Medicine*, *164*(1), 9–15. https://doi.org/10.1001/archpediatrics.2009.240.

Eckenrode, J., Ganzel, B., Henderson, C. R., Smith, E., Olds, D. L., Powers, J., & Sidora, K. (2000). Preventing child abuse and neglect with a program of nurse home visitation. *JAMA*, *284*(11), 1385–1391.

Ellenbogen, S., Klein, B., & Wekerle, C. (2014). Early childhood education as a resilience intervention for maltreated children. *Early Child Development and Care*, *184*(9–10), 1364–1377. https://doi.org/10.1080/03004430.2014.916076.

Eyberg, S. M., Nelson, M. M., & Boggs, S. R. (2008). Evidence-based psychosocial treatments for children and adolescents with disruptive behavior. *Journal of Clinical Child and Adolescent Psychology*, *37*(1), 215–237. https://doi.org/10.1080/15374410701820117.

Felitti, V. J., Anda, R. F., Nordenberg, D., Williamson, D. F., Spitz, A. M., Edwards, V., & Marks, J. S. (1998). Relationship of childhood abuse and household dysfunction to many of the leading causes of death in adults: The adverse childhood experiences (ACE) study. *American Journal of Preventive Medicine*, *14*(4), 245–258. https://doi.org/10.1016/S0749-3797(98)00017-8.

Fergusson, D. M., Grant, H., Horwood, L. J., & Ridder, E. M. (2005). Randomized trial of the early start program of home visitation. *Pediatrics*, *116*(6), e803–e809. https://doi.org/10.1542/peds.2005-0948.

Filene, J. H., Kaminski, J. W., Valle, L. A., & Cachat, P. (2013). Components associated with home visiting program outcomes: a meta-analysis. *Pediatrics*, *132*(Suppl(Supplement_2)), S100–S109. https://doi.org/10.1542/peds.2013-1021H.

Finkelhor, D. (2017). Screening for adverse childhood experiences (ACEs): cautions and suggestions. *Child Abuse & Neglect*, *85*, 174–179. https://doi.org/10.1016/j.chiabu.2017.07.016.

Finkelhor, D., Shattuck, A., Turner, H., & Hamby, S. (2013). Improving the adverse childhood experiences study scale. *JAMA Pediatrics*, *167*(1), 70–75. https://doi.org/10.1001/jamapediatrics.2013.420.

Follett, C. C. (2004). *Implementation and process evaluation of starting early starting smart*. ProQuest Dissertations Publishing, University of Michigan. Retrieved from: https://search.proquest.com/docview/305180741.

Garbarino, J., & Kostelny, K. (1992). Child maltreatment as a community problem. *Child Abuse & Neglect*, *16*(4), 455–464. https://doi.org/10.1016/0145-2134(92)90062-V.

Garbarino, J., & Sherman, D. (1980). High-risk neighborhoods and high-risk families: the human ecology of child maltreatment. *Child Development*, *51*(1), 188–198. https://doi.org/10.1111/j.1467-8624.1980.tb02525.x.

Garner, A. S. (2013). Home visiting and the biology of toxic stress: opportunities to address early childhood adversity. *Pediatrics*, *132*(Supplement), S65–S73. https://doi.org/10.1542/peds.2013-1021D.

Garner, A. S., Shonkoff, J. P., Siegel, B. S., Dobbins, M. I., Earls, M. F., Garner, A. S., & Wood, D. L. (2012). Early childhood adversity, toxic stress, and the role of the pediatrician: translating developmental science into lifelong health. *Pediatrics*, *129*, 224–231. https://doi.org/10.1542/peds.2011-2662.

Gershater-Molko, R. M., Lutzker, J. R., & Wesch, D. (2002). Using recidivism data to evaluate project Safecare: teaching bonding, safety, and health care skills to parents. *Child Maltreatment*, *7*(3), 277–285. https://doi.org/10.1177/1077559502007003009.

Gershater-Molko, R. M., Lutzker, J. R., & Wesch, D. (2003). Project safe care: improving health, safety, and parenting skills in families reported for, and at-risk for child maltreatment. *Journal of Family Violence*, *18*(6), 377–386. https://doi.org/10.1023/A:1026219920902.

Gershoff, E. T., & Grogan-Kaylor, A. (2016). Spanking and child outcomes: old controversies and new meta-analyses. *Journal of Family Psychology*, *30*(4), 453–469. https://doi.org/10.1037/fam0000191.

Gershoff, E. T., Lee, S. J., & Durrant, J. E. (2017). Promising intervention strategies to reduce parents' use of physical punishment. *Child Abuse & Neglect*, *71*, 9–23. https://doi.org/10.1016/j.chiabu.2017.01.017.

Glazner, J., Bondy, J., Luckey, D., & Olds, D. (2004). *Effect of the nurse family partnership on government expenditures for vulnerable first-time mothers and their children in Elmira, New York, Memphis, Tennessee, and Denver, Colorado*. Retrieved May 14, 2018 from:https://www.acf.hhs.gov/sites/default/files/opre/effect_nursefam.pdf.

Gomby, D. S., Culross, P. L., & Behrman, R. E. (1999). Home visiting: recent program evaluations—analysis and recommendations. *Future of Children*, *9*(1), 4–26. https://doi.org/10.2307/1602719.

Gorski, P. A., & Kuo, A. A. (2013). Community pediatrics: navigating the intersection of medicine, public health, and social determinants of children's health. *Pediatrics*, *131*(3), 623–628. https://doi.org/10.1542/peds.2012-3933.

Gottlieb, L., Cottrell, E. K., Park, B., Clark, K. D., Gold, R., & Fichtenberg, C. (2018). Advancing social prescribing with implementation science. *Journal of the American Board of Family Medicine*, *31*(3), 315–321. https://doi.org/10.3122/jabfm.2018.03.170249.

Grimes, D. A., & Schulz, K. F. (2002). Uses and abuses of screening tests. *The Lancet*, *359*, 881–884. https://doi.org/10.1016/S0140-6736(02)07948-5.

Gurwitch, R. H., Messer, E. P., Masse, J., Olafson, E., Boat, B. W., & Putnam, F. W. (2016). Child-adult relationship enhancement (CARE): an evidence-informed program for children with a history of trauma and other behavioral challenges. *Child Abuse & Neglect*, *53*, 138–145. https://doi.org/10.1016/j.chiabu.2015.10.016.

Guttentag, C. L., Landry, S. H., Williams, J. M., Baggett, K. M., Noria, C. W., Borkowski, J. G., & Ramey, S. L. (2014). "My baby & me": effects of an early, comprehensive parenting intervention on at-risk mothers and their children. *Developmental Psychology*, *50*(5), 1482–1496. https://doi.org/10.1037/a0035682.

Haire-Joshu, D., Brownson, R. C., Nanney, M. S., Houston, C., Steger-May, K., Schechtman, K., & Auslander, W. (2003). Improving dietary behavior in African Americans: the parents as teachers high 5, low fat program. *Preventive Medicine*, *36*(6), 684–691. https://doi.org/10.1016/S0091-7435(03)00053-7.

Haire-Joshu, D., Elliott, M. B., Caito, N. M., Hessler, K., Nanney, M. S., Hale, N., & Brownson, R. C. (2008). High 5 for kids: the impact of a home visiting program on fruit and vegetable intake of parents and their preschool children. *Preventive Medicine*, *47*(1), 77–82. https://doi.org/10.1016/j.ypmed.2008.03.016.

Hakman, M., Chaffin, M., Funderburk, B., & Silovsky, J. F. (2009). Change trajectories for parent-child interaction sequences during parent-child interaction therapy for child physical abuse. *Child Abuse & Neglect*, *33*(7), 461–470. https://doi.org/10.1016/j.chiabu.2008.08.003.

Hall, J., Porter, L., Longhi, D., Becker-Green, J., & Dreyfus, S. (2012). Reducing adverse childhood experiences (ACE) by building community capacity: a summary of Washington family policy council research findings. *Journal of Prevention and Intervention in the Community*, *40*(4), 325–334. https://doi.org/10.1080/10852352.2012.707463.

HealthyPeople.gov. (2014). *Determinants of health | healthy people 2020*. Retrieved April 13, 2018 from: http://www.healthypeople.gov/2020/about/foundation-health-measures/Determinants-of-Health.

History of the Center for the Study of Social Policy. (2018). Retrieved May 9, 2018 from: https://www.cssp.org/about/history.

Holtrop, J. S., Rabin, B. A., & Glasgow, R. E. (2018). Dissemination and implementation science in primary care research and practice: contributions and opportunities. *Journal of the American Board of Family Medicine*, *31*(3), 466–478. https://doi.org/10.3122/jabfm.2018.03.170259.

Home Visiting Evidence of Effectiveness. (2018). Retrieved May 10, 2018 from: https://homvee.acf.hhs.gov.

Jacobs, F., Easterbrooks, M. A., Goldberg, J., Mistry, J., Bumgarner, E., Raskin, M., & Fauth, R. (2016). Improving adolescent parenting: results from a randomized controlled trial of a home visiting program for young families. *American Journal of Public Health, 106*(2), 342–349. https://doi.org/10.2105/AJPH.2015.302919.

Kamerman, S. B., & Kahn, A. J. (1993). Home health visiting in Europe. *The Future of Children, 3*(3), 39–52.

Karoly, L. A., Greenwood, P. W., Everingham, S. S., Houbé, J., Kilburn, M. R., Rydell, C. P., & Chiesa, J. (1998a). *Investing in our children: What we know and don't know about the costs and benefits of early childhood interventions*. Santa Monica, CA: Rand Corporation. Retrieved from: http://www.rand.org/pubs/monograph_reports/MR898.html.

Karoly, L. A., Greenwood, P. W., Everingham, S. S., Houbé, J., Rebecca, M., Rydell, K. C. P., & Chiesa, J. (1998b). *Investing in our children: What we know and don't know about the costs and benefits of early childhood interventions* Santa Monica, CA. Retrieved from:https://www.rand.org/content/dam/rand/pubs/monograph_reports/1998/MR898.pdf.

Kempe, C. H. (1976). Approaches to preventing child abuse: the health visitors concept. *American Journal of Diseases of Children, 130*(9), 941–947. https://doi.org/10.1001/archpedi.1976.02120100031005.

Kennedy, S. C., Kim, J. S., Tripodi, S. J., Brown, S. M., & Gowdy, G. (2016). Does parent-child interaction therapy reduce future physical abuse? A meta-analysis. *Research on Social Work Practice, 26*(2), 147–156. https://doi.org/10.1177/1049731514543024.

Kitzman, H. (1997). Effect of prenatal and infancy home visitation by nurses on pregnancy outcomes, childhood injuries, and repeated childbearing. A randomized controlled trial. *JAMA: The Journal of the American Medical Association, 278*(8), 644–652. https://doi.org/10.1001/jama.278.8.644.

Kitzman, H., Olds, D. L., Sidora, K., Henderson, C. R., Hanks, C., Cole, R., & Glazner, J. (2000). Enduring effects of nurse home visitation on maternal life course: a 3-year follow-up of a randomized trial. *Journal of the American Medical Association, 283*(15), 1983–1989. https://doi.org/10.1001/jama.283.15.1983.

Klein, M. D., Beck, A. F., Henize, A. W., Parrish, D. S., Fink, E. E., & Kahn, R. S. (2013). Doctors and lawyers collaborating to HeLP children: outcomes from a successful partnership between professions. *Journal of Health Care for the Poor and Underserved, 24*(3), 1063–1073. https://doi.org/10.1353/hpu.2013.0147.

Lane, W. G., Dubowitz, H., Feigelman, S., Kim, J., Prescott, L., Meyer, W., & Tracy, J. K. (2007). Screening for parental substance abuse in pediatric primary care. *Ambulatory Pediatrics, 7*(6), 458–462. https://doi.org/10.1016/j.ambp.2007.07.007.

Langford, J., & Ahsan, N. (2005). *Protective factors literature review: early care and education programs and the prevention of child abuse and neglect, social and emotional development in the strengthening families approach*. Retrieved May 10, 2018 from: http://matrixoutcomesmodel.com/EvaluationMenu/Protective_Factors_Literature_Review.pdf.

LeCroy, C. W., & Krysik, J. (2011). Randomized trial of the healthy families Arizona home visiting program. *Children and Youth Services Review, 33*(10), 1761–1766. https://doi.org/10.1016/j.childyouth.2011.04.036.

Lee, E., Mitchell-Herzfeld, S. D., Lowenfels, A. A., Greene, R., Dorabawila, V., & DuMont, K. A. (2009). Reducing low birth weight through home visitation. A randomized controlled trial. *American Journal of Preventive Medicine, 36*(2), 154–160. https://doi.org/10.1016/j.amepre.2008.09.029.

Lenze, S. N., Pautsch, J., & Luby, J. (2011). Parent-child interaction therapy emotion development: a novel treatment for depression in preschool children. *Depression and Anxiety, 28*(2), 153–159. https://doi.org/10.1002/da.20770.

MacMillan, H. L., Wathen, C. N., Barlow, J., Fergusson, D. M., Leventhal, J. M., & Taussig, H. N. (2009). Interventions to prevent child maltreatment and associated impairment. *The Lancet*, *373*(9659), 250–266. https://doi.org/10.1016/S0140-6736(08)61708-0.

Magruder, K. M., Kassam-Adams, N., Thoresen, S., & Olff, M. (2016). Prevention and public health approaches to trauma and traumatic stress: a rationale and a call to action. *European Journal of Psychotraumatology*, *7*, 29715. https://doi.org/10.3402/ejpt.v7.29715.

Matone, M., O'Reilly, A. L. R., Luan, X., Localio, A. R., & Rubin, D. M. (2012). Emergency department visits and hospitalizations for injuries among infants and children following statewide implementation of a home visitation model. *Maternal and Child Health Journal*, *16*(9), 1754–1761. https://doi.org/10.1007/s10995-011-0921-7.

McKelvey, L. M., Selig, J. P., & Whiteside-Mansell, L. (2017). Foundations for screening adverse childhood experiences: exploring patterns of exposure through infancy and toddlerhood. *Child Abuse & Neglect*, *70*(June), 112–121. https://doi.org/10.1016/j.chiabu.2017.06.002.

McLeroy, K. R., Bibeau, D., Steckler, A., & Glanz, K. (1988). An ecological perspective on health promotion programs. *Health Education Quarterly*, *15*, 351–377. https://doi.org/10.1177/109019818801500401.

McLintock, K., Foy, R., House, A., & Alderson, S. L. (2016). A policy of universal screening for depression: caution needed. *BMJ*, *353*(April), 2174. https://doi.org/10.1136/bmj.i2174.

Mejdoubi, J., Van Den Heijkant, S.C.C.M., Van Leerdam, F. J. M., Heymans, M. W., Crijnen, A., & Hirasing, R. A. (2015). The effect of VoorZorg, the dutch nurse-family partnership, on child maltreatment and development: a randomized controlled trial. *PLoS One*, *10*(4), e0120182https://doi.org/10.1371/journal.pone.0120182.

Mejdoubi, J., Van Den Heijkant, S., Struijf, E., Van Leerdam, F., Hirasing, R., & Crijnen, A. (2011). Addressing risk factors for child abuse among high risk pregnant women: design of a randomised controlled trial of the nurse family partnership in Dutch preventive health care. *BMC Public Health*, *11*, 823. https://doi.org/10.1186/1471-2458-11-823.

Mikton, C., & Butchart, A. (2009). Child maltreatment prevention: a systematic review of reviews. *Bulletin of the World Health Organization*, *87*, 353–361. https://doi.org/10.2471/BLT.08.057075.

Miller, T. R. (2015). Projected outcomes of nurse-family partnership home visitation during 1996–2013, USA. *Prevention Science*, *16*(6), 765–777. https://doi.org/10.1007/s11121-015-0572-9.

Minkovitz, C. S., O'Neill, K. M. G., & Duggan, A. K. (2016). Home visiting: a service strategy to reduce poverty and mitigate its consequences. *Academic Pediatrics*, *16*(3), S105–S111. https://doi.org/10.1016/j.acap.2016.01.005.

Morone, J. (2017). An integrative review of social determinants of health assessment and screening tools used in pediatrics. *Journal of Pediatric Nursing*, *37*, 22–28. https://doi.org/10.1016/j.pedn.2017.08.022.

Niec, L. N., Barnett, M. L., Prewett, M. S., & Shanley Chatham, J. R. (2016). Group parent-child interaction therapy: a randomized control trial for the treatment of conduct problems in young children. *Journal of Consulting and Clinical Psychology*, *84*(8), 682–698. https://doi.org/10.1037/a0040218.

Nurse-Family Partnership—Helping First-Time Parents Succeed. (2018). Retrieved May 10, 2018 from: https://nursefamilypartnership.org.

Odgers, C. L., Caspi, A., Russell, M. A., Sampson, R. J., Arseneault, L., & Moffitt, T. E. (2012). Supportive parenting mediates neighborhood socioeconomic disparities in children's antisocial behavior from ages 5 to 12. *Development and Psychopathology*, *24*(3), 705–721. https://doi.org/10.1017/S0954579412000326.

Olds, D., Henderson, C. R., Cole, R., Eckenrode, J., Kitzman, H., Luckey, D., & Powers, J. (1998). Long-term effects of nurse home visitation on children's criminal and antisocial behavior. *JAMA*, *280*(14), 1238–1244.

Olds, D. L. (1992). Home visitation for pregnant women and parents of young children. *American Journal of Diseases of Children*, *146*(6), 704–708.

Olds, D. L. (2006). The nurse-family partnership: an evidence-based preventive intervention. *Infant Mental Health Journal*, *27*(1), 5–25. https://doi.org/10.1002/imhj.20077.

Olds, D. L., Eckenrode, J., Henderson, C. R., Kitzman, H., Powers, J., Cole, R., & Luckey, D. (1997). Long-term effects of home visitation on maternal life course and child abuse and neglect: fifteen-year follow-up of a randomized trial. *Journal of the American Medical Association*, *278*, 637–643. https://doi.org/10.1001/jama.278.8.637.

Olds, D. L., Henderson, C. R., Phelps, C., Kitzman, H., & Hanks, C. (1993). Effect of prenatal and infancy nurse home visitation on government spending. *Medical Care*, *31*(2), 155–174.

Olds, D. L., Henderson, C. R., Tatelbaum, R., & Chamberlin, R. (1986). Improving the delivery of prenatal care and outcomes of pregnancy: a randomized trial of nurse home visitation. *Pediatrics*, *77*(1), 16–28.

Olds, D. L., Henderson, C. R., Tatelbaum, R., & Chamberlin, R. (1988). Improving the life-course development of socially disadvantaged mothers: a randomized trial of nurse home visitation. *American Journal of Public Health*, *78*(11), 1436–1445. https://doi.org/10.2105/AJPH.78.11.1436.

Olds, D. L., Robinson, J., O'Brien, R., Luckey, D. W., Pettitt, L. M., Henderson, C. R., … Talmi, A. (2002). Home visiting by paraprofessionals and by nurses: a randomized, controlled trial. *Pediatrics*, *110*(3), 486–496. https://doi.org/10.1542/peds.110.3.486.

Ownbey, M., Ownbey, J., & Cullen, J. (2011). The effects of a healthy families home visitation program on rapid and teen repeat births. *Child and Adolescent Social Work Journal*, *28*(6), 439–458. https://doi.org/10.1007/s10560-011-0235-z.

Pai, N., Kandasamy, S., Uleryk, E., & Maguire, J. L. (2016). Social risk screening for pediatric inpatients. *Clinical Pediatrics*, *55*(14), 1289–1294. https://doi.org/10.1177/0009922815623498.

Parents as Teachers. (2018). Retrieved from: https://parentsasteachers.org.

Peacock, S., Konrad, S., Watson, E., Nickel, D., & Muhajarine, N. (2013). Effectiveness of home visiting programs on child outcomes: a systematic review. *BMC Public Health*, *13*(1), 17. Published Online https://doi.org/10.1186/1471-2458-13-17.

Prinz, R. J., Sanders, M. R., Shapiro, C. J., Whitaker, D. J., & Lutzker, J. R. (2009). Population-based prevention of child maltreatment: the U.S. triple-P system population trial. *Prevention Science*, *10*(1), 1–12. https://doi.org/10.1007/s11121-009-0123-3.

Prochaska, J. O., & Norcoss, J. C. (2011). Stages of change. *Journal of Clinical Psychology*, *68*(2), 143–154.

Proctor, E., Silmere, H., Raghavan, R., Hovmand, P., Aarons, G., Bunger, A., & Hensley, M. (2011). Outcomes for implementation research: conceptual distinctions, measurement challenges, and research agenda. *Administration and Policy in Mental Health and Mental Health Services Research*, *38*(2), 65–76. https://doi.org/10.1007/s10488-010-0319-7.

Puliafico, A. C., Comer, J. S., & Pincus, D. B. (2012). Adapting parent-child interaction therapy to treat anxiety disorders in young children. *Child and Adolescent Psychiatric Clinics of North America*, https://doi.org/10.1016/j.chc.2012.05.005.

Reynolds, A. J., Mathieson, L. C., & Topitzes, J. W. (2009). Do early childhood interventions prevent child maltreatment? *Child Maltreatment*, *14*(2), 182–206. https://doi.org/10.1177/1077559508326223.

Reynolds, A. J., Temple, J. A., Robertson, D. L., & Mann, E. A. (2001). Long-term effects of an early childhood intervention on educational achievement and juvenile arrest. *JAMA*, *285*(18), 2339. https://doi.org/10.1001/jama.285.18.2339.

Robling, M., Bekkers, M. J., Bell, K., Butler, C. C., Cannings-John, R., Channon, S., & Torgerson, D. (2016). Effectiveness of a nurse-led intensive home-visitation programme for first-time teenage mothers (building blocks): a pragmatic randomised controlled trial. *The Lancet*, *387*(10014), 146–155. https://doi.org/10.1016/S0140-6736(15)00392-X.

Sampson, R. J., Raudenbush, S. W., & Earls, F. (1997). Neighborhoods and violent crime: a multilevel study of collective efficacy. *Science*, *277*(5328), 918–924. https://doi.org/10.1126/science.277.5328.918.

Sanders, M. R. (2012). Development, evaluation, and multinational dissemination of the Triple P-positive parenting program. *Annual Review of Clinical Psychology*, *8*(1), 345–379. https://doi.org/10.1146/annurev-clinpsy-032511-143104.

Sanders, M. R., Kirby, J. N., Tellegen, C. L., & Day, J. J. (2014). The Triple P-positive parenting program: a systematic review and meta-analysis of a multi-level system of parenting support. *Clinical Psychology Review*, https://doi.org/10.1016/j.cpr.2014.04.003.

Sanders, M. R., Turner, K. M. T., & Markie-Dadds, C. (2002). The development and dissemination of the Triple P-positive parenting program: a multilevel, evidence-based system of parenting and family support. *Prevention Science*, https://doi.org/10.1023/A:1019942516231.

Schilling, S., French, B., Berkowitz, S. J., Dougherty, S. L., Scribano, P. V., & Wood, J. N. (2017). Child-adult relationship enhancement in primary care (PriCARE): a randomized trial of a parent training for child behavior problems. *Academic Pediatrics*, *17*(1), 53–60. https://doi.org/10.1016/j.acap.2016.06.009.

Scribano, P. V. (2010). Prevention strategies in child maltreatment. *Current Opinion in Pediatrics*, *22*(5), 616–620. https://doi.org/10.1097/MOP.0b013e32833e1688.

Shanley, J. R., & Niec, L. N. (2010). Coaching parents to change: the impact of in vivo feedback on parents' acquisition of skills. *Journal of Clinical Child and Adolescent Psychology*, *39*(2), 282–287. https://doi.org/10.1080/15374410903532627.

Shonkoff, J. P., Garner, A. S., Siegel, B. S., Dobbins, M. I., Earls, M. F., Garner, A. S., & Wood, D. L. (2012). The lifelong effects of early childhood adversity and toxic stress. *Pediatrics*, *129*(1), e232–e246. https://doi.org/10.1542/peds.2011-2663.

Sinyor, M., Rezmovitz, J., & Zaretsky, A. (2016). Screen all for depression. *BMJ*, *352*(March). https://doi.org/10.1136/bmj.i1617 [Online].

Social Programs That Work Review: Evidence Summary for the Nurse Family Partnership. (2017). *Social programs that work review: Evidence summary for the nurse family partnership*. Retrieved May 7, 2018 from:http://evidencebasedprograms.org/document/nurse-family-partnership-nfp-evidence-summary/.

Stack, D. M., Serbin, L. A., Enns, L. N., Ruttle, P. L., & Barrieau, L. (2010). Parental effects on children's emotional development over time and across generations. *Infants & Young Children*, *23*(1), 52–69. https://doi.org/10.1097/IYC.0b013e3181c97606.

Stamuli, E., Richardson, G., Duffy, S., Robling, M., & Hood, K. (2015). Systematic review of the economic evidence on home visitation programmes for vulnerable pregnant women. *British Medical Bulletin*, *115*(1), 19–44. https://doi.org/10.1093/bmb/ldv032.

Starmer, A. J., Duby, J. C., Slaw, K. M., Edwards, A., & Leslie, L. K. (2010). Pediatrics in the year 2020 and beyond: preparing for plausible futures. *Pediatrics*, *126*(5), 971–981. https://doi.org/10.1542/peds.2010-1903.

Stephanie, L., Steve, A., & Marna, M. (2008). *Evidence-based programs to prevent children from entering and remaining in the child welfare system: Benefits and costs for washington. Vol. 202.* Olympia, Washington. Retrieved from: http://www.wsipp.wa.gov/ReportFile/1020.

Straus, M. A., & Kantor, G. K. (1994). Corporal punishment of adolescents by parents: a risk factor in the epidemiology of depression, suicide, alcohol abuse, child abuse, and wife beating. *Adolescence*, *29*(115), 543–561.

Straus, M. A., Sugarman, D. B., & Giles-Sims, J. (1997). Spanking by parents and subsequent antisocial behavior of children. *Archives of Pediatrics & Adolescent Medicine*, *151*(8), 761–767. https://doi.org/10.1001/archpedi.1997.02170450011002.

Sweet, M. A., & Appelbaum, M. I. (2004). Is home visiting an effective strategy? A meta-analytic review of home visiting programs for families with young children. *Child Development*, *75*(5), 1435–1456. https://doi.org/10.1111/j.1467-8624.2004.00750.x.

Swick, K. J. (2009). Promoting school and life success through early childhood family literacy. *Early Childhood Education Journal*, *36*(5), 403–406. https://doi.org/10.1007/s10643-009-0305-4.

The Duke Endowment. (2018). Retrieved May 9, 2018 from: http://dukeendowment.org/.

Thomas, R., & Zimmer-Gembeck, M. J. (2012). Parent-child interaction therapy: an evidence-based treatment for child maltreatment. *Child Maltreatment*, *17*(3), 253–266. https://doi.org/10.1177/1077559512459555.

Timmer, S. G., Urquiza, A. J., Zebell, N. M., & McGrath, J. M. (2005). Parent-child interaction therapy: application to maltreating parent-child dyads. *Child Abuse & Neglect*, *29*(7), 825–842. https://doi.org/10.1016/j.chiabu.2005.01.003.

Washington State Institute for Public Policy. (2018). Retrieved July 12, 2018 from: http://www.wsipp.wa.gov/BenefitCost?topicId=9.

Weintraub, D., Rodgers, M.a., Botcheva, L., Loeb, A., Knight, R., Ortega, K., & Huffman, L. (2010). Pilot study of medical-legal partnership to address social and legal needs of patients. *Journal of Health Care for the Poor and Underserved*, *21*(2 Suppl), 157–168. https://doi.org/10.1353/hpu.0.0311.

Weiss, B., Dodge, K. A., Bates, J. E., & Pettit, G. S. (1992). Some consequences of early harsh discipline: child aggression and a maladaptive social information processing style. *Child Development*, *63*(6), 1321–1335. https://doi.org/10.1111/j.1467-8624.1992.tb01697.x.

Weitzman, C., & Wegner, L. (2015). Promoting optimal development: screening for behavioral and emotional problems. *Pediatrics*, *135*(2), 384–395. https://doi.org/10.1542/peds.2014-3716.

Wichstrøm, L., Berg-Nielsen, T. S., Angold, A., Egger, H. L., Solheim, E., & Sveen, T. H. (2012). Prevalence of psychiatric disorders in preschoolers. *Journal of Child Psychology and Psychiatry, and Allied Disciplines*, *53*(6), 695–705. https://doi.org/10.1111/j.1469-7610.2011.02514.x.

Wilson, P., Rush, R., Hussey, S., Puckering, C., Sim, F., Allely, C. S., & Gillberg, C. (2012). How evidence-based is an "evidence-based parenting program"? A PRISMA systematic review and meta-analysis of Triple P. *BMC Medicine*, *10*(130), https://doi.org/10.1186/1741-7015-10-130. Published Online.

World Health Organization. (2013). *WHO backgrounder 3: Key concepts*. Retrieved April 13, 2018, from http://www.who.int/social_determinants/final_report/key_concepts_en.pdf?ua=1.

Wuthnow, R. (1991). *Acts of compassion: Caring for others and helping ourselves*. Princeton University Press.

Zigler, E., Pfannenstiel, J. C., & Seitz, V. (2008). The parents as teachers program and school success: a replication and extension. *Journal of Primary Prevention*, *29*(2), 103–120. https://doi.org/10.1007/s10935-008-0132-1.

Zubrick, S. R., Ward, K. A., Silburn, S. R., Lawrence, D., Williams, A. A., Blair, E., & Sanders, M. R. (2005). Prevention of child behavior problems through universal implementation of a group behavioral family intervention. *Prevention Science*, 6(4), 287–304. https://doi.org/10.1007/s11121-005-0013-2.

Further reading

Child Welfare Information Gateway. (2017). *Child maltreatment prevention: Past, present, and future*. Washington, DC: Child Welfare Information Gateway. Retrieved from: https://www.childwelfare.gov/pubPDFs/cm_prevention.pdf.

Maternal and Child Health Bureau | Maternal and Child Health Bureau. (2018). Retrieved May 16, 2018 from: https://mchb.hrsa.gov/.

CHAPTER

13

Neurodevelopmental mechanisms linking ACEs with psychopathology

*Margaret A. Sheridan**, *Katie A. McLaughlin*†

*University of North Carolina, Chapel Hill, NC, United States, †Harvard University, Cambridge, MA, United States

Introduction

Exposure to childhood adversity is common, with more than half of children in the US experiencing at least one form of adversity by the time they reach adulthood (Green et al., 2010; McLaughlin et al., 2012). These experiences are strongly associated with risk for psychopathology and other negative outcomes in childhood, adolescence, and adulthood (Cicchetti & Toth, 1995; Green et al., 2010; McLaughlin et al., 2012). Exposure to childhood adversity increases risk for onset of both internalizing (Edwards, Holden, Felitti, & Anda, 2003) and externalizing psychopathology (Biederman, Petty, Clarke, Lomedico, & Faraone, 2011; De Sanctis, Nomura, Newcorn, & Halperin, 2012), with effects that persist into adulthood (Kessler et al., 2010). In studies that experimentally manipulate adversity exposure via early intervention that removes children from adverse rearing environments, causal evidence for an effect of adversity on psychopathology has been observed (e.g., Humphreys et al., 2015; Muennig, Schweinhart, Montie, & Neidell, 2009; Nelson et al., 2007). Given this robust evidence base, the field is well poised to move beyond questions of whether adversity influences psychopathology to those that focus on the pathways through which this impact occurs. Here we briefly review the history of how the developmental effects of childhood adversity have been conceptualized before presenting a new theory—the dimensional model of adversity and psychopathology (DMAP)—proposed by the authors of this chapter (McLaughlin, Sheridan, & Lambert, 2014; Sheridan & McLaughlin, 2014).

https://doi.org/10.1016/B978-0-12-816065-7.00013-6

Cumulative risk model

Seminal work on childhood adversity focused on linking single types of adversity, such as poverty, abuse, and neglect (e.g., Brooks-Gunn & Duncan, 1997; Cicchetti & Toth, 1995) to health and developmental outcomes. This work was central to demonstrating the importance of these early adverse experiences for shaping psychopathology, but was largely abandoned after evidence for the strong co-occurrence of different adversity types emerged (e.g., Dong et al., 2004). Children are often exposed to multiple forms of maltreatment (e.g., Vachon, Krueger, Rogosch, & Cicchetti, 2015), and many kinds of adverse experiences, such as poverty and abuse co-occurr in the same children (Barnett, Manly, & Cicchetti, 1993). Importantly, this co-occurrence is greatest in nonrepresentative or clinical samples. For example, in the National Comorbidity Survey Replication—Adolescent Supplement (NCS-A; Merikangas, Avenevoli, Costello, Koretz, & Kessler, 2009), a nationally representative survey of adolescents, poverty and physical abuse were correlated at about $r = .20$ (McLaughlin et al., 2012). A more macroview of adversity examines associations between number of early adversities and psychopathology or other developmental outcomes (Edwards et al., 2003; Felitti et al., 1998). The resulting prevailing approach used to examine the consequences of adversity exposure for negative health outcomes is a cumulative risk model (Evans, Li, & Whipple, 2013; Felitti et al., 1998). At the core of this approach is a focus on the amount of exposure to adversity, but not the kind of exposure a child has experienced.

Evidence for this approach has been robust. The cumulative risk model has been useful in highlighting the strong links between adversity exposure and many negative health outcomes and has pushed the field toward reducing exposure to adversity and providing intervention to the most vulnerable. A robust set of studies taking a cumulative risk approach has shown a dose–response relationship between exposure of adversities with negative physical and mental health outcomes, such that increasing exposure is associated with elevated risk both physical and mental health problems (Chapman et al., 2004; Dube, Felitti, Dong, Giles, & Anda, 2003; Edwards et al., 2003; Felitti et al., 1998; Green et al., 2010; Hakulinen et al., 2016; McLaughlin et al., 2010, 2012; Vachon et al., 2015). This equifinality, whereby the multiple forms of adversity are associated with virtually all commonly occurring mental health outcomes in both childhood and adulthood, is well established (e.g., Green et al., 2010; Kessler et al., 2010; McLaughlin et al., 2012).

What we review now is evidence concerning the mechanisms through which this link is forged. The cumulative risk model points clearly to the fact that individuals with multiple forms of exposure are at highest risk for negative health outcomes; however, it also implicitly suggests that all forms of adversity function through the same underlying mechanisms.

This has a less well-developed evidence base. One mechanism that could account for this equifinality has been proposed; specifically, disruption of the physiological stress response system or increases in allostatic load. Evidence for the stress pathway is robust in rodents (Eiland & McEwen, 2010; Francis, Champagne, Liu, & Meaney, 1999; Liu, Diorio, Day, Francis, & Meaney, 2000). In humans, exposure to multiple forms of adversity in childhood is consistently linked with disruptions in stress physiology and related immune dysfunction, particularly when these outcomes are measured in adulthood (Danese et al., 2009; Danese & McEwen, 2012; Seeman, Epel, Gruenewald, Karlamangla, & McEwen, 2010). When these mechanistic links are measured in childhood, disruption of the stress response is often observed, but less consistently and these associations do not closely mimic the work in rodents, even in well-controlled studies where the adversity exposure to rodents and humans is equated (e.g., McLaughlin, Sheridan, Tibu, Fox, Zeanah, & Nelson, 2015).

Most importantly, the single stress pathway is problematic because it ignores numerous other known developmental mechanisms through which early experience shapes brain development, which is experience-dependent and maximally plastic during early life (Fox, Levitt, & Nelson, 2010). Decades of work in human and animal models have established the presence of sensitive periods for sensory modalities (Collignon et al., 2013; de Haan, Johnson, & Halit, 2003; Hensch, 2004, 2005; Wiesel & Hubel, 1965). These periods of increased plasticity function to allow the developing brain to adapt to the environment in which it will grow, resulting in long-term change that shifts fundamental capacity and developmental trajectories lasting into adulthood. Developmental plasticity functions through basic learning mechanisms, where iterative experience, or a lack of experience, shapes the neural substrate, which supports functioning of a particular type. Although stress is one mechanism through which adversity impacts neural development, it is likely not the only mechanism, and we argue that learning processes supporting developmental plasticity should be considered as candidate mechanisms through which adversity comes to impact neural development and, subsequently, a range of negative health outcomes. The introduction of developmental plasticity as a mechanism through which adversity comes to impact health allows for more specific links between types of adversity exposures and developmental outcomes as we describe now.

Dimensional model of adversity and psychopathology

In recent work, we have examined developmental mechanisms related to early learning and specific forms of adversity. This complement to the cumulative risk model—the DMAP (McLaughlin et al., 2014; Sheridan &

McLaughlin, 2014, 2016)—is based on the principle that across the range of adverse childhood experiences (ACEs; e.g., maltreatment, community violence), different types of adversity share common features that can be conceptualized along specific dimensions of environmental experience. Two initial dimensions proposed in our model are threat, which encompasses experiences of interpersonal violence involving harm or threat of harm to the child, and deprivation, which involves an absence of expected caregiver inputs from the environment, resulting in a reduction in cognitive, social, and emotional stimulation. Although other core dimensions of environmental experience likely exist, we chose these two dimensions because they have been well studied in relation to childhood adversity. The history of research into the impact of maltreatment, as an example of threat, on psychopathology is extensive, wide ranging, and robust (e.g., Cicchetti & Toth, 1995; Vachon et al., 2015). A similarly robust literature with an equally long history has examined lack of cognitive stimulation as one pathway through which poverty impacts developmental outcomes (e.g., Bradley & Corwyn, 2002; Brooks-Gunn & Duncan, 1997). In addition, these dimensions reflect a core aspect of environmental experience for a number of commonly studied adversities (e.g., threat encompasses both experiences of violence in the community and violence occurring within the family, such as abuse and domestic violence), allowing us to rely on existing measures of adversity to investigate the dimensional model. A dimensional approach allows investigation of differences between distinct types of environmental experiences (i.e., threat and deprivation) without relying on overly specific comparisons of particular adversity types (e.g., comparing neglect and physical abuse), as was historically done prior to the development of the cumulative risk approach. Finally, ample evidence in both humans and animals already exists, which links threat and deprivation with neurobiology in a way that allows us to propose clear neural mechanisms that are likely to be influenced by these exposures.

In the following sections, we articulate the predictions of the DMAP with regard to the neurodevelopmental mechanisms that are likely to be differentially influenced by experiences of threat and deprivation. These predictions are also outlined in greater detail elsewhere (McLaughlin et al., 2014; McLaughlin & Sheridan, 2016; Sheridan & McLaughlin, 2014, 2016).

Threat

Exposure to threat is conceptualized within DMAP as the presence of a specific type of aversive learning experience that occurs during periods of peak developmental plasticity. Repeated exposure to threat (e.g., interpersonal violence) during childhood, when neural systems that support learning about threat and safety are maximally plastic, will alter these neural systems in ways that facilitate the rapid identification of threat in the environment and mobilize strong emotional and behavioral responses to potential threats. This reflects an adaptive response to living in an environment characterized by danger, but may contribute to the emergence of psychopathology later in development. Consistent with these ideas, existing evidence demonstrates that exposure to threats early in development alters neural circuitry underlying fear learning in animals, including lasting changes in hippocampus and amygdala structure and function. In animal models, early-life exposure to stress has been associated with earlier development of fear learning (Callaghan & Richardson, 2012, 2013). For example, rodent pups who experience maltreatment by dams show avoidance of shock-associated odors earlier in development than standard-reared pups (Moriceau, Shionoya, Jakubs, & Sullivan, 2009). These findings in fear learning are related to changes in amygdala and ventromedial prefrontal cortex (vmPFC) function. The neural circuitry underlying fear learning is well characterized in animals (Johansen, Cain, Ostroff, & LeDoux, 2011; Kim & Jung, 2006). The amygdala underlies the acquisition and expression of conditioned fear (Phillips & LeDoux, 1992). In contrast, fear extinction, the process which allows the decrease of learned fear, relies on the hippocampus and vmPFC, the latter of which directly inhibits the amygdala (Bouton, Westbrook, Corcoran, & Maren, 2006). Thus, early threat exposure is linked with increased dendritic spines in the amygdala, elevated amygdala activity, and deficits in inhibitory pathways regulating the amygdala as well as dendritic atrophy in vmPFC and poor vmPFC-amygdala synaptic transmission (Eiland & McEwen, 2012).

Few studies in humans have examined early threat exposure to fear learning across development, due in part to challenges in developing paradigms that can be ethically used in children (Pine et al., 2001). However, in two studies, we have shown that children and adolescents with a history of trauma exposure demonstrate disrupted fear learning, reflecting difficulty discriminating between threat and safety cues (McLaughlin et al., 2016) and developmentally earlier fear acquisition (Machlin, Miller, Snyder, Mclaughlin, & Sheridan, 2019), findings that are remarkably consistent with the animal literature.

While few studies to date have examined the neural correlates of fear learning in children exposed to adversity, a robust literature has demonstrated that other processes, which rely on the same underlying neural circuitry, are disrupted in children with a history of threat exposure. For example, previous studies have linked violence exposure in childhood with altered patterns of information processing that prioritize threat-related information, including heightened perceptual sensitivity and attentional biases to negative emotional stimuli (Pollak & Sinha, 2002; Pollak & Tolley-Schell, 2003). In addition, multiple studies have demonstrated heightened amygdala reactivity to negative stimuli in children exposed to threat (Heleniak, Jenness, Stoep, McCauley, & McLaughlin, 2016; McCrory et al., 2013, 2011; McLaughlin, Peverill, Gold, Alves, & Sheridan, 2015), along with a wide range of difficulties with emotion regulation (Heleniak et al., 2016; Milojevich, Norwalk, & Sheridan, 2019; Weissman et al., 2019). Childhood threat exposure is associated with reduced volume of and thickness of the vmPFC (Gold et al., 2016; Hanson et al., 2010) and reduced resting-state amygdala-vmPFC connectivity (Burghy et al., 2012).

In sum, there is robust evidence in animal models and in human studies examining discrete adversity types (e.g., abuse, violence exposure) that threat exposure during childhood is associated with heightened emotional reactivity, poor emotion regulation, and disruptions in fear learning. In subsequent studies, we attempted to demonstrate that these effects are relatively isolated from the impact of deprivation, which we argue impacts health outcomes via different neurocognitive pathways.

Deprivation

Deprivation refers to an absence of social and cognitive stimulation and constrained opportunities for learning among children whose interactions with supportive caregivers are limited. Because most types of early learning occur in the context of interactions with caregivers, learning opportunities are constrained among children who experience less frequent and stable caregiving. The absence of consistent interactions with a caregiver deprives children of sensory, motoric, linguistic, and social experiences that caregivers provide as fodder for early learning. This kind of deprivation has frequently been observed among children who experience neglect and institutional rearing (Kaufman Kantor et al., 2004; Smyke et al., 2007). One of the primary drivers of experience dependent plasticity is the developmental process of synaptic pruning. Through pruning, the environment directly impacts neural structure such that the most efficient neural connections are preserved across development and the least efficient pathways are pruned away (Bourgeois, Goldman-Rakic, & Rakic, 1994; Huttenlocher, Levine, & Vevea, 1998). The neural system that emerges is designed to be maximally efficient within the environment in which it developed. If the environment in which a child develops is rich with complex cognitive stimulation from age-appropriate cognitive and social interactions, the emergent neural systems are likely to require many redundant and complex connections between neurons to navigate this environment. In contrast, if the environment is lacking in stimulation, the resulting neural system may be less redundant, the cortex would be thinner, and behavior relying on those redundant inputs would be impaired. The DMAP hypothesis suggests that reduced or low complexity inputs hijack the typical pruning process, resulting in early and extreme synaptic pruning in circuits that are not receiving complex input expected from the environment, and ultimately producing a neural system adapted to a less complex environment. In support of this possibility, animal models demonstrate that global deprivation in rodent models leads to widespread decreases in cortical volume (Bennett, Diamond, Krech, & Rosenzweig, 1964). Similarly, institutional rearing in humans, which is associated with reduced social and cognitive inputs of numerous kinds, is associated with global decreases in gray matter volume (Sheridan, Fox, Zeanah, McLaughlin, & Nelson 3rd., 2012).

We argue that early deprivation in cognitive and social stimulation will have pronounced effects on children's cognitive development, particularly in the domains of language and executive functioning (Sheridan & McLaughlin, 2016). Poor performance on tasks of expressive and receptive language and executive functioning has been consistently observed among children who experience deprivation related to neglect (Allen & Oliver, 1982; Culp et al., 1991; Spratt et al., 2012) and these impacts are over and above the impact of other forms of maltreatment on cognitive function (Hildyard & Wolfe, 2002). Severe forms of deprivation, such as institutional rearing, are also consistently linked with deficits in linguistic and executive function (Albers, Johnson, Hostetter, Iverson, & Miller, 1997; Bos, Fox, Zeanah, & Nelson Iii, 2009; Colvert et al., 2008; Pollak et al., 2010; Tibu et al., 2016; Windsor et al., 2011) as have adversities associated with deprivation such as low family socioeconomic status (SES; Blair, 2002; Farah et al., 2006; Fernald, Marchman, & Weisleder, 2013; Noble, McCandliss, & Farah, 2007; Noble, Norman, & Farah, 2005; Raver, McCoy, & Lowenstein, 2013). Altered function in the neural networks that support language and executive functioning, particularly the lateral prefrontal cortex, has also been observed in children who have experienced deprived early environments, including institutional rearing (Mueller et al., 2010) and low SES (Kishiyama, Boyce, Jimenez, Perry, & Knight, 2009; Raizada, Richards, Meltzoff, & Kuhl, 2008; Sheridan, Sarsour, Jutte, D'Esposito, & Boyce, 2012). Lower SES is additionally associated with thinner cortex and reduced surface area broadly across numerous areas of association cortex (Mackey et al., 2015; Noble et al., 2015; Noble, Houston, Kan, & Sowell, 2012).

This variability in cognitive development related to neglect, institutionalization, and low SES is likely shaped by early learning opportunities and environmental stimulation. The degree of stimulation in the home and the amount and quality of maternal language predicts children's language skills (Farah et al., 2008; Hoff, 2003) and the degree of enrichment and stimulation in the early caregiving environment is associated with cognitive outcomes, including executive functioning and school achievement (Crosnoe et al., 2010; Duncan & National Institute of Child Health and Human Development Early Child Care Research Network, 2003; Sarsour et al., 2011). SES-related differences in both language ability and executive functioning are mediated by language complexity and enrichment in the home environment (Hoff, 2003; Sarsour et al., 2011; Sheridan, Sarsour, et al., 2012). Interventions that increase children's access to learning opportunities and provide more consistent and structured interactions with adults improve cognitive development among children growing up in low-SES families (Campbell, Pungello, Miller-Johnson, Burchinal, & Ramey, 2001; Schweinhart, Berrueta-Clement, Barnett, Epstein, & Weikart, 1985), providing additional support for the role of cognitive and social stimulation in shaping children's cognitive development.

In sum, existing data support the hypothesis that deprivation is linked with thinning in cortex, reductions in surface area, and impairments in complex cognition such as executive function. These patterns are notably distinct from those most commonly observed among children exposed to threat, which primarily involve alterations in emotional processing, regulation, and learning. Together, existing studies are consistent with the notion that distinct types of adversity may have differential influences on aspects of cognitive, emotional, and neural development.

Current evidence for the dimensional model

Reflecting existing evidence related to both threat and deprivation, the DMAP proposes that these two dimensions of adversity exposure have distinct influences on developmental pathways that can be delineated in statistical models. We expect threat to primarily influence the development of emotional reactivity, emotion regulation, and fear learning processes as well as associated neural substrates such as the amygdala and vmPFC. In contrast, we expect deprivation to primarily influence the development of complex cognition, such as language and executive function, and associated neural substrates, such as the frontoparietal network.

Given that threat and deprivation-related adversities often co-occur (Green et al., 2010; McLaughlin et al., 2012), it is essential to examine their unique effects by adjusting for exposure to both forms of adversity simultaneously. The goal is not to identify children who have only experienced one particular form of adversity in isolation, but to demonstrate that despite the co-occurrence of adversity experiences, there is at least some specificity in the mechanisms that link particular forms of adversity with downstream outcomes. Such an approach is critical for isolating whether developmental processes are influenced by adversity globally or are specific to particular adversity dimensions. Thus, the primary prediction of the DMAP is that experiences of threat will have stronger influences on circuits involved in fear learning and emotional processing than experiences of deprivation and will persist after controlling for co-occurring deprivation; in contrast, experiences of deprivation will be more strongly associated with neural circuits underlying complex cognitive abilities than experiences of threat and will persist even controlling for exposures to threat.

Recent work has supported these hypotheses. We have demonstrated that associations of threat with emotional reactivity, emotion regulation, and fear-learning processes are robust to controls for exposure to deprivation and find no associations of deprivation with these outcomes. Specifically, we have demonstrated that exposure to abuse and community violence is associated with elevated emotional reactivity (Weissman et al., 2019), heightened amygdala reactivity to negative emotional stimuli (McLaughlin et al., 2015), and disruptions in emotion regulation (Lambert, King, Monahan, & McLaughlin, 2017), after controlling for poverty. In all of these studies, markers of deprivation were unrelated to emotional reactivity and emotion regulation. We have also found a similar pattern for fear-learning processes. Specifically, children exposed to threat (abuse or domestic violence exposure) exhibited disruptions in fear learning such that they had difficulty discriminating threat and safety cues during learning, even after adjustment for poverty (McLaughlin et al., 2016). As with the prior studies, poverty was unrelated to fear learning. We have further demonstrated that exposure to abuse and community violence is associated with externalizing psychopathology, and that this association is mediated by blunted physiological reactivity (Busso, McLaughlin, & Sheridan, 2016). These associations were robust to controls for poverty and poverty was unrelated to physiological reactivity after adjusting for threat. In more recent studies, we have found that the associations of threat with amygdala reactivity and emotion regulation are robust to controls for more extreme forms of deprivation, such as neglect (Jenness et al., under review; Milojevich et al., 2019). Finally, in early childhood, we have found that exposure to threat (i.e., a composite measure taking into account abuse and domestic violence) was associated with early fear learning after controlling for deprivation (i.e., a composite measure taking into account family SES, neglect, and lack of cognitive enrichment in the home) (Machlin et al., 2019). Thus, in early childhood and adolescence, we consistently observe associations between threat exposure and heightened emotion reactivity, difficulties with emotion regulation, disruptions in fear-learning processes, and the neural correlates of these processes even after controlling for indicators of deprivation. Importantly, in these same studies, we did not observe associations between deprivation and these processes once we controlled for threat exposure (Busso et al., 2016; Lambert, King, Monahan, & McLaughlin, 2016; Machlin et al., 2019; McLaughlin, Peverill, et al., 2015).

We have similarly found specificity in the associations of deprivation with cognitive outcomes and associated neural circuitry. In a community sample of adolescents, we observed that low parental SES was linked with disruptions in executive function (i.e., performance on an inhibitory control task), even after controlling for exposure to abuse and community violence (Lambert et al., 2017). In a replication of this finding in a sample with high levels of exposure to family violence (~38% of the sample reported clinically significant exposure to maltreatment), we observed that low parental SES predicted poor adolescent executive function measured by either performance on a behavioral task or parental report on a questionnaire measure (Sheridan, Peverill, Finn, & McLaughlin, 2017). In this same sample, low SES was associated with differences in recruitment of the frontoparietal network during a working memory task. These associations were robust to controls for exposure to violence (Sheridan et al., 2017). These initial tests of DMAP revealed evidence consistent with our predictions, but relied on low parental SES instead of a direct measure of deprivation exposure.

While low SES in families has been consistently associated with a lack of opportunity for cognitive enrichment (Bradley, Corwyn, McAdoo, & Coll, 2001), SES remains a risk factor for this exposure and not evidence of exposure. In follow-up analyses, we addressed this concern by directly measuring enrichment in the home environment. We demonstrated that directly measured opportunities for cognitive enrichment in the home environment during early childhood mediated the impact of SES on executive function and cortical thickness in the frontoparietal network (Rosen, Sheridan, Sambrook, Meltzoff, & McLaughlin, 2018) and that exposure to complex language in the family environment mediated the association of family SES with prefrontal cortex function (Sheridan, Sarsour, et al., 2012). In a longitudinal study of young children, we have shown that the degree of cognitive stimulation in the home environment mediates the association of SES with multiple forms of executive functions as well as growth in executive function over time (Rosen et al., in press). In more recent work, associations between a composite score reflecting deprivation (i.e., family SES, neglect exposure, and lack of cognitive enrichment) predicted executive function (i.e., performance on an inhibitory control task), after controlling for exposure to threat (i.e., a composite score of abuse and domestic violence exposure) (Machlin et al., 2019). Finally, we demonstrated that a lack of enrichment in the home environment predicted psychopathology in young adulthood via an indirect pathway through linguistic ability measured in early adolescence, and that this association was robust to controls for family violence exposure (Miller et al., 2018). In sum, in recent investigations, we have accumulated robust evidence that associations between deprivation and complex cognitive function, in particular executive function, are robust to controls for exposure to abuse and other forms of community and family violence exposure. Importantly, these associations have been observed in both early childhood and adolescence, longitudinal predictions of cognitive function, and multiple methods of assessing complex cognitive function, including through parent report, functional activation using fMRI, and direct measures of task performance. Finally, we did not observe associations between threat exposure (e.g., abuse, community violence) and cognitive function in models which included both deprivation and threat (Lambert et al., 2016; Machlin et al., 2019; Miller et al., 2018; Sheridan et al., 2017), even when exposure to threat was significant and more severe than exposure to deprivation (i.e., exposure to physical or sexual abuse versus exposure to low family SES).

The evidence we have collected thus far in our direct tests of the DMAP robustly supports the hypotheses in our originally proposed model (McLaughlin et al., 2014; Sheridan & McLaughlin, 2014) and in subsequently published articulations and extensions of this model (McLaughlin & Sheridan, 2016; McLaughlin, Sheridan, & Nelson, 2017; Sheridan & McLaughlin, 2016). Importantly, we, like others (Farah et al., 2008; Humphreys & Zeanah, 2015; Manly, Kim, Rogosch, & Cicchetti, 2001), have observed multifinality with regards to associations between indicators of deprivation and threat and psychopathology (e.g., Busso et al., 2016). However, none of our existing studies suggests that the same multifinality exists for the more proximal developmental measures (e.g., emotional reactivity or executive function), which we hypothesize and observe to be mechanisms through which different forms of adversity influence risk for psychopathology (e.g., Miller et al., 2018). This distinction is central to DMAP, and makes this model substantively congruent with and complementary to existing cumulative risk approaches. While cumulative risk approaches can facilitate identification of *who* is most at risk, the DMAP approach can help identify *why* these associations exist and, thereby, identify potential targets for early interventions.

Directions for future research

While our existing work robustly supports the DMAP, the findings have primarily relied on self-report and have been in small nonrepresentative and cross-sectional samples. Future work should prospectively link direct measures of both threat and deprivation in the home during early childhood with psychopathology in later childhood or adulthood while demonstrating mediation by separate neurocognitive pathways. This would constitute a full test of DMAP. In addition, timing of both exposure and measurement of developmental outcome will almost certainly affect our observed associations between exposure to adversity and developmental outcomes. As an example of this, we observe that, in adolescence, exposure to threat is linked with a lack of differentiation between stimuli which do and do not predict threat (McLaughlin et al., 2016). In contrast, in early childhood, threat exposure predicts developmentally earlier acquisition of fear learning; that is, younger children (ages 4–5 years) who have been exposed to family violence are able to distinguish between stimuli which do and do not predict a fear-eliciting stimulus, whereas same-age children without threat exposure do not (Machlin et al., 2019). This developmental distinction is consistent with theory, as the fear-learning system is developing during early childhood (Britton, Lissek, Grillon, Norcross, & Pine, 2011; Rudy, 1993), and animal models would suggest that exposure to threat would enhance this learning process early in development (e.g., Gunnar, Hostinar, Sanchez, Tottenham, & Sullivan, 2015). However, across time, iterative exposure to threats and the consequences of disrupted fear learning would likely function to blunt distinctions between fear and safety cues (McEwen, 1998, 2007). It is precisely this kind of interaction between development and adversity exposure that longitudinal studies could better characterize and disentangle.

Policy and practice implications

As we have articulated earlier, we theorize and have empirically observed that different forms of adversity exposure give rise to many forms of psychopathology via separable neurobiological pathways. This observation leads to the novel implication that not all forms of psychopathology related to adversity should be treated similarly. In fact, the etiology of a set of symptoms may influence the way in which those symptoms are treated. For example, a child with emotion regulation difficulties following exposure to traumatic violence and a child with executive function deficits following a lack of cognitive stimulation at home both may display what appears to be similar disruptive behavior; yet, interventions for these two hypothetical children could be very different. In the case of threat exposure, the child may benefit from a trauma-focused therapy designed to increase self-regulatory capacity via emotional awareness, whereas, in the case of an executive function deficit, the child may benefit from increased scaffolded learning opportunities at home and in the classroom. Of course, many children will have multiple exposures and require multiple and varied interventions. Even in these complicated cases, we expect that understanding the etiological "source" of behavioral deficits could enhance and refine future interventions.

Conclusion

The DMAP presents an alternate conceptual model of how adversity comes to influence developmental outcomes and addresses a specific limitation in the cumulative risk approach involving a lack of specificity concerning how early adverse experiences influence developmental processes and, in turn, health outcomes. First, our model encompasses a wide range of adverse experiences. Traditionally, the ACEs model specifically focuses on a set of experiences within the family, which, while demonstrably important in development, are limited in scope (Felitti et al., 1998). Such models do not take into account a robust literature which links early deprivation related to a lack of cognitive stimulation or exposure to violence within the community with negative developmental outcomes (e.g., Bradley, Convyn, Burchinal, McAdoo, & Coll, 2001; Margolin & Gordis, 2000). Second, our model provides a way of distilling complex environmental experiences into core underlying dimensions that can be used to examine multiple adversity types that share core features (e.g., physical abuse and community violence), and evaluating the specificity with which these dimensions relate to developmental outcomes. Third, our model outlines neurobiological mechanisms that are specific to particular kinds of experiences that are both testable and falsifiable. Although adverse experiences co-occur, they can and should be measured separately to identify specificity in the cognitive, emotional, and neurobiological processes that they influence. Importantly, although threat and deprivation each impact psychopathology, they appear to do so through distinct cognitive, emotional, and neurobiological pathways.

DMAP builds on existing models of the impact of adversity on child development. The concept of deprivation is derived from the poverty literature identifying reduced cognitive stimulation as one pathway through which poverty influences education. The concept of threat is related to stress exposure postulated in the traditional ACEs model. Our model brings together multiple dimensions of adversity and pathways through which these adversities could be embedded to yield novel testable hypotheses, which recent evidence supports. This approach is an alternate to existing models of the impact of adversity on psychopathology that promises to generate novel and more targeted intervention strategies, which have the potential to enhance opportunities for our most disadvantaged children.

Conflict of interest statement

The authors have no conflicts of interest, which impact this work.

References

Albers, L. H., Johnson, D. E., Hostetter, M. K., Iverson, S., & Miller, L. C. (1997). Health of children adopted from the former Soviet Union and Eastern Europe. Comparison with preadoptive medical records. *JAMA: The Journal of the American Medical Association*, *278*(11), 922–924.

Allen, R. E., & Oliver, J. M. (1982). The effects of child maltreatment on language development. *Child Abuse & Neglect*, *6*(3), 299–305.

Barnett, D., Manly, J. T., & Cicchetti, D. (1993). Defining child maltreatment: The interface between policy and research. In D. Cicchetti & S. L. Toth (Eds.), *vol. 8. Child abuse, child development, and social policy: advances in applied developmental psychology*. New Jersey: Ablex Publishing Corporation.

Bennett, E. L., Diamond, M. C., Krech, D., & Rosenzweig, M. R. (1964). Chemical and anatomical plasticity brain. *Science (New York, NY)*, *146*(3644), 610–619.

Biederman, J., Petty, C. R., Clarke, A., Lomedico, A., & Faraone, S. V. (2011). Predictors of persistent ADHD: an 11-year follow-up study. *Journal of Psychiatric Research*, *45*(2), 150–155. https://doi.org/10.1016/j.jpsychires.2010.06.009.

Blair, C. (2002). School readiness. Integrating cognition and emotion in a neurobiological conceptualization of children's functioning at school entry. *The American Psychologist*, *57*(2), 111–127.

Bos, K. J., Fox, N., Zeanah, C. H., & Nelson Iii, C. A. (2009). Effects of early psychosocial deprivation on the development of memory and executive function. *Frontiers in Behavioral Neuroscience*, *3*, 16. https://doi.org/10.3389/neuro.08.016.2009.

Bourgeois, J. P., Goldman-Rakic, P. S., & Rakic, P. (1994). Synaptogenesis in the prefrontal cortex of rhesus monkeys. *Cerebral Cortex (New York, NY: 1991)*, *4*(1), 78–96.

Bouton, M. E., Westbrook, R. F., Corcoran, K. A., & Maren, S. (2006). Contextual and temporal modulation of extinction: Behavioral and biological mechanisms. *Biological Psychiatry*, *60*(4), 352–360. https://doi.org/10.1016/j.biopsych.2005.12.015.

Bradley, R. H., Convyn, R. F., Burchinal, M., McAdoo, H. P., & Coll, C. G. (2001). The home environments of children in the United States part II: Relations with behavioral development through age thirteen. *Child Development*, *72*(6), 1868–1886.

Bradley, R. H., Corwyn, R. F., McAdoo, H. P., & Coll, C. G. (2001). The home environments of children in the United States part I: Variations by age, ethnicity, and poverty status. *Child Development*, *72*(6), 1844–1867.

Bradley, R. H., & Corwyn, R. F. (2002). Socioeconomic status and child development. *Annual Review of Psychology*, *53*(1), 371–399. https://doi.org/10.1146/annurev.psych.53.100901.135233.

Britton, J. C., Lissek, S., Grillon, C., Norcross, M. A., & Pine, D. S. (2011). Development of anxiety: The role of threat appraisal and fear learning. *Depression and Anxiety*, *28*(1), 5–17. https://doi.org/10.1002/da.20733.

Brooks-Gunn, J., & Duncan, G. J. (1997). The effects of poverty on children. *The Future of Children/Center for the Future of Children, the David and Lucile Packard Foundation*, *7*(2), 55–71.

Burghy, C. A., Stodola, D. E., Ruttle, P. L., Molloy, E. K., Armstrong, J. M., Oler, J. A., ... Birn, R. M. (2012). Developmental pathways to amygdala-prefrontal function and internalizing symptoms in adolescence. *Nature Neuroscience*, *15*(12), 1736–1741. https://doi.org/10.1038/nn.3257.

Busso, D. S., McLaughlin, K. A., & Sheridan, M. A. (2016). Dimensions of adversity, physiological reactivity, and externalizing psychopathology in adolescence: Deprivation and threat. *Psychosomatic Medicine*, *79*(2), 162–171. https://doi.org/10.1097/PSY.0000000000000369.

Callaghan, B. L., & Richardson, R. (2012). The effect of adverse rearing environments on persistent memories in young rats: Removing the brakes on infant fear memories. *Translational Psychiatry*, *2*(7), e138. https://doi.org/10.1038/tp.2012.65.

Callaghan, B. L., & Richardson, R. (2013). Early experiences and the development of emotional learning systems in rats. *Biology of Mood & Anxiety Disorders*, *3*(1), 8. https://doi.org/10.1186/2045-5380-3-8.

Campbell, F. A., Pungello, E. P., Miller-Johnson, S., Burchinal, M., & Ramey, C. T. (2001). The development of cognitive and academic abilities: Growth curves from an early childhood educational experiment. *Developmental Psychology*, *37*(2), 231–242.

Chapman, D. P., Whitfield, C. L., Felitti, V. J., Dube, S. R., Edwards, V. J., & Anda, R. F. (2004). Adverse childhood experiences and the risk of depressive disorders in adulthood. *Journal of Affective Disorders*, *82*(2), 217–225. https://doi.org/10.1016/j.jad.2003.12.013.

Cicchetti, D., & Toth, S. L. (1995). A developmental psychopathology perspective on child abuse and neglect. *Journal of the American Academy of Child & Adolescent Psychiatry*, *34*(5), 541–565. https://doi.org/10.1097/00004583-199505000-00008.

Collignon, O., Dormal, G., Albouy, G., Vandewalle, G., Voss, P., Phillips, C., & Lepore, F. (2013). Impact of blindness onset on the functional organization and the connectivity of the occipital cortex. *Brain*, *136*(9), 2769–2783. https://doi.org/10.1093/brain/awt176.

Colvert, E., Rutter, M., Kreppner, J., Beckett, C., Castle, J., Groothues, C., … Sonuga-Barke, E. J. S. (2008). Do theory of mind and executive function deficits underlie the adverse outcomes associated with profound early deprivation?: Findings from the English and Romanian adoptees study. *Journal of Abnormal Child Psychology*, *36*(7), 1057–1068. https://doi.org/10.1007/s10802-008-9232-x.

Crosnoe, R., Leventhal, T., Wirth, R. J., Pierce, K. M., Pianta, R. C., NICHD Early Child Care Research Network. (2010). Family socioeconomic status and consistent environmental stimulation in early childhood. *Child Development*, *81*(3), 972–987. https://doi.org/10.1111/j.1467-8624.2010.01446.x.

Culp, R. E., Watkins, R. V., Lawrence, H., Letts, D., Kelly, D. J., & Rice, M. L. (1991). Maltreated children's language and speech development: abused, neglected, and abused and neglected. *First Language*, *11*(33), 377–389. https://doi.org/10.1177/014272379101103305.

Danese, A., & McEwen, B. S. (2012). Adverse childhood experiences, allostasis, allostatic load, and age-related disease. *Physiology & Behavior*, *106*(1), 29–39. https://doi.org/10.1016/j.physbeh.2011.08.019.

Danese, A., Moffitt, T. E., Harrington, H., Milne, B. J., Polanczyk, G., Pariante, C. M., … Caspi, A. (2009). Adverse childhood experiences and adult risk factors for age-related disease: Depression, inflammation, and clustering of metabolic risk markers. *Archives of Pediatrics & Adolescent Medicine*, *163*(12), 1135–1143. https://doi.org/10.1001/archpediatrics.2009.214.

de Haan, M., Johnson, M. H., & Halit, H. (2003). Development of face-sensitive event-related potentials during infancy: A review. *International Journal of Psychophysiology: Official Journal of the International Organization of Psychophysiology*, *51*(1), 45–58.

De Sanctis, V. A., Nomura, Y., Newcorn, J. H., & Halperin, J. M. (2012). Childhood maltreatment and conduct disorder: Independent predictors of criminal outcomes in ADHD youth. *Child Abuse & Neglect*, *36*(11–12), 782–789. https://doi.org/10.1016/j.chiabu.2012.08.003.

Dong, M., Anda, R. F., Felitti, V. J., Dube, S. R., Williamson, D. F., Thompson, T. J., … Giles, W. H. (2004). The interrelatedness of multiple forms of childhood abuse, neglect, and household dysfunction. *Child Abuse & Neglect*, *28*(7), 771–784. https://doi.org/10.1016/j.chiabu.2004.01.008.

Dube, S. R., Felitti, V. J., Dong, M., Giles, W. H., & Anda, R. F. (2003). The impact of adverse childhood experiences on health problems: Evidence from four birth cohorts dating back to 1900. *Preventive Medicine*, *37*(3), 268–277.

Duncan, G. J., National Institute of Child Health and Human Development Early Child Care Research Network. (2003). Modeling the impacts of child care quality on children's preschool cognitive development. *Child Development*, *74*(5), 1454–1475.

Edwards, V. J., Holden, G. W., Felitti, V. J., & Anda, R. F. (2003). Relationship between multiple forms of childhood maltreatment and adult mental health in community respondents: Results from the adverse childhood experiences study. *The American Journal of Psychiatry*, *160*(8), 1453–1460.

Eiland, L., & McEwen, B. S. (2010). Early life stress followed by subsequent adult chronic stress potentiates anxiety and blunts hippocampal structural remodeling. *Hippocampus*, https://doi.org/10.1002/hipo.20862.

Eiland, L., & McEwen, B. S. (2012). Early life stress followed by subsequent adult chronic stress potentiates anxiety and blunts hippocampal structural remodeling. *Hippocampus*, *22*(1), 82–91. https://doi.org/10.1002/hipo.20862.

Evans, G. W., Li, D., & Whipple, S. S. (2013). Cumulative risk and child development. *Psychological Bulletin*, *139*(6), 1342–1396. https://doi.org/10.1037/a0031808.

Farah, M. J., Betancourt, L., Shera, D. M., Savage, J. H., Giannetta, J. M., Brodsky, N. L., ... Hurt, H. (2008). Environmental stimulation, parental nurturance and cognitive development in humans. *Developmental Science*, *11*(5), 793–801.

Farah, M. J., Shera, D. M., Savage, J. H., Betancourt, L., Giannetta, J. M., Brodsky, N. L., ... Hurt, H. (2006). Childhood poverty: Specific associations with neurocognitive development. *Brain Research*, *1110*(1), 166–174. https://doi.org/10.1016/j.brainres.2006.06.072.

Felitti, V. J., Anda, R. F., Nordenberg, D., Williamson, D. F., Spitz, A. M., Edwards, V., ... Marks, J. S. (1998). Relationship of childhood abuse and household dysfunction to many of the leading causes of death in adults. *American Journal of Preventive Medicine*, *14*(4), 245–258. https://doi.org/10.1016/S0749-3797(98)00017-8.

Fernald, A., Marchman, V. A., & Weisleder, A. (2013). SES differences in language processing skill and vocabulary are evident at 18 months. *Developmental Science*, *16*(2), 234–248. https://doi.org/10.1111/desc.12019.

Fox, S. E., Levitt, P., & Nelson, C. A. (2010). How the timing and quality of early experiences influence the development of brain architecture. *Child Development*, *81*(1), 28–40. https://doi.org/10.1111/j.1467-8624.2009.01380.x.

Francis, D. D., Champagne, F. A., Liu, D., & Meaney, M. J. (1999). Maternal care, gene expression, and the development of individual differences in stress reactivity. *Annals of the New York Academy of Sciences*, *896*, 66–84.

Gold, A. L., Sheridan, M. A., Peverill, M., Busso, D. S., Lambert, H. K., Alves, S., ... McLaughlin, K. A. (2016). Childhood abuse and reduced cortical thickness in brain regions involved in emotional processing. *Journal of Child Psychology and Psychiatry, and Allied Disciplines*, *57*(10), 1154–1164. https://doi.org/10.1111/jcpp.12630.

Green, J. G., McLaughlin, K. A., Berglund, P. A., Gruber, M. J., Sampson, N. A., Zaslavsky, A. M., & Kessler, R. C. (2010). Childhood adversities and adult psychiatric disorders in the national comorbidity survey replication I: Associations with first onset of DSM-IV disorders. *Archives of General Psychiatry*, *67*(2), 113–123. https://doi.org/10.1001/archgenpsychiatry.2009.186.

Gunnar, M. R., Hostinar, C. E., Sanchez, M. M., Tottenham, N., & Sullivan, R. M. (2015). Parental buffering of fear and stress neurobiology: Reviewing parallels across rodent, monkey, and human models. *Social Neuroscience*, *10*(5), 474–478. https://doi.org/10.1080/17470919.2015.1070198.

Hakulinen, C., Pulkki-Råback, L., Elovainio, M., Kubzansky, L. D., Jokela, M., Hintsanen, M., ... Raitakari, O. T. (2016). Childhood psychosocial cumulative risks and carotid intima-media thickness in adulthood: The cardiovascular risk in young Finns study. *Psychosomatic Medicine*, *78*(2), 171–181. https://doi.org/10.1097/PSY.0000000000000246.

Hanson, J. L., Chung, M. K., Avants, B. B., Shirtcliff, E. A., Gee, J. C., Davidson, R. J., & Pollak, S. D. (2010). Early stress is associated with alterations in the orbitofrontal cortex: A tensor-based morphometry investigation of brain structure and behavioral risk. *The Journal of Neuroscience: The Official Journal of the Society for Neuroscience*, *30*(22), 7466–7472. https://doi.org/10.1523/JNEUROSCI.0859-10.2010.

Heleniak, C., Jenness, J. L., Stoep, A. V., McCauley, E., & McLaughlin, K. A. (2016). Childhood maltreatment exposure and disruptions in emotion regulation: A transdiagnostic pathway to adolescent internalizing and externalizing psychopathology. *Cognitive Therapy and Research*, *40*(3), 394–415. https://doi.org/10.1007/s10608-015-9735-z.

Hensch, T. K. (2004). Critical period regulation. *Annual Review of Neuroscience*, *27*, 549–579. https://doi.org/10.1146/annurev.neuro.27.070203.144327.

Hensch, T. K. (2005). Critical period mechanisms in developing visual cortex. *Current Topics in Developmental Biology*, *69*, 215–237. https://doi.org/10.1016/S0070-2153(05)69008-4.

Hildyard, K. L., & Wolfe, D. A. (2002). Child neglect: Developmental issues and outcomes. *Child Abuse & Neglect*, *26*(6–7), 679–695.

Hoff, E. (2003). The specificity of environmental influence: Socioeconomic status affects early vocabulary development via maternal speech. *Child Development*, *74*(5), 1368–1378.

Humphreys, K. L., Gleason, M. M., Drury, S. S., Miron, D., Nelson, C. A., Fox, N. A., & Zeanah, C. H. (2015). Effects of institutional rearing and foster care on psychopathology at age 12 years in Romania: Follow-up of an open, randomised controlled trial. *The Lancet Psychiatry*, *2*(7), 625–634. https://doi.org/10.1016/S2215-0366(15)00095-4.

Humphreys, K. L., & Zeanah, C. H. (2015). Deviations from the expectable environment in early childhood and emerging psychopathology. *Neuropsychopharmacology*, *40*, 154–170.

Huttenlocher, J., Levine, S., & Vevea, J. (1998). Environmental input and cognitive growth: A study using time-period comparisons. *Child Development*, *69*(4), 1012–1029.

Jenness, J. L., Peverill, M., Miller, A.B., Heleniak, C., Robertson, M.M., Sambrook, K.A., et al. (under review). Alterations in neural circuits underlying emotion regulation following child maltreatment emerge across adolescence: A transdiagnostic mechanism underlying trauma-related psychopathology.

Johansen, J. P., Cain, C. K., Ostroff, L. E., & LeDoux, J. E. (2011). Molecular mechanisms of fear learning and memory. *Cell*, *147*(3), 509–524. https://doi.org/10.1016/j.cell.2011.10.009.

Kaufman Kantor, G., Holt, M. K., Mebert, C. J., Straus, M. A., Drach, K. M., Ricci, L. R., ... Brown, W. (2004). Development and preliminary psychometric properties of the multidimensional neglectful behavior scale – Child report. *Child Maltreatment*, *9*, 409–428.

Kessler, R. C., McLaughlin, K. A., Green, J. G., Gruber, M. J., Sampson, N. A., Zaslavsky, A. M., ... Williams, D. R. (2010). Childhood adversities and adult psychopathology in the WHO World Mental Health Surveys. *The British Journal of Psychiatry: The Journal of Mental Science*, *197*(5), 378–385. https://doi.org/10.1192/bjp.bp.110.080499.

Kim, J. J., & Jung, M. W. (2006). Neural circuits and mechanisms involved in Pavlovian fear conditioning: A critical review. *Neuroscience and Biobehavioral Reviews*, *30*(2), 188–202. https://doi.org/10.1016/j.neubiorev.2005.06.005.

Kishiyama, M. M., Boyce, W. T., Jimenez, A. M., Perry, L. M., & Knight, R. T. (2009). Socioeconomic disparities affect prefrontal function in children. *Journal of Cognitive Neuroscience*, *21*(6), 1106–1115. https://doi.org/10.1162/jocn.2009.21101.

Lambert, H. K., King, K. M., Monahan, K. C., & McLaughlin, K. A. (2016). Differential associations of threat and deprivation with emotion regulation and cognitive control in adolescence. *Development and Psychopathology*, 1–12. https://doi.org/10.1017/S0954579416000584.

Lambert, H. K., King, K. M., Monahan, K. C., & McLaughlin, K. A. (2017). Differential associations of threat and deprivation with emotion regulation and cognitive control in adolescence. *Development and Psychopathology*, *29*, 929–940.

Liu, D., Diorio, J., Day, J. C., Francis, D. D., & Meaney, M. J. (2000). Maternal care, hippocampal synaptogenesis and cognitive development in rats. *Nature Neuroscience*, *3*(8), 799–806. https://doi.org/10.1038/77702.

Machlin, L., Miller, A. B., Snyder, J., Mclaughlin, K. A., & Sheridan, M. A. (2019). Differential associations between deprivation and threat with cognitive control and fear conditioning in early childhood. *Frontiers in Behavioral Neuroscience*, https://doi.org/10.3389/fnbeh.2019.00080.

Mackey, A. P., Finn, A. S., Leonard, J. A., Jacoby-Senghor, D. S., West, M. R., Gabrieli, C. F. O., & Gabrieli, J. D. E. (2015). Neuroanatomical correlates of the income-achievement gap. *Psychological Science*, *26*(6), 925–933. https://doi.org/10.1177/0956797615572233.

Manly, J. T., Kim, J. E., Rogosch, F. A., & Cicchetti, D. (2001). Dimensions of child maltreatment and children's adjustment: Contributions of developmental timing and subtype. *Development and Psychopathology*, *13*, 759–782.

Margolin, G., & Gordis, E. B. (2000). The effects of family and community violence on children. *Annual Review of Psychology*, *51*(1), 445–479. https://doi.org/10.1146/annurev.psych.51.1.445.

McCrory, E. J., De Brito, S. A., Kelly, P. A., Bird, G., Sebastian, C. L., Mechelli, A., ... Viding, E. (2013). Amygdala activation in maltreated children during pre-attentive emotional processing. *The British Journal of Psychiatry: The Journal of Mental Science*, *202*(4), 269–276. https://doi.org/10.1192/bjp.bp.112.116624.

McCrory, E. J., De Brito, S. A., Sebastian, C. L., Mechelli, A., Bird, G., Kelly, P. A., & Viding, E. (2011). Heightened neural reactivity to threat in child victims of family violence. *Current Biology: CB*, *21*(23), R947–R948. https://doi.org/10.1016/j.cub.2011.10.015.

McEwen, B. S. (1998). Stress, adaptation, and disease: Allostasis and allostatic load. *Annals of the New York Academy of Sciences*, *840*(1), 33–44. https://doi.org/10.1111/j.1749-6632.1998.tb09546.x.

McEwen, B. S. (2007). Physiology and neurobiology of stress and adaptation: Central role of the brain. *Physiological Reviews*, *87*(3), 873–904. https://doi.org/10.1152/physrev.00041.2006.

McLaughlin, K. A., Green, J. G., Gruber, M. J., Sampson, N. A., Zaslavsky, A. M., & Kessler, R. C. (2010). Childhood adversities and adult psychiatric disorders in the national comorbidity survey replication II: Associations with persistence of DSM-IV disorders. *Archives of General Psychiatry*, *67*(2), 124–132. https://doi.org/10.1001/archgenpsychiatry.2009.187.

McLaughlin, K. A., Greif Green, J., Gruber, M. J., Sampson, N. A., Zaslavsky, A. M., & Kessler, R. C. (2012). Childhood adversities and first onset of psychiatric disorders in a national sample of US adolescents. *Archives of General Psychiatry*, *69*(11), 1151–1160. https://doi.org/10.1001/archgenpsychiatry.2011.2277.

McLaughlin, K. A., Peverill, M., Gold, A. L., Alves, S., & Sheridan, M. A. (2015). Child maltreatment and neural systems underlying emotion regulation. *Journal of the American Academy of Child & Adolescent Psychiatry*, *54*(9), 753–762. https://doi.org/10.1016/j.jaac.2015.06.010.

McLaughlin, K. A., & Sheridan, M. A. (2016). Beyond cumulative risk a dimensional approach to childhood adversity. *Current Directions in Psychological Science*, *25*(4), 239–245. https://doi.org/10.1177/0963721416655883.

McLaughlin, K. A., Sheridan, M. A., Gold, A. L., Duys, A., Lambert, H. K., Peverill, M., … Pine, D. S. (2016). Maltreatment exposure, brain structure, and fear conditioning in children and adolescents. *Neuropsychopharmacology: Official Publication of the American College of Neuropsychopharmacology*, *41*(8), 1956–1964. https://doi.org/10.1038/npp.2015.365.

McLaughlin, K. A., Sheridan, M. A., & Lambert, H. K. (2014). Childhood adversity and neural development: Deprivation and threat as distinct dimensions of early experience. *Neuroscience and Biobehavioral Reviews*, *47*, 578–591. https://doi.org/10.1016/j.neubiorev.2014.10.012.

McLaughlin, K. A., Sheridan, M. A., & Nelson, C. A. (2017). Neglect as a violation of species-expectant experience: Neurodevelopmental consequences. *Biological Psychiatry*, *82*(7), 462–471. https://doi.org/10.1016/j.biopsych.2017.02.1096.

McLaughlin, K. A., Sheridan, M. A., Tibu, F., Fox, N. A., Zeanah, C. H., & Nelson, C. A. (2015). Causal effects of the early caregiving environment on development of stress response systems in children. *Proceedings of the National Academy of Sciences of the United States of America*, *112*(18), 5637–5642. https://doi.org/10.1073/pnas.1423363112.

Merikangas, K. R., Avenevoli, S., Costello, E. J., Koretz, D., & Kessler, R. C. (2009). The National Comorbidity Survey Adolescent Supplement (NCS-A): I. Background and measures. *Journal of the American Academy of Child and Adolescent Psychiatry*, *48*(4), 367–369. https://doi.org/10.1097/CHI.0b013e31819996f1.

Miller, A. B., Sheridan, M. A., Hanson, J. L., McLaughlin, K. A., Bates, J. E., Lansford, J. E., … Dodge, K. A. (2018). Dimensions of deprivation and threat, psychopathology, and potential mediators: A multi-year longitudinal analysis. *Journal of Abnormal Psychology*, *127*(2), 160–170. https://doi.org/10.1037/abn0000331.

Milojevich, H., Norwalk, K. E., & Sheridan, M. A. (2019). Deprivation and threat, coping, and psychopathology: Concurrent and longitudinal associations. *Development and Psychopathology*, https://doi.org/10.1017/S0954579419000294.

Moriceau, S., Shionoya, K., Jakubs, K., & Sullivan, R. M. (2009). Early life stress disrupts attachment learning: The role of amygdala corticosterone, locus coeruleus CRH and olfactory bulb NE. *The Journal of Neuroscience*, *29*(50), 15745–15755. https://doi.org/10.1523/JNEUROSCI.4106-09.2009.

Mueller, S. C., Maheu, F. S., Dozier, M., Peloso, E., Mandell, D., Leibenluft, E., … Ernst, M. (2010). Early-life stress is associated with impairment in cognitive control in adolescence: an fMRI study. *Neuropsychologia*, *48*(10), 3037–3044. https://doi.org/10.1016/j.neuropsychologia.2010.06.013.

Muennig, P., Schweinhart, L., Montie, J., & Neidell, M. (2009). Effects of a prekindergarten educational intervention on adult health: 37-Year follow-up results of a randomized controlled trial. *American Journal of Public Health*, *99*(8), 1431–1437. https://doi.org/10.2105/AJPH.2008.148353.

Nelson, C. A., Zeanah, C. H., Fox, N. A., Marshall, P. J., Smyke, A. T., & Guthrie, D. (2007). Cognitive recovery in socially deprived young children: the Bucharest Early Intervention Project. *Science (New York, NY)*, *318*(5858), 1937–1940. https://doi.org/10.1126/science.1143921.

Noble, K. G., Houston, S. M., Brito, N. H., Bartsch, H., Kan, E., Kuperman, J. M., … Sowell, E. R. (2015). Family income, parental education and brain structure in children and adolescents. *Nature Neuroscience*, *18*(5), 773–778. https://doi.org/10.1038/nn.3983.

Noble, K. G., Houston, S. M., Kan, E., & Sowell, E. R. (2012). Neural correlates of socioeconomic status in the developing human brain. *Developmental Science*, *15*(4), 516–527. https://doi.org/10.1111/j.1467-7687.2012.01147.x.

Noble, K. G., McCandliss, B. D., & Farah, M. J. (2007). Socioeconomic gradients predict individual differences in neurocognitive abilities. *Developmental Science*, *10*(4), 464–480. https://doi.org/10.1111/j.1467-7687.2007.00600.x.

Noble, K. G., Norman, M. F., & Farah, M. J. (2005). Neurocognitive correlates of socioeconomic status in kindergarten children. *Developmental Science*, *8*(1), 74–87. https://doi.org/10.1111/j.1467-7687.2005.00394.x.

Phillips, R. G., & LeDoux, J. E. (1992). Differential contribution of amygdala and hippocampus to cued and contextual fear conditioning. *Behavioral Neuroscience*, *106*(2), 274–285.

Pine, D. S., Fyer, A., Grun, J., Phelps, E. A., Szeszko, P. R., Koda, V., … Bilder, R. M. (2001). Methods for developmental studies of fear conditioning circuitry. *Biological Psychiatry*, *50*(3), 225–228.

Pollak, S. D., Nelson, C. A., Schlaak, M. F., Roeber, B. J., Wewerka, S. S., Wiik, K. L., … Gunnar, M. R. (2010). Neurodevelopmental effects of early deprivation in postinstitutionalized children. *Child Development*, *81*(1), 224–236. https://doi.org/10.1111/j.1467-8624.2009.01391.x.

Pollak, S. D., & Sinha, P. (2002). Effects of early experience on children's recognition of facial displays of emotion. *Developmental Psychology*, *38*(5), 784–791. https://doi.org/10.1037//0012-1649.38.5.784.

Pollak, S. D., & Tolley-Schell, S. A. (2003). Selective attention to facial emotion in physically abused children. *Journal of Abnormal Psychology*, *112*(3), 323–338.

Raizada, R. D. S., Richards, T. L., Meltzoff, A., & Kuhl, P. K. (2008). Socioeconomic status predicts hemispheric specialisation of the left inferior frontal gyrus in young children. *NeuroImage*, *40*(3), 1392–1401. https://doi.org/10.1016/j.neuroimage.2008.01.021.

Raver, C. C., McCoy, D. C., & Lowenstein, A. L. (2013). Predicting individual differences in low-income children's executive control from early to middle childhood. *Developmental Science*, *16*(3), 394–408. https://doi.org/10.1111/desc.12027.

Rosen, M. L., Hagen, M. P., Miles, Z. E., Sheridan, M. A., Meltzoff, A. N., McLaughlin, K. A. (in press). Cognitive stimulation as a mechanism linking socioeconomic status with executive function: A longitudinal investigation. *Child Development*.

Rosen, M. L., Sheridan, M. A., Sambrook, K. A., Meltzoff, A. N., & McLaughlin, K. A. (2018). Socioeconomic disparities in academic achievement: A multi-modal investigation of neural mechanisms in children and adolescents. *NeuroImage*, *173*, 298–310. https://doi.org/10.1016/j.neuroimage.2018.02.043.

Rudy, J. W. (1993). Contextual conditioning and auditory cue conditioning dissociate during development. *Behavioral Neuroscience*, *107*(5), 887–891.

Sarsour, K., Sheridan, M., Jutte, D., Nuru-Jeter, A., Hinshaw, S., & Boyce, W. T. (2011). Family socioeconomic status and child executive functions: The roles of language, home environment, and single parenthood. *Journal of the International Neuropsychological Society: JINS*, *17*(1), 120–132. https://doi.org/10.1017/S1355617710001335.

Schweinhart, L. J., Berrueta-Clement, J. R., Barnett, W. S., Epstein, A. S., & Weikart, D. P. (1985). Effects of the Perry preschool program on youths through age 19: A summary. *Topics in Early Childhood Special Education*, *5*(2), 26–35. https://doi.org/10.1177/027112148500500204.

Seeman, T., Epel, E., Gruenewald, T., Karlamangla, A., & McEwen, B. S. (2010). Socio-economic differentials in peripheral biology: Cumulative allostatic load. *Annals of the New York Academy of Sciences*, *1186*(1), 223–239. https://doi.org/10.1111/j.1749-6632.2009.05341.x.

Sheridan, M., & McLaughlin, K. (2014). Dimensions of early experience and neural development: deprivation and threat. *Trends in Cognitive Sciences*, *18*(11), 580–585.

Sheridan, M. A., Fox, N. A., Zeanah, C. H., McLaughlin, K. A., & Nelson, C. A., 3rd. (2012). Variation in neural development as a result of exposure to institutionalization early in childhood. *Proceedings of the National Academy of Sciences of the United States of America*, *109*(32), 12927–12932. https://doi.org/10.1073/pnas.1200041109.

Sheridan, M. A., & McLaughlin, K. A. (2016). Neurobiological models of the impact of adversity on education. *Current Opinion in Behavioral Sciences*, *10*, 108–113. https://doi.org/10.1016/j.cobeha.2016.05.013.

Sheridan, M. A., Peverill, M., Finn, A. S., & McLaughlin, K. A. (2017). Dimensions of childhood adversity have distinct associations with neural systems underlying executive functioning. *Development and Psychopathology*, *29*(5), 1777–1794. https://doi.org/10.1017/S0954579417001390.

Sheridan, M. A., Sarsour, K., Jutte, D., D'Esposito, M., & Boyce, W. T. (2012). The impact of social disparity on prefrontal function in childhood. *PloS One*, *7*(4), e35744. https://doi.org/10.1371/journal.pone.0035744.

Smyke, A. T., Koga, S., Johnson, D. E., Fox, N. A., Marshall, P. J., Nelson, C. A., … the BEIP Core Group. (2007). The caregiving context in institution-reared and family-reared infants and toddlers in Romania. *Journal of Child Psychology and Psychiatry*, *48*, 210–218.

Spratt, E. G., Friedenberg, S. L., Swenson, C. C., Larosa, A., De Bellis, M. D., Macias, M. M., … Brady, K. T. (2012). The effects of early neglect on cognitive, language, and behavioral functioning in childhood. *Psychology (Irvine, Calif)*, *3*(2), 175–182. https://doi.org/10.4236/psych.2012.32026.

Tibu, F., Sheridan, M. A., McLaughlin, K. A., Nelson, C. A., Fox, N. A., & Zeanah, C. H. (2016). Disruptions of working memory and inhibition mediate the association between exposure to institutionalization and symptoms of attention deficit hyperactivity disorder. *Psychological Medicine*, *46*(3), 529–541. https://doi.org/10.1017/S0033291715002020.

Vachon, D. D., Krueger, R. F., Rogosch, F. A., & Cicchetti, D. (2015). Assessment of the harmful psychiatric and behavioral effects of different forms of child maltreatment. *JAMA Psychiatry*, *72*(11), 1135. https://doi.org/10.1001/jamapsychiatry.2015.1792.

Weissman, D. G., Bitran, D., Miller, A. B., Schaefer, J. D., Sheridan, M. A., & McLaughlin, K. A. (2019). Difficulties with emotion regulation as a transdiagnostic mechanism linking child maltreatment with the emergence of psychopathology. *Development and Psychopathology*, 1–17. https://doi.org/10.1017/S0954579419000348.

Wiesel, T. N., & Hubel, D. H. (1965). Extent of recovery from the effects of visual deprivation in kittens. *Journal of Neurophysiology*, *28*(6), 1060–1072.

Windsor, J., Benigno, J. P., Wing, C. A., Carroll, P. J., Koga, S. F., Nelson, C. A., … Zeanah, C. H. (2011). Effect of foster care on young children's language learning. *Child Development*, *82*(4), 1040–1046. https://doi.org/10.1111/j.1467-8624.2011.01604.x.

Further reading

Milad, M. R., & Quirk, G. J. (2002). Neurons in medial prefrontal cortex signal memory for fear extinction. *Nature*, *420*(6911), 70–74. https://doi.org/10.1038/nature01138.

Quirk, G. J., Russo, G. K., Barron, J. L., & Lebron, K. (2000). The role of ventromedial prefrontal cortex in the recovery of extinguished fear. *The Journal of Neuroscience: The Official Journal of the Society for Neuroscience*, *20*(16), 6225–6231.

Quirk, G. J., Likhtik, E., Pelletier, J. G., & Paré, D. (2003). Stimulation of medial prefrontal cortex decreases the responsiveness of central amygdala output neurons. *The Journal of Neuroscience: The Official Journal of the Society for Neuroscience*, *23*(25), 8800–8807.

Raineki, C., Moriceau, S., & Sullivan, R. M. (2010). Developing a neurobehavioral animal model of infant attachment to an abusive caregiver. *Biological Psychiatry*, *67*(12), 1137–1145. https://doi.org/10.1016/j.biopsych.2009.12.019.

Roth, T. L., & Sullivan, R. M. (2005). Memory of early maltreatment: Neonatal behavioral and neural correlates of maternal maltreatment within the context of classical conditioning. *Biological Psychiatry*, *57*(8), 823–831. https://doi.org/10.1016/j.biopsych.2005.01.032.

Tibu, F., Sheridan, M. A., McLaughlin, K. A., Nelson, C. A., Fox, N. A., & Zeanah, C. H. (2015). Disruptions of working memory and inhibition mediate the association between exposure to institutionalization and symptoms of attention deficit hyperactivity disorder. *Psychological Medicine*, 1–13. https://doi.org/10.1017/S0033291715002020.

CHAPTER

14

ACEs and resilience: Methodological and conceptual issues

Assaf Oshri[a,b,*], *Erinn K. Duprey*[a,b], *Sihong Liu*[a,b], *Andrea Gonzalez*[a,b]

[a]Department of Human Development and Family Science, The Youth Development Institute, The University of Georgia, Athens, GA, United States, [b]The Offord Center, McMaster University, Hamilton, ON, United States

Introduction

Children who report adverse childhood experiences (ACEs) are often reared in unstable and unsafe environments, enduring chronic toxic stress that can impair development through the life span and across multiple psychological and health domains (Anda et al., 2006; Dube et al., 2001; Felitti et al., 1998). Despite the psychological and physiological threats presented by ACEs, not all people who are exposed to childhood adversity are at an equal risk for maladaptive developmental trajectories (Masten, 2001). Many youth exposed to ACEs exhibit resilience, a multidomain developmental process eventuating in positive adaptation within the context of adversity (Cicchetti, 2010; Luthar, Cicchetti, & Becker, 2000). Resilience is defined as a process in which the individual who experienced ACEs is able to thrive, or

*This work was partially supported by Clinical and Translational Research Unit (CTRU) at UGA awarded to Assaf Oshri (PI). Also supported by the National Center for Advancing Translational Sciences of the National Institutes of Health under Award Number UL1TR002378 and by a K01 grant funded by The National Institute of Drug Abuse (NIDA; 045219-02; PI Oshri). The content is solely the responsibility of the authors and does not necessarily represent the official views of the National Institutes of Health.

https://doi.org/10.1016/B978-0-12-816065-7.00014-8

at least function with relative success, despite being exposed to an adverse environment (Luthar et al., 2000; Masten, 2014). The concept of resilience draws significant interest across the discipline of human development, given the interest in helping individuals who were exposed to ACEs to attain well-being. Throughout the past several decades, developmental scientists have made significant progress in conceptualizing and studying resilience. In the present chapter, we review the current state of knowledge in theory and research on resilience and end with a review of innovative theoretical directions and their implications for preventive intervention.

Resilience in the context of ACEs: A brief historical recount

Resilience research exists in multiple disciplines, including soil and ocean sciences, economics, engineering (Arthur, Schjønning, Moldrup, & de Jonge, 2012; Moritz & Agudo, 2013; Shropshire & Kadlec, 2012), and various subdisciplines within psychology (Chmitorz et al., 2018; Cicchetti, 2010; Masten, 2014). In this chapter, we will refer to resilience research as it has evolved in the field of child development, specifically in research on individual development from birth to young adulthood. Scientific progress in research on resilience in human development is thought to include four stages (Masten, 2014). The first stage of resilience research started in the early years of the previous century, and was characterized by descriptive research, while the second stage of resilience research occurred in the middle of the 20th century and was characterized by a focus on empirical research on the process of resilience. This second stage lent itself to the third phase of resilience research toward the end of the 20th century, in which the focus was on interventions to promote positive youth development. Lastly, the fourth stage of resilience research started toward the beginning of the 21st century and has been characterized by systems research that incorporates multiple levels of analyses (e.g., biological and genetic [Cicchetti, 2010]) in the study of resilience. In the present chapter, we contend that the fifth generation of resilience theory and research, informed by the evolutionary developmental perspective, is on the horizon (Ellis, Bianchi, Griskevicius, & Frankenhuis, 2017; Oshri, Duprey, Kogan, Carlson, & Liu, 2018).

Current methodological and conceptual consensus

Researchers in resilience have reached a consensus on four assumptions about the conceptualization and methodological examination of resilience. First (assumption 1), resilience is defined in the context of significant adversity that can be in the form of acute trauma or exposure to prolonged stress. That is, resilience cannot be inferred in the aftermath of exposure to an acute but normative stressful situation. For example, a middle school child who successfully passes a math exam despite having difficulty in preparing for the test would not be thought of as exhibiting resilience. Although such an exam may involve significant stress for the child, this type of stressor and the associated stress response is expected, temporary, and rather normative. Therefore, an exam does not constitute a real-life threat to the child. On the other hand, a youth who experiences chronic neglect, yet who is able to perform well academically and attain physical and mental health, can be considered to follow a process of resilience. Second, (assumption 2) resilience is a process and not a predetermined construct or trait that one can possess or acquire (Luthar et al., 2000). Thus, an individual cannot "have" or "own" resilience but, instead, can follow or exhibit the process of resilience through functioning well despite exposure to significant adversity. Third, (assumption 3) because resilience is not a static construct, or trait, but instead, a process that unfolds over time, the empirical examination of resilience requires individual development to be tested over the course of time. This requires the use of longitudinal data. Lastly, (assumption 4) testing resilience among individuals who endured ACEs should entail an examination of multiple domains of functioning (e.g., health, vocational, mental health), including the presence and absence of both positive and negative outcomes. Hence, a study which reports that maltreated youth lack internalizing problems is not necessarily documenting the process of resilience, as these youth may have other psychopathology or unobserved physiological vulnerabilities (Brody et al., 2013).

Common models of resilience

In the resilience literature, researchers have utilized several models to empirically test for components of the resilience process. Common empirical models used to examine resilience include those that test either promotive or protective factors, and models that test both. Methodologically, these include direct effect models (i.e., A→B), indirect effect or mediation models (i.e., A→B→C), and moderation models (i.e., A→C, depending on the level of B). Promotive factors are defined as factors that contribute directly to positive adaptation, whereas protective factors are defined as factors that interact with ACEs to reduce their burden and subsequently enhance positive adaptation. These concepts are discussed in more depth in the following sections. Resilience-enhancing factors can also be categorized into assets (i.e., individual traits and processes) and resources (i.e., external characteristics and processes; Zimmerman, 2013). An example of an asset can be seen in the literature on ego resiliency among maltreated youth (Oshri, Rogosch, & Cicchetti, 2013), whereas resources have been studied in research on vulnerable youth who benefit from distal protective factors such as neighborhood cohesion or supportive adults (Oshri et al., 2015; Oshri, Topple, & Carlson, 2017). Thus, skipping the historical use of case studies and descriptive methodologies, we focus on defining empirical models of resilience and provide brief examples from the extant literature to show the empirical implementation and existing challenges with these models. In the present chapter, we focus on variable-centered models of resilience, which entail the modeling of associations between resilience-enhancing factors and positive outcomes. However, recent methodological and conceptual advances have contributed to the increased use of person-centered methodologies in resilience research (Oshri et al., 2017). These modeling techniques enable researchers to investigate patterns of resilience under the assumption of heterogeneity within a given sample; however, a detailed discussion of person-centered methodologies is beyond the scope of the present chapter.

Promotive factors models

Researchers looking to examine conditions that facilitate positive youth development often test for promotive factors, which have also been referred to as compensatory factors in the literature on resilience (Fergusson & Horwood, 2003). Promotive factors empower vulnerable individuals to pursue positive developmental pathways. These factors may also be salient for youth who have not been exposed to ACEs, making these factors important for universal prevention efforts. Methodologically, promotive factors can be studied by utilizing direct effect models, indirect effect models with longitudinal data, or experimental methodologies that show the direct impact of interventions on youths' competence.

Direct, or main effects, models (Fig. 1) can be used to evaluate the effect of promotive factors on positive outcomes, or to assess interventions (adapted from Masten, 2015). For example, self-esteem may be identified as a promotive factor if it has a significant and positive direct association

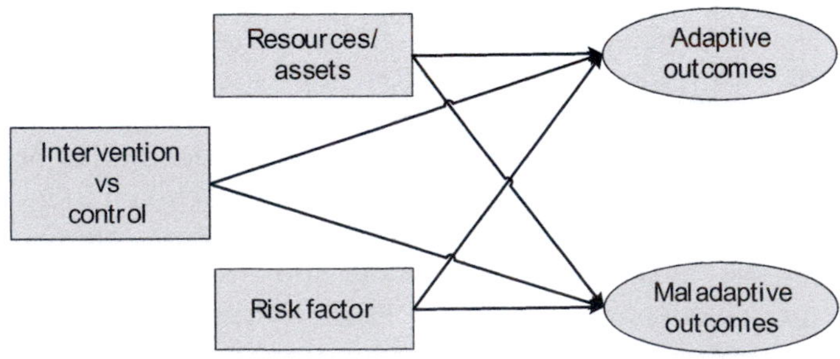

FIG. 1 Direct effects model displaying the impact of resources/assets, intervention, and risk factors on developmental outcomes.

with positive adjustment markers, and a significant and negative direct association with negative adjustment markers.

Main effect models are limited because they are susceptible to confounding variables and spurious effects. For example, self-esteem is an asset that can help reduce substance use behaviors and promote positive adaptation in school among youth who have experienced stress (Byrne & Mazanov, 2001); yet, the association between self-esteem and positive outcomes may be confounded by a third unobserved variable, such as having a close friend, which could be driving the change in adaptation to school. Experimental methodologies (e.g., randomized controlled trials [RCTs]) and longitudinal designs are more empirically sound for testing and deriving inferences about true direct effects. These approaches allow the researcher to avoid confounding effects via the process of randomization, or to parcel out variance associated with confounding variables.

The promotive effect of intervention research is evident in multiple studies. For example, in the Christchurch Health and Development Study, researchers utilized data gathered over 21 years to test the protective and promotive effect of a number of factors on the presence of internalizing and externalizing problems in adolescence and emerging adulthood (Fergusson & Horwood, 2003). Results revealed, unsurprisingly, that ACEs such as socioeconomic distress and family conflict were related to adjustment problems later in life. In addition, several promotive factors (i.e., quality of peer affiliations, self-esteem, and attachment to parental figures) helped to reduce the likelihood of maladaptation following early life adversity. The factors identified were also tested as moderators (i.e., protective factors) in the association from ACEs to adjustment problems and were not significant in this way, suggesting that the promotive factors identified are likely beneficial for all youth, and not just for youth with ACE exposures. Similarly, in a test of a psychotherapy intervention, researchers found that parents and their maltreated infants who were randomly assigned to the intervention group (Cicchetti & Valentino, 2006) were shown to have higher rates of secured attachment, a key developmental factor that promotes positive youth development. This psychotherapy intervention, thus, can be regarded as a promotive factor in youth's positive development.

To test for promotive factors, indirect effect models may also be used in which the promotive factor is modeled as a mediator[1] between a predictor (e.g., intervention) and adjustment-related outcomes (Fig. 2). For example, in a RCT, Schonert-Reichl et al. (2015) reported that a social and

[1]Mediation models are a form of a causal hypothesis, in which the predictor variable A is expected to predict the outcome C, by way of change in variable B. For example, poverty influences parenting behaviors which, in turn, influences youth mental health. In this example, parenting behaviors serve as the mediating variable between poverty and youth outcomes. Mediation models are also commonly known as *indirect effect* models.

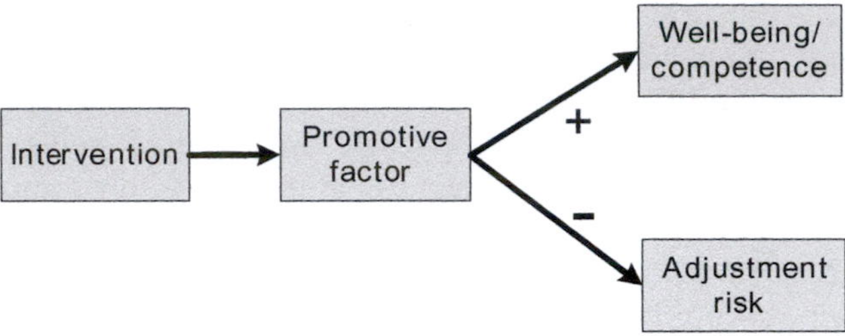

FIG. 2 Indirect effect model of promotive factors.

emotional learning program involving mindfulness was effective in improving elementary school children's cognitive and emotional regulation, mental health status, and prosocial behaviors. Further, Rimm-Kaufman and Hulleman (2015) found that social and emotional learning interventions can improve youth's distal outcomes, such as social and academic performance, through improving proximal assets that include emotional, interpersonal, and cognitive skills. In these two examples, the intervention programs impact youth's proximal and distal positive developmental outcomes indirectly, through improved social and emotional abilities.

Protective factors model

Protective factors are competence-enhancing assets or resources that reduce the harmful impacts of ACEs and subsequently promote positive adaptation (Sameroff, 2006). In the resilience literature, a protective factor is specifically defined as a factor that interacts with a risk factor to moderate the negative effect of that risk factor (see Fig. 3). For example, having a positive adult mentor can help youth cope with the stress of child maltreatment and is negatively associated with risk behavior outcomes (Brown & Shillington, 2017). The effect of protective factors is distinct from promotive factors, because promotive factors have a direct relation to the competency outcomes of interest (Sameroff, 2006). Protective factors are identified empirically by testing for a statistical moderation effect,[2] wherein the outcome of interest is regressed upon an interaction term composed of the risk factor (i.e., ACE exposure) and the protective factor. The identification of protective conditions or traits that enhance youth competence is important for informing prevention efforts for youth exposed to ACEs.

[2] A moderation model is a type of causal hypothesis in which variable A is hypothesized to predict outcome variable C, depending on the level of the moderator B. An example of a moderation hypothesis is that ACEs will predict poor academic outcomes, but only for girls. In this example, gender is posed as a moderator.

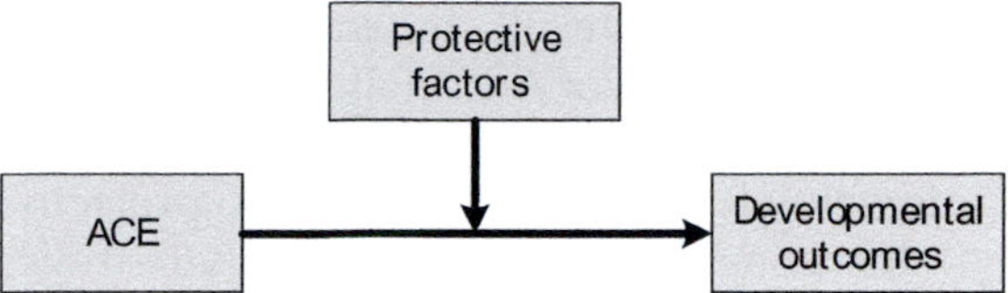

FIG. 3 Effect of protective factors.

Protective factors have been identified at several levels of analysis, including individual-, family-, and community-level traits (Afifi & MacMillan, 2011). Following the emergence of biopsychosocial perspectives in resilience, researchers have also begun to identify biological protective factors for ACEs. For example, El-Sheikh and Whitson (2006) conducted a study examining the longitudinal associations between children's exposure to family conflict and their adjustment, as measured by internalizing and externalizing symptoms. Exposure to marital conflict did indeed predict heightened adjustment problems, although this was moderated by vagal regulation (i.e., a measure of parasympathetic nervous system activity that is related to one's self-regulation under stress). Thus, a youth's ability to physiologically regulate during situations of acute stress may protect them from the harmful impacts of ACEs.

Similarly, to study the effect of child maltreatment on decision making (i.e., delayed reward discounting) and attendant substance use risk among a sample of young adults, Oshri et al. (2018) examined the role of heart rate variability reactivity, a psychophysiological index of self-regulation. The authors reported that increased heart rate variability reactivity buffered the indirect effect of child maltreatment on alcohol use problems through elevated delayed reward discounting. In addition, genetic studies have also found protective effects of certain genotypes against ACEs. For example, Andreou, Comasco, Åslund, Nilsson, and Hodgins (2018) tested the role of the oxytocin receptor gene (OXTR) in the associations between child maltreatment and adolescents' conduct problems and reported that the A allele of OXTR could protect maltreated children from developing conduct problems. These studies suggest that, in addition to behavioral risk and protective factors, neurobiological and genetic protective factors are involved in the process of risk and resilience among youth.

Protective factors are not only aspects of interindividual systems of adaptation (i.e., assets), but can also be components of wider contextual systems (i.e., resources). In addition to individual-level protective factors, Afifi et al. (2016) studied the protective influence of relationship factors in the effect of child abuse on mental health among a large ($N = 23{,}395$) nationally representative sample of Canadians. This study documented a wide range of individual- and relationship-level factors that resulted in enhanced well-being; for example, a higher income and being married were associated with better mental health for individuals who were abused during childhood. The findings of Afifi et al. (2016) identify a broad array of individual and relationship factors that can be useful targets for child maltreatment intervention strategies. In addition, protective factors from even broader contexts have been identified in other studies, including at the community- or neighborhood-level. For example, researchers utilizing a national longitudinal sample of at-risk youth tested the protective role of collective efficacy (i.e., a community's level of informal social control and cohesion) in the association between childhood experiences of maltreatment and level of externalizing behaviors at age 12 years (Yonas et al., 2010). Results showed that collective efficacy moderated the relationship between experiences of child neglect and externalizing behavior problems.

Modeling promotive and protective factors together

Methodological advances in multivariate statistics (Preacher, Rucker, & Hayes, 2007) enable the concurrent modeling of promotive and protective factors. These methodological strategies, such as moderated mediation and mediated moderation (Fig. 4), are often used in a structural equation framework and permit the researcher to simultaneously test a mechanistic model (i.e., mediation) while also testing the condition in which this mechanistic model works (i.e., moderation). For example, in a study by Duprey, Oshri, and Liu (2018), a moderated mediation model was used to examine the promotive effect of self-esteem in the indirect path from child maltreatment to suicide risk. Further, in this study, Duprey et al. (2018) hypothesized that self-regulation (measured physiologically with an index of heart rate variability) would serve as a protective factor in this mechanism. Findings showed that self-esteem indeed served as a promotive factor in reducing the likelihood of young adult suicide risk, and that self-regulation served as a protective factor in the mechanistic pathway from childhood maltreatment to suicide risk through self-esteem. Thus, these findings showed that the promotive impact of self-esteem was dependent on the context of the individual's self-regulation abilities; indeed, youth

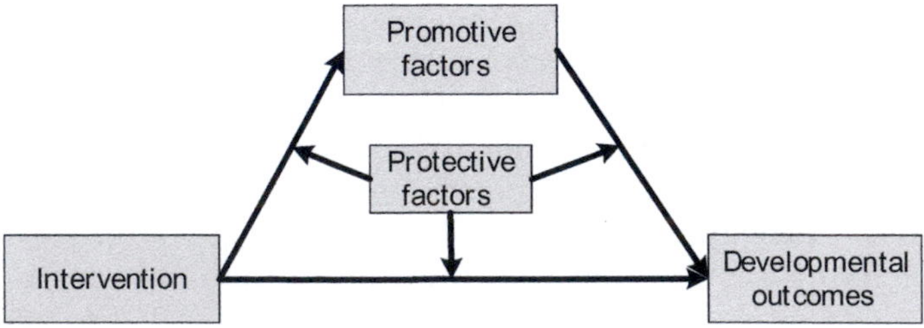

FIG. 4 Moderated mediation models of the effects of protective and promotive factors.

with high self-esteem and better self-regulation were particularly less likely to have any suicidal ideation. In another study by Alink, Cicchetti, Kim, and Rogosch (2009), researchers tested the promotive effects of emotional regulation and the protective effects of mother-child relationship quality on children's development of psychopathology. Findings of the study suggested that emotional regulation mediated the associations between child maltreatment and psychopathology, which was moderated by the mother-child relationship quality. Specifically, youth with better emotional-regulation abilities and good relationship quality with their mothers exhibited lowest levels of psychopathology.

Current state of resilience research

Studying protective and promotive factors can advance basic science of resilience and the development of preventive interventions aiming to promote resilience. However, challenges remain at both the conceptual and methodological levels. In the past several decades, theoretical perspectives (e.g., developmental psychopathology and systems perspectives) and empirical research on resilience have cohered to suggest that resilience is best understood from ecological systems perspectives, in which the dynamic interactions between multiple levels of analyses are examined in relation to positive adaptation (Cicchetti, 2010; Masten, 2001, 2014). For example, developmental psychopathology is a paradigm that has sought to integrate developmental and clinical science to better understand the processes that lead to psychopathology. This is captured by Dante Cicchetti, a leader in the field of developmental psychopathology:

> Understanding the dynamic transactions between risk and protective factors plays a central role in building developmentally informed models of prevention. Through increasing the relative balance of protective processes over risk factors, the potential for righting the developmental course, attaining adaptive developmental pathways, and reducing the emergence of psychopathology may be achieved. ***(Cicchetti, 2010, p. 145)***

Similarly, current perspectives on resilience draw principles from system theories. Developmental systems models are informed by complex systems in the physical sciences; specifically, these developmental models conceptualize the developing child as a complex system that is made of various interconnected and codependent subsystems that influence one another over time (Urban, Osgood, & Mabry, 2011). The developmental systems perspective converges with the developmental psychopathology approach to suggest that resilience is a process that can be better understood through multiple levels of analyses that include molecular and genetic, psychopathological, family, neighborhood, and broader cultural contexts.

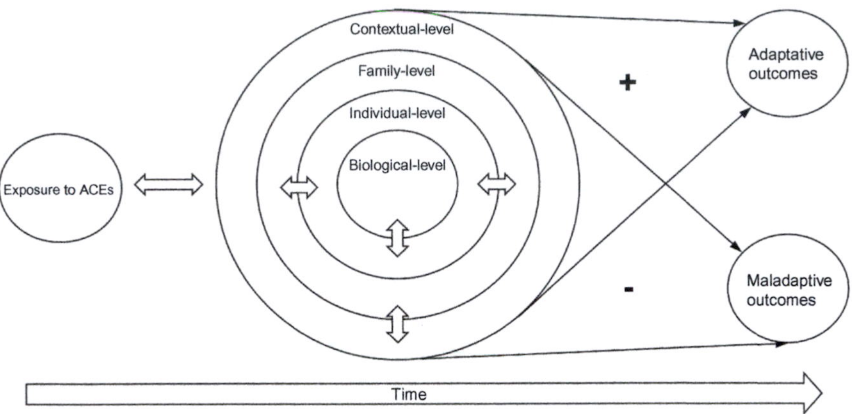

FIG. 5 An ecological systems model of resilience.

The conceptualization of resilience through a systems lens has marked significant progress in moving beyond studies that focus on isolated and static factors of resilience. Placing the individual in a system of risk and protective factors that dynamically influence one another provides an opportunity to examine the process of resilience with greater ecological validity. An ecological systems model of resilience is illustrated in Fig. 5. In this model, exposure to ACEs influences development at the biological, individual, family, and contextual levels. There are reciprocal transactions between ACEs and each of these levels, and also between different levels of analysis. These reciprocal transactions, occurring over time, influence the emergence of resilience (e.g., adaptive outcomes) or risk (e.g., maladaptive outcomes).

The focus on variables from one level of the youth's ecology, as compared to studies of resilience that utilize an ecological systems perspective, is illustrated in studies on resilience and future orientation. Several decades of past research have suggested that future orientation, defined as one's tendency to make plans for the future, is a protective factor for youth who experience ACEs such as and child maltreatment (Cabrera, Auslander, & Polgar, 2009; So, Gaylord-Harden, Voisin, & Scott, 2015). Despite the contribution of this body of work on the role of future orientation in the development of youth resilience, this literature is limited because it views future orientation as an isolated protective factor. In reality, youths' future orientation changes over time, affected by risk and protective factors at multiple levels, including youths' own genetic composition, experiences at home and school, relationships with peers, and broader neighborhood and social environment (Oshri et al., 2018). Here, the ecological systems view assists in delineating the dynamic process of resilience (Cicchetti, 2010; Masten, 2001, 2014; Oshri et al., 2018). To overcome the limitations in the research literature on future orientation, Oshri et al. (2018) utilized a systems approach to examine the development of future orientation as a dynamic protective and promotive factor among maltreated youth. Accordingly, results showed that youths' level of future orientation fluctuated in relation to a constellation of risk and protective factors from other levels of analyses, including family, peers, schools, neighborhood, and social services (Oshri et al., 2018). In this study, the integration of ecological and dynamic system perspectives allowed the authors to model the process of resilience using multiple levels of analysis, while accounting for changes in future orientation and risk and protective factors over time.

Current research in resilience science also includes the development and assessment of prevention programs that enhance positive adaptation following exposure to ACEs. Preventive interventions are key to addressing ACEs by circumventing the transmission of risk across generations and building resilience within vulnerable families. Several parenting programs targeting at-risk families and children have embraced an ecological systems perspective, using it as an overarching framework to guide theory and treatment strategies. The ecological systems approach to prevention recognizes the environment as a system, where features of the environment, as well as the parent and the child, need to be attended to in order to reduce maladaptive outcomes (Dishion & Stormshak, 2007). In the following content, we briefly outline evidence-based preventive programs, which use an ecological perspective to reduce the impact of ACEs and promote resilience.

The Nurse-Family Partnership (NFP) is a primary prevention program of child abuse and neglect risk. The NFP model is a home-visiting program for vulnerable families, often including young, low-income, first-time mothers, beginning in pregnancy and continuing through to when the child is two years of age (Olds et al., 2013). Nurses aim to improve the outcomes of pregnancy, child health and development, and maternal life-course well-being by helping mothers improve their prenatal health and supporting parents' early care of their child. The nurses address social and material conditions in the home that support or undermine mothers' and their children's health, and coordinate their services with other community agencies and office-based staff. Nurses delivering the NFP recognize that diverse factors influence the lives of mothers and their infants. They are trained to identify and address circumstances that affect their clients, including the mother's relations with her partner and other important people in her life, and the impact of the neighborhood where she lives. Armed with awareness of human systems ecology, nurses can help these young mothers navigate challenges at multiple levels of systems (e.g., health, education, and social welfare) that they encounter as new mothers (Olds, 2002; Olds et al., 2013). With over three decades of research, in one or more of three US RCTs, compared to services as usual, the NFP has demonstrated improvements in prenatal health behaviors and birth outcomes, reduction in child mortality rates from preventable causes, as well as improvements in sensitive child care. The NFP has also shown consistent effects in improving child functioning (Donelan-McCall, Eckenrode, & Olds, 2009; Eckenrode et al., 2017; Kitzman et al., 2010). International trials (Denmark and the United Kingdom) have replicated some, but not all, of these findings (Mejdoubi et al., 2013, 2015; Robling et al., 2016). Failure to replicate in the United Kingdom has been attributed to selection criteria of participants, based solely on age (<20 years), and the frequency and intensity of "usual care" (Olds, 2016). In the original US trials, and Denmark, program effects were most pronounced in families with concentrated disadvantage, and for children whose mothers had few psychological resources to cope with adversity (Mejdoubi et al., 2013, 2015; Robling et al., 2016). The United Kingdom is currently collecting follow-up data and may see program effects at later ages.

A second program with an ecological approach to family intervention and treatment to enhance resilience is the EcoFIT model developed by Dishion and colleagues at the Oregon Social Learning Centre (Dishion & Stormshak, 2007). The EcoFIT model is an adaptive, tailored approach to intervening with children and their families. At the heart of the model is the Family Check-Up (FCU), involving three core components: (1) an initial intake interview, (2) an ecological assessment, and (3) a feedback and motivation session, where a menu of intervention options is provided. The FCU comprises an ecologically sensitive, multimethod, multiinformant assessment in which the clinician meets with the family to review strengths and difficulties across multiple domains of contextual risk, family functioning, and child health and development. The assessment incorporates questionnaires, interviews, and videotaped/coded parent-child observational tasks. This enables the parent and clinician to come up with an intervention plan tailored to child and family needs. During the third visit (feedback), parents engage in self-assessment and discussion about motivation and barriers to addressing parenting practices or other factors that may perpetuate risk for their child. The FCU clinician provides structured feedback based on assessment results and engages the parent in a motivational interviewing approach to establish a collaborative menu of available clinical or community-based options. Families may also be offered a suite of sessions from the "Everyday Parenting" (EDP) curriculum, an evidence-based curriculum focusing on parent management training, delivered by FCU therapists, that is tailored to the family and child profile. Several RCTs comparing the FCU to a control group (no intervention) have demonstrated positive effects on child emotional and behavioral problems, parental depression, and positive parenting practices across multiple age groups (preschoolers and school-aged children) and community contexts (Dishion, Forgatch, Chamberlain, & Pelham III, 2016).

The two aforementioned evidence-based programs adopt an ecological perspective framework within their interventions. Although the target population, scope, and implementation of the NFP and FCU are quite different, there are a number of core features common to both programs. First, both recognize that to intervene with vulnerable families and children, one must recognize the system within which they are embedded. Thus, to be truly effective, interventions must address individual, relationship, and contextual systems—multifaceted assessment guides intervention activity. Second, both adopt a strengths-based approach, highlighting resiliency factors within families, and build on these factors to promote continued successes. Addressing areas of challenge involves collaboration between the practitioner and caregiver and assisting clients by linking them to community resources. Finally, motivational interviewing (i.e., a person-centered therapeutic technique; for more information, see Hettema, Steele, & Miller, 2005) is a core component of both interventions, recognizing that motivation and knowledge are active ingredients of effective service delivery.

Future and emerging directions in resilience research: The challenges and promise of evolutionary developmental perspectives

While systems and ecological theories have been informing basic research and clinical practice in the field of resilience, promising new directions in conceptualizing and studying resilience have recently emerged. Specifically, theory (e.g., Ellis et al., 2017) and research (e.g., Oshri et al., 2018) grounded in evolutionary developmental psychology have identified ACEs as a possible source of strength and/or adaptation to one's environment. The following section will review the basic tenets of the evolutionary-developmental approach, including stress-inoculation effects, as it applies to research on ACEs and resilience.

Stress inoculation and the steeling effect

Recent research has concerned the concept of inoculation after exposure to stress; in other words, how are individuals with ACEs able to thrive because of, and not despite, these experiences? Accordingly, the steeling effect (Rutter, 2006) refers to the strengthening effect that stress can have on an organisms' resistance to later stress. The phenomenon of stress-inoculation, or steeling, is evident in biological and psychological research in which animals or individuals are able to surmount past adversity or harsh conditions due, in part, to their earlier experiences of adversity. For example, Parker,

Buckmaster, Schatzberg, and Lyons (2004) tested whether primates' exposure to moderate stress would result in less severe stress reactions later in life, as measured by anxiety level and stress hormone concentrations (i.e., corticotrophin [ACTH] and cortisol). The findings provided preliminary support for the stress-inoculation concept (Parker et al., 2004). Specifically, moderately stressful early experiences strengthened monkeys' socioemotional and neuroendocrine resistance to subsequent stressors in adulthood. Similarly, beneficial behavioral and epigenetic changes were found among young mice that were experimentally exposed to unpredictable maternal separation combined with unpredictable maternal stress for two weeks (Gapp et al., 2014). This experimental manipulation induced a steeling effect in which stress-exposed mice favored goal-directed behaviors, showed behavioral flexibility as adults, and displayed positive epigenetic changes. The steeling effect has also been shown in research on humans; for example, in a longitudinal investigation on the connection between future orientation development and resilience among maltreated youth, Oshri et al. (2018) found a developmental pattern consistent with the steeling effect. Specifically, they found that maltreated youth who held lower expectations for the future when they are children realized unique benefits later on in young adulthood.

Individuals who show a steeling effect are assumed to have adapted to the environment in a way that strengthened them through their development and thereby enabled them to overcome adversity and thrive in later conditions (Rutter, 2006). It is possible that by experiencing ACEs, youth may learn to cope better and adapt to their specific situation. Accordingly, research and theory involving stress inoculation move beyond ecological and systems theories, by considering evolutionary principles such as adaptation and phenotypic[3] plasticity. This trend in studying strengthening effects after adversity has been recently advanced by the call to examine the utility of hormesis in resilience science (Oshri, 2019).

The incorporation of evolutionary theory in resilience science necessitates that, first, several conceptual issues be resolved. According to the classic evolutionary perspective (see commentary by Laland et al., 2014), it is impossible to synthesize theories of individual development with theories of evolution, because evolution is applicable only at the population level, describing changes over generations, and thereby is not pertinent to adaptations during ontology (i.e., the lifespan). This split between ontological development and evolution was debated and was first reconciled by new theories in biological science referred to as evolutionary developmental theories. Subsequently, these principles were carried over to psychological science (Lickliter & Honeycutt, 2003) and by a new school of thought

[3]Phenotypic refers to any observed individual characteristic that is a result from one's genotypic (or genetic code).

referred to as evolutionary developmental psychology (EDP; Lickliter & Honeycutt, 2003). We propose that the integration of developmental and evolutionary principles can be integrated into the conceptualization of the resilience process. We further argue that this synthesis can occur through the implementation of a new paradigm in biology and psychological science named *evo-devo*. Evo-devo principles, which are adopted in EDP, allow for a more precise theorization on the process of resilience by shifting the focus onto a process-oriented framework that integrates development and evolution sciences. In the following section, we delineate several concepts in EDP theory and identify its conceptual potential to advanced understanding of the process of resilience in developmental sciences.

Evolutionary developmental psychology

EDP is a perspective that seeks to resolve the dichotomies between developmental approaches and the classic evolutionary perspective, which assumes that development cannot be explained in evolutionary terms. The dichotomies between these two approaches are apparent in the example of epigenetic research (i.e., studies of heritable and environmentally-induced modifications to ones' underlying DNA sequence, or genotype), in which researchers have discovered environmental influences on gene expression, and which diverges from a strict evolutionary perspective that regards genes as constant determinants of human development (Lickliter & Witherington, 2017). From classic evolutionary biology and psychological perspectives, genes encapsulate information that dictates development, and adaptational changes can occur only over generations of natural selection in response to random mutations. However, recent advances in epigenetics research show that environmental conditions interact with genetic expression during an organism's ontology, explaining adaptational processes within and across generations.

The conceptual advances of EDP are based on assumptions founded in the relational metatheory of development (Overton, 2006). Specifically, Overton's relational metatheory emphasizes that adaptations in human development are a result of a bidirectional process, as opposed to unidirectional or one-way processes (e.g., the genes instruct development). This dynamic account of development refrains from reducing the factors that shape the individual development into separated static entities. Instead, development is perceived as a dialectic integration of nature and nurture (Sameroff, 2010) and is assumed to be an ongoing process that emerges from the bidirectional interactions within and between multiple levels of analysis, from the individual's own genome and biology to the environment, and vice versa (Gottlieb, 2007).

The traditional reductionist view assumes that an organism's development unfolds through predetermined stages that are based on the adult's evolutionary history (referred to as phylogeny). The view that ontogeny recapitulates phylogeny has been contested by evolutionary developmental biology (evo-devo) and psychology. Emerging from theoretical developmental biology, EDP seeks to synthesize developmental and evolutionary components in human adaptations to change (Witherington & Lickliter, 2016). Thus, EDP delineates development in organisms via traditional principles of evolution that were thought to evolve only over generations of species.

Researchers who seek to incorporate evolutionary theory principles to the study of resilience and intervention to promote resilience should consider the inherent contradiction between evolution and development. We will briefly cover two contradicting principles—the modularity and phenotypic plasticity assumptions—that concisely demonstrate the paradox between traditional evolutionary and the new evo-devo perspective. The modularity assumption in evolutionary theory refers to the hypothesis that organisms consist of organic modules that are not malleable during the organism's lifespan, but which can change over generations. Researchers who seek to identify specific brain structures or genetic makeup (e.g., polymorphism in as specific gene) that may "protect" youth exposed to ACEs should avoid this modularity assumption, in which structure is considered to be more important than the environment. For example, one should not assume that a specific genetic polymorphism (e.g., the short allele of the 5HTTPLR-gene) will offer an independent, predetermined, and superior ability to protect individuals who experienced ACEs from developing psychopathology.

In contrast to the modularity assumption, the concept of phenotypic plasticity refers to the phenomenon in which, in response to varying environmental conditions, different phenotypes (i.e., expressed observable characteristics) can be produced from a single genotype (i.e., specific genetic constitution of an organism). This phenomenon has been identified in the field of epigenetics, was coined as the multifinality effect in biological science (Von Bertalanffy, 1968), and was later adopted in psychological sciences (Cicchetti & Rogosch, 1996). The concept of phenotypic plasticity illustrates the need to synchronize principles from evolution and development to explain variation in traits, natural selection, and environmental influences (Honeycutt, 2015; Lickliter & Honeycutt, 2015). Extending this line of thought to the process of resilience, two individuals with an identical genome (e.g., monozygotic twins) who experienced similar severity of ACEs may be affected very differently from these experiences, where one youth exhibits psychopathology and other does not have any socioemotional problems. Accordingly, researchers who seek to elucidate the process of resilience using genetics may benefit from being a priori informed that the resilient individual might go through varying and significant behavioral phenotypic changes.

Summary

In the present chapter, we reviewed empirical progress in resilience science and discussed some methodological issues and advancements. We introduced the utility of, and the conceptual and methodological differences between, promotive and protective factors in the study of resilience. We suggest that attention to the distinction between promotive and protective factors can help advance the field of resilience. Next, we provided a brief review of state-of-the-art preventive interventions that promote resilience, and discussed the utility of these programs in testing principles from ecological and systems theory. We conclude that these interventions are ecologically informed and are beneficial for youth who experience ACEs. Lastly, we presented the evolutionary developmental perspective as a potential new conceptual direction to the study of resilience. While some theoretical and philosophical challenges on the conflict between seemingly dichotomous developmental and evolutionary perspectives need to be addressed, emerging evo-devo principles provide a possible solution. We are hopeful that this chapter elucidates some of the challenges and advantage in studying resilience from an evo-devo perspective, potentially launching the next generation of transdisciplinary research on resilience.

References

Afifi, T. O., & MacMillan, H. L. (2011). Resilience following child maltreatment: a review of protective factors. *The Canadian Journal of Psychiatry*, *56*(5), 266–272.

Afifi, T. O., MacMillan, H. L., Taillieu, T., Turner, S., Cheung, K., Sareen, J., & Boyle, M. H. (2016). Individual-and relationship-level factors related to better mental health outcomes following child abuse: results from a nationally representative canadian sample. *The Canadian Journal of Psychiatry*, *61*(12), 776–788.

Alink, L. R., Cicchetti, D., Kim, J., & Rogosch, F. A. (2009). Mediating and moderating processes in the relation between maltreatment and psychopathology: mother-child relationship quality and emotion regulation. *Journal of Abnormal Child Psychology*, *37*(6), 831–843.

Anda, R. F., Felitti, V. J., Bremner, J. D., Walker, J. D., Whitfield, C., Perry, B. D., … Giles, W. H. (2006). The enduring effects of abuse and related adverse experiences in childhood. *European Archives of Psychiatry and Clinical Neuroscience*, *256*(3), 174–186.

Andreou, D., Comasco, E., Åslund, C., Nilsson, K. W., & Hodgins, S. (2018). Maltreatment, the oxytocin receptor gene, and conduct problems among male and female teenagers. *Frontiers in Human Neuroscience*, *12*, 112.

Arthur, E., Schjønning, P., Moldrup, P., & de Jonge, L. W. (2012). Soil resistance and resilience to mechanical stresses for three differently managed sandy loam soils. *Geoderma*, *173*, 50–60.

Brody, G. H., Yu, T., Chen, E., Miller, G. E., Kogan, S. M., & Beach, S. R. (2013). Is resilience only skin deep? Rural African Americans' socioeconomic status-related risk and competence in preadolescence and psychological adjustment and allostatic load at age 19. *Psychological Science*, *24*(7), 1285–1293.

Brown, S. M., & Shillington, A. M. (2017). Childhood adversity and the risk of substance use and delinquency: the role of protective adult relationships. *Child Abuse & Neglect*, *63*, 211–221.

Byrne, D. G., & Mazanov, J. (2001). Self-esteem, stress and cigarette smoking in adolescents. *Stress and Health: Journal of the International Society for the Investigation of Stress, 17*(2), 105–110.

Cabrera, P., Auslander, W., & Polgar, M. (2009). Future orientation of adolescents in foster care: Relationship to trauma, mental health, and HIV risk behaviors. *Journal of Child & Adolescent Trauma, 2*(4), 271–286.

Chmitorz, A., Kunzler, A., Helmreich, I., Tüscher, O., Kalisch, R., Kubiak, T., … Lieb, K. (2018). Intervention studies to foster resilience—a systematic review and proposal for a resilience framework in future intervention studies. *Clinical Psychology Review, 59*, 78–100.

Cicchetti, D. (2010). Resilience under conditions of extreme stress: a multilevel perspective. *World Psychiatry, 9*(3), 145–154.

Cicchetti, D., & Rogosch, F. A. (1996). Equifinality and multifinality in developmental psychopathology. *Development and Psychopathology, 8*, 597–600.

Cicchetti, D., & Valentino, K. (2006). An ecological-transactional perspective on child maltreatment: failure of the average expectable environment and its influence on child development. In D. Cicchetti & D. J. Cohen (Eds.), (2nd ed.) vol. 3. *Developmental Psychopathology: Risk, disorder, and adaptation*. (pp. 129–201). Hoboken, NJ: John Wiley & Sons Inc. xvi, 944 pp.

Dishion, T., Forgatch, M., Chamberlain, P., Pelham, W. E., III. (2016). The Oregon model of behavior family therapy: from intervention design to promoting large-scale system change. *Behavior Therapy, 47*(6), 812–837.

Dishion, T., & Stormshak, E. A. (2007). *Intervening in children's lives: An ecological, family-centered approach to mental health care*. Washington, DC: American Psychological Association.

Donelan-McCall, N., Eckenrode, J., & Olds, D. L. (2009). Home visiting for the prevention of child maltreatment: lessons learned during the past 20 years. *Pediatric Clinics of North America, 56*(2), 389–403.

Dube, S. R., Anda, R. F., Felitti, V. J., Chapman, D. P., Williamson, D. F., & Giles, W. H. (2001). Childhood abuse, household dysfunction, and the risk of attempted suicide throughout the life span: findings from the Adverse Childhood Experiences Study. *JAMA, 286*(24), 3089–3096.

Duprey, E. B., Oshri, A., & Liu, S. (2018). *Childhood maltreatment, self-esteem, and suicidal ideation in a low-SES emerging adult sample: the moderating role of heart rate variability*. Archives of Suicide Research.

Eckenrode, J., Campa, M. I., Morris, P. A., Henderson, C. R., Jr., Bolger, K. E., Kitzman, H., & Olds, D. L. (2017). The prevention of child maltreatment through the nurse family partnership program: mediating effects in a long-term follow-up study. *Child Maltreatment, 22*(2), 92–99.

Ellis, B. J., Bianchi, J., Griskevicius, V., & Frankenhuis, W. E. (2017). Beyond risk and protective factors: an adaptation-based approach to resilience. *Perspectives on Psychological Science, 12*(4), 561–587.

El-Sheikh, M., & Whitson, S. A. (2006). Longitudinal relations between marital conflict and child adjustment: vagal regulation as a protective factor. *Journal of Family Psychology, 20*(1), 30.

Felitti, V. J., Anda, R. F., Nordenberg, D., Williamson, D. F., Spitz, A. M., Edwards, V., … Marks, J. S. (1998). Relationship of childhood abuse and household dysfunction to many of the leading causes of death in adults: the Adverse Childhood Experiences (ACE) Study. *American Journal of Preventive Medicine, 14*(4), 245–258.

Fergusson, D. M., & Horwood, L. J. (2003). Resilience to childhood adversity: results of a 21-year study. In S. S. Luthar (Ed.), *Resilience and vulnerability: Adaptation in the context of childhood adversities* (pp. 130–155). Cambridge: Cambridge University Press.

Gapp, K., Soldado-Magraner, S., Alvarez-Sánchez, M., Bohacek, J., Vernaz, G., Shu, H., … Mansuy, I. M. (2014). Early life stress in fathers improves behavioural flexibility in their offspring. *Nature Communications, 5*, 5466.

Gottlieb, G. (2007). Probabilistic epigenesis. *Developmental Science*, *10*(1), 1–11.

Hettema, J., Steele, J., & Miller, W. R. (2005). Motivational interviewing. *Annual Review of Clinical Psychology*, *1*, 91–111.

Honeycutt, R. L. (2015). A mouse eye's view of the evolutionary process. In M. Macholan, S. J. E. Baird, P. Munclinger, & J. Pialek (Eds.), *Evolution of the house mouse* (526 pp.). New York: Cambridge University Press. 2012. ISBN: 978-0-521-76066-9. *Journal of Mammalian Evolution*, (1), 125. https://doi.org/10.1007/s10914-014-9260-y.

Kitzman, H. J., Olds, D. L., Cole, R. E., Hanks, C. A., Anson, E. A., Arcoleo, K. J., … Holmberg, J. R. (2010). Enduring effects of prenatal and infancy home visiting by nurses on children: follow-up of a randomized trial among children at age 12 years. *Archives of Pediatrics & Adolescent Medicine*, *164*(5), 412–418.

Laland, K., Uller, T., Feldman, M., Sterelny, K., Müller, G. B., Moczek, A., … Hoekstra, H. E. (2014). Does evolutionary theory need a rethink? *Nature News*, *514*(7521), 161.

Lickliter, R., & Honeycutt, H. (2003). Developmental dynamics: toward a biologically plausible evolutionary psychology. *Psychological Bulletin*, *129*(6), 819.

Lickliter, R., & Honeycutt, H. (2015). Biology, development, and human systems. xxvii, 883 pp. In W. F., Overton, P. C. M., Molenaar, & R. M., Lerner (Eds.), Vol. 1. (7th ed.) *Handbook of child psychology and developmental science: Theory and method*. (pp. 162–207). Hoboken, NJ, US: John Wiley & Sons Inc.

Lickliter, R., & Witherington, D. C. (2017). Towards a truly developmental epigenetics. *Human Development*, *60*(2–3), 124–138.

Luthar, S. S., Cicchetti, D., & Becker, B. (2000). The construct of resilience: a critical evaluation and guidelines for future work. *Child Development*, *71*(3), 543–562.

Masten, A. S. (2001). Ordinary magic: resilience processes in development. *American Psychologist*, *56*(3), 227.

Masten, A. S. (2014). Global perspectives on resilience in children and youth. *Child Development*, *85*(1), 6–20.

Masten, A. S. (2015). *Ordinary magic: Resilience in development*. Guilford Publications.

Mejdoubi, J., van den Heijkant, S. C., van Leerdam, F. J., Heymans, M. W., Crijnen, A., & Hirasing, R. A. (2015). The effect of VoorZorg, the Dutch nurse-family partnership, on child maltreatment and development: a randomized controlled trial. *PLoS One*, *10*(4), e0120182.

Mejdoubi, J., van den Heijkant, S. C., van Leerdam, F. J., Heymans, M. W., Hirasing, R. A., & Crijnen, A. A. (2013). Effect of nurse home visits vs. usual care on reducing intimate partner violence in young high-risk pregnant women: a randomized controlled trial. *PLoS One*, *8*(10), e78185.

Moritz, C., & Agudo, R. (2013). The future of species under climate change: resilience or decline? *Science*, *341*(6145), 504–508.

Olds, D. L. (2002). Prenatal and infancy home visiting by nurses: from randomized trials to community replication. *Prevention Science*, *3*(3), 153–172.

Olds, D. (2016). Building evidence to improve maternal and child health. *The Lancet*, *387*(10014), 105–107.

Olds, D. L., Donelan-McCall, N., O'Brien, R., MacMillan, H., Jack, S., Jenkins, T., … Thorland, B. (2013). Improving the nurse–family partnership in community practice. *Pediatrics*, *132*(Supplement 2), S110–S117.

Oshri, A. (2019, June 27). Resilience in developmental science: A case for hormesis. https://doi.org/10.31234/osf.io/dwsjg.

Oshri, A., Duprey, E. B., Kogan, S. M., Carlson, M. W., & Liu, S. (2018). Growth patterns of future orientation among maltreated youth: a prospective examination of the emergence of resilience. *Developmental Psychology*, *54*(8), 1456.

Oshri, A., Lucier-Greer, M., O'neal, C. W., Arnold, A. L., Mancini, J. A., & Ford, J. L. (2015). Adverse childhood experiences, family functioning, and resilience in military families: a pattern-based approach. *Family Relations*, *64*(1), 44–63.

Oshri, A., Rogosch, F. A., & Cicchetti, D. (2013). Child maltreatment and mediating influences of childhood personality types on the development of adolescent psychopathology. *Journal of Clinical Child & Adolescent Psychology*, *42*(3), 287–301.

Oshri, A., Topple, T. A., & Carlson, M. W. (2017). Positive youth development and resilience: growth patterns of social skills among youth investigated for maltreatment. *Child Development*, *88*(4), 1087–1099.

Overton, W. F. (2006). Developmental psychology: philosophy, concepts, methodology. In *Handbook of child psychology*. Hoboken, NJ: John Wiley & Sons.

Parker, K. J., Buckmaster, C. L., Schatzberg, A. F., & Lyons, D. M. (2004). Prospective investigation of stress inoculation in young monkeys. *Archives of General Psychiatry*, *61*(9), 933–941.

Preacher, K. J., Rucker, D. D., & Hayes, A. F. (2007). Addressing moderated mediation hypotheses: theory, methods, and prescriptions. *Multivariate Behavioral Research*, *42*(1), 185–227.

Rimm-Kaufman, S. E., & Hulleman, C. S. (2015). *Social and emotional learning in elementary school settings: identifying mechanisms that matter*. In *The handbook of social and emotional learning*. New York, NY: The Guilford Press (pp. 151–166). xxii, 634 pp.

Robling, M., Bekkers, M.-J., Bell, K., Butler, C. C., Cannings-John, R., Channon, S., … Kemp, A. (2016). Effectiveness of a nurse-led intensive home-visitation programme for first-time teenage mothers (building blocks): a pragmatic randomised controlled trial. *The Lancet*, *387*(10014), 146–155.

Rutter, M. (2006). Implications of resilience concepts for scientific understanding. *Annals of the New York Academy of Sciences*, *1094*(1), 1–12.

Sameroff, A. (2006). *Identifying risk and protective factors for healthy child development*. (x, 389 pp). New York, NY: Cambridge University Press.

Sameroff, A. (2010). A unified theory of development: A dialectic integration of nature and nurture. *Child Development*, *81*(1), 6–22.

Schonert-Reichl, K. A., Oberle, E., Lawlor, M. S., Abbott, D., Thomson, K., Oberlander, T. F., & Diamond, A. (2015). Enhancing cognitive and social-emotional development through a simple-to-administer mindfulness-based school program for elementary school children: a randomized controlled trial. *Developmental Psychology*, *51*(1), 52.

Shropshire, J., & Kadlec, C. (2012). Where are you going? A comparative analysis of job and career change intentions among USA it workers. *Journal of Internet Banking and Commerce*, *17*(2), 1.

So, S., Gaylord-Harden, N. K., Voisin, D. R., & Scott, D. (2015). Future orientation as a protective factor for African American adolescents exposed to community violence. *Youth & Society*. 0044118X15605108.

Urban, J. B., Osgood, N. D., & Mabry, P. L. (2011). Developmental systems science: exploring the application of systems science methods to developmental science questions. *Research in Human Development*, *8*(1), 1–25.

Von Bertalanffy, L. (1968). General system theory. *New York*, *41973*, 40.

Witherington, D. C., & Lickliter, R. (2016). Integrating development and evolution in psychological science: evolutionary developmental psychology, developmental systems, and explanatory pluralism. *Human Development*, *59*(4), 200–234.

Yonas, M. A., Lewis, T., Hussey, J. M., Thompson, R., Newton, R., English, D., & Dubowitz, H. (2010). Perceptions of neighborhood collective efficacy moderate the impact of maltreatment on aggression. *Child Maltreatment*, *15*(1), 37–47.

Zimmerman, M. A. (2013). *Resiliency theory: A strengths-based approach to research and practice for adolescent health*. Los Angeles, CA: Sage Publications.

CHAPTER

15

ACEs and trauma-informed care

Caroline C. Piotrowski[a,b]

[a]Department of Community Health Sciences, University of Manitoba, Winnipeg, MB, Canada, [b]Children's Hospital Research Institute of Manitoba, Winnipeg, MB, Canada

Introduction

The long-term impact of adverse childhood experiences (ACEs) is well documented; indeed, research has converged in demonstrating that early negative experiences can have significant mental, physical, social, and emotional consequences throughout life (Hughes et al., 2017). The high prevalence of these experiences (Merrick, Ford, Ports, & Guinn, 2018), coupled with our ever-expanding knowledge of their potentially traumatic impact, creates a mounting responsibility for practitioners, researchers, and decision makers to act in a manner that takes trauma into account. While it is important to acknowledge that not everyone who has suffered a childhood adversity will feel traumatized, it is becoming increasingly apparent that not taking ACEs into account may inadvertently contribute to further potential harm. The purpose of this chapter is to provide an overview of trauma-informed approaches for professions and institutions, rather than trauma-specific clinical treatment. The following sections define trauma-informed care (TIC), describe its benefits and outcomes, and point out the unintended outcomes of its absence. Recommendations as well as directions for future research, policy, and practice are also identified.

Adverse Childhood Experiences
https://doi.org/10.1016/B978-0-12-816065-7.00015-X

Origins and definitions: What happened to you?

The term *trauma-informed care* has come to represent a major paradigm shift in the conceptualization, delivery, and evaluation of individual-, team-, and systems-level care and services. It is now implemented by diverse professionals across a wide variety of settings, including healthcare, education, justice systems, mental health, child welfare, crisis and homeless shelters, first-response systems (e.g., police officers, paramedics), and others (Ko et al., 2008). Implications for research protocols (SAMHSA, 2015a) and for policy are also gaining attention (Bowen & Murshid, 2016; Larkin, Felitti, & Anda, 2014). This shift is based on an ever-increasing awareness of the significant impact of trauma, which has historically stemmed from many sources. It initially emerged in shelters for abused women in the 1970s, child advocacy centers, and multidisciplinary teams addressing child abuse in the 1980s, and the treatment of combat-related posttraumatic stress with veterans after the Vietnam war (Sciolla, 2017; van der Kolk, 2014; Wilson, Pence, & Conradi, 2013).

The expanding implementation of trauma-informed perspectives has been supported by the surge of traumatic stress-related research over the past 20 years, particularly in the fields of developmental neuroscience, clinical psychology, psychiatry, genetics, and immune response (Huber-Lang, Lambris, & Ward, 2018; Lupien, McEwen, Gunnar, & Heim, 2009; McCrory, De Brito, & Viding, 2010; van der Kolk, 2014). This body of work has helped to identify the ways in which trauma survivors think, feel, and behave (Levine, 2010; Perry, 2009), and has helped to pinpoint how trauma impacts physical and mental health. Even prior to the current widespread awareness of trauma, many service providers and health professionals intuitively identified gaps in how they were interacting with trauma survivors and responded to a need for an approach that prevented or minimized retraumatization (van der Kolk, 2014).

What exactly is TIC? Definitions have evolved over time; but, it is just as important to clarify what TIC is not. TIC is a broad systemic approach that can be incorporated in a myriad of professional practices and applied in a diverse variety of contexts. It is not a form of trauma-specific clinical treatment such as trauma-focused cognitive behavioral therapy (Cohen, Deblinger, Mannarino, & Steer, 2004). One of the best-known definitions of TIC was proposed by the Substance Abuse and Mental Health Services Administration (SAMHSA):

> It includes an understanding of trauma and an awareness of the impact it can have across settings, services, and populations. It involves viewing trauma through an ecological and cultural lens and recognizing that context plays a significant role in how individuals perceive and process traumatic events, whether acute or chronic. TIC

> involves vigilance in anticipating and avoiding institutional processes and individual practices that are likely to re-traumatize individuals who already have histories of trauma, and it upholds the importance of consumer participation in the development, delivery, and evaluation of services. ***(SAMHSA, 2014, pp. 7–8)***

The National Child Traumatic Stress Network defines a trauma-informed child and family services system as:

> One in which all parties involved recognize and respond to the impact of traumatic stress on those who have contact with the system including children, caregivers and service providers. Programs and agencies within such a system infuse and sustain trauma awareness, knowledge, and skills into their organizational cultures, practices, and policies. They act in collaboration with all those who are involved with the child, using the best available science, to maximize physical and psychological safety, facilitate the recovery of the child and family, and support their ability to thrive. ***(The National Child Traumatic Stress Network, 2018, p. 1)***

It has also been described as "a strengths-based framework that is grounded in an understanding of and responsiveness to the impact of trauma, that emphasized physical, psychological and emotional safety for both providers and survivors, and that creates opportunities for survivors to rebuild a sense of control and empowerment" (Hopper, Bassuk, & Oliver, 2010, p. 82). The essence of TIC involves adopting and expressing an attitude of *What happened to you?* rather than *What is wrong with you?* not only in interpersonal interactions, but also systemically throughout institutions.

Although there are overlaps, there are also important differences between TIC and both person-centered care and family-centered care. Patient- or person-centered care focuses on healthcare providers listening to patients and their families and respectfully engaging them as a member of the healthcare team as much as possible when making care decisions (Canadian Interprofessional Health Collaborative, 2009; Constand, MacDermid, Dal Bello-Haas, & Law, 2014). Family-centered care has been defined as respectful of and responsive to individual families' needs and values (Davidson et al., 2017), and acknowledged as having core principles of information sharing, respect and honoring differences, partnership and collaboration, negotiation, and care in the context of family and community (Kuo et al., 2012). The main difference between these approaches and TIC lies in the explicit recognition of and deliberate effort to understand the impact of past traumatic events, such as ACEs. Therefore, TIC addresses ACEs in ways that person- and family-centered care do not; although, overlapping principles of sensitivity, respect, and partnership would certainly benefit trauma survivors and their families. TIC can provide unique and important benefits to those with a history of ACEs; alternatively, the absence of TIC when needed can also have significant negative consequences for all involved. The core principles upon which TIC is based are outlined as follows.

Benefits and outcomes of TIC

The proposed benefits of a trauma-informed approach stem from 10 key principles, which, according to SAMHSA, include a resilience and strengths-based perspective, acknowledging that change is a process, safety, trustworthiness and transparency, collaboration and mutuality, empowerment, voice and choice, peer support and mutual self-help, inclusiveness and shared purpose, and sensitivity to cultural, historic, and gender issues (SAMHSA, 2014). It is important to note that the benefits resulting from the implementation of these principles have not yet been fully or adequately assessed in a holistic manner; however, there is mounting evidence that many characteristics of a trauma-informed approach have beneficial effects. TIC is designed, first and foremost, to reduce the risk of retraumatization for individuals engaging with professionals. This can include patients receiving care in healthcare settings, clients of social and public health services (e.g., homeless shelters, food banks, crisis shelters, immunization campaigns, home visitation), as well as participants who are recruited to engage with professionals (e.g., participation in a research study, interview with a professional journalist). A trauma-informed approach is also designed to prevent secondary traumatization of family members of trauma survivors, as well as the professionals involved, by providing a physically and psychologically safe setting. It is important to note that physical safety does not guarantee a sense of psychological safety, which is based on the perception of feeling safe (Ward-Lasher, Messing, & Stein-Seroussi, 2017). For those who have experienced ACEs, feeling unsafe may be triggered unexpectedly by a person, place, sound, smell, or event that is reminiscent of a traumatic experience (van der Kolk, 2014). A sense of physical and psychological safety is supported by trustworthiness, in which decisions and operational processes are consistent, reliable, and conducted in a transparent manner (SAMHSA, 2015a).

Transparency by professionals is considered to be an essential component of collaboration and mutuality, because it facilitates shared decision making. Making decisions together is a meaningful form of power sharing between professionals and their clients, patients, and participants, as well as family members. Transparency and shared decision making also facilitate a sense of agency for trauma survivors, which is integrally related to voice and choice. Having a voice reflects not just feeling safe and confident in expressing one's own perspective, but also feeling heard and respected in the decision-making process to the fullest extent possible. This type of context and communication process fosters a sense of inclusiveness and a shared sense of purpose between all involved. Furthermore, empowerment is embodied in having a sense of agency and a voice which, in turn, promote awareness of and motivation for self-help and peer support. Helping others who have also experienced trauma contributes to feelings of connection and support. Finally, an understanding of and sensitivity to cultural, historic, and gender issues are essential components of avoiding retraumatization, in that traumatic experiences can be exacerbated, re-enacted, or prolonged by cultural, historic, and gendered bias and discrimination (Kirmayer, Gone, & Moses, 2014). The importance of this final characteristic of a trauma-informed approach cannot be overstated (Mattar, 2011). Cultural safety is an important recommendation for future work.

These principles have been hypothesized to provide benefit to patients, clients, and participants, as well as to professionals and the organizations within which they work (Fallot & Harris, 2009; Kirst, Aery, Matheson, & Stergiopoulos, 2017; Sciolla, 2017; Wilson et al., 2013). A recent review identified eight studies that focused on TIC benefits to clients; of these, five demonstrated significant improvements (Purtle, 2018). For example, trauma survivors benefit from TIC by a lessened risk for retraumatization when engaging with professionals. Preventing retraumatization encourages better relationships with professionals, and increases the likelihood of self-care, thereby further increasing the likelihood of adherence and accessing services when needed. A review of the healthcare usage of adult survivors of child sexual abuse found that when health professionals facilitated disclosure with survivors, the likelihood of their accessing health care increased (Havig, 2008). Trauma survivors also benefit from TIC with improved health and treatment outcomes (Reeves, 2015). For example, an evaluation of trauma-informed interventions for women with co-occurring mental health symptoms, trauma symptoms, and substance use found that the TIC intervention groups showed greater overall improvement in mental health and trauma symptoms as compared to the usual care group (Morrissey et al., 2005). In sum, patients and clients appear to benefit from TIC in many ways, although research has not yet explored the potential effects of TIC on other common trauma comorbidities, such as chronic pain (Asmundson, Coons, Taylor, & Katz, 2002; Siqveland, Ruud, & Hauff, 2017; Speck, Schlereth, Birklein, & Maihofner, 2017) and depression (Morris, Compas, & Garber, 2012). Using a TIC approach reducing the practices of seclusion and restraint has also been associated with a significant reduction in client and staff injuries, client recidivism, and staff sick time (LeBel & Goldstein, 2005). It is currently unknown if these improved outcomes also contributed to a reduced need for health services by trauma survivors over time. Future research needs to address this issue.

An emerging body of implementation research has begun to address how a TIC approach can be successfully implemented, including specific changes in practice and the benefits of these changes, including improved satisfaction for professionals and improved efficiency for organizations (Vu et al., 2017). A recent review of this body of work found that staff attitudes, behavior, and knowledge improved significantly after training in about two-thirds of the studies identified (Purtle, 2018). TIC self-assessment was implemented in an addictions treatment setting (Brown, Harris, & Fallot, 2013), while others have described the implementation and assessment of TIC in settings for individuals in recovery from addictions, substance use, and homelessness (Hales et al., 2018). Evidence of successful implementation has been operationalized in a variety of ways; for instance, the practices of client seclusion and restraint are considered to be acute catalysts for retraumatization in mental health settings, and a reduction in or elimination of these practices has been defined as one component of successful implementation of TIC (Chandler, 2008; Hales et al., 2018). Preliminary work has supported this premise. For example, a study comparing traditional psychiatric residential treatment for children aged 5 to 17 years with a trauma-informed approach found that young people in the TIC group experienced less seclusion and greater improvement in the remediation of functional impairment. Because of this improvement, they spent significantly shorter time in care than young people in the traditional care group (Boel-Studt, 2015). Qualitative work examining staff perceptions of the transition to a trauma-informed approach in a psychiatric hospital unit identified themes that included a change in staff perspectives toward a more collaborative approach. This resulted in reductions in restraint usage, better self-care, and more peer support among patients, and greater inclusion of patients and their family members in treatment and discharge plans (Chandler, 2008).

The experience of professionals who implement a TIC approach is a key aspect of evaluation research demonstrating feasibility and acceptability. One study investigated staff knowledge, and the use of safety, trustworthiness, choice, collaboration, and empowerment in social service organizations using a web-based survey (Kusmaul, Wilson, & Nochajski, 2015). Results showed that agencies were most likely to address the TIC component of safety (both physical and emotional) and were least likely to address the component of collaboration; however, most TIC components were found to be highly interrelated (Kusmaul et al., 2015). Another study demonstrated that training of child welfare staff was successful in increasing knowledge of TIC practices, particularly those staff with the least formal education and training (Connors-Burrow et al., 2013). An evaluation of staff satisfaction before and after implementing a TIC approach in a residential addiction treatment agency found that workplace satisfaction, organizational climate, and procedures and practices improved moderately, while client satisfaction and client retention improved significantly (Hales et al., 2018; Hales, Nochajski, Green, Hitzel, & Ganga, 2017). However, the authors cautioned that their measure of client retention was based on compliance with treatment goals as reflected by fewer unplanned discharges, rather than by clients spending longer periods in care. Improved adherence is a strongly valued goal that contributes to better outcomes as well as reduced cost (Iuga & McGuire, 2014). Other work that evaluated a substance abuse treatment program for women using a TIC approach as compared to usual care found that the TIC group was 31% less likely to discontinue treatment within 4 months. This was beneficial because mental health symptoms improved with increased duration of treatment, particularly for those with more severe baseline scores (Amaro, Chernoff, Brown, Arevalo, & Gatz, 2007).

Perhaps one of the earliest and best-known TIC approaches is the Sanctuary Model© developed by Bloom and her colleagues (Bloom, 1997; Bloom & Farragher, 2011, 2013). This approach is based on four main pillars that include safety, emotional management, loss, and future (Bloom & Sreedhar, 2008). It involves organizational change at all levels. Rivard and colleagues (Rivard, Bloom, McCorkle, & Abramovitz, 2005) conducted an evaluation of this model at a residential youth treatment facility, comparing treatment and control groups at baseline and at three and six months after implementation. The evaluation included focus groups with youth and with staff, standardized measures of youth adjustment, and a measure of community environment. Focus group findings indicated that the treatment group had a greater awareness of trauma and its effects and more empathy among both youth and staff, as compared to the control group. The community environment measure indicated a greater sense of safety and self-sufficiency in decision-making, better communication, and greater openness to understanding feelings and personal problems in the treatment compared to control group; however, there were few differences in youth adjustment over time.

More recently, an evaluation of a statewide implementation of a TIC approach in the child welfare system indicated that, two years following implementation, there were significant improvements in trauma-informed knowledge, practice, and collaboration across nearly all child welfare domains assessed, which included identification as well as case planning and service delivery for children and families (Lang, Campbell, Shanley, Crusto, & Connell, 2016). Overall, the evaluation indicated many positive changes, but concluded that a 2-year timeframe was not sufficient to become a fully trauma-informed system (Lang et al., 2016). Taken together, these and other results (Brown et al., 2013; Connors-Burrow et al., 2013; Corbin et al., 2011) reflect an emerging body of research that indicates TIC does provide significant benefits for clients, patients, and participants through improved quality of care (e.g., lack of seclusion and restraint, improved adherence, better retention), for staff (e.g., increased sense of safety, increased satisfaction), and for organizations as a whole (e.g., greater cost utility) (LeBel & Goldstein, 2005). Although these findings are promising, many studies to date have been limited to short-term outcomes (Greenwald et al., 2012) or individual components or characteristics of TIC, rather than taking a longer-term comprehensive or holistic approach (Brown, Baker, & Wilcox, 2012; Purtle, 2018). Clearly, more comprehensive implementation research is needed in future to assess the complexity of trauma-informed care.

Unintended consequences: The absence of TIC

It is also important to note that the absence of TIC can pose unintended barriers for patients, clients, and participants to access services or care, or to benefit from their experiences with professionals. For example, a recent review of the healthcare experiences of adult survivors of child sexual abuse in non-TIC environments found they were more likely to avoid or delay healthcare treatment, more likely to fail to adhere to treatment recommendations, and reported having aggravated trauma reactions from their healthcare experiences (Havig, 2008). It is now widely recognized that the long-term effects of trauma and its sequelae are serious and significant if left untreated, as documented in the ACEs literature (Felitti & Anda, 2009). Other work has shown that non-TIC environments increase the likelihood of unnecessary or ineffective treatment strategies, based on mistaken assumptions concerning the origins of illness or maladaptation that stem from trauma. That is, a lack of knowledge concerning trauma history by service and care providers can contribute to misdiagnosis and/or misinterpretation of trauma-based symptoms, as well as their unintended exacerbation (Sciolla, 2017). For example, youth with a trauma history involved in the justice system reported feeling retraumatized by practices commonly used in detention or corrections settings, including strip-searches or pat-downs, placement in secure facilities with limited access to family members or social supports, and use of seclusion or restraint (Branson, Baetiz, Horwitz, & Hoagwood, 2017). A retrospective study of young adults who had been recently discharged from a juvenile justice facility found that seclusion and other potentially traumatic experiences while incarcerated were positively associated with postrelease criminal behavior and posttraumatic stress disorder symptoms (Dierkhising, Lane, & Natsuaki, 2014). These results suggest that non-TIC environments may unintentionally impede recovery or rehabilitation.

Recommendations

Given the wide array of potential benefits of TIC for clients, patients, and participants, and for professionals actively utilizing this approach, as well as the potentially harmful consequences arising from the absence of TIC, a variety of settings have begun implementation (Crosby, 2015; Reeves, 2015). The diversity of settings continues to broaden (Dworznik & Grubb, 2007). Several recommendations regarding the expansion of TIC are provided below.

Recommendation 1. While the core components of TIC can be beneficial in virtually any setting, it is especially recommended in interactions with vulnerable persons who are more likely to have experienced multiple ACEs. This population incorporates a broad spectrum of ages, contexts, and experiences, including but not limited to veterans, refugees, persons who are homeless or incarcerated, those struggling with addiction, survivors of interpersonal violence, survivors of violent conflict and torture, survivors of natural disasters, seniors in care, persons with disabilities in care, as well as others too numerous to list here (Wilson et al., 2013).

Recommendation 2. Implementation of TIC approaches in services and systems for children and youth are an urgent priority for many reasons (Marsac et al., 2016). Preventing retraumatization not only reduces suffering in the short term, but also reduces the effects of ACEs in the long term (Levine, 2010; Perry, 2009; van der Kolk, 2014). While it was often mistakenly assumed in the past that very young children were not aware of or did not remember potentially traumatic events, research has demonstrated this is not the case (Scheeringa, 2009). Therefore, the importance of a trauma-informed approach applies to children of all ages, from birth to adulthood. It should be noted that a trauma-informed perspective was recommended for pediatric primary care in 2012 by the American Academy of Pediatrics in a policy statement. Overall, a TIC approach is more predominant in pediatric settings such as child welfare (Pynoos et al., 2008), but is addressed less often in the education (Crosby, 2015; Walkley & Cox, 2013) and pediatric dentistry (Raja, Hoersch, Rajagopalan, & Chang, 2014) literature. In the Canadian context, the special case of Indigenous children in care is of particular concern (Blackstock, Brown, & Bennett, 2007) and highlights the importance of cultural sensitivity in effective trauma-informed approaches (Canadian National Aboriginal Health Organization [NAHO], 2008). This issue is discussed in further detail as follows.

Recommendation 3. Further expansion of trauma-informed approaches for vulnerable women is also strongly recommended. This expansion would not only directly benefit women, but for those who are mothers, children would indirectly benefit as well. TIC interactions with women also cut across diverse systems, including mental health settings, addictions treatment settings, and welfare systems (Amaro et al., 2007; Havig, 2008; Morrissey et al., 2005; Muskett, 2014). Recently, TIC approaches were recommended as a practical and ethical imperative for women in primary care settings (Machtinger, Cuca, Khanna, Rose, & Kimberg, 2015), in midwifery practice (Sperlich, Seng, Li, Taylor, & Bradbury-Jones, 2017), as well as for incarcerated women (Harner & Burgess, 2011). Surprisingly, the implementation and evaluation of TIC has not been closely studied in crisis shelters and transitional housing for women who have experienced intimate partner violence (IPV; Ward-Lasher et al., 2017; Wilson, Fauci, & Goodman, 2015) or for their children (Stylianou & Ebright, 2018). A recent exception was a case study of a housing insecurity program for women survivors of IPV. Based on semistructured interviews with staff and administrators and surveys of client self-reported outcomes, the researchers argued that using a TIC approach increased the likelihood of successful housing for survivors of IPV (Ward-Lasher et al., 2017). A qualitative review of TIC applied in domestic violence programs identified core themes across programs, but also called for more rigorous evaluation of outcomes (Wilson et al., 2015).

Recommendation 4. As noted, those with a trauma history come into contact with numerous systems (Hopper et al., 2010; Ko et al., 2008; Larkin et al., 2014). The National Traumatic Stress Network in the US has made a significant impact on increasing awareness of TIC since its inception in 2001 and has recommended improved standards of care across all systems (Pynoos et al., 2008). These improvements rely, in part, on the effective continuing education of professionals and paraprofessionals in TIC, as well as the inclusion of TIC in professional training programs. For example, TIC training has begun to emerge in medical and dental schools (Magen & DeLisser, 2017; Raja et al., 2015) and it has also been called for in other health professional training programs (Wheeler, 2018). The American Academy of Pediatrics currently offers a continuing education course in TIC. However, TIC is noticeably absent from the training literature in some areas, including rehabilitation professionals such as physiotherapists, first responders, those who provide care and services to seniors, as well as those who provide care to persons with developmental and intellectual disabilities (Keesler, 2014). A core curriculum for a trauma-informed mental health workforce has been piloted (Layne et al., 2011) and continued expansion of TIC training for diverse practicing professionals who interact with individuals who have experienced trauma is strongly recommended (Dworznik & Grubb, 2007; Keesler, 2014; Magen & DeLisser, 2017).

Recommendation 5. Despite the diverse spectrum of settings and services that have adopted a trauma-informed approach, the implementation science literature continues to build toward a consensus of the core components of TIC (Hanson & Lang, 2016; Hopper et al., 2010). There is also growing agreement across practitioners and researchers concerning how to transform systems and organizational cultures using a TIC approach (Bloom & Farragher, 2013), and how to evaluate essential components of this transformation (Baker et al., 2017; Hales et al., 2018; Purtle, 2018). To this end, several self-assessment tools (Baker, Brown, Wilcox, Overstreet, & Arora, 2016) and planning inventories (Fallot & Harris, 2009) have been created to assist organizations with how to implement and evaluate TIC. In brief, these tools assess service-level changes, such as program procedures, and policy-level changes. They also assess changes in staff attitudes, and the quality of coworker and staff-client relationships. However, more work remains to be done concerning the harmonization of standardized trauma-informed guidelines and approaches across systems and services (Ko et al., 2008; The National Child Traumatic Stress Network, 2018).

Directions for future research

Although many of the core concepts of TIC are decades old, rigorous scientific research on the evaluation of the effectiveness of standardized TIC practice guidelines is currently in its infancy (Hales et al., 2017, 2018; Rivard et al., 2005). As TIC becomes ever more widely adopted across diverse settings with diverse populations, valid and reliable evaluation of TIC implementation grows in importance. Although both physical and psychological safety are included as core concepts within TIC, cultural safety is not. Instead, the role of cultural and historic contexts is acknowledged. It is argued here and elsewhere (Brascoupe & Waters, 2009; Gerlach, 2012; Shimmin, Wittmeier, Lavoie, Wicklund, & Sibley, 2017) that awareness of cultural, historic, and gendered influences on the provision of care and services is a positive first step; but, that awareness alone is not sufficient (Gerlach, 2012; Mattar, 2011). Raising awareness is limited in terms of improving the quality of interactions with individuals with a trauma history and effectively preventing retraumatization. Building on this critique, a conceptual model for cultural safety was recently developed as part of a health sciences curriculum that incorporated four interrelated components, including cultural awareness, cultural sensitivity, cultural competence, and cultural safety (Shah & Reeves, 2015). Originally developed in New Zealand, cultural safety is a concept that does not yet have a universal definition. NAHO (2008) defines cultural safety as:

> … what is felt or experienced by a patient when a health care provider communicates with the patient in a respectful, inclusive way, empowers the patient in decision-making and builds a health care relationship where the patient and provider work together as a team to ensure maximum effectiveness of care (p. 19).

To date, cultural safety has been primarily included as a core TIC concept with Indigenous patients in health settings as a means to address inequities between Indigenous and nonindigenous populations, and to provide better quality of care and optimize health outcomes (Dell, Firestone, Smylie, & Vaillancourt, 2016; Jamieson et al., 2017; Vickers & Wells, 2017). However, this important concept can be applied in virtually any setting with underserved and marginalized populations who have experienced intergenerational trauma and systemic bias (Giles & Darroch, 2014). As with all core components of TIC, future research should address both formative and summative evaluations of cultural safety as part of a TIC approach.

Future research on TIC also needs to address three additional issues. First, as noted earlier, more work needs to address the harmonization of standardized trauma-informed guidelines and approaches across systems and services. While TIC guidelines for practice and standards of care have emerged in differing contexts (Arthur et al., 2013; Kezelman & Stavropoulos, 2012; SAMHSA, 2015b; Walkley & Cox, 2013), research that promotes interdisciplinary and intersectoral collaboration that solidifies globally accepted definitions and standardized state-of-the-art practice guidelines would greatly facilitate the adoption of TIC across professions and professional training programs (Pynoos et al., 2008). The evaluation of the effectiveness of training programs based on these standards of care, both in professional and graduate training programs and in continuing education for practicing professionals and researchers, is needed to advance our knowledge of excellence in TIC practice.

Next, rigorous evaluation of the systems and programs that have adopted TIC based on standardized guidelines should include both process and outcome evaluations. Formative evaluation of TIC processes should not only document a lessened risk for retraumatization when engaging with professionals, but should also address other aspects of quality of care, such as better relationships with professionals, increased likelihood of self-care, and adherence and help-seeking when needed. Summative evaluation of TIC outcomes should investigate a wide variety of physical and mental health benefits, including reduced symptomatology (e.g., fewer trauma-related symptoms) as well as other symptoms that are commonly comorbid with trauma (e.g., chronic pain, depression, anxiety).

Finally, summative evaluation should not only assess outcomes for recipients of TIC, but also for those who engage in TIC approaches. The benefits of engaging in TIC for professionals, semiprofessionals, and other providers is needed to expand the evidence base concerning how TIC positively impacts those who engage with patients, clients, and participants (Chandler, 2008; Hales et al., 2017; Kirst et al., 2017). A comprehensive evaluation should also include how organizations that have adopted a TIC philosophy (Bloom & Farragher, 2013) may have benefited, including a cost-utility analysis. Research investigating the financial benefits of TIC, such as the association between increased adherence to treatment protocols and reduced need for services, and the association between increased staff satisfaction and reduced number of sick days and turnover, should be prioritized. In sum, rigorous formative and summative evaluation research demonstrating the benefits of TIC at multiple levels (e.g., individuals, systems or organizations) across diverse settings would have significant implications for policy and practice.

Implications for practice and policy

The implementation of a trauma-informed approach has taken different forms across settings in terms of practice, from lessened or restricted use of restraint and seclusion to improved adherence, required trauma screening, and more shared decision making (Purtle, 2018). While some shifts in practice toward TIC are subtle, it is widely agreed (Bloom, 1997; Fallot & Harris, 2009; Ko et al., 2008) that adopting a TIC approach requires explicit training and ongoing maintenance. One major shift toward TIC practice has been the implementation of navigation programs that originated in cancer care approximately 20 years ago, and have since become more widespread (Freeman, 2012). In essence, navigation programs provide patients or clients with personalized guidance, support, and assistance with accessing resources from a professional, paraprofessional, or peer familiar with their circumstances. Reviews (Paskett, Harrop, & Wells, 2011; Wells, Valverde, Ustjanauskas, Calhoun, & Risendal, 2018) and systematic reviews (Robinson-White, Conroy, Slavish, & Rosenzweig, 2010) of the effectiveness of navigation programs for cancer patients have consistently shown improved access to and quality of care. Navigation programs are spreading from health care into other areas, including but not limited to mental health (Corrigan, Pickett, Batia, & Michaels, 2014).

Interestingly, although TIC and navigation programs share many practical similarities, they remain conceptually distinct. The benefits of navigation programs could be enhanced by being embedded within a system-wide TIC approach, while navigation programs could be added to many existing TIC systems. A TIC community-focused violence prevention program with a navigation program for youth is one such example. This navigation program targeted youth aged 8 to 30 years who, after being treated for a violent injury at an emergency department, were left with no further follow-up to support their coping with the effects of trauma (Corbin et al., 2011; Fischer et al., 2018), even though fully 75% of participants met full diagnostic criteria for posttraumatic stress disorder (Corbin et al., 2013). A trauma-informed multidisciplinary intervention program was created within the organizational framework of the sanctuary model (Bloom, 1997), built on a collaboration between a university hospital emergency department and community partners to address the needs of injured youth after discharge. The youth navigation program was an important component embedded within this TIC model, wherein a community intervention specialist provided support for several months following discharge to help ensure youth received needed supports and services (Corbin et al., 2011). Evaluation of this type of program has indicated that recidivism rates for violent injury were significantly lower following implementation (Smith, Dobbins, Evans, Balhotra, & Dicker, 2013). More generally, it seems likely the integration of navigation programs into numerous TIC settings could significantly improve the quality of care and relevant outcomes. This question needs to be addressed in future research.

Another important recent development in TIC practice is the increasing recognition of how trauma resulting from violent experiences, particularly those that involve a betrayal of trust and attachment injury within close interpersonal relationships, differ qualitatively from other traumatic experiences, such as natural disasters, military combat, car crashes, or occupational injury (van der Kolk, 2014). Recent work has supported the view that trauma stemming from interpersonal violence is more likely to contribute to feelings of distrust and social withdrawal due to distrust of others than the experience of unintentional injury (Jiang, Webster, Robinson, Kassam-Adams, & Richmond, 2018). An emerging offshoot of TIC, called *trauma- and violence-informed care* (TVIC), is built upon such recognition, and represents a timely advancement in the field. To date, research concerning the implementation and evaluation of TIC has not addressed the unique nature of trauma resulting from violence. TVIC incorporates a more nuanced and comprehensive understanding of the complex interaction between the unique effects of violent trauma within a health equity lens (Ponic, Varcoe, & Smutylo, 2016). This lens acknowledges the effects of institutional violence that are based on systemic discrimination and inequities in services and care (Dickman, Himmelstein, & Woolhandler, 2017; Martin et al., 2018). Violence-informed care expands the core concepts of TIC to include cultural safety (DeSouza, 2008), as well as intersectionality, inclusiveness, health equity, and social justice (Shimmin et al., 2017). This acknowledgement of the interplay between the unique effects of violent trauma and systemic inequities adds complexity to the implementation and evaluation of TVIC. Because of the TVIC emphasis on how system inequities can retraumatize survivors of violent trauma and contribute to further disparities in health and wellbeing, it represents an important new direction for TIC practice and policy.

Trauma-informed principles applied to practice are now being applied to policy in health care, social work, and elsewhere (Bowen & Murshid, 2016; Hecht, Biehi, Buzogany, & Neff, 2018; Larkin et al., 2014). As argued by Bowen and Murshid (2016), these principles reflect "the reality that trauma and its effects are not equally distributed, and offers a pathway for public health professionals to disrupt trauma-driven health disparities through policy action" (p. 223). The European Public Health Association, in collaboration with 17 national associations of public health, created a joint statement calling for political engagement to reduce inequalities in health

(European Public Health Association, 2018). Policies that incorporate a TIC approach offer such an opportunity and have enormous potential to create population-wide benefits. TIC policies are gaining momentum. For example, a policy-mapping investigation of legislative proposals in the US Congress found that the number of trauma-informed bills increased from 0 in 2010 to 28 in 2015 (Purtle & Lewis, 2017). A TIC approach to policy and practice is supported by other governments as well (Public Health Agency of Canada, 2018). Although trauma-informed practice has a longer history, the rising tide of trauma-informed policy that not only promotes TIC principles, but that also supports intersectoral prevention efforts early in life (Larkin et al., 2014), has significant potential to reduce health inequities for the most vulnerable groups (Hecht et al., 2018) and contribute to the prevention of the short- and long-term effects of ACEs across entire populations (Shern, Blanch, & Steverman, 2016; Sorenson, 2002). The next step is to evaluate the impact of these policies on those they are designed to benefit.

Conclusion

The scientific evidence regarding trauma-informed practices and outcomes has begun to demonstrate that TIC has considerable promise to increase access to care and services, improve the quality of care and services, enhance the effectiveness of care and services, and reduce the need for care and services across the entire life course. This promise is becoming a reality in many fields. While ACEs research has clearly demonstrated the long-term and serious impact of childhood adversity, the specific list of traumatic events is limited in that there are many other experiences that are potentially traumatic in childhood and beyond (e.g., natural disasters, institutional racism, workplace violence). It is also important to emphasize that trauma can be idiosyncratic in nature; that is, similar events can be perceived as traumatic by some, but not by others (van der Kolk, 2014). Therefore, TIC principles can and should be applied not only to those who have experienced ACEs, but to anyone with a trauma history. The core concepts of TIC reviewed here reflect parallel theoretical advances in life course health and development (Halfon & Forrest, 2018). Taken together, they provide a comprehensive approach for understanding the complex and interactive nature of trauma and resilience, and provide a blueprint for how to address trauma in everyday interactions. In conclusion, although TIC has a long history, its continued growth and expansion into practice and policy will enhance its effectiveness to save lives, prevent suffering, and increase the cost effectiveness of health and prevention programming far into the future.

References

Amaro, H., Chernoff, M., Brown, V., Arevalo, S., & Gatz, M. (2007). Does integrated trauma-informed substance abuse treatment increase treatment retention? *Journal of Community Psychology*, *35*(7), 845–862.

Arthur, E., Seymour, A., Dartnall, M., Beltgens, P., Poole, N., Smylie, D., … Schmidt, R. (2013). *Trauma-informed practice guide: BC Provincial Mental Health and Substance Use Planning Council.*

Asmundson, G., Coons, M., Taylor, S., & Katz, J. (2002). PTSD and the experience of pain: research and clinical implications of shared vulnerability and mutual maintenance models. *Canadian Journal of Psychiatry*, *47*(10), 930–937.

Baker, C., Brown, S., Wilcox, P., Overstreet, S., & Arora, P. (2016). Development and psychometric evaluation of the attitudes related to trauma-informed care (ARTIC) scale. *School Mental Health*, *8*, 61–76. https://doi.org/10.1007/s12310-015-9161-0.

Baker, C., Brown, S., Wilcox, P., Verlenden, J., Black, C., & Grant, B. (2017). The implementation and effect of trauma-informed care within residential youth services in rural Canada: a mixed methods case study. *Psychological Trauma: Theory, Research, Practice, and Policy*, https://doi.org/10.1037/tra0000327.

Blackstock, C., Brown, I., & Bennett, M. (2007). Reconciliation: rebuilding the Canadian child welfare system to better serve aboriginal children and youth. In I. Brown, F. Chaze, D. Fuchs, J. Lafrance, S. MacKay, & S. Thomas Prokop (Eds.), *Putting a human face on child welfare: Voices from the prairies*. Calgary, AB: Prairie Child Welfare Consortium/Centre of Excellence for Child Welfare.

Bloom, S. (1997). *Creating sanctuary: Toward the evolution of sane societies*. New York, NY: Routledge.

Bloom, S., & Farragher, B. (2011). *Destroying sanctuary: The crisis in human service delivery systems*. New York, NY: Oxford University Press.

Bloom, S., & Farragher, B. (2013). *Restoring sanctuary: A new operating system for trauma-informed systems of care*. New York, NY: Oxford University Press.

Bloom, S., & Sreedhar, S. (2008). The sanctuary model of trauma-informed organizational change. *Reclaiming Children & Youth*, *17*(3), 48–53.

Boel-Studt, S. (2015). A quasi-experimental study of trauma-informed psychiatric residential treatment for children and adolescents. *Research on Social Work Practice*, *27*(3), 273–282. https://doi.org/10.1177/1049731515614401.

Bowen, E., & Murshid, N. (2016). Trauma-informed social policy: a conceptual framework for policy analysis and advocacy. *American Journal of Public Health*, *106*(2), 223–229. https://doi.org/10.2105/AJPH.2015.302970.

Branson, C., Baetiz, C., Horwitz, S., & Hoagwood, K. (2017). Trauma-informed juvenile justice systems: a systematic review of definitions and core components. *Psychological Trauma Theory Research Practice and Policy*, *9*(6), 635–646. https://doi.org/10.1037/tra0000255.

Brascoupe, S., & Waters, C. (2009). Cultural safety: exploring the applicability of the concept of cultural safety to aboriginal health and community wellness. *Journal of Aboriginal Health*, (November), 6–40.

Brown, S., Baker, C., & Wilcox, P. (2012). Risking connection trauma training: a pathway toward trauma-informed care in child congregate care settings. *Psychological Trauma Theory Research Practice and Policy*, *4*(5), 507–515. https://doi.org/10.1037/a0025269.

Brown, V., Harris, M., & Fallot, R. (2013). Moving toward trauma-informed practice in addiction treatment: a collaborative model of inter-agency assessment. *Journal of Psychoactive Drugs*, *45*(5), 386–393. https://doi.org/10.1080/02791072.2013.844381.

Canadian Interprofessional Health Collaborative. (2009). *CIHC Patient Centred Care Factsheet*. Ottawa, ON: Health Canada. Retrieved from http://www.cihc.ca/.

Canadian National Aboriginal Health Organization (NAHO). (2008). *Cultural competency and safety: A guide for culturally safe practice*. Ottawa, ON: National Aboriginal Health Organization.

Chandler, G. (2008). From traditional inpatient to trauma-informed treatment: transferring control from staff to patient. *Journal of the American Psychiatric Nurses Association, 14*(5), 363–371. https://doi.org/10.1177/1078390308326625.

Cohen, J., Deblinger, E., Mannarino, A., & Steer, R. (2004). A multisite, randomized controlled trial for children with sexual abuse-related PTSD symptoms. *Journal of the American Academy of Child & Adolescent Psychiatry, 43*, 393–402.

Connors-Burrow, N., Kramer, T., Sigel, B., Helpenstill, K., Sievers, C., & McKelvey, L. (2013). Trauma-informed care training in a child welfare system: moving it to the front line. *Children and Youth Services Review, 35*, 1830–1835. https://doi.org/10.1016/j.childyouth.2013.08.013.

Constand, M., MacDermid, J., Dal Bello-Haas, V., & Law, M. (2014). Scoping review of patient-centred care approaches in healthcare. *BMC Health Services Research, 14*, 271–280. https://doi.org/10.1186/1472-6963-14-271.

Corbin, T., Purtle, J., Rich, L., Rich, J., Adams, E., Yee, G., & Bloom, S. (2013). The prevalence of trauma and childhood adversity in an urban, hospital-based violence intervention program. *Journal of Health Care for the Poor and Underserved, 24*(3), 1021–1030. https://doi.org/10.1353/hpu.2013.0120.

Corbin, T., Rich, J., Bloom, S., Delgado, D., Rich, L., & Wilson, A. (2011). Developing a trauma-informed, emergency department-based intervention for victims of urban violence. *Journal of Trauma & Dissociation, 12*(5), 510–525. https://doi.org/10.1080/15299732.2011.593260.

Corrigan, P., Pickett, S., Batia, K., & Michaels, P. (2014). Peer navigators and integrated care to address ethnic disparities of people with serious mental illness. *Social Work in Public Health, 29*, 581–593. https://doi.org/10.1080/19371918.2014.893854.

Crosby, S. (2015). An ecological perspective on emerging trauma-informed teaching practices. *Children & Schools, 37*(4), 223–230.

Davidson, J., Aslakson, R., Long, A., Puntillo, K., Kross, E., Hart, J., … Curtis, J. (2017). Guidelines for family-centred care in the neonatal, pediatric, and adult ICU. *Critical Care Medicine, 45*(1), 103–128. https://doi.org/10.1097/CCM.0000000000002169.

Dell, E., Firestone, M., Smylie, J., & Vaillancourt, S. (2016). Cultural safety and providing care to aboriginal patients in the emergency department. *Canadian Journal of Emergency Medicine, 18*(4), 301–305. https://doi.org/10.1017/cem.2015.100.

DeSouza, R. (2008). Wellness for all: the possibilities of cultural safety and cultural competence in New Zealand. *Journal of Research in Nursing, 13*(2), 125–135. https://doi.org/10.1177/1744987108088637.

Dickman, S., Himmelstein, D., & Woolhandler, S. (2017). Inequailty and the health-care system in the USA. *The Lancet, 389*(10077), https://doi.org/10.1016/SO140-6736(17)30398-7.

Dierkhising, C., Lane, A., & Natsuaki, M. (2014). Victims behind bars: a preliminary study of abuse during juvenile incarceration and post-release social and emotional functioning. *Psychology, Public Policy, and Law, 20*(2), 181–190. https://doi.org/10.1037/law0000002.

Dworznik, G., & Grubb, M. (2007). Preparing for the worst: making a case for trauma training in the journalism classroom. *Journalism and Mass Communication Educator, 62*(2), 190–210. https://doi.org/10.1177/107769580706200206.

European Public Health Association. (2018). *Ljubljana statement*. In *Slovenia: 11th European Public Health Conference 2018*.

Fallot, R., & Harris, M. (2009). *Creating cultures of trauma-informed care (CCTIC): A self-assessment and planning protocol*. (Vol. 2.2). Washington, DC: Community Connections.

Felitti, V., & Anda, R. (2009). The relationship of adverse childhood experiences to adult medical disease, psychiatric disorders, and sexual behavior: implications for health care. In E. Lanius (Ed.), *The hidden epidemic: The impact of early life trauma on health and disease*. Cambridge, MA: Cambridge University Press.

Fischer, K., Bakes, K., Corbin, T., Fein, J., Harris, E., James, T., & Meizer-Lange, M. (2018). Trauma-informed care for violently injured patients in the emergency department. *Annals of Emergency Medicine*, https://doi.org/10.1016/j.annegergemed.2018.10.018. November 28.

Freeman, H. (2012). The origin, evolution, and principles of patient navigation. *Cancer Epidemiology, Biomarkers & Prevention, 21*(10), 1614–1617. https://doi.org/10.1158/1055-9965.EPI-12-0982.

Gerlach, A. (2012). A critical reflection on the concept of cultural safety. *Canadian Journal of Occupational Therapy, 79*(3), 151–158.

Giles, A., & Darroch, F. (2014). The need for culturally safe physical activity promotion and programs. *Canadian Journal of Public Health, 105*(4), e317–e319.

Greenwald, R., Siradas, L., Schmitt, T., Reslan, S., Fierle, J., & Sande, B. (2012). Implementing trauma-informed treatment for youth in a residential facility: first-year outcomes. *Residential Treatment for Children & Youth, 29*, 141–153. https://doi.org/10.1080/0886571X.2012.676525.

Hales, T., Green, S., Bissonette, S., Warden, A., Diebold, J., Koury, S., & Nochajski, T. (2018). Trauma-informed care outcome study. *Research on Social Work Practice*, 1–11. https://doi.org/10.1177/1049731518766618.

Hales, T., Nochajski, T., Green, S., Hitzel, H., & Ganga, E. (2017). An association between implementing trauma-informed care and staff satisfaction. *Advances in Social Work, 18*(1), 300–312. https://doi.org/10.18060/21299.

Halfon, N., & Forrest, C. (2018). The emerging theoretical framework of life course health development. In N. Halfon, C. Forrest, R. Lerner, & E. Faustman (Eds.), *Handbook of life course health development* (pp. 19–43). New York: Springer.

Hanson, R., & Lang, J. (2016). A critical look at trauma-informed care among agencies and systems serving maltreated youth and their families. *Child Maltreatment, 21*, 95–100. https://doi.org/10.1177/1077559516635274.

Harner, H., & Burgess, A. (2011). Using a trauma-informed framework to care for incarcerated women. *Journal of Obstetric, Gynecologic & Neonatal Nursing, 40*(4), 469–476. https://doi.org/10.1111/j.1552-6909.2011.01259.x.

Havig, K. (2008). The health care experiences of adult survivors of child sexual abuse. *Trauma, Violence & Abuse, 9*(1), 19–33. https://doi.org/10.1177/1524838007309805.

Hecht, A., Biehi, E., Buzogany, S., & Neff, R. (2018). Using a trauma-informed policy approach to create a resilent urban food system. *Public Health Nutrition, 21*(10), 1961–1970. https://doi.org/10.1017/S1368980018000198.

Hopper, E., Bassuk, E., & Oliver, J. (2010). Shelter from the storm: trauma-informed care in homelessness services settings. *Open Health Services and Policy, 3*, 80–100.

Huber-Lang, M., Lambris, J., & Ward, P. (2018). Innate immune responses to trauma. *Nature Immunology, 19*, 327–341.

Hughes, K., Bellis, M., Hardcastle, K., Sethi, D., Butchart, A., Mikton, C., … Dunne, M. (2017). The effect of multiple adverse childhood experiences on health: a systematic review and meta-analysis. *The Lancet*, 2(8), e356–e366. https://doi.org/10.1016/S2468-2667(17)30118-4.

Iuga, A., & McGuire, M. (2014). Adherence and health care costs. *Risk Management and Healthcare Policy, 7*(35), 35–44.

Jamieson, M., Chen, S., Murphy, S., Maracle, L., Mofina, A., & Hill, J. (2017). Pilot testing an intervention on cultural safety and Indigenous health in a Canadian occupational therapy curriculum. *Journal of Allied Health, 46*(1), 64–70.

Jiang, T., Webster, J., Robinson, A., Kassam-Adams, N., & Richmond, T. (2018). Emotional responses to unintentional and intenional traumatic injuries among urban Black men: a qualitative study. *Injury, 49*, 983–989. https://doi.org/10.1016/j.injury.2017.12.002.

Keesler, J. (2014). A call for the integration of trauma-informed care among intellectual and developmental disabilitiy organizations. *Journal of Policy and Practice in Intellectual Disabilities, 11*(1), 34–42. https://doi.org/10.1111/jppi.12071.

Kezelman, C., & Stavropoulos, P. (2012). *Practice guidelines for treatment of complex trauma and trauma informed care and service delivery.* Department of Health and Ageing, Trans. Sydney, Australia: Blue Knot Foundation.

Kirmayer, L., Gone, J., & Moses, J. (2014). Rethinking historical trauma. *Transcultural Psychiatry*, *51*(3), 299–319. https://doi.org/10.1177/1363461514536358.

Kirst, M., Aery, A., Matheson, F., & Stergiopoulos, V. (2017). Provider and consumer perceptions of trauma informed practices and services for substance use and mental health problems. *International Journal of Mental Health and Addiction*, *15*(3), 514–528. https://doi.org/10.1007/s11469-016-9693-z.

Ko, S., Ford, J., Kassam-Adams, N., Berkowitz, S., Wilson, C., Wong, M., … Layne, C. (2008). Creating trauma-informed systems: child welfare, education, first responders, health care, juvenile justice. *Professional Psychology: Research and Practice*, *39*(4), 396–404. https://doi.org/10.1037/0735-7028.39.4.396.

Kuo, D., Houtrow, A., Arango, P., Kuhlthau, K., Simmons, J., & Neff, J. (2012). Family-centred care: current applications and future directions in pediatric health care. *Maternal and Child Health Journal*, *16*, 297–305. https://doi.org/10.1007/s10995-011-0751-7.

Kusmaul, N., Wilson, B., & Nochajski, T. (2015). The infusion of trauma-informed care in organizations: experience of agency staff. *Human Service Organizations: Management, Leadership and Governance*, *39*(1), 25–37. https://doi.org/10.1080/23303131.2014.968749.

Lang, J., Campbell, K., Shanley, P., Crusto, C., & Connell, C. (2016). Building capacity for trauma-informed care in the child welfare system: initial results of a statewide implementation. *Child Maltreatment*, *21*(2), 113–124.

Larkin, H., Felitti, V., & Anda, R. (2014). Social work and adverse childhood experiences research: implications for practice and health policy. *Social Work in Public Health*, *29*(1), 1–16. https://doi.org/10.1080/19371918.2011.619433.

Layne, C., Ippen, C., Strand, V., Stuber, M., Abramovitz, R., Reyes, G., … Pynoos, R. (2011). The core curriculum on child trauma: a tool for training a trauma-informed workforce. *Psychological Trauma Theory Research Practice and Policy*, *3*(3), 243–252. https://doi.org/10.1037/a0025039.

LeBel, J., & Goldstein, R. (2005). Special section on seclusion and restraint: the economic cost of using restraint and the value added by restraint reduction or elimination. *Psychiatric Services*, *56*, 1109–1114.

Levine, P. (2010). *In an unspoken voice: How the body releases trauma and restores goodness.* Berkeley, CA: North Atlantic Books.

Lupien, S., McEwen, B., Gunnar, M., & Heim, C. (2009). Effects of stress throughout the lifespan on the brain, behaviour and cognition. *Nature Neuroscience*, *10*, 434–445.

Machtinger, E., Cuca, Y., Khanna, N., Rose, C., & Kimberg, L. (2015). From treatment to healing: the promise of trauma-informed primary care. *Women's Health Issues*, *25*(3), 193–197. https://doi.org/10.1177/1524838004272559.

Magen, E., & DeLisser, H. (2017). Best practices in relational skills training for medical trainees and providers: an essential element of addressing adverse childhood experiences and promoting resilience. *Academic Pediatrics*, *17*(7S), S102–S107.

Marsac, M., Kassam-Adams, N., Hildebrand, A., Nicholls, E., Winston, F., Leff, S., & Fein, J. (2016). Implementing a trauma-informed approach in pediatric health care networks. *JAMA Pediatrics*, *170*(1), 70–77.

Martin, D., Miller, A., Quesnel-Vallee, A., Caron, N., Vissandjee, B., & Marchildon, G. (2018). Canada's universal health-care system: acheiving its potential. *The Lancet*, *391*(10131), https://doi.org/10.1016/SO140-6736(18)30181-8.

Mattar, S. (2011). Educating and training the next generations of traumatologists: development of cultural competencies. *Psychological Trauma Theory Research Practice and Policy*, *3*(3), 258–265. https://doi.org/10.1037/a0024477.

McCrory, E., De Brito, S., & Viding, E. (2010). Research review: the neurobiology and genetics of maltreatment and adversity. *The Journal of Child Psychology and Psychiatry*, *51*(10), 1079–1095. https://doi.org/10.1111/j.1469-7610.2010.02271.x.

Merrick, M., Ford, D., Ports, K., & Guinn, A. (2018). Prevalance of adverse childhood experiences from the 2011-2014 behavioral risk factor surveillance system in 23 states. *JAMA Pediatrics, 172*(11), 1038–1044. https://doi.org/10.1001/jamapediatrics.2018.2537.

Morris, M., Compas, B., & Garber, J. (2012). Relations among posttraumatic stress disorder, comorbid major depression, and HPA function: a systematic review and meta-analysis. *Clinical Psychology Review, 32*(4), 301–315. https://doi.org/10.1016/j.cpr.2012.02.002.

Morrissey, J., Jackson, E., Ellis, A., Amaro, H., Brown, V., & Najavits, L. (2005). Twelve-month outcomes of trauma-informed interventions for women with co-occurring disorders. *Psychiatric Services, 56*(10), 1213–1222.

Muskett, C. (2014). Trauma-informed care in inpatient mental health settings: a review of the literature. *International Journal of Mental Health Nursing, 23*, 51–59. https://doi.org/10.1111/inm.12012.

Paskett, E., Harrop, J., & Wells, K. (2011). Patient navigation: an update on the state of the science. *CA: A Cancer Journal for Clinicians, 61*(4), 237–248. https://doi.org/10.3322/caac.20111.

Perry, B. (2009). Examining child maltreatment through a neurodevelopmental lens: clinical applications of the neurosequential model of therapeutics. *Journal of Loss & Trauma, 14*(4), 240–255. https://doi.org/10.1080/15325020903004350.

Ponic, P., Varcoe, C., & Smutylo, T. (2016). *Trauma-(and violence-) informed approaches to supporting victims of violence: Policy and practice considerations, Victims of Crime Research Digest No. 9*. Ottawa, ON.

Public Health Agency of Canada. (2018). *Trauma and Violence-Informed Approaches to Policy and Practice* Retrieved December 11, 2018, fromhttps://www.canada.ca/en/public-health/services/publications/health-risks-safety/trauma-violence-informed-approaches-policy-practice.html.

Purtle, J. (2018). Systematic review of evaluations of trauma-informed organizational interventions that include staff training. *Trauma, Violence, & Abuse*, 1–6. https://doi.org/10.1177/1524838018791304.

Purtle, J., & Lewis, M. (2017). Mapping "trauma-informed" legislative proposals in U.S. Congress. *Administration and Policy in Mental Health and Mental Health Services Reseach, 44*(6), 867–876. https://doi.org/10.1007/s10488-017-0799-9.

Pynoos, R., Fairbank, J., Steinberg, A., Amaya-Jackson, L., Gerrity, E., Mount, M., & Maze, J. (2008). The National Child Traumatic Stress Network: collaborating to improve standards of care. *Professional Psychology: Research and Practice, 39*(4), 389–395. https://doi.org/10.1037/a0012551.

Raja, S., Hoersch, M., Rajagopalan, C., & Chang, P. (2014). Treating patients with traumatic life experiences: providing trauma-informed care. *Journal of the American Dental Association, 145*(3), 238–245. https://doi.org/10.14219/jada.2013.30.

Raja, S., Rajagopalan, C., Kruthoff, M., Kuperschmidt, A., Chang, P., & Hoersch, M. (2015). Teaching dental students to interact with survivors of traumatic events: development of a two-day module. *Journal of Dental Education, 79*(1), 47–55.

Reeves, E. (2015). A synthesis of the literature on trauma-informed care. *Issues in Mental Health Nursing, 36*(9), 698–709. https://doi.org/10.3109/01612840.2015.1025319.

Rivard, J., Bloom, S., McCorkle, D., & Abramovitz, R. (2005). Preliminary results of a study examining the implementation and effects of a trauma recovery framework for youth in a residential treatment. *Therapeutic Community: The International Journal for Therapeutic and Supportive Organizations, 26*(1), 83–96.

Robinson-White, S., Conroy, B., Slavish, K., & Rosenzweig, M. (2010). Patient navigation in breast cancer: a systematic review. *Cancer Nursing, 33*(2), 127–140.

SAMHSA. (2014). *SAMHSA's concept of trauma and guidance for a trauma-informed approach.* Rockville, MD: Substance Abuse and Mental Health Services Administration. (14-4884).

SAMHSA. (2015a). *A guide to GPRA data collection using trauma-informed interviewing skills.* Washington, DC: Substance Abuse and Mental Health Services Administration.

SAMHSA. (2015b). *Trauma-informed care in behavioral health servcies: Quick guide for clinicans*. Rockville, MD: Substance Abuse and Mental Health Services Administration.

Scheeringa, M. (2009). Posttraumatic stress disorder. In C. Zeanah (Ed.), *Handbook of infant mental health*. (3rd ed., pp. 345–361). New York, NY: Guilford.

Sciolla, A. (2017). An overview of trauma-informed care. In K. Eckstrand & J. Potter (Eds.), *Trauma, resilience, and health promotion in LGBT patients*. New York, NY: Springer.

Shah, C., & Reeves, A. (2015). The aboriginal cultural safety initiative: an innovative health sciences curriculum in Ontario colleges and universities. *International Journal of Indigenous Health, 10*(2), 117–131.

Shern, D., Blanch, A., & Steverman, S. (2016). Toxic stress, behavioral health, and the next major era in public health. *American Journal of Orthopsychiatry, 86*(2), 109.

Shimmin, C., Wittmeier, K., Lavoie, J., Wicklund, E., & Sibley, K. (2017). Moving towards a more inclusive patient and public involvement in health research paradigm: the incorporation of a trauma-informed intersectional analysis. *BMC Health Services Research, 17*, 539. https://doi.org/10.1186/s12913-017-2463-1.

Siqveland, J., Ruud, T., & Hauff, E. (2017). Post-traumatic stress disorder moderates the relationship between trauma exposure and chronic pain. *European Journal of Psychotraumatology, 8*(1), 1–9. https://doi.org/10.1080/20008198.2017.1375337.

Smith, R., Dobbins, S., Evans, A., Balhotra, K., & Dicker, R. (2013). Hospital-based violence intervention: risk reduction resources that are essential for success. *Journal of Trauma and Acute Care Surgery, 74*(4), 976–982. https://doi.org/10.1097/TA.0b013e31828586c9.

Sorenson, S. (2002). Preventing traumatic stress: public health approaches. *Journal of Traumatic Stress, 15*(1), 3–7.

Speck, V., Schlereth, T., Birklein, F., & Maihofner, C. (2017). Increased prevalence of posttraumatic stress disorder in CRPS. *European Journal of Pain, 21*(3), 466–473. https://doi.org/10.1002/ejp.940.

Sperlich, M., Seng, J., Li, Y., Taylor, J., & Bradbury-Jones, C. (2017). Integrating trauma-informed care into maternity care practice: conceptual and practical issues. *Journal of Midwifery & Women's Health, 62*(6), 661–672. https://doi.org/10.1111/jmwh.12674.

Stylianou, A., & Ebright, E. (2018). Providing coordinated, immediate, trauma-focused, and interdisciplinary responses to children exposed to severe partner violence: assessing feasibility of a collaborative model. *Journal of Interpersonal Violence*, 1–27. https://doi.org/10.1177/0886260518769359.

The National Child Traumatic Stress Network. (2018). *Fact sheet—Creating trauma-informed systems*. Retrieved Viewed November 26, 2018, from https://www.nctsn.org/trauma-informed-care/creating-trauma-informed-systems.

van der Kolk, B. (2014). *The body keeps score: Brain, mind, and body in the healing of trauma*. New York: Penguin Books.

Vickers, M., & Wells, N. (2017). Nothing about us without us. *Academic Pediatrics, 17*(7S), S20–S21.

Vu, C., Rothman, E., Kistin, C., Barton, K., Bulman, B., Budzak-Garza, A., … Bair-Merritt, M. (2017). Adapting the patient-centered medical home to address psychosocial adversity: results of qualitative study. *Academic Pediatrics, 17*(7S), S115–S122.

Walkley, M., & Cox, T. (2013). Building trauma-informed schools and communities. *Children & Schools, 35*(2), 123–126. https://doi.org/10.1093/cs/cdt007.

Ward-Lasher, A., Messing, J., & Stein-Seroussi, J. (2017). Implementation of trauma-informed care in a housing first program for survivors of intimate partner violence: a case study. *Advances in Social Work, 18*(1), 202–216. https://doi.org/10.18060/21313.

Wells, K., Valverde, P., Ustjanauskas, A., Calhoun, E., & Risendal, B. (2018). What are patient navigators doing, for whom, and where? A national survey evaluating the types of services provided by patient navigators. *Patient Education and Counselling, 101*(2), 285–294. https://doi.org/10.1016/j.pec.2017.08.017.

Wheeler, K. (2018). A call for trauma competencies in nursing education. *Journal of the American Psychiatric Nurses Association*, *24*(1), 20–22. https://doi.org/10.1177/1078390317745080.

Wilson, J., Fauci, J., & Goodman, L. (2015). Bringing trauma-informed practice to domestic violence programs: a qualitative analysis of current approaches. *American Journal of Orthopsychiatry*, *85*(6), 586–599. https://doi.org/10.1037/ort0000098.

Wilson, C., Pence, D., & Conradi, L. (2013). Trauma-informed care. In *Encyclopedia of Social Work*. New York, NY: NASW Press and Oxford University Press.

Further reading

Brewin, C. (2005). Systematic review of screening instrument for adults at risk of PTSD. *Journal of Traumatic Stress*, *18*(1), 53–62. https://doi.org/10.1037/spq0000244.

Dube, S. (2018). Continuing conversations about adverse childhood experiences (ACEs) screening: a public health perspective. *Child Abuse & Neglect*, *85*, 180–184. https://doi.org/10.1016/j.chiabu.2018.03.007.

Eklund, K., Rossen, E., Koriakin, T., Chafouleas, S., & Resnick, C. (2018). A systematic review of screening measures for children and adolescents. *School Psychology Quarterly*, *33*(1), 30–43. https://doi.org/10.1037/spq0000244.

Fallot, R., & Harris, M. (2006). A trauma-informed approach to screening and assessment. *New Directions for Student Leadership*, *2001*(89), 23–31. https://doi.org/10.1002/yd.23320018904.

Finkelhor, D. (2018). Screening for adverse childhood experiences (ACEs): cautions and suggestions. *Child Abuse & Neglect*, *85*, 174–179. https://doi.org/10.1016/j.chiabu.2017.07.016.

Murphy, A., Steele, H., Steele, M., Allman, B., Kastner, T., & Dube, S. (2016). The clinical Adverse Childhood Experiences (ACEs) questionnaire: implications for trauma-informed behavioral healthcare. In R. Briggs (Ed.), *Integrated early childhood behavioral health in primary care* (pp. 7–16). Cham: Spinger.

CHAPTER

16

Safe, stable, nurturing environments for children☆

Melissa T. Merrick, Katie A. Ports, Angie S. Guinn, Derek C. Ford

Division of Violence Prevention, National Center for Injury Prevention and Control, Centers for Disease Control and Prevention, Atlanta, GA, United States

Introduction

Children thrive when their relationships and environments are consistently safe, stable, and nurturing (Mercy & Saul, 2009). Such positive experiences are associated with optimal brain development and developing biological systems, including the nervous, endocrine, and immune systems. While some experiences of adversity are normal and even essential components of human development, exposure to frequent, severe, and/or prolonged adversity can result in *toxic* stress, which can disrupt healthy brain development and function, as well as the function of other biological systems, increasing the risk for cognitive impairment, unhealthy coping behaviors, and disease across the life span. When toxic stress occurs continually, or is triggered by multiple sources, it can have a cumulative impact on an individual's physical and mental health across the life course (Shonkoff, 2016). Indeed, childhood adversity can increase physical and mental health problems, engagement in risky health behaviors, limited life opportunities, and early death by almost 20 years (Brown et al., 2009; Felitti et al., 1998; Font & Maguire-Jack, 2016; Gilbert et al., 2015; Merrick et al., 2017; Metzler, Merrick, Klevens, Ports, & Ford, 2017; Shonkoff, 2016).

☆The findings and conclusions in this report are those of the authors and do not necessarily represent the official position of the Center for Disease Control and Prevention.

https://doi.org/10.1016/B978-0-12-816065-7.00016-1

Much of the research related to the impact of childhood adversity on health and well-being focuses almost exclusively on relational risk and protective factors (Shonkoff et al., 2012). While children learn and grow in the context of their relationships, the conditions within which these relationships occur can confer additional risk or protection. From a public health perspective, then, preventing early adversity before it begins by promoting safe, stable, nurturing relationships *and* environments is strategic in order to achieve multiple health, well-being, and productivity goals across generations [Centers for Disease Control and Prevention (CDC), 2010]. Further, the assurance of the conditions in which people can be healthy and thrive is a foundational principle of public health (Institute of Medicine, 1988).

To assure the conditions that children need to thrive, and that prevent many early adversities like child abuse and neglect from occurring in the first place, comprehensive approaches that minimize risk factors and promote protective factors at all levels of the social ecology are critically important. That is, strategies that address individual- and relational-level risk and protective factors must be complemented by community- and societal-level strategies to achieve broad public health impact (Fortson, Klevens, Merrick, Gilbert, & Alexander, 2016; Frieden, 2010).

The CDC's *Essentials for Childhood* framework proposes four goal areas that communities and organizations can consider when implementing comprehensive approaches to prevent child abuse and neglect, among other childhood adversities (CDC, 2014). These areas include: (1) raising awareness and commitment to promote safe, stable, nurturing relationships and environments and prevent child maltreatment, (2) using data to inform actions, (3) creating the context for healthy children and families through norms change and programs, and (4) creating the context for healthy children and families through policies. Goal 1 suggests adopting the vision of assuring, safe, stable, nurturing relationships and environments to protect children from maltreatment and to share and foster this unified vision by partnering with a diverse set of stakeholders across multiple sectors within the community. Goal 2 requires communities to take stock of existing data and to identify and fill gaps within those data so that they can be used to identify targets for prevention and to evaluate progress toward eliminating child maltreatment. Goal 3 encourages communities to promote positive community norms, such as the recognition by individuals within the community of the benefits of evidence-based parenting and caregiving programs and creating a shared responsibility for the success and well-being of all children. Lastly, goal 4 highlights the importance of thoroughly evaluating and implementing policy to provide the necessary supports for children and families to thrive. Implementation of activities in each of the four goal areas is more likely to assure the conditions within which children can access safe, stable, nurturing relationships and environments.

CDC's child abuse and neglect technical package

While *Essentials for Childhood* provides a general implementation framework to guide communities and organizations in their efforts to reduce childhood adversity and strengthen families, it does not detail specific evidence-based strategies shown to reduce and prevent adverse childhood experiences (ACEs) like child abuse and neglect. However, the CDC's Division of Violence Prevention created a suite of technical packages, collections of the best-available evidence for prevention strategies across five violence topics that can negatively impact children (i.e., child abuse and neglect, intimate partner violence, sexual violence, youth violence, and suicide) (Basile et al., 2016; David-Ferdon et al., 2016; Fortson et al., 2016; Niolon et al., 2017; Stone et al., 2017). These technical packages provide a compilation of strategies that can inform action to prevent ACEs across the social ecology. Since child abuse and neglect is a type of childhood adversity that can have the most profound impact on child health and wellbeing, and because it typically precedes the other violence and victimization types that can impact children and represents a risk factor for the other violence types (Wilkins, Tsao, Hertz, Davis, & Klevens, 2014), what follows in this chapter is a description of the five strategies that have been identified for preventing child abuse and neglect in the US. These evidence-based strategies are prioritized based on their potential for maximal population level impacts (see Table 1). Each strategy is independently important, but is intended to be part of

TABLE 1 Strategies for Preventing Child Abuse and Neglect in the United States

Strategy	Approach	Description
Strategy 1: Strengthen economic supports for families	Strengthening household financial security	Allows parents to satisfy their children's basic needs (e.g., food, shelter, medical care) and provide childcare appropriate to the child's age and level of development
	Family-friendly work policies	Allows parents to improve the balance between work and family
Strategy 2: Change social norms to support parents and positive parenting	Public engagement and education campaigns	Uses communication strategies (e.g., framing and messaging or social marketing), communication channels (e.g., mass or social media), and community-based efforts (e.g., town hall meetings, neighborhood screenings and discussions) to support parents
	Legislative approaches to reduce corporal punishment	Establishes norms around safe, more effective discipline strategies

Continued

TABLE 1 Strategies for Preventing Child Abuse and Neglect in the United States—cont'd

Strategy	Approach	Description
Strategy 3: Provide quality care and education early in life	Preschool enrichment with family engagement	Ensures the provision of high-quality early education and care to economically disadvantaged children; also ensures support and educational opportunities for parents
	Improved quality of child care through licensing and accreditation	Ensures that children's daily experiences are positive and supportive
Strategy 4: Enhance parenting skills to promote healthy child development	Early childhood home visitation	Uses a home setting to provide information, caregiver support, and training about child health, development, and care to families
	Parenting skill and family relationship approaches	Provides parents and caregivers with support and teaches behavior management and positive parenting skills
Strategy 5: Intervene to lessen harms and prevent future risk	Enhanced primary care	Allows for the identification and treatment of problems (e.g., parental depression, intimate partner violence, substance abuse) that serve as risk factors for child abuse and neglect
	Behavioral parent training programs	Allows parents to learn specific skills to build a safe, stable, nurturing relationship with their children
	Treatment to lessen harms of abuse and neglect exposure	Mitigates the health consequences of abuse and neglect exposure and decreases the likelihood of intergenerational transmission of abuse
	Treatment to prevent problem behavior and later involvement in violence	Provides support and treatment for youth in their social networks as a means to address current problems and prevent future violence

Based on Fortson, B. L., Klevens, J., Merrick, M. T., Gilbert, L. K., & Alexander, S. P. (2016). Preventing child abuse and neglect: A technical package for policy, norm, and programmatic activities. Atlanta, GA: Centers for Disease Control and Prevention. Retrieved from https://www.cdc.gov/violenceprevention/pdf/can-prevention-technical-package.pdf.

a comprehensive prevention portfolio that maximizes the potential for impact at a population level. The strategies focus on different levels of the social ecology; but, all are intended to work together and reinforce each other to assure the conditions that prevent children's exposure to adversity and violence. The implementation of each of the strategies requires collaboration across multiple sectors (e.g., public health, healthcare, social services, justice, education), as no one entity has the capacity orexpertise to implement every strategy (Fortson et al., 2016).

Strategy 1: Strengthen economic supports for families

Parental stress is a key, repeatedly documented risk factor for child abuse and neglect (Rodriguez & Green, 1997). As such, one strategy for preventing child abuse and neglect is to strengthen economic supports for families, thereby relieving some of the stress associated with not being able to afford things that satisfy families' basic needs (Fortson et al., 2016). Further, the socioeconomic conditions within which children live and develop can influence health and life outcomes, just as these conditions can and do influence how parents interact with their children (Doepke & Zilibotti, 2017; Metzler et al., 2017). There are two broad approaches that can improve economic conditions for families—policies that strengthen household financial security (e.g., tax credits, nutrition assistance programs) and family-friendly work policies (e.g., livable wages, paid leave). Thus, by strengthening household financial security and supporting family-friendly work policies, parental financial strain can be minimized. Research has demonstrated that a severe form of child physical abuse (i.e., abusive head trauma) actually decreases when certain policies, such as tax credits and paid leave, are provided to families (Klevens et al., 2017; Klevens, Luo, Xu, Peterson, & Latzman, 2016). Also, the Earned Income Tax Credit (EITC), a refundable tax credit for low-to-moderate income working individuals and families with children, in particular, has been associated with reductions in infant mortality, maternal stress, and mental health problems (Klevens et al., 2017). As maternal depression is another well-documented risk factor for child physical abuse and neglect, EITC has the potential to prevent child abuse and neglect long term. When parents are able to afford and address financial necessities (e.g., through the use of EITC, other tax credits, and child support payments to the custodial parent), provide safe and developmentally appropriate, high-quality child care (e.g., through subsidized child care), and provide opportunities to balance work and family life (e.g., through paid leave and livable wages), children are more likely to thrive (Cancian, Yang, & Slack, 2013; Chatterji & Markowitz, 2005; Forget, 2011; Gibson-Davis & Foster, 2006; Klein, 2011; Klevens, Barnett, Florence, & Moore, 2015; Lee & Mackey-Bilaver, 2007; Pressman, 2011; Schnitzer & Ewigman, 2005; Tiehen, Jolliffe,

& Gunderson, 2012). For example, policies that include paid leave upon the birth or adoption of a child for new parents may minimize parental stress and fear about losing their jobs and may prevent parents from returning to work quickly simply because they cannot afford to stay home. By their nature, such policies allow parents to focus on bonding with and nurturing their child. Thus, several risk factors (e.g., parental depression and parental stress) are potentially mitigated when strategies are implemented to strengthen economic supports for families (Aumann & Galinsky, 2009; Cancian & Meyer, 2014; Gordon, Usdansky, Wang, & Gluzman, 2011; Ludwig et al., 2012; Milligan & Stabile, 2011; Morrissey & Warner, 2007; Sanbonmatsu et al., 2012). Family-friendly workplace policies also benefit employers in the form of increased productivity, improved employee retention, and lower absenteeism. In other words, family-friendly workplace policies that prevent early adversity also make good economic and business sense (CDC, 2018).

Strategy 2: Change social norms to support parents and positive parenting

A second strategy that aims to prevent early adversity, including child abuse and neglect, focuses on changing how we think and talk about the topic and how we, as a society, can best support all parents and promote positive parenting techniques. In the US, there is a common belief that what happens in families stays in families (i.e., the family bubble) and others outside of the family are not to interfere (Aubrun & Grady, 2003; O'Neil, 2009). We also tend to blame individuals, parents, and families for their own experiences of violence and victimization when, in reality, we all have a role to play in preventing child abuse and neglect, as children thrive when those around them are also thriving (Carrell & Hoekstra, 2010; CDC, 2014; Kendall-Taylor, Simon, & Volmert, 2014). Public engagement and education campaigns have demonstrated some success in changing norms, reframing how we think and talk about child abuse and neglect, spanking, and harsh discipline techniques, and who is responsible for preventing them (Henley, Donovan, & Moorhead, 1998; Kendall-Taylor et al., 2014; Stannard, Hall, & Young, 1998). However, despite decades of research that finds no evidence of positive impact on child development from spanking (Afifi et al., 2017; Gershoff & Grogan-Kaylor, 2016), 60% of parents in the US think, "it is sometimes necessary to discipline a child with a good hard spanking" (ChildTrends, 2015). At present, 53 countries have bans on corporal punishment (i.e., spanking); however, it is still permissible in much of American culture (Global Initiative to End All Corporal Punishment of Children, 2018) and 19 states still allow physical discipline in schools (Gershoff & Font, 2016). The use of harsh physical discipline strategies remains high, in part, because many parents lack mastery or knowledge of alternative, positive parenting skills and techniques (Knox, 2010; Patton, 2017). While behavioral parent training programs may be helpful for parents in addressing some challenging child behaviors (see Strategy 4 below), changing our narrative about parenting and, subsequently, social norms might lead to even greater impacts, because misperceptions about parental responsibility would be addressed to highlight the fact that responsibility for child wellbeing in general resides with *all* adults (CDC, 2014; Daro & Dodge, 2009). Legislative approaches to reduce corporal punishment have been used in other countries, and over time have resulted in changes in norms about the acceptability of corporal punishment and the availability of more developmentally nurturing and effective behavior management techniques (i.e., positive parenting) (Bussmann, Erthal, & Schroth, 2011).

Strategy 3: Provide quality care and education early in life

Assuring optimal learning environments for young children through quality care and education is the third strategy for preventing child abuse and neglect (Fortson et al., 2016). While much of the research on toxic stress and brain development finds that early adversity is associated with physical differences in brain structure (Shonkoff, 2016) and development (Shonkoff et al., 2012), promoting protective environmental contexts such as quality care and education can help to mitigate these impacts (Fortson et al., 2016). For example, preschool enrichment with family engagement provides a supportive early learning environment wherein there is an opportunity to reverse some of the harm conferred by disadvantage, as these programs can enhance parenting practices and attitudes as well as family involvement in children's education (Reynolds & Robertson, 2003). Research on Child Parent Center and Early Head Start Centers has found associations between participation in these programs and high school completion, lower rates of juvenile and violent arrests, lower rates of grade retention and special education services, and decreases in rates of documented child abuse (Green et al., 2014; Love et al., 2005; Reynolds, Temple, Robertson, & Mann, 2001). A randomized control trial found that parents of children enrolled in Early Head Start compared to children who were not enrolled in Early Head Start were more emotionally supportive, provided more language and learning stimulation, and read to their children more (Green et al., 2014). Quality child care is also important for healthy child development, particularly for children from at-risk backgrounds (Peisner-Feinberg et al., 2001; Pluess & Belsky, 2009; Watamura, Phillips, Morrissey, McCartney, & Bub, 2011). Quality child care is associated with positive social and cognitive development in children, which contributes to better academic achievement and less parental stress and conflict (Mersky, Topitzes, & Reynolds, 2011).

Strategy 4: Enhance parenting skills to promote healthy child development

Much of the research in preventing childhood adversity has focused on parenting behavior. The fourth strategy for preventing child abuse and neglect, thus, capitalizes on this robust evidence base to focus on enhancing positive parenting skills to promote healthy child development (Fortson et al., 2016). Early childhood home visitation (e.g., Nurse Family Partnership) and parenting skill and family relationship approaches (e.g., Incredible Years, SafeCare) provide parents and caregivers with support and teach positive parenting skills to build strong foundations of safe, stable, nurturing relationships and environments and protect children and youth from multiple forms of violence and associated risks (e.g., substance abuse, sexually transmitted diseases, teen pregnancy; Kaminski, Valle, Filene, & Boyle, 2008; Lundahl, Risser, & Lovejoy, 2006; Taylor & Biglan, 1998). These programs have been associated with positive outcomes for children and families, including reductions in child abuse and neglect perpetration, reductions in risk factors for child abuse and neglect (e.g., child behavior problems), and improvements in parenting-related behaviors (e.g., nurturing behaviors, child behavior management; Carta, Lefever, Bigelow, Borkowski, & Warren, 2013; Dodge et al., 2014; Knox, Burkhart, & Hunter, 2011; Olds et al., 1997; Portwood, Lambert, Abrams, & Nelson, 2011; Webster-Stratton, Reid, & Hammond, 2001).

Strategy 5: Intervene to lessen harms and prevent future risk

Intervening to lessen harms and prevent future risks is of paramount importance given that between 50 and 90% of children who experience child abuse and neglect never receive any intervention or treatment (Leeb, Lewis, & Zolotor, 2011). Given the vast short-term and life-long effects of child abuse and neglect on physical and mental health, health risk behaviors, and life opportunity, mitigating these negative health effects is critically important to assure safe, stable, nurturing relationships and environments for future generations. In other words, trauma-informed treatments can be primary prevention agents for the next generation. Some approaches are geared toward high-risk populations to prevent child abuse and neglect (e.g., enhanced primary care with the Safe Environments for Every Kid program), whereas other approaches seek to support families in which abuse has already occurred, such as Parent-Child Interaction Therapy, SafeCare, or The Incredible Years (Chaffin et al., 2004; Chaffin, Funderburk, Bard, Valle, & Gurwitch, 2011; Dubowitz, Feigelman, Lane, & Kim, 2009; Dubowitz, Lane, Semiatin, & Magder, 2012; Gershater-Molko, Lutzker, & Wesch, 2002; Linares, Montalto, Li, & Oza, 2006; Silovsky et al., 2011; Webster-Stratton & Reid, 2010). Collectively, these programs are associated with preventing recidivism for abuse and neglect in families with substantiated cases of maltreatment, and in reducing child abuse and neglect risk factors in high-risk families (e.g., those who use harsh/punitive parenting practices) (Chaffin et al., 2004, 2011; Hurlburt, Nguyen, Reid, Webster-Stratton, & Zhang, 2013; Letarte, Normandeau, & Allard, 2010; Silovsky et al., 2011). Also, these programs have been found to result in fewer occurrences of physical assaults and decreased maternal psychological aggression, among other positive outcomes (Dubowitz et al., 2009, 2012).

Exposure to childhood adversity such as child abuse and neglect has been found to increase risk of a host of negative outcomes across the lifespan and even into future generations, which highlights the necessity of interventions, which may lessen the impact that these events have on children when they occur (Matta Oshima, Jonson-Reid, & Seay, 2014; Milaniak & Widom, 2015; Widom & Wilson, 2015). Trauma-focused cognitive behavioral therapy is one evidence-based approach that has been associated with both short- and longer-term reductions in posttraumatic stress disorder symptoms and short-term improvements in symptoms of depression, and behavior problems (Cary & McMillen, 2012) in young people. Other programs, such as Multisystemic Therapy, have also been used to address behavioral issues (e.g., inappropriate parent-child interactions and parenting behaviors) and psychological symptoms for children and caregivers (Brunk, Henggeler, & Whelan, 1987; Carpentier, Silovsky, & Chaffin, 2006; Schaeffer, Swenson, Tuerk, & Henggeler, 2013; Swenson, Schaeffer, Henggeler, Faldowski, & Mayhew, 2010).

WHO's *INSPIRE* technical package

While the aforementioned strategies are based on the best available evidence for preventing child abuse and neglect in the US, the World Health Organization (WHO) partnered with experts from a number of global agencies, including the CDC, as well as with partners across sectors that touch children and families, to identify seven strategies for preventing violence against children globally (WHO, 2016) (see Table 2). The *INSPIRE* technical package focuses on strategies to prevent all forms of violence against children. Like its US counterpart, the strategies are most effective when implemented as part of a comprehensive prevention plan that includes multiple sectors working together to fulfill a common goal—to prevent and respond to violence against children. Each of the seven strategies is represented by the *INSPIRE* acronym (WHO, 2016). The strategies focus on the *I*mplementation and enforcement of laws, *N*orms and values, *S*afe environments, *P*arent and caregiver support, *I*ncome and economic strengthening, *R*esponse and support services, and *E*ducation and life

TABLE 2 Strategies for Preventing Violence Against Children Globally

Strategy	Approach	Objective
Implementation and enforcement of laws	Laws banning violent punishment of children by parents, teachers, or other caregivers Laws criminalizing sexual abuse and exploitation of children Laws that prevent alcohol misuse Laws limiting youth access to firearms and other weapons	Protect children from all forms of violence and limit youth access to and misuse of alcohol, firearms, and other weapons
Norms and values	Changing adherence to restrictive and harmful gender and social norms Community mobilization programs Bystander interventions	Strengthen norms and values that support nonviolent, respectful, nurturing, positive, and gender-equitable relationships
Safe environments	Reducing violence by addressing "hotspots" Interrupting the spread of violence Improving the built environment	Create and sustain safe streets and other environments where children spend time
Parent and caregiver support	Delivered through home visits Delivered in groups in community settings Delivered through comprehensive programs	Reduce harsh parenting practices and support positive parent-child relationships
Income and economic strengthening	Cash transfers Group saving and loans combined with gender equity training Microfinance combined with gender norm training	Improve families' economic security and stability
Response and support services	Counseling and therapeutic approaches Screening combined with interventions Treatment programs for juvenile offenders in the criminal justice system Foster-care interventions involving social welfare services	Improve access to quality support services (i.e., health, social welfare, and criminal justice)

TABLE 2 Strategies for Preventing Violence Against Children Globally—cont'd

Strategy	Approach	Objective
Education and life skills	Increase enrolment in preschool, primary and secondary schools Establish a safe and enabling school environment Improve children's knowledge about sexual abuse and how to protect themselves against it Life and social skills training Adolescent intimate partner violence prevention programs	Increase access to effective, gender-equitable education and social-emotional learning and life skills training and ensure safe, enabling school environments

Based on World Health Organization. (2016). INSPIRE: Seven strategies for ending violence against children. Geneva: World Health Organization. Retrieved from: http://apps.who.int/iris/bitstream/10665/207717/1/9789241565356-eng.pdf?ua=1.

skills. In sum, *INSPIRE* focuses on assuring conditions and environments, broadly defined, that prevent violence against children. In particular, the recommended strategies reflect the importance of positive parenting, economic security and stability, access to quality response and intervention services, and gender-equitable education and school environments (WHO, 2016).

Directions for future research

Despite the existing evidence demonstrating the positive impact of prevention strategies on the health and wellbeing of children and their families, more work is needed to understand the impact of comprehensive prevention strategies that work across the social ecology. Evaluations of prevention strategies often isolate the unique impact of one strategy as opposed to a collection of strategies that target individual, relationship, community, and societal change. In addition, adaptations for evidence-based strategies among minority populations are needed. For example, we know less about the impact of prevention strategies and potential unintended consequences among sexual and gender minorities, immigrants, people of color, and so forth. An important first step in ensuring that policies support children and families is to identify and assess (within the community) which policies have the potential to positively impact the lives of children and families and make individuals' default decisions healthy ones. Consideration of how policies are implemented (e.g., the coverage, cost, and eligibility requirements) at the appropriate community level is critical in understanding potential impacts of a policy on children and families. Public health and other research fields are in a unique position to provide decision makers and community leaders with information on the benefits of evidence-based strategies and rigorous evaluation to ensure that any activities being implemented, including policies, are providing optimal benefits and worth any investments being made (Kendall-Taylor et al., 2014). For example, health impact assessments and paid leave analyses (e.g., cost-benefit analysis of worker retention and productivity) may be helpful in understanding potential gains and barriers to the provision of family-friendly work supports at the national and local level.

Implications for policy and practice

The technical packages discussed for preventing child abuse and neglect and violence against children are based on the best available evidence (Fortson et al., 2016; WHO, 2016). While everyone has a role to play in promoting safe, stable, nurturing relationships and environment, several of the strategies identified require leadership from various sectors. For example, public health agencies are well positioned to convene leadership and resources for implementation efforts; however, for other strategies, leadership and commitment from other sectors such as business/labor, government, social services, healthcare, education, and justice are most critical to implementation (Fortson et al., 2016; WHO, 2016). Moreover, the sectors that are in the best position to enact and lead implementation of the various strategies and approaches will likely depend on whether implementation is occurring in the US or globally. In most cases, implementation is best when multiple sectors intentionally and strategically collaborate in implementation efforts. For example, although public health will not be directly responsible for changes in policy, public health agencies may provide government leaders with data that can provide support for or against certain policy-level changes. In general, implementation of laws and policies will require commitment and/or support of governments to enact changes at the local, state, or federal/country levels. Organizational policy changes (when occurring without a broader governmental mandate) require the engagement of business and labor. Public health agencies are poised to lead norms change activities focused on supporting parents and positive parenting, whereas commitment and/or support of the government is necessary for legislative approaches to reduce corporal punishment and to improve the quality of child care through licensing and accreditation (Fortson et al., 2016). Everyone can help educate community, state, and national leaders on what policies and programs work to prevent ACEs. Increasing awareness among stakeholders—including policy makers, employers, and the public—about the relationship between family-friendly policies and decreased risk for multiple forms of violence, as well as health and productivity, may be helpful in encouraging buy-in and support for policies that positively impact children and families.

Data can be particularly powerful when highlighting social issues, including ACEs. Data allow communities to identify population needs, gaps in services, high-risk groups, and protective factors, to name a few. Data also help communities understand the size and nature of the problem, how to best direct prevention resources, and monitor the impact of prevention strategies; thus, communities may want to ensure partnerships include those who can assist in gathering and synthesizing data. Once partnerships are established, communities will need to examine what data already exist in the community and identify steps to fill critical gaps in data. Most communities have existing systems that include vital statistics, as well as health, criminal justice, child protection and welfare, educational, and basic demographic (e.g., number of children living in poverty, number of parents unemployed) data. Data from other community/national level surveys or surveillance systems also may be available and customizable to the community. Partnerships may be used to develop new data systems and fill critical data gaps. Once data have been collected, they can be used to support activities that are part of a comprehensive prevention portfolio (CDC, 2014).

Strategies at the outer levels of the social ecology, such as policies and norms change strategies, will likely have greater population impact in preventing child abuse and neglect than programs focused on individuals or families (Fortson et al., 2016). It is more difficult for individual- or family-level prevention and intervention programs to have population impact due to the substantial cost of scaling up to reach a sufficient number of individuals and families. Finally, the costs associated with implementation of programs to prevent child abuse and neglect are often a barrier to implementation. Start-up costs for programs often include the costs of materials, as well as training staff. Agencies with high staff turnover may have to provide training several times a year to ensure staff are trained appropriately in implementing services. To this end, it will also likely be helpful to consider the type and number of policies or programs that are introduced at any one time.

Conclusion

ACEs are a serious public health issue with far-reaching consequences; however, we can prevent early adversity. The policies, social norms, and programmatic strategies and approaches highlighted in this chapter are intended to help guide the creation of neighborhoods and communities where every child has safe, stable, nurturing relationships and environments, and, ultimately, a world where every child can thrive. Together we can assure that all children reach their full health and life potential.

References

Afifi, T., Ford, D., Gershoff, L., Merrick, M. T., Grogan-Kaylor, A., Ports, K. A., ... Bennett, R. P. (2017). Spanking and adult mental health impairment: the case for the designation of spanking as an adverse childhood experience. *Child Abuse and Neglect*, *71*, 24–31.

Aubrun, A., & Grady, J. (2003). *Two cognitive obstacles to preventing child abuse: The "other-mind" mistake and the "family bubble"*. Washington, DC: FrameWorks Institute. Retrieved from http://frameworksinstitute.org/toolkits/canp/resources/pdf/TwoCognitiveObstacles.pdf.

Aumann, K., & Galinsky, E. (2009). *The state of health in the American workforce: Does having an effective workplace matter*. New York, NY: Families and Work Institute. Retrieved from http://familiesandwork.org/downloads/StateofHealthinAmericanWorkforce.pdf.

Basile, K. C., DeGue, S., Jones, K., Freire, K., Dills, J., Smith, S. G., & Raiford, J. L. (2016). *STOP SV: A technical package to prevent sexual violence*. Atlanta, GA: Centers for Disease Control and Prevention. Retrieved from https://www.cdc.gov/violenceprevention/pdf/sv-prevention-technical-package.pdf.

Brown, D. W., Anda, R. F., Tiemeier, H., Felitti, V. J., Edwards, V., Croft, J. B., & Giles, W. H. (2009). Adverse childhood experiences and the risk of premature mortality. *American Journal of Preventive Medicine*, *37*(5), 389–396.

Brunk, M. A., Henggeler, S. W., & Whelan, J. P. (1987). Comparison of multisystemic therapy and parent training in the brief treatment of child abuse and neglect. *Journal of Consulting and Clinical Psychology*, *55*(2), 171.

Bussmann, K. D., Erthal, C., & Schroth, A. (2011). *Effects of banning corporal punishment in Europe—a five-nation comparison*. In E. D. Joan & B. S. Anne (Eds.), *Global pathways to abolishing physical punishment* (pp. 299–322).

Cancian, M., & Meyer, D. R. (2014). Testing the economic independence hypothesis: the effect of an exogenous increase in child support on subsequent marriage and cohabitation. *Demography*, *51*(3), 857–880.

Cancian, M., Yang, M. Y., & Slack, K. S. (2013). The effect of additional child support income on the risk of child maltreatment. *Social Service Review*, *87*(3), 417–437.

Carpentier, M. Y., Silovsky, J. F., & Chaffin, M. (2006). Randomized trial of treatment for children with sexual behavior problems: ten-year follow-up. *Journal of Consulting and Clinical Psychology*, *74*(3), 482.

Carrell, S. E., & Hoekstra, M. L. (2010). Externalities in the classroom: how children exposed to domestic violence affect everyone's kids. *American Economic Journal: Applied Economics*, *2*(1), 211–228.

Carta, J. J., Lefever, J. B., Bigelow, K., Borkowski, J., & Warren, S. F. (2013). Randomized trial of a cellular phone-enhanced home visitation parenting intervention. *Pediatrics*, *132*(Supplement 2), S167–S173.

Cary, C. E., & McMillen, J. C. (2012). The data behind the dissemination: a systematic review of trauma-focused cognitive behavioral therapy for use with children and youth. *Children and Youth Services Review*, *34*(4), 748–757.

Centers for Disease Control and Prevention. (2010). *Preventing child maltreatment through the promotion of safe, stable, and nurturing relationships between children and caregivers*. Atlanta, GA: Centers for Disease Control and Prevention. Retrieved from http://www.cdc.ov/ViolencePrevention/pdf/CM_Strategic_Direction--Long-a.pdf.

Centers for Disease Control and Prevention. (2014). *Essentials for childhood: Steps to create safe, stable, nurturing relationships and environments*. Atlanta, GA: Centers for Disease Control and Prevention. Retrieved from https://www.cdc.gov/violenceprevention/pdf/essentials_for_childhood_framework.pdf.

Centers for Disease Control and Prevention. (2018). VetoViolence. In *Making the case: Engaging businesses*. Atlanta, GA: Centers for Disease Control and Prevention. Retrieved from https://vetoviolence.cdc.gov/apps/child-abuse-neglect-biz/.

Chaffin, M., Funderburk, B., Bard, D., Valle, L. A., & Gurwitch, R. (2011). A combined motivation and parent–child interaction therapy package reduces child welfare recidivism in a randomized dismantling field trial. *Journal of Consulting and Clinical Psychology*, *79*(1), 84.

Chaffin, M., Silovsky, J. F., Funderburk, B., Valle, L. A., Brestan, E. V., Balachova, T., … Bonner, B. L. (2004). Parent-child interaction therapy with physically abusive parents: efficacy for reducing future abuse reports. *Journal of Consulting and Clinical Psychology*, *72*(3), 500.

Chatterji, P., & Markowitz, S. (2005). Does the length of maternity leave affect maternal health? *Southern Economic Journal*, *72*, 16–41.

ChildTrends. (2015). *Attitudes toward spanking: Indicators of child and youth well-being*. Bethesda, MD: Child Trends Data Bank. Retrieved from https://www.childtrends.org/wp-content/uploads/2015/11/51_Attitudes_Toward_Spanking.pdf.

Daro, D., & Dodge, K. A. (2009). Creating community responsibility for child protection: possibilities and challenges. *The Future of Children*, *19*(2), 67–93.

David-Ferdon, C., Vivolo-Kantor, A. M., Dahlberg, L. L., Marshall, K. J., Rainford, N., & Hall, J. E. (2016). *A comprehensive technical package for the prevention of youth violence and associated risk behaviors*. Atlanta, GA: Centers for Disease Control and Prevention. Retrieved from https://www.cdc.gov/violenceprevention/pdf/yv-technicalpackage.pdf.

Dodge, K. A., Goodman, W. B., Murphy, R. A., O'Donnell, K., Sato, J., & Guptill, S. (2014). Implementation and randomized controlled trial evaluation of universal postnatal nurse home visiting. *American Journal of Public Health*, *104*(S1), S136–S143.

Doepke, M., & Zilibotti, F. (2017). Parenting with style: altruism and paternalism in intergenerational preference transmission. *Econometrica*, *85*(5), 1331–1371.

Dubowitz, H., Feigelman, S., Lane, W., & Kim, J. (2009). Pediatric primary care to help prevent child maltreatment: the safe environment for every kid (SEEK) model. *Pediatrics*, *123*(3), 858–864.

Dubowitz, H., Lane, W. G., Semiatin, J. N., & Magder, L. S. (2012). The SEEK model of pediatric primary care: can child maltreatment be prevented in a low-risk population? *Academic Pediatrics*, *12*(4), 259–268.

Felitti, V. J., Anda, R. F., Nordenberg, D., Williamson, D. F., Spitz, A. M., Edwards, V., & Marks, J. S. (1998). Relationship of childhood abuse and household dysfunction to many of the leading causes of death in adults: the adverse childhood experiences (ACE) study. *American Journal of Preventive Medicine*, *14*(4), 245–258.

Font, S. A., & Maguire-Jack, K. (2016). Pathways from childhood abuse and other adversities to adult health risks: the role of adult socioeconomic conditions. *Child Abuse & Neglect*, *51*, 390–399.

Forget, E. L. (2011). The town with no poverty: the health effects of a Canadian guaranteed annual income field experiment. *Canadian Public Policy*, *37*(3), 283–305.

Fortson, B. L., Klevens, J., Merrick, M. T., Gilbert, L. K., & Alexander, S. P. (2016). *Preventing child abuse and neglect: A technical package for policy, norm, and programmatic activities*. Atlanta, GA: Centers for Disease Control and Prevention. Retrieved from https://www.cdc.gov/violenceprevention/pdf/can-prevention-technical-package.pdf.

Frieden, T. R. (2010). A framework for public health action: the health impact pyramid. *American Journal of Public Health*, *100*(4), 590–595.

Gershater-Molko, R. M., Lutzker, J. R., & Wesch, D. (2002). Using recidivism data to evaluate project safecare: teaching bonding, safety, and health care skills to parents. *Child Maltreatment*, *7*(3), 277–285.

Gershoff, E. T., & Font, S. A. (2016). Corporal punishment in US public schools: prevalence, disparities in use, and status in state and federal policy. *Social Policy Report*, *30*, 1.

Gershoff, E. T., & Grogan-Kaylor, A. (2016). Spanking and child outcomes: old controversies and new meta-analyses. *Journal of Family Psychology, 30*(4), 453.

Gibson-Davis, C. M., & Foster, E. M. (2006). A cautionary tale: using propensity scores to estimate the effect of food stamps on food insecurity. *Social Service Review, 80*(1), 93–126.

Gilbert, L. K., Breiding, M. J., Merrick, M. T., Thompson, W. W., Ford, D. C., Dhingra, S. S., & Parks, S. E. (2015). Childhood adversity and adult chronic disease: an update from ten states and the District of Columbia, 2010. *American Journal of Preventive Medicine, 48*(3), 345–349.

Global Initiative to End All Corporal Punishment of Children London. Retrieved from www.end-corporalpunishment.org(2018).

Gordon, R. A., Usdansky, M. L., Wang, X., & Gluzman, A. (2011). Child care and mothers' mental health: is high-quality care associated with fewer depressive symptoms? *Family Relations, 60*(4), 446–460.

Green, B. L., Ayoub, C., Bartlett, J. D., Von Ende, A., Furrer, C., Chazan-Cohen, R., … Klevens, J. (2014). The effect of early Head Start on child welfare system involvement: a first look at longitudinal child maltreatment outcomes. *Children and Youth Services Review, 42*, 127–135.

Henley, N., Donovan, R. J., & Moorhead, H. (1998). Appealing to positive motivations and emotions in social marketing: example of a positive parenting campaign. *Social Marketing Quarterly, 4*(4), 48–53.

Hurlburt, M. S., Nguyen, K., Reid, J., Webster-Stratton, C., & Zhang, J. (2013). Efficacy of the incredible years group parent program with families in Head Start who self-reported a history of child maltreatment. *Child Abuse & Neglect, 37*(8), 531–543.

Institute of Medicine. (1988). *The future of public health*. Washington, DC: The National Academies Press.https://doi.org/10.17226/1091. Retrieved from.

Kaminski, J. W., Valle, L. A., Filene, J. H., & Boyle, C. L. (2008). A meta-analytic review of components associated with parent training program effectiveness. *Journal of Abnormal Child Psychology, 36*(4), 567–589.

Kendall-Taylor, N., Simon, A., & Volmert, A. (2014). *Taking responsibility for solutions: Using values to reframe child maltreatment in the United Kingdom*. Washington, DC: Frame Works Institute. Retrieved from https://frameworksinstitute.org/assets/files/ECD/nspcc_values.pdf.

Klein, S. (2011). The availability of neighborhood early care and education resources and the maltreatment of young children. *Child Maltreatment, 16*(4), 300–311.

Klevens, J., Barnett, S. B. L., Florence, C., & Moore, D. (2015). Exploring policies for the reduction of child physical abuse and neglect. *Child Abuse & Neglect, 40*, 1–11.

Klevens, J., Luo, F., Xu, L., Peterson, C., & Latzman, N. E. (2016). Paid family leave's effect on hospital admissions for pediatric abusive head trauma. *Injury Prevention, 22*(6), 442–445.

Klevens, J., Schmidt, B., Luo, F., Xu, L., Ports, K. A., & Lee, R. D. (2017). Effect of the earned income tax credit on hospital admissions for pediatric abusive head trauma, 1995-2013. *Public Health Reports, 132*(4), 505–511.

Knox, M. (2010). On hitting children: a review of corporal punishment in the United States. *Journal of Pediatric Health Care, 24*(2), 103–107.

Knox, M. S., Burkhart, K., & Hunter, K. E. (2011). ACT against violence parents raising safe kids program: effects on maltreatment-related parenting behaviors and beliefs. *Journal of Family Issues, 32*(1), 55–74.

Lee, B. J., & Mackey-Bilaver, L. (2007). Effects of WIC and food stamp program participation on child outcomes. *Children and Youth Services Review, 29*(4), 501–517.

Leeb, R. T., Lewis, T., & Zolotor, A. J. (2011). A review of physical and mental health consequences of child abuse and neglect and implications for practice. *American Journal of Lifestyle Medicine, 5*(5), 454–468.

Letarte, M. J., Normandeau, S., & Allard, J. (2010). Effectiveness of a parent training program "Incredible Years" in a child protection service. *Child Abuse & Neglect, 34*(4), 253–261.

Linares, L. O., Montalto, D., Li, M., & Oza, V. S. (2006). A promising parenting intervention in foster care. *Journal of Consulting and Clinical Psychology*, *74*(1), 32.

Love, J. M., Kisker, E. E., Ross, C., Raikes, H., Constantine, J., Boller, K., … Fuligni, A. S. (2005). The effectiveness of early head start for 3-year-old children and their parents: lessons for policy and programs. *Developmental Psychology*, *41*(6), 885.

Ludwig, J., Duncan, G. J., Gennetian, L. A., Katz, L. F., Kessler, R. C., Kling, J. R., & Sanbonmatsu, L. (2012). Neighborhood effects on the long-term well-being of low-income adults. *Science*, *337*(6101), 1505–1510.

Lundahl, B., Risser, H. J., & Lovejoy, M. C. (2006). A meta-analysis of parent training: moderators and follow-up effects. *Clinical Psychology Review*, *26*(1), 86–104.

Matta Oshima, K. M., Jonson-Reid, M., & Seay, K. D. (2014). The influence of childhood sexual abuse on adolescent outcomes: the roles of gender, poverty, and revictimization. *Journal of Child Sexual Abuse*, *23*(4), 367–386.

Mercy, J. A., & Saul, J. (2009). Creating a healthier future through early interventions for children. *JAMA*, *301*(21), 2262–2264.

Merrick, M. T., Ports, K. A., Ford, D. C., Afifi, T. O., Gershoff, E. T., & Grogan-Kaylor, A. (2017). Unpacking the impact of adverse childhood experiences on adult mental health. *Child Abuse & Neglect*, *69*, 10–19.

Mersky, J. P., Topitzes, J. D., & Reynolds, A. J. (2011). Maltreatment prevention through early childhood intervention: a confirmatory evaluation of the Chicago child–parent center preschool program. *Children and Youth Services Review*, *33*(8), 1454–1463.

Metzler, M., Merrick, M. T., Klevens, J., Ports, K. A., & Ford, D. C. (2017). Adverse childhood experiences and life opportunities: shifting the narrative. *Children and Youth Services Review*, *72*, 141–149.

Milaniak, I., & Widom, C. S. (2015). Does child abuse and neglect increase risk for perpetration of violence inside and outside the home? *Psychology of Violence*, *5*(3), 246.

Milligan, K., & Stabile, M. (2011). Do child tax benefits affect the well-being of children? Evidence from Canadian child benefit expansions. *American Economic Journal: Economic Policy*, *3*(3), 175–205.

Morrissey, T. W., & Warner, M. E. (2007). Why early care and education deserves as much attention, or more, than prekindergarten alone. *Applied Developmental Science*, *11*(2), 57–70.

Niolon, P. H., Kearns, M., Dills, J., Rambo, K., Irving, S., Armstead, T., & Gilbert, L. (2017). *Preventing intimate partner violence across the lifespan: A technical package of programs, policies, and practices*. Atlanta, GA: Centers for Disease Control and Prevention. Retrieved from https://www.cdc.gov/violenceprevention/pdf/ipv-technicalpackages.pdf.

Olds, D. L., Eckenrode, J., Henderson, C. R., Kitzman, H., Powers, J., Cole, R., … Luckey, D. (1997). Long-term effects of home visitation on maternal life course and child abuse and neglect: fifteen-year follow-up of a randomized trial. *JAMA*, *278*(8), 637–643.

O'Neil, M. (2009). The family bubble, achievement gap, and development as competition: media frames on youth. *New Directions for Youth Development*, *2009*(124), 39–49.

Patton, S. (2017). *Spare the kids: Why whupping children won't save black America*. Boston: Beacon Press.

Peisner-Feinberg, E. S., Burchinal, M. R., Clifford, R. M., Culkin, M. L., Howes, C., Kagan, S. L., & Yazejian, N. (2001). The relation of preschool child-care quality to children's cognitive and social developmental trajectories through second grade. *Child Development*, *72*(5), 1534–1553.

Pluess, M., & Belsky, J. (2009). Differential susceptibility to rearing experience: the case of childcare. *Journal of Child Psychology and Psychiatry*, *50*(4), 396–404.

Portwood, S. G., Lambert, R. G., Abrams, L. P., & Nelson, E. B. (2011). An evaluation of the adults and children together (ACT) against violence parents raising safe kids program. *The Journal of Primary Prevention*, *32*(3–4), 147.

Pressman, S. (2011). Policies to reduce child poverty: child allowances versus tax exemptions for children. *Journal of Economic Issues*, *45*(2), 323–332.

Reynolds, A. J., & Robertson, D. L. (2003). School-based early intervention and later child maltreatment in the Chicago longitudinal study. *Child Development, 74*(1), 3–26.

Reynolds, A. J., Temple, J. A., Robertson, D. L., & Mann, E. A. (2001). Long-term effects of an early childhood intervention on educational achievement and juvenile arrest: a 15-year follow-up of low-income children in public schools. *JAMA, 285*(18), 2339–2346.

Rodriguez, C. M., & Green, A. J. (1997). Parenting stress and anger expression as predictors of child abuse potential. *Child Abuse & Neglect, 21*(4), 367–377.

Sanbonmatsu, L., Potter, N. A., Adam, E., Duncan, G. J., Katz, L. F., Kessler, R. C., … Gennetian, L. A. (2012). The long-term effects of moving to opportunity on adult health and economic self-sufficiency. *Cityscape, 14*, 109–136.

Schaeffer, C. M., Swenson, C. C., Tuerk, E. H., & Henggeler, S. W. (2013). Comprehensive treatment for co-occurring child maltreatment and parental substance abuse: outcomes from a 24-month pilot study of the MST-building stronger families program. *Child Abuse & Neglect, 37*(8), 596–607.

Schnitzer, P. G., & Ewigman, B. G. (2005). Child deaths resulting from inflicted injuries: household risk factors and perpetrator characteristics. *Pediatrics, 116*(5), e687–e693.

Shonkoff, J. P. (2016). Capitalizing on advances in science to reduce the health consequences of early childhood adversity. *JAMA Pediatrics, 170*(10), 1003–1007.

Shonkoff, J. P., Garner, A. S., Siegel, B. S., Dobbins, M. I., Earls, M. F., McGuinn, L., … Committee on Early Childhood, Adoption, and Dependent Care. (2012). The lifelong effects of early childhood adversity and toxic stress. *Pediatrics, 129*(1), e232–e246.

Silovsky, J. F., Bard, D., Chaffin, M., Hecht, D., Burris, L., Owora, A., … Lutzker, J. (2011). Prevention of child maltreatment in high-risk rural families: a randomized clinical trial with child welfare outcomes. *Children and Youth Services Review, 33*(8), 1435–1444.

Stannard, S., Hall, S., & Young, J. (1998). Social marketing as a tool to stop child abuse. *Social Marketing Quarterly, 4*(4), 64–68.

Stone, D. M., Holland, K. M., Bartholow, B., Crosby, A. E., Davis, S., & Wilkins, N. (2017). *Preventing suicide: A technical package of policies, programs, and practices*. Atlanta, GA: Centers for Disease Control and Prevention. Retrieved from https://www.cdc.gov/violenceprevention/pdf/suicidetechnicalpackage.pdf.

Swenson, C. C., Schaeffer, C. M., Henggeler, S. W., Faldowski, R., & Mayhew, A. M. (2010). Multisystemic therapy for child abuse and neglect: a randomized effectiveness trial. *Journal of Family Psychology, 24*(4), 497.

Taylor, T. K., & Biglan, A. (1998). Behavioral family interventions for improving child-rearing: a review of the literature for clinicians and policy makers. *Clinical Child and Family Psychology Review, 1*(1), 41–60.

Tiehen, L., Jolliffe, D., & Gunderson, C. (2012). *Alleviating poverty in the United States: The critical role of SNAP benefits*. Washington, DC: US Department of Agriculture, Economic Research Service.

Watamura, S. E., Phillips, D. A., Morrissey, T. W., McCartney, K., & Bub, K. (2011). Double jeopardy: poorer social-emotional outcomes for children in the NICHD SECCYD experiencing home and child-care environments that confer risk. *Child Development, 82*(1), 48–65.

Webster-Stratton, C., & Reid, M. (2010). Adapting the incredible years, an evidence-based parenting programme, for families involved in the child welfare system. *Journal of Children's Services, 5*(1), 25–42.

Webster-Stratton, C., Reid, M. J., & Hammond, M. (2001). Preventing conduct problems, promoting social competence: a parent and teacher training partnership in Head Start. *Journal of Clinical Child Psychology, 30*(3), 283–302.

Widom, C. S., & Wilson, H. W. (2015). *Intergenerational transmission of violence*. In *Violence and mental health* (pp. 27–45). Dordrecht: Springer.

Wilkins, N., Tsao, B., Hertz, M., Davis, R., & Klevens, J. (2014). *Connecting the dots: An overview of the links among multiple forms of violence*. Atlanta, GA: Centers for Disease Control and Prevention, Prevention Institute. Oakland, CA.

World Health Organization. (2016). *INSPIRE: Seven strategies for ending violence against children*. Geneva: World Health Organization. Retrieved from http://apps.who.int/iris/bitstream/10665/207717/1/9789241565356-eng.pdf?ua=1.

Further reading

Gershoff, E. T., Lee, S. J., & Durrant, J. E. (2017). Promising intervention strategies to reduce parents' use of physical punishment. *Child Abuse & Neglect*, *71*, 9–23.

Heckman, J. J., & Masterov, D. V. (2007). The productivity argument for investing in young children. *Applied Economic Perspectives and Policy*, *29*(3), 446–493.

Peterson, C., Florence, C., & Klevens, J. (2018). The economic burden of child maltreatment in the United States, 2015. *Child Abuse & Neglect*, *86*, 178–183.

The Heckman Equation. (2017). *Heckman. The economics of human potential*. Retrieved from-https://heckmanequation.org/.

CHAPTER

17

Current knowledge and future directions for the ACEs field

Tracie O. Afifi[a,b], *Gordon J.G. Asmundson*[b]

[a]Departments of Community Health Sciences and Psychiatry, University of Manitoba, Winnipeg, MB, Canada, [b]Department of Psychology, University of Regina, Regina, SK, Canada

Introduction

The adverse childhood experiences (ACEs) field as we know it today initially began with the clinical insights of Dr. Vincent Felitti. He discovered that many of his patients who were dropping out of a weight loss program despite weight loss success had a history of childhood sexual abuse. Dr. Felitti along with Dr. Robert Anda and colleagues, and in collaboration with the Centers for Disease Control and Prevention (CDC) and Kaiser Permanente, began an ambiguous data collection of over 17,000 patients to better understand the links between childhood trauma and various aspects of health. Details of this work can be found in Chapter 1 by Dube and Chapter 2 by Ports, Ford, Merrick, and Guinn. Since the first study published by Felitti and colleagues in 1998, the number of studies published on ACEs has grown exponentially.

What we know with certainty from the current evidence base is that ACEs are associated with a number of poor mental health outcomes (Chapter 4 by Sheffler, Stanley, and Sachs-Ericsson), poor physical health outcomes (Chapter 5 by Vig, Paluszek, and Asmundson), poor sexual health outcomes (Chapter 6 by Wekerle, Hébert, Daigneault, and Fortin-Langelier), continuing violence into adulthood (Chapter 7 by Taillieu, Garces Davila, and Struck), and negative impacts on neural development (Chapter 13 by Sheridan and McLaughlin). As detailed in Chapter 11 by Massetti, Hughes, Bellis, and Mercy, we also know that ACEs are

Adverse Childhood Experiences
https://doi.org/10.1016/B978-0-12-816065-7.00017-3

prevalent and associated with negative outcomes across countries and contexts. Although there have been many advances in our understanding of how ACEs can impact an individual across the lifespan, there are still many gaps in knowledge and lack of innovation in some areas of this field. Five critical areas for future directions to advance understanding of, interventions for, and policies surrounding ACEs include: (1) development and validation of ACEs measurement tools, (2) use of empirical evidence to guide definitions of ACEs, (3) evidence-based methods to assess harms and benefits of ACEs screening, (4) continued development and evaluation of ACEs interventions, and (5) an increase in upstream public health approaches and ACEs prevention. These areas are summarized as follows.

Measurement

A limitation of many studies in the field is how ACEs are assessed and measured in research. Over the last two decades, very little advancement has been made in tools to assess ACEs nor has there been proper validation of ACEs tools that currently exist. Interestingly, when reflecting specifically on the issue of child maltreatment, progress over time has been made to improve how child maltreatment is measured. For example, in some earlier studies, child maltreatment was assessed using very simple subjective questions (e.g., *were you ever psychologically abused, physically abused, or sexually abused?*; Afifi et al., 2007) which, over time, evolved to became more objective and focused on behaviors and actions (e.g., asking if the respondent was pushed, grabbed, slapped, shoved, or hit rather than asking if they were physically abused). As well, researchers invested efforts into developing and validating tools to improve how child maltreatment can be assessed (e.g., Bernstein et al., 2003; Dunne et al., 2009; Finkelhor, Hamby, Ormrod, & Turner, 2005; Straus, 2004; Straus & Mickey, 2012). This evolution in measurement has improved the quality of data and our understanding of child maltreatment. Unfortunately, similar advancement in measurement has not occurred in the ACEs literature and, as such, the way we currently measure ACEs is very similar to how we measured ACEs in the late 1990s.

As noted in Chapter 9 by Holden, Gower, and Chmielewski, improving ACEs instruments using sophisticated methods for development along with proper psychometric analyses is needed and should be encouraged. Important considerations are the severity and chronicity of ACEs, something not currently captured with simple dichotomous yes or no response options to single items. Similarly, the common method of adding up the number of ACEs for an ACEs score may be over simplistic. Individuals who have the same ACEs score may have completely different histories, making the score insufficient with regard to understanding one's needs or potential for identifying the intervention strategy. More work is needed in this area.

Definitions

Related to the importance of how ACEs are assessed, it is equally important to consider what it is we are measuring. That is, we need to consider how ACEs are defined and conceptualized. Despite recent recommendations to use empirical evidence for reconsidering the definition of ACEs (Afifi et al., 2017; Finkelhor, Turner, Shattuck, & Hamby, 2013; Finkelhor, Shattuck, Turner, & Hamby, 2015), and even though there are inconsistencies in what are included as ACEs across studies, many researchers still use the 10 original ACEs from the first studies (Dube et al., 2003; Felitti et al., 1998) to guide current research. Similar to the lack of advancement of ACEs measurement, there has been little change in the definition of ACEs overtime. As noted in Chapter 3 by Afifi, changing definitions and conceptualizations of ACEs is not a simple task and is one that is made more complicated when considering ACEs from a global perspective. However, researchers should be encouraged to think innovatively to advance definitions of ACEs and to do so using empirical evidence that is theoretically informed.

Screening

The push for universal ACEs screening has gained momentum over the past several years. It is nonetheless important to carefully understand what an ACEs screening recommendation actually means. On the surface, ACEs screening may seem logical; indeed, there is no dispute that ACEs are related to numerous negative outcomes that continue across the lifespan. However, any decision about implementation of screening needs to be based on whether screening does more good than harm in terms of health outcomes. Simply identifying exposure to adversities within a clinical context should not be an end in itself. The systematic approach to screening in general, as well as a detailed description of how and why ACEs do not meet recommendations for screening, is provided in Chapter 8 by McLennan, McTavish, and MacMillan. At this time, universal ACEs screening may lead to more harms than benefits and should not be recommended. Substantial work using a systematic approach to address the key principles of screening is needed before a recommendation for universal ACEs screening can be reconsidered. As well, it is important that language not conveniently shift from the term *screening* toward less prescriptive concepts like *evaluation* in order to circumvent the need for developing and assessing a systematic approach for ACEs screening. Notably, Finkelhor (2017) has recommended that rather than invest efforts into ACEs screening tools, it may be better to develop and evaluate programs that prevent child maltreatment. We suggest that there is little value in thinking of ACEs screening as a solution and, consistent with Finkelhor (2017), contend that the solution is effective ACEs preventive and therapeutic intervention.

Intervention

Related to ACEs screening, it is necessary to have evidence-based preventative and therapeutic interventions available for those who may be at risk of ACEs or those who are identified as having ACEs by clinicians, other health care providers, teachers, social workers, and so forth. However, this issue is complicated in that ACEs, as currently conceptualized, include a long list of experiences that are quite diverse (e.g., child sexual abuse, child physical abuse, neglect, parental divorce, parental substance use problems). It is not feasible to develop ACEs prevention strategies or therapeutic interventions that can adequately address all of the diverse experiences that are currently considered as ACEs. This issue may become even more complicated if advances to ACEs definitions are made in a manner that leads to the list becoming longer or even more diverse. There are many child maltreatment interventions that currently exist, including strategies for fostering resilience and growth (Chapter 14 by Oshri, Duprey, Liu, and Gonzalez) and provision of trauma-informed care (Chapter 15 by Piotrowski); but, more work needs to be done to ensure that the interventions that we are investing in are proven to be effective in the populations in which they are implemented. We recommend that any intervention be evidence-based and directly related to specific experiences of the target individual or group.

Upstream public health approaches and prevention

ACEs are recognized as a significant public health issue; yet, more needs to be done to address policies and strategies to prevent ACEs. Chapter 10 by Tonmyr, Lacroix, and Herbert provides insights on adopting a public health approach to ACEs and implications of policies and practice that may help reduce the occurrence of ACEs. The current state of knowledge on effective preventions that are relevant to ACEs are described in Chapter 12 by Brennan, Stavas, and Scribano and the impact that positive relationships and environments have on the prevention of ACEs is detailed in Chapter 16 by Merrick, Ports, Guinn, and Ford.

It is important that we invest in efforts to develop upstream preventive strategies for ACEs—strategies aimed at the causes of the problem—that show evidence of effectiveness at a population-level in various countries and contexts. In short, while it is important to have evidence-based and diversity-sensitive therapeutic interventions to help individuals who have been exposed to various forms of childhood adversity, the greatest gains will be realized at a population level if we can be successful in preventing ACEs from occurring in the first place.

Setting the research agenda

In this chapter, we have highlighted what we believe to be the five most critical areas in need of further attention to advance understanding of, intervention for, and policies surrounding ACEs. There are numerous specific priorities for future research that emerge from this discussion—many presented in greater detail in the chapters of this book—and await the empirical attention and scrutiny of investigators working in the ACEs field. The following is a list of what we believe to be some of the most pressing avenues awaiting empirical scrutiny.

1. Large-scale studies designed to systematically evaluate the psychometric properties of various ACEs and ACEs-related measures in diverse population-based and clinical samples are required. Informed by the results of such studies, efforts designed to improve reliability, validity, and measurement efficiency are needed.
2. Systematic development of new measures that provide psychometrically sound evaluations capturing the heterogeneity in the type, duration, and severity of ACEs are needed.
3. Further research is needed to help establish what we define as ACEs and, relatedly, to support empirically driven changes to current definitions.
4. Systematic refinement and development of ACEs measures (i.e., priorities 1 and 2) may be further informed by a better understanding of the mechanisms that lead from ACEs to negative mental and physical health outcomes as opposed to resilience and growth. Such efforts would not only involve more research on basic mechanisms underlying negative cognitive, behavioral, physiological, and social outcomes of ACEs, but also evidence-based refinements to current models and conceptualizations of ACEs and their effects.
5. The heterogeneity of ACEs demands continued research to better understand what intervention strategies are most effective in treating the negative outcomes for children and adults exposed to significant childhood adversity. Researchers need to establish which

interventions work best and, as a means for tailoring treatment and increasing efficiency, whether delivery in individual or group formats is supported. Also, since many children and adults negatively impacted by ACEs live in geographically remote areas where specialized interventions and programs may not be available, research is needed to develop and assess feasibility and efficacy of technology-assisted intervention strategies.

6. Additional systematic evaluation of the costs and merits of universal screening for ACEs, perhaps informed by systematic refinement and development of ACEs measures (i.e., priorities 1 and 2) and availability of evidence-based intervention for ACEs (i.e., priority 5), is certainly warranted; however, given that it is well understood that ACEs lead to numerous negative outcomes, seeking evidence for implementation of universal screening for ACEs may be less relevant than empirical efforts to understand, identify, and promulgate the characteristics and factors that foster resilience to adversity.
7. Additional empirical efforts to better understand the efficacy and effectiveness of ACEs prevention programs are warranted. Likewise, and akin to research needs identified for ACEs interventions, development and assessment of feasibility and efficacy of prevention strategies for populations residing in geographically remote areas is needed.

Conclusion

In this book, we have included contributions from accomplished scholars whose empirical work and practical ideas have contributed significantly to understanding, treating, and preventing the negative consequences of ACEs. The chapters provide a comprehensive and start-of-the-art compendium of current knowledge, key controversies and developments, available and emerging interventions, and lingering issues that remain to be further investigated with respect to ACEs. While there has been a veritable explosion of research on ACEs over the past two decades, and significant advances have been made with respect to understanding and evidence-based intervention, much remains to be learned to further inform definition and conceptualization, screening, therapeutic and preventive interventions, and upstream policies. It is our hope that this book will serve as a useful collection of information that will guide and shape the future ACEs research agenda to further our understanding of this critical issue and, perhaps more importantly, aid clinicians and policy makers in their efforts to deliver highly effective evidence-based strategies to prevent or reduce ACEs-related human suffering and enhance quality of life.

References

Afifi, T. O., Enns, M. W., Cox, B. J., de Graaf, R., ten Have, M., & Sareen, J. (2007). Child abuse and health-related quality of life. *The Journal of Nervous and Mental Disease*, *195*, 797–804.

Afifi, T. O., Ford, D., Gershoff, E. T., Merrick, M., Grogan-Kaylor, A., Ports, K. A., ... Peters, R. (2017). Spanking and adult mental health impairment: the case for the designation of spanking as an adverse childhood experience. *Child Abuse & Neglect*, *71*, 24–31. https://doi.org/10.1016/j.chiabu.2017.01.014.

Bernstein, D. P., Stein, J. A., Newcomb, M. D., Walker, E., Pogge, D., Ahluvalia, T., ... Zule, W. (2003). Development and validation of a brief screening version of the childhood trauma questionnaire. *Child Abuse & Neglect*, *27*, 169–190. https://doi.org/10.1016/S0145-2134(02)00541-0.

Dube, S. R., Felitti, V. J., Dong, M., Chapman, D. P., Giles, W. H., & Anda, R. F. (2003). Childhood abuse, neglect, and household dysfunction and the risk of illicit drug use: the adverse childhood experiences study. *Pediatrics*, *111*, 564–572. https://doi.org/10.1542/peds.111.3.564.

Dunne, M. P., Zolotor, A. J., Runyan, D. K., Andreva-Miller, I., Choo, W. Y., Dunne, S. K., ... Youssef, R. (2009). ISPCAN child abuse screening tools retrospective version (ICAST-R): Delphi study and field testing in seven countries. *Child Abuse & Neglect*, *33*, 815–825. https://doi.org/10.1016/j.chiabu.2009.09.005.

Felitti, V. J., Anda, R. F., Nordenberg, D., Williamson, D. F., Spitz, A. M., Edwards, V., ... Marks, J. S. (1998). Relationship of childhood abuse and household dysfunction to many of the leading causes of death in adults: the adverse childhood experiences (ACE) study. *American Journal of Preventive Medicine*, *14*, 245–258. https://doi.org/10.1016/S0749-3797(98)00017-8.

Finkelhor, D. (2017). Screening for adverse childhood experiences (ACEs): cautions and suggestions. *Child Abuse & Neglect*, *85*, 174–179.

Finkelhor, D., Hamby, S. L., Ormrod, R., & Turner, H. (2005). The juvenile victimization questionnaire: reliability, validity, and national norms. *Child Abuse & Neglect*, *29*, 383–412. https://doi.org/10.1016/j.chiabu.2004.11.001.

Finkelhor, D., Shattuck, A., Turner, H., & Hamby, S. (2015). A revised inventory of adverse childhood experiences. *Child Abuse & Neglect*, *48*, 13–21. https://doi.org/10.1016/j.chiabu.2015.07.011.

Finkelhor, D., Turner, H. A., Shattuck, A., & Hamby, S. L. (2013). Violence, crime, and abuse exposure in a national sample of children and youth an update. *JAMA Pediatrics*, *167*, 614–621. https://doi.org/10.1001/jamapediatrics.2013.42.

Straus, M. A. (2004). Cross-cultural reliability and validity of the revised conflict tactics scales: a study of university student dating couples in 17 nations. *Cross-Cultural Research*, *38*, 407–432. https://doi.org/10.1177/1069397104269543.

Straus, M. A., & Mickey, E. L. (2012). Reliability, validity, and prevalence of partner violence measured by the conflict tactics scales in male-dominant nations. *Aggression and Violent Behavior*, *17*, 463–474. https://doi.org/10.1016/j.avb.2012.06.004.

Index

Note: Page numbers followed by *f* indicate figures, *t* indicate tables, and *np* indicate footnotes.

9780128160657